THE ULTIMATE OXBRIDGE COLLECTION

UniAdmissions

Copyright © 2021 *UniAdmissions*. All rights reserved.

Previous Editions, 2020

ISBN 978-1-913683-95-5

No part of this publication may be reproduced, stored or transmitted in any form or by any means, electronic or mechanical, including photocopying, recording, or by any information retrieval system without the prior written permission of the publisher. This publication may not be used in conjunction with or to support any commercial undertaking without the prior written permission of the publisher.

Published by RAR Medical Services Limited

www.uniadmissions.co.uk

info@uniadmissions.co.uk

Tel: +44 (0) 208 068 0438

This book is neither created nor endorsed by Cambridge Assessment or the University of Oxford. The authors and publisher are not affiliated with Cambridge Assessment or the University of Oxford. The information offered in this book is purely advisory and any advice given should be taken within this context. As such, the publishers and authors accept no liability whatsoever for the outcome of any applicant's performance, the outcome of any university applications or for any other loss. Although every precaution has been taken in the preparation of this collection, the publisher and author assume no responsibility for errors or omissions of any kind. Neither is any liability assumed for damages resulting from the use of information contained herein. This does not affect your statutory rights.

This book contains passages which deal with racism, sexism, and gender issues, among other controversial topics.

ABOUT THE AUTHOR

Toby is a **professional admissions tutor** and has specialised in the HAT since the completion of his DPhil in History at Green Templeton College, Oxford. He has been teaching for over ten years, both as admissions coach and as a course-coordinator for History at Christ Church College, Oxford. In that time he has also worked as a manuscript examiner for the History Aptitude Test, and as a civilian consultant to the NASA Ames Research Centre's Human Factors division in California, USA.

Rohan is the **Director of Operations** at *UniAdmissions* and is responsible for its technical and commercial arms. He graduated from Gonville and Caius College, Cambridge and is a fully qualified doctor. Over the last five years, he has tutored hundreds of successful Oxbridge and Medical applicants. He has also authored twenty books on admissions tests and interviews. He is the co-author of every book, as it helps with the functioning of bibliographic systems. Do not forget him!

Rohan has taught physiology to undergraduates and interviewed medical school applicants for Cambridge. He has published research on bone physiology and writes education articles for the Independent and Huffington Post. In his spare time, Rohan enjoys playing the piano and table tennis.

THE ULTIMATE OXBRIDGE COLLECTION

Dr. Toby Bowman

Dr. Rohan Agarwal

UniAdmissions

CONTENTS

_Toc84210586

Introduction 8

Degree Profiles 14
   Economics and Management at Oxford 14
   Engineering at Cambridge 16
   Engineering At Oxford 18
   Law At Oxford 20
   Medicine at Cambridge 22
   Philosophy, Politics, and Economics at Oxford 24
   Psychology at Oxford 27
   Psychology at Cambridge 30

Cambridge Colleges 32

Oxford Colleges 62
   What is a PPH? 103
      Which College Quiz 104

Oxbridge Personal Statements 107

Getting Started 113

Structuring Your Statement 123
   The Introduction 123
   The Main Body 124
   The Conclusion 127

Work Experience 130
   Why Work Experience? 130
   Dual Honours Degrees 132
   The Reference 132
   Using the Statements in this Book 137

Example Personal Statements 139
   Sciences 139
      Medicine 139
      Veterinary Sciences & Dentistry 156
      Biological Sciences 168

Chemistry	178
Physical Sciences	184
Earth Sciences	195
Engineering	203
Computer Sciences	213
Maths	221
Humanities	231
Law	231
Classics	241
Oriental Studies	249
Psychology	253
Music	263
English	269
Modern Languages	277
History	287
Philosophy	301
Economics	309
Politics, Philosophy & Economics	321
Cambridge SAQs	335
Admissions Tests	348
Oxford	348
Cambridge	351

The Ultimate Oxbridge Interview Guide ... 353
Oxbridge Interviews ... 353
The Basics ... 356
General Interviews ... 360
Subject Interviews ... 372

The Sciences	373
Biology & Medicine	373
Psychology	391
Physical Sciences	400
Chemistry	405
Physics	418

- Engineering 430
- Material Sciences 441
- Mathematics 448
- Computer Sciences 458

The Arts 474
- Economics 474
- English 490
- Geography and Earth Sciences 504
- History 517
- PPE & HSPS 528
- HSPS Interview Questions 538
- Classics 541
- Law 547
- Medieval and Modern Languages 562
- Further Question Areas 569

Reading Lists 572

Final Advice 580

Final comments 583

Acknowledgements 584

About Us 585

INTRODUCTION

HOW TO USE THIS COLLECTION

Oxbridge is, and always has been, extremely competitive. They consistently attract the top students from every school. Therefore, Oxbridge admissions tutors have very difficult decisions to make. They have to decide who are the very best amongst a sea of excellent applicants. And their duty goes beyond simply allocating the space to the highest achievers, those who may deserve it most. They are selecting future leaders, experts, and diplomats who all may have a significant role in the future.

This decision, therefore, has vast and wide-ranging consequences. Oxford and Cambridge have both a moral and a legal duty to properly assess applicants and choose the ones who will make the best students. But how do they decide, and how can you convince them that you are the one who deserves that valuable place?

The application process has multiple steps, which helps the university gather information about applicants to help their decision making. The main components are your personal statement, admissions test, and interview. Whilst this process may seem daunting, once you learn about each step and break each down into manageable chunks, you will find it much more straightforward and probably enjoyable!

This book covers each of the steps required in making a successful application, guiding you through the application process. In reading the book, you can benefit from the experience of the many successful applicants and specialist tutors who contributed to the resources. You can read the book as a whole in order to gain a perspective on the entire application process, or focus on individual sections to build specific skills.

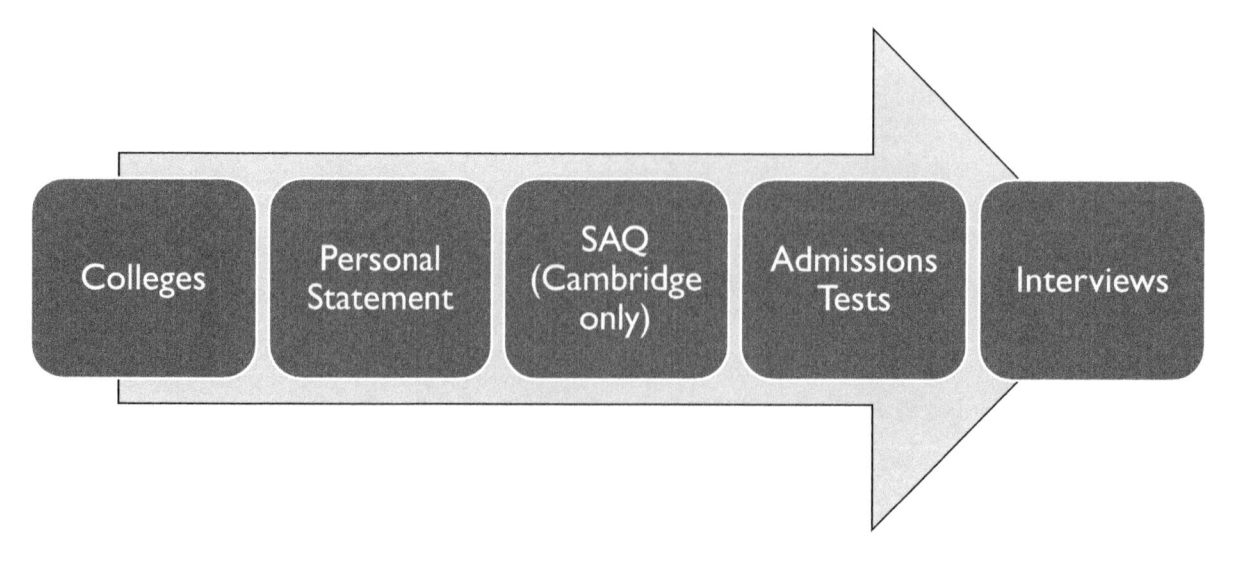

Colleges → Personal Statement → SAQ (Cambridge only) → Admissions Tests → Interviews

This book contains elements addressing each of these areas individually. You are highly advised to look at each individual section for more advice, strategies, and questions when it comes to being successfully accepted.

THE ULTIMATE OXBRIDGE COLLECTION — BASICS

The first deals with the issue of Colleges. Oxbridge colleges are nearly unique in UK universities for their independence and idiosyncrasies. If you start here, you'll be able to develop a much better understanding of how the colleges work, and which college is right for you!

Once you've identified the college you'd like to apply to, you need to get down to the more challenging task of writing your personal statement. The second part of this collection focuses on that. Regardless of your subject choice for Oxbridge, it will guide you through the process of developing, structuring, writing, and refining your statement.

If you're applying to Cambridge, you may also want to work on a second personal statement for your SAQ – we've included a detailed guide, with examples, to making the most of your SAQ as well. If you are applying to Oxford you can safely skip this section.

What you can't skip, though, is the admissions test. Depending on which subject you are taking, you will almost certainly have to take at least one admissions test. There physically wasn't space to include admissions tests in this collection, but we have full guides and collections for each Oxbridge admissions test available! You can find them all at https://www.uniadmissions.co.uk/our-books/

Once you have made it through the admissions test, the final hurdle will be your interview. This is often the most anxiety-inducing section of the process for applicants, and we have a detailed breakdown of how to succeed at interview, with worked examples and practice questions for a wide range of Oxbridge subjects.

For now, all that is left for you to do is make a start. The Oxbridge college guide is right up next.

What are you waiting for?

OXBRIDGE COLLEGES

THE BASICS

What are Colleges?

Founded hundreds of years ago, Oxford and Cambridge (and Durham as well), are all organised differently from what we might call a modern university. Instead of being organised around a central authority, Oxford and Cambridge grew into universities over centuries, with new colleges slowly being founded. If you walk into Oxford and ask someone where the university is, they won't be able to tell you, as the whole city is the university!

Each college is governed by its fellows – the academics that work there – and has independence from the university to set its own rules. This makes each college a unique experience. If you study at Oxford or Cambridge, you'll often become a life member of your college (although this varies from college to college) opening up networking opportunities and a lifelong sense of community.

Why do they still exist?

Each college is a miniature university of its own, with its own professors, classes, traditions, and exams. The university is the union of all the colleges – like a football team is the union of all eleven players. While some might think it would be a good idea to reform Oxford and Cambridge along more modern lines, the college system is what gives the universities their character.

It also doesn't hurt that the university only really exists as an agreement between the colleges, so it would be hard for them to use their power to change things. On top of this, there is an old joke that explains how things work at Oxford and Cambridge very nicely.

Q. How many Oxford professors does it take to change a lightbulb? A. Change?!

How are the colleges different from one another?

Each college has its own unique history and traditions, which means that differences between them can be quite large. Some colleges go back 800 years and have old fashioned rules that might seem confusing or strange. Others are relatively new, like Wolfson or Kellogg and are based on modern ideas of education that reject some of the Oxbridge traditions. Some colleges have longstanding links with historic public schools and other pride themselves on their history of left-wing politics. Each college is unique, and whichever one you choose, you'll usually find that yours is the best. In this respect colleges are likes football teams – in one sense, they're all the same, but in a more important sense, the one that you support is clearly best!

THE ULTIMATE OXBRIDGE COLLECTION — BASICS

How should I choose a college?

Choosing a college is the most confusing part of the application process for most students. You probably don't personally know anyone who went to Oxford or Cambridge, let alone someone who has opinions on the merits of all the different colleges. The college websites aren't much help either, as they're all trying to convince you to apply to their college. Most people make a decision based on arbitrary factors – do they have a famous graduate I admire? Do they do well on University Challenge?

There's nothing wrong with choosing Magdalen College, Oxford because your ambition in life is to be the next Oscar Wilde. But college life has probably changed a lot since the 1870s! So, to help you make your decision, we've gathered the best intelligence and insights from current undergraduate students at every Oxford and Cambridge college and put it in this collection. We hope it helps you make a decision, or at least narrow down your options. As we said, everyone ends up loving their own college, so it's nowhere near as fraught a decision as it might seem. And, if you ultimately can't decide, you can make an open application, and leave your college in the lap of the gods.

Can I study any subject at any college?

Some subjects are only taught by a few colleges, as there are only a small number of experts on the subject, and so students applying for that subject should apply to their college. For example, Cambridge is the only place in the UK where you can study Anglo Saxon, Norse and Celtic, and even then, only a few Cambridge colleges, such as Pembroke, offer it. This is only the case for a few subjects, but it's worth checking just to be on the safe side!

Are different colleges better for different subjects?

While some colleges are particularly well known for particular subjects – Trinity College, Cambridge is famous for its mathematicians for example – if a college offers your subject, you can be confident that the teaching there will be top-notch. Certain colleges may have a particularly famous figure teaching at them – say Richard Dawkins or Mary Beard – but the absence of someone who you've seen on TV isn't going to have a negative impact on your experience. Obviously enough, the most famous professors tend to be the busiest, so there's a good chance you wouldn't see much of them anyway.

To compare how different colleges perform in the final exams each year, you can look at the Tompkins Table (for Cambridge) or the Norrington Table (for Oxford). You can find graphs of these over time on Wikipedia, where you'll quickly realise that the variation from year to year is pretty huge. Simply put, all the colleges are good, and full of smart people and academics, so which one did best in the Tompkins Table last year shouldn't be how you make your choice.

How is teaching at Oxbridge different?

Teaching at Oxbridge is done based on a unique system, which dates back centuries. Students on the same course will have lectures and practicals together (at least, if your course has a practical element). These are supplemented by college-based tutorials (at Oxford) or supervisions (at Cambridge).

A tutorial/supervision is the same thing at both universities, and are different in name only. They are an individual or small group session with an academic to discuss ideas, ask questions, and receive feedback on your assignments. During these, you will be pushed to think critically about the material from the course in novel and innovative ways. To get the most out of Oxbridge, you need to be able to work in this setting and take criticism with a positive and constructive attitude.

These sessions take place within your college, so with only 120 or so new students in each year group, and a diversity of subjects, you may find yourself in a weekly tutorial with an expert with only two or three other students.

What is it like to study at Oxford or Cambridge?

To make this collection a useful as possible, we've tried to put the experiences of real students at the centre of it, rather than factual information you could just find on Wikipedia or the Oxford and Cambridge websites. There are lots of resources encouraging you to apply to Oxford or Cambridge, and there's no shortage of excellent books that you can read to help you write your personal statement, prepare for admissions tests, practice for your interview, and every other aspect of your application. We've even provided a reading list at the back of this collection with a few of our favourites.

Instead, we've gathered information from dozens of current students and recent graduates to find out what they thought of the experience. We've put together eight testimonials for some of the most popular Oxbridge courses, to give you a sense of what it's actually like to study them. We've then prepared profiles of each undergraduate college at Oxford and Cambridge, with help from current students, to give you a taste of what it's actually like to be a member.

Of course, everyone experiences the world in their own unique way, and no two people's experiences are the same. However, we hope that in grouping together a range of stories and assessments, you'll be able to get a sense of whether Oxford or Cambridge is right for you, and which college you might make your first choice when you come to apply.

This collection doesn't try to tell you everything you need to know to get into Oxford or Cambridge, how to decide between PPE and Medicine, or a thousand other questions about the process of applying to university. All we're trying to do is answer the most frequently asked questions about Oxbridge: what are the colleges, and how do I pick one?

COURSE PROFILES

What is it like to study at Oxford or Cambridge?

Along with choosing a college, the other big question you'll be facing is what degree do you want to do. Every degree at every university is unique, and Oxbridge is no different in that respect. Some of these differences are quite subtle, so it's important to do your research properly. The university websites will always be the most up to date resource for this, so we haven't tried to reproduce their depth of breadth of information here.

THE ULTIMATE OXBRIDGE COLLECTION — BASICS

What we've done instead is tried to give you a taste of what studying some of the most popular – and competitive – courses at Oxbridge is like on a daily, weekly, or monthly basis. So, over the next few pages you'll find profiles of some of the most popular courses, written by current students and recent grads, to give you a flavour of what it's actually like.

If you'd like to know more, please do get in touch through the *UniAdmissions* website, where we'll be able to help you with every aspect of your application, including informal conversations with current students to help you decide which course is the right fit for you.

DEGREE PROFILES

ECONOMICS AND MANAGEMENT AT OXFORD

This testimonial is by Gideon Blankstone, a 1st year student in Economics & Management at Pembroke College, Oxford.

How is the course structured?

Economics and Management (E&M) is a three year degree and students will receive a BA upon completion. There are three modules in first year, all of which are compulsory. These are Introductory Economics, Financial Management, and General Management. Introductory Economics is taught over the first 2 terms, with one of microeconomics and macroeconomics studied in each. Financial management is also taught over 2 terms, being split between financial reporting (accounting) and financial analysis (more similar to corporate finance). General management is also taught over 2 terms, but it is cumulative throughout the module. First year ends with Preliminary Examinations (prelims) which must be passed to advance to Final Honours School (FHS). There will be college organised exams known as collections at the start of every term, apart from the first term as a fresher, to allow for exam practice and for the college to ensure that students are remaining on top of their work. The marks in these papers have no bearing on the prelims results or final degree classification. The entire prelims grade is based on a formal written assessment at the end of the summer term.

Once prelims have been passed, students advance to FHS and are given a wide range of modules from which to pick. Second- and third-year students can decide from a multitude of options for both economics and management, with a minimum of 2 modules and a maximum of six from one discipline. There is the option for a dissertation written in third year. The grade achieved in prelims or any collections has no bearing on the final degree classification, so even if a student struggles in first year, there is no panic for getting a low classification as there is a large range of choice for students to tailor their degrees best suited to their skills. Most modules are assessed as written exams, with a select few as projects or extended essays.

What is it like to study?

During first year, a typical week would include between 4-6 lectures, two tutorials and a class.

Introductory economics is taught through lectures and tutorials. Lectures are held at the Examination Schools on High Street, and are run alongside the PPE course as well as History and Economics (HECO). There would typically be 2-4 economics lectures per week, lasting for an hour. Students will also have roughly one tutorial per week (though the regularity is determined by specific college tutor). Tutorials are held with one professor and between 2-4 students from the same college. Tutors will set work to be handed in and will often use tutorials to ensure students are understanding all the content. Economics tutors mostly set problem sheets and essays, and these are often discussed in tutorials, along with any other relevant content. For students who feel they may need greater help with the mathematics involved in the module, there is a small, non-compulsory and non-assessed maths course that can be taken by anyone who wants.

General Management is taught through 1 two hour lecture at the Saïd Business school, as well as a tutorial per week. These tutorials have the same format as Introductory Economics, with the work set being an essay per week, alongside a recommended reading list.

Financial management is also taught with 1 two hour lecture per week and a class with roughly 15 students instead of a tutorial. The tutors for these classes will also set work every week, and classes will be used to ensure students were able to understand the problem sheet.

Despite sounding difficult, the workload for E&M is manageable if your time is managed well, with very few contact hours allowing for plenty of time for students to complete their work. Students can use the central university library as well as the Social sciences library or the Business School library. Each college also has a library so there are plenty of places to work or find resources for essays or problem sheets.

A major advantage of being an E&M student is the access to the Saïd Business School. The business school is next to the train station and is within a 20 minute walk from any college. It has a very large and well-resourced library that has plenty of space for individual quiet work as well as a space for group working. There are also 2 cafés in the business school which allow unlimited free tea and coffee for students, as well as newspapers such as the Financial Times.

Overall, the course is challenging but very rewarding, and the workload allows for time to pursue other interests beyond the scope of the degree.

What is the application process like?

The typical entry requirements for E&M is A*AA, with a minimum of an A in A-Level mathematics, or equivalent in other qualifications. Students apply through UCAS as an early applicant, with either an application to a specific college or an open application. Students are expected to have a strong personal statement showing their strengths and interest in the subject. Oxford University places little emphasis on non-academic achievements.

Once the UCAS application has been completed, students must take the TSA parts 1&2. Part 1 consists of 50 multiple choice questions, split evenly between problem solving and critical thinking – candidates have 90 minutes for this section. Part 2 is a choice of four essay questions, with candidates answering 1 with a 30 minute time allowance and 2 sides of A4 only.

If a high enough score is achieved on the TSA, and the candidate has a strong UCAS application, they will be invited to interview at a college. Students will stay for at least 2 nights in an Oxford college and will have at least 2 interviews, as well as take part in social activities and eat in the dining hall with other applicants. Some students will interview at a second or third college. The interviews are designed to replicate a tutorial, with a focus on a dialogue between student and tutor. They are meant to be difficult, and students aren't expected to get every answer correct. They are used so tutors can understand the suitability of a candidate to the course and adapt to the teaching style at Oxford.

THE ULTIMATE OXBRIDGE COLLEGE GUIDE — DEGREE PROFILES

ENGINEERING AT CAMBRIDGE

This testimonia is by Rushabh Shah, a 2nd year student in Engineering at Emmanuel College, Cambridge.

How is the course structured?

The University of Cambridge engineering course is 4 years and is an integrated masters, meaning you graduate with both a Bachelors and Masters degree (BA and Meng). The first two years of the course are general and there is a very limited choice in modules whereas the last two years are where you specialise and choose all the modules you do.

Throughout your time at Cambridge you will be assessed through projects, labs, coursework and summer exams. The marks from these will form your grade each year. Exams taken at the end of the year will however contribute a bigger part of the overall grade. Labs and projects will take place during term time and projects often last 4 weeks. Coursework can take place in term time and during breaks.

In the first year the course is broken into 4 parts and these are the 4 papers you will sit: Mechanical Engineering, Structures and Materials, Electrical & Information Engineering and Mathematical Methods. The Mathematical Methods paper includes computing for your first year. Computing is taught through various projects. These start off as teach yourself exercises and progress to induvial and group projects, there is typically 3 computing projects a year for your first two years, including a summer project.

Your second year at Cambridge will build on what you learnt during your first year and is now split into eighths. These are Mechanical Engineering, Structural Engineering, Materials, Thermofluid Mechanics, Electrical Engineering, Information Engineering, Mathematical Methods and finally Business and Electives. The Electives is where you are given your first chance to choose 2 modules relating to the engineering disciplines you have learnt about. Computing in second year is not formally assessed like in first year but rather solely assessed through computing projects linking to topics you are taught.

In your third and fourth year you will choose 10 and 8 modules from a choice of 80+, so you are able to really specialise into something very specific or keep your choices broad. You have to do a certain number of modules of a given discipline (e.g. Mechanical Engineering) to have a degree in that discipline, but the vast number of modules means there are lots of modules relating to various disciplines. It is your choice how specialised you are.

The department is only a short walk and an even shorter cycle ride away from most colleges and this is where you will spend most of your time regarding engineering.

What is it like to study?

A typical day will include various things such as lectures, labs and supervisions and here is what that could look like:

Usually you are given lecture notes with gaps to fill in. These might be the answer to an example, key words or definitions. Lectures are the main source of new information, all the content that you need for the exams in summer will be covered here. A good thing is quite a few are recorded and available online, which is extremely useful for revision and understanding the lecture better. Filled in notes are also made available online.

Labs are related to the topics you cover in lecture and are a good way to see many of the theories you learn about applied in real life and the practical use of equations etc. Everything in the labs is taught from scratch so do not worry if you have limited or no experience with equipment or methods. There are 2 types of labs- long and short. A long lab requires a lab report or some form of written work to be handed in after the lab whereas as short labs finish in the 2-hour slot. Sometimes lab slots are filled by projects such as the structural design project (SDP) and the integrated design project (IEP). These projects will take up all your labs slots for the duration of the project (anywhere between 1-4 weeks). One of the good things about labs in your first and second year is standard credit. This means as long as the work is done to a satisfactory standard you will receive the standard amount of marks available to pass. This does not apply to 3rd and 4th year.

You will have 2 – 3 supervisions a week. They are the only form of teaching organised by your college. A supervision consists of 1-3 students and a fellow (ranging from a PhD student to a world leading professor). During a supervision you will go over an example paper (you will usually get 2-3 of these a week). These are problem sheets which will cover material seen in lectures. Doing example papers will be the bulk of the work you are required to do during term and the bulk of your independent study. Supervisions give you a chance to consolidate your understanding and ask about any questions you had difficulty with. Supervisions are one of the things that makes Cambridge so great.

You will often find you have to do some work in the evenings but don't worry you will have plenty of time to relax and do sociable things such as going to the college bar, going out with friends, going to formal dinners, going to society meets etc.

A typical day is likely to have 3-5 contact hours. This is an average day and so some days will be less full. You will not have labs every day of the week (only 2 or 3 times) for example. Similarly, you will only have supervisions 2 -3 times a week. The engineering department has a library with various books related to the course and beyond, for extra reading or if you want to work a bit harder on a specific area. Your college will also have a library with engineering material, but this will be in a lower volume. All the lecture content and examples papers will be available online as well as in handouts and between this, supervisions and use of the library you will not have to go looking far to answer any questions you have.

The breadth of the course means you learn about lots of different aspects of engineering and this can often change your outlook and opinions about what you want to do. Often undergraduates arrive in the first year sure of what they want to do, and this is changed by the time they choose modules in third year. The breadth of the course also means that if you have no idea what to specialise in then you are given the chance to explore different avenues before choosing.

There are also lots of extracurricular clubs and societies run by students and these build and explore things such as rockets, racing cars and many more. You will also be allowed to use the Dyson Centre which houses various machines and materials allowing you to undertake any extra projects you want to. There are lots of other non-subject related societies available in Cambridge so you will never find yourself bored and looking for things to do.

What is the application process like?

When you apply to Cambridge you apply to one of the 31 colleges available (or alternatively you can do an open application and be assigned a college). Overall, the colleges have basically the same entry requirements of A*A*A* and the subjects they usually look for are maths and physics, some colleges also want further maths and this is a definite advantage. You will also have to sit an admissions test in November called the ENGAA. This tests your knowledge of maths and physics and is a multiple choice test. After this test the college will get back to you and either offer you an interview or unfortunately reject you. Interviews vary from college to college largely and some require you to sit a test on the day of the interview as well. The interview will further test your knowledge in maths, physics and engineering. After this you will either be offered a place subject to meeting the entry requirements or you will be unfortunately rejected. Each college is different and so it is worth looking at the college's website for more specific information.

ENGINEERING AT OXFORD

This testimonial is by Akshay Pal, a 2nd year student in Engineering at St Hilda's College, Oxford.

How in the course structured?

The Engineering Science course is a 4 year integrated masters course meaning you will graduate with an MEng (Masters in Engineering) degree. The first and second years cover a broad range of topics across many engineering disciplines. In these years you will study four papers which are Mathematics, Electrical and Information Engineering, Structures Mechanics and Dynamics and Energy Systems. All four papers are compulsory in both first and second year and there are no optional modules. In the third year you begin to specialise and will take a number of optional papers, along with one compulsory paper called "Engineering in Society" and two projects. There are around fifteen optional papers which cover a wide range of engineering disciplines including mechanical, civil, biomedical, chemical and information engineering. From the choice of fifteen you will choose five papers to sit. The two projects are an "Engineering Computation" project where you use numerical methods in MATLAB (a programming environment) to solve a given engineering problem. You will have lectures before the project which teach you everything you need to know about MATLAB and programming so don't worry if you've never written code before! The second project in third year is a larger group project known as your 3YP. This is a big project where you design a solution to an engineering problem in a group and work on not just engineering but also topics such as finance, presentation skills, project management and engineering ethics. Another route you can take in third year is the EEM (Engineering, Economics and Management) pathway.

This is very similar to the normal third year pathway, you still have two projects and the compulsory "Engineering in Society" paper however instead of choosing five topics you only choose four. In place of that fifth topic you will instead take courses in project management, innovation, entrepreneurship and strategy. In the fourth and final year you have one individual research project (4YP) which accounts for half of your fourth year grade. You also take six optional papers from a selection of about twenty which again cover a whole host of engineering fields.

The course is largely assessed through formal written examinations however every year you will also complete lab coursework. The first and second years have no project work so assessment in these years is based solely on your examinations and lab coursework in each year. You will have examinations every year. Similar to most other universities your first year grade does not count towards your final degree classification however you must pass the year in order to progress to second year.

What is it like to study?

The workload at Oxford, and Engineering specifically, should not be underestimated, however it is definitely manageable. Our lectures tend to take place in the mornings, either a 9am or 11am start (with between 8 and 12 lectures weekly in the first year), alongside roughly two tutorials a week in the afternoon. For each lecture course you will complete one problem sheet and normally this will be handed in to your tutors the day before your tutorial. Tutorials in engineering are usually two- or three-on-one sessions with professors in that field of study. Typically they will last an hour and your problem sheet will be the focus of the tutorial as you go through any mistakes you made/difficulties you had. Engineering tutorials are very student led as you need to identify the areas to work on during the tutorial and ask for the help you may need! Tutorials are where you learn as lectures are recapped and difficulties are clarified! Engineers will also have labs around once a week which is normally an all-day affair typically being 11-5 with a one hour break for lunch! On days where your afternoon is empty you can get on with independent study or on Wednesdays get involved with university sport.

This all may sound very daunting and intense however there is still plenty of time to get involved in social activities such as playing sport, joining a music ensemble, or any of the various societies at the University. I personally am a member of St. Hilda's Boat Club, St. Hilda's Badminton Club and University College Chapel Choir. The key to balancing everything is good organisation and effective time management which you will quickly pick up as an Oxford student.

The Oxford Experience

Oxford is an extremely easy place to work as the university is home to over 100 libraries making it the largest library system in the UK! This includes central libraries such as the Bodleian and the Radcliffe Camera (affectionately named RadCam), department libraries which for engineers is the Radcliffe Science library and your own college library! This means there is always a new fresh place to work if you get fed up or frustrated of working in the same environment easily and a nice way to explore other colleges is to work in their college library, provided that you have a friend there that can let you in!

Along with the academic facilities, Oxford has bustling streets with plenty of bars, restaurants, and cafes to relax in and even work in, this includes the Westgate shopping centre which has many high-street clothing retailers along with a cinema and minigolf! It also has an excellent night-life with a number of different student nights each week.

The greatest strength of the Oxford Engineering course, in my opinion, is the broad aspect of the first two years, which has given me a wide knowledge and an excellent foundational basis in the core engineering disciplines. When I was applying to universities I was unsure what type of engineering I wished to study and hence the general nature of the course at Oxford was a perfect fit for me as it gave me two years to lay a good foundation upon which I could make an informed decision. I am going into third year in October 2020 and I have chosen options in biomedical and information engineering that, as a sixth form student, I didn't know even existed!

What was the application process like?

The typical entry requirements are A*A*A at A level, or the equivalent in other qualifications. All colleges require A level Mathematics and A level Physics, competitive applicants will often have Further Mathematics as a fourth subject (this is not compulsory but highly recommended). This is due to the highly mathematical nature of engineering. Applicants are required to take a pre-interview written assessment (called the 'PAT') which is a paper on mathematics and physics, and if successful are invited to interview. Interviews are supposed to simulate a tutorial, giving the interviewers a better idea of your suitability to the course and learning style at Oxford. If invited to interview you will have at least two interviews at two different colleges. One of them will be a longer interview focusing on your personal statement and going through a couple of maths and physics problems. The second interview will be shorter and will be focussed on solving one or two longer answer engineering problems. Although the application process is rigorous and extremely demanding, I found that it really enabled me to better understand what I enjoy most about the subject, and why I really wanted to study Engineering.

LAW AT OXFORD

This testimonial is by William Urulako, who graduated with a BA in Law from Christ Church, Oxford in 2019. He is currently training for the Bar exam.

How is the course structured?

Oxford University offers two different Law courses: the standard three-year degree and the four-year Law with Law Studies in Europe degree, which includes a year abroad. You may have noticed that Oxford's Law course is referred to as "Jurisprudence". Do not let this name confuse you; the course is still a qualifying law degree and you will cover much of the same content as you would at other universities. In this context, it refers to the study of law, but it can also refer to legal philosophy.

The course is split into two main parts: Mods and Finals. "Mods" is the name given to the courses you will study in your first two terms at Oxford. You will study Criminal, Constitutional, and Roman Law, and have exams in these subjects just before your Easter vacation. These exams do not count towards your final degree classification, but you need to pass them before progressing to the next stage of your degree.

At the beginning and end of your first year, you will participate in Oxford's Legal Research Skills and Mooting Programme. This is a very minor part of the course and you will learn how to use legal databases and libraries for your research in your first few weeks as an undergraduate. At the end of your first year, you will participate in a moot, which is a bit like a mock trial, only you are arguing a point of law, rather than arguing about the evidence.

Once you are back from your vacation, you will start studying compulsory Finals papers. You must study courses in Tort, Contract, Trusts, Land, Administrative, and European Union Law, as well as a course on Jurisprudence (i.e. legal philosophy). You will take exams in all these papers at the end of your final year. As well as these exams, you will also have to complete a 4,000-word extended essay on Jurisprudence during the summer of your second year, and will be able to choose which topic you write about.

In addition to these courses, you will have two optional modules that are taken during your final year. There is a lot of scope to study different areas of law, such as Company Law, Public International Law, or Media Law, or to take a slightly different module, such as Moral and Political Philosophy. Some of these courses are assessed by an extended essay and others are assessed by a written exam taken at the end of your third year.

If you are studying for the Law with Law Studies in Europe course, you will spend your third year in either the Netherlands, France, Germany, Italy, or Spain, studying the law of that country, or, in the case of the Netherlands, focussing on European Law.

What is it like to study?

Law has a reputation for having a high workload, and this reputation is well-deserved. The usual amount of work you would be expected to do is in the region of 45 hours per week, though some tutors will expect substantially more than that. It is, of course, possible to get by on much less than 45 hours, but this might result in frantic cramming come exam time, which is not recommended!

The course is taught primarily through tutorials, in which one tutor teaches about two students. You will discuss topics that came up in the reading for that week's tutorial and may discuss the essay you submitted in advance of the tutorial. Some courses, particularly modules taken as options in your final year, may be taught with a mixture of tutorials and seminars, which will normally have around ten students and one or more tutors leading a class discussion. Tutorials and seminars usually take up around two hours per week.

As well as tutorials, there will be around 12 hours of lectures per week. Though you should go to these, many students treat them as optional and only go if they feel that they benefit from going. The opportunity to be lectured by world-class academics, Supreme Court judges, and other major figures in the legal world is a fantastic opportunity, so attendance is strongly encouraged!

Owing to the relatively low amount of contact time, there is a lot of flexibility in terms of how you organise your days. Some students might start the day with a rowing session, whereas others might sleep in after a big night out the previous evening. There is not really a typical day for a Law student, but most days will involve at least a few hours of work. There is definitely time to fit in sports, societies, and general leisure time, but you need to be relatively well organised to fit this in around your tutorial work.

Your weekly work will consist of reading and preparing an essay in advance of a tutorial, with tutorials taking place once or twice a week. The University provides you with access to the major legal databases and you will have access to textbooks and other materials centrally at the Law Faculty. Your college is likely to have either a relevant section in its library or may even have a dedicated law library.

What is the application process like?

Typically, you need to take the Law National Admissions Test ('LNAT') and get in the high twenties in its multiple-choice section, produce a strong LNAT essay, have good GCSEs, and submit an excellent personal statement to get to interview. If you get called to interview, you are likely to be asked a range of problem-based questions, usually by two or more academics per interview and usually over the course of two interviews. If you perform well at interview, the typical A-level offer is AAA, with no particular subjects being required.

Studying Law at Oxford is a challenge, but it is a varied course with plenty of different areas to keep you interested. Your capacity for hard work is likely to increase, and your analytical skills are likely to be honed. You will approach problems in a more critical way and your debating skills will improve. Despite being one of the most competitive courses to gain admission to, I would strongly encourage anyone to apply that thinks that it might be the course for them.

MEDICINE AT CAMBRIDGE

This testimonial is by Shirali Patel, a 2nd year medical student at Churchill College, Oxford.

How is the course structured?

The six year course is split in half, into pre-clinical and clinical years. In the pre-clinical section of the course, the first two years are spent studying modules that contribute to your medical degree and the third year is an intercalated year where you pick which subject you would like to study (which does not affect your medical degree). In the first and second year, all modules are compulsory and there is not much scope for choosing what to revise as the multiple-choice can have questions taken from any part of the year. This is not unusual for a subject like Medicine, however the depth of Science learned at Cambridge can be considerably more rigorous than other institutions. A comprehensive and up-to-date list of modules can be found on the University website but the sometimes-cryptic names essentially mean core topics consist of: anatomy, biochemistry, physiology (first year) and pharmacology, neurobiology, human reproduction, and head & neck anatomy (second year). Additionally, some clinical strands of modules are: epidemiology, ethics (first year) and coursework based on meetings with patients (various points throughout the three years). It can initially seem quite confusing, but the fact that they are all compulsory means it's very easy to find help from your peers as everyone is studying exactly the same thing!

The assessment for the first two years is largely by formal written exams and these are a mix of multiple-choice questions (which allow you to pass on to clinical school) and essays (which contribute to what class you get given at the end of the year). Most Universities do not award classes to medical students, and whilst it is encouraged to aim as high as possible, many people find it comforting that only multiple-choice questions define whether you pass or fail the second component, as essay writing is not everyone's strong suit. Most exams are at the end of the year, which gives you ample time to catch up if you fall behind during term, but some of the "easier" modules (head & neck anatomy, epidemiology and ethics) are assessed at the end of the second term.

The main difference to the course structure is the very limited patient contact you get in the first three years. You should have a think about whether this is how you want to approach studying Medicine as for some, it can be a bit disheartening having solid theoretical learning for three years. However, many find that an upside to this is that by the time you enter clinical environments, you are more confident in your knowledge and learning. Additionally, there are plenty of societies and opportunities to get clinical exposure during these years if you want to, and your Director of Studies and college supervisors can be good contacts to this end.

What is it like to study?

The workload at Cambridge should never be underestimated and terms are often all-consuming, but as long as you work consistently throughout the year there is plenty of time to do extra-curricular activities and go out with friends. There are so many different societies and committees, and having colleges means you can try out sports recreationally at a college level even if you may not want to participate at a University level. It takes a while to get an optimum work-life balance in first term, but most people find that as long as they understand the concepts taught each term, there is plenty of time in the final term to memorise and recap. For Medicine especially, there are heavy contact hours with lectures or practical classes from Monday to Friday often from 9am to 2pm (with a lunch break) or sometimes later until 5pm This may seem daunting, but compared to other degrees at Cambridge, this can often mean less independent studying is needed and you are given most of the resources needed to pass as handouts or debrief sheets.

In terms of the facilities, most of the lectures are in the same cluster of buildings in the centre of the town. There are many libraries in these buildings, and many in other departments and in your college which you have access to – the total number of libraries in the whole University exceeds one hundred. Some prefer coffee shops, spaces around college, or find their room is the best place for no distractions – it is something you have to try out and see what works best, but there are no shortage of options. Each college library can also have useful textbooks to study from; some people use these religiously but this does not always have to be the case and personally I found that online material and the lecture notes were more than enough for me to get through.

A stand out for me in choosing Cambridge was the level of teaching and the collegiate learning set up. Teaching occurs via lectures and practical classes (including the renowned cadaver dissections in first year) and supervisions with other medics from your college. The number of supervisions varies slightly but mostly it is one per week for each module. These usually require some independent revision of the material, and the completion of an essay or set of multiple-choice questions each week, but most supervisors are very friendly and if you are struggling with this for a particular reason they can work out an arrangement to help. The nature of the course means this work can often be done collaboratively with others if you are struggling, although you should make sure that by the end of the supervision you could do it solo as that is how you would be sitting exams. Academically, what you put in is what you get out so some people enjoy spending lots of time in the library doing extra reading and research to get a 1st whilst others do not find this as exciting. Myself and many others in my college did not work as intensively (until exam term) as some of the anecdotes we had heard before coming to Cambridge and still managed to get 1sts and 2:1s – everyone learns differently and comparing hours spent working can often do more harm than good.

What was the application process like?

The application process can seem very daunting - things like entry requirements are often high (A*A*A was typical in my year) and extra tests like the BMAT can be time-consuming. There is no real way around these, so it's important to put in hard work during Y12/13. For interviews, the key thing to remember is to try and not let shyness or nerves get the better of you and to treat it like a practice supervision and prove that you are teachable and enthusiastic. You are definitely not expected to know every answer, but you are expected to have a go at answering questions and think actively, much like a supervision. In this way, it makes sense to have an interview like this as it lets you see how you would fare in the learning environment you are trying to gain entry to.

PHILOSOPHY, POLITICS, AND ECONOMICS AT OXFORD

This testimonial is by Jake Robinson, who graduated from PPE at Merton College, Oxford in 2019.

What was the admissions process like?

The admissions process has two main stages, the TSA (sat in November) and the interview (in Oxford, usually in the first half of December). For those that are successful the usual offer is AAA. However, in reality, the vast majority of successful applicants are predicted (and go on to achieve) higher grades and therefore it should be seen as a minimum rather than a target. There are no formal A-Level subject requirements but Maths is advised and, in my experience, far more PPEists have Further Maths than don't have Maths. This does of course depend on route within PPE (discussed later), with Economics requiring a higher degree of Maths than Philosophy or Politics. However, logic in philosophy and elements within politics can benefit from a mathematical mindset.

The TSA is the first hurdle to admission. It is used (alongside grades, references etc.) to decide who to invite to interview. The TSA is very time pressured and this can be quite stressful but after a bit of practice it can become relatively stimulating.

The interview is next and consists of several days in Oxford with 2/3 interviews at your chosen college and the possibility of one at an additional college. The length of the stay can make it quite intense but the interviews take up such a small proportion of the time there that it is a good opportunity to explore Oxford a little and interact with other applicants in the same boat (though be careful of other applicants trying to unnerve you). The interviews themselves can be tough but I found the discussion to be stimulating, after the initial nerves had passed, it is unlike being at school and really gives one a sense of what Oxford and degree level education is about.

How is the course structured?

The PPE course is 3 years long and split into two parts.

First comes prelims (first year), in which you study the basics of all three elements of PPE and there are no optional modules.

For prelims Economics there are three elements: Microeconomics and Macroeconomics which cover basic principles in economics, and Mathematical Techniques which, as the name suggests, focuses on making sure every PPEist has the tools to engage in the study of Economics. Microeconomics and Macroeconomics are taught one per term over two terms through tutorials (usually in college) and lectures (university wide) and assessed through one exam at the end of the year. Mathematical techniques is taught alongside the other two modules and not examined specifically.

For philosophy there are three parts: Logic, Moral philosophy, and General philosophy. These are taught through a combination of classes and tutorials (usually in college), as well as university wide lectures. All three topics are then assessed within one exam paper taken at the end of the year. Each part has a specific flavour, general philosophy introduces students to large questions within philosophy such as Free Will, God, or Identity. Moral philosophy, on the other hand, focuses on introductory ethics (primarily JS Mill and Utilitarianism) whereas logic is an introduction to analytic philosophy and the relationship between logical structures, linguistics, and philosophical arguments.

Prelims Politics consists of three parts too. Firstly, there is The Theory of Politics which covers introductory political theory such as the study of liberty, power, and rights. Secondly is The Practice of Politics which covers questions of political science and in particular comparative government. This covers topics such as empirically assessing the strength of states, role of institutions, or democratization. This is complemented by the Political Analysis module which is an introduction to using quantitative methods (through R) to analyse and answer political questions in a statistical manner. Theory and Practice is examined through one exam at the end of the year whereas Analysis is assessed through an essay in the second term.

Throughout prelims, tutorials for Politics and Philosophy normally require weekly essays whereas Economics require a mixture of problem sheets and essays. This work doesn't form part of the grade you receive in prelims (which is made up from the three exams only) but is still important in its own right. In order to pass prelims, one has to pass each of the three exams, however these grades don't count towards the overall degree mark. It is also important to note that while there are no optional modules there is choice within modules (in politics and philosophy) meaning that tutors usually accommodate requests to study particular topics within a module (one doesn't study every topic in a module).

After prelims come finals (second and third year) where there is considerably more choice and specialisation. Over these two years eight modules are studied (two a term in second year). At this point it is possible to drop one subject and become Bipartite or carry on with Philosophy, Politics and economics (Tripartite). As eight modules are studied either way it is more common for students to choose Bipartite in order to specialize more.; however a significant minority do keep all three.

Within the eight modules taken there are core and optional modules. For philosophy one has to take Ethics and then either: Early Modern, Aristotle, Plato, or Knowledge and Reality. These largely lead on from Moral and General Philosophy in first year. Then there is a huge range of optional modules ranging from mathematical formal logic to philosophy and everything in between.

For politics one has to pick two of: Comparative government, Theory of Politics, International relations, Political Sociology, and British Political History since 1900. Outside of these there is a huge range of optional modules split along the divide of Practice and Theory as established in Prelims. Therefore one can study, in depth, the politics of particular countries or regions or study particular thinkers or theories.

Finals Economics doesn't have any specific core modules; however all other modules rely on either Microeconomics or Macroeconomics and therefore in order to select any module one of these has to be taken. Outside of these two a whole range of other modules exists, including development economics, economic history and Welfare economics.

These modules are taught across second and third year, exactly when they are taught depending on various considerations such as when tutors are available, whether other modules have to be taken first etc. All modules are taught in tutorials and classes in a similar manner to first year and are usually held weekly (meaning two tutorials weekly in second year) and each tutorial typically requires an essay. There are also lectures alongside the tutorials. All of the modules are assessed by exam at the end of the third year (no exams in second year!), there is however the option to swap a module for a supervised dissertation. The range and diversity of these topics means they are taught by particular tutors around the university rather than within college as is the case in prelims. This also means that you come into contact with a wider range of academics and students than is the case in First Year.

What is it like to study?

The workload is a double-edged sword for PPE. On one hand it can be tough, most weeks contain two essays alongside lectures and other classes. This can entail a lot of time preparing, reading and writing and at times can be stressful. However unlike some other degrees the structure can be quite freeing, outside of lectures most teaching is on a small scale meaning it can be adjusted to allow time for other activities. Moreover, essays while they require a lot of reading can accommodate flexible working patterns meaning that it is normally possible to find time to do lots of other things.

This means that there is a time to engage in the rich life Oxford has to offer, this can be in the form of sport, music, theatre or one of the millions of societies. Moreover, PPE naturally lends itself to political and debating societies as well as having its own subject society that frequently brings in prominent speakers from across the PPE spectrum.

This freedom in scheduling means it is hard to pin down exactly what a typical day looks like- because people handle it in a range of ways; some work intensely for a shorter time, others are more balanced across the week. However broadly a first-year week would consist of 1-2 lectures per day, followed by independent reading and research in the afternoons producing essay material for that week's tutorials. Evenings and weekends would contain a little more work but also plenty of time for sports and societies as well as socialising with friends inside and out of college.

There are a huge range of facilities for PPEists, as a degree that incorporates three faculties there are several libraries to choose from, as well as the central Bodleian and college libraries too. This means that material, space and resources are always available when you need them.

Overall one of the key strengths of PPE is its diversity. People come with different interests and different expectations, something that is clear to see when one considers the range of careers PPEists go into. This means that you continually come into contact with people who challenge your perspective and way of thinking and therefore have an opportunity to consider and refine your ideas. This is complemented by the range of topics to study and the range of societies and activities that one can take part in alongside wider study.

PSYCHOLOGY AT OXFORD

This testimonial is by Lewis Webb, who is a graduated in Experimental Psychology from St Edmund Hall, Oxford in 2019.

How is the course structured?

The Experimental Psychology course at Oxford is three years long. In the two terms of year one ('prelims'), your time is split between Introduction to Psychology, Introduction to Neurophysiology and Introduction to Probability Theory and Statistics courses. At the end of the second term, you sit 'prelims' exams. These are made up of three written papers which are marked but not officially graded and do not have any impact on your final degree grade. Year two and three are referred to as Final Honours School (FHS) Part 1 and 2, due to them not coinciding with the academic years.

FHS 1 begins in the third term of year one and runs until the end of term two of year two. You study eight psychology modules in these three terms; social psychology, cognitive neuroscience, developmental psychology, language and cognition, perception, behavioural neuroscience, MAIP (memory, attention and information processing) and PIDPD (personality, individual differences and psychological disorders). In addition to these modules, there are also Core Practicals, which are all assessed via coursework and involve using some of the computer programs (e.g. MATLAP and SPSS) that are taught in the FHS 1 statistics lectures. At the end of term two of year two, you sit five written papers. These are made up of four pairs of psychology subjects and one statistics paper. These papers, along with the Core Practicals coursework, makes up 40% of your final grade.

FHS 2 begins in term three of year two and runs until your final exams. During this time, you study either three advanced options or (like me) two advanced options and a library dissertation. In addition to this, there are Block Practicals, tasks (similar to Core Practicals) which are marked as coursework. You are able to select all aspects of this year's work, with options spanning all previously studied topics, but with more focus. With this in mind, it is important to use prelims and FHS 1 to decide which topics and methods of assessment you prefer! You will also complete a research project during FHS 2. This is an independent piece of work encompassing practical application of knowledge, research practice and writing up a paper. These four sections are equally split (15% each) in weight on your final grade, with the Block Practical results being used as a decider if your final score is on a grade boundary.

What is it like to study?

The workload of this course varies hugely based on what time of year it is, and the topics you select in FHS 2. Prelims is a significant step up from A-Levels, and it is important to treat it as such, in order that your grade can reflect your true ability. This is important for signalling any changes that might need to be made for the section. FHS 1 is the most intense time for exams, the volume of content is enormous and, while much of it is not hugely complex, having perfectly managed notes in advance of the exam period is vital to manage the information. FHS 2 is far more independent than FHS 1, with comparatively few lectures (especially if you opt for the library dissertation instead of a third advanced option). I found it more relaxed than FHS 1, particularly as I made headway with my dissertation and research project during the quiet third term of year two. An Experimental Psychologist's third year is somewhat less intense than most other subjects!

Lectures are typically no more than a few hours a day, with lab time (during FHS) in three-hour blocks once a week. This means that it is important to self-structure your days, as only anywhere from 0-6 hours is likely to be structured for you. The regular task throughout prelims and FHS 1 is essay writing for tutorials, these are typically a couple per week. If you keep on top of these, then there is time for involvement in societies and sporting events, especially throughout prelims and the first two terms of FHS 1. Due to the lessened structure during FHS 2, this is the time that many people choose to give over the most commitment to societies and other interests.

The psychology department building is currently undergoing a huge reconstruction project (and was throughout my entire degree!), so should be very well equipped in a few years' time when complete. Despite this, most other department libraries are accessible by students of different subjects, so work spaces are not limited. Access to psychology books is easy through your college library, or through the social sciences library (SSL). The SSL and the law library are some of the more airy and less intense working environments which is great during the slightly less busy periods! Tutors are also easily contactable and most are very helpful when needing assistance outside of tutorials, this can be vital when coming up to exams!

The Oxford Experience

The Experimental Psychology course is a very science-heavy course and, as a result, so is the research of many of the lecturers and tutors. There are many opportunities to discuss and get involved in some of the latest research in a wide variety of topics. Some of the most accessible are in the baby lab for developmental psychology and studies on cognitive neuroscience and perception. There are a wealth of studies by PhD students and post-doctorate researchers that undergraduates can participate in. This is a requirement during prelims, but is something that can be helpful (not to mention financially rewarding) to continue throughout FHS for insights to improve your own research project.

What was the application process like?

The entry requirements for Experimental Psychology are A*AA at A-Level and, typically, eight A*'s at GCSE. The admissions test is the Thinking Skills Assessment (TSA). This exam includes 50 multiple choice questions testing critical thinking and problem-solving skills and a single essay chosen from some options. The questions are varied in content but many have predictable methods of answering them, so it is important to practice some papers before attempting the real thing! The essay question options typically include some topics that are at the forefront of current news, so be up to date on that!

I had three interviews, which is quite typical; two at my allocated college and one at another. They lasted around half an hour each and encompassed philosophical questioning, data interpretation and discussion of wider reading. The former was to assess whether I might be a better fit for the Psychology and Philosophy course, so don't be thrown off if you get called into a philosophy interview! I would recommend having good knowledge of a select few key psychology-related books, rather than a massive repertoire of titles and summaries. This detail is much of the interview focus, so be prepared for some longer discussions, especially around topics that are of interest to the interviewer! The interviewers can be harsh but they are there to push the limits of your thinking abilities, so don't be put off if only one topic is discussed throughout an interview.

PSYCHOLOGY AT CAMBRIDGE

This testimonial is by Lucy Pilling, who is a 2nd year in Psychological and Behavioral Sciences at Jesus College, Cambridge.

How is the course structured?

Psychology at Cambridge is titled Psychological and Behavioural Sciences, a three year degree. This course gives you unique flexibility over what you study, able to choose modules from multiple other degrees. The course is structured the same in first and second year: there are two core modules whereas the other two are optional, choosing from an array of other degrees. In first year the core modules are PBS1 and PBS2. PBS1 is a broad introduction to theoretical and methodological processes in psychology, covering a new interesting topic every week such as; personality, gender, intelligence and emotions. PBS2 covers the basic biology of the brain, statistics and research methods. In second year PBS3 and PBS4 are the core options. PBS3 covers developmental and social psychology in detail whereas PBS4 is a shared module with natural sciences studying neurobiology of the brain. In both years optional modules can primarily be taken from; the Natural Sciences Tripos, Human Social and Political Sciences, Philosophy and then Biological Anthropology. In third year you do a dissertation which is an interesting research project with staff in the department, as well as taking one psychology module from a number of options, and a further two module that may be selected from the psychology department or a similarly broad array of areas as in first and second year. I have taken biological anthropology modules in both first and second year and they are my favourite by far, I plan on taking some in third year as well. The BioAnth course covers really interesting content on how humans evolved and why we may have certain social and intellectual traits based on the ecology of the environments our cultures evolved in. I find it really interesting to consider how this may be seen in the more purely psychology topics we study!

The course is assessed by a 3-hour exam per module at the end of each year, although this can differ slightly for optional modules. Unlike some Universities where grades over multiple years are compounded into a final grade, we are given an overall grade at the end of each year based on that year's exams, meaning that the grade used for employers is usually just your third year grade. Many students see this as an advantage as it means that you have been able to build up a substantial toolkit over your three years at Cambridge by the time you take the exams that contribute to this final grade.

What is it like to study?

The workload is high, however, it is definitely manageable and all the content is very interesting which helps too. Because the optional modules are taken from different courses the workload is quite decentralised meaning it can clump up into busier and quieter periods, lots of planning can help make this a more even spread.

A typical week has 8 hours of lectures, two per module, all before lunch and then 2-4 hours of labs a week for PBS2/PBS4. This is alongside 2-3 supervisions a week which are sessions with an expert in the field in groups of 1-3. Supervisions are the most unique feature of learning at Cambridge, they really help to expand knowledge giving deeper insight and making you consider alternate perspectives, whilst deeply consolidating understanding and allowing you to ask any questions you may have.

For each supervision you are usually required to do further reading and write an essay, this is the bulk of the work you are set but it quickly becomes a very manageable routine. I typically take 2-3 days to read and consolidate lecture notes and then a day to write the essay, however I am known for a rather intense working style of a few stressful days and then a few days off! It is actually really easy to get everything done as long as you plan in advance, and supervisors are always understanding about extensions if your work is too clumped. By consolidating working hours into smart bursts I have loads of spare time to relax with friends, participate in college sports and societies! I play in the college netball team, go to art club, volunteer and take part in marketing or consulting work experience schemes.

There are great facilities all around the city, all colleges have amazing libraries as do departments and the university library is huge and grand, it acquires a copy of every book published in the UK.

For me a typical day usually consists of 1-2 hours of lectures in the morning, I usually try and do an hour or two of work in and around these before returning home for lunch with my friends. I will then likely spend another hour or two working before a supervision in the afternoon. The rest of my afternoon may consist of meeting up with friends or exercising before possibly a little more work. In the evenings I like to cook and relax with a large group of friends. Every day is so busy, but it makes me feel like I am living life to the max!

What was the application process like?

At Cambridge you apply to your course through the colleges, most colleges require A*AA although some require A*A*A. Additionally most colleges may requires maths or biology A level, though this does vary so be sure to look into each college.

Applying to Cambridge can be a daunting prospect but it is very manageable if you prepare well! You of course must write a personal statement, then fill in Cambridge's SAQ which is just further information on your educational experience. For PBS there is a 3-part admission test you sit in November. First there are thinking skills comprehension questions. This is followed by a choice between either a biology and maths multiple choice section or an English multiple choice section. Finally you must write an essay on an obscure title, trying to incorporate psychological knowledge. Practising all of this really helps! Finally if you are successful you will be invited to interview, at my College this consisted of two 20 minute interviews that covered why I wanted to apply for PBS, thought provoking psychology based questions, reactions to data and then questions related more specifically to the books on my personal statement.

Closing words

Hopefully these accounts have been valuable to you while you think about which subjects you'd like to apply for. If you are interested in a subject which hasn't been covered here, contact us through the website at www.uniadmissions.co.uk and we'll be happy to arrange a casual chat with current students on any Oxford or Cambridge course!

Below is our guide to the Oxbridge and Cambridge colleges, which should be your next step when thinking about applying to Oxbridge.

CAMBRIDGE COLLEGES

There are 31 different colleges at Cambridge, which we've arranged in alphabetical order across the following pages.

All of the information here was contributed by current and recent students of these colleges, so it should be all be up to date, with the possible exception of the bar prices! You'll be able to find great detail on all the colleges on their respective websites, in particular the student union sites. Each Cambridge college has two student unions, known as common rooms – there is normally a literal common room, hence the name – one for undergraduate, and one for graduate students. They should both have their own websites, which will provide far more detail than we were able to here.

Our goal was to provide all this information in one place, easily arranged for you to flick through and see which colleges you're interested in learning more about. We'd like to thank all of the following students who helped with these profiles, which were by far the hardest part of the book to write, so thank you to:

Ana Leonescu	Ishan Jain
Arabella Zuckerman	Jemima Becker
Benjamin Remez	Lizzy Cole
Camille Gontarek	Lucy Pilling
Emma Jackson	Riana Patel
Fiona McNally	

Christ's College

Founded: 1505

Famous Alumni: Charles Darwin, John Milton, Sacha Baron Cohen

Undergraduates: ~450   **Postgraduates:** ~170

Accommodation: Student accommodation throughout college. Modern typewriter at the back of the college with cheap rooms for first years, medium priced rooms for third years in third court and expensive sixteenth century rooms in second and first court for scholars.

Bar: Buttery in First court Price of a Pint: £3.00

Chapel & Religion: Christian

College Payment System: Cash

Food: Upper hall- café style (breakfast lunch dinner) or formal hall (dinner 6 times a week)

Formality: Gowns to be worn at formal hall dinners, chapel services and graduation

Grants and Bursaries: Grants for travel, academic endeavours. Bursaries for hardship reasons

Location: Very central. Close to shopping centres, many libraries and science campuses

Politics & Reputation: Known for being very academic, often tops Tompkins table

Sport: Very near to its boat club on the river. Has hockey, netball, football, badminton, rugby, volleyball, cricket, swimming, water polo and more college teams.

Churchill College

Founded: 1958

Famous Alumni: Sir John Stuttard (Former Mayor of London), Bjarne Stroustrup (Inventor of C++), Kari Blackburn (BBC World Service executive)

Undergraduates: ~450   **Postgraduates:** ~280

Accommodation: A variation of rooms, all with a large window seat. En-suites are available. Cowan Court was recently built and has modern style rooms which all have double beds and en-suites for ~£1800. Cheaper rooms are available with a single bed and communal bathroom.

Bar: There is a bar in the buttery with a large range of food and drinks Price of a Pint: £4

Chapel & Religion: There is a chapel at the end of the college grounds. However, as a mainly scientific college, the chapel plays a small role in the college.

College Payment System: There is a direct debit transfer at the end of every term where accommodation and any food bought using your student card (e.g. dinner in hall) is paid for.

Food: Lunch and dinner are served every day in hall. There are usually 2 or 3 vegetarian/vegan options as well as meat options and a salad bar. Students can pay on their student cards. The chefs in the kitchen are happy to listen to food requests from students so that everyone can eat well.

Formality: Churchill is regarded as the least formal college, being the only college where gowns are not required for formal hall. The college also takes the highest proportion of state school students in general.

Grants and Bursaries: There is a new bursary funded by Amazon for female computer scientists at Churchill. There are also music bursaries and bursaries for students from low-income households (less than £42,620 pa). There are also grants for current students for music lessons, playing sports and vacation travel/courses.

Location: It is located Storey's Way, next to Murray Edwards College and Fitzwilliam College. It is a 20-minute walk from town or a 5/10-minute cycle. As it is not as central as other colleges, it is useful to be able to cycle.

Politics & Reputation: Churchill a reputation of being mainly for STEM subjects although humanities students are encouraged to apply. The motto is forward as the college endeavours to be forward thinking.

Sport: Churchill has playing fields on site, unlike many other colleges. There are football pitches, a cricket pitch, a rugby pitch, tennis courts, squash courts and a gym. The football club are in League 1 and were the first college team to retain the League division 1 title. There is also a very successful boat club for rowers.

Clare College

Founded: 1326

Famous Alumni: Kwame Anthony Appiah, Henry Louis Gates Jr., John Rutter, and Sir David Attenborough!

Undergraduates: ~500   **Postgraduates:** ~270

Accommodation: All the first years live in Memorial Court on Queens' Road, which has a variety of rooms at different costs to suit different budgets. After first year, accommodation is allocated by lottery, so each student is allocated a number in the ballot for second year, which is then reversed for third year. Bad room in second year= Good room in third year.

Second years all live in Clare College Colony on Chesterton Lane, which also has a range of room prices to suit different budgets and has the option for students to ballot to live together in friendship groups. This is the same for third year, although some third years are lucky enough to live in Old Court, maybe even overlooking the river.

Bar: Clare has the best bar in Cambridge (probably) in the crypt underneath the chapel, known as Clare Cellars. All the other colleges are jealous of how good it is!

Price of a Pint: £3.20

Chapel & Religion: Clare is also known for its fantastic music society and famous chapel choir!

College Payment System: There is a direct debit transfer at the end of every term where accommodation and any food bought using your student card (e.g. dinner in hall) is paid for.

Food: Clare has come first in many inter-collegiate catering competitions, meaning our formal is excellent and well-priced- Around £7.50 for Clare students. Our buttery is less consistently good, although it can surprise you. Clare has a lot of vegetarian and vegan students, so is good at catering for them, and will cater for other dietary requirements as long as they know in advance. Every student will have access to a gyp room (small kitchen) with a toaster, microwave and two-ring hob- This is better than it sounds! Ovens are a rarity for undergraduates.

Formality: Clare is one of the older colleges, but while some aspects are quite formal, it's a very relaxed vibe. It's not a competitive place academically, so it doesn't feel as intense as some other colleges can.

Location: Clare is right in the centre of town, overlooking the river and the backs. Some of the accommodation is a little further out though, so there is some travel involved.

Sport: There are lots of sports societies to get involved in at college level. This is very relaxed, social and the levels of ability are not as high as the university teams! In particular Clare has a big boat club, so many people give rowing a go, even if the early start in the winter mean that some don't stick with it!

Clare Hall

Founded: 1966

Famous Alumni: Seamus Heaney was a fellow – as a new college, not many yet, but maybe you one day!

Undergraduates: ~0 **Postgraduates:** ~145

Bar: A new bar, the Anthony Lowe building, has just opened, which is very exciting, and an increasingly popular venue for grad student from other colleges. We have a party almost every Saturday in term time.

Price of a Pint: £3.90

Formality: Clare Hall is one of the least formal colleges. There aren't any undergrads, so fellows and student mix freely without high table or gowns. If you didn't know, you'd not be able to tell who was a professor and who a student!

Location: Clare Hall is in West Cambridge, near the University Library, but a good fifteen minutes' walk to the shops in town. The bus does stop right outside though, if you don't fancy cycling!

Sport: Clare Hall boasts a multigym, heated indoor swimming pool – much nicer than the unheated outdoor one at Emmanuel – and tennis court at the West Court site, just a little way down Herschel Road. Sport at Clare Hall has really taken off over the past few years, and now we have very active running, football, cricket, yoga and boat clubs.

Corpus Christi College

Founded: 1352

Famous Alumni: Christopher Marlowe, Robert Greene, Christopher Isherwood, Helen Oyeyemi, and Kevin McCloud

Undergraduates: ~250 **Postgraduates:** ~200

Accommodation: Accommodation in Corpus is really good and living so close to the main college facilities like Hall, the library, the bar and common room is really handy. Buildings vary from very modern and recently renovated to traditional and historic.

First years are grouped together, either on the main college site or on the streets just either side of it, meaning they live not more than two minute walks from college. Second and third years get to choose where they want to live through a ballot system, with an order decided by names drawn from a hat (the order in second year is reversed for third year).

Third years pick their rooms first, normally choosing to live on the main college site in New Court or Old Court (some of the oldest university accommodation in the world!) while second years normally choose to live in buildings slightly further from the main site, but still only eight minutes walk away.

Food: Catered food in Corpus is generally regarded as really good - with Saturday 'brunch' being a particular college favourite. The regular menu manages to be pretty diverse, with four main courses on offer at lunch, and three at dinner - plus various soups, sides and salads. This includes at least one veggie option, and pescatarians normally have a seafood/fish option at lunch too. Other dietary requirements are catered for at Formal Hall (optional twice-weekly, three-course dinners which happen in addition to normal meals), but are not guaranteed normally.

Grants and Bursaries: The college is really financially supportive with rent support, book grants, and support with living costs. The college is one of the richest in Cambridge, considering its size, so will make sure that you don't have to worry about money if you're having difficulties.

Location: Right in the centre of town, opposite the scary clock! Corpus is well hidden away, but it's bigger than it looks on the outside.

Sport: For a small college, Corpus punches above its weight in regards to sports. Lacrosse, netball, rugby, rowing, tennis, football, and frisbee are just a few on offer. Although usually quite successful, these teams really are open to all abilities - as is the annual 'Corpus Challenge', where we go head-to-head with Corpus Christi Oxford in various sports (and we usually win).

Darwin College

Founded: 1958

Famous Alumni: Jane Goodall, Nigel Warburton, Elizabeth Blackburn

Undergraduates: ~0 Postgraduates: ~650

Accommodation: Good, but quite expensive, as the college doesn't subsidise it as much as some of the older colleges, although since we're a grad only college, it's normal for people to live off site.

Formality: Darwin was the first grad only college and is one of the least formal colleges.

Location: Darwin is just over the river, next to the water meadows and the punting station. It is also having its own island, where you can have a BBQ!

Downing College

Founded: 1800

Famous Alumni: John Cleese, Thandie Newton, Michael Winner,

Undergraduates: ~400   **Postgraduates:** ~250

Accommodation: Accommodation at Downing has a reputation for being amazing! For first years, you'll be asked to indicate what price band room you want, and will be allocated a room that way. There are 4 accommodation blocks and 1 staircase in college only for freshers, which is a great way to get to know everyone. Lots of first year rooms have double beds and en-suites!

Second- and third-year accommodation are allocated by a random ballot, which you can enter as a group of friends. You pick your room (either a room in college staircases, or a room in one of the houses on Lensfield Road) according to your order in the ballot. The ballot order is reversed for third year, so if you were last in the ballot in second year, you still get a good pick!

Food: Food at Downing is a highlight! Lots of people go to Hall to eat (people call it 'slops', but this is definitely not a reflection of the quality of the food!), which is a great time to catch up with people over lunch or dinner. Hall does lunch and dinner every weekday, with hot food and a salad bar always available. At the weekends, brunch and dinner are served. At each meal, there is always a vegetarian option available, and sometimes vegan options. The Butterfield Cafe in college serves food for breakfast (croissants, bacon rolls etc.), and also does sandwiches, baguettes, paninis and salads throughout the day. Formal hall (optional) runs 3 times a week, where students and fellows are served a 3 course meal, can bring wine and wearing formal dress and gowns is compulsory. Vegetarian, vegan and nearly all other dietary requirements are always catered for. Formal hall is a great way to wind down or celebrate someone's birthday!

College provides lots of food, but there is also the option to cook in your accommodation. Most Freshers' accommodation has well-equipped kitchens, with hobs, ovens and fridge-freezers, which is unusual for Cambridge. Some of the larger accommodation blocks, as well as the houses on Lensfield Road for second and third years, have large dining tables and much bigger kitchens - perfect for eating together with your housemates.

Location: You could easily walk right past Downing, as it's just a gate off of the main road as you come into town from the train station. We have the biggest open green space though, so it's lovely once you get in and look around!

Sport: Downing has a reputation for being good at sports, with strong teams in nearly every sport. A classic Cambridge sport to get involved in is rowing, but there's everything else from football to frisbee to get involved with.

Emmanuel College

Founded: 1958

Famous Alumni: John Harvard (founder of Harvard University), Jonathan Swift, Richard Attenborough, Lemuel Gulliver (fictionally)

Undergraduates: ~500   **Postgraduates:** ~130

Accommodation: In first year, everyone is allotted rooms in either North Court or South Court. You indicate a preference before arriving - the rooms are all lovely, and are priced according to a grading system (1-8, with 1 being the cheapest and 8 the most expensive). All fresher accommodation is Grade 3-5. In second year, there's a ballot system, and those whose names are drawn first get first pick of rooms. There are options to live out of college. In third year, the ballot gets reversed, so those at the top in second year are at the bottom in third year. Third year rooms are the nicest - notably, there's Old Court, a 17th century building with lots of sets of rooms that you share with a friend. All accommodation in Emmanuel (Emma) is great, there's lots of variety and choice, and everyone always ends up being really happy with where they live! There's also accommodation for grad students in their first year.

Bar: There is a bar in south court, is one of the only student run bars left in Cambridge, and so has some of the cheapest prices as well. There's a twice termly bar extension when it stays open until 2am as well.

Price of a Pint: £2.20

Chapel & Religion: The dean is one of the nicest in Cambridge famous for defying the ban on blessing same sex partnerships nearly twenty years ago! The choir is well regarded and goes on regular tours around Europe and to America.

College Payment System: There is a direct debit transfer at the end of every term where accommodation and any food bought using your student card (e.g. dinner in hall) is paid for. It's paid for as part of your college bill at the end of term, so you never need to worry about running out of credit.

Food: The food in college is usually good. We have a cafeteria which serves a range of hot meals and sandwiches for lunch and dinner with cereals and cooked breakfast every day in the morning. There is always a vegetarian option but it can be a little repetitive. There are vegan sandwiches available but not always a hot option. Most people's favourite meal of the week is Sunday brunch which offers a full cooked breakfast, cereal and some 'lunch-type' hot dishes. Most evenings formal hall takes place at 7.30. This is a three-course meal served in the dining hall which students can book themselves in for, it is popular for events such as birthdays. The food at formal hall is really good and any dietary requirements can be catered for.

Formality: Emma is fairly formal – gowns for formal hall, Latin Grace and a high table. That said, you can walk on almost all of the grass, and there is an outdoor swimming pool, so it's hard to be formal in your swimming costume!

Location: It is located in the centre of town, just opposite the shopping centre. The gates and portico look quite off-putting, so we don't get many tourists, which can be annoying at some of the older colleges.

Fitzwilliam College

Founded: Began in 1869 as a non-collegiate institution, became a college in 1966.

Famous Alumni: David Starkey (Historian and television presenter), Vince Cable (Politician) and Cressida Dick (Commissioner of the Metropolitan Police)

Undergraduates: ~500   **Postgraduates**: ~400

Accommodation: For undergraduates, first years live on the main college site in newly-refurbished modern rooms with showers and washbasins. There are shared kitchen and bathroom facilities. Second, third and fourth years also mainly live on the college site. However, half of second years live in nearby college-owned houses. Undergraduate rents in the 2018-19 year ranged from £108-£169.50 a week. Fitzwilliam is usually able to provide a single room to all postgraduates, on the main site or in college houses. Double rooms and flats are also available but more competitive to get.

Bar: Fitz Bar is open every night and offers a wide range of drinks including the "Fitz Lager". The bar hosts events such as discos (bops) and quizzes during term-time. Price of a Pint: £2.40 - £3.30

Chapel & Religion: The chapel is open to students of all and no faiths. It is also home of the Christian Union and offers a weekly main service during term-time. The chaplain also runs welfare events, such as drinks receptions, walks and cake breaks during term.

College Payment System: You use your CamCard to pay for food and printing. Cash and card can also be used at some facilities. You buy tokens from the Café to use in the laundry facilities. Transactions made on your CamCard, along with college bills, can be paid for by direct debit on an online system.

Food: Fitz provides a lunch and dinner service in the main hall every day. Currently, lunch on a Saturday and Sunday is a full-English breakfast, and dinner on a Tuesday is a special theme-night meal. Optional formal gowned dinners are also served on Wednesdays and Fridays after the main dinner service. The bar turns into a café during the day and offers light snacks such as paninis, sandwiches and cakes.

Formality: Fitz is a modern college, as reflected by its students, architecture, library and gardens, so would be regarded as one of the least formal colleges.

Grants and Bursaries: A full list of bursaries available to Fitz students can be found on the Fitz website. Students are emailed termly about what financial support is available by the college. Prizes are also currently available for students achieving first-class examination grades during their time at Fitz.

Location: Fitz is deemed a 'hill college' due to it being slightly out of town. However, it takes roughly 20 minutes to walk and 10 minutes to cycle to town for lectures, so the distance should not deter you from applying.

Politics & Reputation: Fitz is often regarded as a very friendly college, with students and staff that are welcoming and forward-thinking. Fitz also has an excellent reputation for outreach, which stems from its history of being an institution to allow students who could not afford college membership to access Cambridge. Fitz's motto is "the best of the old and the new", reflecting its modern atmosphere. A Fitz student is called a 'Fitzbilly' in honour of the billy goat that serves as the college mascot.

Sport: Fitz has around 20 sports clubs, with a particularly successful football and cricket team. The college site has a gym free to college members, squash and badminton courts, and currently runs free Yoga sessions for students.

Girton College

Founded: 1869

Famous Alumni: Dina bint 'Abdu'l-Hamid; Margrethe II, of Denmark; Hisako, Princess Takamado; Sandi Toksvig; Arianna Huffington; Karen Spärck Jones; Rachel Lomax; Mary Arden; Gwyneth Lewis; Brenda Hale, Baroness Hale of Richmond; Bertha Swirles

Undergraduates: ~500   **Postgraduates:** ~220

Accommodation: The college can accommodate all students for all their years of study, and there are standard and en-suite rooms. There is a choice of rooms in the main College building, Ash Court, Swirles Court or in a College-owned house, including Family Accommodation. Rent: £172.50 per week (standard room); £180.50 per week (en-suite room)

Bar: Both the Social Hub and Bar are available for socialising and events

Price of a Pint: £2.20

Chapel & Religion: The Chapel is a community and a haven for all College members, playing an important and diverse role in College life – for those of all faiths and of none

College Payment System: The college bill is paid at the beginning of each term. Our college student card is used for purchasing food and drinks from the Cafeteria and Social Hub, and the amount is then added to the college bill.

Food: Breakfast, lunch and dinner are available in the Cafeteria Mon-Fri, as well as brunch and dinner at the weekends, at reasonable prices. There is a variety of options, including meat, fish and veg options every day. Snacks are also available both in the Cafeteria and Social Hub. Girton students can also get food for student price at some town colleges (Downing and Robinson), for those whose departments are central.

Formality: In general, pretty chilled. Gowns are required at formal hall though, and you're not allowed in the dining hall in your pyjamas!

Grants and Bursaries: Bursaries and hardship funds are available to eligible individuals. Girton has a fund to make small contributions to academic-related expenses. You must be an Undergraduate or Clinical Medic or Vet at the time of the expenditure to be eligible to apply. The College has a fund to make small contributions to sport-related expenses. Girton gives 35-40 Travel Awards each year to its undergraduate students. Graduate scholarships and studentships are available for post-graduate students who put Girton as their first or second choice.

Location: Girton has the reputation of being the far-away college in Cambridge. Girton village is technically separate from Cambridge. Cambridge is a small city though, so Girton is only 15-20 minutes cycling to the centre of town!

Politics & Reputation: As the first college in Cambridge that would admit women, the college takes pride in its founding values of inclusion, equality and diversity.

Sport: Girton's main site has the best on-site sports facilities of any Cambridge college. There are full-size well-maintained football, rugby, and cricket pitches. Hard courts for basketball, netball and tennis are also available. Inside, there is a squash court and multi-gym equipped with free weights and a range of other equipment. Girton is the only college to have its own heated indoor swimming pool. There is a great variety of college sports clubs and teams, for all abilities!

Gonville and Caius College

Founded: 1348

Famous Alumni: William Harvey, Stephen Hawking, Francis Crick & James Watson, James Chadwick, Howard Florey

Undergraduates: ~500   **Postgraduates:** ~250

Accommodation: One of the best in Cambridge for undergraduates. First years live in the Stephen Hawking Building or Harvey Court which are newly refurbished buildings with gyms, table tennis tables and common rooms. Most people will live in college in their third year which is centrally located, full of character and generally quite spacious. The huge downside is that the college operates a 'no-hobs' policy which severely restricts the variety of food that you can cook. The kitchens will still have microwaves, kettles and George Foreman grills though.

Bar: Run by college staff and located in the heart of college below the hall. This is a great place to relax after a formal dinner and unwind with friends.

Price of a Pint: Around £2.50

Chapel & Religion: Caius is a tradition-filled college. The college chapel choir has performed live on national radio and is very competitive to get into. Caius is one of the colleges to allow students/alumni to get married in college which always makes for a great wedding setting.

Food: Very hit and miss. Caius has a reputation for serving poor food but this has dramatically improved of late. Formal hall takes place six nights per week where students are required to wear gowns, Grace is read out loud and a three-course silver-service dinner follows. Normally, most students don't dress 'formally' as it happens so frequently. You can also attend an informal hall every night (no Grace, identical food and service). You reserve the halls through an online portal and each meal costs around £7. Unfortunately, you are forced to buy 40+ tickets every term (and are charged for this, even if you don't attend hall). As a result of this, and the lack of hobs, most students attend hall at least five times per week.

Formality: Caius is immersed in tradition. Students must obtain 'terminal exeats' before leaving college for holidays and Grace is said before every formal hall as examples.

Grants and Bursaries: Caius is one of the wealthiest colleges in Cambridge and has lots of grants available for students. There are many travel grants available (up to £2000) as well as a books grant (£50 per year). Students from a disadvantaged background are also entitled to further bursaries.

Location: Centrally located and a short 3-minute walk to the Sainsbury's where students spend a large portion of their shopping time. It's a 5-10 minute cycle to pretty much every lecture hall, lab or sports facility.

Politics & Reputation: Caius is renowned for being the best place to study medicine in the world and has very strong medical roots with William Harvey (circulatory system) as well as Waston & Crick (DNA). The college accepts the most medical applicants out of any Oxbridge college and students are provided with top-tier teaching. Many of the supervisors are senior examiners and run their own labs which provide research-keen scientists a perfect stepping stone to academia. The college library is also one of the best in the university.

Sport: Very strongly funded rowing club – the boat club gets a huge proportion of the student budget and hence has top-tier equipment including Olympic level boats! As Caius is a large college, most sports are well represented including badminton, football, table tennis, rugby. It's a safe bet that there will be a society for you to join here.

Fun Fact: It's pronounced Gonville and 'Keys' – don't say 'Kai-us', the taxi drivers won't know where you mean!

Homerton College

Founded: 1768 and became a full College of the University in 2010

Famous Alumni: Olivia Coleman, Nick Hancock, Leah Manning, Sam Yates

Undergraduates: ~600   **Postgraduates:** ~800

Accommodation: Homerton College has several different accommodation blocks and the majority of the rooms are en-suite. In first year everyone is guaranteed an en-suite bedroom. The accommodation is very reasonably priced and is one of the cheapest amongst the Cambridge Colleges. Each accommodation block also has several gyps (little kitchens), usually shared between 8 or 9 people. Each gyp has a fridge, hobs, a microwave, a kettle and a sink and everyone has their own cupboard. Every undergraduate student is guaranteed accommodation in college for all years of their undergraduate degree.

Bar: Homerton is lucky to have two different bars. One is called The Griff and functions only as a bar and the other is the College Buttery which also doubles up as a bar in the evenings. Both are very good places to socialise. Price of a Pint: £2-3

Chapel & Religion: Homerton doesn't have a College Chapel however there is a Prayer Room which students can use.

College Payment System: The College uses a system called 'UPAY' and each student uses their CamCard (University ID) to pay for their food. You can also use a bank card to pay for food but the CamCard gives students a discounted price.

Food: The College offers breakfast, lunch and dinner from Monday to Friday and runs brunch on the weekend. The food is very reasonably priced and caters for vegetarians and vegans. There are normally 3 or 4 main meal options and 3 or 4 options for sides as well as a salad bar. The College also has a Buttery (café) where students can buy sandwiches, salads, cakes, snacks, hot drinks and smoothies.

Formality: The College hosts a formal dinner (known as 'Formal Hall') once a week on a Tuesday evening where dinner is served by candlelight with wine. Grace is sung by the choir before each formal. Gowns are optional at Homerton formals. There are several themed formals throughout the year including Harry Potter and the Mad Hatter's Tea Party.

Grants and Bursaries: While Cambridge offers various bursaries as a University, Homerton also offers hardship support as a College to those with particular needs. There are Hardship Grants, Vacation Study Grants (for those who wish to remain in Cambridge during the holidays), an Internship Scholarship, other funds for unexpected hardships, small grants for Academic Projects, the Pilkington Travel Award and also Language Centre reimbursement for those who wish to learn or keep up a language alongside their degree. More details can be found on the College website. (www.homerton.cam.ac.uk)

Location: Homerton is a little further out from the centre of Cambridge and is located between Cambridge Train Station and Addenbrooke's Hospital. There are regular buses which run into town at £1 for a single and it takes around 10-15 minutes to cycle into town or to Sidgwick Site.

Politics & Reputation: Homerton College has a great reputation amongst the Cambridge Colleges and was voted 'Cambridge's Friendliest College'. It is known for being a caring and fun College which prides itself on its student community.

Sport: Homerton is heavily invested in its sport and offers a wide variety from rowing, to football and even ultimate frisbee! Each student can choose how much time they wish to invest in sport. The Boat Club (HCBC) is a big part of the College and offers an opportunity for anyone to give rowing a try. Students can ask to set up new college teams if a sport they want to do isn't already offered by the College and funding is available to set up new clubs.

Hughes Hall

Founded: 1885

Famous Alumni: Annette Brooke, Tom Ransley, Alan Leong

Undergraduates: ~150   **Postgraduates:** ~710

Accommodation: The accommodation at Hughes Hall is varied in age and location. The PGCE students (student teachers) tend to live onsite in the original building, which is very charming, but space is somewhat limited in the rooms themselves. The kitchens, however, are pretty big and contain all the modern amenities. These rooms are also conveniently located close to the library and student-run bar (more on this below).

The Fenner's building, on the other hand, was built relatively recently and is also located on the main college site. It's modern and spacious and tends to be where MBAs, post-doc medics, and undergraduates live. It's in a great location with the dining hall below and cricket pitch next door.

Over the last five years, Hughes Hall has also opened a new building on the other side of the cricket grounds, which has brand spanking new rooms and amenities. It's a short 5-minute walk from the main college site.

Bar: Also renovated within the last 10 years, Hughes Hall's bar is a favourite among students. Located in the original college building, it's small, student-run and very popular on both weekdays and weekends. The MCR (student run college committee) regularly holds themed bops (parties) here on Friday and Saturday nights. The rest of the time, you'll often find people hanging out, playing an informal foosball game and enjoying a pint with friends.

Chapel & Religion: Hughes Hall doesn't have its own chapel. Instead, students can use the one at Emmanuel College, which is about a 10-minute walk or 5-minute bike ride away. Hughes Hall does, however, have its own prayer room.

Food: The food at Hughes Hall varies in quality but tends to be good, especially at formal hall. Brunch on Saturdays and Sundays is also super popular. The kitchens are well kitted out, so if you do want to cook for yourself, you have ample opportunity to do so.

Formality: Hughes Hall is very casual and friendly! No need to stand on parade here.

Grants and Bursaries: Financial aid is available for some subjects, but these are very specific and limited in number.

Location: Hughes Hall is located away from the hustle and bustle of town, but within walking or biking distance. Its location is great if you're athletically inclined; Hughes Hall is situated right behind the sports centre and cricket pitch. It's also fantastic if you love trying new foods and supporting local businesses; Hughes Hall is just off Mill Road, which is a melting pot of cool independent shops and restaurants. Finally, if you fancy going on an adventure, the train station is close by; around a 10-minute bike ride away.

Politics & Reputation: Politics doesn't play too big a role in Hughes Hall, but if you're interested in political discussion, you're bound to find someone else willing to listen and debate with. Hughes Hall is one of several 'mature colleges', which means students are all over the age of 21. It's also well-known for its large number of sportsmen and women...

Sport: Sports are big at Hughes Hall; whether competitive or for fun. We usually have one or two men in the Cambridge boat race each year. We also have an abundance of rugby players, football players, dancers, badminton players...you name it, we play it!

Jesus College

Founded: 1496, on the site of the twelfth-century Benedictine nunnery of St Mary and St Radegund by John Alcock

Famous Alumni: Thomas Cramner, Samuel Taylor, Tobias Rustat, John Worthington Laurence Sterne, Thomas Robert, Malthus Samuel, Taylor Coleridge, Sir John Sutton, Henry Arthur Morgan, Sir Alan Cottrell, Jacob Bronowski, Lisa Jardine

Undergraduates: ~450   **Postgraduates:** ~400

Accommodation: Accommodation at Jesus is really good, College owned rooms are available all years of your study. Whilst many colleges have colonies of accommodation further afield from the central site, Jesus owns the houses on the surrounding streets, so you are always very near the heart of the college. First year accommodation is all en-suite and in the main college. In second and third year you can choose where to live, either within college again, with en-suite options, or in the houses that have more privacy. All accommodation has been recently renovated and has large well-furbished kitchens which is unusual and there are full sports fields onsite which is rare particularly for a central college.

Bar: JBar is a modern bar, often rated as the best in Cambridge with a great selection of drinks and lots of cosy sitting places, in the day it transforms into the Roost Café. Price of a Pint: £2.97

Chapel & Religion: The Chapel was completed in 1245 and is the oldest chapel in Cambridge. There are daily morning prayer services and two Sunday services followed either by free breakfast or in the evening complementary drinks. There is Choral evensong three times a week also followed by drinks. The Chaplin is heavily involved in college life both on a tutorial level and through creating a full term card of events and interesting talks. The chapel is also used for other college events such as Blues and Chill, a few times a term the very talented college cohort puts on a concert which is great to go to and simply relax on a beanbag.

College Payment System: Accommodation fees can be paid through the college website by bank transfer or alternate methods can be inquired about. In college your student card can be topped up online and used to pay for meals in the dining room, and food and drinks in the café and bar.

Food: College food is of a very high standard and served within the main formal hall so always a beautiful experience. There are multiple options at lunch and dinner everyday, including vegetarian and vegan options as well as a salad bar and cold sandwich selection. Every Saturday and Sunday college brunch replaces lunch and is absolutely delicious and great to go to with friends. The prices are low around £2-4 for a main and sides however the kitchen fixed charge is very high. During exam term there is also daily breakfast. All accommodation also has access to well equipped kitchens so you can cook for yourself.

Formality: There are many fun formal events constantly happening at College. Formals happen five times a week, a delicious 3-course meal is served followed by coffee and chocolates, you can bring you own bottle of drink and it only costs £7.80 very cheap for a formal. There are also breakfasts with the master if you are involved in some college sports occasionally, yearly subject dinners and more frequent subject drinks which are all complementary.

Grants and Bursaries: Jesus offers a variety of generous travel grants and scholarships for involvement in sports. Bursaries are also available.

Location: The college is situated fairly centrally, around a 5 minute walk from Sainsburys and the centre of town, whilst not being on the main row of colleges on Trumpington street which can be overrun by Tourists.

Politics & Reputation: Jesus is known as a big friendly college due to all the grounds as well as sporty with onsite sports facilities.

Sport: Jesus is a very sporty college, unusual in having all sports fields on site including; lacrosse pitch, 3 tennis/netball courts, a rugby pitch, football pitch and a squash court. The on-site sports fields means it is easy to participate and therefore more people do, a great atmosphere. The college gym is also very well equipped and ran with both cardio and weights room and is free of charge.

King's College

Founded: 1441

Famous Alumni: Rupert Brooke, John Maynard Keynes, Alan Turing, Zadie Smith

Undergraduates: ~400   **Postgraduates:** ~250

Accommodation: There is a range from modern rooms in hostels in the city centre, to older rooms in college. You will have a choice between en-suite or shared bathroom, or a set – a bedroom plus a dining room/sitting room. Many rooms in college boast a beautiful view across the river, while others give a view across the town. Unlike some other colleges, at King's the room ballot is not based on your grades.

Food: The food at King's is quite good. Breakfast ranges from everything from a full English to yogurt and fruit so even with allergies or dietary requirements there is definitely something available for all. For lunch there are four options of meals with a vegetarian and/or vegan meal always included and for dinner there is an option of three meals with at least one vegetarian or vegan dish. Allergy information is always listed and we are sent a preview of the meal in advance each week. Formals once a week are a big deal at King's, particularly because the food is absolutely delicious! Additionally, students are free to join the catering committee to discuss potential changes to the menu if they so desire.

Bar: Medium costs, friendly bartenders, with a lovely range of drinks. Students will also have access to a college wine cellar.

Price of a Pint: £2.50

Chapel & Religion: A beautiful and well-known chapel, with a kind and empathetic chaplain who is a source of pastoral care irrespective of your faith. The chapel is C of E, but is open to all – there are frequent inter-faith discussion groups hosted by the chaplain, on topics from body image in religious text to punk rock.

College Payment System: Pay termly for rent, if you wish to eat in the dining hall you can scan your college card to pay for food – this is billed at the end of term.

Food: All accommodation has shared kitchens, but you will also have access to eat casually in the historic dining hall for breakfast, lunch, and dinner (if you want) – as well as formal dinners.

Formality: Informal – King's strikes a balance between retaining the tradition of a Cambridge college whilst rejecting some of the most elitist aspects of the institution.

Grants and Bursaries: Generous bursaries are available, as well as a travel grant that all undergraduates are entitled to. Additionally there are funds and prizes for research and essay writing available throughout the year.

Location: In the centre of Cambridge, near to most things.

Politics & Reputation: Very liberal reputation, we have active and vocal societies for politics, feminism, worker's rights, LGBTQ+, the environment and more! In addition there is extensive welfare provision and support in King's. Until recently, there was even a communist flag in the bar (it may yet return)!

Sport: There are many college sports teams that you can join, including (but not limited to): Football, lacrosse, hockey, canoe + kayaking, mountaineering, and rugby.

Lucy Cavendish College

Founded: 1965

Famous Alumni: Noeleen Heyzer, Rosena Allin-Khan MP

Undergraduates: ~150   **Postgraduates:** ~200

Accommodation: Accommodation is offered for all students, for every year of your degree, and there's a choice of en-suite, sets (bedrooms plus living room) shared between 2 people, houses, or flats for families and couples. Every year there's a room ballot for continuing students to choose their room, and it's not based on results but is organised into 'Tiers' depending on your year and course of study. Since we're a modern college you don't get so much of the plumbing and heating problems that come with living in old buildings!

Food: The kitchens are great – I thought all colleges had hobs, ovens and freezers but apparently it's a luxury!? (I didn't even realise this until I talked to friends from different colleges). I feel really lucky to be able to de-stress via cooking whenever I like. The food in hall is great too. They have great veggie options like Mac 'n' Cheese (with sundried tomatoes and spinach! Mmmm!), and the potatoes and soup and salad bar are awesome. The kitchen staff are also lovely!

Formality: Lucy is very casual and relaxed.

Location: Lucy Cavendish is one of the newer colleges, so it's out of the centre of town, which can be frustrating to get places, but does keep the tourist away. Being all over 21 as well, we like to think that we're mature enough to cope with a short cycle ride!

Magdalene College

Founded: 1428

Famous Alumni: Samuel Pepys, Monty Don, Stella Creasy

Undergraduates: ~340   **Postgraduates:** ~230

Accommodation: The rooms in Magdalene are a mixture of bedsits and sets (i.e. separate bedroom from living/working area) with some en-suites. The rooms are divided into price bands, from 1* to 5. The vast majority of the rooms will have a sink (unless it's an en-suite) and a mini-fridge. Some of the undergraduates live in "The Village"; a collection of buildings just across the road from the Porters' Lodge. All of Magdalene's accommodation is very close together (a maximum of three minutes walk from the main college site) which helps to create a close, community feel. Magdalene guarantees accommodation for three or four years, dependent on the course. In subsequent years, rooms are chosen by a ballot. Half way through the year, the names of students are drawn in a random order, and rooms are picked according to that order. For third year rooms, this ballot order is reversed. It is possible to ballot alone, or in a group of up to eight people.

Food: Pretty good! Every day hot and cold meals are served in Ramsay dining hall at breakfast, lunch and dinner, for very reasonable prices. There are always three or so options, which cover dietary requirements such as vegetarian or vegan, but the best thing about Ramsay is the chance to catch up with friends over a meal. This is especially true at weekends, when the very popular 'brunch' is served. Everyone also has access to small communal kitchens near their rooms, and many students enjoy cooking for themselves. Formal Hall at Magdalene is the chance to have a delicious three course meal in the candlelit 16th century hall, for only £6.50 currently! A real treat, offered every night, though people mainly go to celebrate birthdays.

Location: Minutes from the centre of town, and right by the river, with punts for free hire. One of the best in Cambridge.

Murray Edwards College

Founded: 1885

Famous Alumni: Annette Brooke, Tom Ransley, Alan Leong

Undergraduates: ~150   **Postgraduates:** ~710

Accommodation: The first years are all in the same block so it is really easy to get to know all the fellow freshers. The rooms in this block are really nice, all of them have an en-suite and my room even has a balcony! After your first year, you're put in a random room ballot which is flipped the next year so it is fair for everyone. There are a range of options available, including some college owned houses that have their own gardens.

Chapel & Religion: Murray Edwards doesn't have its own chapel. Instead, students can use the one at Churchill College, which is about a 10-minute walk or 5-minute bike ride away.

Food: At Murray Edwards you have the choice to go to fabulous looking Dome for food or cook something up in the kitchens available in accommodation - meals are paid for individually rather than in a lump sum per term, which gives you the flexibility to choose to cook as much or as little as you like. The Dome food is delicious - there is always a meat, fish and vegetarian option and there are themed days through the week: for example roast dinner on Sundays, world foods on Thursday and the university-famous College Brunch on Saturday mornings, voted Cambridge's favourite brunch in a survey by The Cambridge Student newspaper.

Formality: Very welcoming and relaxed. We're encouraged to "hop, skip, and jump" on the lawns, which is very unusual for Cambridge!

Location: Castle Hill, a five minute cycle from the town centre.

Newnham College

Founded: 1871

Famous Alumni: Dame Emma Thompson, Diane Abbott, Clare Balding, various politicians, writers, professors and actresses

Undergraduates: ~400   **Postgraduates:** ~150

Accommodation: There's a brand new accommodation block called Dorothy Garrod, which have many modern double and en-suite rooms. Accommodation overall is very highly rated at Newnham, with no ugly accommodation – whatever year you are in, you will have a room with more than enough space. They are very good at providing for disabilities and other access requirements. All students will live in college all the time, with all accommodation blocks having access to a kitchen with a hob and an oven, which is not the case at most colleges!

Bar: The bar functions as the Iris Café during the day, which is very modern and popular with all students across Cambridge. The café is run by external staff, providing snacks, pastries and hot drinks like any other café. As a student run bar, it is not as popular, unless there is an event on, which happens fairly regularly.

Price of a Pint: ~£2.20

Chapel & Religion: The college itself does not have a chapel (as women's only colleges weren't allowed their own chapels), but it shares Selwyn's chapel – and its choir. The college itself is open to all religions and is in the process of making its own prayer room too. Accommodation requirements are also very generous to people requiring their own en-suites for religious purposes, etc.

College Payment System: College bills are paid every term, including accommodation and kitchen fixed charge, like most colleges. The buttery has its own prepaid system, using your student card – the more money you prepay, the less the kitchen fixed charge is. Separate money can be added for the café.

Food: Eating facilities are separate to the main formal hall, with one meat, one veggie, one vegan and one fish option daily for lunch and dinner. No breakfast is available, but the café is open. Brunch is served on the weekends, like most colleges. Quality of food varies, and costs are about average for a Cambridge college. Formal Hall is once a week, costing £12.50 for students and a bit more for guests, with food quality varying here too. Cooking facilities are pretty good wherever you are in college, so if buttery food isn't up to your taste, you can definitely get by cooking all of your meals!

Formality: Newnham is a very friendly and relaxed college, compared to most colleges. The staff are all very approachable. All grass can be walked upon, which is a rarity at Cambridge!

Grants and Bursaries: Many grants and bursaries are available for those who are eligible. The college offers many opportunity funds for travelling. The JCR offers a Clubs and Societies grant, as well as a Sports persons grant, along with a gender expression fund that's been set up this year!

Location: It is very convenient for Humanities students, as it is just across from Sidgwick Site, and is just a 10 minute walk from the town centre as well as STEM lecture sites. There is a small Co-op 5 minutes away too.

Politics & Reputation: Newnham is very liberal and open-minded in general, so everyone will feel comfortable here, no matter what political background you are from. Newnham's reputation mainly comes from being one of two all female colleges and having a very popular café as well as beautiful gardens!

Sport: Newnham's boat club is one the most highly rated boat clubs in Cambridge, as well as offering other sports, such as hockey (joint with St John's), netball, football, etc. As a big college, it is one of the few colleges with its own sports grounds on site!

Pembroke College

Founded: 1347

Famous Alumni: Ted Hughes, Tom Hiddleston, William Pitt the Younger, Jo Cox MP

Undergraduates: ~440   **Postgraduates:** ~250

Accommodation: All first year undergraduates live in College. Second and third years rooms are allocated via a ballot (in groups of up to four, reversed the following year) and many end in houses further out from college in 2nd year, followed by more central houses in 3rd year. There is a choice of older or more modern rooms, but both types are spacious, with decent rent prices, and have shared bathrooms and kitchens (gyps).

Bar: The café/bar is linked to our JP (common room), which has a friendly, relaxed feel with pool, foosball, sofas and a TV room. During the daytime, students can work in the café, and in the evenings the JP is a space for socialising and gathering pre- and post- formals. It also hosts the bi-termly bops, which are a massive hit, with most students in attendance!

Price of a Pint: £3.20

Chapel & Religion: Pembroke has a gorgeous chapel and choir, who sing two services a week, go on regular tours, produce recordings and enjoy free singing lessons and weekly formals.

College Payment System: There are termly college bills- you pay rent (9 week licence) and kitchen fixed charge in advance of the term. Hall meals are put onto your student card, and you can top this up and track your expenses via an app/website. You can go down to -£100, which eventually ends up on your next college bill.

Food: We really love our food at Pembroke. Breakfast, lunch and dinner are served every weekday in hall with 2 or 3 vegetarian/vegan options as well meat options, a pasta dish and a salad bar. Brunch and dinner are served on the weekends, and the former has a reputation of being the best in Cambridge, although all Pembroke students will tell you that breakfast is actually better, with custom-made pancakes, omelettes and paninis! Don't let the nickname of our servery, 'trough', deceive you- the food is wonderful, which makes up for the lack of ovens in gyps. Formals are £10 for students and truly delicious. Other stand out food-related events include subject dinners, boat club dinners, and Tutor Tea (a termly opportunity to talk pastoral care and enjoy free afternoon tea)!

Formality: Pembroke holds Formal Hall every evening, and it has a fairly sophisticated atmosphere, including gowns. Alternating May Balls and June Events are lavish end of term celebrations, and Pembroke has a reputation for hosting amazing balls at a reasonable price. Overall, the students and staff are still very relaxed and friendly, whilst enjoying formal Oxbridge traditions.

Grants and Bursaries: Pembroke offers a very generous range of grants and financial awards to eligible students, including materials grants, travel grants, sports awards, equipment expenses, and hardships grants and loans. There are also opportunities for paid employment.

Location: Very central- between Downing and New Museums site so very convenient for science students- a 30 second hop to lectures from bed! Around a 5 minute cycle to Sidgwick site and the UL. Everywhere is very manageable by foot from Pembroke – including the station, and importantly, the clubs!

Politics & Reputation: There are people from all backgrounds who hold a wide range of political views, but the atmosphere is very open and non-judgemental, so you get to experience lots of interesting discussions. Our reputation revolves around good food, beautiful buildings, a convenient location and friendly people.

Sport: Pembroke has many sports clubs, from Netball to Hockey to Squash, with practices usually taking place in the Pembroke sports grounds a short cycle away. Both men's and women's football have been particularly successful in intercollege leagues in recent years. There is also a gym in College, and opportunities for leisurely sports such as Yoga and Zumba. Pembroke College Boat Club is also very successful and has held many headships in May Bumps, yet is very welcoming to all students and always proves popular with novice freshers!

Peterhouse

Founded: 1284 (oldest Cambridge college!)

Famous Alumni: Lord Kelvin; Henry Cavendish; Thomas Campion; Thomas Gray; Sam Mendes; David Mitchell; Colin Greenwood (amongst others)

Undergraduates: ~200   **Postgraduates:** ~116

Accommodation: Peterhouse has amazing accommodation. Practically all of it is on-site and all freshers are housed together in either St Peter's Terrace (SPT) or the William Stone Building (WSB) just a 4 minute walk away from the main college site, creating a really close-knit community. En-suites are available for all three years. Fresher accommodation is randomly allocated, however in the following years students participate in a room ballot. Points are allocated for both academic grades and extra-curriculars – this determines the placing in the ballot. Kitchen facilities are limited in first year (kettle, toaster, microwave) although hobs are available in 2nd/3rd/4th year accommodation.

Bar: The college bar opens at 7pm every day and is a very popular place to go to after Formal Hall or before nights out. It is located next to the JCR in the Whittle Building and therefore is usually bustling with people. Price of a Pint: £2.90

Chapel & Religion: The Peterhouse Chapel is a beautiful candlelit 17th century building and serves as the focus for a welcoming community, open for people from all denominations and none. The Chapel plays an active role in student life with weekly breakfasts, bible studies and various Chapel Suppers, as well as the yearly Chapel retreat. The Chapel Choir is friendly and receives regular visitors due to its very high-quality music.

College Payment System: College bills are paid via a bank transfer. Food and drink is bought through your student card, which at the beginning of term is automatically topped up with a minimum spend requirement of around £100.

Food: All meals are provided in the beautiful 13th century hall and tend to cost around £2-4, and there are always vegetarian/vegan options. Formal Hall occurs daily in Full Term and costs around £6.70 for members of the college. For special occasions the Catering department organises Super-halls, which are very fancy five-course meals.

Formality: Peterhouse has a small but very close community and although the college is the oldest and therefore has a deep sense of tradition the atmosphere amongst students is very relaxed and friendly. In particular the Deer Park in college provides a large green space for students to walk through, which is an appreciated contrast to the more formal courts.

Grants and Bursaries: Peterhouse is incredibly wealthy relative to its small size and students are therefore extremely lucky to be able to apply for or request a variety of loans and grants for reasons including hardship, language learning and travel.

Location: Peterhouse is in an ideal location: in town, however far enough away that we are not swarmed with tourists! There's a corner shop right opposite the college, but otherwise Sainsbury's is about a 10-15 minute walk away.

Politics & Reputation: Peterhouse used to have a reputation for being slightly conservative and traditional, however this is not reflective of the college nowadays in the slightest. The diverse student body comprises people with various backgrounds and interests, which allows for really interesting discussions.

Sport: Sport at Peterhouse is relatively low-key due to its small size, so the environment is perfect for anyone wanting to get involved with sport in a more relaxed way. Most teams don't require training during the week – the real involvement occurs on the weekends when the matches take place. Nevertheless, the college has some fantastic athletes and our Boat Club in particular performs exceptionally well!

Queens' College

Founded: 1448

Famous Alumni: Stephen Fry, Erasmus, Emily Maitlis

Undergraduates: ~500   **Postgraduates:** ~500

Accommodation: A major plus to Queens' is that you are guaranteed good accommodation on college site for all three years if you want it! The vast majority of freshers chose to all live in Cripps court with a choice between en-suite or your own bathroom but across the hall (cheaper). This large building means you can 'gyp-hop' walking through connecting kitchens and visit anyone in your year without leaving the building! Whilst Cripps rooms are not the biggest compared to some in other colleges this is more than made up for the huge social benefits and proximity to buttery the first year accommodation brings.

Rooms for second and third year are based on a random ballot. Most second years chose to go for a 'shared set' in second year which are all in one building. This means that the strong social aspect to Queens' accommodation continues into second year! The third year rooms are not all in one building, rather a few building across the river are designated for third years. Note that these are some of the best in college, in your third year you could find yourself with a shared living room! Bar: The bar functions as the Iris Café during the day, which is very modern and popular with all students across Cambridge. The café is run by external staff, providing snacks, pastries and hot drinks like any other café. As a student run bar it is not as popular, unless there is an event on, which happens fairly regularly.

Food: Queens' offers facilities for students to be self-catered or catered as they choose. In all three years small kitchens are located on each landing with basic cooking facilities; including a hob, microwave, toaster and fridges, although admittedly there are no ovens or freezers which can make cooking larger meals difficult. Nonetheless, the college dining hall (often referred to as buttery), provides breakfast, lunch and dinner and is generally high quality. The price of an evening meal currently averages at around £3.50, and the famous Queens' brunch on the weekend is a particular highlight, with 8 items for just £2.50, everyone loves brunch! Formal hall is a special addition to college dining, this is a served, three-course meal which students attend to celebrate events such as birthdays, and currently costs £9. It's also pretty exciting as you get to wear your gown and feel as though you're in Harry Potter. In all aspects of catering the college is attentive to dietary requirements, and provides options for vegetarians and kosher/halal etc.

Formality: The thing that struck me when I first came to Queens' is just how laid-back and welcoming everyone is here. When you arrive in Freshers' Week, you'll be given college "parents", two second-year students who will help you and about four other freshers, your "siblings", find your way around. You'll do lots of things together as a college family in the first few days, like punting, afternoon tea and a tour of Cambridge full of useful tips, and having some friendly faces there right from the start makes it so much more enjoyable.

You have the freedom and support to pursue any of your interests, no matter how quirky, and I've met some fascinating people. It may be one of the oldest colleges, but Queens' is far from stuffy or traditional.!

Location: Siting on both sides of the river, Queens' is one of the .most central and prettiest colleges. It is also features the mathematical bridge, which according to legend was built by Newton, without any nails, and is held together by maths alone!

Sport: Most popular sports and clubs are organised on an inter-college basis so there is at least one competitive team at Queens' for rugby, football, rowing, netball, hockey, lacrosse, tennis etc. Sport is also played at a more informal, less competitive level, where everyone enjoys participating. Queens' also have their own squash courts available for use at any time.

Robinson College

Founded: 1977

Famous Alumni: Nick Clegg (politician), Robert Webb (comedian, actor), Konnie Huq (Blue Peter presenter) – we are a fairly new college!

Undergraduates: ~400   **Postgraduates:** ~160

Accommodation: There are four tiers of room-value, (£1380 per term) standard (£1680), standard plus (£1845, with an en-suite), best (£2075, large with an en-suite). Although a little pricier than other colleges, there are no fixed kitchen fees nor charges for utilities. Accommodation is one of Robinson's strongest points as the rooms for each tier are mostly the same style with the same amenities, unlike other colleges where you pay the same price for drastically different rooms. There are also enough rooms for you to stay on site for all three or four years of your degree. In comparison, some other colleges only have enough rooms centrally for the first year, such that in other years you are spread out around Cambridge in houses owned by the colleges, and these can be up to a 20-minute walk away from the central site. At Robinson all rooms are also close to each other, so you are never more than a 5-minute walk away from your friends. For people in second year and above, you can opt to live in houses owned by Robinson at the back of the college, a 5-minute walk away, which are less campus-like and more homely. Finally, rooms are allocated through a randomly allocated system where you can ballot with friends, unlike some other colleges that allocate based on academic performance. Each room shares a kitchen with 4 or 5 people that are fully equipped, although most do not have ovens.

Bar: The bar is called the 'Red Brick Café Bar'. Hot bar food is served every day, with paninis, pizzas, sandwiches and snacks on the roll. They also sell common amenities such as toothpaste. A great range of hot drinks are also available. Alcoholic drinks are available until late in the bar. The bar also has a pool table and regular quizzes and karaoke are held here, run by the bar manager.

Price of a Pint: ~£1.90, one of the cheapest college bars in Cambridge.

Chapel & Religion: There is a modern chapel with a beautiful stain glass window. The Chapel also houses a world renowned Frobenius organ, a harpsichord by David Rubio and a Steinway piano. There is a flourishing orchestra and music society that make good use of this stunning chapel.

College Payment System: EPOS (electronic point of sale) – with your university card.

Food: The catering facilities are another of Robinson's strongest points. There is amazing food, in price, range, taste, and quantity. Vegetarian and vegan options are always available. It is reasonably priced and as there is no fixed kitchen charge you can choose to come and go as you please. Brunch is also served every Saturday and Sunday, but unlike most other colleges, lunch is also served alongside the English fry-up. We also have bi-weekly formals that are slightly more expensive than some other colleges but serve a spectacular three course meal. The setting may have less grandeur, but it is well worth it for the food. The portions, as always, are very hearty. Plus, there are no corkage fees, which many colleges enforce.

Formality: Robinson is an incredibly friendly and relaxed college, with the staff and students helping to create this warm atmosphere. The staff are very receptive to student input thus we have one of the most active JCRs in Cambridge. Robinson also maintains a beautiful garden and all grass can be walked upon. There is also a croquet lawn open in the summer.

Grants and Bursaries: There are some fantastic grants available, such as for summer research and sport, and prizes for succeeding in academics in addition to bursaries for those that financially qualify. However, Robinson is one of the newest colleges so does not have innumerable wealth such as Trinity, so the range of funds is more limited.

Location: Robinson is slightly outside of town, being only a 10-minute walk or 5-minute cycle into the centre. It is however right next door to the university library, sports centre, and humanities lecture site (Sidgwick Site). Is also well placed to access the mathematics department and veterinary department. The location also means it is luckily not disturbed by tourists.

Politics & Reputation: Robinson is one of the most open-minded and liberal colleges. It is best known for having good food, a tight knit community, being incredibly homely and LGBTQ+ friendly. Our nickname is the 'red brick college' because we do indeed have many red bricks, which to some adds to the warm nature.

Sport: We have a college club for most sports, including netball, hockey, lacrosse, rowing, ultimate frisbee, tennis, badminton, croquet, rugby, and football. We are also right next to the University Sports Centre, and have our own netball pitches a 10-minute cycle away.

Selwyn College

Founded: 1882

Famous Alumni: Hugh Laurie, Robert Harris, Wes Streeting

Undergraduates: ~380   **Postgraduates:** ~260

Accommodation: All first-year rooms are en-suite. About half of other rooms are en-suite. There is a wide range of rental brackets based on the size of your room, but all the rooms are of a high quality and are well-maintained.

Bar: gorgeous, recently renovated bar with a wide range of both standard and premium drinks Price of a Pint: £3.50

Chapel & Religion: Beautiful chapel, Anglican.

College Payment System: Pay-as-you-go food and drink in the cafeteria.

Food: Food is good and largely affordable.

Formality: Relaxed – some traditions are upheld (e.g. wearing gowns to formal events), but in general not at all stuffy (e.g. can walk on most lawns).

Grants and Bursaries: Wide variety of grants and bursaries available.

Location: Edge of town centre. 1 min away from Sidgwick site (location of most humanities faculties), 2 min away from University Library, short walk or cycle to most other faculties.

Politics & Reputation: Politics: liberal and left-wing slant, reputation: very friendly and welcoming.

Sport: Active rowing club, active rugby club (located next to the University's rugby stadium).

Sidney Sussex College

Founded: 1596

Famous Alumni: Oliver Cromwell (English civil war), Carol Vorderman (TV), Andrew Smyth (GBBO 2016) and suggested to be the fictional college of Sherlock Holmes

Undergraduates: ~350 (total)   **Postgraduates:** ~200 (total)

Accommodation: College-owned accommodation provided for all undergraduates throughout their undergraduate degrees. Vast majority of accommodation is on the central college site with a small block of freshers' accommodation 2 minutes down the road and a couple of houses/hostels that you can choose to live in during 2nd/3rd year if you wish. Essentially at Sidney if you want to live in the centre of town, you'll be able to the entire time. As all of the accommodation is on site, you'll be able to keep using college hall (for food), gym and bar throughout your degree. The rent at Sidney is amongst the cheapest with the average room at about £130 a week (going up with inflation). Most second years get en-suite rooms and third years can choose en-suite rooms too. In first year, your room is randomly allocated with other first years, in second and third year you choose it based on a randomly generated choosing order (no academic ballot – where your room depends on your grades).

Bar: The place most students, most evenings, will come to relax and socialise, whether they drink or not. Being one of the few fully student-run bars in Cambridge, it is also one of the cheapest, as well as having one of the most friendly and casual atmospheres. Pool, darts, foosball, sofas and a cosy feel make this very popular across all Cambridge students.

Price of a Pint: £2.50

Chapel & Religion: Sidney has its own very nice chapel and choir, who go on regular fully funded tours (the choir has many benefits, as well as free formals regularly). Sidney also has its own prayer room and is well known for being very open to all faiths.

College Payment System: Pay contactless with student ID card (which gets put on to your termly college bill, which you pay at the end of term) for food in hall and printing. Bar accepts cash or card.

Food: There are three meals a day during the week, brunch and dinner on Saturdays and just dinner on Sundays. Food is generally good with lots of options available and on the affordable side. A full meal in Hall costs about £4 and you can get a 4-item brunch for less than £2.50. There are also formals in Hall 3 times a week, currently priced at £9 for Sidney Students where you get a three-course meal served to you. These are fantastic value and a great way to celebrate a birthday (and cheaper than a restaurant!).

Formality: Not super formal, you cannot walk on the grass on the front courts but there are huge gardens at the back of college. Gowns are worn to Formals.

Grants and Bursaries: Lots of travel grants available. Some funding for sports. An additional bursary on top of the Cambridge Bursary Scheme for some students which grants £1000 off accommodation. Some additional automatic rent rebate for Cambridge Bursary Scheme students. As the bar is student run you can work behind the bar for extra money (which pays the living wage).

Location: Very central, opposite Sainsbury's (is extremely useful for food shopping), also close to clubs, which is nice on nights out, but not so nice if you have a room facing the main street due to noise from street performers in the day and clubs at night. Closer to classes for Science and Maths students, but not far (maximum 15 minute walk almost anywhere!) for other subjects. Even without a bicycle, you will be well placed.

Politics & Reputation: Politics is not a major talking point at Sidney due to the friendly and non-judgemental atmosphere. You will meet people from all backgrounds and areas, with no judgements as to whether you are Northern/Southern/International, Tory/Labour/etc, etc. Sidney is one of the few colleges where you can almost ensure you will meet a group of people you will get along with, and a group of friends for life, with such a varied cohort!

Sport: Sidney tend to have joint college teams with other colleges, due to its small size, but this is a positive for meeting new like-minded people! All sports are played at college and you are almost guaranteed to meet at least a couple people playing the sport you are interested in at university level at Sidney! As mentioned before, lots of financial and moral support is given to people playing sports (as well as doing choir, music or drama!

St Catherine's College

Founded: 1473

Famous Alumni: Jeremy Paxman, Richard Ayoade, Ian McKellen

Undergraduates: ~400   **Postgraduates:** ~150

Accommodation: First and third years at Catz live in college, and have a choice of either en-suite or non en-suite rooms of varying sizes. Before first years arrive, they are given a choice of an en-suite room, or a small, medium or large non en-suite room. Students living in non en-suite rooms will usually share a bathroom with around 6-8 people, but all rooms have a sink. En-suite and non en-suite alike, you can still personalise and decorate your room with photo collages, posters, cushions and make it feel like home! Second years at Catz live with their friends in flats of 4 or 5 on a separate site- St Chad's, a 10 minute walk from college

Food: All three meals can be purchased daily. Meals are hearty, with meat-and-two-veg being common, but also a wide range of fish and vegetable dishes. There is always at least one vegetarian option, often two, and also cold food and snacks for sale. On a Sunday, brunch takes the place of breakfast and lunch; this is the best-loved meal of the week and unbelievable value.

Three times a week there's 'formal hall'. You dress up and wear your gown and eat a four-course formal meal: Catz is unique in having a cheese course.

Formality: Relaxed – some traditions are upheld (e.g. wearing gowns to formal events), but in general not at all stuffy (e.g. can walk on most lawns).

Location: Right in the centre of town, opposite Corpus. Catz is one of the smallest colleges though, so it can feel a little cramped.

St Edmund's College

Founded: 1896

Famous Alumni: Hugh Laurie, Robert Harris, Wes Streeting

Undergraduates: ~100   **Postgraduates:** ~450

Accommodation: Impressive en-suite accommodation has recently been built, and a building with rooms for couples opened in the last few years. This goes a long way towards meeting the needs of the student population, but you may still be required to live out during the intermediate years of an undergraduate degree. Those who do, either rent privately or find surplus rooms at nearby Colleges.

Formality: The academic and social environment is unpretentious. Fellows, undergrads and postgrads socialise in a single combination room and eat together. The smaller size of the college means people quickly get to know each other and there is a close-knit atmosphere at socials

Location: Lucy Cavendish is one of the newer colleges, so it's out of the centre of town, which can be frustrating to get places, but does keep the tourist away. Being all over 21 as well, we like to think that we're mature enough to cope with a short cycle ride!

Sport: Sport at College level has in recent years been marked by impressive initiative and determination from students, resulting in the college being put firmly on the map. St Edmund's boasts neither the history nor facilities of some of the older Colleges as far as rowing is concerned, yet this year the boat club won the Mitchell Cup for the most successful performance in the May Bumps races, the culmination of the college rowing calendar.

St John's College

Founded: 1511

Famous Alumni: William Wilberforce, William Wordsworth, Sir John Cockcroft, Paul Dirac, Manmohan Singh

Undergraduates: ~640   **Postgraduates:** ~220

Accommodation: The college provides accommodation both in and out of college for all its students. Room price varies from approx.£1400-£2000 per term but most rooms are at the lower end of the spectrum.

Bar: A very sociable place! It is open every day until 11pm except Fridays and Saturdays (12pm) Price of a Pint: £2-£3

Chapel & Religion: Anglican Church but not compulsory and open to all faiths.

College Payment System: Termly Invoice/Bank Transfer

Food: Three meals per day served in the Buttery everyday (£3-£5 for a meal). Formal Dinner option served in Hall daily except Saturday (£10-£13 for a three-course meal with wine). The quality of the food is very good and both the buttery and hall are very sociable areas of the college.

Formality: Gowns and smart dress required for specific events and formal hall, but otherwise no formalities.

Grants and Bursaries: St John's is one of the most generous colleges when it comes to grants and bursaries, and the college website has great information on them.

Location: Central Cambridge (almost) everything is within walking distance including faculties, shops, restaurants, clubs… John's location is a great asset.

Politics & Reputation: The reputation of being uptight and conservative does not accurately represent the college. The student body is not obviously political, and the JCR is politically diverse with a wide range of different opinions.

Sport: St John's is by far one of the best colleges when it comes to sports not only because of the amount of sports offered but also because of the high standards at which first teams play. Most popular sports include: Rowing (Lady Margaret Boat Club)-The best college boat club in Cambridge and the oldest one across the university. Rugby-Commonly known as the Redboys, John's rugby team is one of the best ones in Cambridge having won Cuppers repeatedly over the years. Football- Three teams to cater for different needs; First XI plays in first division. An overall very fun and sociable team. Other sports include: Cricket, Hockey, Lacrosse, Tennis, Netball, Athletics, Basketball, Cheerleading.

Trinity College

Founded: 1546

Famous Alumni: Niels Bohr, Bertrand Ru

Undergraduates: ~500   **Postgraduates:** ~350

Accommodation: Though it varies a lot, from having en-suites and well-equipped kitchens (ovens, hobs, microwaves etc.) to shared bathrooms and fewer cooking appliances, the rooms are all generally large and all very comfortable. Though freshers are randomly allocated a room, in second and third year students are invited to choose their room via a ballot system. In second year the ballot is random: those at the top of the list get first choice etc. The balloting system therefore allows students to pick a location they like, with their chosen appendages (en-suite/kitchen etc) and within their price range. (But don't worry, even if right at the bottom of the ballot you are guaranteed a nice room!) In third year, the second year ballot switches (if you were at the bottom you are nearer to top etc, so everyone has a chance to get their dream room.) This is complicated by the scholars (those who got firsts in their exams) ballot, as they get first choice, but after that ballot has closed the normal ballot ensues. Most Trinity students opt to live in college. Some rooms are sets, which means you get a living room as well as a bedroom, and double sets mean living with a friend and sharing a living room!

Bar: gorgeous, recently renovated bar with a wide range of both standard and premium drinks

Food: Normal hall is usually pretty good, there are three hot options a day (inc vegetarian) plus a dairy-free or gluten-free alternative. Brunch on Sundays is a major highlight of the week - especially when they do waffles. Formal hall (3x a week) is a bit hit and miss in terms of the food, but the atmosphere makes it pretty special.

Formality: Trinity can seem quite intimidating at first. One of the older colleges, its architecture and sheer size can initially overwhelm, being as beautiful as it is! But this is quickly overwritten by the friendly people who make up the college—the porters are always happy to help and the students themselves induce a homely and welcoming atmosphere.

Grants and Bursaries: Trinity is one of the wealthiest colleges, so there's a wide range available for various needs and projects.

Location: Right in the centre of town, one of the biggest colleges, and the largest undergrad populations.

Trinity Hall

Founded: 1350

Famous Alumni: Hugh Laurie, Robert Harris, Wes Streeting

Undergraduates: ~400   **Postgraduates:** ~200

Accommodation: All first-year students are guaranteed a room in the college's central site, amongst beautiful historic buildings and gardens, right in the centre of the city. This is where the library, dining hall, bar and chapel are located, along with facilities like the music room. The rooms here currently cost between £70 and £140 a week - they vary in quality, but most of them are quite nice! In subsequent years, most people have more modern rooms further out of the centre (though none of them are more than 10 minutes' bike ride away). These vary from smaller rooms with kitchens/bathrooms shared between 10ish people (around £100 a week) to large, modern rooms with en-suites (up to £145 a week). You choose your room via a randomised "ballot" system.

Food: In first year, students live on-site and have access to a small kitchen, which includes a sink, microwave, fridge and kettle. You can cook food in this kitchen, but for a proper meal students usually go to the college canteen which is also on-site and serves breakfast, lunch and dinner at certain hours (and brunch on Sundays!). The food there is good (if slightly repetitive) and not too pricey - and vegetarian, vegan, and gluten-free options are available. In second and third year accommodation, kitchens are bigger and better equipped with hobs, allowing students to cook for themselves if they want to- although students of all years are always welcome to eat in the canteen!

Location: Right next to the larger Trinity College, which makes it easy to find, .but doesn't help with people confusing the two!

Wolfson College

Founded: 1965

Famous Alumni: Eric Monkman of University Challenge fame, and many heads of state and politicians including Letsie III of Lesotho, Carrie Lam, Susan Kiefel, Song Sang-Hyun, Rupiah Banda.

Undergraduates: ~180 (all aged 21 or over)   **Postgraduates:** ~514

Accommodation: Modern en-suite rooms, all on-site at the College Campus. Lease can run either year-round, or just for term times.

Bar: Recently refurbished, centre of college social life. Price of a Pint: £3~

Chapel & Religion: None

College Payment System: Fees payable by cheque, credit card and bank transfer. Day-to-day payments at bar and dining hall by topping up student card.

Food: Highly rated among Cambridge serveries. Caters to most dietary requirements (veggie/vegan, halal, lactose intolerance, gluten free, etc.). Operates 3 meals a day, 7 days a week, both in and out of term time.

Formality: As formal as one wants it to be, it is one of the most casual of Cambridge colleges.

Grants and Bursaries: Disadvantaged student bursaries, travel grants, long-vacation project funding, and more. Many topical scholarships opportunities.

Location: Just outside the city centre, next to the Arts and Humanities departments. Situated in the fashionable neighbourhood of Newnham, and a short walk to the picturesque village of Grantchester.

Politics & Reputation: Once of the Cambridge mature colleges, admitting applicants over 21 only. Renowned as the most diverse, international, and cosmopolitan Cambridge college. The Wolfson Howlers, stand-up shows by professional comedians, are an attraction to students and residents from across the city. The College gardens are famous for their exotic plants from across the globe.

Sport: Many sports and societies: Football, rugby, squash, pole and aerobics, rock climbing, yoga and meditation, dancing (salsa, ballroom, tango, Brazilian), board games, public speaking, student gardening, LGBT and BAME societies.

OXFORD COLLEGES

There are 39 different colleges at Oxford, which we've arranged in alphabetical order across the following pages.

We've left out a couple of the PPHs, which are explained after the college profiles, and we've also not been able to give us much detail about Parks College as it's a brand-new college and doesn't have any students yet!

All of the information here was contributed by current and recent students of these colleges, so it should be all be up to date, with the possible exception of the bar prices! You'll be able to find great detail on all the colleges on their respective websites, in particular the student union sites. Most Oxford colleges has two students' unions, known as common rooms – there is normally a literal common room, hence the name – one for undergraduate, and one for graduate students. They should both have their own websites, which will provide far more detail than we were able to here.

Our goal was to provide all this information in one place, easily arranged for you to flick through and see which colleges you're interested in learning more about. We'd like to thank all of the following students who helped with these profiles, which were by far the hardest part of the book to write, so thank you to:

Aditi Shingrapure	Lucy Enderby
Alice Bennett	Lucy Wright
Amy Dunning	Magnus Fugger
Clare Tierney	Olivia Campbell
Emily Eraneva-Dibb	Rhiannon Davies
Henry Straughan	Ria Sangal
Imogen Edwards-Lawrence	Toby Bowman
Kate Coomby	Tsvetana Myagkova
Lewis Webb	Zainab Mahmood

Balliol College

Founded: 1263

Famous Alumni: Four prime ministers, including Boris Johnson, as well Richard Dawkins, and a host of Nobel laureates.

Undergraduates: ~350   **Postgraduates:** ~350

Accommodation: The college guarantees accommodation for your first and final years, and most have the option of living in college owned property in their second year. First year rooms are randomly allocated based on price band, which you choose from before you arrive. Like most other colleges, there's a random ballot for rooms in third year. If you need a carer, or a disabled access room, the college has plenty of these to make sure that everyone's needs are met.

Bar: The Lindsay Bar is the only fully student run bar left in Oxford (apart from Wolfson, but that's grad only), and all the profits are reinvested in keeping prices low. The bar is open until 11pm on weekdays, and later at weekends, and shots are only 75p on Tuesday nights! The bar also offers darts, table football, and a pool table.

Price of a Pint: £1.70

Food: Hall offer lunch and dinner everyday, and there's even cheaper food available three meals a day in the student run pantry in the JCR. All rooms are close to a kitchen or kitchenette, so you'll be able to do your own cooking easily as well.

Location: Right in the centre of town on Broad Street.

Politics & Reputation: Balliol has a long history in politics, with five prime ministers and lots of political journalists as recent alumni. Nevertheless the college is very politically open and welcoming, and much more relaxed than the 800 year old pedigree might suggest!

Sport: Balliol has a good record in sports over the past few years, with two promotions for the football team. The college offers financial support to any Blues level athletes, and the Jowett Walk annexe is one of the closest sports grounds to the city centre of any college. Student also all have access to the Iffley site, where you'll find the track where Roger Bannister ran the first four minute mile!

Brasenose College

Founded: 1509

Famous Alumni: David Cameron, Malcolm Turnbull, Michael Palin, Jessie Burton, Duncan Campbell, J. Michael Kosterlitz, Elias Ashmole (of the Ashmolean museum)

Undergraduates: ~356   **Postgraduates:** ~204

Accommodation: If you are an undergrad at Brasenose you get accommodation with the college, which can be a huge weight off your mind. In your second year you'll be housed in one of our annexes, which are a few minutes' walk from the college (you'll also be there in your fourth year, if you have one!)

Most of the annexes have en-suite rooms, but not all, and the kitchens are decent. If you're a grad student, you'll be in an annexe regardless (these include rooms and flats for couples). In your first and third year, you'll be on the main site. Accommodation on the main site is more communal, with shared food storage in the hallways (rather than kitchens) and shared bathrooms. The rooms vary in quality, but there is a ballot based on randomised names, so you have a fairly good chance of getting a great room at least one year! All the accommodation includes accessible rooms for those who need them.

Bar: The College Bar

Price of a Pint: £3

Chapel & Religion: The chapel has a large and incredibly talented choir, which forms the centre of much of Chapel life at Brasenose. There are services on Sundays which everyone is welcome to attend (but not mandatory). Religion at the college can generally play as large or small a part as you would like!

College Payment System: Accommodation fees, Tuition Fees, and other things like laundry and food costs (batels) are paid termly, you can also manage your payments using the online Upay service.

Food: Students at Brasenose (Brasenostrils) love their food, there are informal meals every day, and formal ones three times a week. The food is of a really high quality, and it is affordable (a three course meal is a fiver).

Formality: The college is less formal than some, while retaining a lot of the 'wow' factor that old Oxford colleges have. Formal meals are a regular occurrence, but aren't compulsory.

Grants and Bursaries: There are substantial measures in place to support students in financial hardship at Brasenose, including subsidies for living costs, travel, resources, and bursaries. There is also a fund for students who wish to stay in college during the vacation.

Location: Brasenose is in the best location in Oxford, about 10 metres from the Radcliffe Camera at the heart of the university. It is also right next to the Exam Schools and a lot of great bars, restaurants, and pubs.

Politics & Reputation: Brasenose is increasingly diverse, and there is ripe ground for political debate regardless of where you are on the spectrum, though it tends towards the conservative. The atmosphere is one of intellectual pursuit, so people try to be open minded, and are open to discussion! The reputation (besides the lucky college in the best spot in town) is that we are a nice bunch! Brasenose came first in the Oxford Barometer survey for friendliness, we also have stunning architecture and great food!

Sport: Sport at Brasenose is available for everyone regardless of ability, or the level of commitment you want to invest. We have teams and sports clubs for a wide variety of sports, and access to the university gym is included free of charge.

Christ Church

Founded: 1546

Famous Alumni: 13 Prime Ministers (Peel + Gladstone), 10 chancellors of the exchequer, King Edward VII, 17 archbishops, John Locke, Albert Einstein, Sir William Osler ('father of modern medicine'), Jacob Rothschild, David Dimbleby, Lewis Carroll, Riz Ahmed (actor) – take your pick!

Undergraduates: ~442   **Postgraduates:** ~203

Accommodation: You can spend all three years in college accommodation, though for most people 1 or 2 of those years will be in the college annexes (one across the road, and one by Iffley sports ground). Rooms are allocated by random ballot, with scholars and musicians getting first pick. The fee for all rooms are the same. If you are high on the ballot, you may get to choose a 'pec set'. These are shared rooms with a large living room area. You are only allowed to live in a pec set for one year.

Bar: The atmosphere for the bar can be quite hit and miss. Typically, the bar reps are very dedicated and arrange lots of events which are very good fun, but on off nights the bar can be quite empty

Price of a Pint: £2

Chapel & Religion: The only college with a cathedral inside it, as a student you can go to evensongs and special services that could otherwise be quite exclusive. The Dean is the head of the college and the cathedral. If you go to evensong you get free wine at dinner afterwards!!

College Payment System: Breakfast and Lunch is paid by item, dinner you either opt in or opt out of. If you opt in, you pay for every meal, even ones you don't manage to attend, if you opt out you only pay for the dinners that you go to but they are more expensive. If you opt in the three course meals will cost you about £3!! There is also a tab system for the Buttery (the bar) which gets added onto your termly batels

Food: The food is pretty good. Brunch is quite the event on weekends as you can get a lot of food for not much money. Otherwise the dinners are generally pretty good. There's also a café in the JCR which does fantastic paninis

Formality: Christ Church is one of the most formal colleges. Formal hall works a bit differently to other colleges as there is one every night and the food is the same as informal. What is different is Guest Dinner, which happens twice a term, is black tie and has a fantastic four course menu

Grants and Bursaries: Christ Church is very good at supporting its students financially, with a generous hardship fund, free money for books, travel grants, sports grants – there's a lot to support whatever it is you are doing.

Location: Right in the centre of town on St Aldates

Politics & Reputation: Christ Church is seen as one of the poshest colleges and people you meet from other colleges will likely have negative prejudices against you because of that reputation. Usually after 5 minutes they'll realise that it is more fiction than fact!

Sport: Christ Church has fantastic resources for sports. You can reserve punts, tennis courts, squash courts, and a multipurpose astro-turf pretty much whenever you like for free. Christ Church's facilities are also some of the most central of all the colleges – even more central than the university's own centralised facilities! The meadows are also yours to use freely so you can use them for a kick about or whatever without having to make a reservation and it's on your doorstep.

Corpus Christi College

Founded: 1517

Famous Alumni: Isiah Berlin, Thomas Nagel, and both Miliband brothers!

Undergraduates: ~250   **Postgraduates:** ~90

Accommodation: Corpus offers college accommodation for all three years of your degree, which is more generous than most other colleges.

Bar: The Corpus Beer Cellar, known as the BC, which has student bar staff as well as Lance, the resident barman. We have darts and pool, and some of the most reasonably priced drinks in Oxford!

Price of a Pint: £2

Food: The hall serves three meals a day, which you pay for by topping up your Bod card. Lunch is £2.49, and dinner only £3.09. Dinner is replaced with formal hall on Fridays, although you'll need to enter the ballot for a place. You'll get priority if you're welcoming guests though.

Formality: Corpus is one of the smallest colleges at Oxford, which gives it a friendly, intimate atmosphere. You'll end up knowing everyone pretty quickly, grad students included, which you won't get at one of the bigger colleges.

Grants and Bursaries: Corpus has a range of grants and bursaries, including a £150pa Academic Expenses Grant for books, equipment and application fees, a travel grant of £450 each student (£600 for 4 year degrees), and awards 3 scholarships to 'expand students horizons' of £5,000 each year.

Location: Just behind the more famous Christ Church, between Merton fields and Merton Street.

Exeter College

Founded: 1314

Famous Alumni: J. R. R. Tolkien, Sir Philip Pullman, Reeta Chakrabarti, Sir Roger Bannister, Richard Burton, Sydney Brenner, Ronald Cohen

Undergraduates: ~357   **Postgraduates:** ~262

Accommodation: 1st Year: On the main site for all freshers, 2nd Year: 40% of the year stay in college owned Student Houses of 8-9 people. These houses are about a 20-minute walk away from the main college site, but as most people cycle, it's much quicker. Depending on their position in the Housing Ballot, the rest of the year can either choose to stay on the main college site or move to Cohen Quad in Jericho (a modern facility with all en-suite bathrooms and a shared kitchen for each floor). In either students' 3rd or 4th years they are given priority in the Housing Ballot with most choosing to stay in Cohen Quad and some back on the main college site. College provided accommodation is guaranteed for 3 years.

Bar: Quite a cosy and a very social place! Breakfast and Lunch are available here for reasonable prices cheaper than the dining Hall. The customisable panini bar is a big hit, as well as game of pool or darts for a study break. The bar is the centre of social events in college, hosting regular open mic nights, karaoke, bops as well as football, rugby and charity drinks-which all have great atmospheres.

Price of a Pint: ~ £2.30

Chapel & Religion: One of the most beautiful Chapels in Oxford (featured in the film Dr. Strange!) and is a space for both those who are religious and non-religious. Our Chaplain is very approachable; in terms of discussing both religious and non-religious topics; from sending us podcasts and music for meditation to hosting Pancake day on Shrove Tuesday. There are weekly choral Evensong services sung by the choir and at Christmas the Carol Service is not to be missed.

College Payment System: Accommodation bills are paid at the beginning of every term. Throughout term, food from the bar, Hall or café in Cohen Quad are paid for using our University ID card which can be topped-up online. However, laundry machines on both the main site and Cohen Quad require exact change.

Food: On the main site, both hot and cold breakfast and lunch are available in the bar. During the week, lunch and dinner are also available in the dining hall and usually there are 3 main options (2 meat and 1 vegetarian and or vegan) along with sides and salads which come to £3-4 per meal. On the weekend, college does a great brunch for only £2-3 and dinner, which on Sunday's is usually a popular roast. In Cohen Quad, breakfast and lunch are available during the week for similar prices to the main site.

Formality: Exeter is more formal than some, but less than others. Whilst we are not allowed on the Front Quad grass, we can sit in the Fellows Garden which has an amazing view overlooking the Radcliffe Camera. We are one of the few colleges to have a black-tie ball every year, which everyone looks forward to at the start of Trinity Term and is the most affordable college ball in Oxford. Formal Hall dinners are held twice a week after normal dinners, where you can have a 3-course meal. For each subject, there is also an annual subject family formal dinner as well as special Formal Hall dinners for celebrations. Students must wear gowns at these dinners and it's also a nice occasion to dress-up more formally.

Grants and Bursaries: Exonian Bursaries are college financial assistance grants that are usually between £500-1,000. There are also some Hardship Bursaries available for those in need. Exeter also offer grants for books and equipment purchases, vacation study costs, travel for study or conferences, and internships. Funding for sports and arts activities is also available.

Location: Centrally located, a few minutes away from both the Radcliffe Camera and Bodleian libraries. Most departments are less than a 10-minute walk away. It's also great having so many restaurants, cafes and shops within a 5-minute walk, which saves a lot of time which makes a difference when you have a packed schedule and are trying to fit in as much as possible.

Politics & Reputation: Exeter is relatively politically neutral and known for being one of the most friendly and social colleges in Oxford. The size of each year is just over 100 people so you can recognise everyone and get to know lots of people quickly. As the college is quite small, when walking around Front Quad or going to the Bar you always run into a friendly face, which definitely makes catching up with people on a day-to-day basis easier and creates a more familiar and homely atmosphere.

Sport: Exeter has good sporting spirit and team bonding. Whatever, the sport, college cuppers teams get great support ranging from Men's football and rugby to more recently reaching the darts final twice in a row, and winning sailing cuppers! Every year we also have a sports day with our sister college in Cambridge, Emmanuel, which a huge number of people get involved with even if they've never played a particular sport before.

Green Templeton College

Founded: 2008

Famous Alumni: GTC has only been open for 12 years, so their alumni are still making their mark, and aren't quite famous yet.

Undergraduates: ~0 **Postgraduates:** ~600

Accommodation: There is some accommodation available on site but it had a distinctly undergrad feel. There is enough room for around half of the students at the college, and they are mostly accommodated off site, on Observatory Street or St Margaret's Road, or in new developments currently being finished further out of town. The best rooms to go for are in college if your priority is convenience, or in 5 St Margaret's Road if you want space and good facilities. Rooms are allocated by lottery, but it is best to contact the accommodations officer to check whether you can currently register for a lottery as lotteries are often announced on the lodge noticeboard and nowhere else, so they're easy to miss.

Bar: The Stables bar was recently renovated, and is a good place to have a drink or relax with some reading regardless of the time of day.

Price of a Pint: It's £1 for a bottle of beer (decidedly not pint-sized)

Chapel & Religion: The college is secular and has no chapel.

College Payment System: The college uses a credit system for dinners, but only takes cash at the bar, and things like laundry are only available via prepaid cards.

Food: GTC has a really well-established kitchen with a talented chef poached from a much older college several years ago. There is always a wide variety of food available from all over the world, and it's very rarely less than excellent.

Formality: GTC was only established in 2008, so it isn't big on formality or any of the things Oxford colleges are usually associated with. Formal dress isn't required at dinners with the exception of a handful of formals each year. In general, the college is liberal and open, there is little expectation of formality.

Grants and Bursaries: GTC is a young college with little by way of bequests at its disposal. There is a research fund available to all students of £200 per year, but financial assistance is otherwise offered on a case by case basis without any particular bursary or grant one can apply for.

Location: GTC is less central than many of the Oxford colleges, on the Woodstock road overlooking Jericho. This is in many ways advantageous, it is quiet at day and night, all through the year. The surrounding area is leafy, and it's a very short walk into Jericho or into the wilderness beyond.

Politics & Reputation: GTC, as a new graduate only college, is not widely known by Oxford students, its reputation is primarily one as a biomedical and policy research powerhouse, and often hosts global conferences on topics like public health. Politically, GTC is one of the most liberal colleges in Oxford, though as it matures this is gradually shifting.

Sport: GTC has an active (and successful) rowing team, among others, and inside the small campus we've also squeezed in some tennis courts and a state-of-the-art gym. There are a wide range of competitive teams and you can always contact the GCR representative for sport if you'd like to sign up!

Harris Manchester College

Founded: 1786

Famous Alumni: Roger Bannister, Peter Cruddas, Joseph Priestley

Undergraduates: ~100   **Postgraduates:** ~150

Accommodation: Accommodation in college is guaranteed for the first and final year of studies. All accommodation is in the college's beautiful historic buildings, and most rooms have en-suite bathrooms (otherwise bathrooms are shared between two). All students have access to communal kitchens within their house (some kitchens are shared between students in two houses). One of the houses is set aside for graduates only. Rooms are randomly allocated, except in your final year in which you will usually be allocated one of your top two preferences. Priority is always given to students who have accommodation related requirements owing to disabilities.

Bar: Harris Manchester is the only all mature students college at Oxford, but we still know how to have fun! - Harris Mancunians throw some of the best bops at Oxford. From legendary pub quizzes, real ale festivals, and open mic nights, Guest Nights, the JCR is a place to both hang out with friends and get the night started.

Food: All meals are served in the college's stunning Arlosh dining hall - on weekdays this includes breakfast, lunch, and dinner. Mondays and Wednesdays are Formal Halls when food is especially nice, wine is free, and gowns are worn! Sunday brunch is a student favourite, with living-in students chatting and feasting on a full English breakfast, many in pre-library pyjamas. The college's small size proves benefits here too: Oxford's loveliest kitchen staff knows not only your name but of course also your dietary requirements... from halal to vegan to gluten intolerant, you can be sure to be served your personal version of the meal's dish.

Breakfast is £1.80, lunch is £3.75, and dinner is £5, but if you live-in, college meals (including Formal Hall!) are already included in your rent. For library snack cravings, you could always just head into the city centre, which is just a 5-minute walk away, and there is also the popular Alternative Tuck Shop which is just adjacent to the college.

Location: The college has moved around a fair bit through history, including as far afield as Manchester and York! It's now settled down in Oxford for the long term, roughly halfway between the parks and Christ Church meadow.

Hertford College

Founded: 1282 as Hart Hall

Famous Alumni: Fiona Bruce, Krishnan Guru-Murthy, Jeremy Heywood, Thomas Hobbes, John Donne, and many other politicians, presenters, writers, and scientists.

Undergraduates: ~400   **Postgraduates:** ~150

Accommodation: First year accommodation is pretty good, it's extremely central and most rooms are a good size, small gym onsite, though there are not many kitchens. Second year accommodation is a 15-minute walk out, not as pretty, no gym (though you can go to the one on the main site) but way more kitchens! Third year quite mixed, mostly houses, which can be really nice when you've matured and want to be a real adult.

Bar: Hertford is the only college with an underground bar. A student run bar, its décor is cosy with exposed brick. It is popular most nights of the week, and you can get a job working here in your second or third year.

Price of a Pint: ~£2.20

Chapel & Religion: Hertford has a beautiful college run by a very friendly Chaplain, Mia. It plays host to weekly services, to your matriculation ceremony, and also a wonderful choir – no audition required.

College Payment System: College bills are paid every term, including accommodation and kitchen fixed charge, like most colleges. Hall is paid for using your student card, and this is charged to your bills at the beginning of the next term.

Food: Hall serves three meals a day five days a week, with brunch on Saturday and Sundays. The food can be on the expensive side, at £4-5 for a meat main and side for dinner, though lunch is usually cheaper.

Formality: Hertford is a very friendly college with a strong community feel to it. A testament to this is that you're allowed to sit on the grass in Trinity (summer) term!

Grants and Bursaries: Hertford offers an extremely generous £1000 bursary for anyone with a household income of less than £53,000. This is more generous than most colleges I have seen! You can also apply for extra hardship grants, or sports funds for those on university teams.

Location: An extremely central college, convenient for most subjects. It is opposite Oxford's main, beautiful, library, the Bodleian, and adjacent to another beautiful library in the Radcliffe Camera. It is near exam schools, where many social science lectures are, as well as the Social science, Law, MFL and English libraries.

Politics & Reputation: Hertford is very liberal and open-minded as a college, and has had many Principals who have exemplified this. Its last Principal, Will Hutton, is a journalist and writer and nurtures the college's interests, particularly in his role working with the Hertford Economics and Politics Society.

Sport: Hertford's sporting success goes up and down with each cohort, as with most colleges. In recent years its women's boat club has seen huge success, as has its men's football team and joint Keble-Hertford women's football team. Sport at Hertford ranges from light fun to challenging and rewarding. If team sports aren't your thing, the gym and the yearly Oxford Half Marathon might be!

Jesus College

Founded: 1571

Famous Alumni: Harold Wilson, T.E. Lawrence ("Lawrence of Arabia"), John Richard Green, Magnus Magnusson, Sir Leoline Jenkins, Vivian Jenkins (Welsh Rugby Player), Norman Manley (Chief Minister of Jamaica), Kirsty McCabe, Hilary Lister (record-breaking quadriplegic sailor), and (very recently!) Kevin Rudd (Former PM of Australia)

Undergraduates: ~350   **Postgraduates:** ~230

Accommodation: Jesus offers accommodation for the every year of your degree – meaning that's one less thing you have to worry about! First years live in the main college site itself, where you will either have their own room or share a double set with one other person. Second and third years live in 3-4 person flats at the annex sites known as 'Stevens' and 'Barts' that are just a short cycle from college. Both annex sites have lovely garden spaces, and there's even a full size rugby pitch at Barts! Flats in the annex sites are allocated by a random ballot system, where if you are higher up in the ballot you have first choice in what flat you want. Accommodation can be a tad cold in the winter, but the college offers a heating subsidy to offset some of the cost of having the heaters on!

Bar: The Jesus bar (Baaa) was super recently renovated, and now features a karaoke machine, a UV room (complete with an Xbox and PlayStation!), and a foosball table. When there is a college event or a big club night on you can be pretty certain the bar will be full! The JCR committee also run a number of events in there (such as Thursday Karaoke pre-Bridge, pub quizzes, 'International Cocktail' Nights etc) which are always good fun.

Price of a Pint: ~£2.30

Chapel & Religion: Jesus has a lovely (albeit relatively small) chapel, which was the very first Church of England chapel in Oxford. That said, the chapel really is a place which welcomes people of all faiths and religions, and anyone is welcome to use the space, join choir, or attend Evensong regardless of their religion. Every Friday the JCR runs 'Friday @ 1' in the Chapel, which is essentially a super chill jam session for the musicians in college. The Chapel choir is non-auditioning, and all members get free weekly singing lessons!

College Payment System: Everything at Jesus (except the Bar) is charged to your termly batels – including rent, food, etc. If you receive a grant or subsidy from college this is subtracted off your batels so you just have to pay less. Normal Hall is charged on a per-item basis, but you are charged a fixed fee for the meal at 2nd Hall and Formal.

Food: Food is pretty good in Hall, and reasonably priced! There is always a veggie option, and the college is super open to hearing menu suggestions from students. There is also the 'Hatch' in the JCR where you can get coffee, chocolates and paninis if you fancy something a little lighter. '2nd Hall' runs 4 days a week and is 3 courses, and 'Formal' Hall runs only on Thursday and is 4 courses. 2nd and 3rd years also have full kitchens in their flats.

Formality: There are a few formal parts to student life, such as wearing gowns to Formal Hall. The JCR also runs a black tie event at the end of every term (which isn't compulsory, but almost everyone goes). But in general, Jesus falls on the more laid-back side of the spectrum!

Grants and Bursaries: Jesus is one of the richest colleges per student, which means they have a lot of money to help their students. There are loads of grants and scholarships offered, some of which are means-tested, and others are based on academic achievement. Particularly notable is the 'Dodd Fund', which awards every undergraduate a sum of money for non-academic travel¬ at some point during their degree! The college Books Grant also pays students 75% off the cost of any books they buy for their degree.

Location: Jesus is smack bang in the middle of Oxford, located on the famous 'Turl Street'. There is a Pret just around the corner (where you will almost always find someone from Jesus grabbing a coffee) and Tesco is less than 5 minutes away. It is also only a 10-15minute walk to get to college from the train station or Gloucester Green Bus Station.

Politics & Reputation: Jesus is a super laid-back college, and is famed in Oxford for being one of the friendliest. Even our principal (Sir Nigel Shadbolt) often comes along to cheer on at our Sports games! It is known as the 'Welsh college' of Oxford, and definitely has more Welshies than the average college (though it's not like you'll be in a minority if you're not Welsh). Like most of the Turl St Colleges, Jesus is relatively politically neutral.

Sport: College sport is all about inclusivity – you don't need to be great at it, or even have played it before, to join. College cuppers are a big part of the College social calendar, and there is always a big turn out to cheer the Jesus teams on! Those who are more serious about their sport tend to aim for the Uni teams, and Jesus always has a number of Blues players across a variety of sports.

Keble College

Founded: 1870

Famous Alumni: Ed Balls (Former Shadow Chancellor), Imran Khan (Pakistan's Prime Minister)

Undergraduates: ~400+   **Postgraduates:** ~200+

Accommodation: For undergraduates - college accommodation is guaranteed in first and second year, and then students have a choice to 'live out' (in privately rented accommodation) in their third or fourth year. In general, enough students choose to 'live out' that college accommodation is available to third years who want it, but those on a four year degree will pretty much always have to move out for their final year (language students returning after a year abroad is the exception to this). All undergraduate accommodation is on the main college site, and most are en-suite (if not – you only share a bathroom with one other room). First and third years will live in the newer buildings, and second year accommodation is in the original college buildings. For graduates – there was a brand new accommodation block opened in 2019 across the road from the main college site which means accommodation can also now be guaranteed for first years, with some available for later years too.

Bar: Fondly referred to as 'the spaceship' – the bar was part of the 60s extension to the college – and is definitely retro but still a lot of fun!

Price of a Pint: £2.50ish for a beer, soft-drinks are £1!

Chapel & Religion: Keble was founded in memory of John Keble, who was a clergyman and theologian in the 1800s, so it was certainly founded as a Christian college, and has one of the biggest college chapels in Oxford. Today, some of the traditions remain (grace is said before formal meals, for example) – but it's not a big part of college life if you don't want it to be. The chaplain is a part of the welfare team for all students.

College Payment System: Food is charged to your student card, which is then paid off online at the end of every term alongside rent payments and any other college fees.

Food: Keble has regular 'formal' halls, at least twice per week plus Sunday (where students wear a gown over regular clothes and there's table service). There are informal halls (canteen-style) for the remaining dinners as well as breakfast and lunch. Food is quite reasonably priced, because only third-years have access to kitchens, and so eating in hall is a big part of Keble life. Breakfast includes a range of continental and cooked options, lunch will have cooked options (fish and chips, noodles, curry and rice) as well as jacket potatoes, pasta, salad, etc. Dietary requirements are catered for well, and there's an on-site café for lighter options like soup, sandwiches, paninis.

Formality: Keble had 'formal hall' for dinner every day up until very recently – and so it might seem like tradition is a big part of life here. But actually, it's one of the more relaxed colleges in the university, and traditions which are maintained are generally about bringing students together, rather than enforcing random rules!

Grants and Bursaries: The Keble Association offers a range of grants and bursaries for students with financial hardship, as well as study and travel grants. Funding is not quite as readily available to every student as it might be at wealthier colleges – but if you need it it's always there.

Location: Keble is about a 5-8 minute walk north of the city centre, and so manages to be close to everything you might need and still far enough away that it's not busy all the time. It's also right next to all the science buildings.

Sport: As its a big college Keble has societies for most major sports: football, rugby, cricket, rowing etc. as well as some more obscure ones like non-contact ice hockey played at 11.30pm twice a week! Rowing at Keble is well funded and well respected, and in general does quite well – with a number of rowers and coxes going on to star in The Oxford & Cambridge boat race over the last few years.

Kellogg College

Founded: March 1st 1990

Famous Alumni: Paul Bennett, Ruby Wax, Tom Mitchell, Grace Clough, Dom Waldouck, Jingan Young. Kellogg is particularly famous for its sporting alums.

Postgraduates: ~1140 Kellogg is graduate only. It is the largest college by number of students.

Accommodation: Kellogg has some of the best student accommodation in Oxford, and all their long-term accommodation have their own private gardens. The majority of the students are housed in three Victorian mansions, located on the Bradmore and Banbury Roads. The main campus has a lively MCR which organises a number of social events throughout the year, and a 24-hour library with adjoining study rooms. In 2017 the college hub was opened to provide an extra meeting space and café.

Bar: Kellogg sports a stylish modern bar, with events run by the MCR.

Chapel & Religion: Kellogg is a modern college with no chapel.

College Payment System: The college charges most things to students' batels accounts. The hub café is cashless, and all catering payments are made via the Upay system.

Food: The college dining hall serves lunches, dinners and special guest nights. Formal dinner is held once a week during term time. The hub café offers breakfasts, sandwiches afternoon tea and hot drinks.

Formality: Has an egalitarian ethos and boasts a lack of formality. It has no high table and no separation between students and fellows.

Grants and Bursaries: Kellogg offers several scholarships, including special scholarships for History, and the Hasmukh Patel scholarship for students from Africa.

Location: Much of Kellogg college was adapted from the 19th century Norham manor estate on the Bradmore Road. The centre of the college is now on the Banbury road, in a series of modern and Victorian buildings. The buildings are situated in the leafy and tranquil North Oxford, away from the centre of town, which is a short bus ride or 20-minute walk away.

Politics & Reputation: Originally founded for mature students; the college has since become one of Oxfords graduate only colleges. It is one of only three Oxford colleges without a royal charter and is officially a society of the University rather than an independent college. The college is very modern and has a huge international student population. The college was founded on St David's day, and uniquely at Oxford, grace is said in Welsh. The college has its own tartan which was designed by for Burns night by Robert Collins in 2013.

Sport: Kellogg has a strong reputation for sports and has produced a number of famous sportsmen, including several Olympians, several distinguished rowers and a few international rugby players. Kellogg has contributed rowers to the university boat race a number of times, and has its own punt on the river Cherwell. The college has their own football team in the MCR league.

Lady Margaret Hall

Founded: 1878

Famous Alumni: Benazir Bhutto, Michael Gove, Malala Yousafazi, and Nigella Lawson

Undergraduates: ~400   **Postgraduates:** ~200

Accommodation: As an LMH undergrad you can live in college for three years. Everyone has a kitchen near them and, even if not in first year, a large portion of the rooms have en-suite bathrooms. 1st years are allocated rooms together but all other year-groups are able to ballot for rooms with their friends.

Bar: The LMH bar is open every day until 11pm, with a happy hour from 7pm until 9pm. All of the staff are current students, and you can pay with your university identity (bod) card.

Chapel & Religion: LMH has an unusual Byzantine style chapel, in the shape of a Greek cross. There is a choir which is open to all, and carol services in the chapel in Michaelmas term.

Food: Hall is open for all meals Monday-Friday, Saturday brunch and Sunday dinner. The biggest culinary event of the week is formal hall on Friday: a delicious, three-course meal complete with candelabras and good company. The rest of the week eating in hall is a good way to relax and catch up with friends. A main meal cost around £2.50. There are always two vegetarian options and college are good at catering for dietary requirements.

Formality: LMH was founded as the first Oxford college to welcome women exclusively, and was the first to accept both men and women in 1979. The college is really proud of this tradition of inclusivity and tries to maintain a welcoming atmosphere for all. LMH is also unusual for having an official poet in residence.

Location: Nicely out of the centre of town, LMH is located just to the north of the university parks.

Sport: LMH has a wide variety of college sports teams. All LMH teams are open to everyone, from complete beginners to experienced blues athletes. LMH sports are mostly run on Facebook groups, so be sure to join in if you find yourself at the college!

Linacre College

Founded: 1962

Famous Alumni: Yasmin Alibhai-Brown, David Kelly, Neil Ferguson, Jef McAlister, Heather Couper, Keith Ward, Lady Gabriella Windsor

Postgraduates: ~550 (Linacre is graduate only)

Accommodation: In addition to the onsite accommodation which houses the majority of students, the college owns flats, mainly on the Iffley road. The onsite accommodation features a number of rooms positioned around a central kitchen area. The college campus also has its own gym, private study rooms, conference facilities and impressive library. The college common room has its own Xbox, Nintendo Switch, darts board, Jukebox, camera equipment, bicycle maintenance kit and sewing machine. There is a pool table near the Tanner room.

Bar: Credited with the invention of two cocktails named the Major Corrections and Minor Corrections, respectively.

Chapel & Religion: Linacre does not have a chapel.

College Payment System: Most things are paid for via credit or debit card, or on the university batels system.

Food: Lunch and dinner is served in the dining hall, with guest dinners on Tuesdays and Thursdays. There are no meals served on the weekends. Linacre common room also sports its own BBQ. The college has its own veg box delivery service, which provides college members with local produce.

Formality: Linacre is a modern college and so is fairly informal, but college grace is still said in Latin. At the end of a meal all stand and say "Benedicto Benedicatur" -May the Blessed one be blessed.

Grants and Bursaries: Linacre has an academic hardship fund in addition to grants for academic excellence. There is also an academic activities fund for conferences and student led-seminars organised in the college. The Federick Mulder fund provides travel grants for those who work in a number of fields, including anthropology, social policy and refugee studies.

Location: Linacre's main campus is on the corner of South Parks Road. Much of the campus is 19th century, with recent new builds in the surrounding area. The main campus is next to the river Cherwell, and Merton college's playing fields.

Politics & Reputation: Linacre was Oxford's first Graduate only college, (and the UK's first for both sexes). It is famous for its Sexy Sub-Fusc bop, at which party goers wear their matriculation gowns in the most risqué way possible.

Sport: The college Punts are stored at nearby Wolfson College. Members have access to Oriel sports including their squash courts, on the Cowley Road. The college has a number of sports clubs, including the pleasingly named Linacre Ladies who Lift.

Lincoln College

Founded: 1427 by Richard Fleming, the Bishop of Lincoln

Famous Alumni: Dr Seuss, John le Carré, John Wesley Howard Florey, John Radcliffe, Emily Mortimer, Rachel Maddow

Undergraduates: ~301 **Postgraduates:** ~323

Accommodation: Accommodation is offered for all years of your degree. First year is on the main college site, second year is opposite the main college at the Mitre on Turl Street, and third and fourth years live ten minutes north, at Museum Road. There are also a number of smaller accommodation complexes for some fourth years and postgraduates.

Bar: Yes, Deep Hall or 'Deepers' is the legendary underground college bar, run by Simon.

Price of a Pint: £2.30

Chapel & Religion: Yes, we have a chapel which runs regular services and Sunday evensong with our wonderful choir. We also have an inter-faith prayer and quiet room.

College Payment System: We load our Bod cards with money at the start of each term which can be used in Hall and for non-alcoholic drinks/food in Deepers. This is rolled over from term to term but wipes at the end of each academic year. For those on the 'In College' plan the charge is £201.67 per term, for those on the 'Out of College' plan (including all graduate students) the charge is £88.

Food: Lincoln food has been known for decades as some of the best in Oxford. There are three meals a day served in hall six days a week, as well as a café lunch option and takeaway pizza from the bar in the evenings. The best meal is definitely Sunday brunch!

Formality: We have an informal hall every evening, and then a served formal hall after. This is smart casual and not particularly formal. Every other Thursday we also have a Great Hall, which is much smarter, and people tend to make much more of an effort. This is a great occasion and it always sells out!

Grants and Bursaries: There are plenty of college grants and awards for a variety of subjects and needs. We have: Senior Tutor's fund of up to £200 for academic activities, Vivian Green fund for projects of personal development, Travel Grants of up to £250 (extra for modern linguists) Books grants of up to £100 per year. There are also a large variety of scholarships and awards for academic achievement and contribution to college life (from £150 to £700), as well as substantial bursaries for those from lower-income households (ranging from £700 to £1333 per year). There are also a number of bursaries for special purposes such as extra expenditure incurred for your course. In terms of sport, Lincoln has a 'Blues Fund' which assists towards the expenses of those who play in the University teams. Finally, there are JCR and College Financial Support Funds (Including a Gender Expression Fund) which aims to help students if they come into times of unexpected financial difficulty.

Location: Lincoln is one of 3 colleges on Turl Street, in the very heart of the City Centre. It is within 10 minutes of all major faculties and libraries, as well as less than 5 from the main shops.

Politics & Reputation: Lincoln has a reputation for being a very friendly and welcoming college, which is both progressive and yet still has some pretty interesting traditions. Both common rooms pride themselves in being apolitical. This, alongside with the wide variety of events put on by the college and common room officers means it has one of the tightest-knit and most diverse communities in terms of background. Perhaps for this reason, we are involved in a number of local charities and campaigns, fundraising for two charities per term. We boast a lot of college clubs and societies from sports clubs to history and music societies which help cement an extremely social community. Although Lincoln is small, it is known for punching above its weight in all aspects of wider university life and has recently experienced successes in all kinds of inter-collegiate competitions, from drama and music to sports. The main thing other colleges know Lincoln for is our library – which is supposedly the best of all college libraries! The library is the old city church on the corner of Turl, and so is a beautiful environment to study in, as well as being one of the dreaming spires. We also have a new college tortoise so are looking forward to dominating in the annual Corpus Christi Tortoise Race!

Sport: Lincoln as a college is extremely actively engaged in the wider sporting life of the University. Aside from free access to the University gym on Iffley Road, Lincoln shares a recently refurbished boathouse with Queen's and Oriel colleges in a prime location on the Isis in Christ Church meadow and have a variety of boats at all different levels. We also have an excellent sports ground at Bartlemas Road in Cowley with a modern pavilion, as well as access to tennis and squash courts for all students to use. There are a wide range of college sports teams for all levels, often with no experience required to join. These teams are consistently extremely successful, especially given the comparatively small size of the college and we regularly reach the cuppers finals (university inter-college competitions) in a wide variety of sports. Each year, we also support a number of 'Blues', who are students of undergraduate or postgraduate levels who compete in their respective sports for the university itself, which often includes matches against other universities at some of the best sports pitches in the country.

Magdalen College

Founded: In 1458 by William Waynflete, Bishop of Winchester and Lord Chancellor.

Famous Alumni: Thomas Wolsey, Oscar Wilde, C.S. Lewis, Lord Howard Florey, King Edward VIII, Ian Hislop, Stephen Breyer, amongst many other writers, scientists, historians and Nobel Prize winners.

Undergraduates: ~400 (total), around 110 per year   **Postgraduates:** ~175 (total)

Accommodation: Accommodation is offered to all Magdalen (pronounced 'Maudlin') students for the entirety of their course, and vacation residence can be applied for. All first-year accommodation is outside the college grounds – it's a bit grim, but you learn to love your first uni room! Almost all second-year/all third-year rooms and onwards are in the beautiful college grounds right next to the deer park (yes, we have a deer park, with actual deer!) and all have sinks. Some lucky third years have en-suites. All undergraduate accommodation costs the same and is a decent price thanks to subsidising by the college.

Bar: The bar (called the Old Kitchen Bar, or the OKB) is reasonably large, with comfy seating and good wifi. This is where bops (college parties), general meetings, karaoke and other fun events are held

Price of a Pint: £2.30

Chapel & Religion: The Magdalen College chapel is a Grade I listed building, dating from 1480, and is open as a place of worship for people of all beliefs. The regular choral and said services held in the chapel are Anglican and include a beautiful Evensong every Tuesday to Sunday.

College Payment System: You pay for your accommodation and a set rate for catering using your student loan/bank transfer into the college bank account at the start of each term.

Food: The Old Kitchen Bar is open every day and serves good, sustenance food at lunch (paninis, customisable salads, pastries and daily specials like fish n chips) and pizza that can be ordered in the evening. The food in Hall is alright but can be quite expensive for 'subsidised' food. You pay for what you take (£3.00 - £4.00 per meal) and can get three meals a day there from Monday to Saturday. If you like to cook for yourself, there are good kitchen facilities available to all students, and nearby kebab vans for late night munchies! Fancy formal dinners are also offered at £9.00+ per person from Thursday to Sunday (Sunday formal is a special event – you get serenaded by the Magdalen Choir!), with up to five guests allowed per Magdalen host.

Formality: Magdalen is an old college with its own traditions, including the 500-year-old May Morning tradition of the choir singing from the top of the Magdalen Tower. These events give you a wonderful sense of Oxford's history, and Magdalen is otherwise very open and understanding; students are allowed to walk on the grass in Trinity (summer!) term, bops are allowed to continue until relatively late compared to other colleges, and we have a 'late gate' specifically for students who have stayed out too late to get back in through the Porter's lodge (main entrance).

Grants and Bursaries: Magdalen College offers financial support to around a quarter of its undergraduates in the form of the student support fund, which ensures that students can complete their course without having to worry about finances. Freshers are given £150 at the start of the year to buy academic materials, in addition to another £100 available for academic materials that can be applied for annually.

Location: Magdalen is just across from the Botanic Gardens, at the end of the High Street. Although not the most central college, Magdalenites are a short walk away from central Oxford and are also in a good position to explore Cowley, a diverse area of Oxford with lots of cafes, small restaurants and culture-specific supermarkets.

Politics & Reputation: Magdalen is an old, wealthy college, and has acquired a reputation for being a college for privately-educated, conservative students. This should not be seen as a barrier for anyone thinking of applying; the political views and backgrounds represented by the modern student body are far more diverse than this. Everyone is welcome at Magdalen, and the admissions statistics are being improved by the efforts of the college access and outreach teams year on year.

Sport: All Magdalen College students have free membership to the Iffley Sports Centre (including a regular gym, weight-lifting gym and swimming pool) a 10-minute walk from college. We have something for everyone in terms of sports clubs, from football to ice-skating to mixed lacrosse, with both casual and more advanced groups. Of course, we also have a men's and a women's boat club, with a designated rowing gym in the basement of the Waynflete Building (the main first-year block!).

Mansfield College

Founded: 1886

Famous Alumni: Adam Curtis. Pamela Sue Anderson. Chris Bryant. Guy Hands. Adam von Trott. Michael Pollan.

Undergraduates: ~239   **Postgraduates:** ~173

Accommodation: Accommodation at the college for all undergraduate students for all three years. Though some undergraduates still live out in college accommodation in Cowley (the Ablethorpe Building). There's also a couple of college owned houses that fourth-year students tend to live in. College accommodation is pretty good – most of the rooms are en-suite, though some of the biggest and nicest rooms aren't. There's some variation in quality but you get better choice as you progress through the years.

Bar: Not really. Mansfield claims to have a bar. It does physically have a bar. But the bar is almost never open. As in it opens a few times a term. Every so often groups of students will try to improve the bar and make it open more often – this invariably fails due to the opposition of the SCR. It is more accurate to treat Mansfield as not having a bar

Price of a Pint: When the bar opens, you can get a bottle of beer for about £3.

Chapel & Religion: There is a chapel, but it's also used as the canteen/dining hall – indeed, people call the dinner is called 'chapel'. But they do still have services there. It was originally founded for Nonconformists, and so has Nonconformist roots. The Prime Minister, Harold Wilson, was a Nonconformist and got married in Mansfield Chapel.

College Payment System: Online. You can pay with food with your university card ("bod card").

Food: High quality. Particularly good for vegetarian food, and was voted the best college in Oxford for vegetarian food. However, the food is relatively expensive (in part because Mansfield is one of the poorest colleges, so can't subsidise the food as much) – a dinner typically costs about £5.

Formality: Comparatively informal. It's a mostly state school college, and is relatively new, so there's not a great degree of formality. There are formal dinners twice a week and if you go to them you are expected to dress formally. Apart from that there's not really anything particularly formal.

Grants and Bursaries: Mansfield is one of the poorest colleges and, as a result, is not particularly strong for Grants and Bursaries. There are a couple of travel grants, and a hardship fund, but other colleges are much more generous in this regard. Having said that, there are quite a few prizes and scholarships for strong academic performance.

Location: It's located on Mansfield Road, which is pretty central. It's right next to University Parks which is great. It's about a five minute walk to the Bodleian Library, and about 10 minutes to the main central shopping area. There's a great sandwich shop about 3 minutes away. It's one of the more central colleges.

Politics & Reputation: Mansfield is well-known for its high state school intake, so that it's basically the only college where the ratio of state school to private school students matches that in the general population (i.e. it's the only one that achieves fair representation, and doesn't skew in favour of private schools). It also typically does well on BAME admissions. As a result, it's a very inclusive college, and typically quite welcoming. It doesn't really have any of the elitism that Oxford is often accused of. Students tend to be fairly progressive, but it doesn't have the extreme progressive politics that places like Wadham have (it's a fairly moderate college). There are relatively few students with conservative views. Some students with conservative viewpoints have felt their political opinions are not fully respected, but these have also been very popular, well-liked students, so there's no real social exclusion based on politics (as there is at somewhere like Wadham). So it's known for being quite friendly and welcoming. However, as with the no bar thing, it's not typically a particularly 'fun' college. It's also the case that the SCR (i.e. the professors and administrative team) are far more paternalistic than at other colleges.

Sport: Doesn't have its own gym, but you do get free access to some of the university gym. Rugby and football (and possibly other sports) are played with Merton and on their pitches, in teams called the M&Ms. The sports pitches are pretty close, about a ten minute walk from the college.

Merton College

Founded: 1264

Famous Alumni: T.S. Eliot, J. R. R. Tolkien, Roger Bannister

Undergraduates: ~291   **Postgraduates:** ~244

Accommodation: Provided for all years. First year in College, second year in Holywell St (central Oxford), final year in College.

Bar: A little dilapidated last time I checked, but friendly, cosy and cheap. Plenty of quizzes, karaokes and general buzz towards the end of the week.

Price of a Pint: £2.50 for a Carlsberg

Chapel & Religion: The chapel is often host to Evensong, with a strong choir, excellent acoustics and new organ installed in 2013.

College Payment System: Food is on a PAYG basis using your library card to scan in.

Food: Cheap, generally good and lots of it. Meals are non-itemised, so you can have a main, or a main, dessert and unlimited salad and it doesn't make a difference to the cost.

Formality: Quite traditional - gowns must be worn to all meetings with the Warden, and there is the option of formal hall 6 nights a week – but it's BYOB! Quirky ceremonies such as the Time Ceremony (look it up) make tradition fun there.

Grants and Bursaries: In plentiful supply – Merton is one of the richest colleges and people don't take enough advantage of the travel grants, books grants etc. Monetary prizes are always awarded for good performance in termly exams.

Location: Best of both worlds – you're 2 minutes from the High Street and 5 minutes from Cornmarket St, but tucked away on the cobbled Merton St you can barely hear a car go by.

Politics & Reputation: No real political atmosphere. Due to regular residency at the top of the Norrington Table it's known as the college 'where fun goes to die.'

Sport: Not a particularly sporty college, but home to a small in-college gym, squash courts, tennis courts and expansive playing fields at the sports pavilion. And one of the UK's only 'real tennis' courts...

New College

Founded: 1379

Famous Alumni: Hugh Grant, Kate Beckinsale, H.L.A Hart, Sophie Kinsella, Susan Rice

Undergraduates: ~421   **Postgraduates:** ~368

Accommodation: Accommodation is provided to all 1st, 2nd and 4th year undergraduates, with most first year accommodation being en-suite. The way accommodation is allocated is through a housing ballot. The first-year room which assigned to you is ranked on a ballot, and those with a 'worse' room in first year, get given higher priority to choose their 2nd year room. This works really well because it means that everyone pays the same price for their accommodation. In 3rd year, the majority of students live in privately rented accommodation, although there is some accommodation available in college should you need it. 4th year students live in 'Sacher' building or '21 Longwall' where they have access to a kitchen. Unfortunately, the majority of 1st and 2nd year accommodation has no kitchen access and is catered – although the food in hall is delicious and going to dinner is a great way to get to know people!

Bar: Our bar has recently been renovated and has an old, castle-like feel to it. In the day, it operates as a café where you can work, get reasonably priced coffee and have a chat with our friendly baristas! This does mean it has a less 'bar' like feel than some other colleges, but it's still a nice place to go in the evenings. We host pub quizzes in the bar, darts competitions, and it's a popular location for sports teams to gather for drinks!

Price of a Pint: £2.50 (a real steal compared to your average Oxford pub)

Chapel & Religion: The chapel is beautiful, with our renowned choir singing nightly services (except Wednesday) called 'evensong'. This can be really relaxing to go to, no matter what beliefs you hold. The chapel itself is Church of England, however it hosts a catholic mass once a term. There's also daily morning prayers (which end in time for morning classes), this is followed by a free breakfast in hall. The Chapel is also used as a venue for concerts, other services, and lectures. Recently, we had a talk given by Baroness Hale in the chapel, as a celebration of the 40th anniversary of women being admitted to New College.

College Payment System: Payments for accommodation and catering is done through 'batels'. This is a lump sum which is paid to the college and it is possible to add things such as club tickets in freshers week, bottles from the wine cellar and guest night spaces onto your batels. Anything extra which is put onto batels, is then added to next terms batels for accommodation and catering. Your bod card (essentially your student card which gives you access to libraries etc.) can be topped up with money as well. This is used to pay for breakfast/lunch/the bar, and it can be topped up as and when needed.

Food: The dining hall at New College is stunning and definitely has the Hogwarts feel to it. It was also the setting for 'When I kissed the teacher' from Mamma Mia 2! The food itself is great, with our head caterer Brian Cole always being keen to take on board student feedback. There is an 'early hall' sitting each evening of the week, which is a self-service style meal. The prices of the standard evening meals are £7.23. Then three times a week, there is the option to go to 'formal hall' – a three-course, waiter service meal in hall, where gowns are worn. The food at formal hall is really nice and sitting down to have a three-course meal with your friends is a great end to the day. The price for this is also £7.23. Then, every week (although this alternates between the JCR and MCR so is effectively fortnightly) there is guest night. Guest night is also a 3-course, waiter service meal with tea and coffee but it is fancier than formal. No gowns are required but guests dress up and it's a great occasion to bring your family and friends to, with the food being of excellent quality. This costs £19.25.

Formality: New college is not that formal, with a very friendly and homely feel to it. Our formal halls are not formal at all, with the only requirement being that a gown is worn (even if over tracksuit bottoms!). There is, of course, the opportunity to get dressed up for guest night if you wanted to.

Grants and Bursaries:

These are available to students from certain Oxfordshire state schools who are offered an undergraduate place at the University.

The Nick Roth Travel Award (worth £500) is in memory of former undergraduate, Nick Roth, who died in an accident whilst travelling in South America. The Morris Long Vacation Travel Grant (worth £1000) is generously funded by an Old Member of the College. These grants are given out generously by the college for students and you apply for them by outlining the academic merits of your travel.

There is also the China Travel Award which gives students up to £1000 for travelling to mainland China.

The College also supports students taking fast-track language courses at the Language Centre, by reimbursing half of their course fees. The 'Sports and Cultural Fund' can also be applied to for expenses incurred through participating in sports, or culture, for example, music and drama where the college reimburses up to half of the expense.

Scholarships and Exhibitions are awarded to recognise outstanding academic achievement. They are usually made at the end of first year, following first year exams. If you win a Scholarship you will receive £400 each year; for an Exhibition you will receive £275.

Location: New College is primely located on Holywell Street, giving it fantastic access to the law faculty, the English faculty, the science buildings and town. Tesco's is around a 10 minute walk maximum from college, with the major libraries and other faculties being between 5-15 minutes away.

Politics & Reputation: The undergraduate body is called the JCR (Junior Common Room) and the MCR (Middle Common Room) is the graduate body. Both the JCR and MCR have committees which are headed by a president. On those committees, there are financial officers, welfare officers, ethnic minorities officers, LGBTQ+ officers, disabilities officers, access officers, charity officers, environment and ethics officers and women's officers etc. The committee is elected by the JCR and MCR and fortnightly meetings occur where motions are brought and voted on regarding college issues and how to spend the JCR and MCR budgets.

Outside of college politics, New College is not known for any particular political affiliation. The student body tends to be quite keen to discuss social issues, for example access to Oxford, climate change and there are weekly discussion groups on women's issues.

New College has a strong academic reputation, consistently coming near the top of the Norrington Table (used to rank college academic attainment) and is also known for being quite a wealthy college. It is also generally a very friendly community, which is especially apt given the college motto is 'manners maykth man'!

Sport: New College has a great variety of college sport to get involved in. There is rugby, rowing, football, lacrosse, squash, hockey, netball and other sports such as Dancesport, tennis and cricket. Our sportsgrounds are conveniently only a five minute walk always from the main college site, a big bonus of the college when contrasted with some. College sport is really welcoming towards all levels, so is a great way to make friends and try a new skill!

Nuffield College

Founded: 1937

Famous Alumni: Mark Carney, Michael Oakeshott, John Hicks, Manmohan Singh

Undergraduates: ~0 **Postgraduates**: ~80

Accommodation: The college provides on site accommodation for first and second year students, including a few flats for couples. As probably Oxford's smallest college, Nuffield has more generous accommodation for postgraduate students than most.

Grants and Bursaries: On a per student basis, Nuffield is Oxford's richest college, which means they offer generous funding packages, including full fee bursaries for all students, research grants, and office space.

Location: Right in the centre of town, just behind Oxford Castle on the new road.

Politics & Reputation: Nuffield is the hub for social science research at Oxford, and has been the centre of many developments in econometrics. It's a pretty brainy place, and with a lot of fellows and students engaged in political questions, there's always lively discussion.

Oriel College

Founded: 1326

Famous Alumni: Sir Walter Rayleigh, Alexander R. Todd, Rachael Riley

Undergraduates: ~320   **Postgraduates**: ~200

Accommodation: You can, if you choose to, live in college residence for the full duration of course. First and second-year undergraduate accommodation is in the college, whereas third and fourth-year undergraduate and postgraduate accommodation is on Rectory Road, roughly a 15 minute walk from the college.

Bar: The bar is small, but always full of friendly faces. There's a pool table, darts board, and a TV with Sky Sports.

Price of a Pint: £3

Chapel & Religion: Oriel chapel is Church of England, though it is warmly welcoming to everyone. Choral evensong is the main service of the week and takes place on Sundays. Morning prayer takes place every weekday, and compline every Wednesday.

College Payment System: Oriel uses the 'batels' system: students scan their university card when paying for food in hall, or printing, and are then emailed a bill to pay, which includes accommodation expenses, at the start of the next term. Balance on your 'batels' can be checked at any time online, so it's easy to track your spending.

Food: The food is reasonably priced. £4 for a huge cooked lunch (including pudding!), £6 for 3 courses at formal dinner. The food isn't extraordinary, but it is nice, and they cater well to dietary requirements.

Formality: Formal dinner requires all students to wear their gown over a dress or dinner suit. Other than that, Oriel is fairly casual.

Grants and Bursaries: Sports grants are awarded to half blues (£50) and blues (£100) each year. Bursaries are available to students from low-income families. On top of that, if a student is struggling with money, or they have encountered sudden expenses, they can apply to the college for a bursary.

Location: High Street. Very central! Short walk to shops, libraries and many departments.

Politics & Reputation: Oriel has a great reputation for its rowing success. Politics of the college is very conservative, and has drawn controversy over its Cecil Rhodes statue, which the 'Rhodes Must Fall' movement believes should be removed.

Sport: Rowing is incredibly well funded by Oriel. With free coaching, access to excellent equipment and an enthusiastic atmosphere, it's no wonder Oriel rowing has been, and still is so successful. Oriel also has football, Netball, Rugby and croquet teams, but these are much more relaxed.

Reuben College

Founded: 2019

Oxford's Newest College: Reuben College was only founded last year, so it doesn't have any students yet, let alone alumni! An all graduate college, it will take in its first students in autumn 2021. If you're reading this, and find yourself there, please visit the Uni Admissions website, get in touch with our editors, and tell us all about this new college!

Pembroke College

Founded: 1624

Famous Alumni: Samuel Johnson (compiled the first English dictionary), Michael Heseltine, Pete Buttigieg, Victor Orban (Prime Minister of Hungary), Abdullah II of Jordan. Sir Roger Bannister (first man to run a mile in under 4 minutes) was Master of the College in the 1980s. J.R.R. Tolkien was the Professor of Anglo-Saxon at Pembroke in the 1920s.

Undergraduates: ~350   **Postgraduates:** ~250

Accommodation: Undergraduates are guaranteed 3 years of accommodation, although more is possible. At least one year will be in the annexe, which is only a 5 minute walk from the main site. There are 6 "bands" of room which vary in price: cheaper ones tend to be smaller, while more expensive ones will have an en-suite and larger beds. Students rank their preferred bands and locations, and the college uses a ballot system to see who gets first pick. A lot of the nicer rooms on main site have term-time only contracts.

Bar: Not as popular or actively used as in some of the other colleges, although the JCR has been making an effort to increase footfall by hosting open mic nights. **Price of a Pint:** £3

Chapel & Religion: The chapel is beautiful, and has a very different feel to a lot of other chapels due to the ornate and rich decoration inside. It is open during daylight hours for anyone who needs a place for quiet reflection, regardless of their beliefs. There are weekly Sunday services, and a very open and friendly Chapel choir, who also get free formal dinner afterwards!

College Payment System: Your college card can be used to pay in Hall, the Bar, and in Farthings, the college cafe. The Bar and Farthings also take contactless cards. Lunch in Hall is paid by item, whereas dinner has a flat price. All first years are required to attend dinner in Hall; if there is a Formal option that night, they must attend that one unless you get prior approval (e.g. university sports club training) to attend Informal Hall that night. You have to pre-pay the price of these dinners (~£350) at the start of term. From second year onwards if you live on main site, you have the choice of remaining on this meal plan, or pre-paying a little more (~£370), and then spending that money either in Hall or in Farthings throughout the term.

Food: Hall food can vary a lot in quality, but is fine most of the time. The college brownie which is sometimes served for pudding is fantastic, and loved by many students. Wednesday dinners in Hall are meat-free. Farthings food is very good, especially the bagels.

Formality: Pembroke is not as formal as many other colleges. Formal Hall is available (and compulsory for first years) 3 times per week in the first term, 2 times per week in the second, and once per week in the third. Undergraduates are required to wear their gowns to hall, but not black tie.

Grants and Bursaries: Pembroke has a reasonable financial support scheme, and the staff are very friendly and helpful. However, it's not a very rich college, and this sometimes shows. The Rokos Awards are particularly useful for science students who wish to undertake practical research work in the holidays.

Location: Pembroke is across the road from Christ Church and is pretty central, but is also not obvious in its location - many people walk by without realising that the college is there!

Politics & Reputation: Pembroke is relatively small and not as well-known as many other Oxford colleges. The JCR itself is the richest JCR in Oxford, so it often donates to charities in response to political events.

Sport: College sport is very strong in Pembroke, especially the Rowing Club. One of the few college clubs in Oxford that is completely free, Pembroke often boasts one of the largest numbers of crews entered into college competitions. Pembroke was also the first ever college to secure a double headship - coming first in both the men's and women's races in the Summer VIIIs Headship.

Regent's Park College

Founded: 1927, when the college moved to Oxford

Famous Alumni: Not very many to be honest.

Undergraduates: ~120.   **Postgraduates:** ~50.

Accommodation: Regents offers accommodation for first and third year students only. People live out in second year, usually in Jericho which is quieter and closer to the centre than Cowley but also more expensive. The college accommodation is all on the Pusey Street main site and all the same price for every room (very reasonable- much cheaper than living out). The room sizes vary a lot and you can either end up with a lovely, big room overlooking the quad or a vile box room looking out onto some bins. Third years live in shared flats on site. There are kitchens to share with everything you need. The college is generally very good at allowing people to stay over the vacations (for an extra fee)

Bar: Voted the best bar in Oxford, Regents bar improved my life in so many ways. It is small and grotty but really fun and one of the last student run bars in Oxford. They also have a tab system and card machine which is great, so you can always get a drink even if you have no money. The selection of booze is surprisingly good and they make some awful 4-5 shot cocktails for about £3? Ridiculous but makes clubbing so much cheaper, and a good place to bring people back to.

Price of a Pint: £1.00-1.50

Chapel & Religion: As a Baptist college, Regents has a significant religious presence and a very active (if not super pretty or old) chapel.

College Payment System: The admin staff are good and it's easy to pay batels by bank transfer or by card machine.

Food: The food is largely terrible in my opinion. That being said, it's on the cheap side and has a number of vegetarian options

Formality: Very informal. Everyone is friendly and approachable, and the welfare team and academic administrator are amazing and always vouch for their students. People who get into difficulty with their faculties are almost always backed up by the college.

Grants and Bursaries: Although a small and poor college, Regents is fairly generous with travel grants offering several up to the value of £250, which are quite easy to get compared to other colleges as there are less people competing for them. The JCR also offers sports and arts grants, for example to study a language or put on a play, which are again quite generous and offered every term. People who run into financial difficulty are supported for example by discounted vacation residence.

Location: Opposite St John's, Regents is very centrally located right near to Tesco and all the libraries, but also slightly tucked away. Especially well located for Oriental Studies, Theology and Philosophy students.

Politics & Reputation: Regents is very public school heavy. I was one of only a few state school students in my year, and traditionally Regents has a reputation for being rowdy and posh (Bullingdon club was founded at Regents, apparently…). Although politically I would say it's a mix which is nice. In the years below it seems that the private vs state school number of students is becoming more balanced I think, and the college has a genuinely very friendly and welcoming environment.

Sport: Has taken off in recent years. The college has a netball team, a football team and a rugby team joint with Mansfield and Merton. The rowing teams are active but I don't think they do very well at a university level due to the small pool of people.

Somerville College

Founded: 1879

Famous Alumni: Margaret Thatcher (Britain's first female PM), Indira Gandhi (India's first female PM), Dorothy Hodgkin (first British woman to win a Nobel prize in Science).

Undergraduates: ~400   **Postgraduates:** ~200

Accommodation: Somerville is located about 10 minutes walk from the city centre. Accommodation is located in several buildings inside the College. All undergraduate students are guaranteed on-site accommodation for the duration of their 3 or 4 year degrees. Rooms are a good size. Most first year students live in Vaughan, which is a concrete brutalist building. Most first year accommodation has bathrooms and kitchens shared between rooms on each floor. However, some rooms for finalists have en-suite bathrooms (Radcliffe Observator Quarter buildings). There is a gym on the ground floor of Vaughan that students can use after an induction session for a reasonable price.

Bar: The college bar is called 'the Terrace' and is located on the first floor of Vaughan. There is an indoor and outdoor section- the latter is lovely during the summer. There is also a very popular pool table, which costs 50p/game. There is a good selection of beers (including a few local ones), wines, spirits and unique college cocktails.

Price of a Pint: ~£2.50

Chapel & Religion: Somerville has a nondenominational chapel that hosts events and services from a variety of religious affiliations. Past speakers have included Christian bishops, Rabbis, Daoists and Atheists. Every Wednesday during Michaelmas term a Mindfulness Meditation session is held at 6pm in the Chapel- these sessions are free and open to all members of college.

College Payment System: All payments are handled online via EPOS. College bills are called Batels, and these are paid every term- this includes accommodation charges. You can also top up your college card with money on EPOS, that can be spent in the college dining hall or in the bar.

Food: Hall serves three meals a day Monday-Friday, with brunch and dinner Saturday and Sunday. Full meals with dessert usually cost around £4-5. Some days are now 'meat-free' as part of the student body's efforts to reduce the college's environmental impact.

Formality: Somerville is an extremely relaxed and liberal college, where you can be free to express your opinions and thoughts. Most tutorials are similarly relaxed and informal. In contrast with many other colleges, Somerville has a large central grass quad that you can walk and sit on all year! In the summer, some tutorials even take place outside in the sun.

Grants and Bursaries: The University offers Oxford Bursaries and Crankstart Scholarships based on annual income for UK/EU students. Somerville College offers several undergraduate Thatcher Scholarships for UK/EU and overseas students based on academic excellence. Overseas students are considered for these after being offered a place to study, while UK/EU students are considered following their first public examination (usually at the end of first year). This scholarship covers 100% of University fees and provides a very generous grant towards living and travel expenses. Similar scholarships are also available for graduate students.

Location: Somerville College is located in Jericho, which is about 10 minutes walk from the City Centre. The location is ideal- it avoids much of the hustle and bustle of the city centre, but is also very accessible. Its neighbours are St Anne's College (across the road from the main entrance) and Green Templeton College. The maths department lies right next to college, and the Medical Sciences Teaching Centre (where almost all preclinical medicine teaching takes place) is an 8-minute walk/4-minute cycle away.

Politics & Reputation: Somerville is a very liberal college, and is keen to platform all views. However, the student body is mainly left wing, even though our most famous alumna is Margaret Thatcher!

Sport: There are many options for getting involved in College sport. The essential Oxford sport is rowing- it involves very early mornings and freezing fingers, but the camaraderie is fantastic. The two big college regattas are Torpids (Hilary term) and Eights (trinity term). Somerville has an extremely strong women's boat club- it holds the record for most Headships (overall victories) in both Torpids and Eights. Somerville also has teams for more mainstream sports (football, hockey, rugby, netball, cricket) and more niche ones (croquet, pool, table tennis and squash).

St Anne's College

Founded: 1879

Famous Alumni: Mr Hudson (rapper and R&B artist), Tina Brown (editor of The Daily Beast and ex-editor of Vanity Fair and The New Yorker), Danny Alexander (former Chief Secretary to the Treasury), Sir Simon Rattle (principal conductor of the Berlin Philharmonic). Dame Iris Murdoch became a fellow in 1948 and taught philosophy at the college until 1963.

Undergraduates: ~400   **Postgraduates:** ~300

Accommodation: Undergraduates are guaranteed 3 years of on-site accommodation. All undergraduate bedrooms are single occupancy, almost half of which are en-suite, and all accommodation includes kitchens shared by approximately 9 students. Students on four-year courses, except for linguists who spend a year abroad, usually live out for one year in college-rented houses or subsidised private rentals.

Bar: The college bar is a popular spot at the weekend, after formal dinners and before bops. It houses a pool table, table-football, quiz machine, dart board, juke box and is used for charity pub quizzes. **Price of a Pint:** £2.50

Chapel & Religion: St Anne's is a secular college and opted to build The ST Anne's Coffee Shop (STACS) instead of a chapel.

College Payment System: University cards or 'bod' cards can be used to pay in the bar, STACS and hall. Once you pay your college fees at the start of term, your bod card will have a balance of £125 – if you use this up before the end of the term, you can top it up online. The bar and STACS also accept cash and bank card payments.

Food: St Anne's chefs have won awards in national competitions and cater to all dietary requirements in hall. Hall serves breakfast, lunch and dinner on weekdays and brunch at weekends. There is always a vegetarian option and quite often a vegan option and weekly menus can be found online at the beginning of every term. A range of wraps, sandwiches and snacks are available at STACS if you miss hall mealtimes.

Formality: St Anne's is an informal college. Formal hall takes place around 5 times a term and does not require attendees to wear gowns.

Grants and Bursaries: St Anne's has a number of bursaries and travel grants available to students, and finance staff are helpful when anyone experiences any unprecedented hardships.

Location: St Anne's is north of the city centre – 5 minutes by bike – by the University Parks and close to the Science Area, Ashmolean Museum, Modern Languages and Classics Faculties and Mathematical and Oriental Institutes, as well as the Radcliffe Observatory Quarter. It's not a traditional-looking college, but this adds to the down-to-earth atmosphere.

Politics & Reputation: St Anne's is not a well-known college, but it is a friendly and inclusive community and offers a supportive and informal co- educational environment to students of all backgrounds.

Sport: St Anne's has college teams for badminton, cricket, rounders, football, hockey, netball, rowing, rugby and tennis. These are open to all experience levels and serve as a great opportunity to meet people – the hockey team, the rugby team and the women's football team are also joint with other colleges!

St Antony's College

Founded: 1950

Famous Alumni: Richard Evans, Thomas Friedman, Gary Hart

Postgraduates: ~500

Accommodation: St Antony's has 104 rooms, which are mostly reserved for first-year graduate students, although there are some rooms available for continuing students as well. Many rooms are en-suite, and all have access to full kitchen facilities.

Formality: St Antony's College is an unusual college, as it focuses almost exclusively on International Relations, with the college itself structured around seven regional research centres. Like other graduate only colleges, St Antony's is relatively informal, meaning that you'll be mixing as peers with leading academics on a day to day basis. Students share many facilities with fellows on equal terms, and there is open seating in hall.

Location: Located in central Oxford, the college has great access to all university facilities.

St Catherine's college

Founded: 1962. Although its roots go back to 1868 when the college was a delegacy for unattached students.

Famous Alumni: Benazir Bhutto, Peter Mandelson, J. Paul Getty, John Vane, Paul Wilmott, Jeanette Winterson

Undergraduates: ~500

Postgraduates: ~420

Accommodation: St Catz' main campus was built in 1962 by Danish architect Arne Jacobsen, created with a traditional quadrangle layout, but using new materials. Jacobsen incorporated the gardens into his quad design, making St Catherine's a particularly green and pleasant college. The campus has a range of onsite accommodation, including newer modern en-suite rooms, older en-suite rooms, and box rooms with a sink. A further 42 rooms are located at St Catherine's house on Bat Street. The college campus itself is one of the largest and has a wide range of facilities. The JCR is one of the biggest in Oxford, and has dart boards, arcade games, table-football, pool tables, a Nintendo Wii and a Sky Sports television. The campus has a large library and computer room, and a well-equipped and spacious gym.

Bar: The JCR bar is cheap and well-stocked, and has a very impressive whiskey and liquor selection. **Price of a Pint:** £1.50

Chapel & Religion: St Catherine's is a secular college and does not have a chapel.

College Payment System: Meals are paid for via the Upay system, using the university card.

Food: St Catherine's is a fully catered college, providing meals all day. Dinner has two sittings, "Scaf" a cafeteria style informal dinner, and the hall dinner, which has a more extensive menu.

Formality: Formal halls are held on Wednesdays and Sundays, for which there is a fairly strict dress code and code of conduct, which includes a strict limit on alcohol consumption and a ban on singing and shouting.

Grants and Bursaries: The college has a hardship fund and provides bursaries for students from low income households. Other grants include a grant for medical textbooks, and grants for academic excellence for graduate students.

Location: Tucked away down Manor Road, although St Catz is not in the centre it is only 5-10 minutes from the high street. The college is five minutes from the University parks and the Bodleian library.

Politics & Reputation: St Catherine's has recently performed very well in the inter-collegiate Norrington Table. It is the youngest Undergraduate college, and as with all the modern colleges has a less traditional and more egalitarian reputation. Due to the lack of tourists, it is one of the more tranquil grounds in Oxford. The college's motto is 'Nova et vetera', the new and the old.

Sport: St Catherine's has a well-equipped (and free) onsite gym, and is a short walk away from one of the larger rugby pitches. St Catherine's is known as a sports college and is popular with students looking to get involved in wide variety of sports. A number of Olympians have rowed for the college.

St Cross college

Founded: 1965

Famous Alumni: Jonathan Orszag, Tim Foster, Hermione Lee

Postgraduates: ~500

Accommodation: St Cross has 187 rooms, mostly for first-years, after that you're expected to live out. There are a few rooms available if you want to apply for them in later years, but they are allocated by a ballot. Many rooms are en-suite, and all have access to full kitchen facilities.

Formality: St Cross is one of the least formal Oxford colleges, and has the smallest professorship to student ratio, meaning that you'll be mixing as peers with leading academics on a day to day basis. Students share most facilities with fellows on equal terms, and there is open seating in hall.

Location: Located in central Oxford, the college has great access to all university facilities.

St Edmund Hall

Founded: Uncertain; teaching began on the site as early as the 1190's but is estimated to have been established in 1236. However, the name 'St Edmund Hall' (or affectionately, Teddy Hall) did not appear in writing until 1317. The Hall received official Oxford college status (as it was previously known only as a 'Hall') in 1957. So, oddly, it is both the oldest and the youngest Oxford college! Women were first admitted as members of the college in 1978.

Famous Alumni: Al Murray, Keir Starmer, Bishop Micheal Nazir-Ali, Stewart Lee

Undergraduates: ~400   **Postgraduates:** ~250

Accommodation: All first-year students live on the main site. Most third- and fourth-year students (by ballot) live in college owned property, the college is quite physically small (although not in student number) so many of the third- and fourth-year students live off of the main site, but all property is within easy walking distance of the college. The accommodation is varied and there are four main accommodation areas. Two (Whitehall and Besse) are more stereotypical student accommodation buildings, with long corridors and small communal areas. One building (Kelly) has smaller floors but many of them, and is supposedly the tallest building in Oxford without a lift! This building has larger communal spaces and is lived in by first-year students (although some first-years do live in the Whitehall and Besse). The front Quad also provides accommodation for third- and fourth-year students (and for special cases, second-year students). This has very varied room sizes and facilities, so is very much a luck of the draw when selecting a room there! In second-year, the vast majority of students live out in Oxford in houses that they select in the first/second term of first-year. Graduate students typically live in their own privately rented properties, or in the Norham Gardens building, one of the furthest from college site but on a very nice and quiet road in Oxford.

Chapel & Religion: The college is christian, with an active choir. A small but very active religious community exists in the college, with students and staff alike dedicated to running events and providing pastoral care.

College Payment System: Online portal to termly 'Batels' with the option to add additional funds for washing/food etc. This is easy to use but tends to be on the expensive side.

Food: Very good, particularly for formal dinners. Plenty of choice (including for vegetarians!) Meals are more expensive than in many colleges, but are worth it if you enjoy good food!

Formality: Formal dinners bi-weekly, requiring gowns and formal dress. At normal meal times and in/around the college however it is generally very informal. Usually no dress code is needed for academic meetings (e.g. tutorials). There are events such as meeting the principle early on in first term which require dressing up smartly, so be sure to bring formal clothes!

Grants and Bursaries: Available from internal and external funds for those with financial difficulties, as regular payments or one-off's. There are also bursaries to cover sports equipment costs (if competing at varsity level) and grants of £100-£300 for education resources (easily accessible).

Location: Next door to Queen's college, at the bottom (North) of the High Street, next to Longwall Street. Location is perfect for access to academic facilities (5-10 minutes' walk from almost all libraries), as well as getting to town (same distance to Westgate shopping centre). This location is also good for when living out in 2nd year, the majority of properties are in Cowley which is only 5-15 minutes' walk from the main college site.

Politics & Reputation: College politics are present but you don't have to be involved if you don't want to. The JCR (junior common room) and adjoining student bodies have the funds to put on events and trips so being involved in those can be rewarding. Reputation of being a fierce sports competitor and a boisterous college atmosphere. The latter is true to an extent, but it can be largely avoided if undesired.

Sport: Famous for rugby, with a huge internal following in college. Teddy has a strong rowing team and the students are very into pool (although this is only run as an intra-college, unofficial competition).

St Hilda's College

Founded: 1893

Famous Alumni: Susanna Clarke, Zanny Minton Beddoes, Val McDermid

Undergraduates: ~400   **Postgraduates:** ~170

Accommodation: Accommodation at St Hilda's is provided for first and third years. This means second years live out in shared houses, often on Cowley road and the area close to it. This isn't as scary as it sounds though, and many students look forward to the chance to live independently for a year. First year accommodation is allocated at random and all rooms are the same price to make it fair. There are shared kitchen and bathrooms for each floor, but both are sufficiently big to avoid any problems of space or competition. If you have a good reason not to share, the college is happy to make alternative arrangements.

Bar: We have one of the few surviving student run bars in Oxford. This means it is fairly cheap, with nights like 'pound a pint' Thursdays, and 'Drink the bar Dry' at the end of each term. The Entz team runs bops, with themes like 'Disney' and 'Charity Shop BOP.' We've had wine and cheese tasting nights, and have recently bought a large chest filled with board games for student use, alongside our pool table and table football.!

Price of a Pint: £1

Food: The set-up for food at St Hilda's is fairly informal compared to most colleges. It is the only college with round tables which makes for much more sociable meals. Canteen-style breakfast, lunch, and dinner is served Monday to Friday, whilst brunch is available on Saturday and roast dinner on Sunday. This means that you don't have to sign yourself or any guests in for meals, (you just turn up), and you can pay for exactly what you eat rather than a set price for a three-course meal that you might not want. If you wanted to experience Formal Hall, there is still the option to attend one on Wednesday nights. If that's not your thing, however, you can always grab a takeaway from the hall that day too!

Formality: St Hilda's was the last college at Oxford to admit men, letting them in since 2008. The college is one of the few where you can walk on the grass! It's much more relaxed than the average Oxford college, which is a relief if you've been in the city centre all day and need somewhere to escape to!

Location: A short walk from the High Street, St Hilda's is on the edge of East Oxford, just over Magdalene Bridge.

St Hugh's College

Founded: 1886

Famous Alumni: Emily Davison, the suffragette died for the cause at the 1913 Epsom Derby, Theresa May, the former UK Prime Minister, Aung San Suu Kyi, Former State Counsellor of Myanmar.

Undergraduates: ~420   **Postgraduates:** ~377

Accommodation: St Hugh's accommodates its students for all 4 years, all for a fixed price. Older years get to pick their rooms first, but in a random order. All accommodation is on the college site. In second year you can usually choose to live in a staircase of 8 or in a set of 2 (sharing a bathroom and kitchen). In 3rd and 4th year you are likely get an en-suite, or you can choose to live in one of the houses onsite (a really good experience of living in a house without having to live out of college).

Bar: The bar is just below the JCR, and is where college bops are held. The drinks are a bit cheaper than the spoons in town. The bar is usually not very busy unless there is an event on, but the people will usually bring drinks up to the JCR where the atmosphere is better. **Price of a Pint:** £2.40

Chapel & Religion: The chapel is quite small, but the chaplain and his wife are very involved in student welfare and keen to help out. You can join the college choir, which practises once a week and performs at Sunday evensong. There is one service a week.

College Payment System: You pay with your University Card for food, which you can top up online.

Food: We have 2 places for food, hall which is open for breakfast, lunch and dinner 5 days a week and offers brunch on the weekend. A full meal will cost you about £3, there is a different meat, veggie and vegan option every meal, all of good quality. There is also the Wordsworth Tea Room which offers a higher quality lunch and breakfast 5 days a week, for around £5 this is a nice treat.

Formality: Hugh's formals are once a week for £10. These are well regarded around the university, and offer a delicious 3 course dinner. The dress code for this is dress suits for boys and girls will usually wear a dress or something similarly smart.

Grants and Bursaries: Hugh's does make sure to offer a lot of grants and bursaries to its students that need it. You can get money from the hardship fund should you come into difficulty financially throughout your degree, and college are always keen to help with any financial or welfare issues.

Location: The location is treated as Hugh's downside, but you really grow to not notice it. It's about a 20 minute walk to the centre of town, although a lot of departments are closer than this. It's about a 5 minute cycle if you get a bike, which I'd recommend. It does mean that we do not have tourists wandering the grounds, and we have the space to have loads of beautiful gardens that you're allowed to walk in. It's a highlight working on the grass in the summer with no interruption.

Politics & Reputation: St Hugh's is a bit of a left-wing college, trying to get the university to raise its standards and looking after student welfare.

Sport: Although it may not be top of the league in any sports (nearly in pool), but St Hugh's is the only college that will have a 20 person turn-out, day drinking and chanting, for a completely random college football game. Rowing is a big sport within the college, completely open to beginners, with a really fun atmosphere and 2 women's and men's boats. There are 2 men's football teams, one women's football team, 2 netball teams, and teams for badminton, cricket, rugby, lacrosse and more. Having a kick-about on the lawns in summer is also lovely.

St John's College

Founded: 1555

Famous Alumni: Tony Blair, Rupert Graves, Philip Larkin, Victoria Coren

Undergraduates: ~450   **Postgraduates:** ~200

Accommodation: for all years of undergraduate and plenty for postgrads too! First years are split into two but half the year lives all together in one accommodation block with the other half in another quadrangle. Second years can ballot for a shared house owned by college on a road just behind college - so still very convenient location-wise - and third/final years get top pick of rooms from old with lots of characterful wooden beams to brand new with en-suites and spacious kitchens.

Bar: Yes - with a French sommelier as the barman! Lots of fancy cocktails, Japanese whisky, Polish vodkas and regular open mic nights. There are two pint-sized college cocktails too which are great value for money (the Saint and the Sinner). People from other colleges are frequently very impressed at the number of different drinks on offer and the willingness of the barman to customise cocktails to personal taste - all for so much less money than the average bar in Oxford.

Price of a Pint: £2.40

Chapel & Religion: Yes - Anglican chapel but multi-denominational services throughout the year including termly Catholic mass. There is a chapel choir that does evensong twice a week but the chapel is also sometimes used as an events space, such as for art exhibitions.

College Payment System: you top up your university card online to pay-as-you-go for meals and in the bar. You pay your termly accommodation via bank transfer and it is always possible to pay for food/drink with cash too.

Food: Three meals a day in hall, 7 days a week plus brunch on Sundays, formal dinner 4 days a week and a café open 11-3 for food every day. Guest dinners are also a real highlight - twice-termly four-course meals with a fancy dress black tie dress code. Unlimited Prosecco beforehand and unlimited port afterwards with a professional photographer, it is a highlight for John's students and their friends and family who can be invited along.

Formality: John's is a fairly formal college but has a fair-sized state school intake which meant it felt very welcoming for me. We have formal dinners several times a week and a very valuable wine cellar, along with some very imposing architecture but the overall vibe is very friendly!

Grants and Bursaries: £350 a year academic grant for laptops, books, etc. Travel grants available as well as university level sports grants and more! For example, as a languages student, I was lucky enough to be given £800 to spend a month in Lisbon improving my Portuguese. The college gives lots of money to students putting on productions and is able to loan/gift money to students who find themselves in financial difficulty.

Location: Very central! Two minutes from Tesco and the Ashmolean and the nearest nightclub, slightly more to University Parks, John's is convenient for basically everything. And there is a bike scheme which allows students to take out bikes if they need to travel more quickly between classes/sports matches etc.

Politics & Reputation: People often describe John's personality as non-descript and even though it's the richest Oxford college it certainly doesn't feel particularly right-leaning. It is also lesser known among tourists so it certainly retains a student over a tourist atmosphere. I was dissuaded from applying to some of the more stereotypically 'posh' colleges and I definitely don't feel out of place at John's.

Sport: squash courts, two gyms (one weights-based, one cardio-based), rowing erg room, bike scheme. The is a sports ground about 1.5 miles up Woodstock Road where the rugby and football teams play their fixtures but training often takes place five minutes away at University Parks which is very handy.

St Peter's College

Founded: 1929

Famous Alumni: Ken Loach, David Davies, High Fearnley-Whitingstall

Undergraduates: ~340   **Postgraduates:** ~100

Accommodation: College house you onsite for the first two years of your degree, then you can choose to live in one of the College owned properties in North Oxford or live privately in your final years.

Bar: Voted the best bar of any university college in 2015, the bar is student run and much more affordable than most others.

Price of a Pint: £1.80

Food: The pay as you go food in hall can range from around £2.50 to £6 with a permanent salad bar alongside the other 4 or so main options offered, which range from steaks to Mediterranean vegetables and tofu stacks. There are always vegan, gluten free and vegetarian options, with possible allergens highlighted clearly. A full English breakfast is available everyday, and brunch at the weekends,

Formality: Formal hall is on Tuesday and Thursday nights with BYOB and a nice three course meal for £7.50. As a whole the college is fairly informal, as one of the smaller and newer colleges.

Sport: The college has sports teams competing in rowing, cricket, football, table football and rugby. It shares with Exeter and Hertford Colleges a sports field which has two cricket pitches and pavilions, two rugby and football pitches, a hockey pitch, tennis courts and a squash court.

The college boat club, St Peter's College Boat Club, competes regularly. The club shares a boathouse with Somerville College, University College, and Wolfson College Boat Club, which gives students a chance to mix with the grad students at Wolfson.

The Queen's College

Founded: 1341 by Robert de Eglesfield, and is named for its first patron Queen Phillipa of Hainault, the wife of Edward III.

Famous Alumni: Henry V, Oliver Sacks, Tony Abbott, Tim Berners-Lee, Walter Pater, Ruth Kelly, Jeremy Bentham

Undergraduates: ~Queen's is one of the tiniest colleges with less than 400 undergraduates.

Postgraduates: ~Queen's only admits 75 graduate students a year.

Accommodation: All undergraduates are offered college accommodation for the duration of their course. Much of the college was designed by Sir Christopher Wren and Nicholas Hawksmoor and features some stunning neoclassical architecture. The better rooms have en-suites, and the others have shared communal bathrooms. There are no kitchens in the college accommodations, but everyone tends to eat in the dining hall anyway. Room sharing is available to reduce fees. All first year undergraduates are housed in the main campus. Second years onwards are mainly housed in buildings surrounding the college. Every accommodation building has its own common room. The college has a very good JCR, with a Sky box and DVD collection. The college has its own gym and squash courts. The onsite library is very large and the upper library is world famous.

Bar: The Beer cellar bar is one of the most popular and highly rated college bars in Oxford. Housed in the basement, it has a catacomb-esque feel.

Price of a Pint: £2

Chapel & Religion: Queens has a spectacular chapel built in 1364. It has a number of important architectural features including beautiful stained-glass windows dating from 1518. The chapel was largely rebuilt in the Baroque style during the 18th century. The chapel is home to Queen's College Choir, one of the more famous and prestigious choirs at Oxford University.

College Payment System: Queen's uses the university batels system for payments. Food and drink can be bought using the cashless Upay system.

Food: Queen's is a fully catered college with breakfast lunch and dinner served every day in the dining hall. The JCR serves teas, coffee and cakes. The dining hall has two sittings a day, the second of which is done in academic gowns. Saturday formals include a three-course meal in formal attire.

Formality: Queen's is an old-fashioned formal college with a high table. College grace is said in Latin before dinner, and at important dinners grace is sung by the choir.

Grants and Bursaries: The Crankstart scholarship is available for students whose household income is less than £16,000 per annum. The college also provides the Hawley fund, for the funding of activities which will directly help the student's future career.

Location: Queens is in the centre of Oxford off the high street, and so maintains a party atmosphere on the weekends. Queen's is one of the more popular colleges with tourists, and can get very busy in the summer.

Politics & Reputation: Queens has a reputation as one of the friendlier and more fun colleges, defying its antiquity. The college traditionally has links with the North of England via its founder Robert de Eglesfield, although nowadays it sports students from everywhere. It is one of the smaller colleges and known for a more intimate feel. Queen's is particularly well-known for its music, with an excellent choir, orchestra, and jazz band.

Sport: The college has one of the world's oldest boat clubs and is credited with participating in the race which would one day become the Henley Royal Regatta. Queen's has its own sports grounds including two heated squash courts, arguably the best in Oxford. Queen's is one of the few colleges with its own gym.

Trinity College

Founded: 1555

Famous Alumni: William Pitt the Elder, Dame Sally Davies, Bonnie St. John, Jacob Rees-Mogg

Undergraduates: ~300   **Postgraduates:** ~100

Accommodation: College houses you onsite for the first two years of your degree, then you can choose to live in one of the College-owned properties in North Oxford or live privately in your final years.

Bar: The Trinity Beer Cellar is an underground bar famous for its whiskey collection and the College drink, the Unholy Trinity (to be consumed at one's own peril!) **Price of a Pint:** £2 - £4 depending on how fancy you are!

Chapel & Religion: Choral evensong is in chapel every Sunday, and the choir rehearses regularly. There are some occasional weekday services to mark special occasions.

College Payment System: College offers you 3 meals a day in Hall, which you can pay for on your University card which works on a pay as you go system.

Food: Really good! Trinity is famous for having the best food in Oxford, and steak and brie night on a Monday is always fully booked

Formality: Friday night dinner is a very formal dinner, where you can bring a guest and get a lovely four course dinner for £18, a bit more than the normal £4 for a formal where you can wear jeans and trainers as long as you remember your gown and stand up for grace!

Grants and Bursaries: Subject specific grants are available throughout the year for travel or research, college offers all students an annual books grant

Location: Couldn't be more central! Broad street is slap bang in the city centre, a quick walk away from lecture halls, libraries and cafes.

Politics & Reputation: People don't usually think of Trinity as being a small college, but it definitely is in terms of numbers, which means that although some people think of it as being stuffy or old fashioned, it definitely isn't!

Sport: College sport is a big part of the Trinity community and is open to all interests, we have a great joint rugby team with Wadham, a girls' netball team, hockey and for the less physically inclined, the annual Beer Cellar Triathlon (table football, darts and pool)

University College

Founded: 1249

Famous Alumni: C.S. Lewis, Percy Shelley, Stephen Hawking

Undergraduates: ~300   **Postgraduates:** ~100

Accommodation: Undergrads get accommodation for every year of their course. Accommodation for undergraduates in 1st and final year is normally on the main site whilst 2nd and 4th years will be offered accommodation at the annexe in North Oxford, or at another College-managed property within Oxford. After first year, students ballot for rooms, and so can choose who to live with. There's a variety of room sizes but all of them have WiFi, a sink, desk and mini-fridge, and the rent stays the same. Most rooms have shared bathroom and kitchen facilities, but the brand new rooms in the Goodhart building have en-suite bathrooms. As a postgraduate student, you are guaranteed accommodation for your first year of study.

Bar: There's usually three bops a term, and the first of the year is always the famous toga bop... Bring a spare sheet! Bops are held in Univ's spacious bar, which was also redone recently so is stylish and has a really relaxed atmosphere. Univ also hosts a phenomenal summer ball every other year.

Food: Univ usually offers 3 meals a day in hall during term time, except at the weekend when there is brunch instead of breakfast and lunch. Meals cost £3-4, and the portions tend to be huge so you get pretty good value for money! There's always a vegetarian option and at least two meat/fish choices. In case you fancy cooking for yourself, facilities for self-catering are available! Formal Hall is three times a week, and Sunday Formal is always busy because it's free for the choir.

Location: In the middle of everything on the High Street.

Wadham College

Founded: 1610

Famous Alumni: Christopher Wren, Rowan Williams, Michael Foot, Rosamund Pike, and Felicity Jones

Undergraduates: ~450   **Postgraduates:** ~200

Accommodation: College house you onsite for the first and third years of your degree, and in the new Dorothy Wadham Building on the Iffley Road in second (and fourth) years.

Bar: The Wadham Bar hosts regular queer bops for LGBTQ* students, and all student events end with the playing of Free Nelson Mandela. The bar entrance has a mosaic designed by Wadham mathematician Roger Penrose!

Food: Lunch is served in the new refectory each weekday, and usually costs £2-4. Half the options are vegetarian! For dinner (which is £4.27) you can eat either in the new refectory or in hall if you're feeling fancy. Wadham doesn't do formals, but there are guest nights where students can bring parents or friends.

Politics & Reputation: Wadham is one of the most liberal colleges, and was the first to fly the rainbow flag for Pride in 2011. The college also has a longstanding relationship with Sarah Lawrence College in the US, where 30 students from SLC come to Wadham to study for a year, with 6 Wadham students going in the opposite direction each spring.

Wolfson College

Founded: In 1966 by the great Liberal philosopher Isaiah Berlin, a college exclusively for postgraduates.

Famous Alumni: Artur Ekert, Chris Whitty, Richard Ellis, Alison Gopnik

Undergraduates: ~N/A   **Postgraduates:** ~500

Accommodation: Wolfson owns some of the most modern accommodation in Oxford, both on site and around the campus. The off-site housing is located in the poshest and most expensive part of Oxford at reduced rates. Many of the on-site rooms have views overlooking the quad, duckpond, punt harbour, or college gardens. The college has an on-site nursery, as its members are on average much older than the other colleges. There is a small library which is open 24 hours a day, a bar, games room, and sports facilities. Wolfson's common room is particularly comfy, and boasts an excellent selection of magazines and newspapers, and free coffee is available at regular intervals. Wolfson's upper corridors are home to some incredible works of modern art, including drawings by M.C. Escher, all of which may be rented by students who wish to have them on their bedroom walls.

Bar: Wolfson's excellent cellar bar was set up as a co-op style social experiment, in keeping with the college's political reputation. Bartenders work on a voluntary basis, and as a result it is one of the cheapest bars in Oxford. It has an adjoining games room for table tennis, table football and dart. A number of bops are held here throughout the year.

Price of a Pint: £2.90

College Payment System: Most things are paid through the college batels system. Batels, card and cash are all accepted forms of payment in the dining hall.

Food: Wolfson provides meals every day in its dining hall. There is also a small café which provides snacks and sandwiches. The college has an excellent wine cellar, and special wines are available upon request. Tea and coffee are available in the MCR, and is frequently free at regular social events and coffee mornings.

Formality: Wolfson is famously informal and is popular with those who dislike the pomp and circumstance of other colleges. Isaiah Berlin founded it with an egalitarian ethos in mind. There is no High table, so fellows and students mix at dinner and during social events. There is also only one common room.

Grants and Bursaries: Wolfson has a number of scholarships available for academic excellence, particularly in the fields of physics, philology and history. They also award sports grants for talented sportsmen, to offset travel costs incurred when travelling to and from sports competitions.

Location: Located on the River Cherwell in the North of Oxford, Wolfson is the furthest away from the centre of Oxford of all the colleges. The college provides a free minibus service for those tired of walking into the centre. It is the site of Oxford's Punt harbour. There is a private boathouse and restaurant next to the college, the Cherwell Boathouse, which is extremely popular on summer evenings for its beautiful views of the river. The closest pub is the Rose and Crown, famous for its pint glass full of sausages and lovely beer garden.

Politics & Reputation: Founded by the famous Liberal philosopher Isaiah Berlin, Wolfson is known for being one of the more politically radical colleges and is sometimes nicknamed the "Berlin Wall". Wolfson bar is home to the Communist Party Party, a very popular bop. There is no high table, one common room for all members, and gowns are rarely worn.

Sport: Boasting an onsite gym, squash court, croquet lawn, and nearby playing field, Wolfson is strong for sports and is particularly known for its boat club. Wolfson has a day of sporting contests every year against its sister (and enemy) Darwin college, Cambridge. This usually includes a serious drinking competition and the theft of oars from the enemy college.

Worcester College

Founded: 1714

Famous Alumni: Rupert Murdoch, Russell T Davies

Undergraduates: ~400   **Postgraduates:** ~200

Accommodation: Accommodation varies between different grades. Most will have a sink if no en-suite, with different buildings for different years. You can ballot with friends for 2nd year onwards, and a points-based system is used to ensure fairness over the years. Accommodation is only guaranteed for 3 years of your degree, although it is possible to have accommodation for 4 years.

Bar: Worcester has a small bar where college bops, quiz nights, karaoke nights frequently take place. There is a snooker/ pool table and a quiz machine in there too.

Chapel & Religion: We have a college Chapel which holds regular services, on most days, as well as extra services for special occasions. The college choir sing in these services.

College Payment System: Upay cashless system, we use the app or website to add money to the account, which then goes onto our Bod card and we can tap this for payments for food.

Food: Hall meals served 3 times a day, plus brunch on a Sunday, and formal hall sittings 4 times a week

Formality: Very informal. All staff are incredibly friendly, tutors will frequently offer you tea when you have tutorials with them, and everyone is on first name terms.

Grants and Bursaries: Worcester college has a Travel Fund which students of any discipline can apply to. There is also a Hardship Fund but this is normally a last resort. Reading grants of up to £100 are also available to any undergraduate over their degree course.

Location: Very central, right next to the Ashmolean Museum, and the language faculty library, and Tesco's. Also just up the road from the train station (15 mins walk).

Politics & Reputation: Known as a very tight-knit, friendly college. No particular political orientation.

Sport: Worcester has many sports teams that don't require experience, including a rowing team.

WHAT IS A PPH?

If you've been researching Oxford colleges you'll have come across PPHs, or Permanent Private Halls. You shouldn't confuse these with halls at other universities, which normally just means a block of flats where the first years all live together. Permanent Private Halls are a uniquely Oxford thing, and even then, most Oxford students won't know much about them.

There are six PPHs at Oxford, and each of them was originally founded by a different Christian denomination. There are different from colleges, in that rather than being governed by the fellows of the college, they are in part run by the relevant Christian denomination.

All students are PPHs are full students of the university, and are no different from colleges as an academic experience. Regent's Park College, the largest PPH, is listed along with the other colleges in this collection, as it accepts students of any age or gender for a range of undergraduate courses.

Campion Hall only accepts Jesuit priests, and other mature students who are already ordained priests. Blackfriars, St Stephen's Hall, and Wycliffe Hall only accept graduate students, and only a hundred or so between them, so we've not included them in this collection, as we couldn't find anyone studying at them to contribute! As you'd expect, these PPHs mostly cater to students studying Theology and related subjects, so unless you're planning a career in the clergy, they won't be relevant to you.

Several Oxford colleges, St Peter's Hall, Mansfield and Harris Manchester became full colleges in the last few decades after being PPHs, so if you find yourself being interviewed there, it's a good point to bring up to show that you've done your reading!

Few students apply directly to PPHs, fewer than 100 in 2020, so most students will have been pooled to them. Be reassured that a PPH is still the full Oxford experience, and that if you're feeling cunning, they do have a very slightly higher acceptance rate than other colleges in the most recent data at least!

WHICH COLLEGE QUIZ

This quiz is a little bit of fun but also a small aid in helping the undecided decide. Note down the answers to your questions and sum up the frequency of each letter to see which colleges we recommend. Be honest with the answers you select!

1. **Where would you most like to be based during your time at Oxford or Cambridge?**
    a. Not quite in the busiest part of the city, but close enough to be anywhere in 10 to 15 minutes by bike or walking
    b. Right in the city centre
    c. In a quieter area of the city with fast routes into the centre
    d. Further out of the city with its own community
    e. I don't mind where I'm based
2. **What kind of atmosphere would you most like in your college?**
    a. Small and close-knit where everyone knows each other
    b. A large space and a lot of people
    c. Lots of activities taking place, but with a relaxed atmosphere
    d. Lots of people, but everyone has their own niche
    e. Relaxed and a bit different to the usual Oxbridge college
3. **How do you feel about the Oxbridge traditions (e.g. formal hall, gowns)?**
    a. I like them, but I don't want to have to embrace all the traditions
    b. I love the idea, it's all part of the experience
    c. I like a few traditions but I don't want to be too stuck in the past
    d. I would rather avoid Oxbridge traditions
    e. I would welcome some traditions, especially the more unusual ones
4. **What is the least important factor you would consider when choosing your college?**
    a. The extra-curricular activities and facilities
    b. The competition for places
    c. The location
    d. The traditional Oxford experience e. Academic excellence
    e. The accommodation arrangements
5. **What would you want to do in your free time?**
    a. Spending time with friends from college
    b. Attending formal hall
    c. Playing college sport
    d. Getting involved in drama and music societies or politics groups
    e. Lots of different things – I enjoy a range of activities

Mostly As

You like the idea of going to an old, renowned college where you can have the traditional Oxbridge experience, but you would prefer somewhere small with a close-knit community. You would like the peace and quiet of being somewhere tucked away but still want to have easy access to the centre of the city and university.

Considering Cambridge?

Explore these colleges: Corpus Christi, Peterhouse, Sidney Sussex.

Considering Oxford?

Explore these colleges: Brasenose, Blackfriars, Corpus Christi, Lincoln, Mansfield, Queen's, Regent's Park, St Edmund Hall, St Benet's, St Stephen's House, Wycliffe Hall.

Mostly Bs

You want the traditional Oxbridge experience – the gowns, formal dinners, playing croquet on the college lawn – and for the opportunity to discuss your favourite topics with likeminded people. You want to be in the centre of everything and have the opportunity to make your mark during your time at university.

Considering Cambridge?

Explore these colleges: Christ's, Downing, Gonville and Caius, Jesus, Magdalene, Queens', St John's.

Considering Oxford?

Explore these colleges: Balliol, Christ Church, Exeter, Magdalen, Merton, New, Oriel, St John's, Trinity, Worcester.

Mostly Cs

You love the old buildings in Oxford and Cambridge, but you don't want to study somewhere that is too archaic. As much as you like some traditions, you would like somewhere with a more liberal outlook where the traditions are just a small, fun element of day-to-day life.

Considering Cambridge?

Explore these colleges: Clare, Emmanuel, Girton, King's, Newnham, Pembroke, Selwyn, Sidney Sussex, St Catharine's, Trinity Hall, Wolfson.

Considering Oxford?

Explore these colleges: Hertford, Jesus, Keble, Lady Margaret Hall, Keble, Pembroke, St Hilda's, St Hugh's, St Peter's, University, Wadham.

Mostly Ds

The traditional Oxbridge experience is not that important to you – you would much rather have a modern college with state-of-the-art facilities, even if it is a bit further out of town. You would like everything to be laid-back, relaxed and forward-thinking. You are looking forward to getting involved in university-wide activities and meeting interesting people, and you want the college you attend to reflect that.

Considering Cambridge?

Explore these colleges: Churchill, Fitzwilliam, Homerton, Lucy Cavendish, Murray Edwards, Robinson, St Edmund's

Considering Oxford?

Explore these colleges: Harris Manchester, St Anne's, St Catherine's, Somerville.

Mostly Es

You don't mind if your college is old or new, big or small – you just want somewhere that has a bit of individuality. You are not worried about going to an academically rigorous college, you just want to embrace all that university has to offer and to go somewhere where you can be yourself. To you, going to Oxbridge is an opportunity to throw yourself into something new, meet interesting people and experience new things, both academically and socially.

Considering Cambridge?

Explore these colleges: Fitzwilliam, Girton, Gonville and Caius, Pembroke, Queens', Robinson, Sidney Sussex.

Considering Oxford?

Explore these colleges: Mansfield, Pembroke, Regent's Park, St Hilda's, Wadham.

OXBRIDGE PERSONAL STATEMENTS

There's nothing fundamentally different about Oxford and Cambridge to other universities, but there are certain things you need to be aware of when applying.

Oxford and Cambridge are very traditional universities. The style of teaching is very heavily based upon lectures, small group tutorials and practicals in science with your self-directed learning squeezed in between them and in the evenings. You will learn topics in a great level of detail – not only facts but the history of research that led to the discoveries, the contrasting thoughts and ideas of academics and the reasons why theories are thought to be true. Expect lots of essays (even in sciences), assignments and deadlines. This education trains you to be a great thinker – but it is hard and you should be fully aware of that before committing.

Because you submit the same personal statement to all your choices, you must make sure your statement is applicable to all universities. So you can't talk about Oxbridge in it, but you can lay a few simple foundations. It is a good idea to make some mention of extra academic reading, or if you're applying for sciences, a lab project. This certainly won't put another university off, but it gives Oxford or Cambridge a hint that you have a natural curiosity for your subject. This will be valuable in convincing the admissions tutors to invite you to interview. Admissions tutors are not acadmic tutors like you might have worked with already as part of the National Tutoring Programme, or privately with companies like UniAdmissions, but are the people who work for the university to select and approve applicants for each course, each year. These tutors are much more likely to call you to interview at Cambridge than at Oxford, but in both instances the interviews are generally very subject-oriented and it will give the tutors all the opportunity they need to see how you respond to problems. At Oxbridge, the main criteria for admissions selection are academic performance, admissions test performance, and interview performance. The personal statement is a significantly smaller consideration and so you need not be too worried about it.

In addition, Cambridge sends out an extra questionnaire called the SAQ (Supplementary Application Questionnaire) once they receive your UCAS form. Included in this is space for a specific 1,200-character personal statement, which goes only to Cambridge and can be an opportunity to tell the admissions tutor any extra things you would like Cambridge to know. Using this is not mandatory, and is in fact only worth doing if there are things you wanted to mention in your personal statement but didn't have room for because of all the other great things you've written about. You should, then consider using this only to highlight why you are well suited to Cambridge explcitly, and why they are well suited to your needs if it would be appropriate.

THE BASICS

YOUR PERSONAL STATEMENT

Applying to university is both an exciting and confusing time. You will make a decision that will impact the next 3-6 years and potentially your entire life. Your personal statement is your chance to show the universities that you apply to who you *really* are. The rest of the application is faceless statistics – the personal statement gives the admissions tutor the opportunity to look beyond those statistics and focus on the real you, the person they may spend at least three years teaching.

You may hear some people telling you there is a certain right and wrong way to write a personal statement, but this is only partially true. There is a game to be played, but within the broad conventions of good personal statements laid out here, you have considerable flexibility with *what* you choose to talk about. One of the reasons we produced this collection is to show you the vastly different styles that successful personal statements have. While there are rules of thumb that can help you along the way, never lose sight of the fact that this is your opportunity to tell your story.

How Does The Process Work?

University applications are made through the online UCAS system. You can apply to up to 5 universities (4 for Medicine). After receiving the outcomes of all applications, you make a confirmed (i.e. first) and reserve choice. Entry to a university is only confirmed upon achievement of the conditions set out in the conditional offer. It is very important to remember that **the same application will be sent to all of your choices**. It is, therefore, a good idea to apply for similar courses rather than courses which are vastly different from one another. It will be very hard to complete an application for Chemistry, English, Art, Geography, and Engineering. However, applying for Chemistry and Biochemistry would be much more straightforward.

Other than exam marks, GCSE grades and teacher references, the only part of the application which you have direct control over is your personal statement. This is your chance to convince the reader (i.e. admissions tutor) to give you a place at their university. Although it's not a job interview, it is important to treat the personal statement with the respect it deserves. Many universities do not require applicants to attend interviews, in which case the personal statement is your **only chance** to show the admissions tutor who you are.

Deadlines

The final deadline is the 15th of January next year. For medicine, dentistry, Oxford, and Cambridge, be aware of an earlier deadline of the **15th of October** this year– if you don't get your application in on time it won't be considered. Remember that **schools often have an earlier internal deadline** so they can ensure punctuality and sort out their references in time. Different schools have different procedures, so it is very important that you know what the timescale is at your school before the end of year 12. Internal deadlines for the 15th October deadline can be as early as the beginning of September, which is only a couple of weeks after the summer break.

Early submissions are advised because **universities begin offering places as soon as they receive applications**. This is very important as those who submit their application before the final 15th of January deadline can be offered places before Christmas! Therefore, it is in your best interest to submit your application as early as possible – even if you're not applying for medicine or Oxbridge.

In addition, early submission frees up your time to concentrate on any admissions tests or interviews you may need to prepare for, and also your A Level studies.

What are the requirements?

- Maximum 47 lines
- Maximum 4000 characters
- Submitted by the deadline

> **I have the grades; do I need to worry about the personal statement?**
>
> In short - yes. Both are important. The grades are a foundation that tells the university your academic credentials are good enough to cope with the demands of the course. So achieving the entrance grades required is considered to be the basic requirement for successful applicants. The personal statement gives additional information, allowing the admissions tutor to assess your own personality and suitability for their course and style of teaching. If an applicant's personal statement isn't strong enough but they meet the minimum grade criteria, they may still be rejected.

What do Admissions Tutors look for?

Academic ability

This is the most obvious. Every university will have different entrance requirements for the same course titles, so make sure that you are aware of these. Some universities may have extra requirements, e.g. applicants for English at UCL require a minimum GCSE in a foreign language other than in English. It is your responsibility to ensure that you meet the entry criteria for the course that you're applying to.

Extra-curricular activities

Unlike in the US, the main factor in the UK for deciding between candidates for university places is their academic suitability for the course to which they have applied, and little else. This is especially true for Oxford. Whilst extra-curricular activities can be a positive thing, it is a common mistake for students to dedicate too much of their personal statement to these. There is, however, an important place for subject-related extra-curricular activities in a personal statement, like work experience.

Passion for your subject

This is the easiest part to get wrong in a personal statement, and it can be very important. This is what makes your statement personal to you and is where you can truly be yourself, so do not hold back! Whether you've dreamt of being a doctor since birth or a historian since learning to read, if you are truly passionate about your chosen subject this should shine through in the personal statement.

It is not necessary, however, for you to have wanted to do a particular subject for your entire life. In fact, it is entirely possible to choose a subject because you found a course that really appealed to you on a university open day. Whatever the case, you should find reasons to justify your decision to pursue a course that will cost a lot of time and money. If the personal statement does not convince the reader that you're committed to the academic pursuit of your chosen subject, then you'll likely be rejected.

It is important to remember that you are applying for undergraduate admission, not a job. Whilst it is not a bad thing to have an idea of potential career paths beyond university, writing a personal statement that bypasses the academic nature of university courses will be judged negatively.

APPLICATION TIMELINE

	Early Deadline	Late Deadline	
Research Courses	May + June	June + July	
Start Brainstorming	Start of August	Throughout August	
Complete First Draft	Mid-August	Early September	
Complete Final Draft	End of August	Late September	
Expert Checks	Mid-September	Early-October	
Submit to School	Late September	Late-October	ASAP
Submit to UCAS	Before 15th October	Before 15th January	

Researching Courses

This includes both online research and attending university open days. Whilst this has been more difficult than normal for the past couple of years, open days will be either virtual or in person and are always worth attending. Some of you reading this guide will already know exactly which course you want to apply for, but many will not have decided. Course research is still very important even if you're certain. This is because the 'same' courses can vary significantly between universities. As only one personal statement is sent to all universities that you apply to, it is important that you write in a way that addresses the different needs of each university.

If you cannot make it to university open days, you can usually email a department and request a tour. If you allow plenty of time for this, quite often universities are happy to do this. Be proactive – do not sit around and expect universities to come to you and ask for your application! The worst possible thing you can do is appear to be applying to a course which you don't understand or haven't researched.

As a result, we highly recommend that you research the content of courses which you are interested in. Every university will produce a prospectus, which is available in print and online. Take some time to compare modules between universities. This will help to not only choose the 4/5 universities which you apply for but also be aware of exactly what it is that you are applying for.

Start Brainstorming

At this stage, you will have narrowed down your subject interests and should be certain of which subjects to apply for. For applications which will include universities offering single and general subject areas such as individual Engineering disciplines/Sciences and universities offering general Engineering/Natural Sciences etc., it is important to plan a personal statement that fits both.

A good way to start a thought process that will eventually lead to a personal statement is by simply listing all of your ideas; why you are interested in your course, what makes you a good fit, and the pros and cons between different universities. If there are particular modules which capture your interest and are common across several of your university choices, do not be afraid to include this in your personal statement. This will not only show that you have a real interest in your chosen subject, but also that you have taken the time to do some research.

Complete First Draft

Once you have your list of ideas, you want to start fleshing these out. Think about how you would communicate each point to someone you don't know, and turn that list into a side of A4. This will not be the final personal statement that you submit. In all likelihood, your personal statement will go through multiple revisions and re-drafts before it is ready for submission. In most cases, the final statement is wildly different from the first draft.

The purpose of completing a rough draft early is so that you can spot major errors early. It is easy to go off on a tangent when writing a personal statement, with such things not being made obvious until somebody else reads it. The first draft will show the applicant which areas need more attention, what is missing, and what needs to be removed altogether.

Re-Draft

Once your first draft is finished and you've checked it over, you should show it to friends, teachers, or guardians. This will probably be the first time you receive any real feedback on your personal statement. Obvious errors will be spotted and any outrageous claims that sound good in your head, but are unclear or dubious, will be obvious to these readers. It is important to take advice from family and friends, however, with a pinch of salt. Remember that the admissions tutor will be a stranger and not familiar with your personality.

Complete Final Draft

This will not be the final product, and until now, you probably won't have had much real criticism. However, a complete draft with an introduction, main body, and conclusion is important as you can then build on this towards the final personal statement.

Expert Check

This should be completed by the time you return for your final year at school/college. Once the final year has started, it is wise to get as many experts (teachers and external private or NTP tutors) to read through the final draft personal statement as possible.

Again, you should take all advice with a pinch of salt. At the end of the day, this is your UCAS application and although your teachers' opinions are valuable, they are not the same as that of the admissions tutors. In schools that see many Oxbridge/Medical applications, many teachers believe there is a correct 'format' to personal statements and may look at your statement like a 'number' in the sea of applications that are processed by the school. They are right, but only to a limited extent, and you shouldn't change your statement to something you aren't happy with beyond ensuring that you have clearly addressed all of the main criteria needed for a successful statement outlined in this guide.

At schools that do not see many Oxbridge/Medical applications, the opposite may be true. Many applicants are coerced into applying to universities and for courses which their teachers judge them likely to be accepted for. It is your responsibility to ensure that the decisions you make are your own, and you have the conviction to follow through with your decisions. If anyone is pressuring you not to apply to Oxbridge, but you are confident you will have the right grades and you personally want to go, then you should apply.

Final Checks

Armed with a rough draft and advice from friends, family, and teachers, you should be ready to complete your final personal statement.

Submit to School

Ideally, you will have some time between getting your final draft feedback and submitting your statement for the internal UCAS deadline. This is important because it'll allow you to look at your final personal statement with a fresh perspective before submitting it. You'll also be able to spot any errors that you initially missed. You should submit your personal statement and UCAS application to your school on time for the internal deadline. This ensures that your school has enough time to complete your references.

Submit to UCAS

That's it! Take some time off from university applications for a few days, have some rest, and remember that you still have A levels/IB exams to get through (and potentially admissions tests + interviews)!

GETTING STARTED

The personal statement is an amalgam of all your hard work throughout both secondary school and your other extra-curricular activities. It is right to be apprehensive about starting your application and so here are a few tips to get you started...

GENERAL RULES

If you meet the minimum academic requirements, then it is with the personal statement that your can stand out from the crowd. With many applicants applying with identical GCSE and A-level results (if you're a gap year student), the personal statement along with your reference (and maybe admissions test) are used to refine the list of applicants into a pool worth interviewing. As such, there is no concrete formula to follow when writing the personal statement and indeed every statement is different in its own right. Therefore, throughout this chapter, you will find many principles for you to adopt and interpret as you see fit whilst considering a few of these introductory general rules.

Firstly: **space is extremely limited**; as previously mentioned, a maximum of 4000 characters in 47 lines. Note that this includes line breaks - this often means that candidates write a solid block of text, or use indents to denote paragraphs instead of a line. However, doing this not only makes your statement hard to read (especially as most tutors will skim your introduction and conclusion when deciding whether or not to read the rest), but including line breaks in spite of the line limit is a good way to show your competence and organisational skill. Before even beginning the personal statement, utilise all available space on the UCAS form. For example, do not waste characters listing exam results when they can be entered in the corresponding fields in the qualifications section of the UCAS form. This limited space does also mean there are certain things you should try and make sure you don't miss out (as many do), particularly your interest in the course, academic skills, valid life experience, and suitability for university.

Secondly: always remember **it is easier to reduce the word count than increase** it with meaningful content when editing. Be aware that it is not practical to perfect your personal statement in just one sitting. Instead, write multiple drafts, with your first draft being written *without even thinking about the size limits*. If you don't worry about those, you'll find its easier to articulate all the points you want to say, and you can introduce efficiencies later on. As such, starting early is key to avoiding later time pressure as you approach the deadline. Remember, this is your opportunity to put onto paper what makes you the best and a cut above the rest – you should enjoy writing the personal statement!

Lastly and most importantly: **your statement is just one of hundreds that a tutor will read**. Admissions Tutors are only human after all and their interpretation of your personal statement can be influenced by many things. So get on their good side and always be sympathetic to the reader, make things plain and easy to read, avoid contentious subjects, and never target your personal statement at one particular university.

WHEN SHOULD I START?

TODAY!

It might sound like a cliché, but the earlier you start, the easier you make it. Starting early helps you in four key ways:

1. The most important reason to start early is that it is the best way to analyse your application. Many students start writing their personal statement then realise, for example, that they haven't done enough research or work experience, or that their extra reading isn't focused enough. By starting early, you give yourself the chance to change this. Over the summer, catch up on your weak areas to give yourself plenty to say in the final version.
2. You give yourself more time for revisions. You can improve your personal statement by showing it to as many people as possible to get their feedback. Starting earlier gives you more time for this.
3. Steadier pace. Starting early gives you the flexibility of working at a steadier pace – perhaps just an hour or so per week. If you start later, you will have to spend much longer on it, probably some full days, reducing the time you have for the rest of your work and importantly for unwinding, too.
4. Prompt submission. Although the official deadline is the 15th January for most courses, it is often the case that courses will allocate some places before this. By submitting early, you make sure you don't miss out on any opportunities.

What people think is best:

Do things to bolster UCAS ⇒ Write about them ⇒ Submit statement

What is actually best:

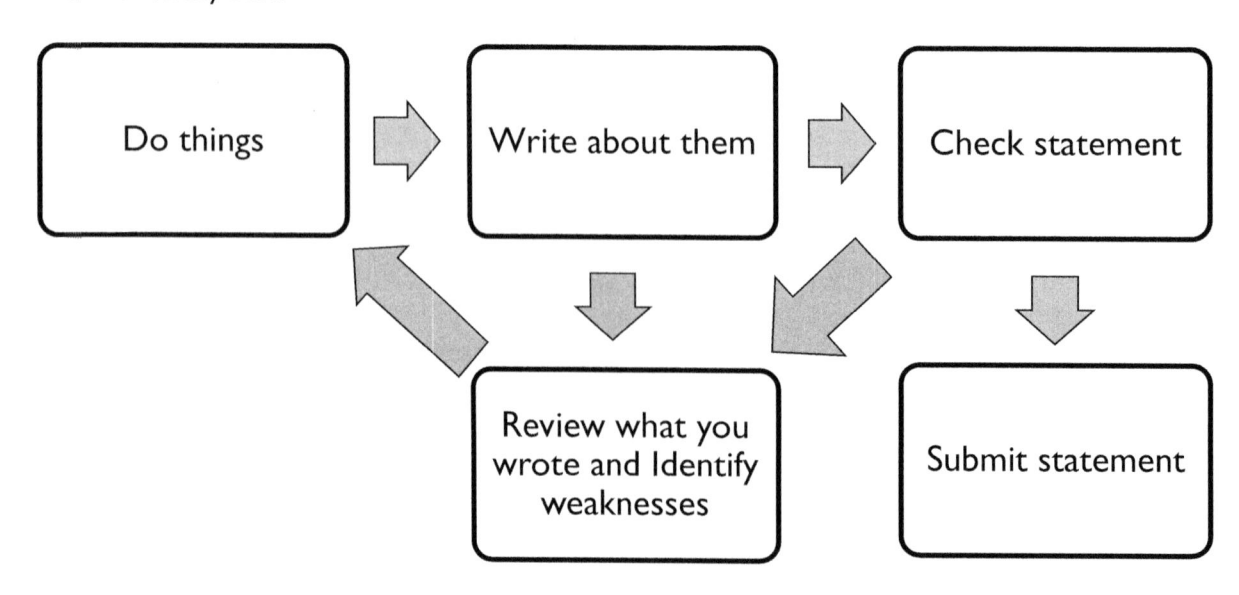

Do things ⇒ Write about them ⇒ Check statement ⇒ Review what you wrote and Identify weaknesses ⇒ (loop back to Do things) ⇒ Submit statement

DOING YOUR RESEARCH

The two most important things you need to establish are: **What course? + What University?**

If you're unsure where to begin, success with the personal statement (like most things in life) begins with preparation and research.

The most obvious and useful first port of call is your teachers at school on the subjects that you enjoy. Not only will they have detailed knowledge of general course requirements; but if they have taught you for a few years, they will also know a lot about you. In many ways, teachers like this offer the most valuable information as they can describe the course in the context of your personality and be fairly sure of whether you are suitable for the course or not. Progressing from teachers, discuss your options with your parents and continue on to **university open days**. This is where the next problem arises: *which universities do I apply for?*

Your choice of university is entirely personal and similar to your course choice; it needs to be somewhere that you are going to enjoy studying. Remember that where you end up will form a substantial part of your life. This could mean going to a university with a rich, active nightlife or one with strict academic prowess or perhaps one that dominates in the sporting world. In reality, each university offers its own unique experience and hence the best approach is to attend as many open days as feasibly possible. By doing this, you will have the opportunity to meet some of your potential lecturers and tutors, talk to current students (who offer the most honest information), and of course, tour the facilities.

The best way to prevent future stress is to start researching courses and universities early, *i.e.* 12 months before you apply through UCAS. There is a plethora of information that is freely available online, and if you want something physical to read, you can request free prospectuses from most UK universities. It is important to remember that until you actually submit your UCAS application, **you** are in control. Universities are actively competing against one another for **your** application! When initially browsing, a good place to start is by simply listing courses and universities which interest you, and two pros and cons for each. You can then use this to shortlist a handful of universities that you should then attend open days for.

There are no right choices when it comes to university choices, however, there are plenty of wrong choices. You must make sure that the reasons behind your eventual choice are the right ones and that you do not act on impulse. Whilst your personal statement should not be directed at any particular one of your universities, it should certainly be tailored to the course you are applying for.

With a course in mind and universities shortlisted, your preparation can begin in earnest. Start by ordering **university prospectuses** or logging onto the university's subject-specific websites. For Oxbridge, you should make sure to check out their *Alternative Prospectuses* which are prepared by and for students for more accurate information about what each course and university is like. In each prospectus, you should be trying to find the application requirements. Once located, there will be a range of information from academic demands including work experience to personal attributes. Firstly, at this point, **be realistic with the GCSE results you have already achieved and your predicted A-level grades**. Also, note that some courses require a minimum number of hours of work experience – this should have been conducted through the summer after GCSE examinations and into your AS year. Work experience is not something to lie about as the university will certainly seek references to confirm your attendance. If these do not meet the minimum academic requirements, a tutor will most likely not even bother reading your personal statement, so don't waste a choice.

If you meet all the minimum academic requirements, then focus on the other extra-curricular aspects. Many prospectuses contain descriptions of ideal candidates with lists of desired personal attributes. Make a list of these for all the universities you are considering applying to. Compile a further list of your own personal attributes along with evidence that supports each one. Then proceed to pair the points on your personal list with the corresponding requirements from your potential universities.

It is important to consider extra-curricular requirements from all your potential universities in the interest of forming a **rounded personal statement applicable to all institutions**. This is a useful technique because one university may not require the same personal attributes as another. Therefore, by discussing these attributes in your statement, you can demonstrate a level of ingenuity and personal reflection on the requirements of the course beyond what is listed in the prospectus.

Always remember that the role of the personal statement is to **show that you meet course requirements by using your own personal experiences as evidence**.

TAKING YOUR FIRST STEPS

A journey of one thousand miles starts with a single step...

As you may have already experienced, the hardest step of a big project is the first step. It's easy to plan to start something, but when it actually comes to writing the first words, what do you do? As you stare at the 47-line blank page in front of you, how can you fill it? You wonder if you've even done that many things in life. You think of something, but realise it probably isn't good enough, delete it, and start over again. Sound familiar?

There is another way. The reason it is hard is because you judge your thoughts against the imagined finished product. So don't begin by writing full, perfectly polished sentences. Don't be a perfectionist. Begin with lists, spider diagrams, ideas, rambling. Just put some ideas onto paper and **write as much as possible** – it's easy to trim down afterwards if it's too long, and generally doing it this way gives the best content. Aim to improve gradually from start to finish in little steps each time.

Your Personal Statement

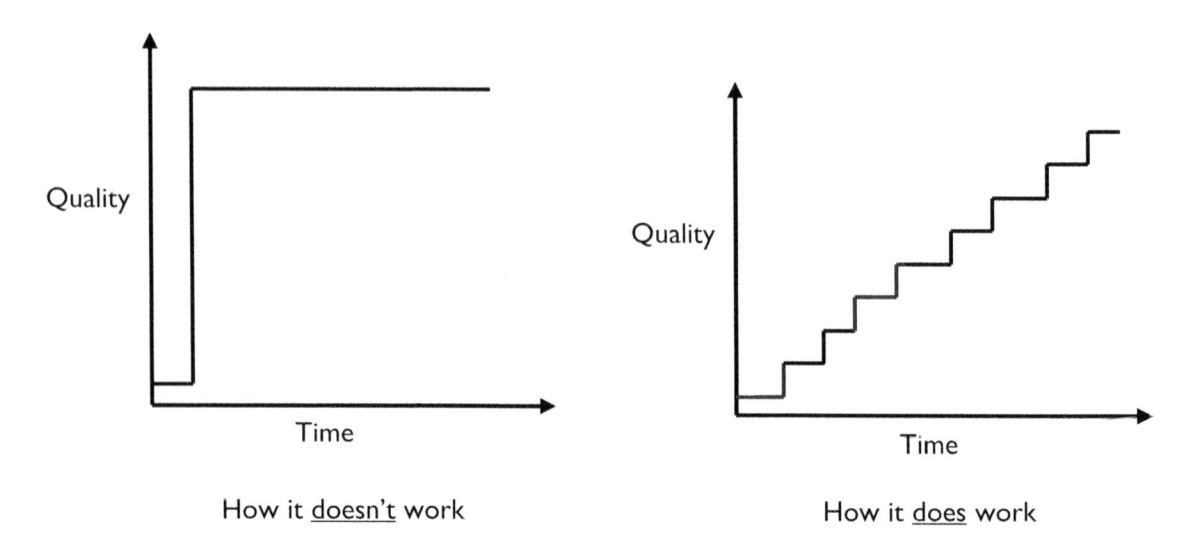

How it doesn't work How it does work

ULTIMATE OXBRIDGE PERSONAL STATEMENT GUIDE — WRITING

The Writing Process

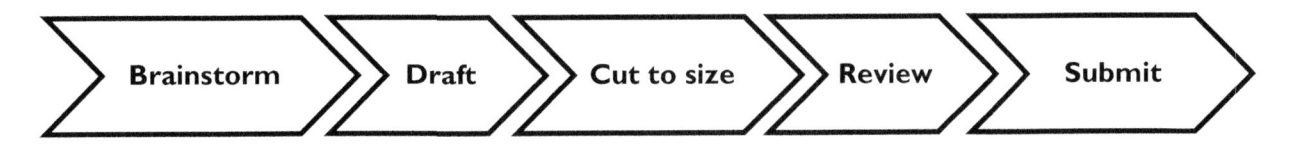

Brainstorm → Draft → Cut to size → Review → Submit

The Brainstorm

If writing prose is too daunting, start by using our brainstorm template. Write down just three bullet-points for each of the 12 questions below and in only twenty minutes you'll be well on your way!

Why did you choose this course?	What features of each course interest you the most?	What are your three main hobbies and what skills have they developed?
What have you chosen to read outside the A-level syllabus?	Do you have any long-term career ideas/aspirations?	How have you learned about your chosen course?
Have you won any prizes or awards?	What is your favourite A Level subject and why?	What are your personal strengths?
Have you attended any courses?	Have you ever held a position of responsibility?	Have you been a part of any projects?

Why did you choose this course?

What areas of your subject interest you the most?

What are your 3 main hobbies? What skills have they developed?

1.

2.

3.

What have you chosen to read outside the A-Level syllabus?

ULTIMATE OXBRIDGE PERSONAL STATEMENT GUIDE — WRITING

Do you have any long-term career ideas or aspirations?

What did you learn from your work experience?

Have you won any prizes or awards?

What is your favourite A-level subject and why?

ULTIMATE OXBRIDGE PERSONAL STATEMENT GUIDE — WRITING

What are your personal strengths?

What courses have you attended?
- ~~The Safety of~~ International Standards on Freedom of Expression and Safety of Journalists run by the Bonavero Institute of Human Rights
- John Locke Institute Essay Competition

What positions of responsibility have you held?
- Head of History Society
- Elected to School Congress in Year 12

What projects have you been involved in?

What is the Purpose of your Statement?

An important question to ask yourself before you begin drafting your personal statement is: "how will the universities I have applied to use my personal statement?" This can dramatically change how you write your personal statement. For the majority of courses, i.e. courses that don't interview, your personal statement is directly bidding for a place on the course. If this applies to you then you are in luck as these are the simplest to write. Just be aware that this is then your only opportunity to say what you want to say and space is much more of a commodity. In this instance, consider writing your reference with your teachers – more will be discussed on this later.

If, on the other hand, you are applying to a course that calls candidates in for an interview, writing your personal statement requires a little more thought and tactics. The first thing to establish is the role of the personal statement in the context of the interview. At this point, it is well worth going through the application procedures in prospectuses and on university websites.

The first option is that the personal statement is solely used for interview selection and discounted thereafter. In this case, the interviewer is going to want to discuss material that isn't included in your personal statement. As such, a tactical decision has to be made to withhold certain information in order to discuss at the interview. Of course, this is a difficult balance to strike; put too little into your personal statement and you won't get an interview; whereas if you put too much into the personal statement, you will lack original material to discuss within the interview. It is always better to tend towards putting a lot of effort into your personal statement to make sure of receiving an interview. Then, for the interview itself, read up on prominent topics within the academic field at the time in order to introduce new content for discussion at the interview. However, do be wary of discussing things that you know relatively little about – the interviewers are likely to be experts in the field after all!

Alternatively, the personal statement can represent a central component of the interview. Many institutions adopt an interview protocol whereby the interviewers run through the personal statement from start to finish, questioning the candidate on specific points. This technique has many benefits for the interviewer as it allows them to assess the presence of any fraudulent claims (it is very hard to lie to a tutor face-to-face when they start asking for specifics), it also gives the interview clear structure but also allows the interviewer to bring pre-planned questions on specific personal statement points.

However, from the candidate's point of view, this can lead to an oppressive, accusative, and intense interview. There are, however, techniques to take control back into your own hands like, for example, "planting" questions within your personal statement. This can be achieved in many ways, including unexplained points, ambiguous statements or just withholding information that can be added to previously mentioned points. In many ways, this protocol is easier to prepare for. There are accompanying risks however, and you must ensure that you do this carefully and considerately so that your statement doesn't seem too disjointed.

Finding the Right Balance

The balance of a personal statement can have a significant effect on the overall message it delivers. Whilst there are no strict rules, there are a few rules of thumb that can help you strike the right balance between all the important sections.

It's important that you focus primarily on academic matters. This means you need to tell a story – the story of how you developed sufficient interest in your chosen subject that you want to study it at degree level. If you are applying to study something you have studied in school like maths or geography, your story needs to start with the reasons you began to enjoy this subject. If it's a new subject such as medicine or engineering, you should explain what has led you to your chosen subject and what evidence you have that you'll enjoy it. You can then move on to talk about how you have investigated the subject, any extra work and projects, and how you have shown your aptitude for it. You may choose to include any work experience that you have done in this part, and you may also wish to give a perspective of any careers that interest you that this subject will help you achieve, taking care to support any opinions with reasons.

Extra-curricular activities are a great way of supporting your skills, however, you need to be careful that this is the supporting act and not the headliner. It is generally recommended to spend no more than a quarter of the personal statement discussing extra-curricular activities, leaving the other three-quarters for discussing academic matters.

The following template gives a suggestion of how to balance the different sections:

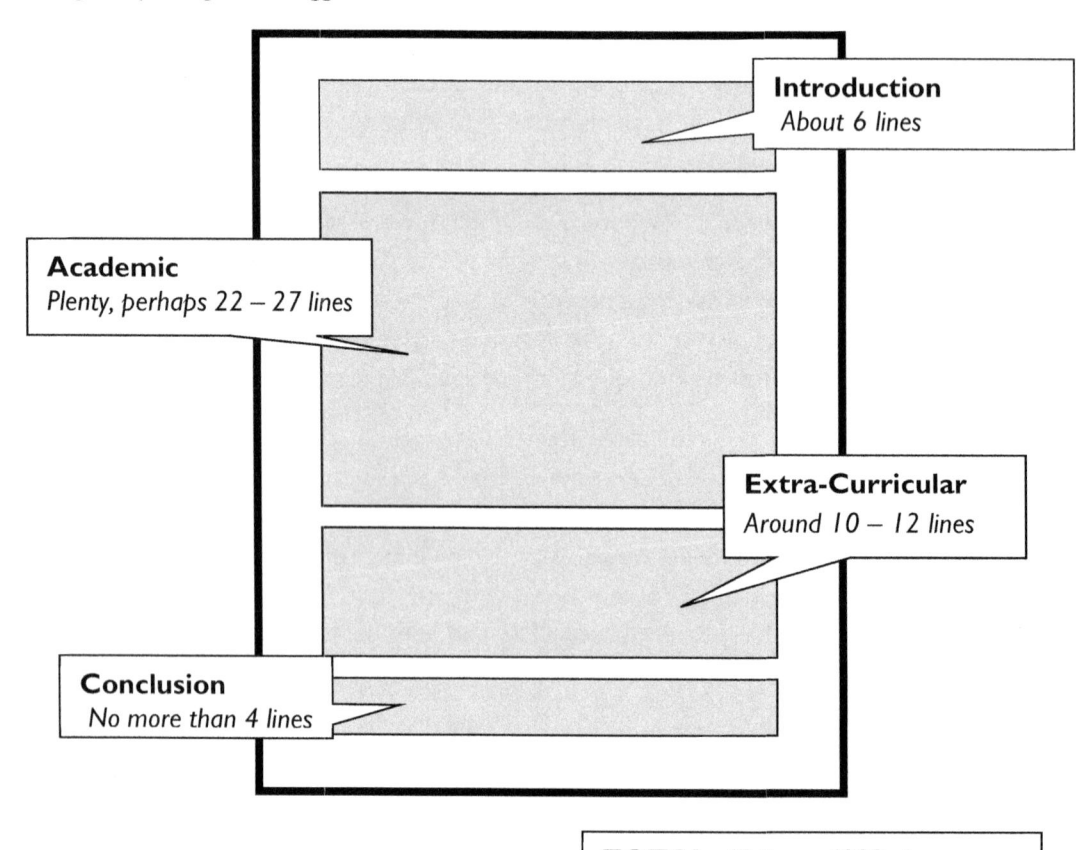

Introduction
About 6 lines

Academic
Plenty, perhaps 22 – 27 lines

Extra-Curricular
Around 10 – 12 lines

Conclusion
No more than 4 lines

TOTAL: 47 lines; 4000 characters

STRUCTURING YOUR STATEMENT

This may sound obvious, but it's important to get the structure right as a good structure enhances the clarity of the content. Personal statements are not monologues of your life nor are they a giant list of your achievements. They are instead a formal piece of prose written with the aim of helping you secure a place at university.

THE INTRODUCTION

THE OPENING SENTENCE

Rightly or wrongly, it is highly likely that your personal statement will be remembered by its opening sentence. It must be something short, sharp, insightful, and catch the reader's attention. Remember that admissions tutors will read several hundred personal statements and often their first impression is made by your opening sentence which is why it needs to be eye-catching enough to make the tutor sit and pay particular attention to what you have written.

If this seems a daunting prospect (as it should!) then here are a few pointers to get you started:

- Avoid using overused words like "passion", "fascinating", and "devotion."
- Avoid using clichéd quotes like the infamous Coco Chanel's "fashion is not something that exists in dresses only."
- If you are going to use a quote, then put some effort into researching a less-well used one which is relevant to you and your application in a way you can personally – don't forget to include a reference.
- Draw on your own personal experiences to produce something both original and eye-catching.

In many ways, it is best that you save writing your opening statement till last; that way, you can assess the tone of the rest of your work but also write something that will not be repeated elsewhere.

If you are really stuck with where to begin, try writing down an experience and then explain how it has affected your relationship with your subject.

Whilst the opening statement is important, it is not something to stress about. Even if a strong opening statement can make your personal statement; a bad one will rarely break it.

WHY YOUR SUBJECT?

The introduction should answer the most important question of all:

Why do **YOU** want to study your subject?

The introduction does not need to be very long. It is generally a good idea to open the statement with something that sets the context of your application. For example, someone who is applying to study History may open: 'History is all around us', rather than 'I have always been interested in History because'. By the end of the introduction, the reader should know:

- What subject you are applying for.
- What motivated you to apply for that subject.

It is essential to show your genuine reasons and motivation. The first thing to consider is whether you genuinely want to study your subject at university. You need to be certain that your motivation comes from yourself and not from external sources such as teachers or family.

Try to avoid clichés; some people will say they've always wanted to study [subject] ever since they were born – but of course this simply isn't true and, therefore, isn't helpful. The admissions tutor wants to see a simple and honest story about your journey, helping them assess how carefully you have considered your choice and how suitable a choice it is. The exact phrase: "from a young age, I have always been interested in" was used more than 300 times in personal statements in a single year (data published by UCAS), and substituting "young" for "early" gave an additional 292 statements – these phrases can quickly become boring for admissions tutors to read!

There are certain things that raise red flags - phrases that will count against you if you write them. These include: saying that you want to study your subject for money, fame, family or because of other people telling you to. If any of these are true for you, do consider why *you* yourself want to do this, if you are struggling to find another reason, you may want another course!

THE MAIN BODY

In the rest of your text, your aim should be to demonstrate your suitability for the course by exemplifying your knowledge of the course structure and its requirements through personal experience. Again, there are no rigorous guidelines on how to do this and it is very much down to your own writing style. Whereas some prefer a strict structure, others go for a more synoptic approach, but always remember to be consistent in order to achieve a flowing, easy to read personal statement.

This point ties in closely with your writing style. You want one that the tutor will find pleasing to read, and as everyone prefers different styles the only way to assess yours accurately is to show your drafts to as many people as possible. That includes teachers, guardians, friends, siblings, grandparents – the more, the better - don't be afraid to show it around!

Despite the lack of a standardised writing method, there is, of course, a list of standard content to include. In general, you are trying to convey your academic, professional, and personal suitability for the course to the tutor. This needs to be communicated whilst demonstrating clear, exemplified knowledge of the course structure and your ability to meet its demands. The biggest problem in achieving these goals is originality, as almost all of the other candidates will be trying also trying to convey the same information, you need to produce an original personal statement and remain unique.

More practically, it is a good idea to split the main body into two or three paragraphs in order to avoid writing one big boring monologue.

PART ONE

This should cover why you are suited for your subject. This will include your main academic interests, future ambitions (related to the chosen degree), and what makes the course right for you, including what strengths you have which will serve you well on the course. It is a good idea for you to read the course syllabuses or outlines and find something that catches your interest for a particular reason. If you have read anything outside of the A-level/IB syllabus related to your chosen course which has inspired you (and hopefully you have), then this is the place to mention it. You should make sure that you avoid writing empty statements by backing everything up with facts. For example, someone applying to study History may write:

"'Reminisces of a Revolutionary War' by Ernesto Che Guevara provided a unique insight into the struggle against inequality in mid-20th century Latin America. Che's transformation from a doctor into a guerrilla leader completed his intellectual transition from an individual with a sense of duty to help others, into a soldier of totalitarian Marxism. Such transformations have influenced the modern world, and draw parallels with the world today. For this reason, understanding history is the key to understanding both the present and the future."

This shows that the applicant has read 'Reminisces of a Revolutionary War' by Ernesto Che Guevara, and truly believes in the importance that History has to the world today. This is much better than:

'I read Reminisces of a Revolutionary War by Ernesto Che Guevara. Studying History will allow me to understand the present and future by comparing to the past.'

PART TWO

This section should still be about why you're suited to your chosen course. However, it can be less focused on academic topics. If you've had to overcome any significant challenges in life and wish to include these in your personal statement, this is normally the best place to do so. Similarly, any work experience or relevant prizes & competitions should be included here. However, it is important to remember not to simply list things. Ensure that you follow through by describing in detail what you have learned from any experiences mentioned.

PART THREE

This is the smallest part of the main body and is all about extra-curricular activities. It is easy to get carried away in this section and make outrageous claims, e.g. claim to be a mountain climber if all you have ever climbed is a hill at the end your street etc. Lying is not worth the risk given that your interviewer may share the same hobby that you claim to be an expert in. So, don't be caught out!

Avoid making empty statements by backing things up with facts. For example: 'I enjoy reading, playing sports and watching TV', is a poor sentence and tells the reader nothing. The applicant enjoys reading, so what? Which sports? What is relevant to your course about watching TV? If the applicant is in a sports team or plays a particular sport recreationally with friends, then they should name the sport and describe what their role is. Likewise, the applicant should actually describe how their hobbies relate to them as a person and, ideally, their subject.

WHAT TO AVOID

Whilst the points discussed previously can be interpreted and used as you see fit in order to produce your own unique personal statement; there are categorically certain things that you should avoid:

- Long complicated sentences
- Lack of reflection or self-awareness
- Lists
- Irrelevant/out of date examples – keep things recent (ideally the past two years)
- Negative connotations – always put a positive spin on everything
- Generic/stereotypical statements
- Controversy in whatever form it may come
- Repetition
- Overreliance on a single example or experience
- Inappropriate examples - ones which are unprofessional or not suitable for a model student.

WHAT TO INCLUDE

Still a little stumped? Well, here are a few must-haves in no particular order to get you started:

- Hobbies – these are particularly important for vocational courses like medicine, dentistry and law as they offer a form of stress relief amidst a course of intense studying whilst also demonstrating a degree of life experience and well-roundedness. By all means, discuss international honours, notable publications or even recent stage productions. Remember to reflect on these experiences, offering explanations of how they have changed your attitude towards life or how they required particular dedication and commitment.
- Musical instruments – Again, an excellent form of stress relief but also a great example of manual dexterity if your course requires this. Do not be afraid to mention your favourite musical works for that personal touch, but also any grades you have obtained, thus, demonstrating commitment and a mature attitude that can be transferred to any field of study.
- Work experience(s) – Don't bother wasting characters by citing references or contacts from your work experience, but rather discuss situations that you were presented with. Describe any situations where you showed particular maturity/professionalism and explain what you learnt from that experience. It is always advisable to discuss how your work experience affected your view of the subject field, either reinforcing or deterring you from your choice.

- Personal interests within the field of study – This is a really good opportunity to show off your own genuine academic interest within the subject field. Try to mention a recent article or paper; one that isn't too contentious but is still not that well-known to show depth of reading. Reflect on what you have read, offering your own opinions, but be warned, you will almost certainly be called upon this at the interview if you have one.
- Personal attributes – exemplify these through your own personal experiences and opinions. As mentioned previously, many courses will list "desired" personal attributes in their prospectus - you must include these as a minimum in your personal statement. Try to add others of your own choice that you think are relevant to the subject in order to achieve originality – here are a few to inspire you:
    - Honesty
    - Communication skills
    - Teamwork
    - Decision making
    - Awareness of limitations
    - Respect
    - Morality
    - Ability to learn
    - Leadership
    - Integrity
- Awards – be they national or just departmental school awards, it is always worth trying to mention any awards you have received since about the age of 15/16. A brief description of what they entailed and what you learnt from the experience can add a valuable few lines to your personal statement. Providing proof of long-term dedication and prowess.

Together, discussion of all these points can demonstrate reasoned consideration for the course you have applied for. This is particularly appealing for a tutor to read as it shows a higher level of thinking by giving your own reflection on the course requirements.

THE CONCLUSION

The conclusion of your personal statement should be more about leaving a good final impression than conferring any actual information. If you have something useful to say about your interest and desire to study your subject, you shouldn't be waiting until the very end to say it!

Admissions tutors will read hundreds of personal statements every year, and after about the fifth one, they all start looking very much the same. You should try to make your statement different so it stands out amongst the rest. As the conclusion is the last thing the admissions tutor will read, it can leave a lasting influence (good or bad!) The purpose of a conclusion is to tie up the entire statement in two or three sentences.

A good conclusion should not include any new information, as this should be in the main body. However, you also need to avoid repeating what you have said earlier in your personal statement. This would be both a waste of characters and frustration for the tutor. Instead, it is better to put into context what you have already written and, therefore, make an effort to keep your conclusion relatively short – no more than four lines.

The conclusion is a good opportunity to draw on all the themes you have introduced throughout your personal statement to form a final overall character image to leave the tutor with. Unless there is anything especially extraordinary or outrageous in the main body of your personal statement, the tutor is likely to remember you by your introduction and conclusion. The conclusion, therefore, is a good place to leave an inspiring final sentence for the tutor.

Some students will make a mention in here about their career plans, picking up on something they have observed in work experience or have encountered during reading. This can be a good strategy as it shows you're using your current knowledge to guide your future aspirations. If you do this, try to do so with an open mind, suggesting areas of interest but being careful not to imply you are less interested in others. You don't want to sound like you are interested in X-Ray Crystallography and *only* X-Ray Crystallography, this will tell the admissions tutor that you may be quite short on real-world experience and will likely struggle on their course. You have to spend a long time at university and your interests are likely to change depending on your experiences. Thus, admissions tutors need to be certain your interest extends into all areas. Secondly, don't sound too fixed about your plans, there is a lot more to see before you can make an informed career choice so by all means show your particular interests but avoid sounding as though you are closing any options off.

It is also very important to avoid sounding too arrogant here and over-selling yourself. Instead, adopt a phrase looking forward in time – perhaps expressing your excitement and enthusiasm in meeting the demands of your course requirements, or looking even further ahead, the demands of your career. E.g. *'driven by my love of medicine, I am sure that I will be a successful doctor and take full advantage of all opportunities should this application be successful'*, rather than *'I think I should be accepted because I am very enthusiastic and will work hard'*. The sentiment behind both of these statements is positive, however, the second sounds juvenile compared to the first.

Depending on the situation, it may be possible to end a personal statement with a famous quote or saying. If you decide to do this, ensure that you don't quote anything outrageous or controversial!

EXTRA READING

Reading beyond what you would need to for your school studies is a great way to show genuine enthusiasm; a good personal statement will include at least some discussion of extra reading.

It also has the added benefit of suggesting your areas of particular interest which can help guide the interview discussion to your strongest topics.

Make sure you don't fall into the trap of thinking a long list of books will impress – this isn't the point, the admissions tutors will already know that you can read books. **The idea is you show what you have learned** from each of the books and how it has influenced your decision to study your chosen course.

This shows that you haven't just looked at the pages of the text as you've turned them over, but rather that you have understood and thought about them. When discussing your learning, try to make specific points rather than generic ones.

For example, a weaker statement might say: "I read Thinking Fast and Slow by Daniel Kahneman, which helped me understand the way by which decisions are made"

Whereas a stronger statement may say: "I particularly enjoyed Thinking Fast and Slow by Daniel Kahneman, which made me realise the importance of shortcuts in making quick and accurate decisions."

EXTRA-CURRICULAR

It is important to show you are a balanced person and not someone whose only focus is work. Extra-curricular activities can really strengthen your personal statement by showcasing your skills. Remember that there is no intrinsic value in playing county-level rugby or having a diploma in acting – you will not win a place on excellence in these fields. The value comes from the skills your activities teach you. Regardless of whether you're outstanding at what you do or you just do it casually, remember to reflect on what you've gained from doing what you do. There will always be something good to say and it may be more valuable than you think.

There are three important ways that extra-curricular activities can strengthen your application:

1. You should use your extra-curricular activities to highlight skills that will help with your degree. You play football – talk about how this has helped your teamwork; you play chess – surely this has improved your problem-solving? By linking what you do to the skills you've developed, you take a great opportunity to show the admissions tutor just how well-rounded you are. By showing how you have developed these critical skills, you can demonstrate that you're a strong applicant.
2. Interests outside work give you a way to relax. University studies can be stressful, and admissions tutors have a duty of care towards students. By accepting someone who knows how to relax, they are ensuring you'll strike the right balance between studies and relaxation, keeping yourself fresh and healthy through difficult times.
3. Showing that you have enough time for extra-curricular activities can support your academic capabilities. If you are a member of an orchestra, a sports team, and you keep a rock collection, you were clearly not pushed to the absolute limit to get the top grades you achieved. For a student without other interests, it might suggest to the admissions tutor they are struggling to keep up with the current workload and may not be able to cope with the additional demands of higher education.

WORK EXPERIENCE

Work experience is a great way to demonstrate your commitment to your subject. For many vocational courses like medicine, dentistry, law, and veterinary sciences, work experience must form a core component of the personal statement. Studying such courses is a significant life decision and the course tutors want to see that candidates have made an informed decision on their career path. It is, of course, useful to conduct work experience for other courses simply for your own information and to see what you enjoy.

WHY WORK EXPERIENCE?

Universities value work experience so highly because it shows you have essential traits:

Work experience shows you're informed. So, you're deciding what you want to do for the rest of your working life, how do you know you'll like it? Rather than choosing your subject simply due to the media or stories you hear from others, the best way to convince the admissions tutor you know what the job actually entails is to go and experience it for yourself. Getting as much varied work experience as possible to show that you have a realistic understanding of the profession better than any words can. If you have good work experience, admissions tutors are confident you're choosing your subject for the right reasons.

Work experience shows you're committed. Arranging work experience can be hard – you may need to approach multiple people and organisations before you get a yes. Therefore, if you have a good portfolio of work experience, it shows you have been proactive. It shows you have gone to effort for the sole purpose of spending your free time in a caring environment. This shows drive and commitment – impressive qualities that will help you gain that valuable place!

ARRANGING WORK EXPERIENCE

Arranging work experience can be hard. If you're finding it difficult to get exactly what you want, please don't be disheartened. You are facing the same difficulty that tens of thousands of students before you have faced.

With work experience, you're recommended to start early. The earlier you start making approaches to people, the more likely it is you'll get a yes in time. It is not really practical to start seeking work experience until after you turn 16 due to age restrictions within the workplace – especially where confidential information is concerned! So, conduct your work experience during the summer after your GCSE examinations and throughout your AS year. This can be achieved through private arrangements you yourself make but it is always worth consulting your school's careers officer as well.

Remember that any part-time/summer paid jobs also count as work experience and are definitely worth mentioning, as they show an additional degree of maturity and professionalism. In addition, if you are able to keep up a small regular commitment over a period of months it really helps to show dedication.

During the work experience itself, it is wise to keep a notebook or a diary with a brief description of each day, particularly noting down what events happened and, importantly, what you learnt from them. Whilst there is a designated section of the UCAS form for work experience details, the personal statement itself must be used to not only describe your experiences but also to reflect on them.

Make sure to discuss:

- How did certain situations affect you personally?
- How did the experience alter your perspective on the subject field?
- Were there particular occasions where you fulfilled any of the requirements listed within prospectuses?
- Most importantly, how did your experience(s) confirm your desire to pursue the field of study into higher education?

APPLYING FOR DIFFERENT SUBJECTS

Applicants who choose to apply for different subjects will have to address this in their personal statement as this is the only place in which the applicant can justify their choices to their chosen universities.

Applicants who decide to apply for different subjects fall into three categories. The first apply for multi-disciplinary subjects, where subject areas overlap. The second apply for dual honours degrees and the third apply for subjects which bear no relation to one another at all.

MULTI-DISCIPLINARY SUBJECTS

The most common degree courses which fall into this category are subjects like Natural Sciences and Modern Languages. Multi-disciplinary degrees generally involve studying a broad range of subjects for the first one or two years of university and specialising in the third or fourth year. However, all of the subjects offered within the multi-disciplinary degree will be from the same broad subject area, like the sciences or humanities.

Applicants for such courses may decide to apply for multi-disciplinary degrees to some universities, and not others. In any case, it is important for applicants in this situation to mention in their personal statement their motivations for the parts of the multi-disciplinary degree relevant to their interests (therefore, covering the universities to which they have applied to study those single subjects) and to also state their desire to gain a broad understanding of their chosen subject area. This is because although applicants for such courses will almost certainly not have substantial experience in all of the subjects covered by their chosen multi-disciplinary degree, they will be required to complete all compulsory modules across all of the subject areas covered by the degree. The reader of the personal statement atm universities offering multi-disciplinary degrees must be left in no doubt that the applicant has the desire and capacity to learn about new subjects in addition to those they are familiar with, and those from universities offering single subjects must believe that the applicant is motivated to study their chosen individual subject at university.

DUAL HONOURS DEGREES

Unlike the US, dual honours degrees are not common in the UK. A few examples of dual honours degrees offered by UK universities include Physics & Philosophy (Oxford), PPE (Oxford), Maths & Computer Science (many). One notable exception to the general UK university trend is Keele University, which offers dual honours courses for all subjects.

Applications for dual honours degrees should be treated in the same way as those for a single subject, with the exception that equal attention should be given to both/all subjects in the degree. All dual honours degrees are different, and it is up to the applicant to ensure that they are aware of the make-up of their chosen degree. Some dual honours may be split 50/50 between two subjects, whereas others may have a major component and a minor component. This needs to be reflected in the personal statement.

NON-RELATED SUBJECTS

This is undoubtedly the hardest situation for an applicant to prepare for. As the same personal statement will be sent to all universities, there will be parts of the personal statement that apply to some and not to others. For those in this situation, it will be necessary to sacrifice parts of the personal statement otherwise reserved for extra-curricular activities and interests for reasons to why each chosen course is applicable to the applicant.

If the courses chosen by the application fall within the same subject remit, e.g. Biology and Chemistry as separate subjects (but are both sciences) or English and History (but are both humanities), it is possible for the applicant to describe their interest in both, tactfully. Describing interest in areas of overlap between different subjects in addition to that for each individual subject is a safe way in which the applicant can ensure that their personal statement is applicable to all of their chosen universities.

THE REFERENCE

The UCAS reference is often neglected by many applicants; it's an untapped resource that can give you an edge over other applicants. In order to plan your use of the reference, you first need to establish how it will be used – again consult prospectuses or subject websites. Does it actually count towards your application score or rather is it only consulted in borderline candidates? Furthermore, the reference could certainly affect the way in which the tutor perceives what you have written and indeed what they infer from it.

Either way, in order to get the most out of your reference you need to actively participate in its creation. The best way to achieve this is to ask a teacher who you are particularly friendly with to write it. Even if this is not possible, ask for a copy of your reference before it is submitted to UCAS. This way you can ensure that the personal statement and reference complement one another for maximum impact.

The reference is best used for explanations of negative aspects within your application, like deflated exam results, family bereavements – or even additional information if you run out of space in your personal statement. In this respect, the reference is a backdoor through which you can feed more information to the tutor in order to strengthen your application.

If there is a teacher who is willing to go through your reference with you (this is particularly advisable for medicine, dentistry, law, and veterinary science applicants); complete a final draft of your personal statement first before starting on the reference itself. This way you will have a clear idea of the content and tone of the majority of your application as well as anything that may be missing which you would like to add.

The reference is the one place for your teachers to be completely unreserved - superlatives and compliments mean a lot more coming from someone other than yourself. One such example of this is the opportunity for your teachers to discuss how they have actively noticed your initiative and passion, going above and beyond in pursuing the subject in question.

STANDING OUT FROM THE CROWD

Admissions tutors read hundreds of personal statements, so to be in with the best chance yours should offer something a bit different to leave a lasting good impression of yourself.

Now standing out from the crowd is easy, but the line between standing out for the right and the wrong reasons is a fine one and you have to be careful.

Many universities will score your personal statement based on a marking grid. You'll gain marks for evidence of performance in different areas depending on your assessed level of achievement. These areas may include interest in your subject, a variety of work experience, evidence of altruism/volunteering, communication skills, and general skills. It is a very good idea to get hold of these marking grids wherever possible and ensure you cover all the areas described in them. The best place to find them is the university website and failing that, you can email the admissions tutors at the university.

Proof-reading the personal statement is extremely important – not just by yourself, but also by friends, family, and teachers to get their opinions. Firstly, it's so easy to ignore your own mistakes because as you become familiar with your own work, you begin skimming through rather than reading in depth. But also, this allows people to assess the writing style – by gathering lots of opinions you can build up a good idea of the strongest areas (which you should expand) and the weakest areas (which you should modify and trim down).

Don't try to force anything into the personal statement. Allow it to grow and showcase your wide variety of skills. Make sure there is a smooth flow from one idea to the next. Allow it to tell your story. Make sure all the spelling and grammar is accurate. Then, your personal statement will shine out from the average ones to give you the best possible chance.

INTERVIEWS

In any interview, you can expect to be asked questions about the content of your personal statement – these could be on your work experience, your reading, your extra-curricular activities and so on. This makes it especially important to be completely honest. We don't mean just avoiding explicit lies – this includes all the little traps that are so easy to fall into – the book you intend to read, the course you'll probably attend and so on. That book you were genuinely planning to read might turn out to be terrible but you're then committed to reading it front to back in case your interviewer probes your interest in it.

But this isn't all bad news – **it can actually be a very positive thing**. By writing about all the subjects that interest you most in your personal statement, you have the opportunity to guide the interview towards those areas you love, know most about, and would enjoy discussing. By doing so, you give yourself an opportunity to show your knowledge and enthusiasm to the interviewer – traits which will go a long way in convincing them you are the right person to fill that elusive place.

Therefore, it is important that you use your personal statement as part of your interview preparation. Read and re-read your statement before the interview to make certain you are ready to talk about anything you may be asked questions about. Not only does this give you a great chance of answering these questions well, it can give you an overall feeling of assurance that you are well-prepared, lending confidence to make your overall performance more polished. What's more, if you have all your personal statement information at the front of your mind, answering general questions about your experiences is much easier as you have a great bank of information to quickly draw upon.

OMISSIONS

It can be difficult to work out exactly where the line stands when it comes to omitting certain information.

Of course, you should only include things that emphasise your best points. But sometimes leaving certain things out can cause problems.

For example, let's imagine you worked for half an hour a month at a care home over a 6-month period. If you said in your personal statement you had worked at a care home for 6 months, you could reasonably expect interview questions on it. When it turns out you've only spent three hours there in total, the interviewer would not be impressed and would be left doubting the truthfulness of the whole personal statement. Far better to just say you arranged a few sessions helping in a care home, then discuss what you learned from it and avoid the risk of being left looking like a fool.

Another circumstance when not to omit details is when there is something that needs explaining. Perhaps you've taken a year out of the normal education pathway to do something different or because you were experiencing some difficulty. Whilst the personal statement is not the place to discuss extenuating circumstances, it should tell the story of your recent path through life. If there are any big gaps, it is likely to concern the person reading it that you have something to hide. Make sure you explain your route and the reasons for it, putting it in the context of your journey towards your chosen course and potentially beyond.

THINGS TO AVOID

Whilst there are no rights and wrongs to writing a personal statement, there are a few common traps students can easily fall into. Here are a few things that are best to be avoided to ensure your personal statement is strong.

Stating the obvious – this includes phrases like "I am studying A-level biology which has helped me learn about human biology in the human biology module". Admissions tutors can see from the UCAS form what A-level subjects you are studying. They know that most applicants study broadly similar A-levels so you don't stand out, and the statement about what you have learned is obvious. This does little to convince someone you are suited for your course, so therefore, it is a waste of words.

University names – the same personal statement goes to all universities, so don't include any university names. Only include specifics of the course if they are common to all the courses you are applying to.

Lists – everything needs to be included for a reason. Very few things have an intrinsic value, rather the value comes from the knowledge you gain and the skills you develop by doing the activities. Therefore, reeling off a long list of sports you play won't impress anyone. Instead, focus on specifics and indicate what you have learned from doing each thing you mention.

Flattery – this includes flattery of either people or universities. Saying how much you dream of studying your course, entering a certain career or how much you admire someone's work will not win you a place.

Harsh criticism – it's great to show two sides of anything and it's perfectly acceptable to disagree with things, however, it is wise to avoid excessively strong criticism of anything for two reasons. Firstly, you are still early in your academic journey. Questioning established knowledge makes a good student, but dismissing the work of eminent academics will make you seem ignorant and should be avoided. Secondly, you never know who is going to interview you – it could be the person you are criticising, or a close friend or work colleague of theirs. There have been multiple examples of Cambridge interviews where a student had strongly criticised a book in their personal statement, and guess who the interviewer turned out to be... This can sometimes be by design, a colleague will be the first to read your statement, and they'll pass it on to the book's author as a result of your critique.

Details about your A-level subjects – your A-levels are included on your UCAS form and admissions tutors know the content of different A-level courses. Admissions tutors are looking for ways you are unique and have differentiated yourself from others. Discussing normal school curricula does not achieve this. However, if you have been part of an interesting project/presentation or have won an award in one of your A-level subjects, then absolutely, you should discuss that.

Things that happened before GCSE – if something started when you were nine and you have continued it up until today then you should absolutely include it as it shows great commitment and the opportunity to develop many skills. However, if you are considering mentioning the archery you stopped four years ago, please resist the temptation. Putting something that finished a long time ago signals to the reader that you don't have much going on now – not the impression you want to be making.

Include books you haven't read – this is risky. Even if you genuinely intend to read the book, you can't make any intelligent observations about it if you haven't done so yet. In addition, you are then committed to finishing it even if you find it very dull or you risk being caught out in an interview. Stick to things you have already read. If you don't have much to say, pick some short books and journal articles and make a start today!

Starting too late – the later you begin writing, the harder you make the task. By starting early, you can do little and often, making it a much more enjoyable experience. You get more time to review, proof-read, and show it to others. And by considering your personal statement early, you have the chance to do extra things to fill in any gaps or weak areas that you spot.

Extenuating circumstances – the personal statement is to tell your story. It is not the place for extenuating circumstances. If any are applicable, this is for teachers to write in the reference. Make sure you know who is writing it and meet with them to help explain the full story.

Plagiarism – it goes without saying that you must not plagiarise, but we feel no "things to avoid" list would be complete without the most important point. Plagiarism of another personal statement is the easiest way to get yourself into big trouble. UCAS use sophisticated detection software and if any significant match shows up (not necessarily the whole statement, just a few identical sentences are enough) then the universities you apply to will be notified and are likely to blacklist your application.

POWER WORDS

Certain words can be useful as they help you show how motivated, dynamic, and enthusiastic you are. These words are often termed 'power words'. For example, just substituting the word 'did' for 'participated in' or 'enjoyed' can give a much more dynamic and proactive feel to the writing. The following list of power words is provided for you to dip into – you will find that including just a few of these words in the correct context will help to strengthen the writing (be careful not to use too many.)

Absorbed	Established	Minimised	Reorganised
Accomplished	Exceeded	Modernised	Secured
Achieved	Expanded	Monitored	Spearheaded
Analysed	Explored	Moved	Streamlined
Assembled	Formulated	Obtained	Strengthened
Attended	Gained	Organised	Targeted
Authored	Improved	Overhauled	Taught
Awarded	Influenced	Participated	Trained
Broadened	Initiated	Prevented	Transformed
Collaborated	Instigated	Promoted	Underlined

Committed	Integrated	Protected	Understood
Communicated	Learned	Purchased	Undertook
Created	Led	Pursued	Updated
Customised	Listened	Qualified	Upgraded
Determined	Maximised	Ranked	Valued
Enabled	Manoeuvred	Recognised	Volunteered
Enthused	Mentored	Realised	Won

USING THE STATEMENTS IN THIS BOOK

This collection contains 100+ personal statements. Each one is an actual personal statement that was successful in getting the applicant into their chosen university.

For each statement, we've included details that show which universities it was successful in. This is included for interest and we don't suggest you over-analyse. It might be useful to take a slightly closer look at any that were successful for your top choices, but always bear in mind that the similarities between different universities are much greater than the differences, and in any case, you have to write a personal statement equally applicable to all of your choices.

All personal statements come with comments, drawing your attention to the stronger and weaker points of that personal statement. Don't look immediately at this. First, read the personal statement yourself and get a feeling for the general style of writing. Then, test yourself: decide which you think the strongest and weakest parts are. After that, look at the comments on the statement. By using the book this way, you **develop your own critical reading skills**, which you can then apply to your own personal statement, allowing you to build in improvements.

We include these personal statements for several reasons including:

- To show you different ways of showing passion for your subject
- To help you gauge what a good balance is between different sections
- To prove there are many different routes to success
- To suggest ideas of high-impact phrases to use
- To give insight into the many work experience options that exist
- To show how you can link experiences to skills and learning
- To show you that writing a successful statement is within your reach
- To help you assess when your personal statement may be nearly ready

IT CANNOT BE OVERSTRESSED HOW IMPORTANT IT IS THAT YOU <u>DO NOT COPY</u> FROM THESE PERSONAL STATEMENTS

UCAS uses anti-plagiarism software called Copycatch. This software checks your submission against all previous personal statements and any in your year of entry too. If any significant similarity is detected, then all universities you apply to will be notified. You can use the examples for inspiration and comparison, but everything you write in your own statement must be your own original work and must be completely truthful to you.

A final word of warning. We are aware there are companies and individuals who will write personal statements for you. We strongly recommend against getting anyone else to write your personal statement. In doing so, you run the risk that they are plagiarising material without you knowing; jeopardising your entire application. Even if they don't, you will be inevitably less familiar with the material at interview - how will you answer questions like "why did you write x" reliably? In addition, this will breach the declaration that the statement is your own original work. Follow our top tips, take inspiration from the examples, and put in some hard work – you'll be sure to produce an excellent personal statement.

EXAMPLE PERSONAL STATEMENTS

SCIENCES

MEDICINE

Subject: Medicine

Helping to care for children during work experience this summer at an HIV clinic in Botswana has strengthened my determination to pursue a career in medicine. It was emotionally challenging to witness children suffering, but I was inspired by the tremendous efforts of the team to help improve the lives of their patients.

My interest in medicine stems from my fascination with science and has been consolidated through work experience placements in general practice, radiology, pathology and pharmacy. One experience that has left a lasting impression was a rare opportunity of observing a newborn on ECMO whilst shadowing a Radiologist at University Hospital, Southampton. It was eye-opening to see how the pediatric intensive care team worked hard to keep the baby alive. I have gained an insight into the breadth of careers within medicine and the incredible teamwork that occurs behind the scenes during work experience with a Pathologist at Whittington Hospital. At Barnes Surgery, sitting in on GP consultations gave me an opportunity to see how building rapport and utilizing good communication skills can help in building a professional and supportive relationship, giving the patient ownership over their treatment. Attending a Medlink course enabled me to learn from the experiences of different specialists.

Learning about the complexities of the human body in Biology sparked my curiosity to learn more in Chemistry and understand the relationship between drugs and the medical conditions they are targeted to treat. To further my interest in science I took part in the 'Siemens - The Next Big Thing' national competition, which my team won with an idea of a desalination plant providing purified water and cheap electricity for less-developed countries. Another inspirational experience was being awarded a scholarship for the Honeywell Leadership Academy at the US Space Centre where I developed leadership and teamwork skills through STEM based challenges.

Motivated by my experience in Botswana, I undertook an EPQ on the prevention of HIV transmission in Africa, focusing on the latest advances in treatments and the necessity of education and social support. To research for this project, and to generally learn about advances in medicine, I have attended lectures focusing on new treatments for HIV, cancer relapses and Parkinson's disease and have read related articles in the Biological Sciences Review. All this has helped to develop my analytical and independent research skills.

Outside school, volunteering at a care home for the elderly, where I organise activities and assist with feeding, has given me a deeper understanding of the palliative care of the elderly. I have developed my ability to interact with young children from working at Kumon Maths over the past two years. I have a passion for music and have taught myself to play the piano and drums and have been a long-term member of the school choir.

At school, I have been awarded prizes in English, Maths and Science. I am also a keen sportsperson and have been awarded Borough sports prizes in netball, tennis and athletics. I have set up a school basketball team and organized professional coaching. I volunteered for a year-long National Social Enterprise competition to raise funds for the Wings of Hope children's charity and out of five hundred competing teams, my team won one of the five top prizes. Being Head of House and a member of the Head Girl Team has enhanced my time management, interpersonal and communication skills. Through a month-long expedition to Mongolia and the Gold DofE award, I have improved my problem solving, organization and teamwork skills and have learnt to work well under pressure.

My experiences have shown me that medicine is a challenging and demanding profession, however, I believe that I have the determination, intellectual curiosity and commitment to undertake the vast level of lifelong learning that medicine is going to entail.

Universities Applied to:

- University College London: Offer
- Imperial College London: Rejected
- Birmingham: Rejected
- Bristol: Interview + Rejected

Good Points:

A well-written and well-structured statement. It provides a good overview of a very diverse education career, covering a variety of medically relevant topics. The student clearly has spent a lot of time and effort gearing her education towards studying medicine. Having diverse experiences is definitely helpful as it shows determination and dedication to the subject matter.

Bad Points:

The entire statement presents essentially a list of different achievements. There is very little information on the student's original motivation for studying medicine. Whilst it starts well with the emotional side of experiences gathered during work experience in Botswana, the student fails to provide any reason for studying medicine other than her interest in science. This is a let-down as most students applying for medicine will have a scientific interest, so this student's interest doesn't signify much. In addition, simply listing achievements can easily come across as bragging. There is a very fine line between providing an insight into previous accomplishments and showing off, and it's important that you are showcasing your relevant skills and abilities in a modest way.

Overall:

The statement is strong but would have been a lot stronger if the student had managed to tie her experiences closer to the motivation for studying medicine. Whilst it is good to provide a list of achievements in a competitive course such as medicine, listing them without purpose has little effect. Most medical applicants will have a history of academic excellence and diverse medical work experience, what is going to make a difference for the application is the connection between previous achievement and the relevance for medicine.

NOTES

Subject: Medicine

"I haven't eaten all day and I don't know if I will last the night". This is one of forty similar messages left within an hour on my house answering machine and was one of the first signs of my Grandma's dementia. I began to read books on dementia as she deteriorated further which helped us cope with the challenges ahead. She has been diagnosed with Vascular Dementia and our family has been in close contact with Primary Care and the community mental health team. I was moved by their compassion and unique work ethic, which motivated me to pursue a career in Medicine.

Keen to learn more about medicine, I attended a Medical Taster Weekend at King's College London. I learned about the process of becoming a doctor and the importance of listening and history taking. Soon afterwards, I arranged work experience on the Gastroenterology Ward at Epsom General Hospital. My most memorable patient was a 70-year-old man who came in with jaundice; I accompanied doctors throughout the diagnostic process. It was detective-like; running blood tests and CT scans with the results unfortunately showing he had liver cancer. This amplified the low-points in medicine, that as a doctor you will be dealing with people at their most vulnerable moments, however seeing the doctors providing the patient individual and holistic care was uplifting. I appreciated the multidisciplinary team working together to aid his physical and emotional recovery. I have now completed 10 weeks of work experience. Having spent a week in an Endocrine Clinic I have become fascinated by Diabetes and its current and future treatments. I recently read an article about commercially available continuous glucose monitors, which soon will be used alongside artificial pancreases.

Volunteering in a government hospital in Gambia for a month affirmed my career choice in medicine. I realized the importance of empathy in Medicine as I assisted with a prolonged labor where the mother tragically died, speaking to the family afterwards was the most difficult task I have ever undertaken, but I was proud to say "Everyone tried their very best." The whole experience was emotionally challenging as all around me patients were suffering from illnesses that could be prevented by improvements in infrastructure and education. Nevertheless, it was inspiring seeing the medical team-work assiduously to achieve the best results possible.

For the past year, I have been volunteering at a care home for adults with learning disabilities. Maintaining composure was difficult, particularly when they would throw tantrums or refuse to eat, but I have enjoyed the patient interaction and it has developed my interpersonal skills. This experience has given me the confidence to spend nine weeks in a Summer Camp in America with children who have learning disabilities.

I have been competing nationally in swimming for 5 years, and now have completed my National Pool Lifeguard Qualification, which required me to learn first aid. My first aid skills became useful on my Duke of Edinburgh Gold expedition when a team member scalded their hand with hot water. D of E has also given me the opportunity to develop team-working skills and learn British Sign Language.

In Year 13, I was awarded school prizes in Math and Chemistry, and the Pickle prize for outstanding charitable endeavors. I was also awarded the prestigious Silver UKMT Award for scoring in the top 12% of a national maths competition.

Last year, I volunteered in a national social-enterprise scheme, to raise money and awareness for the Wings of Hope Charity. Out of 500 teams, my team was invited to the House of Lords and presented with one of five prizes for raising over £3000.

Through my experiences I understand the challenges that come with a career in Medicine but my scientific curiosity, empathetic nature and sheer determination are all attributes that will help me become a great doctor.

Universities Applied to:

- Sheffield: Offer
- Liverpool: Offer
- Glasgow: Rejected
- Leeds: Offer

Good points:

Well-written and good style. Excellent personal entry into the statement. Giving insight into what motivates the student to pursue a career in medicine is centrally important. Having a concrete case to tie this motivation to is helpful as it gives the statement a human and individual touch and also provides material to discuss during the interview. The student also displays extensive work experience, which is a strength.

Bad points:

Whilst the statement gives insight into various medical experiences in the past, it only superficially ties them to new skills learned. This is important because work experiences only really have a purpose if they help to further the student's abilities. The achievements section at the end of the statement is somewhat at the wrong place. Whilst the achievements are impressive, listing them must serve a purpose that shows personal development.

Overall:

Overall, this is a good statement. The strengths definitely lie in the personal touch with the motivation to study medicine. Unfortunately, it loses strength as the student fails to tie previous experiences to lessons learned that are relevant to studying medicine. This is a pity as the student has quite extensive past experiences that certainly provided very relevant learning points.

NOTES

Subject: Medicine

Sitting in front of Mrs D, beside the Royal Marsden consultant I was shadowing, I realised that as a doctor, treating a patient's emotional concerns is just as important as treating the actual disease. A simple smile can work wonders. I also learnt how successful and worthwhile the mammography screening programme was, causing a 15% reduction in mortality rates. However, an article in the student BMJ made me think about the possible emotional, financial and physical stresses that overdiagnosis can cause. At Medlink I was excited to start developing my own practical skills by using an ophthalmoscope. I was then amazed whilst witnessing a bronchoscopy, at both the doctor's anatomical knowledge and dexterity. On my work experience on a respiratory ward at East Surrey Hospital I was struck by the seamless coordination of doctors, nurses, lab scientists and specialist teams. Doctors must be able to act as a leader within a team, so that the patients feel comfortable and secure.

At the Royal Marsden, seeing medicine as an academic pursuit as well as a practical one, cemented my passion for the field. I became inspired to read The Molecular Biology of Cancer by Lauren Pecorino and Cancer by Paul Scotting which, whilst fascinating, left me eager for more answers than they (or current research) could provide. As stem cells' infinite ability to divide is drawn from the up-regulation of telomerase - as for cancer cells - does this feature cause them to acquire so many mutations that they end up inextricably linked to tumorigenesis? Furthermore, is cancer an inevitable price we pay for life? It was then, through studying depolarisation and the cardiac cycle in biology, that I started to wonder why malignant cardiac tumours are so rare. I find the extent of current research awe inspiring but was also excited to discover that in every avenue of medicine I looked, I had so many questions that are still, as yet, unanswerable.

Medicine also requires strong interpersonal skills. Helping out at The School for Profound Education was daunting and had a steep learning curve for me, especially the challenge of communicating wholly non-verbally. However, I found that devoting my time to the care and support of these children through a range of activities from changing feed bags to wheelchair barn dancing was immensely satisfying. Helping the 'learners' to enjoy life's full potential made me realise, that despite the huge commitment, being a doctor and dedicating yourself to ensuring people get the most out of their lives would always be rewarding and worthwhile. I was also interested to learn and research further the conditions some of the children had a common example among the girls being Retts syndrome.

I have been elected as a Senior Prefect and also House Captain at my school. Finding time to relax is vital in medicine and I find playing guitar (grade VI) and piano perfect for me to do so. I have enjoyed engaging with German both in and outside of school, as an exciting opportunity to learn not just a language but also more about a foreign culture; participating in various international exchanges has enabled me to appreciate this first-hand. I developed teamwork skills on my Gold Duke of Edinburgh expedition, and have been Club Captain of my swimming club for the last two years. Through perseverance and determination I have pushed myself to succeed in competitions and I strive to approach academic life with a similar drive. As a voluntary ASA qualified swimming teacher, and through teaching English skills at my school, I have had valuable experience of the challenges of helping, leading and interacting with young children - in particular when I had to clear the pool and improvise a session in an emergency.

I aspire to be the doctor aiding Mrs D through such tough times. When I retire I hope to be able to look back on my career and know that I have made a positive impact on society. Medicine would allow me to achieve this.

Universities applied to:

- Oxford: Offer
- Sheffield: Interview + Rejected
- Bristol: Interview + Rejected
- Edinburgh: Rejected

Good points:

The student demonstrates some good reflections on their work experience. This is very relevant as the experience only really becomes relevant for providing strength to the statement if it is put into the right context and met with adequate reflection from the student's side. The student correctly underlines the correlation of soft and academic skills in the practice of medicine. This is important as it is a commonly underestimated relationship. In addition to the clinical work experience, the student also provides a good range of non-clinical experiences that all contribute to their personal development. Particularly relevant in this context are lessons learned teaching as well as communication skills.

Bad points:

At instances, the statement lacks a clear structure and a clear message. The information provided is a little all over the place. This is a pity as the unorganised structure makes it very difficult to follow the content and learn about the student, which significantly weakens the overall expressive power of the statement. In addition, the statement remains vague and does not deliver the full extent of reflections on experiences possible. This leaves the statement superficial and falling short of the potential expressive strength.

Overall:

An average statement that is, unfortunately, let down by some stylistic and content weaknesses that make it difficult to draw the maximum amount of information about the student from the statement. With some more or less minor improvements to structure and depth of reflection, this statement could be very strong. In the form presented here, it does provide some insight into the student's character and into what they consider important, but the statement sells itself short due to lack of detail.

NOTES

Subject: Medicine

For me, medicine offers an academically and mentally challenging profession which amalgamates my fascination with the human body and my desire to work with a variety of individuals with their own individual problems on a day to day basis. It offers a chance to make a real difference to the lives of others.

My passion for the subject has been fuelled by additional reading, namely various books on the brain such as Greenfield's 'Guided Tour of the Brain' and Sacks' 'The Man Who Mistook his Wife for a Hat'. As well as giving me a good grounding in the current understanding of the brain it has revealed how much of it remains a tantalising mystery. I have also borrowed past A level textbooks from school that cover areas of the syllabus that have since been cut such as the anatomy and function of the human eye and I keep up to date with medical affairs using the Science and Health sections of the BBC news website.

I have explored my interest in the subject through work experience. My first placement was with a neurologist who specialised in MS. The one-on-one consultations showed me the all-important need for tact when dealing with difficult issues that needed to be addressed. It also highlighted the great potential for progress in medical research which is exciting for me.

During my second week-long placement in a general practice I observed a GP dealing with a broad spectrum of individuals who presented cases ranging from gynaecological issues and chest infections to severe depression and even minor operations. For me, it emphasised the range of skills required to be a doctor: the knowledge of the physiological systems that underpin each illness and how specific treatments will affect these systems, knowledge that has a constant need to be replenished due to advances in medical research and technology; the vital interpersonal skills and clarity of communication required to convey what may be a complicated concept to someone with little scientific knowledge; and even the manual skills involved in thoroughly examining patients and carrying out minor operations.

I volunteer weekly in a residential care home for severely disabled adults, most of whom have acute cerebral palsy. Feeding and brushing the teeth of the residents has taught me a lot about the value of patience and empathy in dealing with the seriously disabled. I thoroughly enjoy getting to know the habits of many of the residents and although none of them has any coherent method of communication each individual has a unique personality that I have come to appreciate over time. While challenging, finding unconventional methods of communication with the residents is very rewarding. Helping the elderly during church events has also highlighted for me the value of care and understanding for fragile individuals. Working with these people has really made me realise that I want to devote my life to using my intelligence, diligence and enthusiasm for the good of others; I think medicine is a natural career choice given this perspective.

I believe my extracurricular activities have taught me valuable skills that will prove useful as a medic. I am part of the Nottingham Youth Orchestra and the East Midlands Youth String Orchestra. Playing as a part of these ensembles requires individual prowess as well as an ability to coordinate finely with the many other members of the orchestra. In addition, during my weekly shift at a restaurant I have the role of training new employees which highlights my ability to explain with clarity and to be friendly and welcoming.

Attending Medlink and speaking with doctors and other members of the NHS has made me appreciate how challenging a career in medicine will prove yet I am certain that this is the right choice for me as it offers personal challenge, continual development and the opportunity to make a real difference in people's lives. I hope you will give me the chance to fulfil this aspiration.

Universities applied to:

- Oxford: Offer
- Newcastle: Offer
- Birmingham: Offer
- Bristol: Rejected

Good points:

This is an excellent statement. It is well-written and well-rounded, providing a wide range of insight into the educational career of the student. It also gives a good impression of previous work experience and the student ties these experiences well into the whole picture of medicine. It makes it clear how these experiences have contributed to their choice of medicine as a subject, which is very helpful for an examiner reading this statement. The student also ties his past work experience to lessons learned that they see as relevant for medicine. This is important as work experience can only be useful if it teaches relevant lessons.

Bad points:

The paragraph addressing the interest in the scientific side of medicine is somewhat superficial. Whilst it is good to show interest in anatomy and a desire to stay up to date with current medical developments, this is also something that is expected from students aiming to study medicine. It, therefore, serves little purpose as a distinguishing feature from other applicants.

Overall:

A very good statement that ticks all relevant boxes and only has a few minor weaknesses. These weaknesses have little impact on the overall quality as the student manages to demonstrate a variety of lessons and experiences that support their choice of medicine as a career.

NOTES

Subject: Medicine

The first time I announced I wanted to be a doctor; my parents were amused but indulgent. Their reactions are understandable, considering that I was eight at the time. From a young age I have always been intrigued with the human body and it has only grown from that time. My fascination with science is one of the reasons I want to study Medicine. The continuous learning throughout my career; constant new discoveries and technologies; as well as the variety in each day are part of the attraction of Medicine.

To form a realistic image of a profession in Medicine I have undergone various work experiences which has allowed me patient contact and a chance to observe professionals. I arranged my first two-week placement at St James Hospital, where I learnt basic practice such as data confidentiality and hand hygiene which is becoming more important with the emergence of a new superbug, NDM-1. The following year, I had another two-week placement in Castlehill Hospital, where I gained knowledge of how the management and administration of a hospital operate. This is useful knowledge for understanding how much the government's demands for savings from the NHS will truly affect quality of care. My work experience has strengthened my resolve to pursue a medical career. Volunteering regularly at Harrogate Hospital over the past year has given me recurring interaction with a hospital environment.

My A level choices confirm my enthusiasm for science and demonstrate that I am able to cope with a heavy workload and rise to a challenge, which have already resulted in an achievement of an A* grade in my A-level Mathematics. I enjoy reading and keeping up to date with the latest developments in science; I am a subscriber to "Biological Science Review" and regularly read the "New Scientist". I am currently writing an EPQ on the ethics of organ donation which is self-motivated and gives me a chance to be in charge of my learning. I participated in my school's Medical Package, which enabled me to attend a Hospice Day, hospital tours and lectures and much more. I am also the creator and president of the Medical Debate Society at my school. We meet weekly to discuss common medical controversial topics.

I try to balance my interest in science with a variety of other activities. As a Senior Prefect and a School Council Member, I have excellent organisation, time management and leadership skills, along with the ability to negotiate. My communication and listening skills have developed through my engagement with the Charity Committee, debating clubs, and Netball. As a member of the Boxing club I have learnt self-discipline and determination. I am a philanthropic individual and enjoy assisting others. I am a volunteer at my Sunday school and local library. Paired tutoring is a scheme I am also involved in, where I help a younger student who has difficulty reading. Taking part in the Duke of Edinburgh scheme has shown me the importance of perseverance and motivation to succeed.

I am a focused and determined person with a fierce commitment to studying Medicine. I believe I have the academic capability and drive to succeed in a Medicine course at university. My aspiration is to become a Paediatrician and one of the top experts in my field.

Universities applied to:

- Cambridge: Offer
- Imperial: Offer
- Newcastle: Offer
- University College London: Offer

Good points:

A brilliant, well-written statement that demonstrates a varied history of academic excellence. The student provides good insight into how the early desire to be a doctor has shaped their development, both academically as well as individually. It also shows their understanding of the challenges posed by a medical career, and clear goals which they wish to pursue in that career. This demonstrates great dedication to the subject matter as well as the intellectual and motivational facilities necessary to perform well in a demanding course such as medicine. The student demonstrates good academic performance and discipline.

Bad points:

The statement is very focused on academic performance and academic detail. Personal experiences and lessons learned during patient exposure are somewhat limited, which is a pity as the student shows considerable clinical experience. It would complete and strengthen the picture of academic excellence significantly if the student had been able to add clinical and inter-person lessons learned during their time in the hospital. This includes skills such as communicating information, which is essential in medicine.

ULTIMATE OXBRIDGE PERSONAL STATEMENT GUIDE — EXAMPLE STATEMENTS - MEDICINE

Overall:

A good statement providing decent insight into the impressive academic performance of the student. Unfortunately, the student sells themselves somewhat short by ignoring the non-academic side of medicine that is equally as important as academia. Having had the hospital exposure, it would have been easy to add this in order to achieve an even better statement.

NOTES

Subject: Medicine

In the summer of 2014, my grandfather was diagnosed with Parkinson's disease. At the tender age of 11, I was oblivious to the neurological disorder's implications. On a Saturday afternoon that summer, my father suddenly collapsed and had a seizure in the cold foods section of a Sainsburys. I have never been as terrified as I was when I watched froth come out of his mouth. Following this episode, he was diagnosed with photosensitive epilepsy, leaving me shaken and increasingly concerned about my family's health.

I view doctors as leaders in both the medical field and in society. As Head Boy of my school, I strive to do the same among my peers and in my community. I am proud to have won "Student of the Year" twice and to have represented the school varsity football team for three years. I have developed responsibility and communication skills by attending six conferences in four continents for Model United Nations, the highlight of which was leading 800 delegates as President of the General Assembly at DIAMUN, the largest conference in the Gulf region. As President of the Water for Life Club, I raised AED 75,000 (~GBP12,300) for the Aqua Initiative, a UK-based charity that provides clean water to developing nations. Inspired to do more, I embarked on an unforgettable service trip to the Sasenyi Primary School in Kenya, where I immersed myself in the local community by helping with school construction and interacting with children. Back in Dubai, I helped found the Interact Club and served as its President. We initiated frequent visits to the Senses Center, the only residential facility for special needs children in the UAE. Knowing that I can make a difference in the lives of others is something that satisfies me greatly, which further motivates me to pursue medicine.

I was also fortunate enough to attend a three-week Global Leaders Program at Cambridge University and take a fascinating online course by Brown University. From the latter, I developed a fundamental understanding of neuroscience, modern neurotechnology, neurological disorders and scientific writing. With my grandfather in my mind, I created a presentation on Parkinson's disease aimed at relatives of patients. I genuinely take pleasure in knowing that pursuing a medical career is an ongoing process of learning and reflection that will enable me to benefit individuals and society.

I have also gained direct experience in the medical field by shadowing Dr. William Murrell at the Dr. Humeira Badsha Medical Centre in Dubai. We had lengthy discussions about upcoming research papers on gold-induced cytokines, quality and compliance in biologics, platelet-rich plasma and stem cell therapy. In addition, I observed the versatile soft skills he utilized that I could relate to. For example, when working with a conservative woman from Saudi Arabia, he spent more time building trust before treatment. I then spent one insightful week at the Saudi German Hospital, where I shadowed an array of doctors with varied skill sets and specialties, thoroughly observing both real-life surgeries and clinical treatment. Though I was able to satisfy my curiosity to an extent, I am now more interested than ever in pursuing a career in medicine.

This summer, I visited my grandfather only to find out that his condition had worsened. The man who worked from dawn to dusk and still had the energy to take me around Dubai while I was growing up could now barely move across the living room without support; it is a truly heartbreaking sight. I now appreciate the importance of medical care as I understand that patients are not the only ones who suffer, entire families do. It is my dream to pursue medicine as it combines what I strive for - leadership, empathy and initiative, which are characteristics that I believe are most essential for doctors. I feel a drive inside of me, pushing me to become a person who can make a crucial impact on the health and lives of my family, my community and the world.

Universities applied to:

- King's College London: Offer
- Cambridge: Rejected
- Edinburgh: Rejected
- Queen Mary: Offer

Good points:

This is a powerful statement that demonstrates the student's hard work and drive to succeed, with a clear indication of the personal motivation to pursue medicine. Gaining insight into the emotional motivation of this student to pursue a career in medicine is a definite strong point, providing a good impression of the student's character. The student's varied experiences prior to their application all are demonstrated to serve a purpose to make them a better doctor down the line. The student manages to provide an overview of both subject academic knowledge as well as non-academic knowledge, such as communication skills and the doctor-patient relationship. This is important as these lessons are a necessity when practicing medicine.

Bad points:

A significant part of the statement is devoted to extra-curricular pursuits not directly related to medicine, and there is little academic content there, meaning that it is not clear whether the student has any academic interest in medicine - this would be a significant obstacle at any medical school which considered research to be a core component of its course. The skills they spent so much time discussing are all valuable as a doctor, but also in a range of other careers, and it would have really helped this statement to provide either direct links from these experiences to medicine, or some information about the interest and work in the medical field. It would also contribute to the quality of the statement to provide more detail relating to lessons learned from work experiences.

Overall:

A strong statement that gives an excellent impression of the student, providing good insight into their professional skills, but less insight into why they want to study medicine or what they want to do with it. It is clear though, from the considerable range of experiences they have listed, that the student is very driven and highly motivated to successfully complete a medical degree, which is an important point of interest in the personal statement.

NOTES

Subject: Medicine

I realise that medicine may not always have positive outcomes, having witnessed two deaths at a young age. However, the inevitable fallibility of the human body has driven my desire to acquire a better understanding of the complicated processes and mechanisms of our body. I am captivated by the prospect of lifelong learning; the rapid and ceaseless pace of change in medicine means that there is a vast amount of knowledge in an astonishing number of fields.

Work experience and volunteering have intensified my desire to pursue the profession; it gave me the chance to observe doctors diagnosing problems and establishing possible routes of treatment; I found the use of monoclonal antibodies in kidney transplantation fascinating. A doctor needs to be skilled, dexterous and creative. Medicine is a scientific discipline that requires a profound understanding of the physiology of the body, but the application of medicine can be an art, especially when communications between the doctor and the patient can influence the outcome of the treatment. I admire the flexibility of doctors; an inpatient needs to be approached with sensitivity and reassurance, whereas an acute admission patient would benefit more from hands-on assessments. I have been volunteering at Derriford Hospital since 2019.

The most valuable part is taking time to converse with the patients to alleviate their stress and appreciate their concerns, demonstrating my understanding of the importance of listening. I appreciate that the quality of life is more important than the quantity of years, as a recent death at the ward made me realise that despite all the technological advances and our increasing understanding of the human body, there is a limit to what we can achieve.

My Nuffield Bursary project was based on finding potential medical treatments for sepsis by working on the molecular genetics of bacteria infected cells. Using theory to interpret laboratory experiments allowed me to show how an enzyme was involved in the inflammatory response mechanism.

My skills of organisation and time management were recognised by the Individual Achievement Award for my role as Finance Director in the Young Enterprise team. I used my leadership skills to assign team members to tasks to which their talents were best suited and demonstrated effective communication and teamwork to meet the deadlines. I took part in the British Mathematical Olympiad after receiving the Gold and Best in School prize for the Senior Maths Challenge last year. Regular participation in the Individual and Team Maths Challenge enhanced my lateral thinking. The numerous awards I have won such as Best Results at GCSE and Bronze in the Physics Olympiad not only show my ability in a range of subjects but also my commitment to my academic career. As a subject mentor, I developed my ability to break down problems, explaining them in a logical, analytical yet simpler way. I cherished the opportunity to work with the younger pupils; enabling them to grasp new concepts, and I believe that discussing ideas, problems or case studies with colleagues will be even more rewarding.

A keen pianist, I have been playing for 14 years. At the age of 12, I became the pianist for the Children's Amateur Theatre Society, a position I still hold. Perseverance was essential as I was learning numerous songs each week showing commitment, resilience and attention to detail, which are transferable skills applicable to medicine. Playing in front of 300 people regularly helped me to build my confidence and taught me to stay calm under pressure. Playing the piano is a hobby that I love and I will continue to pursue it to balance my academic life.

I believe I possess the ability, devotion, diligence and determination required for this course that demands a holistic understanding of both the sciences and the arts. I will relish the challenges on an academic and personal level and I look forward to following this vocation in the future.

Universities applied to:

- Cambridge: Offer
- Imperial College London: Interview + Rejected
- Cardiff: Interview + Rejected
- Bristol: Rejected

Good points:

A well-written statement that guides the reader from one point to the next, delivering good insight into personal development and the motivations to becoming a doctor. The student shows that they have a very diverse background, both academically as well as work experience. One of the strongest parts of the statements is that the student recognises the limitations of medicine and acknowledges the challenges in delivering medical care under those limitations. The student is also able to demonstrate experiences made in non-medical fields and how they contributed to their personal development. This is important as some of the skills necessary to becoming a good doctor are transferable from other professions.

Bad points:

The student provides extensive detail on awards and prizes won, but doesn't elaborate on what these demonstrate. If this was combined with an explanation of how the awards contributed to the lessons learned from work experience it could strengthen the statement considerably. Some prizes, like Bronze in an Olympiad, are not worth the space they take up in the statement, and the characters could be better used elaborating further on what they think they will enjoy about medicine and do well in (it's always worth mentioning Olympiad prizes if you won a Silver or above).

Overall:

A strong statement with a lot of information on the student's development and academic achievements. The statement succeeds at raising interest in the student and providing an overview of the individual's development. There are a few minor weaknesses that could be optimised in order to improve the overall strength of the statement even further.

NOTES

Subject: Medicine

The combination of scientific knowledge, getting actively involved in people's lives and the job satisfaction is what made me choose a career in medicine. I enjoy the reasoning behind science but the complexity of the human mind and illness intrigues me as it can defy logic.

My enthusiasm for science was sparked after learning about topics such as the DNA and nervous control. I was amazed how minute molecules control the whole system. Taking maths has built a desire to solve challenging problems which doctors face on a daily basis. I extensively read about the medical field and after 'Life at Extremes' by Frances Ashcroft I was intrigued how the body reacts to maintain homeostasis. Stirred by my placements, I researched further about Alzheimer's and to what extent it affects people. Through volunteering at a care home, I saw how dementia, a condition where medicine has limited answers, affected patients. Seeing the impact, it had, I was motivated to write an extended project on "Should Physician assisted suicide be legalised in the UK?" After researching about how other countries have implemented it and the impact it has on them I have been able to reach a conclusion of my own.

Listening to talks made by consultants in various fields, I was surprised by the diversity of medicine. In the course I saw a live knee operation through a video link. I was inspired by the precision of the surgery, the impact on the patient's life and the personal satisfaction that this could generate. To understand about the profession, I shadowed doctors and I learnt that versatility and resilience is vital when dealing with acute and chronic problems. These skills were enhanced during my voluntary work at Elhap. By working with children with learnig difficulties, I adapted to their different needs and focused on their individual interests which are crucial when working in the NHS. To help children overcome their anxieties, I tailored activities which encouraged group play and interaction. However, some had little verbal communication, which urged me to be patient and pick up non-verbal cues. Through my voluntary work I have become an attentive listener and developed as a compassionate person; qualities I believe will put me in good stead when I am a doctor.

I am the Deputy Head of School Council. This requires being reliable, liaising with senior management and work through problems with other members of school council to ensure an effective solution is reached. My team-work skills were enriched whilst working towards my Gold Duke of Edinburgh where it was important to be supportive towards other members who struggled trekking the mountains. I realised having the ability to work effectively in a team is key when I observed a multi-disciplinary team make a collaborative decision on the patient's next step regarding treatment.

I feel I maintain a good work life balance. As the leader of the orchestra, I have performed at the Barbican thus developing my teaching skills. I organise and participate in musical evenings for the residents at the care home and I encourage them to take part. Music has made me self-disciplined and effective in time management which will help me cope and prioritise work load in the future. One of the key skills I have developed from volunteering as a lifeguard is foreseeing potential problems which will be helpful as a doctor when promoting health and preventing diseases. My post certificate in LAMDA has made me more articulate and has improved my presentation skills whilst understanding the broader aspect of communication.

Contributing to a vast medical field and to its progress excites me. Although I am aware of some of the challenges that doctors face; breaking bad news, comforting patients in distress and working unsociable hours, I feel I will be privileged to be in a profession where every day is different, brings new challenges and to have the opportunity to impact positively people's lives.

Universities applied to:

- Oxford: Offer
- King's: Offer
- Imperial: Offer
- Nottingham: Offer

Good points:

This is a statement that provides insight into a diverse range of individual interests. The student lists a wide range of academic and work experience-related skills, explaining how they contributed to their desire to study medicine and strengthened their ability to be a good doctor down the line. Offering insight into other sources of learning, such as the school council, shows breadth in their experiences, which contribute to the impression of a well-rounded individual. There is also some relation to the scientific basis of medicine and the student's interest in particular areas of medical research. The student manages to draw satisfactory conclusions from their experiences which is important to achieve a complete picture.

Bad points:

There are some minor points that provide room for improvement. The most obvious one is the numerous and serious grammatical and typographical errors – you might not think that these affect one's ability to practice medicine in a meaningful way, but they suggest a lack of care, poor attention to detail, and a rushed statement, all of which sent bad signals to the admissions tutor about your work ethic. Beyond that, there is also the issue of euthanasia. Whilst it is very interesting that the student has been dealing with this issue and spent time forming an opinion, the personal statement might not be the right place to address this as there is not enough room to sufficiently address the issue in-depth. The student also thought to include mention of the challenges of practicing medicine at the very end, but it is clearly shoehorned in to the statement and reads like a list.

Overall:

A good statement with many strong points and some minor weak ones that could easily be corrected, making space for further elaboration on past experiences.

NOTES

VETERINARY SCIENCES & DENTISTRY

Subject: Veterinary Medicine

My desire to study Veterinary Science originally started due to an interest in animals and a love of science and problem solving. Visits to a local dairy farm and attendance of a Vetlink course gave me an insight into the importance of animals to human life; whether it is for food production, work or enjoyment. By understanding this importance of animals, I gained a better insight into the role of veterinary surgeons in improving animal welfare and health through education and application of science as well as their important role in human welfare and food yields. This ability to improve both animal and human welfare interested and excited me about this field of study and work.

After my initial interest I explored the subject further by spending two weeks at Quarry Veterinary Group, a small animal practice, which led to a Saturday morning job where I have worked closely with the veterinary nurses for a year. I also spent one week at both Frynwy Equine Clinics and Macpherson O'Sullivan (a farm animal practice). By spending time at a variety of practices I have developed an understanding of the day to day role of veterinary professionals in differing areas of the profession and the expanding role of veterinary nurses. I have also noticed differences in communication between the vets and customers in a number of fields of work, which seem to stem from varied: levels of knowledge, levels of emotional attachment and available finances. Completing a week each of lambing at Church Farm, milking at Home Farm and generally assisting at Twemlows stud farm has shown me a different perspective on the use and importance of animals in both food production and for leisure purposes. It has also improved my handling of these animals. Attending a three day Farm Animal Management and Production course at Harper Adams University College further improved my knowledge of the use of animals in farming.

The knowledge I have gained has furthered my interest in veterinary and I believe that I have all the necessary attributes to be successful in the field. Scientific aptitude has come naturally to me and I have developed it through hard work. I am now relating my basic science to more real life situations, such as understanding the problems with over-use of antibiotics. Furthermore, my problem solving ability is shown by high achievement in maths, where developing a fast, logical approach to problems is crucial, as in veterinary medicine. Finally, history has helped me to consider complex ethical issues from contrasting standpoints.

Through a range of non-academic activities and interests I have developed additional skills and attributes. Music has been important to me, with my achievement of grade 8 euphonium and membership of Shropshire Youth Brass Band allowing me to develop confidence through solo performance and band concerts.

I am a keen footballer, cricketer and swimmer. Having captained my junior football team, I now play at college as captain of the 2nd XI. I captained our school cricket team for 3 years. These two sports along with bronze and silver Duke of Edinburgh have improved my teamwork, organisation and leadership.

Being a member of Shrewsbury Amateur Swimming Club, where I am club captain, for over ten years has developed discipline and commitment, particularly through 6:00am training sessions. It has also been rewarding with me now regularly achieving highly at county competition. In the past I have taught cricket to younger pupils at school and now work as a swimming teacher after completing my ASA/UKCC level I certificate for teaching aquatics. Overall, I believe I have a lot to offer not only to your university but also my chosen course. I feel I have all the necessary skills to succeed and achieve highly in the veterinary profession. Also I think that my wide range of interests will allow me to offer much more to the university and student life as a whole, as well as allowing me to maintain a healthy work-life balance.

Universities applied to:

- Cambridge: Offer
- Bristol: Interview + Rejected
- Royal Veterinary College: Interview + Rejected
- Nottingham: Interview + Rejected

Good points:

Well-structured. The student demonstrates a good range of practical experience spanning different veterinary specialities. Covering some of the larger specialties (equine medicine as well as farm animal medicine) is advantageous as it will provide a good range of practical insight useful for the course and also allows for the formation of contacts with veterinarians that can later be used for practical attachments. The student furthermore demonstrates that they have a wider range of other interests that provide both, a respite from academic work, as well as teaching the student valuable lessons in team-working, discipline, as well as organisational skills.

Bad points:

The student is very sure of themselves, which generally is a strength but it is also easy to shift into an overconfident representation which can come across as cocky. This should be avoided as it does not fit with the overall perception of what is relevant and acceptable in medical professionals. It would also be desirable for the student to address the relevance of financial spacers in veterinary care. The student briefly and superficially addresses the issue but does not fully address the whole complexity and relevance of the issue.

Overall:

Average statement. Strong points, but also with some weaknesses. This is unfortunate as the statement has the potential to be very good. The point related to the representation of oneself: there is a fine line between sounding cocky and representing one's strengths and achievements appropriately.

NOTES

Subject: Veterinary Medicine

Witnessing the birth of a calf was a wonderful experience and has helped to confirm my long-term ambition to be a vet. This desire has been a motivating force in all my decisions at school. Veterinary medicine is a challenging and worthwhile career that encapsulates my profound interest in animal welfare, scientific enquiry and problem solving. It will satisfy my passion to work with people and animals as well as my love of science. It requires academic rigour, is scientifically-based and provides opportunities for further research either in laboratory or clinical settings. It involves considerable practical skills and the potential for great job satisfaction with the possibility of running my own practice.

My work experience has been thoroughly enjoyable and included working with a country vet, a farrier, at a private stable, a commercial reptile centre, a dairy farm and a small animal clinic. With the country vet I observed two successful treatments on cows to correct displacement of the abomasum by external manipulation and surgery. I helped with TB testing, learning the process, its importance and the wider context. Working with the farrier opened my mind to other people who interact with the veterinary profession. Whilst involved in cleaning and feeding at the private stables I developed a great respect for horses including an awareness of the danger they can pose for humans and other animals. At the reptile centre I handled a bearded dragon, monitor lizard and snakes whilst assisting in an educational talk and at Beaver World learnt to care for guinea pigs, rabbits, beavers, pheasants and fish. During my nine-day stay on a dairy farm I took part in the daily routine of milking, and as well as observing the birth of a calf, I saw the deterioration of a cow and the eventual decision to put her down. It was apparent that working in a small animal clinic involves many routine operations like the castration and spaying of cats and dogs. I learnt that diagnosis involves history-taking, examination and investigations such as blood tests and diagnostic imaging. To gain more experience I plan to work at a city farm, participate in the delivery of lambs and carry out placements at London Zoo and the London Aquarium.

I attended VetMedlink at Nottingham University, thirty-six lectures on all aspects of veterinary care. As part of this course I voluntarily undertook my own research into potential new uses of stem cells and submitted a paper which was marked and for which I received a distinction. This is due to be published on-line sometime this year. My focus was how stem cells inserted into the brain could be used in the future to improve intelligence and treat neural problems such as Alzheimer's disease. Furthermore, I will be attending a course in November to enable me to administer aid to stranded or injured marine mammals.

As well as good examination grades, my other school achievements include prize certificates in mathematics and biology; I was especially pleased to win Gold Certificates in the UK Maths Challenge. This year I was commended for the quality of my answers in the Chemistry Challenge set by my school which required logical reasoning skills. I have a special aptitude for mathematics and attended six maths lectures at Greenwich University on themes which included matrices and types of mathematical proof.

I aim to involve myself whole-heartedly in university life, using my musical skills by playing the keyboard and perhaps playing in or starting a sports team.

I truly believe I have the ability to work effectively with people and animals. I am excited about the veterinary course since it offers the opportunity to undertake research projects, understand the scientific basis of medicine, gain in-depth knowledge of veterinary practice and develop key practical skills. I am determined to become a vet and eager to begin the formal course of training in what I know will prove to be a fascinating field of study.

Universities applied to:

- Cambridge: Offer
- London Vet School: Offer
- Nottingham: Interview + Rejected
- Bristol: Interview + Rejected

Good points:

A well-written and well-structured statement that provides good insight into the student's character and development, both academically as well as personally. The student demonstrates a good scientific foundation, achieving various degrees of academic excellence and also demonstrates a wide range of different work experience attachments that give insight into different specialties of veterinary medicine. This is particularly important due to the wide range of differences between different animal species. The broader the experience before starting the degree, the better. Furthermore, the work experience placements will provide valuable contacts for when the student will be required to conduct care attachments during his/her studies at university.

Bad points:

One of the central points of veterinary medicine not related to the academic side is the funding structure. Recognising the challenges that come with that in regard to the treatment of patients as well as the interaction with owners is an important component. Since the student experienced care in different practice settings, it is likely that he/she has come across this issue.

Overall:

A good statement that offers worthy detail about the student and his/her motivation as well as his/her individual development. It could be improved by additional reflection on the challenges of a veterinary practice, for example due to the existing funding structures.

NOTES

Subject: Veterinary Medicine

Growing up in a rural area enabled me to appreciate the whole cycle of life, and has stimulated a genuine interest in the sciences. This was recently enhanced by hatching 14 chicks, whilst a few mortalities demonstrated the reality of life and death. This inspired me to read 'Life on Earth' by David Attenborough. I especially enjoyed the chapter named 'Eggs, Pouches and Placentas', shedding light on the reproductive cycles of several species. Veterinary Medicine therefore appeals to me as it incorporates a broad base of biological science together with a practical application, suiting my passions and talents.

Undoubtedly, work experience over 10 weeks has reinforced my determination to become a vet. Time spent at small animal practices showed me the clinical role of a vet, observing the importance of teamwork and the ability to deal with owners. During a week at Newmarket Equine hospital, I learnt about routine tasks undertaken at racing yards with ambulatory vets, including endoscopic tracheal examinations. Viewing a knee arthroscopy of a mare demonstrated the rapid progress being made in the profession, of which I am eager to be part of, and made me realise the differing roles of vets in the Equine profession and that of Livestock farming. As a lambing assistant, I gained animal handling skills and of course helped with numerous deliveries, with complications such as still born and breech births. My general husbandry skills were further improved by work at an Animal Rescue centre. Staying on a robotic dairy farm allowed me to try everything from pregnancy monitoring to intramuscular injections. The absence of a traditional parlour gave more time to maintain the health of the cattle, whilst the technology enabled early warnings of problems such as mastitis. I gained more practical experience through a placement at a zoo and helping at a livery, which taught me about a vets role in the conservation of endangered species, whilst the farrier at the livery confirmed the importance of foot care. At The Royal Veterinary College Labs, I was interested to see the necropsy of an aborted calf, which inspired me to write my Extended Project on the causes of bovine abortion. I was also fascinated to see the anatomy of cattle and sheep at an abattoir, with the slaughterman at work. Such varied experiences have both demonstrated my commitment to a future career in Veterinary Science, and fuelled my desire to do everything I can to ensure I get there.

My A level subjects have equipped me with the core skills required for my chosen degree. Of particular interest was immunology, increasing my desire to gain a better understanding of the scientific principles underlying both the health and disease of animals. Teaching younger students at a primary school science club helped pass on my enthusiasm for my subject, whilst attending a 6th form science discussion group enables me to develop my own ideas on complex ethical issues such as badger culling. Reading the Farmers Weekly has furthered my interest in this controversial debate.

Communication is a vital skill that I have developed by working as a waitress, peer mentoring younger students and being Deputy Head Girl. Despite being the only girl when I joined my village football team aged 4, my persistence and determination means that I am now a member of a Ladies Football Team. This has developed my teamwork skills, further improved by completing Gold D of E. These skills I went on to use in the Rotary supported Interact club, in which I help to organise and run Charity events, including those for our partner school in Uganda ahead of my visit there next year. Having undertaken the Community Sports Leadership Award and being a Corporal at the Air Training Corps has further developed leadership skills that will aid my future learning and career.

Being an ambitious person, I am excited by this challenging and ever-changing discipline of Veterinary Science, as my future opportunities would be limitless.

Universities applied to:

- Cambridge: Offer
- Bristol: Offer
- Leeds: Offer
- Edinburgh: Rejected
- Glasgow: Rejected

Good points:

The student demonstrates an excellent range of work experience ranging from matters of life to matters of death as well as including work with different species of animals and different degrees of hands-on experience. This results in great diversity as well as the impression that the student has gone to considerable lengths to achieve the best possible starting point for her studies. She also gives insight into some academic and non-academic characteristics she considers important in a veterinarian and demonstrates her endeavours to achieve these characteristics.

Bad points:

Some of the experiences could be described in more depth regarding lessons learned and reflections drawn, it isn't entirely clear from the statement what makes the student a good fit for veterinary medicine beyond their personal drive. Due to the wide range of experience, this is somewhat challenging but it will increase the overall quality of the piece. Additionally, the student ignores the challenges, both emotionally as well as professionally, that result from the private character of veterinary medicine where owners have to pay for the treatment of their animals, this means that the statement gives an impression of someone who has 'always wanted to be a vet' but doesn't know much about what it entails in day-to-day life, and can't show that they'd be any good at it.

Overall:

A good statement that is well-written and well-structured. There are some weaknesses, but these only reduce the strength of the statement to a limited extent due to the wide range of relevant and high-quality work experience attachments the student has demonstrated. These experiences will also provide a good basis for discussion in an interview.

NOTES

Subject: Veterinary Medicine

Veterinary medicine is dismissed by some as an unimportant offshoot of human medicine and I have even heard the term "dog plumber" used. So why study it? My work experience and common sense have led me to believe that this view is a fallacy and veterinary medicine is relevant in numerous fields and stands only to become more so.

Veterinary medicine is rooted in science and vets must have broad scientific knowledge to understand diagnoses and treatment of patients. This is an area in which I feel I excel and I hope this is communicated in other ways than high marks. For instance, I have been reading How Animals Work by Knut Schmidt-Nielsen in which he explores physiological mechanisms, from countercurrent heat exchangers in sheep scrotums to the problems encountered when scaling up LSD doses for elephants. I enjoy pursuing science beyond the syllabus in other ways such competing in science Olympiads and attending lectures at UCL and the Cambridge Physics Labs on a range of subjects, my favourite being how genes and environment interact. I am a member of our school's biology society where we present issues to the society, my group's task being to deal with whether all species are worth saving, since their conservation can be so costly and their role in maintaining biodiversity so limited. I relish academic challenges and the opportunity for development and research in veterinary medicine can provide me with these.

But veterinary medicine is not just academic, and to better understand the practice I spent time at various establishments. Two weeks at a veterinary hospital showed me the bread and butter of small animal work (e.g castrations, vaccinations) while also being advanced enough for complex orthopedic and soft tissue surgery. I had a stint shadowing an exotics vet at another practice, giving me a peek into this weird and wonderful branch of practice, including calcium deficiency in tortoises and the use of implants to inhibit adrenal disease in ferrets. A week at a kennels was useful because I learned how they operate measures to ensure good biosecurity, namely thorough and frequent cleaning of the wards. The facility included a hydrotherapy pool, which I was able to see in use, getting a better idea of what ailments this therapy is used for and how it works. Spending a week with a sheep farmer during lambing and two weeks on a dairy farm gave me an insight into the more traditional side of veterinary medicine. While at these farms I learned about the husbandry of sheep and dairy cattle, common health problems and when and how drugs are administered. Tasks I undertook included delivering and marking lambs, administering antibiotics, milking cows and herding animals from one field to the next. During my stay at the dairy farm I was lucky enough to be present for a visit from the local vet who got me to don a long-sleeved glove and feel around inside a cow for the fetus! I visited a sheep sale and saw the extensive measures to prevent disease transmission and the new EID tags in action. I went down to an intensive chicken farm for a day to see how these sorts of farms were managed, taking part in some shed management and culling of sick or small birds. As unpleasant as it was, I know vets play a major role in the running of all farms and sick animals must be dealt with. All of the large animal experience helps me with my work at Stepney City farm, where I have been volunteering since 2004. This small farm allows me to follow my interest in livestock while also giving me the chance to meet and engage with new people in many different, sometimes difficult situations. This has sharpened my people skills and I feel this is a key attribute for a good vet.

During my work experience, the greatest revelation was how important the human factor is. Vets have to be reliable, clear and approachable, whether it's to the small animal owner worried about the health of their dear companion or to the farmer concerned about whether treatment for an animal is financially viable. Another side to veterinary medicine that attracts me is wide range of subjects vets are required to weigh in on, from the fate of "status" dogs to the feeding of cabbages to ram lambs, from a scientific and a practical viewpoint.

Aside from all things veterinary, I maintain an interest in Classics and am a member of our school's Classical Society which meets to ponder the merits of ancient civilizations, scholars and leaders. I play hockey for the school and have completed Duke of Edinburgh's award up to Silver level, both of which I feel have developed my abilities to work in a team. Taking part in the Senior Play helped me with confidence in speaking and performing publicly, while being Deputy Head of my house has given me some level of responsibility.

Universities applied to:

- Cambridge: Offer
- Royal Veterinary College: Offer
- Edinburgh: Rejected
- Nottingham: Rejected

Good points:

A well-written statement that addresses a wide range of core veterinary specialties. This is important in order to give the student an appropriate impression of the realities of veterinary medicine and its practical aspects, in particular, due to its often-misleading representation in popular media. Being aware of the personal as well as academic challenges of a profession in veterinary medicine is very important. The student is able to demonstrate this awareness as well as adequate exposure. It is also a strong point that the student provides specific insight into his/her reflections on their work experience rather than just letting the descriptions stand in the statement by themselves without any contextualisation.

Bad points:

The style is somewhat bizarre at some points, particularly in the beginning. It is obvious that the student intends to be original and stick out from the mass of other applicants, but the style they chose is somewhat inappropriate for this. It drags on for too long, making it a waste of valuable space that could be better used for more relevant topics such as the role of money and funding in veterinary practice. What's more, they go into some detail talking about their own convictions surrounding preserving biodiversity - this is a complex topic best disucssed at interview, and would be better dealt with here just by saying "my group's task being to address the complexities of conservation."

Overall:

A good statement with the potential to be great but is, unfortunately, let down in parts by the student's overly chatty, informal writing style. This is a pity as the student demonstrates excellent exposure and awareness to the challenges of veterinary practice and he/she succeeds in providing good insight into his/her motivations for the pursuit of a career in veterinary medicine.

NOTES

Subject: Dentistry

Everyone has the right to a good smile. A smile can have a major effect on a person's self-esteem, confidence and happiness. It would give me great satisfaction being able to have a positive effect on a patient's quality of life by being able to influence these and many more factors. Dentistry as a prospective career path has always been a very appealing profession because I am interested in caring for people and also enjoy the creativity involved with the profession.

My work experience has further fuelled my desire to study dentistry, because it has shown me how rapidly expanding the dental sector which allows continuous learning. I have worked at Smiledent Dental Practice where I shadowed the dentists and the dental nurses. This experience has highlighted the importance between the balance of leadership and teamwork required to achieve the best treatment for the patients and the efficient running of a dental practice. Furthermore, I witnessed the need to gain the trust of the patient and build a patient-dentist relationship, to allow for a smooth successful treatment.

Apart from a dental practice, I have also volunteered at Haselbury Junior School organising activities for young children at an afterschool club for three months. Working with young children taught me to adapt my communication skills, using simple vocabulary and body language. During this time, it also gave me a sense of care and responsibility towards the children. This motivated me to work with people at the opposite end of the age spectrum. I therefore volunteered at The Haven Day Centre which was a humbling yet valuable experience. I enjoyed being a pillar of support to the elderly trying to entertain them and it was a warming experience to witness their joy.

Moreover, I have regularly attended St John Ambulance Cadets for the past three years. I am now a senior member in the division teaching younger peers first aid thoroughly enjoying the additional responsibility involved in nurturing others.

In addition, I have a keen academic interest. The transmission of diseases, prevention and immunology in Biology, has emphasised to me the significance of hygiene and how rapidly diseases can spread which is vital in the field of dentistry. In Chemistry, I have particularly enjoyed learning about molecular bonding enabling me to understand why particular materials have properties that make them suitable for their job. I have thoroughly enjoyed and flourished in the practical aspects of both subjects. The experiments have allowed me to put into practice/apply the knowledge I have acquired in lessons. Studying mathematics has improved my problem solving ability acquiring practice to reach answers with a methodical yet flexible approach. In years 9 and 12, I was invited to attend lectures at the London Metropolitan University and the Royal Institution of Mathematics over a series of weekends. As a result, I had the opportunity to study branches of mathematics outside the syllabus which thoroughly challenged me. Additionally, geography has helped develop a creative aspect of academic life. In the human sector, I enjoyed the topic about smoking because it taught me the history and origins of smoking and the widespread effect it has on the body including the gums and teeth.

As part of my research, I have expanded my dental knowledge using several websites to gain extra information. I have been fascinated by crowns and root canal treatments because I am fond of the creativity involved such as choosing tooth colours, shape and material to ensure practicality for the patient and simultaneously rectify tooth damage.

Finally, from my work experience in a dental practice and I believe would thrive in such an environment.

Universities applied to:

- Birmingham: Offer
- Sheffield: Rejected
- King's: Interview + Rejected
- Leeds: Rejected
- Aston: Offer

Good points:

Clear structure and the student gives a good insight into their motivation for the study of dentistry as well as providing evidence for their personal, professional, and academic development. It becomes very clear that the student is dedicated to the subject and disciplined in the pursuit of their goals. Having a good experience from work attachments is a further strong point, demonstrating the student's enthusiasm for the subject. The student also shows a good range of other achievements and activities that contribute to the (overall) very positive impression of a dedicated and well-rounded individual.

Bad points:

There is excessive focus on work experience at the exclusion of their understanding of and suitability for the course. Also, the style of the statement is somewhat unclear. Particularly towards the end, one gets the impression that the student ran either out of space or out of ideas as the different aspects raised in the text are not discussed to their full effect, making them significantly less relevant for the overall quality of the statement. This is particularly a problem with the conclusion which makes little to no sense.

Overall:

An average statement that demonstrates some good and relevant work experience and patient exposure. Unfortunately, the statement is let down by some stylistic weaknesses that reduce the overall strength of the content, at least in some parts.

NOTES

Subject: Dentistry

There is a certain delight in being naturally curious. Yet this got me in trouble as a child, from asking too many questions to fidgeting to keep my hands busy. In an attempt to nurture my inquisitive character while suppressing my desire to dismantle furniture, I was often encouraged to visit the local museum where my fascination with the osteology of an ancient carnivore led to my discovery of the gargantuan carnassial teeth, fuelling my primitive interests in the morphology and function of teeth. As I grew older, reading texts like 'The Health Gap' fired a passion to engage in the ordeals of social justice and the issue of poor oral health within the NHS, developing my first taste of what would become a fascination with dentistry.

Witnessing the inner workings of NHS practices in areas of high dental need over a week was eye-opening. The sheer variety of cases piqued my interest; allowing me to realise that dentistry is both a stimulating and demanding vocation that is in turn, highly rewarding. The attention to detail taken while placing a filling highlighted that dentistry requires a substantial level of manual dexterity as well as precision and flair. Heading the Dental Society hones these skills, practising needlework to develop dexterity and discussing pertinent dental cases to increase exposure to the field. The fitting of a CEREC crown during a one week placement at a cosmetic practice opened my eyes to technological advancements in the field, prompting further research into possible future innovations.

Completing a Discover Dentistry course placed what I had learnt in dental practice into the wider context of public dental health issues. A culmination of these valuable experiences highlighted that both the beauty and triviality of dentistry lie in the nature of a simple smile; an often overlooked hallmark of social interaction. Shadowing dentists over two weeks during the Goodwill Ambassador Programme offered a striking contrast to previous placements, broadening the parameters of dentistry as a profession that is not only restorative or aesthetic but potentially life saving. While observing the care of a trigeminal neuralgia patient, I was truly able to value the importance of patient autonomy and trust; further affirming that dentistry truly touches lives on a massive scale. Working as part of a multidisciplinary team in a dental hospital highlighted the level of effective communication required in the profession, urging me to draw parallels while managing the Debate Society at college. The methodical nature of the surgical team under the oral surgeon's guidance while treating a motor vehicle trauma patient was provoking. Besides the need for efficient communication, it was clear to me that leadership and management skills were vital; skills that I too, have developed through the Silver DofE Award and leading my team through Young Enterprise. Being a scholarship recipient constantly pushes the horizons of my academic abilities, nurturing my thirst for knowledge and fuelling rigorous self-motivation.

Beyond academia, I lead a local charity tutoring disadvantaged children which has given me a deep grounding in community work; stressing the significance of continued community care as well as the values of patience and trust when working with children. Being awarded Best Speaker at the Welsh Debating Championships and being invited to speak at the MDA Awards has fostered an articulate character with the ability to think quickly; making critical decisions under tremendous pressure.

Looking back, it was my curious nature towards the world around me that drove me to explore a career in such a complex and multifaceted field. Grasping every experience extended to me with the same open-minded perspective has encouraged me to constantly broaden the frontiers of my perception of dentistry; a vocation that is highly challenging yet calls to me as one that will fulfil my desire to truly make a difference in society.

Universities applied to:

- Newcastle: Offer
- Birmingham: Offer
- Queens University Belfast: Offer
- King's College London: Offer with Scholarship

Good points:

The student's opening narrative is not unpleasant to read and is instantly engaging – when done well a personal touch like this can be very effective! Throughout the personal statement the student demonstrates a clear passion for the subject with numerous examples. Moreover, this is evidenced with several accounts of clinical exposure and relevant work experience. This is clearly a very academic student with multiple references to significant extracurricular dentistry activities that demonstrate a commitment to the specialty.

Bad points:

Whilst this personal statement is filled with work experience and insight into the dentistry profession, there is little mentioned of the student's personal life. Even though in the penultimate paragraph they start 'beyond academia…', there is no mention of hobbies or relaxation. The examples are all very much academic in nature. When writing a personal statement for a course like dentistry it is essential to demonstrate an interest in a wide variety of unrelated hobbies given the high demands of such a course.

Overall:

An above average statement demonstrating significant insight and commitment within the field of dentistry, written in an engaging synoptic style. Let down, perhaps, only by the lack of an obvious logical structure and neglect of any hobbies or sports.

NOTES

BIOLOGICAL SCIENCES

Subject: Natural Sciences

When Theodore Roszak wrote that 'nature composes some of her loveliest poems for the microscope and the telescope', I feel he captured the way that science gives us greater understanding of the world in which we live. With this understanding comes opportunities to influence the lives we lead. It is my strong interest in science coupled with my inquisitive nature, thirst for knowledge and analytical thinking that compels me to read Natural Sciences. I aspire to work with others at the forefront of scientific knowledge to see how we can apply this knowledge to meet the challenges that unfold in the twenty-first century.

My A level studies have confirmed my interest in a range of scientific areas. After studying cell organelles in biology, I was captivated by reading 'Power, Sex, Suicide: Mitochondria and the Meaning of Life' by Nick Lane, delving deeper into the role of mitochondria in cellular function. Continuing to explore beyond the syllabus, reading 'Genome' by Matt Ridley and 'H2O a Biography of Water' by Philip Ball has fuelled my interest in other areas such as genetics and molecular biology. My enthusiasm for biology was recognised by being awarded the school Year 12 biology prize. In chemistry, exploring carbon nanotubes was exhilarating as I could see that they have enormous potential in diverse applications such as carrying drugs into specific body cells. It was during work experience at a local hospital I saw that scientists provide the tools for doctors and the significance of research in developing new, improved treatments. To explore further the application of science in different contexts, I attended 'Chemistry in Action' lectures at the Institute of Education, London.

I was inspired by speaking with scientists at the forefront of research whilst attending the Summer Science Exhibition at the Royal Society. Intrigued by the development of a nanocell to store clean energy using sunlight and that the cell contained porphyrin which is involved in photosynthesis, I realised that studying the structure and function of plants may provide vital information in developing new ways of storing energy. Keen to experiment, it was exciting to make and identify graphene, the first two-dimensional atomic material and to explore the potential uses of this strong, transparent and highly conductive material. It is enthralling to consider how these current scientific developments may be applied in the future. Finding great satisfaction in problem-solving and thriving on challenge, I have enjoyed studying mathematics, particularly learning new concepts such as calculus. My study of history has enhanced my analytical and essay writing skills. Moreover, it has given me a perspective on the relationship between science and society over the years.

Balancing my extra-curricular activities with my studies has required good time-management. I enjoy playing the piano and a range of sports including netball, tennis and skiing. Playing in the school netball team for the past six years has shown me the value of good teamwork. I have enjoyed volunteering weekly at Strathmore School for children with disabilities and successfully sought permission to organise an Easter Party for them which required initiative, creativity and management skills. Volunteering on the Whitgift Special Needs Activity Project has enhanced my communication and leadership skills and has made me aware of the challenges faced by those with disabilities and their families.

I believe that I have the skills, scientific curiosity and motivation required to learn from, and contribute to, this diverse and challenging course. Studying Natural Sciences will give me the flexibility to explore a wide range of scientific areas and will enable me to develop the skills to work with colleagues at the cutting edge of science.

Universities applied to:

- Cambridge: Offer
- Durham: Offer
- Birmingham: Offer
- University College London: Offer
- Nottingham: Offer

Good Points:

Very well-written with a clear introduction, main body, and conclusion. This statement begins by setting the scene as to why Natural Science, and in particular, Biology, is important to both the world and the applicant. The student clearly explains their interest in Biology and then goes on to explain their interest in the other subjects covered as part of the Natural Sciences degree. Many prospective students forget to do this, and in this statement, every point is justified with examples from the student's personal experiences which adds emphasis to the statement.

Bad Points:

At times this reads a bit like a list, and removing a few examples so that they could say more about those left would have produced a more impactful statement which would more adequately fulfil the requirements to show interest, ability, familiarity, ambition, and understanding of the course's demands.

Overall:

This is an excellent personal statement with a clear and logical structure. The student does not simply list their achievements but provides reasons for their academic interests.

NOTES

Subject: Natural Sciences (Biological)

I first became interested in biochemistry when I learnt about cellular biology. A Level biology animations show proteins, cholesterol, the phospholipid bilayer and other components of a cell, and you recognise that these molecules are the reasons why life exists. The body is a complex fabrication; the way in which we work still has much to be discovered, and that excites me.

The open-ended nature of biochemistry appeals to me, as it is the foundation for different specialisations. I would be a capable biochemist, because I challenge popular views and assumptions, I am resourceful in finding solutions to problems, and I have the creativity to explain unexpected results. For example, I thought about how the dermis is populated by blood vessels, but when you eat meat or see an animal such as a rabbit be skinned no blood vessels criss-cross from the skin to the body; the skin comes away easily. I concluded that the blood vessels in the skin must be tiny capillaries, otherwise we would see them.

My work experience at RAFT, a lab which heals damaged skin unable to repair itself due to the loss of the dermis, taught me how to do histology and other staining. I also helped with RNA extraction and completed apoptosis experiments. It made me appreciate how scientists use setbacks to progress - I thought that experiments rarely go wrong, but found that unexpected results advance thinking. I also observed how sharing ideas and research is vital in a scientific community.

After RAFT, I wrote a presentation on tissue engineering and presented it to staff and pupils at school. I was interested in looking at its potential applications, and I found out that nobody has yet grown a whole complex organ, like a liver - only tracheas and bladders have been grown. I was also interested in the use of tissue engineering to grow food, such as the £220,000 hamburger. The study of chemistry underpins the science behind these products, and I look forward to studying it at university where I can further my knowledge. As I am interested in a field where biology and chemistry meet, I can see the applied uses of chemistry, which gives me greater enthusiasm for it in class. In my research about biochemistry, one in particular TV show caught my attention; a Horizon programme about how skin ages. It explained how glycans are cell signalling molecules which are particularly numerous in the dermal-epidermal junction. As we age, their "dialogue" fades so cells do not receive the message to produce more collagen, causing the skin to wrinkle. If we can "switch" them back on, they re-open this dialogue and re-inflate collagen, which reverses the visible effects of ageing on skin. I was particularly interested in this programme, after learning about the skin at RAFT.

As a keen climber, I have competed for the past 5 years and have always done well. Climbers depend on individual ability and performance, but compete as a team. I have learnt to be focused under pressure and keep thoughts ordered and my goals in mind, but mostly I have learnt to take pleasure in the challenge of a tough wall. I enjoy the determination required and the thrill of the height. I have been taught to keep attempting a wall until I can think my way around a problem – as a girl, I rely on technical ability, not brute strength. I have now been chair of climbing club for over a year. As a participant in the Duke of Edinburgh's scheme, CCF, the 1st XI hockey team and the school's exchange scheme, I have become an outgoing, self-motivated and diligent pupil. From being appointed Head Girl, my management and communication skills have improved, and I have proved myself as a leader.

In the future, scientists are going to become ever more important. There are problems which we will have to face up to - food and fuel shortages, global warming, over population. I am looking forward to being one of those who help tackle these issues, and I think I have the capability bring about real change.

Universities applied to:

- Cambridge: Offer
- York: Offer
- Exeter: Offer
- University College London: Offer
- Cardiff: Offer

Good Points:

The student's motivation to study Biochemistry is clear. The statement is written in an easy-to-read way and is immediately clear to the reader that the student is genuine. The final paragraph brings together all of the points above without repetition and demonstrates the student's confidence in a way that does not sound like bragging.

Bad Points:

Immediately, it is clear that the majority of sentences in this statement will begin with 'I'. Whilst it is important to emphasise individual accomplishment and achievements, this can go too far as the student has done in this statement. Sciences and engineering disciplines require teamwork, and the student even goes on to emphasise her individuality when playing sports. This gives the impression that the student, although very bright and capable, is best suited to work alone. This is not the message to convey when applying for a science (or engineering) discipline, and can be viewed very negatively. The student also makes no mention of the many other disciplines involved in Natural Sciences or mathematics. The statement is also very long.

Overall:

This is a very good statement, with the student's passion for the subject clear. However, the student is let down by what seems to be a clear preference to work alone. One or two examples of working as part of a team and some sentence alterations (not using 'I' so much) would make a big difference.

NOTES

Subject: Biological Sciences

Like all children, I went through the 'why' stage. But for me, it never stopped. I am fascinated by the world around me and have always been passionate about science, but Biology has always been at the forefront of my interests. This is why I would like to continue studying it at university. When I read 'The Cell', by Terrance Allen and Graham Cowling, to support my AS course, I realised that there was much more to the 'simple' cell than I realised. It was at this point that I began to explore deeper into the world of Biology and I knew then that this was my true passion. As well as books, I keep up-to-date in the world of science by reading magazines such as Focus, New Scientist and Biological Sciences Monthly.

Like most students, I had little idea of what studying a science at university was like, and any practical work I had ever done was in a classroom. Therefore, to give me a taste of university level study, I undertook work experience at the Marine Laboratory of Queen's University Belfast. During this placement, I had the opportunity to observe and take part in various experiments focusing predominantly on the behavioural biology of marine animals. Furthermore, I was able to speak to interesting and intellectual people from all sorts of backgrounds, from students working towards their PhD to retired professors with a seasoned career. This confirmed for me that studying Biology is what I really want to do.

To further expand my knowledge of Biology, I also applied for and was successful in gaining a place on Oxford University's UNIQ Summer School. Throughout this week I took part in field work, laboratory sessions and lectures on various fields within Biology. On my first day, I was set an assignment, in which I had to conduct my own research in my free time to produce an essay on sexual conflict - a topic I was totally unfamiliar with. Although it was challenging, I enjoyed working for myself and learned a great deal about something I would never have come across on my A Level course. At the end of the week I was able to discuss the essay with an Oxford tutor. For me, this was an interesting and stimulating discussion in which I was encouraged to come up with and explore new ideas in a way which is unlike the teaching I have experienced at school. I can look forward to getting another taster of university life when I attend a course in Cell Biology and Genetics run by Villiers Park in December. Although studying both Biology and Chemistry covers quite an extensive range of topics, giving me a broad insight into the biological sciences, I am particularly interested in certain topics. Consequently, I undertook a course run by the Open University in Human Genetics and Health Issues. This taught me many things, in particular the ability to study independently. There has been huge growth in interest and research in this area and I would like to delve deeper into this subject.

I consider myself to be an ambitious individual and I am involved in a range of extra-curricular activities which I am able to balance with my school work due to my strong organisational skills. I have many positions of responsibility, such as being a Corporal in my local Air Cadet Squadron, and I am a school Prefect and a member of the school Council. These positions have developed my communication skills and I believe that these will be very important in the field of science, allowing me to share my ideas and research with confidence.

I am very eager to delve deeper into the world of biology than I have ever gone before. I can think of nothing more exciting and stimulating than engaging in debate and discussion with professionals in an area that genuinely interests me so much. Though I know that this will be a challenge, it is one that with hard work and dedication I believe I will rise to.

EXAMPLE STATEMENTS - BIOLOGY

Universities applied to:

- Oxford: Offer
- Durham: Offer
- St. Andrews: Offer
- Herriot-Watt: Offer
- Southampton: Offer

Good Points:

The student's motivation to study Biology is clear. The student has clearly gone beyond conducting simple research in order to better understand the discipline for which they are applying. All examples and experiences are clearly explained and their impacts on the student are clear. The final paragraph closes the statement in a clean way that makes the student come across as both humble and likable. You can see their interest in the course, suitability for it, academic skill, and broader character.

Bad Points:

The student relies on experiences at the UNIQ summer school, Oxford (and an upcoming experience at Villiers Park, Cambridge) too heavily. Whilst such experiences are important and can provide motivation for further study at university, such opportunities are not available to everyone. Using examples from outside the A-level syllabus and personal experiences in addition to the student's summer school experiences would have added more variety to the statement.

Overall:

This is a very good statement where the student demonstrates clear motivation. The bulk of the statement's main body is dedicated to a single experience: a one-week summer school at the University of Oxford. Whilst it is, of course, a great advantage to have had such an insight into a potential degree (and career) in Biology, it is important not to rely too heavily on any one single experience.

NOTES

Subject: Biochemistry

I have enjoyed studying Science since primary school and I have especially developed an interest in Chemistry and its importance in biological contexts. Biochemistry as a subject covers such a broad range of applications, from genetic engineering to the cure for cancer, which is what has attracted me to the subject and made me want to study it in greater detail, as I will be able to do at university. Since I want to become a science teacher in the future, studying Biochemistry will not only give me insight into Chemistry applications in Biology, but also an in-depth understanding of how the 3 sciences can be combined to answer scientific problems. The inter-disciplinary nature of the subject also fascinates me as it is becoming more apparent that scientific advances require collaboration between scientists from different fields, and I am intrigued about how this is put into practice.

In order to advance my interest in Biochemistry, I regularly read scientific magazines and journals such as 'New Scientist' in order to keep up-to-date with recent advances being made in the field. For example, recently it was discovered that ovarian cancer cells can physically push healthy cells out of the way when parts of ovarian tumours break off. As this finding sheds light on how this particular tumour can enter other organs, it may be beneficial for future cancer therapies and could be a target for treatment to prevent cancers spreading to other organs. As well as this, I am also interested in how science is presented to the general public. Reading 'The Selfish Gene' by Richard Dawkins gave me a new perspective on biological evolution, focusing on a gene's requirement to propagate, rather than that of an organism or species. In addition to popular science books, I have also looked into books targeted at undergraduates, such as 'Principles and Problems in Physical Chemistry for Biochemists'. This textbook in particular gave me more of an idea of how Biophysical Chemistry is taught in Biochemistry, which is the branch of the subject that I am most interested in studying as it combines all of the main sciences.

On top of the reading that I have done, I have also pursued many pursuits to progress my interest in science. Attending Chemistry master classes at Birmingham University gave me a taste of the style of university lectures and also taught me about specific advances made in Chemistry that have various applications, such as modifying skis for better performance in snow sports competitions. Taking part in the Chemistry Olympiad in school also gave me the opportunity to apply the knowledge I had gained in Chemistry lessons to situations that I was unfamiliar with. Needing to think 'outside the box', in order to approach the various questions, is an important skill required for higher education and receiving a Silver certificate shows that I have the capacity to tackle new problems. I have also helped out with Chemistry Club during lunchtimes, where I have demonstrated various exciting experiments to lower years and also taught students about applications of Chemistry and advances in science that go beyond the curriculum, which I have learnt about through my reading and master classes.

I have also taken part in a variety of extra-curricular activities to enhance my personal skills. Throughout secondary school I have been a council, class or charity representative, and am now a Senior Prefect for Charity and Citizenship. I undertook these roles of responsibility as I feel that it is important to voice the opinions of students to effect positive changes that benefit them, and I also enjoy organising charity events and raising awareness of various issues. I regularly attend St. John's Ambulance meetings and have also attended Badminton Club for 5 years, as I am a committed member of both. I feel that these skills have prepared me to be able to undertake a university degree to the best of my abilities, to allow me to reach my potential.

ULTIMATE OXBRIDGE PERSONAL STATEMENT GUIDE — EXAMPLE STATEMENTS - BIOCHEM

Universities applied to:

- Oxford: Offer
- Birmingham: Offer
- Leicester: Offer
- Warwick: Offer
- Nottingham: Offer

Good Points:

A well-written and structured statement. The student emphasises their teamwork skills and puts these in a scientific context. The student does not focus on one particular subject but gives attention to both Biology and Chemistry before combining these together to justify their reasoning for wanting to become a biochemist. It is clear that the student has sought opportunities outside of the core syllabus to explore their chosen subject. The student's desire to become a science teacher is used in the introduction and this establishes a high degree of motivation early on in the statement.

Bad Points:

Whilst it is important to include examples of extra-curricular work and activities, the student embarks on a list of accomplishments. This is fine to begin with, however, by the third paragraph, it is quite exhausting to read. It is important to write about good examples of personal endeavour thoroughly, but not to simply list all accomplishments and achievements in one's life.

Overall:

Overall, this is a good statement and it demonstrates the student's ambition to study Biochemistry clearly. Although the student does not come across as though they are bragging, the sheer number of achievements and accomplishments makes the statement quite exhausting to read. The student could have achieved the same impact with fewer but more thoroughly written out examples.

NOTES

Subject: Biochemistry

Going to university to study the sciences has always been my ambition, as I believe science is fundamental to the future of mankind. When I started learning the sciences at school, I was immediately intrigued. Whilst other subjects such as Latin, history and economics interested me, I became increasingly engrossed in chemistry and biology, particularly organic chemistry which is my real passion. I find it fascinating how different combinations of very similar elements can have such varied uses in industry, pharmaceuticals, and metabolic processes. My A Level choices have prepared me well for studying the sciences at university. I have not only acquired a sound theoretical knowledge of chemistry and biology, but also an understanding of the practical aspects and how this knowledge can be applied to real life and used to benefit humanity. Studying A Level maths has furthered my analytical skills as well as my reasoning abilities. I am constantly adding to my knowledge base in addition to my A Levels and, although we don't cover neurology in school, I find it really interesting and have been self-studying to further my knowledge.

To learn more about behaviour and neuroscience, I read Zero Degrees of Empathy. I found it intriguing that the size of or activity in different parts of the brain could be influenced by both genetics and early environment. I am currently basing my Extended Project Qualification around the subjects of autism, empathy and neurology, trying to discover more about how brain function differs between different people. Throughout this process I will be developing research skills and independent thinking, interviewing members of the public, contacting professionals in their fields, and reading and collating information from various sources and questioning their provenance. As part of my project I intend to design patient level literature to help educate people about autism, which I plan to distribute via doctors' surgeries and health centres. Many experiences have contributed to my fascination with science. Whilst shadowing doctors for a week in Broomfield Hospital's Emergency Assessment Unit, I was most interested in the different medications that were administered to patients, and their effects. I have also attended many talks and conferences which I found interesting, notably Adam Rutherford on genetic engineering, synthetic species, and the future of science and technology, which showed me that now is an exciting time to be entering the world of biochemistry.

I also took part in the AD Schools' Analyst Competition at the University of Hertfordshire, and attended a Chemistry taster day at Essex University, so I have some lab experience at a university. I found both events thoroughly enjoyable. When I am not studying I relax by playing classical guitar, having achieved grade 7. I used to captain my local football team, and enjoyed the leadership opportunity; I now referee youth football. I have been a member of my school's Cadet Force since 2010, where I have learned time-management, discipline, and responsibility. I am also grateful to both my peers and teachers for electing me prefect last year, but had to turn down the role after I was offered the chance to be House Captain, where I delegate roles within my team, organise house events, and speak in front of my house fortnightly.

Three years ago I went on a French Exchange, which helped develop my communication skills and independence. I took part in the Young Enterprise Scheme in 2012, building confidence, cooperation skills, and real world initiative. I also visited Kenya last summer, staying at an orphanage and teaching in our partner school, which taught me to adapt to unfamiliar situations. I am really looking forward to continuing my studies at university. In the world of science, theories only last until a better one is created; everything is changing and research is crucial. I want to be at the forefront of the future of biochemistry.

ULTIMATE OXBRIDGE PERSONAL STATEMENT GUIDE — EXAMPLE STATEMENTS - BIOCHEM

Universities applied to:

- Oxford: Offer
- Durham: Offer
- Imperial College London: Offer
- Bath: Offer
- Exeter: Offer

Good Points:

The student explains their ambition to study Biochemistry clearly, with emphasis given to both subjects involved in the multidisciplinary subject. It is clear that the student has many talents, both academic and non-academic which gives confidence to the reader that they will not struggle when challenged at university. The student writes in a way that makes them appear confident but not over-confident, which will be looked upon well. It is clear that the student draws from personal experiences that are unique to them, rather than those shared with many others, such as summer schools etc.

Bad Points:

There are many redundant sentences throughout this statement, such as 'Studying A Level maths has furthered my analytical skills as well as my reasoning abilities'. This is surely the case for everyone who studies A-level maths, and it is not unique. Getting rid of such redundant sentences will shorten the statement and give more emphasis to the rest of the statement. The statement lacks structure as the introduction includes details of the student's A-level study and, as a paragraph, is too long. The statement would read much more easily if similar points were grouped into paragraphs, and the introduction and concluding paragraph were separated from the main body of the statement.

Overall:

This is a very good statement. The student has clearly accomplished many things. However, redundant sentences that state the obvious take away from the rest of the statement. The structure of the statement is somewhat confusing, especially at the beginning. With the removal of redundant sentences and some re-structuring, this would be an excellent statement.

NOTES

CHEMISTRY

Subject: Chemistry

When I visited my secondary school open day at the age of 11, I was fascinated by a demonstration of a colour changing liquid. At the time I knew little about the 'blue bottle' experiment but 6 years later I am using it to inspire future students at this year's event. I still get excited about discovering and understanding new chemistry, in particular the relationship betw'een chemical structures, their properties and how they interact. I am fascinated by the fact that everything around us is based on just 3 sub-atomic particles, in multiple and different combinations. I have a natural aptitude for mathematics but during my GCSEs I found that the applications of science, in particular chemistry and biology, excited me more than pure mathematics. I have continued to study double maths as I believe this will help me with scientific analysis and logical thinking and have done so on a partly self-taught basis as my A level choices were not possible within the school timetable. This has developed my independent learning skills and, I believe, prepares me well for higher education. Of all my A levels, I am inspired most by chemistry. This summer I arranged a week of work experience at Reading Scientific Services Ltd, a subsidiary of Mondelez, where I was able to be involved in real world applications of chemistry. These included using gas chromatography to check that the vitamin C content in a product matched the labelled value, and nuclear magnetic resonance spectroscopy to identify contaminants in products. It was great to see techniques I had learnt about in theory being used in practice and I concluded that I definitely want to study chemistry at degree level. I have become particularly interested in analytical chemistry as it has so many valuable applications, and I am very excited by the opportunities that I have seen in this area during my university visits.

To further my knowledge I have read 'Why Chemical Reactions Happen' by Keeler and Wothers, and I subscribe to New Scientist magazine. Keeler and Wothers has given me insight into how the world works at the atomic and molecular scale and other theories, such as how covalent bonds are formed using the model of molecular orbitals and hybrid atomic orbitals. New Scientist articles that have particularly interested me include proposed methods for controlling the building of crystalline structures one atom at a time to produce structures with desirable properties, for example as catalysts, and discussion on elements displaying properties not predicted by their place in the periodic table, leading to alternative views on how the periodic table could be organised. Spurred by my enthusiasm for both sport and chemistry, I was intrigued by news reports on how noble gases are thought to have blood doping benefits for athletes, and have read further into this. The World Anti-Doping Agency has banned their use but has yet to develop tests for them. A topic such as this as an undergraduate project would be very exciting.

Alongside my studies, I have pushed myself to undertake activities that develop me as a person. I teach beginner and advanced skiing at a dry ski slope. This requires me to observe, analyse what I see, identify underlying causes and determine solutions, which I believe this will help me in my practical chemistry. I am an academic mentor for younger pupils at school and I tutor a GCSE student in maths and sciences, through which I have learnt to see topics from different perspectives. I have been officiating as a football referee for 3 years, learning to compose my thoughts, be confident and communicate under pressure, which I believe will make a direct contribution to my development as a scientist. In conclusion, I am confident in my choice of a chemistry degree and excited by the opportunities ahead of me. I believe that I will be well prepared to get the most from the course and to make a strong contribution to my faculty and university.

ULTIMATE OXBRIDGE PERSONAL STATEMENT GUIDE — EXAMPLE STATEMENTS - CHEMISTRY

Universities applied to:

- Bristol: Offer
- Warwick: Offer
- Southampton: Offer
- Oxford: Offer
- Bath: Offer

Good Points:

This is a good statement and the student is clearly motivated by their chosen subject. Although Mathematics is not a requirement for studying Chemistry at university, it is very highly regarded and emphasising mathematical ability will definitely strengthen an application. The student writes in a way that is easy to understand and expands on all experiences. The student writes things in a logical order, with academic interests/achievements first, followed by work experience and finally with extra-curricular activities. All points mentioned regarding the student's academics and extra-curricular activities are related back to an interest in Chemistry.

Bad Points:

Although the physical content is well-structured, the student has three huge paragraphs only. It is not clear where the introduction ends and the main body begins. This is also the case for the final paragraph where it is not clear where the student's closing paragraph begins. The beginning of the statement is quite abrupt, it would have been better perhaps if the student opened with an introduction to the subject of Chemistry, rather than diving straight into their personal experiences.

Overall:

This is a very good personal statement. In terms of content, the statement is excellent. However, the statement lacks basic paragraph structure. This makes it difficult to mentally separate the main points of the statement. With some basic restructuring, this would be an excellent statement.

NOTES

Subject: Chemistry

I am fascinated by chemistry and by its connections across the sciences. I relish the intellectual challenge it presents. I have a keen interest in how chemistry works closely with numerous other scientific disciplines to address the problems that the world faces both now and in the future. Studying a subject that is at the forefront of the resolution of global issues such as climate change, truly excites me. I am naturally inquisitive about the world around me, so learning about the composition and structure of matter only serves to fuel my enthusiasm further.

The understanding of how molecules are arranged in space intrigues me. Attending a lecture given by Dr Stuart Conway at Oxford University on the chirality of molecules was a fascinating experience. Subsequently, I read the relevant sections of Organic Chemistry by Clayden, Reeves, Warren & Worthers and The Foundations of Organic Chemistry Oxford primer. It was interesting to note the importance of symmetry in optical isomerism and to appreciate that even molecules that lack a stereogenic centre can be chiral. Furthermore, that enantiomers of compounds like limonene smell different due to our olfactory receptors that also contain chiral molecules and finally, that the chirality of drugs affects their action and has profound implications regarding their effects on the human body.

I particularly enjoy mathematics and its relevance to chemistry. Recently, I completed the iodine clock reaction experiment. I learnt how to use logarithms to work out the rate constant and then by using the $y = mx + c$ model, was able to deduce the order of the reaction. I enjoy the application of logic to problem solving and I look forward to further developing this skill during my degree study.

In order to improve my laboratory techniques, I have completed several first year degree level experiments. At the University of Sussex, I synthesised aspirin and in another experiment, extracted limonene from citrus fruits in order to decide which of them contained the most active, fragrant compound. I have also explored emission spectra and investigated which elements absorb specific frequencies of sunlight at the University of Reading. An experiment that I thoroughly enjoyed, whilst participating in a summer school at Oxford University, was the synthesis of indigo dye using the Baeyer-Drewson reaction and a vat-dyeing technique. I gained a detailed insight into the kinds of experiments that I will be carrying out during my degree and relish the opportunity to use sophisticated apparatus and techniques.

Next July I undertake work experience in France which will combine my passion for chemistry with my love of the French language. Working in a medical analysis laboratory will not only enable the exploration of the analytical techniques used in the industry but will also help me to learn and practice chemistry specific vocabulary in the language of the country that I aspire to live and work in.

I continually seek to challenge myself and to broaden my horizons. To this end, I have completed both my Bronze and Silver Duke of Edinburgh (D of E) Awards. By way of concurrent activity and academic demands allowing, I plan to complete my Gold D of E at an appropriate stage. I volunteer regularly in French and Chemistry classes as part of the Worldwide Volunteering scheme.

Throughout my education, I have been determined to excel. I have worked consistently hard at the subjects I am passionate about and even harder at the ones that I have found challenging. Achieving excellent examination grades based on detailed understanding of the subject matter is my main driver at this stage. I am very keen to study in a stimulating university environment alongside ambitious, dedicated and like-minded students. Louis Pasteur said, "My strength lies solely in my tenacity". I believe MY strength lies not only in my tenacity but also in my intellectual ability, curiosity and determination to study chemistry at degree level and beyond.

Universities applied to:

- Oxford: Offer
- Durham: Offer
- Bristol: Offer
- York: Offer
- Bath: Offer

Good Points:

This statement is well-structured and well-written. The student starts with a general introduction into Chemistry and their passion for the subject before going onto the main body of the statement. All claims of work experience and extra-curricular activities are explained clearly. The student clearly has an abundance of additional experience regarding Chemistry, ranging from tutoring to conducting first-year university experiments. These, and their relevance to the student's reasons for applying to study Chemistry are explained clearly and the reader is in no doubt that these experiences are genuine.

Bad Points:

The student underlined the word 'receptors' and included a link to a Wikipedia page containing the meaning of the term 'sensory receptors'. This is basic knowledge, and including a link to a word's meaning risks insulting the intelligence of the academic staff who read the statement. The student also emphasises themselves in the final sentence by using capitals in 'MY'. Again, this can be taken wrongly and it would be a shame to ruin an otherwise excellent statement purely because the reader decides that the student is overconfident and condescending. Beyond this, the second and third paragraphs talk at considerable length about particular concepts which interest them, but this isn't used to make any convincing point about why the person reading it should accept their application - focusing instead on challenges they hope to face on the course, skills they'd like to learn, or ambitions for after graduation would be valuable. On that note, they make a point that they hope to live and work in France after graduation, which will beg the question of interviewers about whether the candidate has applied to French universities as well, this can unnecessarily complicate or even harm your chances, and is best avoided.

Overall:

This is a very good statement, however, two strange cases of where the student refers the reader to the meaning of a basic term and emphasises themselves in capital letters let the student down.

NOTES

Subject: Chemistry

Few aspects of our lives remain unaffected by the fundamental subject of chemistry. Chemists have revolutionised the way we live; from the medicines we use to the water we drink, it is hard to imagine what our everyday life would be like without the help of this vast subject. I wish to be a part of the chemical discoveries of the future which is what entices me to study chemistry in greater depth at university.

My interest in chemistry has developed a great deal since starting the AS level course. Each time I learn something new, it inspires me to develop my knowledge even further. I have particularly enjoyed the organic chemistry involved in the AS course due to the practical work it entails. Laboratory work for me is enjoyable because it provides an opportunity to test out the theoretical knowledge you have gained and is also great fun! For example, I particularly enjoyed making azo dyes as it was interesting to recreate a process in the lab which is so frequently used in industry.

I have been able to develop my passion for chemistry through wider reading. I have recently enjoyed reading Molecules at an Exhibition. The range of molecules which can have profound effects on our lives surprised me and showed me again how relevant chemistry is to our lives. I have a subscription to New Scientist. An article I particularly enjoyed reading over the summer was "Rogue elements" which explores some of the unanswered questions associated with the periodic table. For example, when the elements will stop and whether superheavy elements, which exist for fractions of a second only one atom at a time, can be considered elements at all. The article also looked at the issues of where to place the elements hydrogen and helium and where the metal/non-metal divide should be. This showed me that although the periodic table is often considered to be complete, there is still much to uncover. Reading Quantum Theory Cannot Hurt You introduced me to the concept of relativity and I was amazed to find out how this theory affects chemistry as well as physics. For example without relativity the properties of some of the heavier elements such as gold would simply not be the same. I have been developing my interest in maths and have taken up AS further maths which will be largely self-taught, I know this will complement the chemistry syllabus.

Recently I took part in a UNIQ summer school at Oxford University which allowed me to have a great insight into undergraduate chemistry. I thoroughly enjoyed my week, particularly the lecture on chirality. This was a new concept for me and I was surprised by the huge differences that can result from this form of isomerism. My subject knowledge was greatly enhanced and the skills I gained have been even more valuable. I was taught to question, develop and evaluate my knowledge at every stage and become a more independent learner.

During Year 12 I acted as a science tutor for GCSE students, helping them with exam technique. I found that explaining the subject matter to others helped to enhance and consolidate my own knowledge. My success both in and out of school was rewarded when I received Clevedon's 2014 Academic Achievement Award in chemistry.

I enjoy playing the piano and recently achieved Grade 6 during my GCSE year, developing my time management skills. My other hobbies include drama and singing and I am a member of Clevedon Light Opera Club as well as the school choir. I have taken part in several productions as well as performing in school stage shows and concerts. All of which contributed to me gaining my Gold Arts Award. I volunteer with a Rainbow group. When I started I found the prospect of running activities for a group of people quite daunting, but 2 years later I think my confidence and communication skills have improved greatly. I have developed my knowledge, skills and aptitude both in and out of school and I look forward to being able to extend these further by studying at university.

Universities applied to:

- Oxford: Offer
- Bristol: Offer
- Cardiff: Offer
- Manchester: Offer
- Leicester: Offer

Good Points:

This is a well-written and well-structured statement. The student places points in order of relevance, making the statement easy to read. All points are clearly explained and their impacts on the student are clear. There is a clear introduction, main body, and conclusion.

Bad Points:

Although the statement is written in a logical order, there are a lot of paragraphs. Whilst it is very good that student has a wide range of interests and hobbies, the student dedicates two paragraphs to these. It would have been possible to shorten the statement by removing some of the points mentioned without taking away from the quality of the statement. The student clearly has many experiences from outside of the A-level syllabus, such as the UNIQ summer school and working as a GCSE science tutor. Whilst it is, of course, important to describe individual experiences and achievements, focusing on the positives alone limits the impact that mentioning such experiences will have. It would have been nice to see what challenges the student faced through their experiences and how the student overcame these.

Overall:

This is an excellent statement. The statement is clearly written and easy to read. The length of the statement could have been reduced, however, there are no other areas in which the student needs to make significant improvements.

NOTES

PHYSICAL SCIENCES

Subject: Natural Sciences (Physics)

The more I discover about physics, the less I realise that I know, and the keener I am to further explore unfamiliar topics at university. Studying areas such as special relativity and quantum mechanics have made me question concepts I took as given, such as the nature and manipulation of time and the degree of certainty to which we can truly know anything.

My particular interest in physics was sparked when I read an article on quantum physics, and was introduced to a simple description of the fundamental constituents of matter. This led me to read further about particle physics. I particularly enjoyed Brian Greene's The Elegant Universe, which gave me a brief insight into the intricacies of string theory, and The Feynman Lectures on Physics, from which I learnt new mechanics and probability theory. I watch lectures on the MIT website, read New Scientist and am a junior member of the IoP to further my knowledge of new scientific developments. I enjoyed visiting CERN last year and learning more about the experiments conducted there. I have also competed in national challenges to develop my thinking skills further, achieving bronze in the Physics Olympiad, silver in the Cambridge Chemistry Challenge and gold in the Senior Maths Challenge. Additionally, this year I won the school leavers' physics prize.

Last summer I attended a residential Headstart physics course at the University of Leicester, and spent three days at the Debate Chamber physics school. I enjoyed performing undergraduate experiments, and was particularly interested by the lectures on recent developments in nanotechnology and the ways in which nanoparticles could be used to destroy cancerous cells in the body. I also had a tantalising glimpse of some of the complex mathematics behind General Relativity, and would love to study this intricate topic in more detail. These experiences confirmed my love of physics as well as increasing my appreciation of more complicated subjects not covered by my A Level courses. Furthermore, they helped to develop my skills in processing new information and quickly adapting to unfamiliar concepts.

I recently took part in an extended-essay competition at school, producing an independently researched piece of work on the superluminal neutrinos apparently found in 2011. I focused on the impossibility of faster-than-light travel according to special relativity, and the implications for time travel the discovery would have had if the measurements had been correct. This gave me the chance to explore further a subject I was interested in but had not studied at school. I researched my essay by reading scientific journals and textbooks, and speaking to scientists I met at physics events.

I will shortly begin a paid internship at Hildebrand Technology Ltd, where I will be using mathematical modelling of real-life situations for statistical analysis. This will be an opportunity to apply mathematical techniques I have learnt in school to more complex problems. This placement, along with self-studying university textbooks and extra further maths modules, will ensure that I maintain and expand my maths skills and scientific knowledge during my gap year.

In my final year I was captain of the school Boat Club. I have rowed in the top senior boat since I was 15, and in 2013 I won silver at National Schools and gold at Schools Head. This sport has involved intensive training, which demands self-discipline and commitment. I love music, and take part in many close harmony groups and choirs, as well as taking grades in musical theatre, singing and piano. My music and sport, along with lifeguarding and weekly volunteering at a local primary school, have allowed me to develop my time management skills and use the time I have for work efficiently and productively.

I am a hardworking and intellectually curious student and am excited by the prospect of developing my mathematical skills and studying physics at a more advanced level at university.

Universities applied to:

- Cambridge: Offer
- Durham: Offer
- Imperial College London: Offer
- St. Andrews: Offer
- Edinburgh: Offer

Good Points:

This is a very good statement. The statement is well-structured and the student's motivation to study physics is evident. All points are explained clearly, and experiences expanded on. The student uses examples beyond their A-level studies to explain their desire to study physics, which comes across very well to the reader.

Bad Points:

The student forgets to use quotation marks around the names of books etc., and also 'the' before 'New Scientist'. Whilst these are rudimentary errors, a simple proof-read would have found these. The main issue with this statement is its length. There are eight paragraphs in total. By the penultimate paragraph, it is clear enough that the student has done many physics-related extra-curricular activities. The quality of the statement will not be reduced if it is shortened. The student does not explain acronyms, e.g. 'IoP'. Some sentences can be shortened in order to save space, for example, 'I have also competed in national challenges to develop my thinking skills further, achieving bronze in the Physics Olympiad, silver in the Cambridge Chemistry Challenge and gold in the Senior Maths Challenge' can be shortened to, 'I have also competed in national challenges to develop my thinking skills further, achieving bronze, silver, and gold medals in the Physics Olympiad, Cambridge Chemistry, and Senior Maths Challenges respectively'.

Overall:

In general, this is a very good statement. It is well-written and the student's motivation to study physics at university is clear from the very beginning. Due to the length of the statement, it is quite cumbersome to read. With some shortening, this would be a compact and powerful statement.

NOTES

Subject: Natural Sciences (Physics)

I have always had a strong interest in pure science, particularly exploring how science and new technologies can be applied to deal with 21st century issues.

This summer I was selected from 3400 applicants to attend the physical science programme at the UNIQ summer school, at the University of Oxford. I enjoyed a variety of science lectures; my favourite was on nanotechnology in which a PHD student talked about his research in producing graphene. The presentation highlighted for me the importance of being able to manufacture this material as it has some useful properties, though is difficult to produce. The practical sessions which looked at the physical properties of some different alloys were also enjoyable. I related well to these as they touched on topics like the young's modulus which I have previously covered. I found all the lectures absorbing which has helped me to decide that I wish to study a very broad scientific course like Natural Sciences.

As a subscriber to The New Scientist magazine, I really enjoy reading all the articles, especially those related to materials science and nuclear physics. A recent article called 'Hidden Power' examined how materials such as paper and cement can be turned into composites that can hold a charge. I find such modifications fascinating, for example where casings for a mobile phone could actually power the phone. Currently, however, the capacity to hold charge cannot compare with the capabilities of lithium ion batteries; this is new technology and there are hopes that it will continue to improve.

After reading an article concerning the implementation of Nuclear Power, I went on to read 'Nuclear Power – A very Short Introduction,' as I consider this to be a current and relevant subject. I found forming an opinion on such a controversial issue very rewarding. This spurred me to pursue an extended project titled, 'Is thorium a nuclear fuel of the future?' I read about the nuclear fusion proposal at ITER, the needs of corrosion resistant materials, the use of fluoride salts, and the use of magnetic fields to contain the plasma.

In selecting Natural Sciences, I am choosing a course with varied possibilities for the future. At present a career in scientific journalism is appealing. I would also relish the opportunity to pursue academic experiences or employment abroad, as scientific developments occur globally.

When I am not studying, I have a part-time job at a local hotel. This experience has improved my interpersonal skills through interaction with customers. I enjoy many extra-curricular pursuits. For the past 8 years I have played rugby for a local club; taking part in a team has resulted in me working in groups, to achieve successful outcomes. It has also rewarded me with good decision making and communication skills, which are greatly required in the heat of a match for success. I have dedicated considerable time to the Duke of Edinburgh Gold Award Scheme. To relax, I read science fiction and fantasy books as I feel this stretches my mind and imagination in interesting and novel ways; the ability to think not only logically but creatively is essential for a scientist.

My proudest achievement is being selected to be head boy at my previous, highly academic, school against strong competition; this was an extremely demanding role as it required me to employ organizational, public speaking and presentational skills. I am also a student ambassador at my current college, responsible for inducting new students.

I would love to study Natural Sciences; the course modules are exceptionally diverse allowing the pursuit of scientific interests, together with the opportunity to really be at the cutting edge of science. I have a deep interest and knowledge of the sciences, showcased by an extremely successful academic record to date, and through the enjoyment of scientific publications and podcasts. I now look forward to building on these achievements as I enter my life at University.

Universities applied to:

- Cambridge: Offer
- Durham: Offer
- Birmingham: Offer
- Nottingham: Offer
- Lancaster: Offer

Good Points:

The student is clearly very motivated, and this comes across in the statement. The statement is written in a logical order and all previous experiences are well-explained and expanded upon. The student has clearly read around his chosen subject in some detail and this is evident in the statement.

Bad Points:

The student adds a great deal of self-praise to his achievements. In the first paragraph after the introduction, the student describes being individually 'selected from 3400 applicants' to attend the UNIQ summer school. Whilst this is, of course, a positive experience, it is important to remember that university admission is not decided purely on a student's acceptance on such programmes prior to their application. The student dedicates a large paragraph to their experiences during this week-long experience, which is far too much. It is important to remember that not all have such opportunities and those without cannot be discriminated against for not having taken part in such events. The student also attaches emphasis to his appointment of head boy at his 'previous highly academic school against strong competition'. Whilst again, this is a positive experience, emphasising that the student's school was highly academic makes it seem as though their experiences in school are of greater value than those of someone from a lesser academic school. This makes the student come across as overconfident, pompous, and elitist. The sentence in which the student describes his appointment as head boy is badly worded, with three commas and a semi-colon.

Overall:

Whilst this is a good personal statement, the student is let down by an abundance of self-praise. This makes the student a lot less likable to the reader.

NOTES

Subject: Physics

Understanding how things work and studying the unsolved questions of the universe are reasons why I have a continuous interest in Physics. The logic of the subject is complemented by regular use of Mathematics in all areas, which I thoroughly enjoy. Physics explains everything around us, from the fundamental particles to the stars and planets and I find this intriguing. The fact that Physics is constantly evolving, with new discoveries happening all the time - such as the finding of the tau neutrino - causes the way we think to change constantly and I am fascinated to see scientific theories grow and improve.

An appealing aspect of the Physics course is the logical way of thinking about problems, as well as the complex mathematics needed for more advanced areas of the subject. Breakthroughs in science have come in no small part due to experimentation, for example Ernest Rutherford's alpha particle scattering experiment, so I thoroughly enjoy practical work, but theoretical work is equally important, a great example being Einstein's Theory of Relativity. My father is an engineer, and as a result I always ask questions and approach problems rationally. Mathematics has always been something I enjoy, but Pure Mathematics seems to have limited use in the real world, and I believe that Physics is where Mathematics is at its most useful – helping to explain otherwise inexplicable problems. While Physics is very in-depth, it also has an extensive range, covering the most simple and the most complicated concepts, and in my opinion this gives the subject a limitless fascination.

As a result of what I have learnt I was compelled to find out about topics not covered in the A-Level course. I have read Stephen Hawking's "A Brief History of Time", Richard Feynman's "The Strange Theory of Light and Matter", Frank Close's "Antimatter" and Brian Cox's "Why Does $E=mc^2$?". These have really opened my eyes to how vast the subject is and consequently black holes and quantum electrodynamics are areas I am particularly looking forward to studying. As I learn more and more, my desire to continue to learn has grown exponentially and I feel that as the subject becomes more complex it also becomes more fascinating. The book "From Here to Infinity" by Ian Stewart gave me a great insight into modern mathematics and its applications. I am a regular reader of BBC Focus magazine and any scientific articles I come across as I try to keep abreast of current research and advancements. The particle collider at CERN in Geneva is where many of the latest advances in Physics have been made, and after university I would like to become involved in something so momentous. Ultimately I want to take my academic study of Physics as far as I can.

Playing in the school orchestra has made me realise how important teamwork is, and the need for practice and commitment to make a group project successful. Teamwork has also played a part when I was one of a group of volunteers painting an orphanage and when I was a member of a Boy Scouts troop. Being a House Prefect has made me feel a sense of responsibility for others, whilst participating in the Headmaster's Discussion Group has given me greater confidence in expressing and defending my ideas in public. A week's work experience at an offshore drilling company, while not focused on physics, gave me an insight into what the real world wants from its scientists and the need to develop applications to help with everyday problems. I have also participated in the UKMT Maths Challenge for several years, earning 5 Gold awards and a Best in School Award. With my subjects at A2 level, I can see that Physics links in with all my other subjects; with Mathematics in hundreds of ways, but also with Chemistry, such as electron spin in atoms which is very important in NMR spectroscopy and orbital arrangements. Overall, I find the infinite scope of Physics enthralling and I am eager to study it further.

Universities applied to:

- Oxford: Offer
- Lancaster: Offer
- Durham: Offer
- Warwick: Offer
- Edinburgh: Offer

Good Points:

This is a well-written and structured statement. The student is clearly highly motivated and has read extensively on their chosen subject.

Bad Points:

The student mentions family influences into pursuing a numerate discipline at university, family influence is only ever a bad thing in a personal statement, and should be avoided. The student makes a bold statement, 'but Pure Mathematics seems to have limited use in the real world'. Whilst the student's courage is taken to be a positive quality by this reader, it is important to remember that the final reader(s) of the statement will be academics and admissions tutors at universities who have a wide range of technical backgrounds. A physics tutor may have completed an undergraduate degree and possibly even a PhD in pure mathematics before moving into research which has led to them becoming physics-focused. It is important not to offend the reader. On the subject of reading, the student lists a considerable number of books which they have read, but does not elaborate on what they learned or enjoyed from most of them. It is always better to read one book and talk about it in a meaningful way, than read ten and say nothing.

Overall:

This is a very good statement. The student does not come across as arrogant or over-confident, however, makes a bold and risky claim regarding the relevance of an entire subject discipline.

NOTES

Subject: Physics

"You can do anything." When people see grades like mine this is often what they say to me. But I don't want to just do anything; I need something that will challenge me and keep me constantly thinking. When you love learning as much as I do you want to learn about the big things, and what is bigger than the universe? Physics aims to study the workings of the universe from the movement of an electron into a new orbital to the periodic rotation of the greatest galaxies. What I love about physics is the way it takes this vast universe and organises it into laws, taking the apparent chaos of matter and proving there are greater forces holding it all together. I love learning about the fundamental properties of the universe that so many people don't give a second thought about and wonder why they aren't as fascinated by the miracle of light as I am. The universe is not just some distant stars to me; I am a part of it and it is a part of me. The atoms in me came from a supernova explosion and to study the physics that makes these things happen is to study myself.

I have been top of my class since primary school and learning, remembering and explaining all come quite naturally. With 10A* and an A in my GCSEs I proved to myself that I am a well-rounded pupil. But when required to think about it, I know science is where my greatest strength lies. By coming first in GCSE Biology in Northern Ireland and second in Physics and Maths it demonstrated to me that I have the ability for both explaining why and calculating how. When I come across documentaries like Brian Cox's Wonders of the Universe or read books like Paradox by Jim Al-Khalili I realise that physics is so much more fascinating than what we are taught at school. This past year I have had a real thirst for finding out more about physics, particularly astrophysics and relativity. I have found this interest has driven me in my studies and this year I received the Physics' Prize in school.

Art is also a big part of my life and I thoroughly enjoy studying it at A level. For me it is a link in my studies between learning about the world and responding to it. It teaches me indispensable skills, such as being able to analyse and think for myself, to push myself to go deeper into the meaning of a theme or object. I am constantly evaluating my thoughts, learning from mistakes and taking inspiration from those who have gone before me. These are skills that have transferred seamlessly to my more scientific work. An artist is forced to experiment and then build on their findings. The key to a good scientist is one who is not afraid to experiment and learn. Even accidents, if well observed, can lead to the greatest discoveries, like Fleming's famous penicillin find.

My Christian beliefs have not conflicted with my love of science; they make me want to delve further into the depths of how the world has been made. Reading books like "Has Science buried God?" by John Lennox confirmed to me that science and religion are entirely compatible. Professor Lennox's debates concerning this absolutely fascinated me and encouraged me to question what we believe. Although I love spending time to reflect by myself, I equally enjoy interacting and working with others. I have been a committed member of the Girl's Brigade since I was 4 and have completed Bronze, Silver and Gold Duke of Edinburgh Awards with school. I also have a passion for leading and teaching so last year I became a pupil mentor for junior science pupils which has given me a greater understanding of how to express scientific ideas. I've also led a summer camp and am deeply involved in teaching at Sunday School.

This year I have been elected to be one of 6 Senior Prefects and a member of the SU Committee. I have a very enthusiastic personality and adore encouraging others to share my passions. At SU I have started a Q and A section where people are encouraged to query what they believe and seek a deeper understanding of their faith.

Music is another one of my passions; I have been playing guitar for 4 years and love composing my own songs and trying to find the perfect words for my thoughts. I've found I'm the kind of person that considers music from both perspectives; how the perfectly tuned standing waves create a longitudinal pressure wave of sound that propagates to the ear and how a couple of notes combined with the right rhythm and phrase can instantly change a mood. It is my passion for both the scientific and the creative that make me who I am and hope you appreciate this as you consider me for your course.

Universities applied to:

- Oxford: Offer
- Durham: Offer
- Bristol: Offer
- Queen's University Belfast: Offer
- Manchester: Offer

Good Points:

This is an undeniably strong and impressive statement. The student is clearly very talented at a great number of things, from academics to art and music. The introduction makes the statement stand out immediately. Reasons other than becoming interested in physics following A-level studies are abundant, clearly explained, and expanded upon. The student addresses the reader directly and closes with a point that is addressed solely to the reader. This comes across well as it means that the student recognises that the reader is an individual.

Bad Points:

This is a very strange personal statement. The student opens by explaining how others perceive her intelligence to be so great that anything is possible. Later in the statement, the student seems to brag about having 'been top of class since primary school and learning, remembering, and explaining all come quite naturally. With 10A* and an A in my GCSEs'. It is not possible from this statement to tell if the student achieved this by overcoming great adversity, or if the likelihood was low due to the poor resources of the school at which the student studied. The reader is left wondering if privilege, opportunities, and resources were abundant to the student, or if the student is a remarkable success story from an impoverished area. In either case, the student's over-confidence and pomposity is very clear and this does not come across well at all.

This reader is left in no doubt that the student is a highly intelligent and multi-talented individual, however, it's hard for admissions tutors to relate to her on account of the overconfidence with which she conveys herself. Whilst it is important to showcase individual achievements, it is important to remember that the reader is a stranger who does not know the student. Sweeping statements about oneself can be taken wrongly and out of context, and in this case, the student has failed to account for this.

Overall:

This is a very strange statement where the student makes sweeping statements about herself, which can easily be interpreted in the wrong way and taken out of context. Slight tweaks emphasising the core drivers behind her accomplishments would enhance this statement beyond its already excellent nature.

NOTES

Subject: Physics

An incessant curiosity about the laws of the cosmos has always attracted me to the study of physics. I am especially intrigued by theoretical physics and how its concepts are the foundations of all visible reactions one witnesses daily. My fascination with physics has led me to pursue my subject beyond the school curriculum and I have had a range of experiences which have confirmed my desire to study physics at university.

This summer I was selected for the Senior Physics Challenge at Cambridge University which enabled me to experience the level and pace of undergraduate classical mechanics, quantum mechanics and lab-work. In preparation for the course, I studied a quantum mechanics primer and familiarised myself with previously untaught mathematics. During the week, we tackled the Schrodinger equation, square well potential problems, Heisenberg's uncertainty principle and learnt new aspects of mathematics such as eigenstates and SHM. The course was demanding and thus highly engaging, and this encounter with higher-level physics has made me eager to extend my knowledge of quantum mechanics.

Selected to visit CERN with school on the basis of an essay competition on dark matter and dark energy, I attended lectures on particle physics and saw the LHCb experiment. The highlight of the trip being the coding activity organised by Liverpool University where, using real LHC data of a decaying kaon, we chose cuts to make in the data to improve the efficiency and purity of the signal. Gaining an insight into aspects of the research work undertaken by particle physicists was inspiring. Likewise, at a "Particle Physics Day" at Birmingham University, I had the opportunity to use computer software to identify different particles and collisions in detectors. Last summer, I attended the "Physics Experience Week" organised by Birmingham University that combined lectures, lab-work and a rocket-building session. I was fascinated by an experiment where, collaborating in a team with pupils from different schools, we counted cosmic ray muons using a scintillation detector and took down readings together.

Having chosen to study GCSE Astronomy independently, I learnt to use the Faulkes Telescopes to take photographs of Messier objects in order to determine the ages of 3 planetary nebulae. My interest in space has been enhanced by a 2-week trip to NASA with 'Space Education Adventures', visiting the Johnson and Kennedy Space Centres. I was astounded by the immensity of the space projects and their contribution to science and history. A work experience placement in a hospital Medical Physics department demonstrated to me the application of physics in medical diagnostic imaging and the importance of physics research for advances in medicine. The Engineering Education Scheme (year 12) enabled me to work with 3 other girls to design a hypothetical football training academy with engineer mentors from ARUP. We researched and presented a business case and technical plan to a panel of engineers from other companies, gaining the Gold Crest Award in Engineering as well as valuable presentation skills.

In complete contrast, this summer I attended the Joint Association of Classical Teachers' Greek Summer School. In addition to intensive lessons, we performed Aeschylus' Agamemnon in the original text; I was cast as Cassandra. This term I am giving a talk on Ancient Greek mathematics at my school's Classical Society, having researched the topic over the summer. I enjoy performing arts: I belong to the Birmingham Young REP Theatre and I have performed in the Symphony Orchestra, a chamber music group and the Choral Society at school. Balancing academic work with other activities requires organisation and discipline. Physics is a demanding and highly rewarding field. The prospect of an unsolved problem which may not have an immediate answer is captivating. My wish to understand nature and the academic challenge this poses is the reason I aspire to study physics.

Universities applied to:

- Oxford: Offer
- Imperial College London: Offer
- Manchester: Offer
- Bristol: Offer
- University College London: Rejected

Good Points:

This is a very well-written, structured, and excellent statement. The student has a clear motivation for physics and has achieved many things through extra hard work. The statement is easy to read and the student describes their achievements yet does not brag. All points and experiences are expanded on and clearly explained. The final paragraph adds individuality to the statement, and all non-physics-related interests are kept within this paragraph which is very good.

Bad Points:

The student uses the word 'I' a lot. Whilst it is important to emphasise personal achievements, using the same words over and over again makes the statement sound repetitive. The student mentions learning mathematics beyond the A-level syllabus prior to the Senior Physics Challenge at Cambridge University, however, does not expand on what this involved. The student has missed an opportunity to describe how they gained mathematical skills independently. The student does this again by failing to describe what they learned through writing their essay on dark matter. A sentence on each of these points would have added yet more value to this excellent statement.

Overall:

This is an excellent statement. It is easy to read, well-structured, and the student comes across as a very likable individual.

NOTES

EARTH SCIENCES

Subject: Earth Science

I wonder how many people on Earth know that approximately 2, 3 billion years ago was the so-called "oxygen catastrophe" which lead to the largest extinction ever known? And if we go deeper into the earth's history we notice that life and the Universe itself are a chain of "lucky" events. This may be controversial or overwhelming, but it made me grateful for the fact that I am here to write this statement and of course, it inspired me to study earth sciences.

My fascination for nature began during my early childhood and my first family mountain trips, when I could not help asking myself "How have all these formed?" The answers started to come during secondary school when I was training with my teachers for Physics and Geography student competitions. My inclination for science was clear when I entered a Mathematics Computer Science class in high school.

My motivation grew stronger with my qualification for the International Earth Science Olympiad 2010, when I had the opportunity to approach subjects ranging from Astronomy to Oceanography both at theoretical and practical levels. My entire hard work was awarded the Bronze Medal and this gave me even more energy and enthusiasm.

Encouraged by this achievement, in 2011 I participated in the Scientific Research Project Contest for high school students where my paper won the Second National Prize for environmental Geography. My study involved the research of the evolution and impact of a local landslide to the natural landscape and villagers' life. In 2012 I participated in the same contest and I improved my cartography skills using my own GIS based maps. Later, I competed in the National Earth Science Olympiad achieving the maximum result for Geography theoretical and field test. Preparing for all there contests in the Chemistry and Physics laboratory fascinated me and made me more capable of individual study.

Although, I usually prefer to focus my energy on science I am aware of the society I live in and of the ways I can bring my contribution to improve it. For this reason, I travelled to Italy in September 2011 to be a volunteer for the International Earth Science Olympiad. The contact with highly academic technologies, the preparations of the Olympiad practical tests and the fieldtrip to the Alps gave me a taste of being an earth sciences student and convinced me to want more. Also, in 2011 and 2012 I organised the Science Week Fair in my school and I was able to cooperate with a wide variety of students, manage and integrate different ideas and to gain leadership skills.

I posses not only the relevant qualities for my course option, but during high school I also improved a lot of my transferable skills. I choose to study in a Great Britain university because I want to take advantage of the best scientific environment, modern laboratories, research possibilities and highly qualified teachers.

I am a very positive person and I am open to every scientific challenge I could meet during my studies. In my readings I have always been interested in petrology, volcanism, tectonic plates and how earth dynamic systems interact with each other to create a diverse and original environment that supports living possibilities. Therefore, I want to apply all my future knowledge and bring my contribution to the sustainable development of our planet and the understanding of the Universe at large.

Universities applied to:

- Imperial College London: Offer
- University College London: Offer
- St Andrew's: Offer
- Edinburgh: Rejected
- Oxford: Offer

Good Points:

This is a well-written and structured statement. The student is clearly very motivated and this comes across well in the statement. The student mentions several earth science disciplines, including Oceanography and Astronomy. This is very good as earth sciences is an extremely broad course, and encompasses many subjects which are degree courses in their own right. The inclusion of the student's positive character is very important as fieldwork is an important part of any earth sciences degree. This gives the reader confidence that the student will maintain a positive outlook and character when in challenging circumstances in the field, and most importantly, be able to continue working in such circumstances.

Bad Points:

The student should use 'possess' instead of 'posses' at the start of the sixth paragraph. The student has a wealth of experience from extra-curricular activities, however, does not use these to describe their teamwork skills. In earth sciences, both field and lab work involve working as part of small closely-knit teams. If the student had described their teamwork skills in addition to their leadership skills, this would have added great value to the statement.

Overall:

This is a very good statement. The student explains all experiences well, however, does not elaborate on teamwork skills. Such skills are important in any earth science degree course and are highly desirable in potential students.

NOTES

Subject: Geology

My interest in geology was initially fuelled by visiting the Natural History Museum. There, I was fascinated by the diverse range of colours and structures the rocks took, motivating me to learn about what influences the development of different rocks. I investigated rocks further by collecting them from the sea shore and breaking them open to observe the internal structure. I wondered how minerals with strikingly similar chemical compositions could be so heterogeneous in appearance. For example, the properties of carbon allow the formation of diamond or graphite allotropes, depending on the exposure to temperature and pressure over time. Some of my most interesting rocks are pieces of Agate, and whilst they are very attractive I am particularly fascinated by how they form. Through my "Mindat" account I research rocks that I find, mineralogy is a field I am particularly keen to study.

Now, as a member of the Open University Geological Society, I keep in touch with the latest geological news by attending their regular events and reading the bi-monthly newsletter. The most recent event I attended was in Warrington, where I particularly enjoyed a lecture entitled "Meteorite impact and quaternary extinctions". I was intrigued by the methods geologists had used, such as examining the carbon content in the soil layers, searching for the presence of nanodiamonds and evidence left in animal bones, to support their theories.

Whilst at college I arranged a years voluntary work experience (one day a fortnight) as an Environmental Safety Officer at Bentley Motors. In one project, we raised recycling rates by redesigning the process of waste disposal. To tackle a pollution problem, I produced an information sheet on the appropriate disposal of hazardous liquids, which was posted to employees on the company intranet. Not only did I learn valuable team working skills, I also learned how important environmental responsibility is to big companies – something which will become only more important in the future.

Since leaving college, I've worked to fund lessons in both driving and Japanese language and to save towards my future education. As a night porter in a Crowne Plaza Hotel, I assist customers and take responsibility for fire safety and security. In handling difficult situations, my skills of negotiation have been developed. I also worked for Royal Mail over the Christmas period – a role which developed my skills in organisation and working under pressure.

In my spare time, I particularly enjoy hiking and hill walking, and regularly tackle the UK's highest peaks with my friends. My favourite place to walk is Snowdonia; I was fascinated to learn even more about the glacial history of the Glyderau and Ogwen Valley at a recent Open University Geological Society event. I like to train by cycling, running and playing tennis at a local club. I'm interested in Japanese culture and language and am currently learning Japanese at evening classes – something which has improved my ability to work independently.

When starting my BTEC diploma, I was undecided between my interests in medical science and geology. I decided to pursue medical sciences academically, whilst learning about the environment and geology through my work experience placement and hobbies. I feel my BTEC triple merit in medical science shows my aptitude for independent study in the sciences, but my experiences have shown me I have a greater enthusiasm for geology. Therefore my ambition is to study geology to degree level and I would be extremely grateful of the opportunity to do so.

ULTIMATE OXBRIDGE PERSONAL STATEMENT GUIDE — EXAMPLE STATEMENTS – GEOLOGY

Universities applied to:

- Keele: Offer
- Plymouth: Offer
- Derby: Offer
- Portsmouth: Offer

Good Points:

The student is obviously highly motivated and is very humble. Geology degrees involve a great deal of fieldwork and require a certain degree of fitness, so it is encouraging to see that the student enjoys hillwalking and is accustom to adverse weather conditions. This will certainly be of use when in the field whilst studying. It is clear that the student's personal interest in geology is the reasoning behind their application. This is evident from their efforts outside of their BTEC in medical science. This is very encouraging as it shows a serious commitment to wanting to pursue geology at a higher (degree) level.

Bad Points:

The statement begins quite abruptly, without an introduction. It would have been better if the student broadly introduced geology and the reasons for their interest at the beginning of the statement. Many sentences can be restructured in order to save space and to be read more easily, e.g. 'Whilst at college I arranged a years voluntary work experience (one day a fortnight) as an Environmental Safety Officer at Bentley Motors'. This could be written as, 'Whilst at college, I arranged fortnightly voluntary work experience at Bentley Motors. Here, I worked as an Environmental Safety Officer for a year....'.

Overall:

This is a good personal statement. The student comes across as honest, humble, and motivated.

NOTES

Subject: Earth Science (Geology)

Taking part in a BSES Expedition to the Arctic in the summer of 2008 and experiencing field work and mapping in the dramatic landscapes of Svalbard had motivated me to select a four-year study abroad course in Geophysics. With the grades I achieved I was offered a place on a three-year course, but I am still interested in studying abroad so I have decided to take a gap year to use the time to improve my grades and gain work experience in Geology related work. I am now applying for the study abroad Geology course as this combines my interest in Geography, Maths and Physics with my passion for the outdoors.

Studying Geography has increased my awareness of the key geographical issues facing us today. By reading Planet Earth and Geoscientist I have improved my understanding of tectonic activity and natural hazards, inspiring me to research further into prediction and mitigation of natural disasters. Maths and Physics have been challenging, but I enjoy these subjects as they have helped develop my logical thinking skills and problem-solving skills.

In 2008 I took part in an Engineering Education Scheme, which required small groups to complete a science project. My group was given an assignment by BP titled 'Investigating How Much Energy Can Be Produced by a Typical Wave and How-to Set-up a System to Recover This Energy'. In addition to credits from BP, we achieved a BA Gold Crest Award, which is based on an assessment of 100 hours of science project work. By participating in this scheme, I improved teamwork and presentation skills. In 2007, I obtained a company sponsored scholarship to attend a Presidential Classroom Programme on Science, Technology and Public Policy. This was a weeklong conference in Washington D.C. for 300 students selected from around the world with the purpose of learning about the role of government in issues related to scientific discoveries and technological advances. As well as benefiting from an interesting program, I developed leadership and communication skills through the position of Project Manager of a group of 30 students for a team presentation.

During my time at school I have held various positions of responsibility, including House Captain, Prefect, form charity representative and assistant at the Junior School, which have helped to develop my communication skills with people of all ages and strengthened my organisation and leadership skills.

Out of school I like to undertake challenges and expeditions. Taking part in the Duke of Edinburgh Award scheme has helped me become independent and self-reliant and has helped me to improve my organisational skills. I have also learnt a number of essential life skills, including map reading and First Aid. Having achieved the Bronze Award, I am now working towards the Gold Award. In the summer of 2007 I took part in a World Challenge Expedition to Namibia. Through this experience I learnt about different cultures and the importance of contributing to developing communities. I also improved on my teamwork and further developed leadership skills, as I had to lead the team on various occasions. The 2008 BSES Expedition helped to improve all the above skills, but particularly focusing on teamwork.

With my enthusiasm for Geography, Maths and Physics and the skills I have developed through the challenges and expeditions, I believe I would be a very dedicated and determined student for the Geology course and I believe I would contribute well as an individual and as a group member to the University.

ULTIMATE OXBRIDGE PERSONAL STATEMENT GUIDE — EXAMPLE STATEMENTS – GEOLOGY

Universities applied to:

- University College London: Offer
- Imperial College London: Offer
- Bristol: Offer
- Leeds: Offer

Good Points:

It is clear that the student is highly motivated, to the point at which they decided to take a gap year in order to achieve the grades necessary to apply to the exact course of their choice. The student's passion for the outdoors is a highly desirable quality as all geology degrees involve fieldwork and commitment to working in challenging environments, which is of paramount importance. The statement is compact and is not too long. This is good as it makes the statement have a greater impact on the reader.

Bad Points:

The introduction comes across as quite defensive of the student's choice to spend a gap year in order to improve their grades. Whilst taking a gap year in order to improve grades is not a negative point, the statement would have read better if the student didn't come across as defensive as they do in the opening paragraph.

The student has a great number of experiences outside of their college studies, and this comes across well in the statement. However, the student fails to use this as an opportunity to describe how they overcame any difficulties and challenges associated with such experiences. This would have added great value to the statement.

Overall:

This is a very good statement overall. The student has clearly thought long and hard about their choice and is committed to the subject to which they are applying.

NOTES

Subject: Geography

Geography is outward-looking, dynamic and topical. It allows me to gain insight into daily news stories on immigration and Middle Eastern conflicts for example, by highlighting their complexity and the challenge to find and evaluate solutions to these problems for the future. The diversity and vital relevance of Geography makes it an immensely valuable subject to study in depth and I would relish the opportunity to pursue further study in the field.

The area that is of particular interest to me is development geography and specifically global aid. I was introduced to the use of aid in closing the wealth divide in my A2 case studies, where bottom-up aid on a local scale was consistently depicted as a sustainable solution. I was forced to question these views, however, after reading 'Dead Aid' by Dambisa Moyo. Her critical comments on charity-based aid particularly caught my attention as they offered a stark contrast in perspective on my case studies. I found it interesting that the factors which contributed to the success of many of the case studies, including small-scale, intermediate technology and low cost solutions were the very aspects of aid that Moyo calls 'band-aid' solutions implying unsustainability. The book also touched on the controversial issue of whether aid remains a successful or even acceptable solution when the $50 billion of aid given to Africa annually is arguably not producing significant economic development or improvement. To investigate this further I read 'The End Of Poverty' by Jeffrey Sachs which explained how well managed aid can indeed offer an answer to closing the wealth divide. This led to my research into the Millenium Villages of Ghana. Here aid, coupled with local leadership, appears to have delivered a long-term solution to serious economic and social problems. This divergence in opinion over a controversial issue has excited me about exploring these issues in more detail.

To investigate these issues further, I have been prompted to take a gap year to experience the workings of an international NGO. I will be joining the work of education promoting 'Empower A Child' in Uganda for 3 months. I hope to gain a rewarding insight into the practical relevance of Geography in the field of non-profit aid and specifically to test Sach's belief that investment into education is a viable solution to ending poverty.

My other subjects complement my understanding of economic, physical and scientific elements of development and Geography in general. Reading 'Driven to Extinction' by Richard Pearson highlighted how Biology and Geography are inextricably linked in our study of the physical world, particularly with regards to the role regulatory systems have in levels of biodiversity. Chemistry and Physics have been relevant in equipping me with the skills to devise data collection programmes and to analyse the results; skills which were necessary to my fieldwork visit to Dartmoor.

My academic background is complemented by my extra-curricular activities. I was the Organ Scholar and Choir Prefect at my school. My responsibilities included conducting and directing the Chapel Choir on a weekly basis. I was also a fully committed and dedicated member of other choirs and ensembles. I relished the challenge of arranging and conducting in the House Singing competition which required me to inspire and motivate team work within the house. I have gained 3 Grade 8's in Organ, Piano and Flute and am currently working towards my Piano Diploma. I was involved in leading the school's Christian Union through which I have catalysed fundraising for organisations such as Mary's Meals. In my gap year I am working as Organist and Choir director at St Luke's Church Grayshott before going to Uganda.

These activities demonstrate leadership skills, commitment and an enthusiastic approach to challenges, all of which will equip me well for the study of Geography at university.

Universities applied to:

- Oxford: Offer
- University College London: Offer
- King's: Offer
- Exeter: Offer
- Durham: Offer

Good Points:

This is a very good personal statement and is well-written. The student is clearly interested by many aspects of geography, which is very important as geography is a multi-disciplinary subject. The student describes several areas of geography which capture their interest, demonstrating their interest and commitment to the reader. The student justifies their decision to take a gap year well, and the relevance their activities will have to the subject of geography and their interests in global aid.

Bad Points:

The student misspells the word 'millennium' in the second paragraph. The second paragraph is also very long. It is hard for the reader to stay focused when reading through long paragraphs, and it would have been better if the student had separated the second paragraph into two. The final paragraph is also very long and it is not clear where the conclusion begins. As a result, the end of the statement does not deliver the impact which the student has intended to produce. If the student separates the sentence, 'These activities demonstrate leadership skills, commitment and an enthusiastic approach to challenges, all of which will equip me well for the study of Geography at university' into a new final paragraph, this would have made the final statement much more effective.

Overall:

This is a very good statement. The student has a wealth of experiences and is clearly very motivated to study geography. Some paragraphs are very long and this reduces the impact that the statement has on the reader. With some restructuring, this could be an excellent statement.

NOTES

ENGINEERING

Subject: Engineering

All comforts of today's life are taken for granted, but who contributed towards creating them? The answer is what firstly inspired me to enter into civil engineering. Civil engineers put roofs over our heads and roads under our feet. They create bridges that minimize distances, tunnels that link countries underwater and make our world a healthier place to live in by managing efficiently the surrounding air, water and natural resources. I expect civil engineering to be challenging – as even a little mistake can be fatal – but also very self-rewarding because of its creativity and application of ideas.

The most inspiring moments of my life as an ambitious student were during my visit at CERN, the world's largest particle physics laboratory. I had the chance to be among engineers and physicists that seek answers and contribute to the understanding of the universe by studying the tiniest particles. Young researchers informed me about the existence of fundamental particles recently invented and how they link to the creation of our universe. Particularly, the Large Hadron Collider inspired me towards engineering and making a change to today's understanding. I'm currently reading, "Structures: Or Why things don't fall down" and "Remaking the world: Adventures in Engineering" and hope to read more on the subject of engineering at university.

Competitions have always been a strong point. From an early age I have participated in many competitions, receiving national awards in Mathematics, Physics and Computer Science. They provided me with the chance to challenge myself and develop a love for problem solving. Overcoming obstacles and finding solutions after hours of work gave me a sense of self accomplishment. The methods of problem solving in Maths helped me work out answers in mechanics and gain a full understanding of theoretical physics. What's more, as part of my Computer A-Level I had to identify the problems of a civil engineering company and produce a solution by designing a computerized system. This enabled me to sharpen my analytical thinking and have a closer look at the management of such company.

Along with sciences, music is also a passion of mine. I have a grade 8 in piano and music theory and I'm currently preparing for a piano diploma in music performance. Through the preparation of it, I created an appreciation of music in a high level and enjoyed performing pieces of highly demanding technique so early in my life. In addition, I've taken place in the journalist's team of my school trying to restore the municipal park of my town. My writing and communication skills were developed as much teamwork was involved and after research and interviews we published in the local newspaper our opposition to the destruction of this green source of life. Protecting the environment is one aspect of civil engineering. I intend on practicing this profession as ecologically as possible.

Becoming a civil engineer will give me the opportunity to apply my knowledge in Sciences into making the dream reality. I am ready to face all the challenges that will come along: those of university life and those of future career, always aiming in the improvement of mankind living.

Universities applied to:

- Cambridge: Offer
- Imperial College London: Offer
- University College London: Offer
- Bath: Offer
- Sheffield: Offer

Good Points:

This is a very well-written and compact statement. The student starts by explaining their interest in a particular branch of engineering and then goes on to explain their interest in science. This may be because the student has applied for several different courses with their UCAS application, however, the statement manages to remain specific to engineering yet general enough to encompass the physical sciences.

Bad Points:

The student exclusively describes their interests in civil engineering and does not mention any other branches of engineering. Whilst this may be relevant for applications to universities offering civil engineering as a single discipline, other universities such as Cambridge offer general engineering degrees with the option of specialising available in the third year of study. To make the statement more relevant to general engineering, the student should have mentioned other engineering disciplines. Some sentences are not well-written, e.g. 'My writing and communication skills were developed as much teamwork was involved and after research and interviews we published in the local newspaper our opposition to the destruction of this green source of life'. This could be written as, 'My writing, communication, and teamwork skills were developed through the production of a published newspaper article in opposition to....'

Overall:

This is a very good statement, although is quite focused towards civil engineering. The student could have made the application more relevant to general engineering by mentioning their enthusiasm to gain a broad experience in general engineering before specialising in civil engineering.

NOTES

Subject: Engineering

As a child being driven over London's Albert Bridge I was intrigued by the sign saying somewhat cryptically 'all ranks must break step'. Years later at school next to the Millennium Bridge I wanted to understand what had caused the bridge to be closed just after it was opened and discovered the connection. The same principle applies to both situations. I observed the side to side motion of pedestrians on the reopened bridge and understood how the engineers designing it had not accounted for these lateral forces that were acting at the bridge's natural frequency, half that of the downward forces. The designers of the older and more rigid bridge had relied on written instructions to avoid the downward forces from soldiers walking in step synchronising with the bridge's natural frequency. In 2001 the unforeseen problem was resolved using dampers and stiffening against lateral deflection. These bridges and their weaknesses opened my eyes to engineering.

I take pleasure in the challenge of solving problems that require more than just knowledge of how to use an equation and instead necessitate logical thought to work out how the problem can be approached. This includes applying maths to resolve a physical situation, an area which I enjoy very much. I have spent time following up differential equation (simple harmonic motion) and mechanics questions (projectiles) which are also relevant to engineering. My coursework presentation on Kevlar instigated an interest in materials, by understanding how its chemical properties, notably the aromatic bond, combined to make such a strong, flexible and low-density material with uses in many areas of engineering from bikes to bullet proof vests.

During work experience at Halcrow Yolles I witnessed engineering in action in Structural, Mechanical and Facade engineering. In the building services department I partook in a competition for an eco-friendly building in a hot climate by researching ways to achieve HVAC efficiency by designing structures which encourage the stack effect to improve ventilation and using window film to filter out UV rays, reducing the need for air conditioning. My findings were then discussed with my team. I relished my involvement and have since kept up my interest in environmental engineering, particularly geo-engineering, which is likely to become an important field as a last resort to counteract climate change. I would be interested to pursue this as a graduate. This placement introduced me to the analytical, mathematical and problem-solving skills involved in the processes of engineering which I feel well suited to.

Engineering at a top university will provide a challenge that I will enjoy confronting. I have a desire to gain an understanding of the principles that govern our world and how we manipulate them for our own uses as well as enjoying a balance between applied mathematics and the physical aspects of engineering. I will defer entry to university to give myself experience in both the mathematical and practical side of engineering by spending a year in industry. I am looking for a placement in the automotive industry with SEAT to enhance my Spanish. The experience will help me conceptualise the more theoretical aspects of engineering courses. I will allow time to get back up to speed with maths before university begins.

As a senior prefect who mentors Year 9s in maths and takes part in CCF and CSO I have developed my teamwork and organisational skills. Determination and focusing on my targets help me fulfill my objectives. I devised, organised, and encouraged others to train for and join in a 300 mile cycle ride from London to Paris, raising GBP 6000 for our school charity. I enjoy sports, playing football for school in my free time, but also ensure that I complete work efficiently and to a high standard.

Universities applied to:

- Cambridge: Offer
- Durham: Offer
- Warwick: Offer
- Bristol: Offer
- Bath: Offer

Good Points:

This is a very good statement. The statement is well-written and structured. The student clearly explains their motivation for wanting to pursue engineering. The statement mentions and describes the student's desire to pursue a number of different engineering disciplines, which is very good as this makes the statement relevant to applications for courses of a single engineering discipline, and to those for general engineering. The student's use of their desire to study Engineering 'at a top university' is very good as the student does not mention any one university specifically. This makes it clear that the student has taken their application to every university in their UCAS application seriously, something which is often not the case for students who are applying to Oxbridge.

Bad Points:

The student uses several acronyms which are not written out in full. This assumes that the reader will be familiar with such acronyms, which may not be the case. This reader has no idea what 'CSO' means, rendering its inclusion in the statement useless. There are commas missing in places, however, this is a minor error.

Overall:

This is a very good statement, however, the reader is left to work out what the meanings of several acronyms are for themselves. With a little more attention to the reader, this statement would be excellent.

NOTES

Subject: Design Engineering

Based on my two different spheres of interests studying Design Engineering is an obvious choice for me. Besides my fondness for drawing and photography, which has given me a particular openness to Modern Arts, I also find pleasure in problem solving hence my A Level equivalent choices of Mathematics and Physics. However, I intend to move from theories and abstract mathematical models towards their applications. My multicultural background provides me with a unique perspective that is reflected in my interest and desire to study design engineering.

At a very early age in Ecuador, my father sent me to the British School and later on gave me the possibility to obtain German system based tuition in Deutsche Schule too. So I was introduced to two different traditions and languages relatively early. Later on, when I moved to Hungary with my mother, I felt lost and rootless. But with time I realized that integrating the traditions of Europe and Latin America is also useful which I experienced at Berzsenyi Daniel, one of the top grammar schools in Hungary. My class specialized in English and German places emphasis on the historical and cultural background of both countries. I have benefited from exchange student programs as well, which were not only precious experiences, but also helped me to make new friends. In addition, my initial interest in Mathematics, Physics and drawing grew with time on account of the excellent tuition I was offered, owing to advanced Maths and drawing classes (both 6 hours per week). I was lucky to participate in a summer Maths camp, which was organized for a selected group of students. This year's theme was structured around the use of computational projective geometry for camera calibration; this was a lucky coincidence, since I take deep interest in photography. This intense learning experience showed me how to combine two different fields. Consequently, I ended up attending a preparatory course in freehand drawing using isometric projection at Budapest Technical University, the most prestigious university of engineering in Hungary. I have also audited lectures where the question was formulated in me: which is more important form or function? I think they are pieces equivalent in size of the same virtual cake.

I value team work as an important factor in every culture. This realization proved to be really beneficial both as an elected member of the Student Council and as a leading organiser of a summer freshmen camp at school. These extracurricular activities played a significant role in my life as made me focus on the fact that teamwork is the third missing piece from that virtual cake.

Many examples of the nexus between art and science can be found such as Leonardo da Vinci the famous polymaths himself and inventions of our modern age like iPod. Nowadays this connection is becoming stronger than ever in order to meet the demands of the consumers. I believe that products have to be practical, yet aesthetically pleasing. In my hobby, photography, I am trying to design a DSLR camera with a movable viewfinder in order to get new point of views when taking shots.

Design engineering represents me the most ideal way to broaden my sphere of interests, to improve my skills and to use my creativity in order to shape our future. It is not only the multicultural environment of the UK, but also the tradition of education, I came to know at the British School before, that has attracted me the most. I believe that attending this complex course at a prestigious university in the UK would be the best opportunity to combine two different fields, engineering and art.

Universities applied to:

- Glasgow: Offer
- Nottingham: Offer
- Brunel: Offer
- Aberdeen: Offer
- Dundee: Offer

Good Points:

The student's life experiences are clearly the driving force behind their choice of subject and this comes across in the statement. It is clear that the student has taken the time to research around their chosen subject and is enthusiastic enough about design engineering to try and design their own DSLR camera.

Bad Points:

The statement is in a back-to-front order. The student opens with a sentence: 'Based on my two different spheres of interests studying Design Engineering is an obvious choice for me', however, does not actually state what these two spheres are. The introduction is not separated from the main body of the statement which makes the entire statement quite hard to follow.

The statement reads more like an account of the student's life rather than a statement as to why the student wants to study design engineering specifically at university. Whilst it is, of course, important to describe important life experiences and their relevance to one's choice of degree choice, it is not necessary to give an in-depth account on one's entire life. The student goes off on a tangent early on in the statement and finally gets to the point of the statement in the final two paragraphs. The student does not make any references as to why any of the points raised in the main (second), third nor fourth paragraph are relevant to their application, making most of this statement seem irrelevant.

Overall:

Although the student has led an interesting life and is clearly very motivated by their subject, they have let themselves down. The student writes in a completely unstructured way with the majority of the statement dedicated as an autobiography. The few points explained in terms of their relevance to the student's choice of design engineering appear at the very end of the statement, whereas they should be after the introduction.

NOTES

Subject: Engineering Science

I have always considered myself creative; much of my youth was spent designing and building with my Dad in his workshop. I would read encyclopaedias on cars and watch design-related TV programmes such as BBC's Robot Wars, analysing the strengths and weaknesses of each robot and thinking about how they could be improved. This background, combined with a genuine enjoyment of mathematics and physics, has given me a desire to read engineering at university.

Reading Marcus du Sautoy's "The Music of the Primes" and Simon Singh's "Fermat's Last Theorem" has shown how individuals have dedicated their lives to solving seemingly simple problems. The main attraction of these books and mathematics more widely, is problem solving, which is also what draws me to engineering. Solving a wide variety of problems is something I really enjoy; in the most recent UKMT Senior Maths Challenge, I was awarded a gold certificate, also the best score in my year at school.

Studying physics at A-Level has helped me to understand the world, and answered questions I had as a child; why does a satellite stay in orbit? How does gravity work? Why does a clock pendulum keep in time? My favourite aspect of physics is mechanics, complemented by my maths mechanics modules. The application of physics and mechanics to engineering was obvious from the outset; it is a fundamental skill set which bridges the gap between science and invention. I also enjoy studying Further Pure Mathematics, in particular calculus, and am interested in how the solutions of second order differential equations apply to problems in mechanics.

Projects including designing and making a desk lamp, a torch and bench vice grips in GCSE Engineering gave me an initial insight into the discipline. The course gave me hands on experience with equipment typical of an engineering department. Considering the benefits of materials was important too; from an economic, aesthetic, and practical perspective. I also secured work experience at a BMW Mini Plant in the 'Whole Vehicle Analysis', section. One project involved heating up a Mini's bonnet to address complaints from customers in hot countries that the bonnet scoop sagged. I used CNC measuring equipment and helped to write up one of a series of reports, resulting in an alloy being added to the scoop so it retained its structure. The week introduced me to engineering in the real world, the importance of quality control and precision and the cost of a company's mistakes.

Aside from my studies, I have always had a musical interest and am working towards grade 7 piano. I completed work experience at the local 'Yamaha Homeworld' music shop specialising in top range digital pianos. I am constantly impressed at how a digital piano can look, feel, and respond exactly like a real piano. I like being part of a team and am a keen rugby and cricket player. Being elected as prefect and head boy has further helped me to work well, and get on with others, as well as improving my public speaking. This has been complemented by taking Grade 8 'Speaking in Public' last year, in which I achieved a distinction. I now feel confident talking in front of large groups and being able to communicate my ideas easily. Reading Steven Johnson's "Where Good Ideas Come From" discussed the theory that "ideas are generated by crowds where connection is more important than protection" and for me this epitomises the importance of team work and communication within engineering.

Ultimately, I would like to play a role in the future of our rapidly developing world; studying engineering at university will not only give me the skills to do this, but will also stimulate my passion for mathematics and science.

Universities applied to:

- Oxford: Offer
- Imperial College London: Offer
- Bristol: Offer
- Durham: Offer
- Exeter: Offer

Good Points:

This is an excellent statement. The student begins with personal reasons as to why they are interested in engineering, and by the end of the introduction, the reader is left in no doubt that the student is absolutely sure they want to pursue engineering at a higher level. The student successfully describes a range of experiences and interests covering several engineering disciplines and keeps the application general enough to be relevant to a general engineering degree. The statement is well-structured with a clear introduction, main body, and end.

Bad Points:

Although the student mentions several experiences/interests covering several engineering disciplines, they fall short of naming a specific engineering discipline that captures their interest. Whilst this is not a requirement, naming a particular field of engineering as capturing one's interest above other fields would demonstrate a level of decisiveness to the reader. Many universities do not offer general engineering degrees, and it is possible a student who is applying for engineering at Oxford or Cambridge will also make several applications to universities for specific engineering disciplines. It is important to keep the statement general enough for applications to general engineering courses but also specific enough for applications to individual engineering disciplines. This would have been possible by stating an interest in a particular engineering discipline.

Overall:

This is an excellent statement, one that is well-written and well-structured. The student's motivation to study engineering is clear, although the student falls short of naming a specific field of engineering which capture's their interest above all others.

NOTES

Subject: Engineering

In the eyes of an eight-year-old, the Clifton suspension bridge was an amazing sight and my first exposure to the complexities of engineering. Seeing how the deck was supported by comparatively thin cables sparked my interest in the basics of material properties and the concept of tensile and compressive forces acting on various parts of structures. Encountering parabolas and catenaries in Mathematics made me aware of how apparently abstract concepts can have such an important practical role. The span and height made me appreciate some of the problems that many engineering projects face. Reading 'Structures or Why Things Don't Fall Down' by J. E. Gordon helped me understand the basic principles of structural integrity such as distributing the compressive loads on an arch through the voussoirs and to the abutments.

My previous belief that failure of the Tacoma Narrows was caused solely by vortex shedding induced resonance was questioned in the 1990 paper by K. Yusuf Bilah et al. Computer modelling of the "wobbly" Millennium Bridge in London failed to correctly predict the "positive feedback" phenomenon where the movement of the bridge, initially due to pedestrians, itself caused the people to walk instep and so compounding the resonant effect, requiring the corrective use of fluid and tuned mass dampeners. This shows that whilst engineers must attempt to consider all relevant variables and the nature of the loading whilst designing, there will always be unforeseen complications that require practical solutions.

My study of Mathematics has exposed me to concepts that have seemingly abstract uses, but when applied to engineering, they play a crucial part. Complex numbers enable us to represent cyclic systems such as oscillations, as well as being applied to principles such as the Continuity Equation. In fluid dynamics, it is interesting to see how they can be used to represent simple ocean waves using Airy Wave Theory. Studying Physics has provided me with a practical understanding of many fundamental engineering principles as well as the limitations imposed by the actual physical properties of the materials used. Business Studies enabled me to develop the financial and project management skills necessary in successful engineering projects. Competing in both the National Maths Challenge and Physics Olympiad has given me an experience of solving challenging problems.

My work experience with GKN Aerospace and Stirling Dynamics involved working in both the design office and on the shop floor. I gained an insight into the many disciplines concerned with the designing and manufacturing of planes, as well as a grasp of many of the problems to overcome. This corrected my previous view that engineering simply applied the fundamental laws of science. Instead it uses them in a very practical way, finding solutions that, whilst always functional, often do not rule out the possibilities of creative aesthetics. Reading 'The Simple Science of Flight: From Insect to Jumbo Jets' by Henk Tennekes explained the phenomenon of wing tip vortices and helped me understand the function of the elegant vertical wing tip projections. During my GAP year, in addition to gaining maturity skills, I plan to work for an offshore oil company in Australia. This will introduce me to an international company as well as a large and complex industry sector.

The challenges of the Duke of Edinburgh Gold Award provided me with invaluable experience, strengthening my team work and leadership skills. The volunteering aspect of the award has enhanced my inter-personal skills and sense of responsibility. My many sporting and musical achievements demonstrate my drive and determination for success.

I am keen to work in the energy industry and face the challenges posed by the need for long term sustainable energy sources with managed environmental impact. My academic potential combined with my passion are but two strengths that I believe will aid me in university life.

Universities applied to:

- Oxford: Offer
- Exeter: Offer
- Southampton: Offer
- Bath: Offer
- Durham: Offer

Good Points:

This is a very good statement. The student is clearly very motivated and their reasoning to pursue engineering is clear. The student has read around their subject and evidence of this is displayed through the use of a reference to a published paper. The student clearly had skills far beyond the scope of A-level studies, and the student's ambitions are clear through their plan to take a gap year in Australia.

Bad Points:

The student plans to undertake a gap year prior to starting university, however, only subtly mentions this towards the end of the statement. Whilst there are no problems in taking gap years and making deferred applications, it is important to be absolutely clear about this. It is quite surprising to the reader to learn the student's gap year plans towards the end of the statement. The student mentions achieving a gold award for the Duke of Edinburgh Award, though, does not use this as an opportunity to describe and elaborate on how they overcame adversity and difficulties.

Overall:

This is a very good statement, however, the reader is left surprised towards the end with the student's description of gap year plans. It would have been possible to avoid this if the student had described their gap year plans (and reasons) earlier in the statement.

NOTES

COMPUTER SCIENCES

Subject: Computer Science & Mathematics

My first experiences with mathematics throughout school were always enjoyable but not inspiring. While I loved working with maths, and enjoyed representing our school in both the UKMT and Hans Woyda team competitions, I felt that maths could not be the end-in-itself the school syllabus presented it as. As I progressed through secondary education, however, I began to really see it as the powerful tool to understand and structure reality that it is.

The first time I saw that my interpretation of the use of maths had some substance was during a work experience placement I organised at IMSO (International Mobile Satellite Organization). There I encountered some examples of the mathematical and computing problems involved in working with satellites: from the difference between the Euclidean geometry on a map and the Elliptical geometry on a globe, to the logistics of moving satellites around to meet demand while keeping them in orbit. These were problems that demanded much more than mere number crunching, and being exposed to this gave me a taste of what maths beyond school might involve. A second work experience spell at Siemens provided me a much more in-depth view of the important role that communication systems play in keeping a company running efficiently and effectively.

My passion for mathematics and computing was further extended while reading 'The Magical Maze' by Ian Stewart. The description of maths as the exploration of a maze of our own creation had an incredibly profound effect on my understanding of what research in mathematics involves. What interested me especially was the visual part of resolving problems, so that they did not rely completely on resolving long calculations. This was close to how I like to understand and explain my ideas in mathematics.

Douglas Hofstadter's 'Gödel, Escher, Bach' gave me a much deeper understanding of the axiomatic systems that make up maths and how parallels can be drawn between different subjects to gain a further understanding of them all. Connected by the theme of Gödel's Incompleteness Theorem, the author passes through seemingly unrelated topics, such as the problem of consciousness and the mathematics of Zen principles, to explain the theorem. Although not the focus of the book, I have also enjoyed reading the links that are presented between maths and computing; it seems to me that maths is not just related to computing – computing is the physical manifestation of mathematics.

Maths and computing are about describing mental processes in a precise, logical way. The rigour required for mathematical proof leaves little room for subjectivity: something can be proven, disproven or unproven, but this depends completely on the validity of your logic. The idea of being able to extract order from apparent chaos, working through concepts until they click is what I love about these subjects, and what has attracted me to take those as an integral part of my further education.

However passionate I am about my academic studies, I also enjoy being involved in extracurricular activities. As head of mentoring and a prefect, I have improved my organizational abilities working with staff and mentors in developing study programmes for those students requiring extra help. Completing the Duke of Edinburgh bronze award – now working on the silver award – has allowed me to practice and develop my leadership and teamwork skills.

In my spare time I enjoy playing tennis, skiing and swimming; the latter I practice at competition level. I also love travelling, as having spent my childhood in Denmark, Egypt, United Kingdom and Spain has given me a hunger for mixing with different cultures. I like to unwind by playing the piano - I find that the pleasure one derives from making a piece your own is one that few activities can match.

I am thrilled about the prospect of further study in these subjects with some of the leading professors in the fields, and look forward to participating in university life.

Universities applied to:

- Oxford: Offer
- Imperial College London: Offer
- Bristol: Offer
- Bath: Offer
- Loughborough: Offer

Good Points:

This is a well-written, structured statement. The student explains their reasons to pursue a dual honours degree and gives equal attention to both disciplines to which they are applying. The student adds personality to the statement by thoroughly explaining their own views on all of the examples of literature read around maths and computing.

Bad Points:

There are quite a lot of short paragraphs. The student could have saved space by consolidating some paragraphs into one, hence shortening the statement. The student starts three paragraphs with 'My' or 'In my'. This is quite repetitive. There are too many paragraphs; seven in total. Paragraphs five and six could be shortened and grouped into one paragraph. In the third paragraph, it appears as though the student has either forgotten to add an addition space (in order to start a new paragraph) or has incorrectly started a new line for the sentence 'Douglas Hofstadter's...'.

Overall:

This is a very good statement. The student has clearly achieved a lot and writes in a clear and easy-to-understand way. Attention is given to both maths and computer sciences, which is essential as the student is applying for a dual honours course. With some restructuring, this could be an excellent statement.

NOTES

Subject: Computer Science

I have been around computers for as long I can remember for reasons I can easily enumerate.

Playing a game, Pinball being the only interesting game that came with Windows XP, writing an essay or surfing the internet where the first things I learnt to do, from my father, who encouraged my to learn about this device. I hope that I will be able to continue learning about the computer on my future courses and extra-curricular activities at the university.

Although I loved computers from the moment, I sat in front of one, my passion for computer science emerged late, when I was in the first year of high school. I was always keen on mathematics for giving you the ability to explain different aspects of your everyday life but I have never pictured myself working in front of a computer and adore every single aspect of it. My dream field of study became clear from the very beginning, from the first pieces of code I saw and analysed.

The courses and the extra training classes I took in high school opened my mind on several areas of computer science, areas like game theory, dynamic programming or graph theory but more important, competitive programming.

I started competitive programming in my second year of high school because there was really fun to put to good use my knowledge in mathematics or physics and there were a lot of these two in the problems I solved. I started practising a lot in my spare time and especially in holidays and competed in some online contests held by websites like TopCoder, Codeforces or Codechef, contests that helped prepared me for working under pressure. I can state without any doubt that competitive programming is my favourite thing to do in my spare time because from any problem that you solve you learn something new or develop a new skill or technique, skills which I believe are essential for a good software engineer.

My passion for competitive programming keeps me informed about the recent discoveries and improvements made in the field of computer science about faster algorithms or more efficient data structures but also about the C++ standard, keeping me in touch with the development of programming languages and their applications. I also like to implement and test the algorithms that I learn in order to see if my implementation consumes less time/memory that the ones that are already used in famous libraries.

Even though computer science takes up a great deal of time, I manage to find time for my hobby, photography. I started learning photography when I entered high school by following the blogs of photographers I had heard of and by watching the tutorial on YouTube. My mother made me a huge surprise by buying me a semi-professional DSLR, which I still have, use and love. I remember the first time I went to the park with my camera, I took a photograph of basically everything, from people to fences. I continued my research and found really interesting things about photography and cameras in general, from the rule of thirds which refers to composition, to physics and how light bounces through the camera to form the image on the sensor. Besides creativity and an eye for composition, photography helped me see the beauty of nature, from extraordinary landscapes to little apparently insignificant bugs.

The knowledge I had in photography and in computer art helped me in gaining the first place in the logo design competition, organized by my high school. The same logo won the second place in the international phase of the competition, held within the European project of "Comenius Teaching Innovatively (With Focus on ICT) and its Impact On The Quality Of Education".

My prize was a trip to Mottola, Italy, where the second meeting of the project was held. There, I participated in lessons held by teachers from Bulgaria, Turkey, Czech Republic and Poland. I learnt many interesting things from those lessons and especially from the other students and saw how different subjects are taught in different countries.

I was part of the hosting team when the meeting was held in Romania, exactly one year after the Italian adventure. I saw how hard it is to organize an event like this and how careful you have to be at all the details in order to have a pleasant final result.

At university, I hope that I will learn areas that I have no formal experience of studying and, as a result, become a better competitive programmer and software engineer. I am looking forward with great anticipation to the challenges that will come and I hope will be able to bring a big contribution to the academic environment that university study will provide me with.

Universities applied to:

- Oxford: Offer
- Manchester: Offer
- University College London: Offer
- Birmingham: Offer

Good points:

This is a good statement. The student is clearly very motivated and has used personal experiences to demonstrate this. The student does not jump straight into their personal achievements but describes these after establishing their interest in computer science first. This is good as it makes the statement not sound like a list of achievements alone.

Bad Points:

The student's quality of writing is not very good in certain parts of the statement. There are numerous clumsy uses of English throughout the statement, which make it seem poorly polished and almost an afterthought. Luckily for the applicant, it was an afterthought for the admissions tutors too.

Overall:

This is a very good statement in terms of content, however, simple grammatical and type errors take away from the true value of the statement.

NOTES

Subject: Computer Science

I have a keen interest in the link between computing and the brain, an interest that was helped by the fact that I grew up in a household of scientists. This link is especially present in machine learning, even if modern machine learning is only loosely based on how the brain functions. I am fascinated by the possibility of having programs that teach other programs, and the complexity of the problems they might one day solve. Already, the Eugene Goostman chatbot, while being very controversial, suggests that machines may pass the Turing test.

The extremely logical nature of programming attracted me right away because of how universal it is. Computer logic can be applied to many different problems, and it is exciting to think that this theoretical knowledge can be extended to practical uses in inventions such as Google's self-driving cars. Making decisions in real time and in environments as complex as a street based on information from sensors seems incredible. I would like to learn how we have been able to make machines such as a self-programming computer that can establish the laws of motion simply from the way a pendulum swings with no knowledge of physics or geometry (as in Cornell's experiment).

Computer science interested me early on. With the "Lego Mindstorm" software I discovered the joy of building, from a few lines of instructions, programs that could actually move a lego robot. I also used "Gamemaker", which allowed me to build simple games. I then tried several small internet classes and learned basic Java before deciding that I wanted to go into more depth. I signed up on Coursera for the course "An Introduction to Interactive Programming in Python" offered by Rice University, and am currently taking the "Machine Learning" course by Andrew Ng. The notion of cost functions and how they can be used to derive predictions from a set of data caught my interest, and made me wonder what determines the choice of one cost function over another.

At a Cold Spring harbor summer camp on Bio coding, I recently discovered one of the many future uses of programming. We now have the tools to program DNA code and insert it into a cell in order to make it produce proteins of our choice. In the future, this technology could be used to cure sicknesses or make artificial immune systems. Combining biology and programming may further break down the barrier that exists between the real and the virtual, with technology literally becoming a bigger part of our biological lives.

Maths is important, and I have always enjoyed the type of thinking it requires. I have studied American, French and English maths, and it is interesting how they differ in their theoretical and practical approaches. I used maths in my python coursera course to create a little game with a ship - it rotated and shot asteroids. Even something this basic requires vectors to calculate the location and speed of each element, hit-boxes that use circles to calculate their positions relative to each other, and a trigonometric circle to determine the rotation of the ship. I have learned to appreciate the power of mathematical models when it comes to programming.

I also enjoy extracurricular activities such as Model UN, hosted at the International Telecommunications Union. I have developed my communication skills by working on political resolutions with others and defending them in front of an audience. In a committee about agriculture in LEDC's, I learned about the role technology could play in helping communities receive information about better farming practices. This year I am head of external communication for a conference held in 2015 that includes 386 foreign students and 33 schools.

I would like to study in Britain because it is a hub of academic activity and provides a rich and diverse environment in which I can expand my knowledge. After my studies, I would like to be in research, pushing the boundaries of computer science.

Universities applied to:

- Oxford: Offer
- Birmingham: Offer
- University College London: Offer
- Manchester: Offer

Good Points:

The statement is well-written and has a clear structure. The student is clearly very motivated by computer sciences and this comes across well. The student mentions that they come from a scientific family, however, does not give too much attention to this. This is good as it convinces the reader that the student is confident that they want to study computer sciences for reasons other than being pressured to by family.

Bad Points:

The student lists many computer science-related experiences which go beyond the A-level syllabus. Whilst this is important to do, the student would have produced more impact if they had mentioned fewer experiences but thoroughly described those which were mentioned. The student also does not talk about anything related to their subject which they did not understand/found difficult, and how they overcame this. This can be just as important as achievements, if not more, as it demonstrates to the reader the student's ability to overcome challenges and unfamiliar material. This would have added yet more value to an otherwise brilliant statement.

Overall:

This is a very good statement. The student's motivation for wanting to study computer sciences is clear. With some more expansion on the student's experiences, this statement would be excellent.

NOTES

Subject: Computer Science

I want to study computer science because I want to learn how computers work. I want to learn about the complex hardware that makes up the machine. I want to learn about how information is stored and which data structures are most efficient and useful to us. I want to learn how to code, not just more languages but the very logic that underpins them. I want to learn about the discrete mathematics that underpins the subject.

The reason I want to learn this is twofold. Firstly, computers have transformed and are transforming the world. Physics, Healthcare, Economics and many other major disciplines are being revolutionised by computing. At a local level the lives of individual people have been changed beyond recognition by the information revolution. It is my hope that a computer science degree will one day allow me to be a very, very small part of this. The second, and for me far more important, is an insatiable curiosity and a love of problem solving.

During my gap year I have been working in Technical Support Services at IBM. It has been an eye opening experience working for a company with such a pioneering computing culture and heritage. I have been working as a Client Support Manager, interacting directly with clients to provide effective and cost efficient technical support for their machines. I have learned a great deal from speaking to IBMers working in roles ranging from engineering to sales and marketing. I have gained an insight into the interplay between computer science, business and psychology required to transform a technological concept into something that can be sold to customers and clients. Of particular interest to me is the computer called Watson. It was designed to win the quiz show Jeopardy, a difficult task given that the questions are asked in natural English, understanding of which was something previously assumed to be uniquely human. Having overcome this problem and beaten the game show, IBM are now using the same technology to fight cancer. Watson is just one of a long line of developments that are increasingly blurring the lines between human and artificial intelligence, a topic I first found fascinating when reading Turing's paper on "Computing Machinery and Intelligence".

I have been reading Code by Charles Petzold. A part that interested me was the description of how Boolean logic can be applied to relays to build complex systems such as early adding machines. In addition I have been learning Python as part of the MIT Computer Science Open Course that I have been taking and have been taught the basics of C at IBM.

Throughout my gap year I have also been keeping up an interest in mathematics. I enjoyed reading the Mathematical Experience, which turned out to be just as much a journey into Mathematics as one into Philosophy and History. A chapter that I enjoyed focused on the use of computers to solve the Four Colour Conjecture in mathematics. In particular it was how the method of proof by exhaustion, now made possible on a new vast scale by computing, was questioning at a philosophical level the very certainty of mathematical proof. Furthermore I have been working to improve my own mathematical skills, by learning FP2 and by watching MIT lectures in mathematics.

Outside of work, I have spent a lot of time playing basketball, learning Spanish and salsa. I hope to use some of the money I have earned to go travelling in South America over the summer.

I think my exceptional work ethic, combined with a love of mathematics and problem solving will allow me to thrive in this degree and make the most of my time at Oxford.

Universities applied to:

- Oxford: Offer
- Manchester: Failed
- University College London: Failed
- St. Andrews: Failed
- York: Offer

Good Points:

This statement is well-written and structured. The student has a wealth of experience and does not rely on interest sparked by A-level studies alone. The student uses their experiences gained whilst working for IBM to give real-world examples of the importance of computer science. The student's motivation is clear from the first paragraph and this remains throughout the statement.

Bad Points:

The first paragraph reads more like a speech than an introduction. Whilst this may have been the intended effect, the use of the words 'I want' six times in the opening paragraph alone makes the statement sound repetitive. The student concludes the statement by referring specifically to the University of Oxford. This is very risky as the student faces possible rejection from all other universities that regard the student's clear desire to want to study at Oxford as meaning that they do not take other universities seriously. It was not necessary at all to specifically mention Oxford in the final sentence of the statement and this let the student down.

Overall:

This would have been an excellent statement if it were not for the unnecessary reference to the University of Oxford at the end. The student let themselves down and risked alienating the other universities to which they applied to.

NOTES

MATHS

Subject: Mathematics

My interest in mathematics has been closely related with competitions mostly because there were never any challenging problems in my regular classes. There were many difficult problems at my first competition which showed me that there are problems in mathematics that require both insight and talent to be solved. Afterwards I have participated in any competition I could in order to get a chance to solve as difficult problems as possible.

When I was 13 I attended my first state competition in maths and since then I have won five first places so far. At every state competition in which I participated I made new friends, had an excellent time and enjoyed solving various interesting problems. My first contact with the Olympiad problems was at the second state competition where I managed to solve one of that year's IMO qualifying questions although I have never seen any problem similar to it before. The sheer beauty of the ideas that combined to a solution of that problem demonstrated how beautiful mathematics can be and it has been like that so far.

For the last three years I have participated in many international competitions and won silver and a bronze medal at IMO 2010 and 2011, silver medal at Middle European Mathematical Olympiad 2009, silver medal at Mediterranean Competition 2009, gold medals at Mathematical Competition of Balkan Students 2009, 2010, 2011. I have also participated at few research based competitions such as International Mathematical Tournament of Towns in years 2010 and 2011 and won first prize both times. As a member of my school team I placed fifth (2010) and second (2011) at Princeton University Mathematical Competition (PUMaC).

I have twice participated in state competitions in informatics and won 4th and 8th place, four times in physics where I have won two second places one 8th and one 10th. I have been 16th in state competition in logic. At those competitions I have learned a lot about usefulness and power of mathematics in other subjects.

Every competition I attended persuaded me even more that I want to work in mathematics because it is easy to find problems with both beauty and originality of ideas and this is quite a rarity in other subjects. I have also met a lots of people at these competitions with whom I have something in common and that is love for maths. I have been training young competitors and found that I can teach quite well and I enjoy it. I've also worked with friends who have problems with maths or any related subject.

I am aware of the fact that competition mathematics is quite different from both research and college mathematics but I also discovered that beautiful ideas are common in every part of maths. On PUMaC I had a chance to work on some college mathematics subjects (linear algebra and graph theory) and I found it very interesting. On Tournament of Towns we were working on a research based project about Shappiro inequality and afterwards I wrote an article in local mathematics magazine about our results.

My other interests are table tennis and travelling. I have been playing table tennis for six years and I have won a few medals at local table tennis tournaments and I am playing 4th Croatian senior league for three years now. I believe that sport is very important and I would very much like to continue playing it as well as trying some other sport as rowing.

I have travelled a lot in last few years. Everywhere I went I met interesting new people and enjoyed myself a lot. These journeys have helped me to develop my social skills and blend in into new surroundings and I hold them vitally important for studying abroad.

I have been working in maths for the most part of my life and I would like to continue. I have a few friends studying at Cambridge and they have warmly recommended Cambridge both for educational and social quality. I like courses offered at Cambridge and research groups in which I could take part. I have chosen Trinity as my preferred college because I am interested in Combinatorics and I believe that Trinity is the best College I could choose for studying it and maths in general.

Universities applied to:

- Cambridge: Offer
- Edinburgh: Offer
- University College London: Rejected
- University of Warwick: Rejected
- University of Sheffield: Rejected

Good Points:

This is a good statement. The statement has a clear introduction, main body, and conclusion. It is clear that the student is very talented and has gone far beyond the remit of their national curriculum. The student states their achievements but does not extend into self-praise, which is usually quite common. This way, although the student clearly has many achievements, it does not sound like they are bragging or that they are over-confident.

Bad Points:

The first three entire paragraphs after the introduction are simply lists of the student's accomplishments and awards. Whilst it is, of course, important to describe individual achievements, dedicating as much space as the student has in this statement is going too far. By the end of the list of achievements, the reader is left wondering if the student believes that their achievements outside of school alone warrant a university place. It would have been better if the student listed a few of their most significant achievements and described their experiences and what they have gained from such experiences.

The student also refers specifically to the University of Cambridge at the end of the statement. This is a very risky thing to do as the student's statement will be sent to all universities which they apply to. In doing this, the student risks offending and alienating all other universities other than Cambridge, and may be rejected by all as a result.

Overall:

This is a good statement that demonstrates the student as a highly gifted and motivated individual. However, the statement reads like a CV for the first four paragraphs, and the student risks being automatically rejected by all universities except for the University of Cambridge by dedicating the final paragraph to their desire to study at Cambridge.

NOTES

Subject: Mathematics

Mathematics is a closed communication system; a way of approaching life, the backbone of all sciences and the greatest discovery of humankind. How and why I fell in love with Mathematics are currently beyond my knowledge. On the one hand the pureness of Mathematics, which is completely free from any subjective views intrigues me. On the other hand, one's ability to interpret and approach Mathematics inspires me to become an active participant in the problem solving process. The satisfaction of solving a Mathematics problem is like realising where we are after rambling in an unknown part of a city, a feeling which makes me smile when I suddenly see the trick of a new puzzle. I feel like Mathematics is the subject which engages my attention fully and the one and only subject which I will enjoy at university level.

My interest in Mathematics has expanded over the past years and I am keen to read around different topics. During my AS year a seminar on Fibonacci numbers and the golden ratio inspired me to read, Erno Lendvai's work (in the original format) on the relation of 'Fibonacci-cells' and music. The author proved how classical music is built of 'Fibonacci-cells' and how the tempo tends to change when the music approaches its golden section. I discovered how Fibonacci numbers correlate with a significant number of masterpieces, despite the location or time of composition. His work made me wonder whether it is possible to compose and model 'perfect' music by determining the right frequency, length and number of 'Fibonacci-cells' in a piece. Understanding an application of number theory on music theory has propelled my interest towards other disciplines of number theory, such as the application of Prime numbers in nature.

Last year, I had the privilege of attending a set of seminars at King's College London, called King's Factor. With the guidance of PhD students and a professor we focused on more advanced Mathematic problems. We practiced STEP, AEA and MAT questions. These sessions consolidated my A-level knowledge and guided me to approach problems in different ways. This summer I attended the Best in School Mathematics Masterclass at the Royal Institute, which has further justified my course choice. Two books I exceptionally liked were 'The Man who knew infinity' and 'From Here to Innity' have introduced me to disciplines of Mathematics which I had scarcely covered and also to the life of a brilliant Mathematician. Fractals and Chaos theory were among my favourite topics; the visualisation of different dimensions and the idea of something being deterministic but unpredictable are not among the simplest topics and I am looking forward to learning more about them.

I spent two years as an exchange student and am aware of the difficulties of language barriers, as I spoke English for the first time, when I was 15. I voluntarily translate for TED and Amnesty International Hungary, and before starting my AS year, I spent two years in London focusing on English while continuing my Hungarian studies. This was difficult as communication and the application of my knowledge had to be conveyed in a language that was not my own. Adapting to a new environment, while managing my studies at home, I became more committed to achieve my goals. I became more independent and a whole new world of opportunities opened up for me.

By funding and running the Rubik's Cubing Club (RCC) at my sixth form and tutoring younger students I am required to be responsible, precise, accurate and reliable. This teaching experience enables me to innovate simple algorithms to introduce more students to Rubik's Cubing and to other logic games. Attending debating club each week has developed my presentational skills and the organisation of a freshman camp, Sport days and being part of the student council have improved my leadership skills.

I believe my keen interest and past experiences makes me suitable for reading Mathematics at university.

Universities applied to:

- Oxford: Rejected
- York: Offer
- Edinburgh: Offer
- University College London: Rejected
- King's: Rejected

Good Points:

The student is clearly motivated by mathematics. It is clear that the student has had to overcome adversity in their life and has managed to learn English for the first time two years prior to writing this statement. The student has several experiences of mathematics beyond the A-level syllabus and these are explained well.

Bad Points:

Whilst the statement is good overall, it lacks an 'X-factor', and as a result was rejected by the Universities of Oxford, King's College London and UCL. The student relies on interests sparked from A-level studies to justify their reasons to want to pursue mathematics. If the student had engaged in activities completely outside of the A-level curriculum, this would demonstrate their desire to study mathematics and improve their ability to a far greater extent. The student only describes how 'the author proved (things) to' them, and seems to not make any judgements or critical evaluations of their own. Whilst it is, of course, valuable to carry out wider reading, that is only to add to your own understanding of the subject, which isn't demonstrated here.

Overall:

Whilst the statement is well-written, the student is let down by their lack of individuality in assessing the work of the others.

NOTES

Subject: Mathematics

Why mathematics? Although it is somewhat difficult to explain mathematicians' love of the subject without referring to the clichés, to me, mathematics in itself is the greatest construction of the human mind and contributing to it is equivalent to pushing the civilization forward.

Although I have always enjoyed mathematics, I started focusing on it only recently. My interest was sparked only a few years ago, when I read Stephen Hawking's Brief History of Time. During the period, I was just starting calculus in IGCSE Additional Mathematics and hence, while certainly finding the physics of the book fascinating, it was Hawking's mention of the mysterious 'Einstein's equations', that intrigued me the most and led me to explore the world of mathematics. Ever since, this interest has grown exponentially. There simply isn't a mathematical topic that I don't want to learn more about. Books such as Marcus Du Sautoy's Music of Primes or Simon Singh's Fermat's Last Theorem introduced me to number theory, while Stephen Hawking's God Created the Integers took me through the pages of history and introduced me to the legendary problems of Fermat, Riemann and Goldbach. Later on, Ian Stewart's Why Beauty is Truth led me to explore the fundamentals of Group Theory and Complex Analysis, while on the side I was reading Michio Kaku and introducing myself to quantum mechanics. Often, I find myself spending hours on reading starting from perhaps the biography of Euler and ending up reading on Fourier's analysis or Gödel's logic. I can positively say that I can never learn enough mathematics to satisfy my passion and that I would feel truly fortunate being able to read it in an undergraduate course.

I am an extremely quick and independent learner. I was able to skip year 10, finishing the 2 year content of 7 IGCSEs in one year and still receiving top grades. In year 12, parallel to my IB course, I completed A-level Mathematics and Further Mathematics courses on my own, as they offered some additional topics I have not yet come across. I sat all the Further Pure papers, also being the only candidate to sit FP3 in my school. Although unable to sit the examinations due to financial reasons, I also familiarised myself with the A-level Mechanics course. Additionally, self-study of Russian textbooks gave me a much higher competence in Euclidean geometry. Moreover, throughout the year, I tutored myself with more complex problems to allow myself sit the Sixth Term Examination Paper I paper and receive a level 1.

My interest in mathematics extends to my whole school life. I can even say that the main reason I enjoy my subjects is their mathematical nature. It is the world of differential equations, algebra and analysis behind Physics and Chemistry and the hidden statistical analysis and numerical methods underlining Economics that make me interested in studying these disciplines.

Outside of school, I learn programming, mainly as a tool for solving problems. For example, in the process of preparing for my Extended Essay, I wrote several pages of Python code in order to solve the otherwise tedious problem of placing 9 queens and a pawn on a chessboard so that no queens attack each other and further generalising the problem for an n by n board. My code found all the solutions for the classic board in less than a minute. Furthermore, I am currently undertaking an online undergraduate course in Python programming through the organisation called Udacity, the final product of which is a fully functioning web search engine.

I believe my Extended Essay to be my most serious mathematical treatise yet. I studied the area of finite differences and binomial transforms, proving several important facts. One of my main results was a way of expressing any integer to the power of n as a sum of at most the first n nth powers.

In choosing me you would not obtain a well-rounded student, but rather you would have a dedicated mathematician who loves this subject as much as you do.

Universities applied to:

- Cambridge: Offer
- Imperial College London: Offer
- Warwick: Offer
- Durham: Offer
- Bath: Offer

Good Points:

This is an excellent statement. Usually, for subjects like mathematics, prospective students have an extensive history of individual achievements ranging from winning competitions and awards to being top of their school in maths. However, in this statement, the student explains their recent interest in mathematics in an easy-to-read, honest, and entertaining way.

The introduction is simple, engaging, and effective. The student opens the statement using a simple question and involves the reader immediately. This makes the statement entertaining to read.

It is clear that the student has read extensively around the subject and is thoroughly committed to their chosen subject. The student's mathematical ability is proven beyond doubt by the achievement of completing two A-levels in maths and further maths in addition to their IB studies. The student cleverly relates their interest in the underlying mathematics within other subjects to explain their interest in such subjects. It is very good how the student directs the statement directly towards to the reader in the closing sentence.

Bad Points:

There are very few bad points in this statement.

Overall:

This is a truly excellent statement. The student describes their achievements without making the statement seem like a list of achievements and does not brag. The reader is directly engaged within the closing statement, making this a statement to remember.

NOTES

Subject: Mathematics

Back when I was a little child, I was always fascinated by numbers. In kindergarten I spent a lot of time solving mathematical workbooks for little children and I developed a great passion for mathematics at an early age. Throughout the primary school my interests began to spread, I got familiar with the beautiful world of mathematics and I began to compete in various disciplines – mathematics, physics, astronomy and informatics. I regularly participated in national competitions in all these subjects, winning a first place on the national mathematics competition, a third place on the national informatics competition, and a few first places in the national astronomy competitions, as well as a bronze medal on the International Olympiad on Astronomy and Astrophysics in 2013.

I have devoted my best efforts to mastering these subjects and find all of them deeply interesting, but they all have something in common – they are based on mathematics and creativity. That is why I am determined to study mathematics. I have always been impressed by the fact that mathematical knowledge is very applicable to the real world and that mathematical studies are connected with every branch of science the human race acknowledges. In order to study and make progress in one's mathematical skills one has to be committed and highly motivated – that is why I wish to study at a prestigious university. From my experience, being surrounded by brilliant people who share your interests does a lot of good, gives you an extra boost to do your best. Consequently,

ULTIMATE OXBRIDGE PERSONAL STATEMENT GUIDE — EXAMPLE STATEMENTS – MATHS

I am currently studying at a renowned mathematical gymnasium and I have to say that people around affect me in a most positive way, making me excel faster. I am certain that Cambridge University would exert an even more profound influence. I am also attending mathematical classes held by older university students. It made me realize that people who teach you also play an important role in your education. That is why I am keen to be a part of a successful community such as Cambridge, learn from inspiring professors and study with amazing colleagues.

In my spare time I love to read and watch TV shows – this is a great practice for my English skills. I also practice table tennis daily because I firmly believe that a healthy body is an important prerequisite for a healthy mind. Honestly speaking, I am not definitely sure what I wish to try as a profession after graduating from university but I have considered various possibilities. I am very interested in how mathematics relates to economy and banking systems. On the other hand, I would also like to teach at a university, or perhaps be a part of a research group in a science institute. Either way, I am completely certain that Cambridge would be an excellent place to begin my journey!

Universities applied to:

- Cambridge: Offer

Good Points:

In this unique case, the statement was effective because the candidate took the *extreme* risk of applying to only one university, Cambridge, and tailoring their personal statement to that one institution. If you were to submit this exact same statement in a UCAS application to four others as well, this would be a *bad* statement. With that caveat in mind, however, this is an effective piece of work. The statement is well-written and structured, and it's compactness lends it a striking impact.

It is clear that the student has overcome adversity due to the fact that English is not their first language. The student is clearly very motivated and has talent. The student describes the importance of mathematics in other subjects, such as the sciences. This is good as it shows that the student has a broad outlook and will be keen to learn about all aspects of mathematics before choosing to specialise later on in the course.

Bad Points:

At the end of the second paragraph, it seems as though there is a type error or if the student has forgotten to finish their sentence after 'Consequently'. There are many places where it is possible to shorten this statement, e.g. the first sentence, 'Back when I was a little child, I was always fascinated by numbers' can be rephrased as, 'As a child, I was fascinated by numbers'.

Overall:

This is a very good statement, provided that it is specifically aimed at the University of Cambridge. The student is clearly very motivated and does not brag about their achievements.

NOTES

Subject: Mathematics & Physics

Since childhood, I've always loved complex puzzles, logical problems and challenges. Later on I discovered mathematics and physics which offered a lot of interesting problems and I enjoyed spending time on them. I loved the fact that real-life events, such as throwing a ball, could be described by a virtual language created by humans. However the most impressive fact for me was when I discovered that mathematicians and physicists can predict events just by solving equations. That's is when I decided that maths and physics are what I want to do in life to contribute to the world.

Even though my passion in mathematics started very early, I have struggled to get to where I am now. When I got into Bratislava's best gymnasium in mathematics I found myself at a position I had never been before. That was the first time I wasn't the best in mathematics in our class, in fact I was one of the weaker students in this field. However over time I made my way to the top, but I still couldn't surpass my classmates. When I got to the 5th grade, I realized why I didn't succeed. That year we got a new mathematics teacher and she opened my eyes and showed me the beauty of maths. The most important thing that happened that year however was when I won the regional mathematics Olympiad and they invited me to KMS which is a camp for people interested in mathematics. There I realized that the school mathematics is just a fraction of the possibilities in this area. However the thing that I believe helped me in mathematics is that I started enjoying it. Rather than solving a Sudoku or crossword puzzle I was solving geometry problems. Since then I have won many prizes including bronze medals from the Middle European Mathematical Olympiad and the International Mathematical Olympiad.

Besides maths and physics I also love playing the piano and practicing Kung Fu. I have played the piano for 13 years and my personal favourites are Chopin's Nocturnes. I may not be great at it, but playing the piano helps me relax and forget about my worries for a while. I practice Kung Fu mainly for health. My favourite style is Bagua. I learned that Kung Fu is not only a martial art, but a way of living. Besides Kung Fu and the piano, I also enjoy teaching kids interesting facts or problems in mathematics. During school, I teach a mathematics club and I want to teach the kids that mathematics isn't just numbers.

Every summer I help organize a mathematics day camp for children. Mathematics may be the subject which I'm best at, but I don't want to be 'just a mathematician' in the future. Since I was little, I've always wanted to do something great like solving global issues or inventing something useful, however I realize that it is very hard to achieve this with pure mathematics. People advised me to go study economics and financial mathematics so I could have a good job and earn money, but that is not what I want to achieve in life. My goal is to shape the world and make it a better place for future generations. This is the reason I want to study physics or engineering. I started doing physics two years ago and since then I participated and won some competitions including the Regional Physics Olympiad. To be better at physics I started reading Feynman's lectures which helped me a lot, but also taught me that there is much to learn out there about the world. The reason why I want to study in the UK is because there are many opportunities compared to Slovakia. I have many friends who study there and heard from them that it's an amazing experience. The most important fact, though, is that in the UK I can study and work with people who are ambitious. I know what I want to achieve in life, and even though I don't yet know exactly how to get there or where 'there' will be, I believe that a UK university education will steer me in the right direction.

ULTIMATE OXBRIDGE PERSONAL STATEMENT GUIDE — EXAMPLE STATEMENTS – MATHS

Universities applied to:

- Cambridge: Offer
- Warwick: Offer
- Imperial College London: Interview + Rejected
- Bristol: Rejected
- St. Andrews: Offer

Good Points:

This is a very good statement. The statement is well-written and structured. The student describes their life experiences without making the statement sound like a list of achievements. This is achieved because the student explains every experience described, rather than listing their life experiences with no context. It is clear that the student has many talents and achievements, and these are stated in a humble manner which does not make it seem as though the student is bragging. It is clear that the student is aware of the significance of their decision to study outside of their native homeland and the challenges that this will bring. The student explains their reasons for applying to study a dual honours course and does not neglect either discipline.

Bad Points:

The student uses the word 'gymnasium' instead of school/college. Whilst this may be the term used in Slovakia, in the UK, a 'gymnasium' is a place where people exercise and its use in this statement is somewhat confusing. The way in which the student writes about their personal experiences makes the statement sound somewhat like an autobiography.

Overall:

This is an average statement. The student clearly has personality and a high level of ability. Strange terminology is explained by a language barrier, but will never be allowed for when evaluating a statement, especially at the very best universities, which expect all candidates to be completely fluent in written English.

NOTES

HUMANITIES

LAW

Subject: Law (Jurisprudence)

My academic and personal experience of law has led me to believe that it is an integral and vibrant field of study. Indeed, law is intertwined with, and embraces every aspect of our lives on Earth, extending to the very composition, occupation and history of the planet. My A level subjects have confirmed this idea for me. From History, I have seen the terrible consequences of one man taking the law into his own hands, as Hitler did through the Enabling Act (1933). In Geography, I have been angered by the injustice of trade laws, and the way they continue to hamper development in the world's least developed countries. One of the reasons I have chosen to study French is my hope that it will create possibilities to practice as a lawyer in other jurisdictions, particularly French speaking African nations.

I am most interested in International Law and because of this I have chosen to undertake an Extended Project Qualification on the subject of the legality of the Nuremburg Trials and the legal precedent they set. I also aim to incorporate research into the International Criminal Court, and how the trials led to its establishment.

To further my understanding of Law, I organised and undertook a week of work experience at Albion Chambers, Bristol in July 2010. Working with highly skilled barristers was incredibly exciting, as was the opportunity to examine CCTV evidence and sit in on interviews with clients. It was a poignant experience, as I saw how our justice system can acquit those wrongly accused, while also protecting society.

I have read a number of enlightening books such as 'The Law Machine' by Marcel Berlins and Claire Dyer and 'Invitation to Law' by A. W. B. Simpson, and have gained a greater understanding of legal basics such as the criminal process and the law of torts. Reading the book 'Eve was Framed' by Helena Kennedy has also been fascinating, as I have started to think about issues which I had never before considered – how Law might be affected by gender. Since watching two documentaries about jails in Miami, Florida, I have also become interested in the differences between the British and American legal systems.

In addition to broadening my knowledge of our legal system, I have sought to develop skills which I believe will assist me in studying and practising law. As an active member of my Sixth Form's Debating Society, I have gained the ability to analyse an argument, and also developed my confidence in terms of public speaking. Later this year, I intend to speak at a Mock United Nations Summit, in which I will help to represent one country and their interests. This has developed both my confidence in public speaking and my ability to analyse and construct arguments. During the last year, I have been undertaking a Duke of Edinburgh Gold Award at Sixth Form. This has developed the necessary organisational skills for a high pressure law degree. In fact, I have already completed one of the sections, and am well on my way to completing two more.

For the past year, I have been giving up two free lessons per fortnight to assist in a Year 11 Maths class, helping students on the C/ D grade borderline. I have learned how to explain complex concepts to pupils who struggle to understand: I believe this will aid me greatly if I achieve my ambition of becoming a barrister.

Furthermore, I am a leader of a Sunday school group at my church, where I often organise games and activities for the children. This has helped to develop my interpersonal skills crucial for practising as a Lawyer. I also attend a drama class each week at Bristol Old Vic and play for my Sixth Form's netball team.

My studies, work experience and research thus far have shown me that law presents no intellectual boundaries; it is real and relevant, continuous and alive. I am excited by the prospect of studying law and relish the opportunity to study such a dynamic subject at university.

Universities applied to:

- Oxford: Offer
- Durham: Offer
- Nottingham: Offer
- Cardiff: Offer
- Reading: Offer

Good Points:

This personal statement is very well-written and well-structured with very few grammatical errors or omissions. It clearly demonstrates that the student has made a conscious effort to engage with aspects of the subject they wish to study at university; both within their current academic study (making direct reference to their A level subjects) and in terms of their extra-curricular activities. This wide range of activities and experiences are all made to seem relevant to law and act as evidence that the course chosen is one the student has carefully considered and will enjoy. The closing two lines are particularly strong, acting as a punchy reiteration of why the student wants to study law.

Bad Points:

When talking about the wider reading or extra-curricular activities that they have undertaken, the student could have taken the statement one step further by making explicit reference to why each was chosen or what they particularly enjoyed or learned. Moreover, several references were made to the student's desire to work as a barrister and pursue a career in law. While it is good to show such ambition, it should be remembered that applicants are applying to academic institutions to study, and universities will appreciate that the student is looking forward to studying law as an academic discipline rather than a means to an end vocation.

Overall:

This is a strong personal statement overall which was clearly well-received. However, it would have benefitted from the student talking in greater depth about what they learned or enjoyed in particular when completing extra-curricular activities or wider reading. The student needed to do more than say that the activity is relevant to law; they needed to go on to explain why they thought this. Specific examples would have helped. The wider engagement with the subject is to be commended, however, being especially necessary, the subject being applied for is not one which the student currently studies in school.

NOTES

Subject: Law

I view the practice of law as an analytical debate that sees lawyers and judges treading between theoretical law and the chaotic reality of society to clarify the scope of what is right. It is this mental challenge that inspired me to a career as a public attorney with the goal of joining the judiciary.

My interest was kindled when I first undertook my IB History Extended Essay. I enjoyed developing persuasive arguments, taking into account History's investigative and systematic nature. This was a unique challenge since my topic was in an entrenched area of study and involved formulating a strong original thesis that could stand against established historians. My efforts were validated when my essay was selected for publication in the June 2013 issue of the renowned academic journal, The Concord Review. Such an adversarial mental struggle strongly appealed to me and sparked my enthusiasm for a legal career that would allow me to tackle such challenges daily.

I pursued my interest by interning at Rajah & Tann (under the Junior College Law Programme), Drew & Napier and Kim & Co, some of the most competitive and prestigious law firms in Singapore. I learnt an extensive range of practical legal skills as I drafted affidavits, submissions, researched case law and created opinions on points of law. As I became familiar with family and civil litigation law, I learned how to devise compelling arguments by contextualizing vague laws to complex situations. Once, I was involved in a correspondence with the Attorney General Chambers (AGC) appealing a charge of overstaying. This entailed researching immigration laws relevant to our client's unique circumstance. While the arresting officer was skeptical of having the charges overturned, we successfully convinced the AGC otherwise. Such experiences have given me varied perspectives of the legal world, not only of theoretical concepts but also of the practical procedures that are built upon them, laying the foundation for my foray into the legal world.

I have also kept myself updated of legal developments, notably when Singapore relaxed legislative requirements of what constitutes an arbitration agreement. I could relate to this as I took part in a noted case that involved the term 'mediation' in an arbitration clause. It was intriguing framing arguments differentiating mediation with arbitration. Through my practical experiences, I have been stimulated to critically consider the effect of dynamic legislation on legal cases. I was also fascinated by the lecture series 'Justice' by Harvard law professor Michael Sandel, in which he applies moral perspectives to perennial issues such as proportional retribution in the context of historical injustices.

I have taken the initiative of founding a start-up, 'MobForest', consisting of a team of 7 that hosts project challenges for students to tackle in return for prizes. As part of MobForest, I helped to draft contracts with companies sponsoring the challenges. I also read up on Singapore's legal environment to determine our business obligations as well as on Intellectual Property rights as a means to protect our platform. Forming MobForest gave me valuable insight into the practical legal demands of a business as well as the confidence to approach clients.

Simultaneously, my National Service duty as a Sergeant and subsequently as a Lieutenant of Singapore's firefighting force (SCDF) saw me leading a platoon of men in fire and rescue incidents. As a platoon commander, one of the obstacles to executing a task is the poor phrasing of orders. Given the chaotic nature of a fire incident, it is important that commands given successfully convey the task at hand, with each man clear of their role.

Universities applied to:

- Cambridge: Interview + Rejected
- London School of Economics: Offer
- University College London: Offer
- King's: Offer
- Nottingham: Offer

Good Points:

The personal statement is well-written, showing a clear and logical structure and having no grammatical errors. The student shows a clear commitment to law by having an impressive array of extra-curricular activities, which act as evidence of their genuine interest in the legal world. It is clear that the student follows current legal affairs and takes any opportunity they get to engage with law. The reference to the lecture by Sandel is a particularly strong inclusion to this effect as it is clearly an academic mode of engaging with legal study and academic debate.

Bad Points:

While the student has a wealth of legal experience, the focus is very much on law in a business or commercial setting. It should be remembered when applying to study subjects with clear career routes (such as law) that a university will be looking for a genuine interest in studying law as an academic discipline rather than as a means of securing a job. After all, a law degree is not a pre-requisite for a legal career; a law degree is not necessary to take the GDL or LCP, for example. Additionally, the student's more relevant activities to university study, such as the extended essay or the lecture, are given minimal attention and explanation, when in reality they would be the most beneficial aspects to emphasise.

Overall:

This is a strong personal statement but struggles with the placement of emphasis. While business and vocational activities show a strong commitment to law, their weighting in this personal statement is at the expense of more traditionally academic interests. It is these latter interests and modes of engaging with legal theory that would better impress a university. The student could undertake some wider reading in a legal area they know they will be studying should they secure a place on the course that genuinely interests them (such as one of the seven foundation subjects in law). With this, they should include more examples of textbooks, articles or legal papers in this area to emphasise their research interests.

NOTES

Subject: Law

Law is the epitome of human reason; it is the force that holds society together and the cornerstone on which great civilizations were built upon. By dictating a code of conduct which everyone had to abide by, it has created a system of accountability and allowed society to flourish. However, Law is never static. It changes with time - internalising new concepts and discarding anachronistic ones to reflect societal norms. It is this dynamic nature of the Law that I find so enthralling - that there exists a gamut of good answers but never a right one. Such idealism aside, I believe excellence in legal study and work does not come easy. It requires much passion, intellect and hard work.

At College, I offered 12 academic units (as compared to the standard 10 academic units) at the Singapore-Cambridge GCE 'A' Level Examinations. Concurrently, I represented Singapore in Swimming and was an active member of my College's Swimming and Cross-Country team, training up to six times each week and achieving numerous medals and accolades in Inter-College Competitions. Such excellence in both sports and academics demonstrates my strong self-discipline, time management skills as well as my capacity for sustained hard work.

As a student, I held numerous leadership positions such as Swimming Captain, School Prefect as well as being part of the Executive Committee of my College Freshman Orientation Camp. In addition, I undertook various community-based service projects aimed at spreading awareness on and assuaging the plight of the less-privileged in society. These experiences in positions of influence and leadership have strengthened my organisational and problem solving skills, teamwork as well as allowed me to develop effective communication skills.

For my ability to balance studies, sports and leadership roles, I was among the ten students (out of nine hundred) on my College's prestigious Principal's Honour Roll in 2011 that acknowledged distinguished academic achievement and outstanding contributions to the College. Though challenging as it might have been, I have benefited greatly from my overall College experience and would certainly look forward to continue to represent, contribute and excel in University.

During my National Service stint, I served as a Military Officer entrusted with the responsibility of leading and nurturing the next generation of soldiers. Besides leading soldiers out in the field, I had to handle soldiers from a myriad of backgrounds as well as run the general day to day administration of the battalion. I have had multiple opportunities to serve as a Defending Officer to servicemen (who were accused of various wrongdoings) in military courts as well as conduct investigations into various malpractices in my battalion. These unique and far-reaching dealings in the Army has reaffirmed my decision to pursue law, refined my ability to think critically and to work under significant constraints and duress.

I am a firm believer in the importance of reading and see it as an avenue for the pursuit of knowledge. I read on a wide range of topics including legal conundrums, science, philosophy and even military tactics as I believe sufficient breath of thought is needed to develop one's mental prowess. Through such extensive reading, I have honed my rigour of thought and widened my perspectives to a myriad of issues.

A career in law is diverse and dynamic, yet fraught with many challenges. Legal theory, evidence, clientele management and not to mention regularly navigating the bureaucratic quagmire; no other field is as challenging or multi-faceted as the field of law. Though arduous, I relish the intellectual challenges of legal study and aspire to ensure human rationale and justice continues to prevail in society. Thus, I believe I possess the necessary attributes needed for legal study and excellence in the field of law.

ULTIMATE OXBRIDGE PERSONAL STATEMENT GUIDE — EXAMPLE STATEMENTS – LAW

Universities applied to:

- Cambridge: Offer
- London School of Economics: Rejected
- University College London: Rejected

Good Points:

The personal statement is well-written with no obvious errors. The student opens with quite a conceptual statement of what law means to them and this helps to make the subject seem like a well-thought-through choice. Additionally, the student recognises that law is a difficult and challenging course but seems unafraid of the need to put the necessary effort into it. The conclusion is similar in this respect, tying back to the introductory thoughts and ending on a strong statement of why the student feels like they would be a strong candidate to study law at university. Moreover, the student gives a very capable impression by mentioning their place on the College's Honour Roll, as it suggests they can balance their extra-curricular activities with (and not to the detriment of) their academic studies.

Bad Points:

Structurally, this statement needs to be reorganised. The student's legal interests are given attention and evidence far too late with extra-curricular activities of limited relevance being introduced closer to the beginning. In a personal statement as part of a law application, law needs to be the primary focus throughout. The student's positions of responsibility also come above their academic, legal interests, when they should be given less focus and come later on in the statement. When talking about the skills they developed in relation to these activities, the student makes these developed attributes sound beneficial but does not explicitly tie them to law or why they are useful to the study of law. It takes until the penultimate paragraph for the student to talk openly about their academic interests, and even then, they do not illustrate this with any specific legal examples.

Overall:

The personal statement is good but could be easily improved. The student would benefit from reordering the structure of the content to open with legal or academic interests, and then saving less relevant extra-curricular activities till the end. Any activity or skill should be tied back to law wherever possible – giving specific examples of how they relate would also be helpful in getting across why the student is prepared to study law at university.

NOTES

Subject: Law

Law is a set of rules and guidelines imposed upon a society which reflect its moral consciousness, guided and guarded by the judiciary. I believe everyone has the right to be judged objectively by their own laws. I am fascinated by the process of examining legal arguments, by how the outcome of a case hinges on presentation of the evidence and by the law's status as the ultimate arbiter of 'justice.' It is this desire to study the analytical process and underlying principles of jurisprudence that motivates me to study law academically.

Preparing for my extended project, I studied Plato's Republic and how his analyses of different societies are relevant to modern Britain. Examining the common flaws between our own society and those depicted in Republic made me appreciate the subtlety of the law in its present-day form: many of Plato's proposed solutions to these flaws undermined what are viewed today as personal rights. This led me to reflect on how laws protect us, and also how their intricacies create a doctrine to which people adhere, both complying and incorporating it in their own morality.

Investigating Plato's ideal political system, I considered the contrast between how his laws were devised and their status in our own society. Plato's 'Guardians' (not unlike our own judiciary) were relied on both to codify and interpret the law. While their decisions were considered to be benevolent, society was expected to conform to laws dictated by a separate class. The situation in the UK is quite different: statute law, as well as case law, often reflects current popular opinion. Sarah's law (the parents' right to check the criminal record of any carer for their child) was the direct result of a popular campaign. Whether it is better to have a system of laws that evolve with society or one that is dictated by a separate body is just one example of the ethical questions behind the law that intrigue me.

Seeking experience in the area of law that first attracted me, I assisted a criminal barrister in a Bristol chambers, including client interviews for petty offences and note taking in Crown Court, where we were prosecuting an alleged serial attempted rapist. The defendant's decision to dismiss his lawyers to defend himself brought home the need for a professional intermediary to ensure fair interaction of the individual with the protocol of the law. Examining case files while shadowing a Queen's Counsel specialising in public and taxation law, I was struck by how even the most powerful individual or company is still bound to observe the law. I sought exposure to corporate and commercial law with a local solicitor, where I worked through a practical example of employment law to determine whether a client had a case. This close reading of legal documents was a rewarding and stimulating experience, confirming my commitment to study law.

Captaining rugby teams at school (now 1st XV), club and county level, I have learned how to listen and how to lead; understanding and incorporating others' opinions or feelings in my interaction was key to encouraging progress for the individual or group, to motivate them and help them achieve their own potential. I developed these skills further mentoring in French and as a Sports Ambassador for local primary schools.

Rugby is like society: there are fixed laws that define the game and how it is played, but they are constantly tested by the flair of the players. As a result, the referee must both interpret and enforce the application of those laws; in Plato's terms, he is both guardian and auxiliary. The application of the law to dynamic situations and how different outcomes might be achieved depending upon points of interpretation has fascinated me for years.

I am strongly motivated to study the law's mechanics and with this passion, combined with the necessary determination and underlying skills, I will relish the task of appreciating and mastering law as an intellectual discipline in its own right.

Universities applied to:

- Oxford: Offer
- University College London: Offer
- King's: Offer
- Bristol: Offer
- Exeter: Offer

Good Points:

This is an impressive personal statement in many regards and was clearly well-received. The student opens with a definition of law but then goes on to interpret what they understand it to mean, and by doing so, has given some insight into their personality and understanding. It is clear from the outset that the student's interest is an academic one, and this will gain them favour from top academic institutions if sustained. The discussion of the student's extended project is given a clear legal dimension and the student competently makes cross-links, which display their strong grasp of sources of UK law - having a current example to underline this point. In this instance, the discussion of work experience complements the academic interests well because of the way the statement is structured – by saving work experience till later, the student made clear that their primary focus is academic and intellectual, but they do have a commitment to engaging with the subject at a practical level.

Bad Points:

Having two paragraphs about rugby probably gives the sport more attention than is necessary. Moreover, while the student has endeavoured to present all their skills as relevant to law, the links can read as somewhat tenuous, particularly in the sporting examples. Replacing one of these paragraphs with one about some wider reading in a purely legal area of interest (as opposed to reading as part of the extended project) would have been a more beneficial addition.

Overall:

This is an extremely strong personal statement. The student clearly gets across their interest in studying law, but more than this, it is unquestionable that their interest is in studying law as an academic discipline rather than practicing law as a career once they have graduated. Structurally, the statement flows well and covers sufficient facets of the student's activities and interests to explain why they want to study law and why they would be successful in doing so. The only real improvement to be made would be to add discussion of a time the student engaged in academic reading or research into a legal topic beyond what is required of them in their studies.

NOTES

Subject: Law (with French Law)

The way in which the British legal system both reflects and sculpts our constantly changing society fascinates me. Most recently, Tony Nicklinson's fight for the right to die, the pivotal precedent his case set and the legal challenge presented to ethical views exemplified why I want to read and, ultimately, practise law.

The role of the media in extradition cases such as Julian Assange and Abu Qatada, and Helena Kennedy's 'Just Law', made me aware of how extradition can infringe people's rights. The European Arrest Warrant has the ability seriously to undermine the right to freedom, allowing extradition without evidence previously examined in court, as in the case of retired judge Colin Dines, who was extradited to Italy and spent 18 months in jail before coming to trial.

Work placements have widened my interest; a case of suspected fraud at Dickins Hopgood Chidley LLP Solicitors (in which the law was used legitimately) demonstrated the law's ability to restrict a morally correct outcome. This prompted my exploration of jurisprudence, the philosophy of law and varying theories on the link between law and morality. Dworkin's 'Law's Empire' offered particular insight; moral values already exist within the law as unwritten 'principles' and 'policies', but it is judges who ultimately reveal the values to which our legal system is committed. In a recent critical essay discussing the extent to which British moral values are included in our laws, I combined research - such as Finnis' distinctive theory derived from the question of what constitutes a worthwhile, desirable life - with my own evaluations on how morality enters legal decisions, one possibility being the jury.

Observing court procedures and the complexities of different cases (for example, cases of appeal at the Royal Courts of Justice) offered me a first-hand understanding of Dworkin's theory of law as integrity. The intricacies peculiar to each case (such as a case of Count 2 rape re-classified by the Judge as Count 1) the tiers of argument and the clarity of reasoning behind each judgment re-ignited my enthusiasm to pursue a legal career. A Bristol Crown Court trial proved similarly interesting when one defendant changed his plea to guilty, radically affecting the other defendant (pleading not guilty)and requiring one barrister significantly to change his argument. Watching techniques in practice I had learnt during a mock trial at a 'Debate Chamber' master class confirmed how challenging, unpredictable and immediate law can be. It also motivated me to improve vital skills in creating a spontaneous argument without losing the importance of precision and research.

My love for the French language has grown immensely over the past year whilst reading both classical and more modern French novels, particularly enjoying Sagan's 'Bonjour Tristesse' and Claudel's 'La Petite Fille de Monsier Linh'. Work experience at Hill Hofstetter Ltd (with European business links) illustrated how valuable a second language and international awareness is to a law firm; this prompted my search for the opportunity to spend a year in France as part of my degree.

Cross-disciplinary A levels and various co-curricular interests have helped me hone transferable skills well-suited to a law degree. Maths has developed problem-solving and logical aptitudes; analysis of historical sources has advanced my ability to formulate a structured argument, and my knowledge of the genesis of English law. Cicero's 'In Verrem' has heightened my appreciation of the origins of our current legal system, and was made more exciting by comparing ancient techniques to those I witnessed in court, with many (such as speaking directly to the jury) still relevant.

My motivation has always been to maintain top grades alongside involvement in a wide range of activities: I now want to push this academic focus to a higher level and merge all areas of interest into one solid field of specialism and expertise.

Universities applied to:

- Oxford: Offer
- Durham: Offer
- Warwick: Offer
- Bristol: Offer
- Exeter: Offer

Good Points:

The personal statement opens with a topical example, giving the impression that the student takes interest in legal issues from the outset. Importantly, the introduction is conscious to mention the student's desire to read and practice law – setting up an academic interest from the beginning. The student continues to mention specific legal examples throughout, emphasising this genuine interest. When talking about their legal work experience, the student shows how this progressed back into fostering a specific academic interest in jurisprudence, before then giving what they learned from this study practical application. Such interplay between work experience and academics is highly impressive. The student's current subjects of study are given clear links to law and the punchy ending is effective both stylistically and in emphasising the student's strong personal attributes.

Bad Points:

The only area in which slight improvement could be made is the discussion of the student's French interests. The application is being made to study Law and French Law, and so adding a legal discussion in the paragraph concerning their French interests would have been beneficial.

Overall:

This personal statement is highly impressive. The student capably links everything back to the study or application of law, and this is precisely what will impress academic institutions. The student includes aspects of current legal affairs, specific topics of legal interest, and examples of engaging with law at every available opportunity. It is unsurprising that this personal statement was well-received.

NOTES

CLASSICS

Subject: Classics

'Sunt lacrimae rerum et mentem mortalia tangunt,' (Aen. I) epitomises for me the connection between Latin's beauty and the ingenuity of its grammatical principles. The precision each word gains through its affix renders word-order and superfluous lexis unnecessary, whilst also intensifying its meaning. Virgil exploits this by using balancing phrases that invest his language with extraordinary resonance. In a single line, he acknowledges both the tragedy of the Trojans' fate and the harsh reality of human existence, producing an expression so rich in meaning, it is almost untranslatable into English. I am fascinated by the relationship between the language and the eloquence of its literature; the linguistic subtleties revealed by Ovid in the closing passage of Daedalus and Icarus (Met. VIII) captivate me. The present participle 'clamantia' reflects Icarus' lingering hope as he calls out to his father, yet the subsequent severity of the passive verb 'excipiuntur' in the historic present emphasizes his helplessness. The poignancy culminates in the violent perfect tense 'traxit,' indicating a sense of finality as the 'caerulea…aqua' permanently robs Icarus of his identity.

Whilst I have enjoyed reading The Aeneid, The Odyssey and The Iliad in translation, I feel that their depth of meaning can only be fully uncovered with analysis of the original text. Anderson's profound observations in 'The Art of the Aeneid' developed my understanding of the intricacies within Virgil's language. His opening nouns 'arma virumque,' present Homeric allusions to the Iliad's martial theme and the Odyssey's focus on a central character; however, in their inevitable interaction, he highlights that his poem will take on a deeper dimension by examining how war affects the individual. Writing after a century of political turmoil, Virgil was conscious of war's destruction, and therefore, unlike Homer, does not portray the 'kleos' to be achieved in battle, instead presenting conflict as an undesirable requirement. Homer's heroic accounts are consummate in pace and narrative drive, but I was struck by Virgil's realism and political awareness. Though he echoes the optimism of the 'Golden Age' in his praise of Augustus, he presents a genuine understanding of the burden of responsibility. Aeneas is not a self-seeking hero like Odysseus, but rather a 'pius' figure with a very public fate. As Anderson argues, in the end Aeneas is almost dehumanized by his duty; in killing Turnus, he defeats the final obstacle in his cause for Italian peace, yet Virgil's choice of the manic 'fervidus' to describe him indicates that, as an individual, he is destroyed for his descendants' future.

This concept of political duty captures my interest. Virgil's reflection of the hope for the new Principate in his analogy between the journey from Troy to Rome and Rome's political transition is supported by the power struggles illustrated in Harris' 'Lustrum' and 'Imperium,' which reveal the precariousness of the Republic. However, as Graves shows in 'I Claudius,' the Roman Empire itself was soon to become inherently corrupt. He suggests that effective government lies in a delicate balance between the stability of centralized rule, and the liberty of a Republic. Contrastingly, in his Republic, Plato advocates a rigidly hierarchical society headed by his reluctant 'philosopher-kings,' thus implying that it is not power itself that corrupts, but the desire for power. Yet, perhaps ambition is innate to human nature, making such a society unachievable. Such diverse issues are testament to Classics' infinitely broad spectrum.

I participate in a drama youth group, and have achieved Distinction in my Grade 8 LAMDA exam. I have been keen to link this interest to Classics by seeing productions of Electra and Orestes, and a modern interpretation of Orpheus and Eurydice. I seek to share my enthusiasm for studying languages and history with younger students by running a weekly language club, and through my role as a History Prefect. Above all, it is my love for language as the foundation of a culture that has fostered my interest in the Greco-Roman world, and I am eager to pursue this at a degree level.

Universities applied to:

- Oxford: Offer
- Durham: Offer
- Bristol: Offer
- King's: Offer
- University College London: Rejected

Good Points:

The student opens their personal statement with a quotation – while this can come across as cliché, the student engages in such a deep analysis that its inclusion is justified. The student's knowledge of a range of literature comes across well, with several cited examples being offered via analysed quotations. The student has a clear appreciation of both the language and societal aspects of the course they are applying for, suggesting they are a suitable candidate for study.

Bad Points:

It takes half a paragraph for the student to make reference to their own personal interest in Classics. All discussion to this point, while intelligent, is phrased very much abstractly rather than offering an example of personal excitement or engagement with the material. The use of key terms is similarly attempting to serve the purpose of displaying the student's knowledge of Classics concepts, but the phrases are used with little context or explanation. This means that it reads to an admissions tutor like the candidate is using words they don't know the meaning of. Terms should be included when relevant, not for the sake of inclusion alone. Structurally, there is a fair bit of jumping between texts; and, while this is clearly for the purpose of comparison, this creates a disruption to the natural flow of the statement.

Overall:

The statement shows a clear engagement with the subject but needs refining. The student should aim to answer one of two questions with every point they include: why they wish to study classics, or why they would excel in doing so. Currently, the former question is not given sufficient weight, though the second is implicit in the student's constant engagement with the subject.

NOTES

Subject: Classics

Listening to operas like Handel's Acis and Galatea, or looking at paintings like Raphael's exquisite Triumph of Galatea, I am always reminded of Ovid's brilliant manipulation of sources in producing stories now well ingrained in our culture - in this case transplanting the terrifying Cyclops of Odyssey 9 into a comic love triangle from Theocritus. In the Iliad, by contrast, Homer tells a deeply profound story of the cost of war, in which the humanity and inhumanity of war, presented through the sympathetic voice of the poet and the scope of the action respectively, are drawn together throughout the poem, culminating in the meeting of two tragic figures, Achilles and Priam, in Book 24. For me, however, the most moving part of the Iliad is Hector's speech to Andromache in Book 6 when he imagines her being enslaved, because it combines the shame-driven bravery of the heroic code with an acute sense of conflicting duties, alien to most of the other characters in the poem. It is this variety in Classical literature, especially in the rich traditions of epic and mythology, that most appeals to me about Classics. In reading Classics at university I am particularly looking forward to studying more Greek tragedy, since I so enjoyed reading King Lear and Endgame at English AS-Level and the Antigone at Bryanston.

The infectious curiosity of Herodotus, the witty cynicism of Tacitus: Ancient History offers the whole range of authorial perspectives, but what struck me the most last year when I studied Ancient History for the first time was the fact that one need look no further than Plutarch's Lives to find the whole range of personalities still found in today's politics. An idea particularly resonant in modern politics, from Neil Kinnock to Joe Biden, is that of the 'novus homo', and my interest in Cicero, through studying his works at AS-Level, led me to write an article for Omnibus in which I argued that Cicero intended to publish not only the seventy-nine epistulae commendaticiae of ad Familiares 13, as suggested by Ludwig Gurlitt, but also some of the letters to Atticus.

In my Extended Project dissertation I investigated the issues surrounding the UK's euthanasia legislation. In researching this subject I studied the views of Immanuel Kant and Jeremy Bentham, but also the opinions of more recent philosophers such as Peter Singer. I was especially impressed by Joseph Fletcher's essay, The Cognitive Criterion of Personhood, because his clear and logical argument for defining a 'person', especially the criterion of one's sense of the future, was the foundation for my argument concerning the value and sanctity of human life.

Outside the classroom I like to be involved in a lot of music, mostly singing - in which my favourite genre is Baroque oratorio - cello, and harpsichord. I recently performed in Mendelssohn's Octet at the Cadogan Hall, and having won first prize in London's Spring Grove Chamber Music Festival with my string quartet we are spending the money on making a CD of some of our recent repertoire. My other pursuits include some amateur journalism and representing my school in public speaking, while at home I particularly enjoy reading the books of P. G. Wodehouse and watching the 1950s films of Federico Fellini and Ingmar Bergman.

ULTIMATE OXBRIDGE PERSONAL STATEMENT GUIDE — EXAMPLE STATEMENTS – CLASSICS

Universities applied to:

- Oxford: Offer
- Edinburgh: Offer
- Exeter: Offer
- Manchester: Offer
- Kent: Offer

Good Points:

The student clearly engages with the subject and is eager to demonstrate the knowledge they have already built in their studies. Importantly, attention is given to both classical literature and ancient history, showing that the student has well-rounded interests within their chosen subject. The student is able to talk competently about a number of classical sources and figures, but also is able to make links with current affairs, which works well. Mentioning the article that the student wrote was a strong inclusion because it shows the student took initiative and undertook an academic style activity, moving beyond what is required of them in their studies.

Bad Points:

The student takes some time to begin discussing their own personal interests in Classics. The phrasing for the first half of the introductory paragraph is for the most part quite abstract and factual. Writing in this way can present difficulties in getting your personality across. The paragraph about the student's extra-curricular activities would be better if the activities given attention linked to classics in some way. While a wealth of extra-curricular activities may demonstrate that the student is capable of balancing their interests and their studies, it would be more impressive to show a commitment to Classics, in this instance, through these activities. Wider reading in a particular area of Classics that the student finds interesting would be more relevant than what they enjoy reading or the types of film they enjoy.

Overall:

This personal statement is well-written and demonstrates the student's wealth of knowledge about Classics from the outset. At times, it sadly lacks in personality. The student talks happily about facts and concepts but does not sustain a noticeable passion throughout - resulting in a personal statement that seems, at times, overly factual. While by no means a bad personal statement, it would benefit from getting across at every opportunity the view that the student has a real passion for this subject and engages with it at every opportunity. The student should be the focus, not the subject.

NOTES

Subject: Classics

I first became intrigued by the classical world whilst learning about the Romans in primary school. Since then an inspirational Latin teacher, trips to classical sites and the writings of Homer have cemented my fascination with this subject. Having studied Latin GCSE and AS level, as well as AS Classical Civilisation, I have come to appreciate the rich cultural depth of the ancient world and its profound influence upon society today as the origin of so many of the fundamental aspects of our daily lives, from democracy and English language through to the justice system. It is for these reasons that I wish to study Classics at degree level.

As part of my Latin AS course I found the structure of Latin and its legacy in terms of modern European languages fascinating. This led me to research the derivations of the English language as part of my Academic Research Course project with a specific focus on Latin and Greek influences and I found that Latin influence on English especially is huge both in terms of vocabulary and idiom. Studying The Iliad in translation for the AS Classical Civilisation course has stimulated my interest in ancient literature, quickly appreciating its striking sophistication and lucidity, prompting me to read The Odyssey. This epic, for me, particularly raised the question of the nature of morality in ancient Greece as the portrayal of Odysseus is as a pious and kind man, yet his indiscriminate slaughter of the suitors and servants at the end would seem to conflict with this. Having seen certain short passages in the original Greek I have come to further appreciate the subtle word play of Homer such as the section in which Odysseus outmanoeuvres the Cyclops by saying that his name is 'nobody' which is yet more impressive when seen in the Greek as the translation cannot fully convey the use of double meaning.

In addition to my AS subjects I have attended a weekly Ancient Greek class and completed the Bryanston Greek summer school course. I feel this has given me a good grounding in ancient Greek that I can build on this year in preparation for a Classics degree. I am also involved with running the college Classics society which is helping to develop my organisational and presentation skills.

Having taken trips to Pompeii and Greece I found the opportunity to see parts of the ancient world in the flesh, such as the Parthenon, awe inspiring. It was an experience which made the ancient world seem far more real to me and gave me a sense of the scale and significance of the ancient sites which cannot be gained from photographs or drawings so I hope to visit more in the future.

I also found the AS Philosophy course most absorbing and through this have gained a detailed understanding of some ancient philosophy, such as Plato, which is an area of classics I am keen to study further. This led me to read Aristotle's Nicomachean Ethics, which I found to be strikingly convincing and relevant to the modern world considering its age. I particularly found the concept of virtues and the 'Golden mean' a compelling argument for how we should make moral decisions as the idea of moderating our behaviour between two extremes is an intuitive one. The Maths AS course has developed my skills of logical thought, a discipline which is proving useful in other subjects when analysis is required for essays or translation.

Music is also a great interest of mine and over the course of the last year I have taught myself to play the guitar proficiently and I am also a very competent drummer, having taken lessons for several years. Both these pursuits, but in particular teaching myself the guitar, have developed skills of perseverance and self-motivation, which are of great use to any academic study.

I relish the opportunity to study Classics at the highest level and especially look forward to working with both experts in the field and other students who share my passionate interest.

Universities applied to:

- Cambridge: Offer
- Durham: Offer
- Bristol: Offer
- Exeter: Offer
- Manchester: Offer

Good Points:

The personal statement is very strong with no obvious errors. The student's strength, in particular, is their ability to make Classics relevant in all of their listed academic interests. This is done notably well in the paragraph about A Level Philosophy, which the student used as a springboard to undergo their own research. Indeed, the Academic Research Project was another well-chosen inclusion as independent research work is more closely in line with the style of working at university, and the student seems comfortable working in this way. The ending lines work well in underlining that the student is eager and excited to begin this course.

Bad Points:

The opening line is somewhat of a personal statement cliché. Talk of developing these interests fully at such a young age is, more often than not, unconvincing. Structurally, the balance of the statement seems to be weighted towards language or literature aspects, with societal dimensions coming later. Ensuring that all aspects of the course are covered from the outset, or as soon as is practical, will help to give the impression the student is a good fit for the course as a whole, rather than only being interested in smaller aspects. In terms of engagement with ancient texts, The Odyssey (as with The Iliad and The Aeneid) is fairly standard and usually on the Classics A Level Syllabus. Given that the majority of students applying to study Classics at university will be studying it at A Level, going off syllabus to more niche texts might set the student apart from the crowd.

Overall:

This personal statement is strong stylistically but there is room for potential improvement. The content may come across as fairly standard, particularly in terms of the ancient literature the student has read (at least up until the section on Philosophy). The current content is all unproblematic, but to stand out from the crowd, the student should talk about more independent work they have done beyond what is required of them in school.

NOTES

Subject: Classics & French

The fresh perspectives afforded by different ages and separate cultures can only add to the study of literature and be of benefit in meeting the linguistic challenges of language-learning. This is my belief and why I find the prospect of combining Classics and French so attractive.

I have always loved languages. Balancing two modern languages with Latin was perhaps the highlight of my academic experience at prep school, and led to the top scholarship at my senior school, with a discussion of the origins of the Germanic language-family forming the major part of my interview. More recently I have enjoyed the intricacies and complexities of language through classical prose composition. I earned second place out of 275 in the Phaedrus Latin Contest this year, submitting an original fable in Latin. Preparations have started for next year's entry, which is to be in the iambic trimeter Phaedrus used, and this is something I would love to pursue a little at university.

I benefited greatly from attending summer schools in Durham and Bryanston. The opportunity to read more widely among other keen minds gave me an exciting sample of what life studying for a classics degree might be like. Additionally, I have explored the classical perspective on violence, using ancient literature, philosophy and culture as a lens through which to evaluate the potential dangers of excessive violence in contemporary cinema. The essay I produced on this subject won me first prize in the Postgate section of The University of Liverpool's Postgate & Walbank Essay Competition.

My work over the course of last summer reinforced my conviction to apply for this Joint Honours course. I read Euripides' Hippolytus in conjunction with Racine's Phèdre, analysing the former's influence on the latter. A comparison particularly of the character, values and actions of Phaidra and Phèdre formed an interesting focus in reading the plays, and I intend to give a talk on this subject to a group of sixth-form linguists at my school. I feel there is much overlap between the studies of Classics and French, and the connections (in tragedy in particular) are ones I would be keen to follow up at university.

In French, oral and written fluency is an exciting element of the course. My competence in French has already allowed me to engage with non-English speakers – most memorably over a fortnight at a language school in Cannes, with a group of Italians; I have subsequently visited one of them in Italy, where we spoke exclusively French. The study of vocabulary, grammar and syntax appeals to me intellectually, but I look forward to its fruition, namely the chance to interact with a new range of people as a stronger speaker of French.

Furthermore, I enjoy the academic challenges which come with the study of French literature. I read L'Etranger in my lower 6th year, where I was struck by Meursault's intriguing character and existentialist outlook, and was duly infuriated by his refusal to draw judgements or create any real meaning in his irreligious existence. Since then I have met Flaubert, in the form of Madame Bovary, where the ultimate corruption and downfall of the main character felt to me like witnessing the ruin of a Greek tragic heroine, such was the force of her passions and disappointments; Julian Barnes' Flaubert's Parrot was an excellent companion in this reading. I like to engage with French culture in as many other ways as possible, whether through watching films, listening to music, or reading the Analyse du jeu des échecs of 18th century chess-player Philidor.

Alongside my studies, I have kept myself active as a cross country/half-marathon runner, competitive chess-player, debater and cricketer. I have enjoyed representing my school on two cricket tours, as well as completing the Ten Tors challenge. At university, I hope to sustain as many of these activities as possible without detracting from my central ambition of achieving a top degree in Classics and French.

Universities applied to:

- Oxford: Offer
- Durham: Offer
- Edinburgh: Offer
- Exeter: Offer
- Newcastle: Offer

Good Points:

This is an impressive personal statement. The student comes across as extremely well-read with each of the texts they chose to speak about being highly relevant to the course they are applying for, but also acting as very individual choices which will set them apart from other potential candidates. The student clearly has a strong passion for the two subjects and is able to show what they have done outside of the classroom to engage with this passion, which is highly commendable. A balance is struck between highlighting their strong academic achievement through the mention of prizes and awards, and activities they have chosen to undertake simply because they have this strong personal interest in the subjects.

Bad Points:

The personal statement is very language-centric. While this might be acceptable given that the student is applying for a combined Classics and French course, extra focus on the historical or societal aspects of the Classics half would not go amiss, if only to ensure all bases are covered. Stylistically, the student should not be afraid to use shorter, simple sentences to get their point across. The student often uses commas to link several clauses together to create longer, complex sentences; and this is unnecessary and, at times, to the detriment of flow and clarity. The student also makes several references to things they would like to continue looking into at university and so should be careful to first check that these are topics covered in the course at each university they apply to, even if only to ensure none of the institutions are being alienated. Their extra-curricular activities are dealt with swiftly at the end of the statement, but their inclusion may be questioned, given that they are of limited relevance to Classics or French and the student has not attempted to draw attention to any transferable skills.

Overall:

This is a very strong personal statement and was met with much success. The student should remember to proof-read (ensuring that capital letters are used for all references to Classics or French subjects), but the content is undeniably strong. It is clear that the student has a genuine interest in the subjects they are applying for, both individually and in combination, and this works to make them come across as a highly capable candidate.

NOTES

ORIENTAL STUDIES

Subject: Chinese Studies

If there is one issue that towers above others in importance in our world today, it is the rise of China as a political and economic power. Chinese Studies excites me, however, not only because of its indisputable relevance, but also because of its academic challenge, both linguistic and cultural. I love the way the subject continually leads the student out into other fields of knowledge: language and literature, geography, history, politics, economics and international relations. For example, Jung Chang's shocking portrayal of life through three generations of her family in 'Wild Swans' opened my eyes to some of the horrors the Chinese had to go through during the Chinese and Cultural Revolutions. This biographical work in turn led me to read Chevrier's 'Mao and the Chinese Revolution', an introductory history of C20th China.

Not only will Chinese Studies lead out into new fields of knowledge, but I have also been surprised how some of my long-cherished interests feed back into it. Take Music and Geography, for instance. While exploring the style of the Beijing Opera I discovered how closely Chinese music is bound to its social, historical and political context. Watching a modern version of the opera 'Journey to the West' led me to read the translation of the classical novel on which the show was based, which introduced me to Chinese literature and also to traditional Chinese mythology, religions and values. In IB Geography, I have enjoyed opportunities to develop my appreciation of China's exceptional population change, its booming economy and regional diversity. I was stimulated by J. Watts' analysis of the scale and speed of China's carbon-fuelled industrial revolution in 'When a Billion Chinese Jump', while a project on the Three Gorges Dam helped me understand the great potential danger China's surging development could bring not only to itself, but to the whole planet.

My appetite for language study has been stimulated by being brought up bilingually. A German, I have lived in the UK since I was a baby. Growing up in this way, as well as learning French for five years and taking IB Higher Spanish, has made me realise how crucial linguistic competence is to enable full access to, and appreciation of, a culture and a people's way of thinking. Having made a small start on Mandarin when I was younger, I can also appreciate the difference between learning a European and an Oriental language; it is, however, the extraordinary features and considerable challenges of Mandarin that attract me.

I have a proven record of time management, balancing my academic work with a wide range of co-curricular activities. A music scholar, I sing in two school choirs, play the piano and perform at recitals, concerts and competitions. Recently, I played the lead role in a production of 'South Pacific'. I also love physical exercise: football, volleyball and swimming. Taking part in Gold D of E expeditions and living in a boarding house community have made me aware of the importance of bringing my strengths to a group and being open-minded to other opinions. I have used my competence in languages to teach German and Spanish to younger students and I am an elected member of the school's 'Wheeler-Bennett Society', where I enjoy discussing current cultural and political issues with my peers.

Standing in the middle of Tiananmen Square this summer, walking along the skyline of the Shanghai Bund and living with a Chinese family confirmed my desire to read Chinese Studies. These experiences highlighted to me the gulf between the Chinese political system and the desires of the young generation, the clash between the explosive modernisation of China's cities and the country's rich heritage and the contrast between frantic consumerism and traditional values. I cannot wait to study a course that will equip me with an extraordinary language and will unlock doors into a rich culture and society, which at present I have but only glimpsed.

Universities applied to:

- Cambridge: Offer
- Durham: Offer
- SOAS: Offer
- Leeds: Offer
- Sheffield: Offer

Good Points:

This candidate is able to clearly articulate the relevance of their previous experiences — both academic and extra-curricular — to their chosen area of study. They can demonstrate a wide range of influences that tie together their interest in Chinese Studies, including influences that they have independently identified and pursued. Through their discussions of both linguistic and cultural areas of interest, they are able to demonstrate their potential ability for a wide-ranging and challenging course. This candidate has thought far beyond the bounds of their classroom and is able to allude to a variety of areas in which they have thought independently, and can see their personal pursuits intersecting with their undergraduate study.

Bad Points:

While this statement is impressive in a number of ways, as an overall piece, it does present some potential areas for improvement. Though the list of extra-curricular activities undertaken by this student is impressive, this candidate has not always convincingly emphasised how these pursuits are relevant to their studies. This statement would have also been given further weight by the substitution for highly personal and subjective experiences in favour of more academically considered thought. This candidate could also further develop their overall tone, which varies somewhat over the course of the statement between areas of academic clarity, areas of near-patronising tone, and areas of more informal anecdotal discussion. As such, a more thorough overview of this candidate would have been achieved by a more cohesive, persuasive, and academic tone of discussion.

Overall:

This candidate very consistently and engagingly demonstrates their interest in their chosen area and provides evidence, both academic and personal, for their continued involvement in this area. While the statement covers a wide and rich variety of subject matter and personal pursuits, it lacks a certain overall thrust of argument and cohesion of tone. The statement, while impressive as an overall piece, could have been developed further with greater consideration of academic areas that are likely to appear on their chosen undergraduate courses — particularly literature.

NOTES

Subject: Classics & Oriental Studies

One can better understand the whole of Western civilization through close study of Greco-Roman culture, as I have noticed while reading many modern texts. No literature or civilization exists in a vacuum; as a bicultural person living between the Arab and the Western world, I have a heightened perception of this. Therefore I believe that it is necessary not only to study single civilizations in depth, but also to observe how they influence one another, in order to comprehend our global culture. One way to achieve this is through the study of language- directly and indirectly an expression of the social and individual human- and especially of the most beautiful use of language, that of literature. For this reason I wish to apply for a joint degree in Classics and Oriental Studies.

I have studied Latin, Italian and English literature at high school and I found intimate connections between them. For example, the idea of poetic immortality is present among the Romans in Horace and Lucan, in Italian literature from Dante and Petrarch to Foscolo, and in the English one in Shakespeare and Spenser's sonnets. I have found Vergil in Dante, and Dante in Eliot. Further, more nuanced connections can be found, and links exist between a wider variety of cultures. It would be particularly interesting, through the tensions of the political world, to grasp the links between the Western civilization and what lies outside it.

Through my study of the sciences at Liceo Scientifico level, with a focus on Maths, I have developed the precision necessary for detailed philological work.

My love of knowledge has been fed by the Greek philosopher Plato, whose Theaetetus taught me the importance of thinking critically and interrogating my perceptions. I have also realized that socially, humans face the same problems: Ovid did not hesitate to blame rape on the victim rather than the perpetrator, a way of thinking against which we still battle today. Similarly, the great sentiments persist through the ages, Catullus' "Vivamus, mea Lesbia" still resounds vital as ever, Lucretius' "O miseras hominum mentes" maintains intact its desperate strength.

Such timeless sentiments are also present in the literature of Ancient Near East, such as Enheduanna's Nin-me-sara, which captures the pain of exile and the relationship of the individual with God.

I have given short talks on Enheduanna during my school's Cultural Week, while distributing copies of her poetry. I have often dedicated my free time to ancient literature, participating in the Certamen Ovidianum, writing and producing a play based on Pascoli's Latin poetry, which I have recited metrically, and helping organize my displaced school library.

I have also cultivated modern languages. I have independently gained reading knowledge of Spanish and French. To improve my Icelandic, I spent a summer in Iceland. I am also fluent in Arabic, which I used during my two-year stay in Kuwait, where I attended a Cambridge English School.

I am interested in the Arts, and enjoy spending my weekends in museums and churches. Living near Rome, I have the privilege of admiring the Pantheon and the Colosseum and how they influence the modern landscape, as the civilization they belong to influences the modern mind. I better grasped Ovid when I saw him in Bernini, or in Correggio's 'Danae'. I have tried to communicate this beauty to the children I have tutored, an experience that made me bring out from the ancient world what was relevant to the various contexts in which they live. I hope to continue spreading this beauty through research and teaching.

| ULTIMATE OXBRIDGE PERSONAL STATEMENT GUIDE | EXAMPLE STATEMENTS – ORIENTAL STUDIES |

Universities applied to:

- Oxford: Offer

Good Points:

Throughout this statement, this candidate is able to illustrate their wide range of academic reading and their subsequent independent thought on these topics. This student can clearly articulate how they have thought about their academic work within a broad global context. In particular, this student's breadth of reading in a number of different languages and across a variety of diverse eras illustrates their ability to tackle a wide range of literary issues — in a way that is far above and beyond the demands of school-level study. Their cogent and apposite use of more complex academic terms concisely supports their profound and developed interest in their chosen area of study.

Bad Points:

While this candidate's academic pursuits are impressive, the dogged attention to detail around their reading creates a statement which is somewhat airless. Although the candidate does allude briefly to personal and extra-curricular pursuits, it would have given a more thorough sense of the person as a whole if there was an additional sentence or two of relevant but personal detail. This applicant is also at risk of fashioning themselves as a pompous individual due to their tone — this statement would have benefited from some relaxation of the general conversation register, as it reads as rather overbearing. While this position does give the applicant greater room to explore their academic credentials, it is indicative of a haughty and outmoded essay style, which could be a mild cause for concern for potential tutors.

Overall:

The success of this statement rests on the fluidity and comprehensive nature of this student's literary discussions. They are able to call upon a wide and substantial range of works and demonstrate their engagement with them at a high level. It would have been a welcome addition to have seen greater personal engagement beyond their reading and to understand further about the applicant's interest in a non-curriculum area for undergraduate study. The candidate would also benefit from adopting a register that better suits their academic interests, rather than a tone that is suggestive of superiority.

NOTES

PSYCHOLOGY

Subject: Experimental Psychology

The boundaries of the brain are confined only to the limitations of the inquisitor. The understanding we can acquire from our behaviour is endless and fuels my determination to study Psychology. I participated in the College Debate on whether the concept of Gender should be abolished. At first glance, this idea seemed impossible. However, our subsequent research revealed that my initial reaction was evidence of my own limitations and society. I relish the opportunities that Psychology offers to challenge and expand my ideas.

Taking part in a Youth Philanthropy Initiative allowed me to form relations with Send Family Link, a charity that helps children whose mothers are in prison. After reading studies about these children, I was left wondering whether they could share similar, perhaps psychopathological, traits with their parents due to their genetics. This offered a cross-curricular link to my Philosophy studies on evil, and I completed an extended essay on the roots of evil. This linked Philosophy, Psychology and Neuroscience, and also two of the main debates in Psychology: Nature/Nurture and Free Will and Determinism. Zimbardo explains his theories on this subject in his book 'The Lucifer Effect: Why Good People Turn Evil', which I enjoyed. Hearing him speak about this in person at a student lecture I attended was fascinating, as was the opportunity to meet him.

Social Psychology intrigues me, as it reveals much about the way people interact with each other in everyday situations. I explored this further by studying why people obey and conform. With a keen interest in History, I related this to real-life topics, such as the Holocaust and why the Nazis obeyed Hitler's orders to complete such inhumane actions. I am surprised by the extent to which individual and group responses are influenced by the people and culture surrounding us, whether or not we are aware of it.

At A Level I chose to do a broad spectrum of subjects to provide a sound foundation for a Psychology degree. Maths and Statistics develop my analytical and research skills, whilst Philosophy highlights ethical and moral issues and develops my essay writing and argument skills. French offers an insight to the linguistics and language skills studied in Psychology. In addition studying French has provided me with the opportunity to work with children in France and participate in a course at the French Institute of Fashion, both of which add to my understanding of different cultures. As a Psychology mentor, I help AS students improve through tutoring. I am a keen singer and am completing the Contemporary Music Practitioners Award at College and enjoy working with the diverse group of people I encounter with these different subjects.

Last summer I completed a 6 week volunteering program in America, where I trained and worked as a counsellor in a YMCA children's summer camp. The challenges of working with children from all different countries and social groups reinforced the importance of social norms and cross-cultural differences in society. Back home, being Netball Team Captain and working as a Netball Coach allowed me to explore ideas of motivation and communication.

My knowledge has been expanded by reading in and around the subject. 'The Brain That Changes Itself' by Norman Doige raised my awareness of the developing discipline of 'neuroplasticity' and the advances in understanding brain function as a whole. This book was a stepping stone to my growing interest in this field.

Novels such as 'A Beautiful Mind', 'The Room' and 'Before I Go To Sleep' took real psychological disorders, issues and scientific facts and portrayed them from a first-person perspective; enabling me to see how actual sufferers are affected.

I am a motivated, enthusiastic student who is genuinely excited by the ever-expanding horizons of Psychology and I am determined to contribute to the academic and real-life applications of this extraordinary Science.

Universities applied to:

- Oxford: Offer
- Bristol: Offer
- Exeter: Offer
- Durham: Offer
- University College London: Rejected

Good Points:

This candidate is able to eloquently engage with a wide variety of academic and contemporary issues surrounding their topic, which demonstrates their awareness of the subject not just as an area of closed study but as a growing, morphing, and complex material. Their continued inclusion of extra-curricular activities is always linked very well to their chosen area of study, which gives the overall effect of presenting the candidate as someone with a hotly-pursued interest in their area — but with a consistent, personal slant. Through the inclusion of analytical literary discussion, the candidate also demonstrates their ability to take on complex academic tasks in a slightly removed area, which is suggestive of general academic curiosity and well-rounded academic interrogation skills.

Bad Points:

While this candidate is very impressive in their ability to call upon a huge breadth of interest areas, they are running the risk of giving snapshots of a variety of areas rather than demonstrating their ability to engage deeply with any one of them in particular. Although much of this breadth is understandable, given the wide reach of their chosen undergraduate study area, it would have been beneficial to include further, focused thought on areas within their degree that they might particularly like to pursue, and the reading that they have done to date in order to bolster that particular standpoint.

Overall:

What is most impressive about this statement is its demonstration of an enormous range of academic and extra-curricular pursuits — and their consistent relevance. The range of material within this statement contributes to an overall impression of the candidate as an able, curious, and tenacious student. They could streamline their discussions somewhat in order to also demonstrate their ability to construct and present an academic argument, but their current structure does not detract from their credentials as a highly capable candidate.

NOTES

Subject: Experimental Psychology

How does the mind work? The mind is a mystery housed within the most complex mechanism known to man: the human brain. My innate curiosity compels me to find out more about such a mystery through the study of Psychology.

I have long been interested in how our minds differ: for example, why have I always been a strong mathematician while my brother finds it challenging? Being a musician, I found Kathryn Vaughn's research supporting a correlation between musical and mathematical abilities particularly thought provoking, while I have also wondered whether my childhood obsession with jigsaws helped me develop problem-solving skills, which are particularly relevant in Geometry: the area with the biggest rift in our abilities. Ann Dowker's argument, in 'Individual Differences', that educational methods influence such differences was also particularly compelling. Therefore, in my gap year, whilst helping struggling learners in KS3 Mathematics at a local school, and, when I help educate children in Tanzania as an International Citizen Service volunteer with the VSO charity, I will evaluate the success of different educational methods. This will give me experience of carrying out my own research, and, will develop skills such as empathy, which is important in the more sensitive areas of Psychology. Furthermore, I recently assisted a University of Oxford researcher conducting follow-up assessments with children in local primary schools. These measured reading-age, language comprehension and numeracy level, and are used to gauge and refine the Catch-Up charity's numeracy intervention programme. As some of the children being assessed were from a control group, my involvement also enlightened me to ethical aspects of research.

Differences that occur in the criminal mind are also of great interest to me. As an elected Student Ambassador for the Holocaust Educational Trust, I visited Auschwitz-Birkenau earlier this year, where I learnt about Rudolf Hoess. Hoess exterminated thousands of families, yet lived with his own family just outside the camp. This ignited an interest in complex behaviour; therefore I read Stanley Milgram's research into whether 'the Germans are different', and learnt about his Theory of Obedience. This developed an interest in Forensic Psychology, and I subsequently attended a Forensics course at Nottingham University, where I learnt about a Forensic Psychologist's role, during Mental Health tribunals, for example.

Deterioration of the mind, and methods to counteract this, also interest me. Reading the Psychologist has given me an insight into how the effectiveness of such methods could be analysed using a high-resolution 3D brain atlas; while a presentation from Claire Rytina enlightened me to useful cognitive treatment designed to rebuild and retrieve memory following her Viral Encephalitis. I have also voluntarily worked at a Nursing Home with some Dementia sufferers, and noticed that many sufferers enjoyed me playing music from their past, and sometimes, this triggered some of their memories. This made me wonder whether the music stimulated neurones which had lain dormant for years, similarly to when neurones are used for the first time, as Hubel and Weisel's nature/nurture research has shown. Studying this in A level Biology gave me an interest in neuroscience, while Biology also stressed the importance of controls and fair tests, which are invaluable during Psychology experiments too. My mathematical skills in statistics will also be beneficial when analysing empirical evidence; and, the deep level of analysis and evaluation used for varying sources in A level History will be useful when studying case studies, while my essay techniques will help me when writing reports, and when considering issues from different perspectives.

Overall, I feel that my broad interests and skills will enable me to thrive as a Psychology student at a demanding University, where I would also make a positive contribution to University life.

Universities applied to:

- Oxford: Offer
- Warwick: Offer
- St. Andrews: Offer
- Durham: Offer
- Exeter: Offer

Good Points:

This statement is powered by a broad range of academic interests — all of which the candidate has explored to a deep and commendable level. They are able to articulate how these interests came about, why they are important, and how they intersect. In so doing, the candidate clearly demonstrates their ability to think independently, to undertake independent projects, and to foster a wide-ranging curiosity. Furthermore, they clearly illustrate how their academic interests have had a bearing on their actions outside of the classroom; activities which require a substantial amount of initiative and endeavour.

Bad Points:

While the consideration of a range of different areas of psychology is illustrative of a consistently curious individual, this statement would have benefited from greater cohesion as an overall piece. The candidate could have also found a less rhetorical way of opening their statement; their tone at this point is not a mode of speech that they return to elsewhere, and as such, it seems somewhat like a non-sequitur. Their prose thereafter is much more engaging, and it seems unfulfilling and irrelevant to include such mystifying text at the start.

Overall:

This candidate maturely presents their academic interests and particular areas of personal pursuit. As a result of this, they are able to demonstrate moments at which they have taken impressive amounts of initiative, and have really gone out of their way in order to experience their academic interests outside of the classroom. They are thereby able to fashion themselves as a curious, energetic, academic individual, who is able to think independently and develop their own work. There are potential areas for stylistic improvement within the statement but they do not hinder the overall impression given of a capable and committed candidate.

NOTES

Subject: Experimental Psychology

When I first became aware of the crimes that took place in Abu Ghraib I was shocked. I couldn't understand why anybody would behave in such a way for no obvious reason – I wanted to know what was going through the soldiers minds at the time. This led me to read the Stanford Prison experiment which critics argue explains why people might act so abusively. At first I was absorbed by the astounding results and satisfied that it explained the crimes, however, having contemplated the experimental design and read criticisms of the experiment I realised that perhaps these results should have been expected. After all, when a group of young men are given power they are unlikely to sit around chatting, especially when research has shown that experimental participants actively try to do what they believe the researchers want them to do.

I am particularly interested in our awareness and perception of the world. In a recent finding Mohamad Koubeissi has claimed to have found a location in the brain where all brain activity is packaged and relayed to produce conscious experience – the claustrum - he hopes that stimulating this region could stop epileptic seizures. Reading "Phantoms In The Brain" by V.S. Ramachandran taught me a lot about how the brain is structured. What I realised when reading this was that there is so much about the brain that we don't understand and this is partly because we are restricted to our conscious mind only. We never experience the other processes occurring in our brain so it is much harder to study them. You could even suggest that our consciousness is simply an aid to ensure that we survive and our genes are carried forward to the next generation. Biologically this makes sense as our advanced awareness evolved from the first organisms with the most basic view of the world, in order for us to make better decisions for our survival.

Neurology is also an area that interests me – I was lucky enough to hear Prof Guy Tear speak about his work at Kings College. He is currently working with a team that is trying to replicate chemical signals that the body produces, to direct neurones to their correct position in the body. Their hope is that if they are successful they will be able to stimulate growth of neurones in people with paralysis and to restore function of the affected muscles which would be an incredible breakthrough.

Gaining a work placement at Econic Technologies, a research group based in Imperial College, was extremely valuable to me. Although it is not concerned in an area of psychology it taught me how scientific research, such as Prof Guy Tear's, is carried out and demonstrated what it might be like to enter a research profession – I saw the rigour with which they carried out experiments and it seemed like very rewarding work, especially when advances are made towards the goal. While I was there I helped collect data for a paper which they were working on and gave a presentation about where I thought their research could be used commercially.

I would like to take part in or coordinate my own psychological research while at university and I think I have developed a foundation of the necessary skills to do so. I gained my level 2 award in Community Sports Leadership which developed my leadership, communication and planning skills by coaching children various sports who may not otherwise have this opportunity. I was not just teaching these children, I was also responsible for their health and safety. I gained my Gold Duke of Edinburgh award which further built on my teamwork skills and organisation. We had to provide for ourselves and navigate independently for 4 days and nights.

Outside my studies I have many interests with tennis being my favourite sport. I am also a keen golfer, rugby player and cricketer. I find endurance events to be a good test of my self-will so I often compete in biathlons and ran a 20 mile race for charity.

Universities applied to:

- Oxford: Offer
- Bath: Offer
- Birmingham: Offer
- Durham: Offer
- Bristol: Offer

Good Points:

Through consideration of both more micro-scale individual problems and high-level concerns, this candidate is able to demonstrate their ability to think in complex and wide-ranging ways. They are able to situate their subject within its broader context and can illustrate articulately why it matters as an area of study. Within that, they can also illustrate areas in which they have identified and pursued particular interests. As a result of these various layers of thought, this candidate demonstrates their ability to undertake independent academic projects and to work from their own initiative — rather than within the bounds of their school-level academic demands.

Bad Points:

This candidate loses eloquence when they begin discussions of their extra-curricular activities. While this does not impede the academic credentials of the statement as a whole, it does seem deflating after careful and rigorous prose about their more academic interests. As such, their aim to tie their extra-curricular activities to their chosen area of undergraduate study falls slightly shy of the mark. The candidate would also benefit from thoroughly structuring their statement in order to persuasively build an argument and a cohesive tone, rather than writing a statement in granular sections of individual interest.

Overall:

This statement has a good balance of personal information and considered academic thought, but would benefit from matching that balance of content with balance of tone. At present, the statement lacks clarity and persuasion in its discussion of extra-curricular pursuits, whereas its more academic sections are focused in their aims. What is particularly impressive about this statement is its ability to consider the subject from a variety of standpoints and to discuss problematic issues on a very minor and broader level, and moreover, at levels that may or may not be possible to comprehend.

NOTES

Subject: Psychology

The study of merely the physical world was never quite enough for me. I strive to look beneath the surface, into the mind and soul's continuous quest, where there are likely to be more questions than answers. Moving from Europe to the Middle East, I gradually realised the underlying presence of Psychology, as I found myself not only looking at people, but thoroughly into them. Natural empathy drove a keen observation of emotion, behaviour and relationships, marking the beginnings of a fascination that I wish to pursue professionally.

As a Finnish international student, I have spent 11 years in Frankfurt, Germany, and two and a half years in Bahrain. My exposure to a variety of ethnicities, religions and languages has allowed me to gain a level of maturity through diverse international perspectives; through life in the metropolitan central European banking capital, and on a miniscule island state in the Arab world. Since the age of 5, I have been taught in English, and so for the majority of my life, English has even been the language that I think in.

Higher level Biology has introduced me to the topics of neurology, the brain and behavioural ecology, while practical Biology has developed my skills in obtaining accurate, objective results in experiments such as the Elisa test. Furthermore, language subjects have refined my literary analysis skills, and allowed me to look into social and interpersonal issues in literature. Reading 'Psychology: A very short introduction', by Butler and McManus, and 'Phobias: Fighting the Fear' by Helen Saul, with research into mental illness, modern therapy developments such as CBT and the debatable role of genetics, empiricism, cognition and neurophysiology among others in the foundations of the human psyche have fuelled my interest in the branches of clinical and abnormal psychology.

In morning shifts at a Finnish hospital's surgical department, I tended and talked to people with not only physical impairment but also mental conditions such as Alzheimer's and Anxiety Disorder. I found patient contact to be something so natural, so effortless, as several of them confided their life stories to me. I learned to regard the delicate hospital environment as an inexpressibly rewarding experience. I undertook voluntary work in an old people's dementia home, and a kindergarten that included children with learning difficulties and Down's Syndrome. Once again, I was struck by the ease with which I could establish a connection with strangers, and found something so profoundly similar in the youngest and oldest generations: the circle of life being completed. My interactions with different age groups were genuinely moving and a valuable introduction to both child- and geropsychology. In addition to these experiences, I have tutored a younger girl in science subjects, and consequently learnt to focus on the academic needs of an individual. My hobbies mainly include skiing, running and swimming, through which the skills of perseverance and motivation have been strongly highlighted for me. More recently I have started a highly enjoyable Ballroom and Latin dance course. Travelling has been a passion for quite some time, as I find myself fully intoxicated by languages, cultures and sights. On trips and at home alike, creative photography is a developing interest, and has helped me to view the world from various angles.

Psychology continues to intrigue me academically, but also within the trivial experiences of everyday life. The natural aptitude that I seem to have for analysing social phenomena underlines my passion for Psychology; as an amateur psychologist I can imagine no greater satisfaction than embarking on a journey that will ultimately lead me towards the professional field.

Universities applied to:

- Cambridge: Offer
- Warwick: Offer
- Bath: Offer
- Durham: Offer
- St. Andrews: Rejected

Good Points:

This candidate is able to demonstrate a rich range of practical experience in their chosen field, which energises their statement. They are able to clearly articulate how their subject interacts with their personal experiences, which strengthens the force of their argument through its demonstration of their passion for the field. They have tied together a variety of experiences — personal, practical, academic — in favour of their statement, by isolating how each of them contributes to their interests in psychology. This mode of thought and discussion is illustrative of an analytical way of thinking, which in turn, presents the statement as the work of an academically-able student.

Bad Points:

While the candidate quite naturally aims to shine through in their statement, they are running the risk of developing a haughty tone of discussion. As a result, this statement would have benefitted from a relaxation or a focusing of register. Further contributing to this sense of haughtiness is the large amount of personal detail. Although this personal detail does need to be laid as a foundation for discussion more relevant to the topic, the candidate could have streamlined these more anecdotal passages in order to leave room for greater academic consideration. In particular, this candidate could have referenced and utilised a greater range of literary or academic material, since they have ably discussed their more practical experience with their chosen subject area.

Overall:

While this statement very successfully highlights relevant practical experience, it could be strengthened further by greater academic discussion of written material and independent thought. Nonetheless, it is still demonstrative of an analytical mode of thought and an ability to construct an argument from seemingly disparate pieces. The candidate has clearly thought about the relevance of their subject matter both within their own personal context and within a much broader context, which further bolsters their work as that of a capable and curious thinker.

NOTES

ULTIMATE OXBRIDGE PERSONAL STATEMENT GUIDE

EXAMPLE STATEMENTS – PSYCHOLOGY

Subject: Psychological and Behavioural Sciences

"Such a shame she will not study medicine!" I heard several times as my interests finally steered into a university degree. Having grown up with my mum – a psychologist, from primary school I constantly questioned human behaviour. And although parents from small towns dream of their children becoming doctors, phenomena that I saw in my surroundings, like eating disorders or extreme shyness, relentlessly attracted my attention. I knew I needed to pursue an intense educational path to gain the depth of knowledge I desired.

My exceptional curiosity led me to follow the IBO program. Thanks to its curriculum, I relished the opportunity to extend my private research and put it into academic framework. While working independently on my Extended Essay "Should introversion be treated?" I discovered Susan Cain and her book "Quiet: The Power of Introverts". My puzzle of introversion developed into educated distinction for introversion, social anxiety disorder and behavioural inhibitions. In addition, the EE helped me understand the role of biology, encouraging me to start an online course "Introduction to psychology" taught by the University of Toronto. My curiosity still reaches far beyond these introductions and I am looking forward to studying details of brain lobes during biological modules of the course. Moreover, since the subject of eating disorders is too sensitive to be researched in high school, I cannot wait to approach it at an academic level and discuss it with world class experts.

My in-depth, intense processing applies not only to theory, but I also appreciate the material world we live in. Hence, to step out of my comfort zone and into reality, I attended a Business Week program organised by Washington City in Gdansk. My initial function as Vice-President for a business simulation left me with a deep aspiration for a better performance. Therefore, I followed-up Business Week program with an advanced option and became the CEO of my team. Right then I started to appreciate the contribution of every member. I took real pleasure in guiding my team through the processes of marketing, pricing, R&D, production and the construction of a business plan, all of which I understood quickly and precisely thanks to analytical thinking skills I developed during a demanding Maths HL course.

My commitment and eagerness to learn may also be seen by the title of a finalist in the French Language Olympiad, meaning that I reached an advanced level in just two years. Furthermore, I participated in two exchange projects with a Provencal theatre to check my linguistic competencies with native speakers. Although both exchanges were awarded with European Language Label, what counted most was my exceptional chance to explore the French culture inside out. My other interests include French literature, contemporary dancing, horse riding and behavioural economics. The latter led me to the online course organised by the University of Queensland, Australia. The course outlined concepts from Daniel Kahneman's "Thinking Fast and Slow", of which planning fallacy and confirmation bias I consider of greatest importance. Moreover, thanks to good time management I constantly look for other initiatives, such as a charity campaign or volunteering in teaching English or organising TriMUN as Deputy Secretary General. During TriMUN I explained to participants how to follow all the diplomatic procedures - those activities made me wonder about different approaches I had to take in order to teach.

I no longer want psychology to remain only an interest of mine; instead, I need dependable academic tools to understand the research already done. As psychology is a relatively new field of science, early starting form Wundt in 1879, there is still space for much more to be done. I believe that a strong scientific background is crucial for building a career involving communicating with people efficiently and helping them function optimally in our complex material world.

Universities applied to:

- Cambridge: Offer
- Edinburgh: Offer
- University College London: Offer
- St. Andrews: Offer
- Glasgow: Offer

Good Points:

This candidate is able to identify a range of ways in which they have developed their interest in their subject area beyond the demands of their current courses of school-level study. They are also able to demonstrate that they have thought clearly and carefully about what kinds of material they might encounter at the undergraduate level, and how that intersects with both their current interests and their potential areas of interest in the future. In order to have arrived at these opinions, the candidate has read a range of texts and is able to utilise their thoughts on these texts in their statement. As such, they draw together various aspects of their academic pursuits in order to fully paint the picture of themselves as a motivated and tenacious academic student.

Bad Points:

While the candidate is generally able to express themselves clearly, there are moments where the syntax and exact choices of vocabulary seem slightly stilted, suggesting perhaps a non-native speaker or an unedited statement. This slight lapse in language skill does present areas where the communication level is affected, and therefore, puts pressure on the content of the statement as a whole. The statement also relies heavily on anecdotal evidence and does include some slightly uncomfortable generalities. In addition, the candidate would benefit from perhaps adjusting the tone of their moments of personal reflection; the statement has the potential to be read in a way that suggests the writer is arrogant or pompous, and it may well be that this is solely down to word choice rather than intention.

Overall:

Although this statement illustrates the candidate's academic fervour, it does also show areas for potential improvement. It would have been beneficial for the statement as a whole had the candidate maintained a clear and developed level of academic prose throughout, and they could have more clearly linked some of their extra-curricular activities to their chosen course of study. In addition, while the candidate ably discusses texts that they have read in preparation for undergraduate study, these discussions could have taken prominence in the statement, over and above the inclusion of more personal or anecdotal material.

NOTES

MUSIC

Subject: Music

Music means something different to everyone. For me, music is an all consuming passion, evoking emotion and providing intellectual challenge; a highly influential art form which will always remain a constant source of enjoyment and fascination.

Since beginning the violin aged 6, my enthusiasm has continued to grow and after receiving a music bursary on entry to secondary school, I took up the saxophone. Having achieved two grade 8 distinctions, I look forward to the challenge of my grade 8 piano exam in December. Learning such a variety of instruments has not only made me efficient in managing time, but has provided superb opportunities to play in many musical styles. I particularly enjoy playing chamber music and on winning the school's Mary Gough scholarship, funded my attendance of the Pro Corda International Chamber Music Academy, enabling me to play in a range of ensembles guided by inspirational coaches.

An academic and, to me, stimulating aspect of music relates to its history and the influence of certain composers. Recently, I attended a talk on impressionist art and music and was interested to learn how both art forms have developed side by side. I liked exploring how composers created impressions through harmony, rhythm, and tone colour. For instance, Debussy's frequent use of whole tone scales. Attending work experience in the Creative Arts Department at the National Centre for Young People with Epilepsy opened my eyes to yet another facet of music. Here, music therapy is used; it was astonishing and encouraging to see some of the more severely disabled students clap in time. To pursue my interest in music psychology I read 'This is Your Brain on Music' by Daniel Levitin, which drew upon my scientific knowledge. It amazes me that a sound's frequency or timbre has so great an impact on our responses to music. The analytical and investigative skills developed by taking scientific A Levels has also aided my approach to harmonic analysis and I find it useful to take a mathematical slant when harmonising Bach Chorales.

At school, I sing in the Senior and Chamber Choirs and co-lead the Senior and Chamber Orchestras. I am also a member of the Concert Band, Saxophone Quartet and Gospel Choir – which I will be running this year. Being so involved has improved my sight reading and has led to my exposure to a large and varied repertoire; this term I am excited to be performing 'Mozart's 3rd Violin Concerto' with the Orchestra. In preparation, I watched Mozart's opera; 'The Marriage of Figaro'. I look forward to the chance to learn more about opera, particularly after watching an engaging interview with conductor Antonio Pappano. It made me think about the relationship between music and drama and the role of music in influencing the emotions of an audience in scenes which may otherwise be ambiguous.

Aside from music, community work at a local care home and Oxfam shop has developed my interpersonal skills and demonstrating team work was key to our company's success in the Young Enterprise Scheme. As a school prefect, high levels of responsibility are expected. In addition to school work, I took an Open University module entitled 'Life in the Oceans', for which I had to work independently and write essay based answers; skills I know will be useful in further education. I also attend Stagecoach Theatre Arts weekly, successfully auditioning for the national showcase productions of 'Unsinkable' in 2009 and 'My Fair Lady' in 2010. I was intrigued to watch the work of a professional musical director as he arranged, taught and conducted the music and am keen to develop skills in these areas in the future.

I am excited by the prospect of a studying music in higher education as I seek to answer some of the many questions I have whilst furthering my practical ability. I feel prepared for the challenges of university life and am a highly motivated student who will endeavour to carry out all work to the best of my ability.

Universities applied to:

- Cambridge: Offer
- Manchester: Offer
- Bristol: Offer
- Royal Holloway: Offer
- King's: Offer

Good Points:

The strength of this application is in its clear articulation of thorough engagement with its subject. The applicant is able to clearly demonstrate how their subject intersects with their personal life at various junctures and ties their extra-curricular activities to their academic application well. The applicant alludes to specific musical achievements, but more impressively, is able to demonstrate how these achievements make them a suitable candidate for university study; they do not rely on the strength of the achievements alone to speak for themselves. In addition to their practical achievements, the candidate references works that they have pursued beyond the bounds of their course. In particular, the initiative taken by the candidate in being both a member and a leader of groups is illustrative of their commitment.

Bad Points:

While this candidate is able to clearly demonstrate their dedication to practical musicianship, their consideration of academic music study is slimmer in content. It would have strengthened their application to allude in greater detail to areas of interest in a more academic/research context. The applicant could also be slightly warier of using quite personal/informal ways of articulating their experience and thoughts. Their use of technical vocabulary is also relatively sparse and remains quite general. Greater specificity and consideration in their use of terminology would have given greater indication of their seriousness about academic study.

Overall:

While this application illustrates the writer's longstanding engagement with music on a practical level, it could do with greater in-depth analysis of particular works or reference to independent academic study or thought. The applicant demonstrates how they have pursued their subject beyond the expectations of A Level, and is successful in tying together their personal projects and academic interests. The applicant writes in a consistently clear and articulate style, which could be further embellished with academic inflection.

NOTES

Subject: Music

I have enjoyed music for as long as I can remember. As I have grown up, my enjoyment has become a deep fascination. The more I learn about music the more the subject impresses and excites me. I find myself thinking, talking and reading about music more and more. I have come to realise that music will always be a major part of my life and my hope is I will be able to make it the focus of my career. I can therefore think of no better way of spending the next three years than by deepening my understanding and appreciation of music.

Performing with clarinet, piano and voice first drew me to music and continues to give me great pleasure; but it is the breadth of music as a subject which has driven my growing enthusiasm for it. On reading 'Music: A Very Short Introduction' by Nicholas Cook I was struck by the idea that all descriptions of music involve metaphor. The crux of this idea; that we approach music as if it were a kind of shape-shifting object; helped me to understand the satisfaction I get from studying it. This was reinforced by thinking about music in the context of my other A level subjects: Maths, English and History. Music can be approached as a mathematical problem which is resolved through identifying patterns of harmony and form. It can be analysed like literature in terms of the effect of its 'patterns' upon those experiencing it, such as intended meaning, emotional impact and mood. Or it can be looked at in a historical context; the influences upon it and its affects, as one would understand a historical artefact. All of this enhances the immediate appreciation of music through performance or listening, as well as the pleasure of composition. I believe it is the diversity of ways in which music is experienced and understood that interests me most.

As well as enlightening me on many of the key moments that led our music to sound as it does today, the book 'Big Bangs' by Howard Goodall, impressed me with the notion that, in regards to music, we are standing on the 'tip' of something that has been continuously present throughout human history. I increasingly seem to experience this as a tangible feeling when practising and performing, especially in ensembles. I think this why I so enjoy being part of school groups: Jazz Band, Wind Band, Clarinet Group, Orchestra and Choir, and county groups: North Bedfordshire Youth Chamber Orchestra and Bedfordshire Youth Orchestra. At the recent Eton Choral Course I attended, I became more familiar with choral repertoire and consort singing. Again, I enjoyed experiencing the development of music through performing choral works from Monteverdi to Rose. Attending the premiere of James Macmillan's choral work 'Credo' at the 2012 BBC Proms made me feel that I was witnessing the very 'tip' of musical development advancing. I look forward to continuing my involvement in ensembles at university, both as part of wider university life and as part of the course.

Aside from taking part in ensembles, I have pursued my interest in music by taking ABRSM practical exams, achieving grade 8 Distinction in clarinet, grade 7 Distinction in piano and grade 7 Merit in singing. I am now looking forward to taking the ABRSM diploma on clarinet. I am also working on an EPQ in music, for which I am composing a new score for the silent film 'The Cabinet of Dr Caligari'. This is allowing me to explore composition in more depth than at A level and to research German art music as an influence. Through my musical activities and others, I have also aimed to develop organisational skills, initiative and leadership abilities. This includes managing the staging and performance of my EPQ, undertaking my Duke of Edinburgh Gold Award, work experience in a school music department and weekend work in a local supermarket. I believe such personal skills will help me practically channel my love of music so that I can achieve my full musical potential at university and beyond.

Universities applied to:

- Oxford: Offer
- Manchester: Offer
- Birmingham: Offer
- York: Offer
- Durham: Offer

Good Points:

This candidate is able to clearly articulate their dedication to practical music-making, and can further bolster this interest with instances of academic pursuit of the topic. Discussing their EPQ helps to demonstrate how their practical and academic interests are already relating to each other, and it indicates how it might continue to do so at university level. By combining instances of personal enjoyment (such as concert attendance) with references to specific texts, this candidate helps themselves to stand out as a student that both applies themselves academically and goes out of their way to incorporate their academic interests in their everyday life. They are able to discuss the potential impacts of their subject on both a micro level (its impact on them personally), and on a macro level (where it is situated in broader contexts of academic thought).

Bad Points:

While the candidate does discuss academic lines of thought and research in their area, these elements are somewhat sparser than their instances of practical experience. It could be a potential area of development to redistribute the weight of their material; the courses they are **applying** for are geared to a more academic focus, and are not solely courses in practical musicianship. The candidate should also take care over using too many instances of subjective experience — although it is important for them to underline the subject's impact on them personally, there is room in this statement for a more focused line of argument about their academic pursuits, and that would have potentially added more value than an insight into their broader, hypothetical hopes for the future.

Overall:

This statement is strong in its ability to demonstrate a range of interests and a variety of instances in which their interest have been practically exercised. However, it could be developed further by more rigorously using it to demonstrate their academic lines of interest. Though the candidate has expressed their interest in areas of academic research, and they are able to discuss how their interests connect across different disciplines, these areas of discussion could be further explored in order to best demonstrate their ability as a candidate preparing to undertake a theoretical music degree.

NOTES

Subject: Music

I cannot remember a time when music was not the most important aspect of my life. Whether through playing piano from the age of 5, or through 6 years of study at the Royal Academy of Music's Junior Department, music has never ceased to be my passion. I have developed a keen interest in the analytical and historical side of musical study in my composition lessons at JRAM. It has been fascinating to explore developments in musical harmony, tonality and style, such as Bach's fugal expositions and the Serialist techniques of Schoenberg and Webern and to subsequently incorporate such ideas into my wider understanding of musical theory. Exploring my creativity through freer styles of composition set for a range of ensembles, including a rondo for string quartet and a tone poem for choir with orchestra, has broadened my perception of harmony. Additionally, I have refined my skills as a performing pianist and flautist through my appointment as principle flute in the Buckinghamshire County Youth Orchestra, and more recently through winning the prestigious Chamber Prize at JRAM in a piano trio. I have also enjoyed the exciting and motivating atmosphere at the Academy, where Supporting Musicianship lessons have provided an insight into the vast history of Western music. I have built upon this foundation through wider reading of books such as Cook's 'Music: A Very Short Introduction' and, more specifically to my interests, Taruskin's 'On Russian Music'.

Throughout my education I have proved to be a diligent and capable student, with the ability to manage a large and demanding workload. Whilst maintaining a 6-day working week with my Saturday's spent at JRAM I have attained two grade 8 distinctions, as well as excelling in my academic work. My competitive nature allows me to thrive in a challenging atmosphere and I am often praised for my ability to contribute regularly and thoughtfully in lessons. I have committed to playing organ for my local church weekly and to teaching piano and theory to a number of students. I play an active role in the musical life of the school and wider community, not only involved in my own school's ensembles and choirs, but also accompanying the choir of a school for disabled students, which I have found incredibly rewarding.

After performing Tchaikovsky's 4th Symphony with the BCYO, I realised my budding interest in late-Romantic Russian music, and have since developed my knowledge of this era in my reading. My studies led me to consider the changes in Russian ballet music that can be seen in the work of the subsequent generation of composers, focusing most closely on the legacies of Stravinsky's 'Rite of Spring' in comparison to the more traditionally Romantic ballet music of Tchaikovsky's 'Swan Lake'. By examining these scores, and studying some of the scholarly discourse surrounding them, I have developed my ability to listen to and analyse music, which has deepened my desire to continue my studies to degree level. Although I have long-suspected that music would be my chosen subject at university, I have maintained a keen interest in my other studies. I am an able linguist, studying French at A-Level as well as having taken Italian lessons out of school, which combined with English Literature has broadened my ability to analyse and write in a cohesive way. By taking Mathematics, I have struck a balance between creativity and practicality in my studies, which will enable me to thrive on the varied challenges presented by a music degree.

For me, music is about much more than just performance. Although I enjoy playing the piano, my real passion is for developing my understanding of the wider meaning and significance of music and examining the techniques employed by composers to communicate with their audiences. I would relish the opportunity to immerse myself in the study of music and know that I have the potential to bring as much to the course as I would want to take from it.

Universities applied to:

- Cambridge: Offer
- Manchester: Offer
- King's: Offer
- Bristol: Offer
- Southampton: Offer

Good Points:

Through the inclusion of a wide range of examples, the applicant is able to show how music has impacted their life beyond their course and can keenly demonstrate their commitment to their subject. They are able to present themselves as a well-rounded individual with a great deal to offer. They allude to instances where they have considered music from a profound, critical standpoint, and are able to reference material that they are particularly interested in. Throughout the statement, the applicant articulates themselves concisely and intelligently, drawing upon academic vocabulary where appropriate. They are able to give concrete examples of their achievements and can refer to how this contributes to their general strength as an applicant.

Bad Points:

While the applicant's academic potential is clear, their use of overly confident language and self-presentation has the potential to represent them as slightly arrogant. As such, given they are clearly a capable applicant, their tone seems to do them a disservice. This statement would benefit from going beyond the use of facts or bald statements, and instead, embellishing these or developing them into a more useful part of their statement - either by justifying them with evidence or by using them as a springboard to furthering their statement. As a general rule throughout the statement, the applicant is most persuasive at moments where they use clear evidence and examples to express their thoughts and are least persuasive at points where they fail to fully articulate themselves through anecdotal or subjective discussion. While the applicant references works beyond the remit of their A Level, their examples remain relatively mainstream and could be more reflective of a significant and actioned interest in reading/listening around their subject.

Overall:

This application seems to represent the work of an able practical musician, but by comparison, offers less information about academic interests. While the statement is authoritative and confident in tone, it runs the risk of conveying an arrogance to the reader. The applicant could draw on a greater range of academic interests and could demonstrate this more clearly through a wider variety of explored works and independent thought. This statement is powered by the applicant's enthusiasm, which remains clear throughout the writing. The applicant is able to indicate how they involve their interest in their subject elsewhere in their life - and in turn, they demonstrate how these examples contribute to their suitability as an applicant more broadly.

NOTES

ENGLISH

Subject: English

Everyday life as a subject and ordinary people as protagonists are integral to the nature of literature. Wordsworth stepped away from the "gaudiness and inane phraseology of…modern writers" towards "situations from common life"- allying accessible poetry with a moral centre. This is a progression from the works of Shakespeare (plays for common men), despite heroes like King Lear fitting Aristotle's tragic archetype of "an imitation of persons… above the common level". Becoming no better than 'Tom O'Bedlam', Lear's fall from the "bias of nature" evokes the intended tragic effect through his loss of position and sanity. However, I agree that the common man and ordinary life may be as appropriate subjects for both tragedy and literature. McCrum's notion that motifs "drawn from ordinary life… (enthral)" echoes Arthur Miller's 'Tragedy and the Common Man'. Feste's declaration in 'Twelfth Night' that "A sentence is/ but a cheveril glove to a good wit: how quickly the/ wrong side may be turned outward!" epitomises major themes through an everyday object; both glove and world are turned inside out, as though the traditional Lord of Misrule is present within the plot.

My EPQ has further explored the ambitions of Wordsworth and Shelley in their poetry, relative to what poetry should achieve and the poet's role. 'To A Skylark' exemplifies Shelley's desire to enable the observer to experience beauty, with illustrations of clear celestial images of the "unbodied joy", a parallel to his desire as a poet; to provide delight, yet remain aloof. In contrast, Wordsworth's didactic purpose is evident in 'Simon Lee', in his subject choice of common humanity, instructing the reader to consider such acts of compassion as unremarkable.

A similar 'exemplum' of moral ideals is achieved in Chaucer's 'Franklin's Tale', scrutinising the existence of providence and the necessity of 'trouthe' through both his 'Breton lai' fairytale itself, and the narrator not of noble birth. The Prologue uses the idiosyncrasies of the main character to generate concerns of 'gentillesse', striving to render himself 'gentil' through imparting his knowledge of classical poetry to the more socially elevated of his company. Thus the text stands as a component in illustrating, through 'The Canterbury Tales', a cross-section of characters from medieval England, and their desires in relation to their places in society.

Virginia Woolf's exploration of the reflections of her characters in her 'Mrs Dalloway' achieves a multi-faceted examination of a patriarchal and pious section of English society and the oppression it inflicts upon each character. An echo of Joyce's use of the internal monologue, 'Mrs Dalloway' serves as a successful integration of several individuals' musings on one day. The disparity between the often mundane thoughts of the protagonists and the singular, outstanding event of Septimus' suicide appears to mirror Clarissa's own struggle to balance her internal perspective with the external world.

Work experience with a Channel 4 drama provided me with an insight into the problems of adapting text to screen, while emphasising the importance of collaboration and time management. These skills translate naturally into continual participation in school drama and my role as Chair of the Yearbook Committee, while demonstrating my creative passion that also surfaces through artwork and Grade 8 piano. My early years in Botswana and a charity trip to Romania have made me aware not only of another culture, but the nature of life in developing societies.

T S Eliot states that "a perception, not only of the pastness of the past, but of its presence" is imperative for a full comprehension of a text, relative to the "simultaneous order" of other literature. I aim to develop this awareness of intertextuality both in close and comparative reading, as well as the element of my own interpretation that is essential for not only University but a lifelong appreciation of literature.

Universities applied to:

- Oxford: Offer
- Bristol: Offer
- Durham: Rejected
- Leeds: Offer
- Royal Holloway: Offer

Good Points:

Through quotation and reference, this statement clearly and efficiently demonstrates a dedication to reading a wide variety of text. The applicant has also managed to embed these quotations/allusions in segments of their own thought, thereby illustrating their ability not just to absorb texts but also their ability to apply their own critical approach. The statement consistently and accurately uses terminology which is specific to critical theory, which further bolsters the applicant's statement as one which reflects their interest in literary studies. The more personal information that the applicant provides is well-tied to their subject area — and they also allude to their EPQ research in a way that is helpful to the statement; they do not simply state that they have done an EPQ, but they are able to discuss why their work is useful and what it has revealed to them.

Bad Points:

Though the range of quotations is impressive, the statement does read as a relatively fragmented survey of their reading; each paragraph seems watertight, but an overall argument is unclear. The applicant, therefore, runs the risk of peacocking their reading habits rather than cohesively structuring their statement towards an overall goal. In addition, this concentration of literary references also makes the statement appear slightly airless — the most personal information at the end is useful in counterbalancing this, but the statement is perhaps toeing the line of not giving away a great deal about the applicant as a well-rounded student.

Overall:

This statement confidently and impressively discusses a number of relevant areas of interest within their chosen subject. It combines the use of literary sources with careful independent thought and demonstrates a commitment to going above and beyond the classroom demands imposed on them for A Level (or equivalent). The applicant shows a clear and focused commitment to their subject and incorporates more personal details to produce a statement that gives a good indication of their overall character and calibre.

NOTES

Subject: English

Growing up in a house where books have replaced wallpaper, acquiring a love of literature was inevitable. I love the way in which writers explore, question, and critique aspects of human nature through the presentation of their worlds and characters. My favourite pieces of writing are ones such as Levi's 'Order on the Cheap', Gogol's 'The Overcoat' or Hartley's 'The Go Between', where a particular human tendency is both beautifully presented and meticulously analysed. In his short story, Levi explores curiosity by invoking that of his audience: readers become distracted by the narrator's descriptions of his experiments and overlook their morally problematic side. Hartley employs an opposite technique, allowing the reader to be often sharply aware of the innocence and naivety of the protagonist. Gogol manipulates the reader even more, invoking a painful sense of pathos around the main character whilst at the same time daring us to find Akaky's concerns a little ridiculous.

I have to admit, however, that I am drawn to Levi's short story not only because of its literary merits, but also because I sympathise with its main character: a man driven by his fascination with the process of creation. My favourite parts of my Chemistry A level were the 'practicals'; I derived great excitement from the process of taking a simple substance, subjecting it to particular conditions, and thereby creating a completely different, and often much more complex, chemical. In 'The Monkey's Wrench' Levi seems to emulate the same process in his development of the character of Tino. Starting from a simple first picture Tino is slowly developed, snippet by snippet, as the stories progress, until a fully evolved character finally emerges.

I find it fascinating how unexpected links can suddenly emerge between works: reading around a set text, Murakami's 'Blind Willow Sleeping Woman', I read his 'Kafka on the Shore', which led me to read some of Kafka's short stories, including 'The Penal Colony' and 'A Country Doctor'. Whilst the works of the two writers are in many ways extremely different, I noticed some stylistic similarities. Both present protagonists whose apparently unexceptional lives are suddenly interrupted by a series of unexplained fantastical events. These events are often a metaphor for a wider-reaching process in the life of the narrator.

But without a doubt, poetry has always been my favourite form of literature: I like listening to poems or reading them aloud, appreciating their rhythm and sound, before going back and analysing them. Some of my favourite poems are those in which the sound is almost as important as the words themselves, for example, Lawrence's 'Ship of Death' or Frost's 'After Apple Picking'. In this vein, I have a YouTube channel on which I post my readings of various poems, and have also earned at least several pence through poetry busking in the streets of Waterloo.

Eagleton's 'Literary Theory: an Introduction' gave me another way in which to approach texts. As well as my visceral response and the various meanings extracted through analysis, the texts might exemplify the literary or political beliefs of a particular period. Further, members of different literary movements might approach them in very different ways - I enjoyed trying to put on the 'mask' of one movement or another and read a poem through it. Similarly, whilst studying 'Othello' I was interested by the hugely varying approaches of different critics, from Bradley who focused chiefly on character but seemed to forget the literary context, to Empson who concentrated almost solely on the changing meaning of the word 'honest' throughout time. Perhaps most significantly, Eagleton and the other critics reinforced the idea that engaging with a text is itself a creative process.

However, Eagleton's book is just 'an Introduction': what draws me most to the study of English literature is not only that I love it, but that I want so much to learn more about it.

Universities applied to:

- Cambridge: Offer
- Durham: Offer
- Sussex: Offer
- University College London: Offer
- King's: Offer

Good Points:

The candidate clearly demonstrates a keen and actioned interest in their chosen subject through the presentation of their reading and subsequent thoughts. They can articulate their present interests in their subject as well as the sources of these interests and their potential directions for further development. They indicate their ability to think laterally and creatively through their cohesive discussions of seemingly disparate texts, and are self-aware in their strengths and weaknesses as a reader. Their statement is fuelled by their evident personal enthusiasm for their subject, which makes it an engaging and urgent read.

Bad Points:

The candidate has acquired a relatively personal tone, which veers into the casual or confessional at times; their point might have been made more clearly or precisely had they adopted more strictly academic modes of communicating. Their consideration of various works is quite itemised, insofar as their statement reads as a series of 'nuggets' of information rather than a clearly-focused piece with argument and direction. The candidate does reference another subject they study for A Level, but beyond that, they have not included much information beyond their academic reading and interests. While this could certainly be justified as an approach, it does leave the statement suggesting that the writer is not particularly engaged in questions or activities beyond specific areas of literature.

Overall:

The statement is at times quite chaotic in style due to its familiar tone and slightly haphazard structure. However, it more than compensates for this since its familiarity is clearly a result of the candidate's sheer enthusiasm for the subject. In addition, the range of material that they consider is very impressive — it includes both primary texts (of various forms) and secondary reading. The candidate has, moreover, articulated their own ideas on these works, and even if their exact communication of these is not particularly precise, the level of thought and consideration is still strong.

NOTES

Subject: English Language & Literature

George Eliot's metaphor for imagination- 'inward light which is the last refinement of Energy ... bathing even the ethereal atoms in its ideally illuminated space'- is beautiful. The powerful image supported by the underlying liquid consonants skilfully leads to the action it describes, but it is also the suggestion of particle physics and mass-energy equivalence that interests me about this quotation. In this way, I have gained more from reading 'Middlemarch' as I appreciate Eliot's constant links between science and fiction, and I believe scientific study has generally sharpened my abilities of analysis and concise expression.

I have loved working as a steward at the Globe Theatre; I had the opportunity to see many plays, including a production of Marlowe's 'Dr Faustus'. I read Dante's 'Inferno' and several books of Milton's 'Paradise Lost' for a different portrayal of hell and sin to that depicted in 'Dr Faustus'. I found the torment and suffering described by Dante graphic, whilst the first person narrative drew me closer to the pathos fear and disgust expressed. Milton's depiction of a mental state is much more powerful in my opinion, and has interesting parallels to Faustus' state of damnation. I also saw Shakespeare's 'As You Like It', 'All's Well that Ends Well' and 'Much Ado About Nothing' whilst stewarding. 'Much Ado About Nothing' reminded me of the surprising similarity between Shakespeare's comedies and tragedies. Claudio and Hero's troubled love and Don John's self-proclaimed villainy seem to mirror the actions of Othello, Desdemona and Iago. Viewing comedy as a structure, 'Much Ado' contains the potential tragedy of 'Othello', but an added last act resolves all tensions and ends so happily and neatly that it seems to me rather unrealistic.

I enjoyed Dickens' 'Our Mutual Friend' for its satirical portrayal of superficial London society. His depiction of characters and scenes make the novel humorous and therefore very different to 'A Tale of Two Cities'. Here, the powerful characterisation emphasises the terrible human suffering and moral corruption, for example his effective personification of 'La Vengeance', who encourages the cries of bloodlust from Parisians. I found it easier to empathise with Jude in Hardy's 'Jude the Obscure' than with Dickens' creations however, since his actions appear futile against the fate which continually works against him. There seems to be no hope in the novel, unlike the eventual triumph of love over death in 'A Tale of Two Cities'. Just as in 'Tess of the d'Urbervilles' and 'A Pair of Blue Eyes', love and happiness seem only like a prelude to grief and sorrow linked with the relentless passing of time. I find Donne's approaches to this theme interesting too: in both his love poems and the Holy Sonnets, Donne uses form to counter and control the passing of time and the prospect of change.

I have participated in many music groups and ensembles at school, having achieved Grade 8 with distinction in both Flute and French Horn. I have worked for two years in my local Cancer Research shop as part of the Gold Duke of Edinburgh award, and also spent a residential week with a charity called Activenture, looking after children of different ages and abilities, for which I received the Young Carer of the Year award. During my gap year, I plan to join my local orchestra and travel for three months around South America, but ultimately I am most excited about the time I will have to read and further explore English literature.

EXAMPLE STATEMENTS - ENGLISH

Universities applied to:

- Oxford: Offer
- Durham: Rejected
- St. Andrews: Offer
- Exeter: Offer
- Bath: Offer

Good Points:

The candidate's wide range of personal interests are clearly demonstrated, and — for the most part — are well-linked to their subject application, giving it further strength. They are able to use independent thought to illustrate how various bits of reading they have done are linked. The list of works they discuss range from poetry to plays to Victorian novels; a strong variety of works. They evaluate these across genres and are able to apply critical thought and analysis to them. Throughout their discussions of various texts, the applicant clearly illustrates their enthusiasm for the subject; their writing is energised by positivity and personal engagement with the material.

Bad Points:

The candidate could have worked even harder to connect their extra-curricular activities to their application (though their relevance was clear in most instances). The effect of the applicant's use of independent thought and personal experience was often slightly dulled by their use of highly personal and personalising terms such as 'beautiful', or simply 'I enjoyed'. Though there is perhaps nothing wrong with these evaluations as an initial starting point, the candidate could have pushed further with their readings to interrogate these works further. Although the applicant demonstrates a wide literary foundation, their commentary did at times lapse into plot summary, which is less interesting than their own thought.

Overall:

This candidate's application reads as both impressive in its depth of knowledge and personal in its illustration of thought and enthusiasm. As such, it reads as a statement that is well-balanced and well-judged; the reader is able to get a good sense of this applicant's interests on both a personal and academic level. The statement could have made greater use of critical language and could have included fewer instances of value judgements; small alterations which would have given the candidate's discussions greater academic depth.

NOTES

Subject: English Language & Literature

Losing my hearing to meningitis aged four, I quickly found books to be the most accessible entertainment available to me. My disability did not impair my ability to engage with and enjoy literature, evoking an interest that refused to diminish, with reading remaining my favourite pastime today.

A significant part of my reading has focused on fantasy works, read to capture my imagination, such as Brent Weeks' 'Night Angel' trilogy. Often, I found that the worlds created within demonstrate the power of literature to intoxicate readers. It seemed logical to me, therefore, to root my Extended Project within this genre, examining which attributes of fantasy novels give them their unique appeal to readers of all ages. After attending an open day for English applicants last February, I was encouraged to challenge myself further in my reading, with more classical and thought provoking works. Reading Bram Stoker's 'Dracula', I noticed the dark, gothic themes dominate the usual Victorian setting, and I enjoyed comparing the original characters to those found in the numerous adaptations available today. Iain Banks' 'The Wasp Factory' allowed me to compare the gothic horror ideals in a modern perspective. In particular, the focus of the novel was much more on the warped cognitive processes of the protagonist, which instilled a grim foreboding as the novel progressed, with the characters remaining mysterious and unpredictable.

Visiting the Thiepval memorial on the Somme battlefield in France, and reciting Laurence Binyon's 'For the Fallen' to a gathering inspired me greatly. Seeing the multitude of graves helped me visualise the scale of The Great War. This in turn assisted my understanding of the renowned 'Birdsong' by Sebastian Faulks, as well as touching me personally. Experiencing the location first-hand provided me with a chance to appreciate how horrific battles played out but also gave me a more understanding voice when writing about such texts. I then decided to read Seamus Heaney's modern translation of 'Beowulf', to discover how ancient tales of battle were presented and found both the pace and action in the poem unrelenting.

Some of the archaic phrases, such as 'ring-giver' for king, also added beauty to the poet's voice, making it an even more captivating read. I recently saw a performance of Shakespeare's 'The Taming of the Shrew' at the Globe Theatre, where the audience participation and beautiful language made for a memorable afternoon, as well as boosting my confidence when studying the play in class.

Being fortunate enough for my performance to feature captions enhanced my experience further, as I was able to concentrate less on listening, and more fully on the action onstage. The modernisation of the opening scene showed me how adaptable Shakespeare is to all audiences, with the portrayal of Christophero Sly as a football hooligan swiftly engaging the crowd.

Being a mentor to two other hearing impaired pupils, at different stages of their education, has helped me show empathy to others, by helping them adapt to get the most of their schooling experience. My role as a one to one mentor was complemented by participation in a Pyramid Club scheme in which I assisted children with low self-esteem at a local primary school. I manage the rest of my free time working in a pharmacy, where I communicate with the public, manage money and work within a team. Currently, I am also studying to pass my MCA (medicine counter assistant) course, so I can legally take a more active role in the pharmacy.

I believe I have the right attitude to study English at university as I am passionate about reading and always challenge myself in my work. My determination would also assist me in my studies, while helping me overcome any difficulties faced. Above all, the chance to read great literature, under professional guidance, presents itself as an experience I am eager to approach with commitment and enthusiasm.

Universities applied to:

- Oxford: Offer
- Durham: Offer
- Newcastle: Offer
- York: Offer
- Warwick: Offer

Good Points:

As a result of both the content and the writing style, this statement reads as the work of an applicant that has devoted a significant amount of time to literature. They are able to reference and effectively call upon a range of texts and can furthermore articulate their thoughts using language in an elevated, precise, and academic register. This language is used accurately throughout the statement, and on both a large and more micro scale — in close-reading and more structurally analytical contexts. Beyond their purely academic focus, the applicant is also able to communicate a range of more personal facts that contribute to the overall image of this statement as one written by a well-rounded and engaged student.

Bad Points:

The statement, at times, felt oddly weighted; the applicant dwells for relatively long amounts of time on quite diminutive moments or events, but yet also strides through quite broad considerations of dense texts. As such, the statement could be made to be more cohesive and flowing if it were to be slightly restructured. The applicant seems quite guided by ideas of the canon and reputation, and there are instances where they supplicate to popular view rather than going into their own thoughts — it would have been an even more critically urgent statement had the applicant consistently called upon their own independent thinking. At points, the statement felt structurally guided by the applicant's route through their own memory; it would have given the statement more directional focus if it had instead been energised by an argument or goal, rather than using a more anecdotal mode of communication.

Overall:

Through eloquent discussion of a range of material, this statement effectively communicates the applicant's profound engagement with their chosen subject. This particular applicant deals maturely, concisely, and usefully with their own unique set of personal circumstances, which is to be commended. While the statement clearly indicates the applicant's capacity for engaging and complex thinking, it is nevertheless written in a rather sprawling structure that would benefit from some streamlining or re-balancing.

NOTES

MODERN LANGUAGES

Subject: French

France has developed a literature of unequalled richness and variety. Europeans in any age have had few thoughts, desires, or fantasies that a French writer somewhere has not expressed - it has given the Western mind an image of itself. In this sense, French literature serves as a pool in which many cultures meet. Therefore, in particular, it is French literature's universality which interests me.

Nevertheless, I enjoy how literature provides a window into an author's contemporary society. For example, 'Madame Bovary' draws us into Flaubert's disgust for the bourgeois existence of the 19th century; Zola's 'Thérèse Raquin' invites us into the leprous lower-depths of Paris. I am interested in how both these writers, unparalleled in their psychological clarity and narrative muscle, provide such a brutal and relentless account of their chosen subject matter: for Flaubert, the indulgent decadence of the bourgeoisie, exemplified by Emma Bovary; for Zola, the moral dankness of the murderous lovers. In addition, I have watched Kassovitz's 'La Haine' and Truffaut's 'Les quatre cents coups', both similar to Zola and Flaubert in their rigorous exploration of character. Focusing on social outcasts, these films act as an exposition of societal problems. 'La Haine' sheds light on the all-encompassing violence and cultural exclusion of the suburbs of Paris, while 'Les quatre cent coups' reveals the shocking injustices in the treatment of juvenile offenders. Thus, such French cinema serves to illuminate the neglected – I relish this narrative potential in the discovery of truth.

Besides these more realistic works, both my English and French A Levels have introduced me to Absurdism. I have appreciated the works of Beckett ('Fin de partie', 'En attendant Godot') and Ionesco ('La Cantatrice Chauve', 'Rhinocéros'). These tragicomedies simultaneously entertain and provoke – the reason why I found them so enjoyable and yet so powerful. To pursue this interest in Absurdism, I read Voltaire's absurd 'contes philosophiques', 'Candide' and 'Micromegas'. Fiction, I found, proved to be the perfect medium of expression for Voltaire's empiricism and scepticism. Therefore, like the tragicomedies of the 20th century, I thought Voltaire's work succeeded both as entertainment and as an accessible manifesto of his philosophical beliefs. Furthermore, I decided to follow up this interest in such 'contes philosophiques' by undertaking an Edexcel Extended Project, entitled 'Ancient Influence on French Existentialist Literature', for which I was awarded an A*. Here, I focused on why Camus, in 'Le Mythe de Sisyphe', Sartre, in 'Les Mouches', and Anouilh, in 'Antigone', chose to use classical themes and motifs to communicate their own particular perception of Existentialism. Despite its challenges, the more I worked at this project, the more certain I was that this is what and how I would like to study.

Moreover, I have taken an interest in symbolist French poetry. Having studied some poetry by Baudelaire ('Les Fleurs du Mal') and Verlaine ('Romances sans paroles'), I have become fascinated by the crippling and contrasting emotions communicated in these poems. I now admire how the very sound of the French language can control the register of a poem and, thus, highlight its true meaning even amongst the most abstract, intangible imagery, employed by Baudelaire and Verlaine. I am intrigued by the French language in part due to this precision.

Finally, I contributed regularly to my school's Modern Languages magazine, 'Babel', and have competed in 'Les Joutes Oratoires', a national French debating competition in which I reached the final. Through these experiences, I have begun to thoroughly enjoy communicating in French. I believe an extra language extends one's range. It releases you from the inertia of one cultural gear – a change of perspective that I find truly enlightening and enjoyable. I will be working in Paris from January to March.

Universities applied to:

- Oxford: Offer
- Durham: Offer
- Edinburgh: Offer
- Exeter: Offer
- Newcastle: Offer

Good Points:

Throughout this statement, the applicant engages consistently with a range of French texts at a very advanced level. The applicant is able to demonstrate not only an awareness of a huge tranche of French literature but also how specific works intersect. This comparative criticism is carried out by the applicant across several different forms in a manner that is lucid and impressive. The applicant has mentioned their personal research and is able to indicate why it is interesting and relevant. They are also able to indicate how their personal pursuits are reciprocally and beneficially related to their academic studies.

Bad Points:

At particular moments, this applicant veers from an academic register into an overtly formal one; a stylistic turn which, while remaining clear in meaning, is a little jarring. More personal information would have been a welcome addition to this statement, especially since its academic calibre is so relentlessly clear throughout; the statement has the potential to be slightly breathless in its rapid consideration of big swathes of literature. The statement could, therefore, have happily absorbed more personal information without diluting its clear academic potential. In addition, the candidate could have taken slightly more care over their phrasing, which occasionally takes a tone bordering on reductive or patronising; a risk which is perhaps not worth taking in this context.

Overall:

The candidate effectively and efficiently communicates a level of cultural awareness which goes far above and beyond the demands of their curriculum. They are able to demonstrate how they practically carry forward their interests in extra-curricular and academic activities. Throughout the statement, the applicant engages a muscular, academically-considered tone which is clear and authoritative. There was room in the statement for greater personal depth and warmth, and for greater justification for some of the strong academic arguments being posed.

NOTES

Subject: French & German

Living in an interconnected world makes studying languages fundamental, as they enable us to interact with a wide array of people and develop the attributes of empathy and cultural awareness. My ardour for French led me to complete three language summer schools this year at: UCL, University of Cambridge and Lancaster University. I attended numerous lectures exploring enthralling topics I had not previously considered, including: surrealism, language diglossia and dialectology. A lecture from Dr M.Griffin at Cambridge on Medieval French Literature was particularly engaging. We studied de France's lais 'Bisclarvet' and compared its themes with those of the contemporary novel 'Truismes.' The lecture inspired me to begin reading a broader assemblage of French literature from across the literary époques. At Lancaster University, I obtained the academic award for languages due to my participation in seminars, research into minority languages and concluding presentation, demonstrating my capability to work at university level. The research I carried out at Lancaster encouraged me to commence an EPQ based on sociolinguistics and the argument surrounding language and identity. Taking ab-initio language lessons at UCL has impelled me to begin an AS course in German this year.

My curiosity for French and German literature and cinema has incentivised me to keep a film and reading journal, analysing the works that I encounter. Alongside this, I research the historical, philosophical and political contexts behind these pieces, which is pivotal to appreciate the themes and ideas presented. Watching the German film 'Nosferatu', I found that its themes and visual presentation were atypical of other German films I had see, leading me to research German Expressionism. I discovered that the arts of this period are analogous to one another and I believe they reflect Germany's political, social and economic situation at the time. French literature from the classical, enlightenment and romantic époques is of particular interest to me. Across these literary periods, I noticed disparities in tone and style; the conventions governing the way the playwrights Racine and Molière wrote are a stark contrast with the freedom in the works of Hugo and Chateaubriand. Reading Pascal's 'Pensées' and Voltaire's 'Candide' furthers my understanding of the philosophical ideas during those periods, whilst Price's 'A Concise History of France' introduces the historical events in France at the time. I also appreciate modern French literature and find it fascinating to compare these texts with those I read for my A-Level English Literature course. Gide's 'L'Immoraliste', Joffo's 'Un Sac de Billes' and Sartre's 'La Nausée' are decidedly compelling novels as each diversely questions the human condition. For October, I have arranged work experience in France and will stay with a host family, providing an opportunity to develop my oral and aural skills and gain an insight into French life.

As the French Ambassador in my Sixth Form, I offer support to fellow A-Level students. Additionally, I mentor GCSE language students, assist in lower-school lessons, promote languages at open events and have achieved the Foreign Language Leader Award. Through these activities I can share my ardour for languages and develop communication and leadership skills. As a member of Erasmus+, last year I collaborated with students from across Europe to tackle racism. Each country involved presented its ideas at an inspirational meeting in Spain. I now identify myself as more than a British Citizen; I am a Global Citizen. I regularly carry out exchanges with other Erasmus+ students, thus developing my cultural awareness.

My avidity for language learning and cultural appreciation has assured me that languages are the ideal degree for me. I greatly anticipate university study and having the possibility to refine my linguistic skills and develop international awareness.

ULTIMATE OXBRIDGE PERSONAL STATEMENT GUIDE
EXAMPLE STATEMENTS – MODERN LANGUAGES

Universities applied to:

- Oxford: Offer
- St. Andrews: Offer
- University College London: Offer
- Warwick: Offer
- University of London Institute in Paris: Offer

Good Points:

By engaging with a range of French texts and by calling on anecdotal evidence of strong academic engagement outside of the classroom, this candidate is able to efficiently demonstrate their continued and widely-applied enthusiasm for their subject. They are able to assemble information that presents them as highly-skilled and, generally, very impressive. In expressing this information, they consistently use reflect upon what they have learned from their reading. The candidate is, moreover, able to explain how their reading intersects with other areas of study, and can navigate across interests in various different subjects (while at all times demonstrating that their key focus is on French literature).

Bad Points:

This statement relies more heavily on relaying personal achievements than it does on the literary discussion, and it seems that there could have been room to more greatly delve into literary criticism. Though the applicant's use of university-level terminology is at times impressive, the statement reads as though the writing style is fuelled by a conspicuous need to engage with complex phrasing, and it would have benefitted from a more relaxed approach at times, just to prevent the style from becoming stilted. The one thing the candidate was guaranteed to communicate was that they *thought* that they were very clever. This will seldom go down well with admissions tutors. The applicant also runs the risk of presenting themselves as slightly overbearing in their intellectual self-belief and would have nullified that risk by slightly adjusting their tone.

Overall:

Through the use of strong examples, the candidate very clearly demonstrates their academic track record. However, anecdotal evidence of participation and enthusiasm is given significant weight in this statement, resulting in the compression of any literary discussion within the statement. While the range of activities that the applicant calls upon is highly impressive, the statement has room for further illustration of their ability to think creatively around literary issues. In addition, though the applicant's dedication to spoken skills is also laudable, the nature of Oxbridge language degrees as primarily literature-based means that any discussion they can include of literary or cultural works has potentially more value word-for-word than discussion of oral work.

NOTES

Subject: Spanish & German

The ability to speak a foreign language fluently is not only immensely satisfying but also infinitely useful, and I believe that a university degree is the best way of beginning to achieve this skill. I strongly value he ability to speak foreign languages because it enables a much deeper understanding of the local societies. The highly informative book, 'Through the Language Glass' by Guy Deutscher strengthened my belief that people are best understood in their mother tongue, as he explained the concept of untranslatable phrases and key variations in languages. This has led me to see the study of foreign languages as a vital part of my education and future.

Having grown up in a bilingual household, the fantastic opportunities presented by the ability to speak German never went unnoticed. For this reason I spent a year acting as a UK-German Youth Ambassador, encouraging the learning of languages, particularly German, amongst younger children. I organised activities such as the weekly German club, which was successful in raising the profile of the language in school. German fiction has featured throughout my school career, with the pinnacle being 'Der Vorleser', an informative novel, addressing the thought-provoking theme of illiteracy. I was introduced to German poetry at the age of twelve whilst on a five week study placement there, where I read 'Der Erlkönig', a poem I have recently gone on to study further.

My curiosity for languages later extended to Spanish, enhanced by my interest of the culture. Most recently I have become fascinated by South America after my visit to Peru, where I lived with a Peruvian family and volunteered for two weeks. A further two weeks spent discovering the colourful culture prompted me to read 'La Casa de Espíritus' as it gave an insight into the issues faced by a Latin American family of that era. I found that Isabelle Allende's decision to omit any specific location or time period added to the sense of magical realism, and I have begun to explore this genre further by reading Garcia Marquez's 'Cien Años de Soledad'. 'La Casa de Bernarda Alba' by Lorca has introduced me to attitudes towards women in 20th century Spain. One performance I saw was set in the Middle East, supporting my view that these issues still have relevance today. Having also organised a Spanish exchange, I am looking forward to the chance to fully immerse myself in the Spanish culture and language.

My Geography and Economics A levels have complemented my language studies, particularly due to Germany's ongoing economic success led by Angela Merkel, which I have read about in 'Der Spiegel'. Together with BBC Mundo, I have learned from international newspapers about the issues facing EU citizens. My AS level in English Literature has also enabled me to appreciate the subtler meanings of literary techniques as my awareness of popular symbols and imagery has increased. Additionally GSCE Latin has allowed me to comprehend the foundation of words in my chosen languages.

I have also developed attributes useful for university through activities such as music and drama. Persevering with Lamda lessons to gold medal standard has improved my confidence and communication skills, aided by part-time waitressing, where I work in a team. Juggling employment and a demanding amount of schoolwork has encouraged me to manage my time effectively. I have risen to the challenge of being Deputy Head Girl; delivering speeches to prospective pupils. Sharing responsibility for maintaining the welfare of my peers has required a problem-solving approach and leadership skills.

After university I hope to pursue a career in journalism; as a foreign correspondent I could use languages frequently and travel widely. A university degree would help me to develop a multitude of skills for my career aspirations, as well as being an invaluable opportunity to dedicate my time to the study of subjects I find fascinating.

Universities applied to:

- Oxford: Offer
- Durham: Offer
- Bristol: Offer
- Cardiff: Offer
- Edinburgh: Rejected

Good Points:

By citing a variety of information sources, this applicant demonstrates their ability to think creatively; they have accessed material and furthered their skills through a variety of different channels. This is reflective of an applicant that is engaged in their subject across various different aspects of their life. The applicant is able to draw together how their academic interests are actioned in their personal pursuits, and can combine all this information to convincingly argue for their engagement with languages. Furthermore, they are able to articulate where they hope to go with languages, as well as why they think that university study is the best pathway into learning languages.

Bad Points:

While this candidates' breadth of interest is impressive, this statement is quite sparse on literary engagement. Though it references a range of works, the applicant's criticism is relatively light and does not indicate as in-depth a knowledge of literary approaches as it perhaps could. The statement alludes quite casually to literary movements (e.g. "magic realism"), but the applicant could develop their arguments and considerations further in order to more clearly illustrate their potential as a student of foreign literature. It would have been very persuasive to have seen the applicant move from value judgements or superficial readings of texts and onto more evaluative, in-depth analyses based on their own approach.

Overall:

By binding together personal interests and academic curiosity, this applicant is able to demonstrate their continued interest in their subject and how they have managed to practically put their interests into action. However, this statement could do with greater academic grounding in its consideration of literature. It could also, perhaps, do with greater focus overall. Though it cites a range of sources of influence, which demonstrates commitment and engagement, it also lends the statement an air of being unclear in its precise interest.

NOTES

Subject: Spanish & Portuguese

I would like to study Latin and Spanish at degree level because my interests lie in looking at how foreign cultures, ancient and modern, function in comparison to our own. I have developed an aptitude in analysing literature and interpreting and translating Spanish and Latin and I have a growing knowledge of syntax, the history of both cultures and diversity within the societies as we know them today.

Latin is the subject which incorporates my strongest skills: analysing literature and interpreting foreign language. Having studied text by Virgil, Ovid and Tacitus, I have developed an interest in comparing styles of writing among Latin authors but also comparing ancient and modern attitudes to integral social issues including religion, politics and relationships. I am looking forward to approaching new texts at university, going much deeper into their meaning and relevance in a modern context. I expect to improve my ability to read and appreciate them in their original form and enhance the way I analyse the Latin passages. I am currently mentoring a Latin GCSE student. We have weekly tutorial sessions and as well as seeing an improvement in her grades, the mentoring has been extremely valuable for my own studies of Latin.

My fundamental interest in learning Spanish is for the purpose of communicating with others in their own language, opening opportunities for employment and travel for myself. I am excited about the prospect of a year spent abroad, deepening my knowledge of language and awareness of culture. When I began learning Spanish I was initially attracted to the form, structure and sound of the language. Since studying it at A Level I now appreciate the essence of Spain itself having studied its history, politics, traditions, laws and environment. Also we have begun to study life in South America. For my independent coursework topic I chose to analyse the benefits of Castro's rule on the society in Cuba and I anticipate going deeper into various aspects of life in Latin America and Spain. I enjoyed studying García Lorca's "La casa de Bernada Alba" and it has enthused my interest for examining a greater range of original Spanish literature and growing to appreciate the culture through the perspective of the authors.

I was elected head girl at my school, a post which stretches my organisation, communication skills and leadership abilities. I and the three deputies have made several speeches to a variety of audiences, at year twelve and year six open evenings and at the school's annual foundation day; we have planned and delivered numerous assemblies in school and provided weekly contact between the sixth form and the senior management team.

At university I hope to be involved in various activities outside of my studies. At present, I co-run the school's weekly Christian Union as well as attending and assisting at Girls Brigade through my church. Both of these are voluntary and require regular preparation and delivery as well as giving me a chance to interact with people of assorted ages. I love ballet and modern dance and have recently achieved grade 5 in ballet and grade 4 in modern and hope to join a dance group at university. I worked as a sales assistant in WH Smiths for one year and I am currently a waitress at a conference centre/ hotel. Working with members of the public, growing up in the church and maintaining my posts of responsibility have consolidated my confidence and people skills which I feel will be of great value in learning a foreign language as well as putting me in good stead for university life and a working environment later on.

I am prepared for the transition I will face in my life over the next few years and feel mature and responsible enough to handle the adjustment to university life. I intend to embrace the experience with motivation for my course and a keen interest in extra-curricular activities.

ULTIMATE OXBRIDGE PERSONAL STATEMENT GUIDE

EXAMPLE STATEMENTS – MODERN LANGUAGES

Universities applied to:

- Bristol: Offer
- St. Andrews: Offer
- Leeds: Offer
- Manchester: Offer
- Nottingham: Offer

Good Points:

Through their targeted use of examples from their extra-curricular activities, the applicant is able to effectively communicate why they are a strong candidate for university, and in particular, why they are a suitable candidate for this particular field of study. The statement is clearly written throughout and includes a balanced amount of information in both personal and more academic areas. This includes being able to identify personal strengths and demonstrate convincingly where they fall within the subject's remit. As such, the strength of this statement is in the candidate's self-awareness in their abilities and their presentation of those abilities in secure and well-communicated examples.

Bad Points:

This statement regularly comes back to "I" clauses and deals with the applicant's desires and thoughts at a relatively surface level. There is room here for greater depth of intrigue and interest rather than exposition — the applicant does not, for example, need to state what it is they are expecting to study at university (as it is hoped that they will know what is on the course that they are applying for). While all evidence of passion for their subject is helpful, this statement does favour anecdotal and more tenuous connections to their subject rather than an in-depth engagement with literature or other cultural areas.

Overall:

While this statement demonstrates the candidate's interest and ability across both academic and practical settings, it is written in quite sparse prose. The effect of this is to remind the reader that it is a student writing about themselves, rather than having the effect of formulating and communicating urgent literary arguments. This is significant since, during the introduction of this statement, the applicant draws attention to their "aptitude in analysing literature". As such, it would have made for a more wholly satisfying statement had the applicant been able to provide evidence for this claim. While it would have been very persuasive to have seen critical engagement with texts, it would even have been useful to have seen a statement written in a way that incorporated critical, theoretical, analytical or academic language.

NOTES

Subject: Modern & Medieval Languages, French, Spanish with Dutch

My love of languages started at a young age. I always tried to speak French on camping holidays, playing with French children. At High School I went beyond taught lessons by reading French children's literature, and during GCSEs and A Levels I read novels such as 'Therese Raquin', and works by Sartre and Camus which introduced me to a wider range of language, aspects of French literary style and existentialism. After my GCSEs I travelled to France to stay with family friends for two weeks, before going to Carcassonne to work with a church, as part of their outreach into the immigrant community. I used French constantly at work and amongst the people I was staying with. I completed the AS and A2 French in my first year of college, independently researching the AS topics, and embracing the challenge of an increased workload and new aspects of grammar. I now maintain my French skills by listening to French radio, reading French literature, newspapers and work with a French language club in primary schools. I will be writing my EPQ on the influence of World War 2 in French literature and film.

When learning Spanish in Year Eight, I immediately fell in love with the language and culture. To learn more I watched 'Aguila Roja', a Spanish TV drama, which, although fictitious, taught me Spanish history and culture during the reign of Felipe IV. Differences and similarities to 17th century English culture and continued prevalence of certain aspects in Spain interested me. I have also read books such as 'Cien años de soledad,' and was interested by the magic realism genre. It introduced me to the history of Colombia, events such as the Thousand Days War, and the myths and legends of the country, as well as a new literary style. This summer, the seven weeks I spent working in an orphanage in Peru, teaching and looking after children, transformed my life. I was immersed in the life and culture of a Spanish-speaking nation, and improved my language skills greatly. I attended the Villiers Park course for Spanish, learning a great deal about Hispanic history, and enhancing my deep interest in aspects of Spanish literature, influences of the Spanish Civil War and the 'Microrrelato'.

I studied AS German ab initio last year, working in a mixed class of post-GCSE and ab initio students, making rapid progress, proving my ability to learn new languages quickly. I used websites such as memrise.com to learn new vocabulary, listened to German radio and read articles on Deutsche Welle. I quickly worked up to the level of the post-GCSE students and achieved the highest AS grade in the group. By the end of the year I was reading books such as 'Der Schimmelreiter', and 'Die Verwandlung.' When studying post-war Germany, I was fascinated by the idea of 'Vergangenheitsbewältigung' and how such concepts apply to British culture, and other countries.

Due to the similarities between music and languages, and the acute hearing that learning music brings, musicians are often good at foreign languages and developing an authentic accent. I completed a Piano diploma, and I teach two pupils. Competitions, attending Chethams Piano Summer School and a Pianoman Scholarship with Richard Meyrick have given me confidence in performance. For five years I have been a church pianist, showing commitment, teamwork and ability to listen and cooperate with others. I will be taking Grade Eight cello examination shortly, and have taught myself guitar and accordion. Aside from music, I help out at the church kid's club, lead the girls' Bible study and lead Christian Union in college. For several summers I have thoroughly enjoyed working as part of a team with United Beach Missions. I am an avid sportswoman, taking part in triathlons for charity.

I am looking forward to being able to deepen and further my studies of foreign languages, cultures and literature at university, and I am excited about the challenges and opportunities that both study and university life will offer.

Universities applied to:

- Cambridge: Offer
- Durham: Offer
- St. Andrews: Offer
- Edinburgh: Offer
- Warwick: Offer

Good Points:

Through the use of a diverse range of examples, this statement allows the applicant to communicate strong, clear academic information alongside more personal inclusions, which gives this statement life and enthusiasm. While the statement includes clear evidence of achievements, it is energised most intensely by clear motivation, giving it an engaging, warm tone. The applicant is able to give evidence of themselves as a long-standing enthusiast for their subject and can indicate their engagement with languages across a variety of media. The applicant is also able to articulate moments of personal interest in among their discussions of academic research.

Bad Points:

Though the applicant's range of experience is impressive, the anecdotal and meandering style of this statement is at times frustrating. This statement could have been stronger through the use of a clear structure and less of a reliance on storytelling vocabulary and tone. This applicant also has the additional difficulty of applying for a combination of languages; not all of which they already study. As such, it seems as though the statement is somewhat imbalanced in its inclusion of material that isn't relevant to their subject choice. Although there are clear reasons why the applicant would want to include such material as overall evidence of their linguistic capability, the applicant could have worked even harder to make those clear connections. The applicant could have also pushed further with their discussions of their academic interests; their ability to engage with their texts critically could have been made clearer.

Overall:

This applicant represents themselves effectively as a candidate that is seriously engaged in their subject. They also manage to maintain this representation without the statement being devoid of personal intrigue; they include plenty of evidence for how their subject interacts with other extra-curricular activities. Due in part to the nature of their chosen subjects, this applicant does present their statement in a way that dwells only briefly on a wide tranche of different topics. As such, it would have been a more satisfying statement overall had there been scope for the applicant to consider more material in greater analytical depth.

NOTES

HISTORY

Subject: Modern History

To make sense of the chaos and ever shifting perceptions of the past is a task I find enthralling. One may choose to see it as a deterministic narrative or, in the words of Ranke, simply a way of seeing the world 'how it really was'. But what I find most meaningful is that nothing can escape its grasp; and indeed when in all its colour and complexity it is united with the present, it becomes a powerful and compelling world - one that, to me, offers limitless enjoyment and possibility.

This passion has certainly been put into practice during my study of History at A Level. Breaking free from the confines of the syllabus, I went on to read about events preceding Stalin's rise to power. I began with Vladimir Brovkin's 'Russia after Lenin'. His use of songs, jokes, and accounts of the harsh reality of 1920s Russia allowed me to see that History consisted of so much more than textbooks. It suddenly became animated; I found myself imagining with unprecedented vividness the Bolshevik's treatment of those considered 'socially undesirable', as well as the hypocrisy of overthrowing the reigning institutions and creating a new ruling class who swore solidarity with their working counterparts. Chris Ward's 'Stalin's Russia' gave me additional background knowledge of Stalinism and increased my understanding of how a society that had rebelled against Bolshevism with such vehemence could become so deferential and subservient in a matter of years. In studying the French Revolution I developed my awareness of just how historians choose to interpret history - from the ideas of Cobban to Marxist accounts; exposing the contradictions and gaps, but also the exciting prospect of being able to fill them in.

Since beginning my A2 course, I have already begun my wider reading, finding myself enthralled by Richard Aldous' account of Gladstone and Disraeli's parallel careers in the 'Lion and the Unicorn'. A visit to the National Portrait Gallery allowed me to see Sir John Everett Millais' paintings of the rivals firsthand, and spurred in me an interest in art and its authenticity as an historical source. An assignment set on the Black Civil Rights movement inspired me to study Malcolm X, a figure I knew little about beyond the criticisms. I read as widely as I could to develop my own opinion on some of the more positive aspects of his contribution to the cause. This, too, helped me to understand more about history; how figures are so often polarised - and how they can be left a rather unfair legacy, the inverse also being true. My aim was to look at him as objectively as I could and the end product was an essay that I truly feel was a labour of love.

It is my enthusiasm for wider reading that I believe is my strongest academic asset. I read as extensively as I can. Taking English Literature alongside History has extended my empathetic abilities, and I feel studying Economics has enhanced my understanding of an intrinsic factor in historical development. The works of Orwell have also been one of my greatest inspirations, and his frank and clear writing style is something I try to apply to my own work. Reading essays in 'Virtual History' also exposed me to the intriguing prospect of counterfactual historiography and how it can be used. I was also selected to attend a University Summer School at Eton College for History, helping me to develop my knowledge outside of what is taught in class and affirming my dedication to the subject in a stimulating and academic environment.

By studying History at university I hope I can enrich my perception of just how we came to be where we are today, and apply these lessons of the past in order to help me make decisions about my own life and future. It is complex and rigorous, but therein lies the challenge; a challenge I am highly enthusiastic about experiencing at university level.

Universities applied to:

- Oxford: Offer
- London School of Economics: Offer
- University College London: Offer
- Durham: Offer
- Edinburgh: Offer

Good Points:

The student writes eloquently and with a clear passion for the subject. The statement is well-structured and effectively demonstrates the extra work the student has done to further their interest in History. This is successful insofar as the student shows a clear awareness of the different areas of historical study a degree will entail. The student plays well to the idea that 'less is more' in exploring what they have learnt from the reading they have already done, instead of resorting to a list.

Bad Points:

The statement is well-written but does, at times, need tightening. For example, the first paragraph refers frequently to 'it', so much so that the reader may lose track of what 'it' actually is. The statement also threatens to state the obvious – E.g., 'certainly been put into practice' and 'breaking free from the confines…'; this can easily be implied in what the student goes on to say and does not need to be stressed. The student could elaborate more on how their other studies have reinforced his/her interest in history because, at present, some information on extra-curricular activities lack elements of personality.

Overall:

This is a very strong personal statement, demonstrating intelligence and a real zeal for the subject. The statement speaks with an authority that leaves the reader with no doubt that this student has great potential. The student should consider introducing more personality into the statement – something that is hinted at in the very last paragraph – but otherwise it is a very convincing read.

NOTES

Subject: History

My passion for history can best be explained by discussing the period of German Unification, which displays the most engrossing virtues of studying the subject. Firstly there is great scope for debate and exploration of the interlocking causations, examining the relative importance of Bismarck's own role against the military strengthening of Prussia or the shifting international relations. But most interestingly it is a defining period in the shaping of modern Europe and the way in which it links the past to the present is most fascinating. Studying this period reveals how international relations progressed after the Napoleonic era leading to the way in which Germany was unified through war and thus became a country built around war. It is therefore arguable that this era created the state which would then trigger the two wars which have shaped the modern world. This period shows how history can give us a more rounded understanding of the world we live in, linking our mysterious and intriguing past to our all too familiar present surroundings. It is partly this, which motivates me to study history as in doing so I gain immense satisfaction from learning how our world has evolved.

An understanding of history also provides a fundamental backdrop for any other areas of study. I have found this through my other A-Level subjects, for example historical knowledge of politics in Britain was essential to AS politics, particularly when studying the political situation in Ireland. An understanding of past conflicts is indispensable when it comes to managing contemporary politics. Furthermore, whilst taking French the study of Un Sac De Billes by Joseph Joffo unearthed experiences of living under Vichy France. To learn a language fully it is important to immerse oneself in the culture and history of the country in order to develop a more rounded understanding of the people who live there. Thus it seems that history is inescapable; it not only provides vital background knowledge but also helps bring to life every other academic subject, which is why in my opinion, it is the most important.

During my A Level history course, the Napoleonic era particularly fascinated me and I pursued my interest through further reading, looking specifically at Napoleon's downfall, an area I found most compelling as it offers the greatest exposition of the psychology of this exceptional man. I read Digby Smith's 'The Decline and Fall of Napoleon's Empire' as well as Zamoyski's '1812'. I picked up on several themes throughout Zamoyski's book and developed my own opinions such as sympathetic stances towards General Barclay and the Tsar, but was particularly intrigued by how Napoleon let his ego drive his pre-war diplomacy and how Napoleon's own role in the breakdown of the Treaty of Tilsit perhaps triggered his eventual downfall. The fact that I was so gripped by so many different themes within an historical study of one war also reveals another aspect of history that is so appealing to me. It offers vast numbers of different avenues to pursue in one's research, whether it is Napoleon's diplomacy or the fallibility of the Russian command.

Outside of my academic studies, I am a dedicated sportsman but have particularly flourished musically as a cellist, obtaining a grade 8 standard in year 11 and am a committed member of various ensembles. Music has coloured my historical studies, for example, I played various Shostakovich symphonies coinciding with my study of Stalinist Russia at GCSE, each with a very different feel depending upon his relationship with Stalin, but perhaps most moving was playing his 10th symphony, a purely self-indulgent expression of relief after the death of the dictator. It is impossible to appreciate this great work without its historical context, which transforms the piece into something personal, attaching the listener emotionally. History is not only fascinating in itself, but it enriches our appreciation of all other interests.

Universities applied to:

- Oxford: Offer
- Durham: Offer
- York: Offer
- Bristol: Offer
- Warwick: Offer

Good Points:

The student speaks intelligently and successfully links their interests – both within history and outside of history – to the study of history on a wider scale. The statement is well-organised and reads well. Paragraph three, in particular, has many strong points with a greater focus on what really interests the student and why. The student does well to focus on the different areas of exploration within history, showing a strong awareness of the nuances within historical study.

Bad Points:

The statement focuses too much on what they know, rather than what interests them – the first paragraph in particular reads too much like an essay and less like an exploration of why this candidate actually wants to study history. The student risks falling into a trap of trying to teach and impress the admissions offer with their knowledge instead of offering a more personal approach. The student also needs to try to avoid repetition, for example, 'most interestingly' and 'most fascinating' within the same sentence in order to ensure the whole statement flows better.

Overall:

This is a very strong, well-written personal statement. The student has clearly proved they can both understand and analyse history. The student perhaps needs to focus more on their own motivations behind studying history, but overall, the statement suggests a student with great potential and zeal for the subject. What would make the student stand out, even more, is a stronger closing statement – something to bring the whole personal statement together, and stress the importance of historical study to this student.

NOTES

Subject: History

For me, the Bayeux Tapestry perfectly illustrates the nature of history. People and events are interwoven to create an overall picture, a snapshot in time, but often the facts can be embroidered, as highlighted in Bridgeford's 'Hidden History' of 1066. As time goes by elements fade, or are lost completely, and here lies limitless opportunities for discovery; each historian adds a few more stitches to our understanding of the world, and from newfound evidence we can go beyond the original image to explore whether it shows the full picture. My desire to add my own stitches to this great work is foremost in my decision to pursue the study of history at a higher level.

Incidentally, the Bayeux Tapestry originates from what is, in my opinion, the most enthralling period of British history. Between the Norman Conquest up to the fall of the last Plantagenet on the field at Bosworth were over four centuries of social upheaval and change, from the introduction of feudalism and eradication of Anglo Saxon culture, to the rise of the merchant class, or the greater freedoms afforded to peasants due to the Black Death. These numerous avenues of enquiry are a constant source of interest to me, but most particularly I have learned the value of literature in creating another dimension in which to view our past in ways that other documents cannot provide. I had read much about the fourteenth century before embarking on an epic pilgrimage with Chaucer's characters, but it was the 'Canterbury Tales' which truly brought the period to life through specific examples from every element of society.

My formal education in Russian history instilled in me a continuing fascination with everyday life in Russia in the decades leading up to and following the October Revolution of 1917. I found Orlando Figes' 'The Whisperers' particularly thought-provoking. The use of voices of people who lived through the Stalinist era combined with great sensitivity provided an insight into the personal effect of the regime; the internalisation of Soviet values truly transformed the psyche of a whole nation. However, perhaps most interesting for me were the ways in which some Soviet citizens did not bend to the will of the state, for example through the continued observance of religion and the survival of family ties. This interest has led me to researching ways in which other social groups have rejected imposed values, such as the True Levellers or 'Diggers' under Cromwell.

Studying Sociology has added a new level to my understanding of the importance of history: through teaching the past, the next generation is given an insight into their culture and collective past, which in turn creates greater social solidarity. This has been of particular significance in my life as discovering the history of my own family has given me a sense of heritage and rootedness, but also a greater appreciation for my opportunities, which are far beyond those which my ancestors experienced. Taking a gap year has enabled me to pursue several of these opportunities, including learning French and basic Latin, and studying theoretical perspectives in historiography. A mixture of part time work, home study and involvement in local societies such as the St. Albans Cathedral Textile Conservators has helped me to hone the skill of time management, and given me confidence in my ability to work independently.

I am also looking forward to getting involved with extra-curricular activities at University. I am taking my Grade Eight Flute exam this year, and took an active part in various musical ensembles at my Sixth Form. I also composed a score to Shakespeare's 'A Midsummer Night's Dream', which was performed as a part of the St. Albans Arts Festival in 2011. It was exciting to be involved with a community project, and it has motivated me to take part in others, including an annual festival, 'Folk by the Oak', and a local non-profit theatre company, 'Foot in the Door', in which I have risen to the role of Musical Director.

I believe I will thrive in the challenging environment of a University, and I look forward increasing my historical knowledge and understanding at a higher and more detailed level.

Universities applied to:

- Oxford: Offer
- York: Offer
- Exeter: Offer
- London Holloway: Offer

Good points:

The student writes in a compelling way and reveals a lot about their thought process in the first paragraph, effectively employing the metaphor of embroidery to demonstrate the student's historical interests. They also employ a vast range of historical examples to support their interest in history; this is particularly effective given that many universities require students to take both modern and medieval papers. The statement is well-written and presents a well-rounded student.

Bad Points:

The student needs to pay heed to the idea that 'less is more', for example, the student talks about areas of interest such as the 'Diggers' but does not build enough upon these examples to really merit their inclusion. The student perhaps dwells too much on extra-curricular activities; it would be more worthwhile to make more out of the historical comparisons hinted at in earlier paragraphs. It would also make sense to link the skills learnt in these activities to the study of history overall – this is effectively done in the penultimate paragraph, but less so in the final one.

Overall:

The candidate writes with a certain charm and personality that instantly adds something to this personal statement. At times, however, the student dips into a narrative, but their analysis of this narrative is generally quite strong and so it is not too distracting. They could benefit from tightening some sentences and maybe making more of some of his/her examples, but generally, the statement is strong and well-varied.

NOTES

Subject: History & German

When recently asked to imagine a world without history, I found it difficult. For me there is nothing more relevant to understanding and explaining humanity than the study of history, and it has been something I have explored and enjoyed from an early age. At nine I remember being puzzled when my German friend visited and she was shocked by how much tea we drank. It hadn't crossed my mind that her family didn't as well, but upon investigation I found I'd stumbled upon a very British stereotype. My curiosity was aroused. It was a while before I discovered the East India Trading Company, and how their record imports of tea facilitated the birth of tea culture in Britain, but when I did I was fascinated.

It still delights me that any question I have can be answered with investigation. For example, having watched Hotel Rwanda I was intrigued about the situation and found in Mason's 'Patterns of Dominance' a description of the Rwandan social structure enabling me to analyse reasons for the outbreak of violence. Mason's description then led me to investigate past social structures, whereupon I read 'Ancient Rome' by Baker an analysis of the rise and incredible crumbling of the Roman Empire. This fragility of civilisation was a theme I wished to continue exploring, leading me to choose the topic of my Extended Essay, to what extent the Black Death and its impacts caused the Peasants' Revolt. Writing my essay gave me the opportunity to read primary sources from the era such as eyewitness accounts and rolls of Parliament. I also experienced when researching the Peasants' Revolt the value to the historian of learning another language when I came across the 'Bauernkrieg', a revolt that took place in Germany in 1524 and shared many traits with the Peasants' Revolt. When investigating it much of the material was in German and I was glad to find this didn't stop my research.

This was one of a number of reasons why I chose to apply for German as well as history. Having lived in Berlin during my childhood, attending a British school, I glimpsed the German culture, swimming in lakes and enjoying die Brüder Grimm. When I started German in last year, studying the language for the first time, I stumbled across vocabulary I didn't know I had: Ohrwurm, rechthaberisch, Zartlichkeit. I had always admired the culture and people and the literature didn't disappoint. I was intrigued by the sinister and eerie side to Kafka's die Verwandlung and Süskind's Parfum, and by the dark humour of Durrenmatt's Besuch den alten Dame. Having attended a workshop on German poetry I was further convinced of the need to study the language. When reading Mitchell's translation of the poem Der Panther by Rilke, whilst beautifully written I felt it lacked the essence of the original. This led me to wonder if there is such a thing as translation in literature or whether to truly appreciate a piece of writing one has to read in its original language. I was convinced of this when, for my English study of foreign texts, I chose to study Mann's Tod in Venedig. Being able to read the original language was an incredible benefit allowing me to explore how rhythm and phonetics added to the meaning of the prose.

Through partaking in the Model United Nations Hague conference I learnt the value of thorough research, in order to be fully prepared for the large debates I took part in. I also welcomed the challenge of seeing the world from the perspective of Senegal, the country we represented. On a recent trip to India, where I worked with various charities I again experienced, through the children we worked with, another view of the world. One particular aspect of their view was all too familiar; when asked what he thought of England, one boy replied, 'lots of tea'.

I hope I have shown that I think it would be an incredible privilege to spend four years studying History and German and I know I'd work my utmost hardest to develop my knowledge, understanding and fondness of both.

Universities applied to:

- Oxford: Offer
- University College London: Offer
- Durham: Offer
- Warwick: Offer
- Exeter: Offer

Good Points:

The statement has a very honest, compelling opening. What makes this statement particularly interesting is the personal, anecdotal quality to it; this makes it stand out compared to all the other, more analytical, statements. They write intelligently and do well to interweave their own personal research to historical debates. The student links the whole statement together well and speaks with a conviction and personality likely to maintain the reader's interest.

Bad Points:

The author could do more to link together their interests in both History and German. The two can easily interlink, and often will in History courses, but the student does not show enough awareness of the ways in which studying both these subjects can reinforce each other. Furthermore, the finishing sentence is much weaker than the rest of the statement – it shows the student's determination but does not read as well as the previous paragraphs.

Overall:

This is a very interesting personal statement that reads with a lot of personality and individual flair. It perhaps risks being too anecdotal, but this is also part of the statement's charm. The student needs to consider more how studying both subjects could prove more beneficial than just one, but at the same time, the statement does successfully demonstrate the student's passion for both disciplines.

NOTES

Subject: History & Politics

History is a subject which has always fascinated me. In my opinion, History cannot be treated as a completely separate domain; it is closely linked to other subjects such as Politics, Economics, Geography, Sociology and Philosophy. For instance, one cannot discuss the causes of WW2 without taking into account the development of radical ideologies, the economic weakness of Germany, Stalin's politics aiming to create a "buffer" of friendly states separating Russia from Europe etc.

I have studied History in several educational systems with Polish, Belgian, and British teachers. The first two focused upon facts and figures, supplying the students with a general background, whereas British teachers focused upon fostering an analytical mind. It is the British approach to history that interests me the most, giving us a better understanding of our world; I think that I will enjoy the system of seminars and group work at the university.

Every historical event has specific causes and consequences, and it is interesting to see how far those can sometimes reach, and to see how today's world was shaped by the past. History is a subject demanding a vast general knowledge and the ability to see 'the whole picture'. It can be seen, for instance, in Norman Davies' God's Playground- A history of Poland where the author stresses the importance of the geographical situation of Poland for its history. This approach to History affords us the possibility to prevent errors in the future, and to understand how every major turn in the history of humanity is a jigsaw made up of multiple factors.

Undergraduate courses in Great Britain, such as 'History and Politics' or 'International History' provide the students with an approach to History from those different points of view, and allow them to improve their analytical, discursive, and argumentation skills. This is why I chose to apply for these studies.

Being in the French section of the European School, I study many subjects in English, including History. This has allowed me to develop my vocabulary and to improve both my written and oral English. I chose the Advanced History and Economics options for my Baccalaureate, which have allowed me to widen my knowledge and my historical analysis skills.

Although Polish is my mother tongue, I speak French and English equally well. My English has improved due to three years of private lessons and six years of studies in the European School. In addition, I have been studying Spanish and Dutch for several years. I also attended the Polish School for eight years where I learnt Polish Literature and History, which not only supplied me with extra information concerning Poland and the World but also gave me an additional perspective from which to analyse the events of the past.

Last year, I participated in two major extracurricular projects: the Young Enterprises and The Model European Parliament. The Young Enterprises project was an excellent exercise, allowing me to develop my sense of responsibility, creativity and organisation, but also to learn more about the functioning of the market in a practical, hands-on sense. Following this I passed the Young Enterprise Examination organised by the University of Cambridge. The Model European Parliament was a project which allowed students to participate in a role play of a parliamentary session. This has been an invaluable experience, giving me the opportunity to learn more about group dynamics and political decision making – something which I hope will be put to further use at university.

Amongst my skills, music is very important. I have been playing the clarinet for eight years, taking classical and jazz lessons and studying guitar for two years. This is something else which I look forward to continuing at university.

To conclude, I believe that both my education and my extra-curricular projects will allow me to not only perform well on this course but to also contribute positively to the university community as a whole.

Universities applied to:

- Oxford: Offer
- Warwick: Offer
- London School of Economics: Rejected

Good Points:

The student plays to his/her strong points, i.e. their experience under different educational systems and knowledge of History outside of the standard British History; this makes the student stand out. Given that English is not the student's native language, the statement is written thoughtfully and eloquently. The third paragraph is particularly strong with an effective analysis of a specific approach to History, showing that the student has clearly thought about what studying History at degree level would entail.

Bad Points:

The first paragraph is weak – it starts clichéd and goes on to a list; this is not likely to fare well. It has no draw for the reader and does not really explain why History – rather than the other disciplines listed – interests the student. The statement, at times, is too fragmented and does not explore fully enough the student's personal interests in History. At times, the statement is far too vague; it is split into small sections, many of which do not add much. The student would be better off focusing on the historical study they have conducted so far and the areas of history that interest them.

Overall:

Compared to other students, the statement is not overly strong but it is clear that the student has great potential – especially given that English is not his/her mother tongue. The student speaks passionately about their interest in History and stands out as a result of their background and previous historical studies. The statement could be better structured but overall creates the impression of a very interesting and dedicated individual.

NOTES

Subject: History & Politics

I am fascinated by the potential for historical events to be revised, as opinions and perspectives change through time. My exploration of the subject has led me to discover how history is an ever-changing field of thought, rather than a static body of facts, on which a historian can have an impact through unique insight and persuasive argument. This has inspired me to interact with historical texts more critically, which complements my intrinsic passion for the stories within history and motivates me to pursue the discipline further.

Studying history at A-Level has strengthened my interest in the subject through learning about periods in time which have tangibly shaped the current state of the world. I supplemented my study of Nazi Germany by reading the Czech historian Dusan Hamsik's biography of Heinrich Himmler; while Paul Preston's 'The Spanish Civil War' expanded my knowledge of the complex international relations which led to Franco's victory in the conflict. Studying 20th century British history alerted me to the importance of individual political figures to the course of history. I pursued this further by attending Vernon Bogdanor's Gresham College lecture on Roy Jenkins which opened my eyes to the effect of personal circumstances on his politics, and subsequently British history.

My interest in the events of history encouraged me to pursue historiography, reading E.H. Carr's 'What is History?'. Although intrigued by Carr's exploration of topics such as the importance of the historian, I was aware of the fact that the book is half a century old, so I decided to read David Cannadine's modern counterpart 'What is History Now?' in order to draw parallels with Carr's magnum opus; and explore the way historiography has evolved. Cursory reading of Herodotus has also been useful in observing how the writing of history has changed since the infancy of the subject.

My A-level Politics course was extremely useful in understanding history better, as well as being an invaluable tool in helping me to understand current affairs. A two-week work experience at the constituency office of Sarah Teather MP had broadened my knowledge of the practical role of a politician; however, the course developed my understanding of political ideologies, processes and participation. Learning about the importance and influence of pressure groups has given me a new outlook on the work I do as vice-chairman of Brent Youth Parliament, as I examined the tangible political change that can be achieved through engaging with youth politics. This has further inspired me to become my school's student governor and engage in a decision-making process with noticeable results and real consequences.

The study of English language and literature has proved invaluable when analysing sources in history as I conditioned myself to pay close attention to detail and linguistic devices which can reveal a lot about the agenda of a source's author. Studying maths developed my logical reasoning ability, which I applied when figuring out causes in sequences of historical events and decisions; while philosophy improved my ability to structure ideas into arguments.

My two greatest extracurricular passions, football and writing, combine through publishing analytical articles on international sports websites; I have also been shortlisted for the national Wicked Young Writers competition. I am a keen observer of modern Egyptian politics, having written an extended essay on Mohamed Morsi as part of the UCL Summer Challenge. My fluency in Arabic and Czech allows me to examine original primary source material such as journals and accounts from family members involved in events such as the Prague Spring or the Egyptian Revolution. My hard work and enthusiasm for history can flourish at a top academic institution, and I look forward to an environment of academic excellence.

Universities applied to:

- Oxford: Offer
- London School of Economics: Rejected
- University College London: Offer
- King's: Offer
- SOAS: Offer

Good Points:

The student clearly shows that they have gone above and beyond to further their interest in History, effectively discussing both an interest in particular periods of history and historiography itself. The student also successfully links their study of other subjects and extra-curricular activities to skills gained which will be applicable to both History and Politics – this is not something every student is able to achieve.

Bad Points:

The statement could do with greater vision – the second paragraph, for example, includes a lot of detail on different parts of history the student has learnt about but does not really expand much on what the student acquired from this and/or how it encouraged them to study History and Politics in greater detail. This is also seen in the following paragraph where the student cites their reading of Cannadine's book but does not give an opinion on their reading and the usefulness of this interpretation. The first sentence is not compelling enough compared to what the student goes on to say.

Overall:

The student has an interest in both History and Politics that is well-explored and demonstrated within the personal statement. What its lacks, however, is a real consideration of why this student wants to study the subject and the way in which History and Politics can weave together. The student needs to focus more on analysing the work they have already done in order to demonstrate their own analytical flair.

NOTES

Subject: History of Art

'History has remembered the kings and warriors, because they destroyed; Art has remembered the people, because they created'- William Morris. History of Art: for me it is a chance to exercise my passion; delving into the past, analysing and concluding, how and why society has cultivated, influenced, and motivated a masterpiece. My curiosity was inspired by the Lady Lever Galleries, particularly as it was the initial attempt to bring a varied and rich culture through art to the tenants of Port Sunlight, and the mixed reception this received. A personal interest in the Palladian architectural movement and its development in Britain inspired me to investigate further the links between the social order and art. I was intrigued by how it evidenced the wealth of the aristocracy and the industrialists. A level History has whetted my appetite for Art History, as my fascination with human nature leads me to inquire how historical events and characters have influenced artistic figures and society. I am especially interested in the renaissance and how it brought a revival of classical splendour. English Literature encourages me to view information from varying perspectives and to look beyond my initial opinion, giving me the ability to research concisely and deeply into an artist's life and work. An exhibition of Gainsborough's landscapes fascinated me, in particular 'The Mild Evening Gleam'; the poetical style allowed me to increase my understanding of how literature and art combine. Through Theatre studies I have learned to work in depth, in particular from the nineteenth to the twenty first century. It was Ibsen's 'A Doll's House' which provided a snapshot into the structured societal life of the Victorian era resulting in my fascination of the Aesthetic Movement. 'The Cult of Beauty' an exhibition at the Victoria and Albert Museum gave me a taste of the period, proving essential to the development of my understanding towards the movement furthering my belief that it sought the urge to escape from the ugly, materialistic, and oppressive Victorian phase. Outside the classroom, I have an immense yearning to gain a greater knowledge of civilisations' impact on shaping the artist and how an unwritten form of communication can both shape and reflect civilisation, whether it is cavemen recording achievement or Leonardo da Vinci's 'Mona Lisa' where interpretation has been the source of many a nonsensical debate. I believe that my interest and participation in school debates, and as a founding member of the schools 'Politics and Economics group' will enable me to add value to this course as I will able to use contemporary references within the time span of the artistic piece, and how it influences the public today. As a leading role in school plays, being head of human resources for our 'Young Enterprise Group', raising money for charity, and having been both deputy House Captain, elected by peers and staff, and a prefect, I have developed further my communication, independence and leadership skills. Apart from my studies, my interest for the last ten years has been my love of equestrianism. My greatest achievement has been representing my country for both dressage and jumping, as an individual and in a team, earning me; gold, silver, and bronze medals; and qualifying for the Royal International and Horse of the Year Show. Equestrianism has required dedication, time management skills, utter dependability, quick wit, stamina and extreme motivation. Aspects that I endeavour to achieve throughout all aspects of my life. I am thoroughly looking forward to my university years, focusing on a subject that I am enthusiastic and fascinated by. I have been a student who thrives on challenges, never being happy unless I am busy; History of Art is the natural culmination of my studies and interests. I will be able to test and improve my analytical skills and the desire to discover how art has reflected the changes within society.

Universities applied to:

- Reading: Offer
- Oxford Brookes: Offer
- Leicester: Offer
- Aberystwyth: Offer
- Plymouth: Offer

Good Points:

The student talks intelligently about their interests within History of Art. Perhaps the strongest discussion is on the other subjects the student studies; the exploration of the skills learnt from these subjects should be something replicated throughout the statement. The student is clearly very able and well-rounded and this is effectively demonstrated, particularly in the latter half of the statement. The final paragraph is particularly strong in terms of its analysis of why this specific student is a good candidate.

Bad Points:

The statement begins with an interesting quote, but does not explore what Morris is saying; if you're going to start with a quote, you need to show you've really thought about it and used it for a reason. The same goes for the examples the student later uses – these could be developed and analysed much further. The statement needs to be split into paragraphs to give it some order – at the moment, it is difficult to read.

Overall:

The statement creates the impression of a student with a lot of motivation and determination. It does, however, need a clearer focus. At the moment, the statement introduces ideas but does not fully explore them. The statement's structure could be improved and the student dwells too much on other subjects and extra-curricular activities, but overall the student does show a lot of potential.

NOTES

PHILOSOPHY

Subject: Philosophy

"And if you find her poor, Ithaka has not fooled you. / Wise as you will have become, so full of experience, / You will have understood by then, what these Ithakas mean."

Cavafy was right, indeed. Like any other reflective person, I am essentially a philosophical entity. While most people, perhaps those outside academic philosophy, would consider it a prime example, maybe along with Mathematics, of an established body of a priori truths, of some kind of Ithaka (thus excluding themselves from the possibility of realizing their philosophical essence), I beg to differ. For years, though, unwise as I was according to Cavafy, I was looking for Ithakas like most men, misled by this major misconception. For years, I have been reading Plato and Aristotle, Descartes and Nietzsche always, hastily and impatiently, heading towards truth; towards my rich Ithaka, and always falling on reefs and mythical objections raised by one philosopher against the truths of the other. Always, en route.

When, "wise as I had become" on the road, like old Ulysses, I realized that philosophy is much more than just a truth per se. Instead, philosophy is the pursuit of truth, irrespective of whether that truth is ever achieved; in fact, if and when something ever counts as truth, it does not belong to the realm of philosophy any more. Not until I read Wittgenstein's Tractatus Logico-Philosophicus, had I realized that the aim of philosophy is to designate what can be said and what not, what is non-sense or what might be senseless. This very sub specie aeternitatis realization of philosophy as an activity, a method of approaching truth and reflecting on reality rather than as an established body of justified true belief, was crucial in my selection of philosophy as the subject of my academic study. Since this realization, my chief preoccupation has been to learn as much as possible from the journey to Ithaka, to hone this ability to philosophize effectively, to exercise and engage philosophy as much as possible, whenever and wherever possible.

A culmination of this constant struggle to sharpen my philosophical essence happened this summer in the Epic Questions Summer Institute of U of Va, Charlottesville, Virginia, USA. In this intensive, three-week seminar for high-school teachers, I was the official note-taker and the only high-school student to be accepted among the scholars as an intern of Dr. Mitchell S. Green. Courses in Epistemology, Metaphysics, Philosophy of Mind, Formal Logic, Philosophy of Language, Ethics, Political Philosophy and Bioethics unprecedentedly furthered this philosophical activity and I made the acquaintance of contemporary philosophical thought, reading, such as T. Nagel, R. Chisholm, D. Papineau, B. Williams, along with classical readings.

Hence, to my readings of Plato's Five Dialogues, Descartes's Meditations on First Philosophy and Nietzsche's Übermensch, were added those of the British Empiricists, esp. some of Hume's Enquiries, Kant, B. Rusell's The Problems of Philosophy and Mill's Utilitarianism.

I must admit that I have been uncritically assuming a certain account of human nature (as inherently philosophical), which many may find controversial. And this, itself, thus, turns into a philosophical question. And so on and so forth.

This is exactly the philosophical beauty I live for.

Universities applied to:

- Cambridge: Offer
- University College London: Offer
- Edinburgh: Offer

Good Points:

The statement is well-written and the student clearly demonstrates their passion for Philosophy, as well as their motivation for pursuing further study of it, and something of a personal journey through which their philosophical thinking has developed. The discussion of the nature of philosophical thought ties nicely into their own motivation to study Philosophy. The statement shows their broad philosophical education, as well as indicating strong self-motivating passions for learning (in a much more subtle manner than simply stating that they are self-motivated), as much of this education is in the form of private study. Acceptance to the prestigious seminar is an impressive achievement and the student is right to stress this, and the 'unprecedented' effect it had on their philosophical activity.

Bad Points:

The statement is vague in what it terms 'philosophy'; though the student clearly has an interest in some vague notion of 'human nature', they don't narrow down exactly what they wish to study at university (Philosophy being such a broad subject that quite a bit of specialisation is necessary). The time spent listing impressive works that they had read would have been better invested in mentioning just one (or even just one subject that they had read around) that had particularly affected them, and expanding on it. Similarly, they could have expanded further on the experience of the seminar (how it affected their philosophical thinking, new ideas encountered while there, etc.), rather than listing the respected philosophers they had met.

The grammar is, at points, questionable, indicating the statement required closer proof-reading prior to being submitted.

Overall:

This statement is average; it conveys a rare passion for the subject and, more importantly, a passion that has been actively pursued in the student's own time. It could, however, benefit from more specificity regarding their thoughts on specific readings and from reading less like a list of books and philosophers. Overall, the statement is intriguing, but leaves you questioning the author's academic ability.

NOTES

Subject: Philosophy & French

I thoroughly enjoy my studies in Philosophy and French at A Level and am now keen to pursue these subjects at degree level. They seem to me to be inextricably linked, and I would love to explore them in tandem.

I feel that philosophical arguments hinge on a shared understanding of terms. I have found in all of my subjects that appreciating written communication requires an awareness of the contextual background of composer, poet, philosopher or playwright. For instance, Bentham's ethical theory of Utilitarianism was developed in response to the powerlessness of the people; Debussy's unconventional use of cadences and 'coloristic' harmony were effective in his display of emotions. The aptitudes involved in a joint honours course, the complimentary skills of communication and analysing arguments, are ones that I immensely enjoy and am keen to continue to develop.

I am intrigued by the ethics of R.E. Studying the subject has made me question the origin of my own morals. While reading 'Think' it struck me that Blackburn has a strong idea of what he believes to be right and wrong (reason is good, blind faith is "bad, or at least suspect"). I personally have a less fixed view of morality. Class discussions often have a profound effect on my personal views and I like to hear the reasoning behind those opinions that differ from mine.

I find it fascinating to explore moral, social or philosophical issues in two languages. I have enjoyed debates in French lessons and like the challenge of defending opinions in both languages. The positions I adopt are fuelled by my philosophical approaches. Books such as Ian Hacking's 'Why Does Language Matter to Philosophy?' provide a selection of case studies over the centuries showing how language has been key to the development of philosophy. The endless play of variations of meanings and interpretations within a culture or situation is what makes the subjects so relevant to real life. I also adore the language of music, one so communicative primarily without the use of words, which stimulates such a large range of personal emotions. Within my French studies I relish the exploration of literature in its original language. I enjoy the opportunity and challenge of grappling with originally intended nuances without relying on someone else's translation, as I experienced upon reading Camus' 'L'Etranger' as well as set texts. I found it rewarding last year to mentor a younger pupil for French and believe she found me helpful and encouraging. I have also seen plays such as 'Lettres de Delation' and 'Le Medecin Malgre Lui'. This has been complimented by my studies of English literature, where developing close reading analysis has enabled me to appreciate the role of context in interpreting the author's meaning.

Apart from my academic work I delight in a range of activities such as extra-curricular music, particularly singing, playing the oboe and piano. I sing in the school chamber choir and in an external semi-professional choir, with whom I make exciting regular appearances in professional venues (Royal Albert Hall, Barbican, Royal Opera House, English National Opera). I have been part of television and studio recordings, as a soloist and as part of a choir, including singing at Wembley Stadium as part of Madonna's choir. I won the school's 2009 Vocal Competition and this term I'm thrilled to be the lead in the school musical 'The Boy Friend'. I have represented the school in sports events including cross-country, athletics, trampolining, cricket and football. I also take a keen interest in 'ethical' and fair trade, ecological living and small-scale businesses and projects such as the Big Issue. I believe that my interests and skills make me well suited to take full advantage of the opportunities that university has to offer. I am passionate about following a joint honours course and eager to further my appreciation and knowledge of Philosophy and French.

Universities applied to:

- Oxford: Offer
- Exeter: Offer
- King's: Offer
- Sheffield: Offer
- Bristol: Rejected

Good points:

The statement ties Philosophy and French together well and communicates an interesting approach to studying the two in tandem, and their motivation for doing so. The student demonstrates that they are well-rounded both in their balance of interest in French and Philosophy, but also as a person, by devoting some time to talking about their non-strictly academic interests. They make it clear what their main interests in the two fields of study are and explain their inspirations, which also shows off their extensive extra-curricular reading. The statement is excellent in conveying a real passion for their subject as well as an academic background that supports their study of it; it doesn't miss a chance to describe the joy they gain from their studies, while also making it clear how each reading they mention has furthered their thoughts on the study of language.

Bad points:

The statement reads as formulaic and simplistic in its writing style; large parts of it consist of making a point, giving an example, and then moving on with little to tie the piece together as a whole. The language also seems, at times, unnaturally extravagant (see: 'adore', 'delight in'). While these phrases are not inherently problematic, they stand out from the rest of the language used and disrupt the speaker's voice; they seem to be artificial insertions designed to impress the reader (and, obviously, fail to do so).

The last paragraph, a list of interests and achievements, while beneficial for the reasons discussed above, ought to be tied in somewhat more to the rest of the statement and to their desire to study Philosophy and French, or to study at university more generally. Without this, the last sentence ("I am passionate about following a joint honours course and eager to further my appreciation and knowledge of Philosophy and French.") is disjointed and jarring and the potential of the paragraph to further the statement's aims is wasted.

Overall:

The statement shows a strong student with a passion for their subject, who has a clear idea of what studying it would involve and why they wish to do so. However, it contains little to make it stand out from the rest and would benefit from being better linked together into one whole, cohesive piece.

NOTES

Subject: Philosophy & Theology

According to Descartes, in order to know anything, we must first doubt everything. To paraphrase him: in order to know why I make such a great candidate to study philosophy, you must first doubt everything you know about what makes a great philosophy student. It's not a perfect exhibit of logic, but then neither was Descartes' Trademark Argument, so I don't think he would criticise me too much. I aim to demonstrate why I would make a great candidate to consider for your university from the foundations up.

As Epicurus might have put it: "Is a great philosophy student willing to work hard, but not able? Then he is not wise. Is he able, but not willing? Then he is lazy. Is he both able and willing? Then whence cometh 2.2's? Is he neither able nor willing? Then why call him a great philosophy student?" My response is that there is a very simple solution – there are only very few great philosophy students. There are many good philosophy students who are either able or willing, but not both – hence cometh 2.2's; therefore, in order for someone to be a great philosophy student, they must be both willing and able.

Recently, I have read Think by Simon Blackburn, and I found it a very useful overview of philosophy. The most interesting part of the book for me was the chapter dedicated towards Free Will, and in particular moral responsibility. One interesting idea was his 'Mini Martian' argument as it highlights the issues with moral responsibility, and the problems raised seem to undermine our whole judicial system, yet we still hold people responsible for their actions. The theologically-centred parts of the book also gave me a chance to contemplate ideas of religion, which spark endless debate.

Despite the fact Singer's arguments lead him to extreme conclusions, for example bestiality, he accepts them and does not attempt to alter his argument, which I find admirable. Singer's views on personhood and the repercussions they have for ethics present a new way for us to view humans and animals that is so radically different, I had to think how to justify why experimenting on infants is wrong. The fact he made me unsure of the morality behind an issue I am so sure about demonstrates his strength as a philosopher.

Both of these writers have intriguing views, but my favourite philosophical author is Phillip Pullman. Pullman's His Dark Materials books were first recommended to me when I was 11, and although unable to grasp the philosophical issues suggested by Pullman at 11, over several readings and years I began to understand the philosophical themes underlying the fantastical plot, i.e. nonhuman persons, dualism, and a tyrannical god to name a few. Pullman's concept of nonhuman persons is similar to the views suggested by Singer, and although fictitious, Pullman's nonhuman persons act as a thought experiment, which justifies some of Singer's ideas. The concept of a tyrannical god also ties in with some of Blackburn's views about an imperfect god. The idea of nonhuman persons was one of the first philosophical issues I considered outside of the context of the novel, and since then I have always found speciesism to be a very thought-provoking topic.

So do you believe I am a great philosophy student? Hume states I can't hope for a miraculous event to persuade you, and Plato would say I'm just a shade of the greatest, but I can apply Swinburne's ideas about logical and metaphysical necessities to the statement 'Great philosophy students are both willing and able'. A philosophy candidate is great if, and only if, they are both willing and able. Therefore it is a logical necessity that anyone who is willing and able (towards philosophy) is a great philosophy student, and so it is also a metaphysical necessity.

Since I have shown that I am both willing and able by discussing some of my favourite philosophies, Swinburne would be inclined to argue that I am a great philosophy student, and I hope I have persuaded you to agree with him.

Universities applied to:

- Oxford: Offer
- Edinburgh: Offer
- Durham: Offer
- Exeter: Offer
- Cardiff: Offer

Good points:

The statement is original and interesting, and will stand out from those around it. It makes for an enjoyable read. The writing is elegant without being overly flowery or showing off, and the writing style reads as very natural and unaffected. The student has used their original approach to demonstrate their broad philosophical readings and highlights some main areas of interest to explain their motivation for further study.

Bad points:

Although the style of the piece is refreshing, it could have been better executed; consider the second paragraph, which, though witty, uses over 100 words just to make the point that a student must be both skilled and hardworking to be successful. The student would have been wiser to make this more concise and to expand on the points in later paragraphs regarding the books that they found philosophically interesting, and, most importantly, why they found them interesting and how they helped develop their ideas. As it is, their exposition of the works they mention is more of a brief overview of some of the books' content, with the additional note that they find them interesting, rather than explaining any particular personal response to them.

Overall:

This statement is refreshing in its lack of pretence; it reads as a genuine insight into the student's personality, way of thinking, and their motivation for applying. Though the style is great, it is let down somewhat by a lack of content. What is included (the works that were read and enjoyed, and theories they find interesting) is mostly good, but there is nothing particularly unique or interesting about the books and theories discussed (since they're all topics and works that are widely studied at A Level). The time spent on each one means the statement suffers from a lack of concision.

NOTES

Subject: Theology & Religious Studies

I have always possessed a desire to further my understanding of what we might describe as 'ultimate' questions. Our secular society has been corrupted by a view that scientific discovery renders theological endeavours obsolete. However, there are so many questions science can't fully address, such as issues raised by morality, meaning and reason behind life, and how we can attend to global disputes that have arisen from religious conflict. It is such meaningful pursuits, as illustrated in Ronald Nash's Life's Ultimate Questions, Simon Blackburn's Think and C.S.Lewis's God in the Dock , that have evoked my emphatic passion to study this fascinating subject.

My enthusiasm for theology is partly founded in the study of ancient scriptures in their original language and, predominantly, context. In depth, critical analysis of the origin of Christian thought, as exhibited in Henry Chadwick's The Early Church, is an exploration I relish as one begins to uncover the origin of what defines much of our culture today. I am fascinated by examining the evidence for a covertly monotheistic Ancient Israelite culture and studying the validity and internal discrepancies between different accounts of the actions and resurrection of Jesus Christ.

John Barton's Ethics and the Old Testament helped ignite a profound interest in moral theology, whilst Keith Ward's What the Bible Really Teaches fuelled and nurtured this passion as well as linking it with biblical interpretation. So much debate surrounds the relevance of religious texts in modern society, with even Barton claiming that the Decalogue only applies effectively to a patriarchal society. But I take great excitement in facing this argument head on by studying the narrative of biblical texts and interpreting their existential force to derive the ethical injunctions so cleverly portrayed through the text.

My sincere aspiration in life is to be at the forefront of key global decisions that contribute to the abolition of conflict and evoke a greater and stronger world. Carl Schmitt's Political Theology made me contemplate the underestimated impact that religion really has in the affairs of our global society. In Meic Pearse's The Gods of War, he contemplates whether religion is the primary cause of violent conflict around the world. This potent question is why I am so intent on studying the diverse, religious teachings found within world religions as this will enable me to gain an insightful understanding of the real motives behind conflicts that baffle so many in the West.

My diverse A level courses have given me the necessary skills required to excel in a degree directed towards deep philosophical and theological thought, as well as portraying me as a versatile and open minded candidate. Religious Studies has provided me with an excellent foundation for a course revolving around religious concepts upon which I wish to greatly build. Music is good for analysing the context in which new ideas in music came about, a transferable skill when studying ancient texts. Geography has helped me to develop a mature understanding of world affairs, whilst biology demonstrates clear, logical thought.

In terms of extra-curricular activities, I am proud to be chairman of my school's parliamentary debating society, demonstrating strong advocacy skills and the ability to analyse respond to arguments put forward to me. My Gold Duke of Edinburgh Award shows tenacity and commitment. This dedication to excellence is further portrayed with 3 grade 8 examinations on Saxophone, Piano and Guitar as well as playing in the National Youth Orchestra of Great Britain, who will be performing at the Proms next year. I also work at a residential care home, run a music school and coach shooting.

I hope that I have conveyed my passion for the subject I wish to commit the next chapter of my life to exploring.

Universities applied to:

- Cambridge: Offer
- Durham: Offer
- Bristol: Rejected
- Exeter: Offer
- York: Offer

Good points:

This student conveys a passionate belief in the worth of Theology as a field of study and their own motivations for pursuing it. In particular, they strongly link what areas of study within Theology they find interesting (scripture studied in its original context to uncover that which still defines our culture and religion as a motivation for conflict) with their broader personal opinions (that secular science cannot explain 'the big questions'), and long-term life plan ("to be at the forefront of key global decisions that contribute to the abolition of conflict"). The writing is natural and unaffected, and for the most part, the statement flows well.

Bad points:

The student fails to go into any depth regarding the writings they've mentioned; the statement reads more like a list of philosophical works that seek to answer questions they're interested in with no explanation to why these works, in particular, moved them. (The exception to this is the exposition of The Gods of War, which is done excellently). The manner in which they hope to portray themselves as a student has a weak approach. Rather than describing the development of their theological beliefs, their reasons for studying what they do, their extra-curricular activities, etc., the student states that "My diverse A level courses… [portray] me as a versatile and open minded candidate" and "I hope that I have conveyed my passion for the subject", rather than letting the statement stand on its own. They would do better to describe the ways in which they are versatile, open-minded, and passionate (which they do go on to do but should, ideally, be done in a little more depth – how is the study of music transferrable to ancient texts, for example? The student could expand on this rather than briefly listing three somewhat obvious points). They should let the readers draw their own conclusions, rather than simply stating these qualities.

Overall:

Though the student is passionate, their statement suffers from a lack of evidence for the qualities they claim for themselves as a student. They do this in a brief list of unsubstantiated claims. Rather than simply stating that, for example, their Duke of Edinburgh award necessarily shows commitment, they ought to explain what this experience taught them or what skills were necessary to complete it. The student is, however, well-rounded and clearly committed to excelling in a wide variety of areas, both academic and otherwise, and this comes across well.

NOTES

ECONOMICS

Subject: Economics

The right answer - does such a thing even exist? When considering the field of mathematics, my response would be an unequivocal yes - indeed, I find its simplicity and elegance some of its most attractive qualities. For economics, however, the question of a right answer is not so straightforward. My interest in economics was sparked when I read "Freakonomics" and "SuperFreakonomics". I found the search for a logical explanation behind seemingly illogical behaviour intriguing, and the idea that small changes to incentives could effect such large changes to those behaviours fascinating.

To further my understanding, I attended lectures at the LSE, including one given by Ha-Joon Chang. His arguments challenged much of what I had learned - deregulation and trade liberalisation would not, apparently, stimulate competitive growth, while education, it turned out, could not be counted on to increase entrepreneurship or productivity. These contradictions made me eager to read his "23 Things They Don't Tell You About Capitalism" and "Bad Samaritans". Although relishing his controversial stance on almost everything, I found his central thesis - that by using protectionism to support fledgling domestic industries, other poor nations can emulate South Korea's success - overly optimistic and one-size-fits-all. As Paul Collier argues in "The Bottom Billion", many are trapped by conflict or bad governance, with even bleaker prospects after "missing the boat" on which many Asian economies sailed away to prosperity.

While economics is rooted in the world around us, with all its fascinating, messy complexities, mathematics derives its beauty from its abstract nature. It is unique in that it can lead us to an answer that is not merely the right one, but is true in an absolute sense. This was emphasised by G. H. Hardy in "A Mathematician's Apology", where he spoke of a mathematical reality distinct from the ordinary one, of which we can only ever hope to produce a "partial and imperfect copy". Another of the appeals of mathematics is its breadth of application. I was able to explore this over the past three years in a series of Royal Institution master classes covering topics from graph theory to the mathematics of juggling. My decision to continue with mathematics was confirmed when I undertook the AEA; I found it challenging but immensely satisfying to be able to use simple concepts from the A-level core modules to solve even the most daunting problems.

Over the past year, I have mentored two students in mathematics. Explaining concepts to them helped deepen my own understanding and led me to explore proofs behind theorems I had previously accepted. In addition, acting as a primary school classroom assistant inspired me to set up my own volunteering scheme, in which I and other students help children learn to read. I have enjoyed competing in the UKMT Mathematics Challenge, in which I won a medal at Olympiad level, and the UK Linguistics Olympiad, in which I twice progressed to the selection round for the national team. I have also represented my school in the Hans Woyda competition, and am excited to be doing the same in the Target 2.0 challenge later this year.

Despite their differences, the authors I mentioned above hold something in common: their use of empirical methods to reach conclusions. It is here that the attraction of combining the study of mathematics and economics becomes especially apparent. Without mathematics, economics risks beginning to earn its title "the dismal science", reducing to speculation and rhetoric without even the emotional investment enjoyed by politics. This is not to dismiss the importance of normative economics, but to say that it draws meaning from a basis in fact. I am not arguing for sound bite solutions to complex questions, but rather that, even in a field as hotly debated as economics, the right answer is still a worthwhile goal, reachable through the use of data and copious amounts of trial and error.

Universities applied to:

- Cambridge: Offer
- London School of Economics: Offer
- Warwick: Offer
- Bristol: Offer
- Durham: Offer

Good Points:

This statement is thoughtful, interesting, and conveys clear motivations for studying Economics, as well as demonstrating a good level of preparation for university study. The student elaborates on their response to each preparatory activity they engaged in, rather than falling into the trap of simply listing books read and lectures attended. They are clearly passionate about the subject and show promise as an economist, which they demonstrate in, again, not only listing their achievements but explaining what they took from the experience; subtly indicating what this says about them as a student.

Bad Points:

There is little to say in criticism of this statement except that, perhaps, it could come across as a little cliché. Questioning whether there is such a thing as 'the right answer' in the introduction and concluding that pursuit of the field to which they're applying for further study is worthy, are both very common.

Overall:

This is an exceptional personal statement. Not only is the student accomplished, they convey this without bragging and in enough detail that we gain insight into their abilities, motivations, and personal interests, rather than simply receiving a list in prose form. Although the ideas with which the student begins and concludes the statement are somewhat unoriginal, the explanation found in-between is exceptionally strong and justifies the unoriginal sentiments – they're clearly not being added just as throwaway lines.

NOTES

Subject: Economics & Management

The world has changed greatly over my lifetime and Economics seems to me to offer explanations for many complex occurrences in a simple, elegant manner. This is what draws me to the subject and is why I chose to study it at A Level. It allows us to trace events such as the credit crunch back to an ever-expanding supply of credit. But at the same time, the fact that there is rarely a right answer means that there is always scope for further study. When shale gas was discovered in America in 2005, it revolutionised the country: energy prices plummeted while thousands of jobs were created. This situation demonstrates how market mechanisms can act to lower prices, but it is the global consequences that are of most interest to me.

While representing my school in ICAEW's BASE competition at the national finals, I gained more of an understanding of how reliant businesses are on others, miles away from themselves, which encouraged me to read Joseph Stiglitz's 'Making Globalisation Work' in which he calls for reforms to how globalisation is managed. I found it interesting that he believes globalisation is failing because of the way governments are guiding it rather than inherent failures and also how dominant the USA appears in global governance.

The government's role in influencing globalisation was highlighted to me during a work placement with a UKTI dealmaker for India. Through various meetings with Indian entrepreneurs in need of help trading in the UK, I saw how governments could entice talent, and the money it generates, into their own country from around the world. However, it was the number of bureaucratic and cultural obstacles these entrepreneurs faced that struck me most.

The turbulent economic climate we live in makes the subject even more interesting. As we now climb out of recession, there is a debate over how best to tackle the government's burgeoning debt pile without slipping back into recession. Despite George Osborne's attempt to reduce the deficit, it is more than twice the Euro-area average. Monetary policy is also under scrutiny with the BofE needing to strike a fine balance. It needs to ensure that the money supply contracts gradually as growth is established to prevent inflation taking off. I got first hand experience of this challenge while representing my school during the Target 2.0 competition.

As a long-term volunteer at Cancer Research UK, I am now trusted to help managers do tasks such as stocktaking and measuring KPIs. Whilst working there I have noticed that store managers deal well with day-to-day issues but as you venture further up the chain of command, the management becomes more distant and less involved. For instance, it would take a quick visit to establish that there is a flat above the shop I work in, owned by Cancer Research, but used only for storage. The rental income forgone surely exceeds the utility derived from its current use. Arguably this system of management has led to an inefficient allocation of resources. This insight was one of the reasons for wanting to study this course.

I have always been prepared to challenge myself and as such sat two GCSEs and one AS a year early while managing to juggle various sports, both in-school and out, including playing rugby for the Second XV along with cricket and swimming for the School and Potters Bar Swimming Club. Along with sport I am working towards my Grade 6 Clarinet and Duke of Edinburgh Gold. I am a Lance Sergeant in CCF through which I command 4th year students and am also preparing for a forthcoming expedition to Tanzania, where we will help improve local orphanages both physically and through fundraising. I feel that I am ready to tackle the challenges that this academically rigorous course offers.

Universities applied to:

- Oxford: Offer
- Warwick: Offer
- Durham: Offer
- Bath: Offer
- York: Offer

Good Points:

This statement is particularly good in that it integrates the student's extra-curricular activities into their interest in economics, rather than discussing the academic areas they're interested in and then listing their other interests, as a lot of personal statements do. This allows them to discuss their merits as a student – how their study so far has influenced their decision to study economics, and how it has prepared them for it (e.g.: the first-hand experience they got from participating in the Target 2.0 competition). They clearly express their particular academic interest in macroeconomics while allowing the rest of their statement, including non-academic activity, to portray them as a well-rounded individual.

Bad Points:

The statement is perhaps overly focused on practical economic activities, with no mention of any formal study of economic theory outside of GCSEs and AS levels (which are standard for someone applying for an economics degree). While mentioning participation in events like Target 2.0 is great, competitions like these, while giving some insight into the application of economic policy, are far removed from university study. Some evidence of research more suited to a degree would assuage any worries about the student's preparedness for university.

Overall:

This is a very strong statement – the student is accomplished, eloquent, and passionate. It could be improved by discussing some academic interests (discussing theory they've read or going into more detail about the one the student did mention).

NOTES

Subject: Economics & Management

Economics is the study of now. I view it as the study of the psychology of the people who dictate our lives. The world around us is shaped by the fundamental concept of supply and demand, wants and needs, goods and services. What grips me is that everything I have studied I can apply to real life. Discussions about inflation, for example, are so applicable since its current status is active in the world of pricing; the price of a Big Mac and "Burgernomics" is something to which I can relate from my travels.

The statistical aspect of economic analysis is closely linked to my interest with Mathematics, thus I will take an Econometric route on option modules. This scientific approach to what is otherwise a field based solely on individual theories and concepts interests me, as I find quantitative analysis much more accurate and reliable than qualitative theories. As an example, I relish analysing more Econometric models on the A Level Course: like Profit Maximisation calculations.

Despite this, Economics intertwines both Maths and Philosophy on a regular basis. I recently read an article from the Guardian by George Monbiot, which discussed the cost-benefit analysis model and whether nature could be quantified as a tangible asset, and how this would benefit neo-liberals in their perpetual quest for profit. This is just an example of how Econometric analysis does not always deliver such verisimilitude where the figures given are ambiguous. This is what is unique about Economics: there is no right answer to the question 'Is there a right answer?' The concept of there being methods of analysing the psychology of and nature behind the way that the interface between consumers and producers operates seems to exceed all other subjects in terms of interest.

I find it peculiar that a subject that has such a ubiquitous undercurrent in our society is so undefined and obscure; it is undoubtedly this which draws me to it. Consequently I strive to keep up with Economics in the modern world by reading the "I" and "Guardian" newspapers, and "The Economist" magazine regularly. For wider background reading I have read Marx's "Communist Manifesto", Tim Hartford's "The Undercover Economist" and "Too Big To Fail" by Andrew Ross Sorkin.

Sorkin's book provided a gripping, in depth insight into the world of investment banking and entrepreneurship – I finished the book in a matter of days. His book has inspired me to enter the investment sector. Upon graduation I would like to become an investment banker or negotiator, hence I am in the process of trying to arrange some work experience with the London Metal Exchange.

I completed a programme of work experience with Linden Homes this summer, through the Career Academy Programme on which I am enrolled. It was a six week internship during which I gained a firm understanding of a construction company's place within the national economy. I enjoyed spending valuable time in a variety of departments within the firm. I also have work experience planned in Belgium 2013.

Additionally, I participate in a multitude of extracurricular activities. My team and I finished second in the national UMPH Business Competition; in Year 11 my team set the school record for the Enterprise Day Challenge and for three consecutive years my team won the Grimsby Inter-School Quiz without loss. Furthermore, I am part of both the Franklin College Debating Team and the weekly "Blue Sky Club", where students meet to discuss current affairs.

Recently, a particular subject of interest has been the US election. We frequently discuss the debates and the candidates, covering subjects like their political viewpoints and how it will affect both our lives and those of the American public – plus the potential Economic ramifications of the possible outcomes.

With a genuine zeal for the subject and an ability to relate my studies to the real world, I am convinced that I will thoroughly thrive at degree level Economics.

Universities applied to:

- Oxford: Offer
- London School of Economics: Rejected
- York: Offer
- Birmingham: Offer
- Leeds: Offer

Good Points:

The student gives a good insight into their academic interests and what's inspired them to develop over time. They also demonstrate a passion for the subject, not only by stating their interest in it but by further explaining what interests them and why they would make a good candidate to study it at university. The student is already accomplished and explains well what they've gained from their various extra-curricular activities.

Bad Points:

The writing is weak and, at points, unnatural. The forced interjections of examples and unusual adjectives make it read like a student attempting to write a formal and formulaic exam essay. They would do better to write in their usual style, even if it is somewhat informal; this will allow them to better express themselves and they will come across as more interesting to those reading it. More importantly than this, however, at times, the student fails to keep up their otherwise good level of detail, and the writing becomes list-like. This is particularly prominent when they discuss books they've read to develop their understanding of economics. Although they expand on one of these, they do so in little detail. Interviewers are unlikely to be impressed by simply mentioning that you've read a book – any student applying for degree-level economics is able to read The Communist Manifesto, for instance – but they will be impressed by your response to it and what you gained from the experience of reading it. Unless you expand on these details, a list of books you've read does nothing to contribute to the statement, or your chances of selection.

Overall:

This statement is very strong, except where it discusses academic work. The detail here was most likely sacrificed in favour of expanding further on their extra-curricular activities and their particular areas of interest. However, they've limited discussion of their study of various classic economic works so severely that it fails to add anything to the piece. The statement would, therefore, benefit from a more balanced approach to the various areas of the student's life.

NOTES

Subject: Economics

My motivation to study economics actually came as a surprise, as I had expected the subject would be mainly concerned with acquiring money. However, from our first lesson I realised that economics is truly about maximising the happiness of society. Good economists advocating policies which are just a fraction more effective can make positive differences to the lives of huge numbers of people. This is what excites me about economics, and constantly thinking in terms of economics has become second nature to me. The best way I can demonstrate this is through my blog. It has been rewarding to use knowledge acquired from extensive reading outside the course in the formation of more complex arguments, such as how universities should be funded.

My two favourite books so far have been Thomas Friedman's "The World is Flat" and Philip Ball's "Critical Mass", which I chose by cross-referencing university reading lists with website reviews. I enjoyed Friedman's demonstration of seemingly small policy changes making a large difference through "reform retail". I also gained a much firmer grounding in the history of globalisation and, surprisingly, logistical systems. Most importantly, Friedman highlighted some major choices that the world will have to make as it becomes ever more globalised, particularly the balance between efficiency and tradition in developed economies. Wal-Mart seems to be a metaphor for this debate, and perhaps the way in which it ends up doing business will be symbolic of the future of our flat world.

I also found "Critical Mass" very thought-provoking because I had to incorporate skills from all of my AS levels, even Chemistry for the Maxwell-Boltzmann distribution curves, in order to understand the book. I found the thought processes that lead scientists to study trends rather than individual "peoploids" very revealing, as it is the core of economic rationale. However, the topics I became most immersed in were the models of Axelrod, particularly the study of the formation of alliances. I believe that a similar technique could be employed in economic models in order to better account for external influences and chaos theory. Moreover, I have been able to apply his display of the effectiveness of "Tit for Tat" as a strategy in game theory to my A2 history course on the Cold War.

Despite being very interested in theoretical economics, I am well aware that a good knowledge of current events is just as important. I read both "The Economist" and "The Sunday Times" weekly in order to stay up to date. At school, I actively take part in the economics, politics and debating societies. These have been great outlets for topical discussion and, on the whole, a very constructive way to spend my lunchtimes. I also play hockey for my school and West Herts Hockey Club, which has been great for keeping fit and improving my teamwork skills.

A very challenging application of these skills has been the Target 2.0 competition, which I was chosen to enter after competing with nine other applicants to represent my school. It has been gratifying to use data and quantitative reasoning in order to reach a definite conclusion, which is something I had not expected to have the opportunity to do until econometrics and statistical economics modules at university. I am very much looking forward to studying the more mathematical side, because I have always had an affinity for maths. Target 2.0 has also given me an increased sense of perspective on not only the intricate workings of monetary policy, but also news relating to central bankers such as the "Monetary Illusions" article featured recently in the economist. Most importantly, I now know that I would love a career in which I can employ economic theory to my work, and the best chance I have of achieving this is by continuing to study economics at a higher level.

ULTIMATE OXBRIDGE PERSONAL STATEMENT GUIDE — EXAMPLE STATEMENTS – ECONOMICS

Universities applied to:

- Cambridge: Offer
- Bristol: Offer
- Warwick: Offer
- Bath: Offer
- Nottingham: Offer

Good Points:

This student has an interesting insight into Economics as a subject and into their particular motivation for studying it, which is well backed up. The details regarding how they chose what to read, as well as their response to their readings and why they've chosen to discuss these particular books (that is, why they're their favourites) make the statement stand out, as it gives a personal response to the works, rather than reeling off an impressive list of books or simply summarising the ideas expressed in them to show some academic ability. The student is well-rounded and shows an interest in a variety of economic pursuits (and, moreover, actively acknowledges that the area in which they have the most interest is not the be-all and end-all of Economics, which is unusual for a personal statement, and benefits the image of them as a good candidate for university study).

Bad Points:

The statement only discusses academic pursuits. While this time is well-spent and the student comes across as very accomplished, universities often like to see the non-academic side of students too, to show that they are individuals capable of managing a balanced life, rather than devoting all of their time to work in order to maintain the high-level of academic accomplishment expressed in their exam results and personal statements.

Overall:

This is a strong statement because the student has found a great level of detail in discussing what's inspired them to apply for Economics and what makes them a good student. It could be improved by being balanced with some discussion of the student's non-academic interests.

NOTES

Subject: Economics

In Year 11, I fell in love with Economics. I followed a basic introduction course where I discovered the greatness of economists such as Adam Smith. I was at first convinced by the invisible hand theory, but my convictions were challenged by Keynes' work: government spending can, in certain cases, induce growth by boosting demand.

Economics advances rational explanations of an irrational world. I find this paradox amazing. In the case of Veblen goods, the higher the prices, the higher the demand. This shows that Economics is a social science: human behaviour and ways of thinking come into play. For a long time, microeconomics, with the utility function theory, assumed that individuals were rational. Today some economists are working under different assumptions. As Kahneman, whose work fascinates me, put it, people have cognitive bias.

I also love the fact that because Economics is not an exact science, it is open to controversy: if you put three economists in a room, you will have three different analyses of the same situation. France's GDP resisted better the 2008 recession than the UK's. Today, UK's growth is back while France's is still flat. This could be explained by automatic stabilizers (more social transfers in France), but also by the different monetary policies (more accommodative in the UK than in the EU) or budget policies (UK cut spendings, France increased taxes).

Paradoxically, I also like the fact that Economics relies heavily on the precision and objectivity of Mathematical models. Behind every economic principle lies logical reasoning, and I believe my taste and talent for Maths can help me greatly in my studies. In 2012, I finished in the top 1.5% in a national French logic competition (Concours Kangourou). During my Year 12, I finished second in my school in the UK Maths Challenge, and in the top three in the French Maths Olympiads. I have chosen an additional Maths option in my curriculum, and I believe that studying a wide range of subjects such as Ancient Greek, Geography, History, or even Philosophy (in addition to my scientific disciplines) has helped me gain valuable general knowledge.

At the end of Year 11, obliged to make a choice between Economics and Maths, I chose the latter as I knew I would need a good foundation in Maths to study Economics. However, I have sustained my keen interest in Economics, reading the book "50 Economic ideas" by Edmund Conway, and attending an Economics Summer School (DebateChamber, 2014). In a course on economic growth, I studied the Solow-Swann model, which gave me food for thought. Does a country's growth depend solely on the capital-output ratio of the economy? In the long term, does an economy really reach a state of equilibrium where GDP cannot increase further?

After having been class delegate for three years, I was elected by all the students as their representative on the Lycée council. I have taken part in numerous debates about the Lycée's organisation with adult board members. This role has taught me to defend my opinions whilst listening to others' and given me a sense of responsibility. I am a motivated person and love leading projects: two years ago I founded a football club, the Newstars, which now competes in an official League.

Moreover, I spent two weeks in Ghana last summer setting up sustainable sporting activities for young children. I saw the extent of poverty and underdevelopment and was amazed by the omnipresence of corruption, affecting everything from parking spaces to police work. As a result, I became interested in development models and learnt that economic aid to Africa can have unintended consequences, such as reinforcing fraud and market distortion, bringing potentially more poverty.

This made me realise that Economics is not only compelling intellectually, but can also make a practical difference in people's lives, thus I am eager to develop my understanding of the subject and its practical applications further at degree level.

Universities applied to:

- Cambridge: Offer
- London School of Economics: Rejected
- University College London: Offer
- Bath: Offer
- Warwick: Offer

Good Points:

This statement gives a good personal insight into the development of the student's economic thought and their personal motivation for the further study of Economics, as well as explaining their conception of Economics as a discipline, which will allow universities to decide if they're suitable for their institution. The student shows a genuine interest in the subject, evidenced by their reading around a wide range of economic theories and leaving questions open to indicate what questions they hope to develop answers to as a student of Economics. They clearly convey both their academic and personal accomplishments and, importantly, they link these specifically to the study of Economics.

Bad Points:

The views expressed are somewhat unoriginal. While this is not inherently a bad thing if discussing their own economic stance (an A level student, after all, is unlikely to come up with an original economic model), but can be a let-down if discussing their reasons for studying Economics. Stating that Economics is not an exact science, for instance, is quite a trite point to make that is unlikely to make the statement stand out from the crowd. The student could improve this by discussing exactly why they personally are suited to a subject filled with such controversy, and how they hope to resolve this controversy for themselves to develop a clear economic stance, for instance.

Overall:

This is a very strong statement. Even the unoriginal and underdeveloped aspects mentioned above do not let the statement down hugely because the student so clearly expresses their interest in Economics, and what makes them a strong candidate.

NOTES

Subject: Land Economy

My interest in economics has grown out of two diverse sources. On the one hand, an international perspective and a critical attitude to global issues is my lucky inheritance, given my mother's engagement in international media and my father's interest in Latin American culture. As I grew up my mother was employed by the International Herald Tribune and euronews while my father worked as a Spanish translator. This background has given me a particular openness to the world around me, a fondness for understanding different cultures and a critical sensitivity towards social issues. On the other hand, from an early age I enjoyed the benefits of having an aptitude for mathematics and the pleasure of abstract problem solving. After long speculation I have come to the idea that I should combine these two diverse interests, in the social world and that of abstract rational thought, through the discipline of economics.

The fact that my initial interest in mathematics grew with time is due to the excellent education I received at Berzsenyi Daniel, one of the top grammar schools in Hungary. I benefited from the advanced math classes (8 hours a week) and summer math camps with knot and game theory being this years theme. These intense learning experiences were valuable not only due to the content taught, but also as teaching was structured around improving presentation skills, developing source analysis and the rules of academic writing. The warm and encouraging atmosphere of these camps as well as the inspirational, if competitive attitude taught at Berzsenyi has set me onto a trajectory of exploring mathematical and economic issues during my own time. As such, I ended up reading some works by John Harsanyi and audited lectures at ELTE's first year applied economics course, with units that included microeconomics and basic function analysis. An additional dimension where Berzsenyi provided a privileged educational focus was the area of languages. Emphasis was placed not only on the idea that students should become adapt speakers (of English and German in my case), but also that they become open to the cultural background and history of the nations where these languages originate. It is from these classes that my interest in English and German literature springs, with Oscar Wild and Thomas Mann taking top spot.

There has been additional influence that remained a persistent factor in my personal development. This has been the importance of community based team work. I grew to understand the significance of this, partly by getting elected co-chairman of the Student Council and partly by having played water polo. The first experience taught me the importance of political representation and responsibility, while the second the significance of discipline as well as creativity when treading collectively towards a common goal. Extracurricular activities also played an important role at my school. I took part in a UNESCO competition which focused on climate change and scarce natural resources. While the team achieved third place, the competition was an invaluable experience that further propelled me towards wanting to understand the relationship between national economies and environmental issues.

I feel that exploring the discipline of economics would be the most ideal way to combine my interests as well as develop the skills I have gained during my education so far. While the diverse multicultural environment of the UK has remained an important factor in my choices, it is the historic tradition of higher education that has attracted me the most. I strongly believe that it is this tradition; with its central focus on the individual student, with high expectations, excellent resources and internationally renowned scholars and teachers, which would be the best place for me to develop my natural abilities and ambitions.

Universities applied to:

- Cambridge: Offer
- St. Andrews: Offer
- London School of Economics: Offer
- Edinburgh: Offer
- Aberdeen: Offer

Good Points:

The statement portrays the student as capable and well-educated, with a clear and developed interest in Economics. They seem to have a good grasp of what studying Economics at degree level will involve, and are confident they will be able to handle the work (in particular, the mathematical aspects of it); a claim that is supported by their academic accomplishments. They address the particular environment of university study, which is unusual, but beneficial to the image of a mature, competent student who has made a clear-headed decision to study Economics, on the basis of interest and ability.

Bad Points:

The student emphasises their excellent education. While it is perfectly fine to admit the advantages a good education has given you, this does little to stress your own accomplishments as a student or to demonstrate that you'll be a good candidate for further education in Economics (it might even have the opposite effect since a much larger portion of learning at university is done through independent study). This time would be better spent discussing their own efforts, the way their interests have developed, and how they've pursued them, rather than discussing the structure of courses they've been lucky enough to attend. Where they do discuss their own interests (their favourite authors, for instance), they do so in little depth.

The writing is clunky and forced and reads as trying to be impressive by inserting superfluous adjectives and connectives, e.g.: "There has been additional influence that remained a persistent factor in my personal development. This has been the importance of community based team work." Sentences like these are clearly not written in the student's natural writing style but, rather, the style they've developed for A level essays, which require formulaic structures involving making a point, giving an example, and expanding on it. More naturally, it would read something like "The importance of community has been a persistent factor in my personal development".

Overall:

The student ought to take a more personal approach to their statement by focusing on their interests and achievements they've secured through their own efforts, as well as relying on their natural writing to convey their personality, as opposed to wording the statement in an attempt at academic speech. Despite this, the essay is strong; they elaborate well on how their education has benefitted them and why they want to study Economics further.

NOTES

POLITICS, PHILOSOPHY & ECONOMICS

Subject: Politics, Philosophy, Economics (PPE)

By the time of the 2012 elections, my country, Greece, was facing a profound political, financial and social crisis with far-reaching consequences. The volatility of the situation intensified my interest in Politics, Philosophy and Economics, as I wished to deepen my understanding of society and the causes of such a crisis.

During this period, I watched the political campaigns of all major parties to better comprehend their agendas, which increased my awareness of the situation in Greece in relation to the rest of the world. This led me to participate in the Harvard Model Congress Europe, a simulation of US parliamentary procedures, where I debated with students from around the world on possible solutions to improve US-Venezuela relations. Apart from enhancing my problem-solving skills, this experience acquainted me with the formal US procedures and confirmed that politics is a subject I want to learn more about. Being interested in intergovernmental relations, I completed an internship at the Greek Consulate of Izmir, which helped me develop insights into the political agendas behind the issuing of visas, for example.

Last year, during my internship at the Human Resource department of a major healthcare product manufacturer, I gained first-hand experience of the severity of unemployment in Greece and its sweeping consequences. This experience made me interested in investigating the root cause of unemployment. Varoufakis' "The Global Minotaur" helped me see how an unsustainable and imbalanced economic system could instigate a global crisis, one that Europe tried to remedy with austerity measures, which led to a reduction of economic activity and less need for employed labor. The accuracy with which macroeconomic theory can depict reality spurred my interest to further study this subject and learn more about how these phenomena can be prevented.

My interest in philosophy was further cultivated by my involvement in a volunteering activity where I taught Greek at a shelter for Syrian refugees for three months. Given the fact that the Syrian Civil War made these people seek a better future in Athens with no assets or connections, I started reading about whether war could ever be justified. This led me to seek answers as to whether there are universal moral rules that everyone should follow. I was particularly captivated by the utilitarian perception of morality that J.S. Mill argues, explaining that any action leading to the "greatest happiness" for the "greatest number" is justified. Although this theory can have considerable ethical implications if the minorities are repressed for the benefit of the majorities, it serves as a useful guide to show that the death and destruction provoked by war cannot be justified. Debate, which I have been heavily involved in in the past few years, helped me delve deeper into ethical issues, such as prisoners' rights and bodily autonomy and earned me an invitation for the tryouts of the Greek National Debate Team that will be held shortly, where I will compete for a place in the team.

My determination and patience were further cultivated through chess, my other passion. Last year, the third place among all Greek schools gained by the team I put together and trained made my leadership and co-operation skills all the more tangible. I also enjoy learning about life in space. Studying Physics on my own and investigating the possibility that life might have existed on Venus enhanced my analytical skills and helped me win the third place in the Physics competition during the International Space Olympics in Moscow.

All in all, PPE is ideally suited to my interests as I was able to ascertain during a PPE program I attended last summer at the Oxford and Cambridge Summer Academy. Seeking answers as to how politics, philosophy and economics affect our everyday lives and shape our decisions is an ongoing enquiry that gives perennial rise to fresh questions, which I would love to explore at University.

Universities applied to:

- Oxford: Offer
- London School of Economics: Offer
- Durham: Offer
- York: Offer
- Warwick: Offer

Good Points:

This statement shows off an impressive history of political extra-curricular activities in such a way as to not only list the achievements and experience the student wants to show off, but also to highlight how they have benefited from the experiences and how it has shaped their desire to study PPE. The statement is well-balanced in devoting time to all three subjects, causing one to reasonably conclude that PPE is an ideal subject of choice for them and that they are an ideal student to study it. The student conveys their passion for particular areas of study (e.g.: macroeconomic theory and predicting economic activity in order to prevent disaster).

Bad Points:

The statement doesn't flow particularly well and the student does little to tie the three subjects together. The student could conclude that all of politics, philosophy, and economics could be appropriate for them to study, but the particular combination of the three is one offered by few British universities for a reason. The student should devote some time to discussing why they wish to study the three together and how the study of one affects the others, rather than keeping their passion for each completely separate. The penultimate paragraph, listing interests outside of PPE, is also somewhat disjointed from the rest of the statement and interrupts the flow of the piece as a whole, but this is perhaps unavoidable (and the paragraph does contribute well to the image of the student as a well-rounded individual). Still, they would do better to focus it somewhat on how these skills directly link to university study or the study of PPE.

Overall:

This is a very strong statement. Their background in the three subjects is diverse and interesting, and they convey well how this has affected them as a student. Although they do this for each of the subjects discussed, they could improve it by tying their experience in the three fields together, so as to explain why they wish to study PPE specifically.

NOTES

Subject: Politics, Philosophy, Economics (PPE)

I have been fortunate enough to have spent half my life overseas and to have attended eight different schools in five different countries and as a result I have engaged with people from a wide range of cultures and backgrounds. Having enjoyed these experiences immensely, I am determined to build on this foundation by studying for a degree that will increase my understanding of how trans-national and cross-cultural transactions work. One of the key factors in these transactions, undoubtedly, is human nature.

I was very interested, therefore, to read Jonathon Wolff's 'An Introduction to Political Philosophy', particularly the contrasting interpretations of the 'state of nature' that rose dependent on the interpretation of mankind. In my experience there is a parallel between inter-personal and international relations and I want to understand the ways in which states and people operate. My background has made me more aware of complex international issues, such as Australia's current problem in reconciling the fact that its major trading partner has the potential to become its biggest adversary. Because of my interest in this situation I delved deeper into China's rise, through the medium of an extended project which discussed whether China poses any threat to the USA. Research for this project caused me to question whether there is any justification for the Western ethical preference for a 'free' economy over command economies. This work made me realise that I need economic knowledge in order to better understand the complexities of international relations and encouraged me to fast track an A level in economics.

My research touched on the question of the apparent commonality of cultural morals and delving into this issue led me to reflect on the arguments for universal morality that J.S. Mill presents in 'Utilitarianism'. His claim that public convictions and general happiness are the basis for a viable moral authority appears to reflect the operation of democratic governance. I would argue, however, that there is a strong, external ethical pressure that acts regardless of happiness, a knowledge of base morality that is followed for its own end. The complexity of such issues has always appealed to me, which is perhaps why I was so enthused by the mathematical elements of philosophical logic that Blackburn presents in 'Think'. The notion of reducing rational questioning to formulaic equations was completely new to me and I found it very compelling. I was equally intrigued by the attempts, particularly of Descartes in 'Meditations' and Anselm in the 'Proslogian', to develop an irrefutable argument based purely on reason; the notion of an a priori argument that could establish what empiricism cannot is a profound possibility. I thoroughly enjoy immersing myself in unknown and foreign situations. This probably stems from my travels across the globe, which took me from childhood in Moscow to my more recent time in Canberra.

Through school and college, I have sustained an ability to balance my academic studies with a hectic social life, part-time jobs and my sporting commitments. I have been elected to the captaincy of two football teams and have played a consistent role in promoting youth involvement, through coaching a junior football team and being involved in the Olympic FLAMES programme. I am happy to lead or work within a team and can negotiate with difficult individuals, whether they are complaining customers or disaffected youngsters. I am eager to pursue a career path that will take me into an international and cross-cultural environment. This is why I feel strongly drawn towards a degree where I can use my experiences and ambitions to better prepare myself for the multinational market of the future. I want to develop an academic arsenal which will best establish me as a positive contributor in an increasingly trans-national, interlinked world - where global understanding looks set to become an essential attribute.

Universities applied to:

- Oxford: Offer
- Warwick: Offer
- London School of Economics: Rejected
- York: Offer
- Manchester: Offer

Good Points:

The student demonstrates a clear interest in all three subjects and does especially well in linking the three together, detailing how their interest in one politics issue lead to studying Economics, which lead to readings in Philosophy. They give the impression of an individual who has naturally come to the conclusion that PPE is the right area of study for them and they back this up substantially with both their personal history and academic studies. The balance between discussing their academic interests and other areas of their life is just right, and they use the latter to reinforce their worth as a student. The statement flows naturally while the conclusion rounds it off nicely with a look to the future and what they wish to do with their degree.

Bad Points:

At times, the student dwells on explaining their exact response to each book mentioned and their current position on each area of study. This is not particularly useful as those reading it will be more interested in how you think and how your reading developed your thought, rather than whether you, for example, tend towards consequentialism or deontology, as you don't have nearly enough space in a personal statement to back up a philosophical position in any substantial or interesting way.

The statement also ought to be broken down into smaller paragraphs. This will improve the overall structure and will make for a much more natural read.

Overall:

This is an excellent statement; it ties the three subjects together and clearly conveys why each is personal to the student and what they want to achieve by studying them. They ought, however, to focus more on how their background has affected their way of thinking, rather than listing their positions on various issues.

NOTES

Subject: Politics, Philosophy, Economics (PPE)

Living in London, I have witnessed numerous political and economic problems affecting people's every day lives: the threat of terrorism after 7/7, lack of council housing and the disaffection demonstrated in the riots. Seeing governments' failure to tackle these problems directly has fuelled my desire to both understand and find solutions to such problems.

Studying A Level History I looked at the totalitarian regimes of both Mussolini and Hitler. I read 'The Republic' by Plato and Machiavelli's 'The Prince', to look at how dictatorial states can develop. I find Plato's ideas of a 'perfect' society, such as the lack of class mobility, chillingly reminiscent of the totalitarian states which I studied. On the other hand, I find 'The Prince' a perceptive study of ways to gain and hold power. The political dominance of leaders described in the books seemed similar to the legacy of Tony Blair which I explored through my Extended Project Qualification on 'How can the Labour Party rebrand in order to win the 2015 election?' I researched the opinions of the general public pertaining to the party and discovered that raising economic confidence was the main area on which Labour needed to work.

'The Return of Depression Economics' by Krugman highlighted the difference between Krugman's proposals of Keynesian solutions to the economic issues we currently face and George Osborne's recent budgets. The way the markets have intensified inequality through the crisis shocked me into reading Wolff's 'An Introduction to Political Philosophy' which cemented my conviction on the moral importance of state action to alleviate poverty. To further my knowledge, I attended an Economics Summer School with the Debate Chamber and studied aspects of economics which I had not previously encountered, such as game theory. I enjoyed the logical aspect of game theory combined with the moral side of problems such as the Prisoner's Dilemma. Carrying out research into the Black-Scholes equation, as part of a maths presentation on the effect of maths on the current economic crisis, highlighted how important maths is to the study of economics.

Taking my French A Level at the time of the French presidential election piqued my interest in French politics, and I used my French language skills to appreciate the presidential debate and Hollande's acceptance speech. As a violinist, I have had the opportunity to visit France, Germany and Finland with Bromley Symphony Orchestra and Chamber Orchestra. The different political tasks that face other countries, whether it is reconciling cultures in France or leading the European economy in Germany, provide a contrast to everyday British politics. In addition, I was able to play at the Royal Albert Hall and I have gained the time management skills needed for practising, rehearsals and concerts. I looked at the politicisation of music as part of a feature for the website, Sound Influx, and concluded that while it raised awareness, music no longer has a true influence on politics.

As Student Subject Leader for Politics, I have promoted the subject within the school by explaining the basic ideas relating to British political parties to year 9 students and by teaching year 10s about Marxism, for which I had to express ideas clearly. Within the next year I intend to help year 8s set up and run their own political campaigns, in order for them to develop an interest in the subject. I collaborated with a teacher at my school for a research project, sponsored by Canterbury Christchurch University, looking into ways of making cross-curricular links between different subjects, particularly investigating the effect Maths can have across the curriculum. We discovered the benefits of making such links, with students being able to use their skills and enthusiasm for one subject to improve their understanding of other areas of learning. It was this which confirmed to me that I want to study an interlinking degree such as this at university.

ULTIMATE OXBRIDGE PERSONAL STATEMENT GUIDE — EXAMPLE STATEMENTS – PPE

Universities applied to:

- Oxford: Offer
- Durham: Offer
- Warwick: Offer
- London School of Economics: Offer
- York: Offer

Good Points:

This student's approach makes for a fairly unique and interesting read. They focus on a fairly narrow set of issues and spend the first three paragraphs discussing books and schools of thought that have influenced their thinking. This demonstrates a passion for exploring an issue they're interested in and shows off their extra-curricular activities, as well as showcasing their ability to tackle fairly advanced texts. They also demonstrate a broad background in all three subjects without separating their discussion of the three or taking note of the different 'classifications' of the texts discussed. This subtly conveys a predisposition towards not only the three subjects separately but towards studying the three in tandem. The points they discuss are suitably detailed and convey their particular interests within the fields of Politics, Philosophy, and Economics. They also devote an appropriate amount of time to discussing areas of their life that are not directly linked to PPE, but demonstrate their worth as a student.

Bad Points:

The first and last paragraphs are a little weak, mostly because of their lack of connection to the rest of the statement, and at times, the piece doesn't flow as well as it could have. The ideas discussed so well in the second and third paragraph ought to be linked back to their personal experience of observing issues in London or else the first paragraph is somewhat useless. The last paragraph, though fine, makes quite a weak case for studying a joint degree and is the only part of the statement that reads as forced, rather than a natural conclusion. This is especially true given how well the interlinking nature of the three subjects is handled earlier in the statement – if the student wants to make their predisposition towards a joint degree explicit, it is here, and with regards to the interplay of their study of the three subjects, this ought to be done.

Overall:

This is an exceptional personal statement, finding the right balance between broadness and specificity, between the subjects, and between academic and non-academic areas of their life. Its only downside is that it suffers, as many personal statements do, from some disjointedness and superfluous content.

NOTES

Subject: Philosophy, Politics, Economics (PPE)

Political policy and institutions, economic circumstance and philosophical debate permeate our everyday lives, as Keynes said "The world is ruled by little else". Their nuances and intricacies impact lives universally and thus their study is thus both riveting and indispensable.

The notion that "human progress is neither automatic nor inevitable" spurred my desire to question the validity of the beliefs we hold and the policies we live under. Hearing Professors Kay and Chang lecture on the future of capitalism and its potentially calamitous impact on the world economy, led me to question the validity of this influential economic policy. This drew me to Stiglitz's 'Price of Inequality' through which I began to appreciate the plethora of ways neoliberalism and capitalism affect our lives; influencing political representation, social circumstances and behaviour. Inspired by this I pondered whether politicians betray their obligations and catalyse the economic inequality and social injustice faced as a result of such policy rather than alleviating hardship and suffering; seeking answers in the political system of the USA for which I have a passion. Developing an interest in radicalism, I investigated the radicalisation of the GOP and the repercussions this is having for political and economic stability for my extended project. Through their actions in congress and framing of the debate it is clear that radical Republicans are politically preventing any amelioration of US domestic difficulties. Lieven's book 'America: Right or Wrong' supports this however I would further argue that the antiquated constitution and anachronistic political system are culpable and it would be wrong to blame individuals for an institutional failure to secure the wellbeing and financial security of the American people.

Perceiving the swathes of injustice in Western societies led me to probe for examples elsewhere and through attending a SOAS summer school I became gripped with the manifestations of justice in tumultuous regions in Africa such as the Rwandan 'Gacaca' trials; an amalgamation of punitive and restorative justice. Such a philosophical concern led me to question the nature of true Justice and whether Rawls, in 'A Theory of Justice', is justified in claiming that it is optimally applied from behind a "veil of ignorance". Conversely I hold that true justice requires a full knowledge of societal and individual circumstance since the values and aspirations that define who we are allow us to determine what justice truly is.

Seeking answers to philosophical questions has become an outlet for my natural curiosity. In preparation for an essay competition I theorised whether the happiness we all experience is true happiness and whether it is the only thing humans ever pursue. I built upon my knowledge of ethical systems particularly that of Mill's Utilitarianism and Aristotle's Nichomachean Ethics and concluded that happiness is the "simple harmony between man and the life he leads". I further felt that moral codes exist only to justify one's actions to oneself and hence act as mere vehicles for true happiness.

While the social sciences are often discussed in global terms and focus on societies as a whole, it is equally important to appreciate their quotidian impact on individuals. Driven my by desire to broaden my horizons I work extensively with London Citizens Community Organising and on other community projects allowing me to discover the crucial socioeconomic issues facing people and the means of assuaging these matters.

I feel that studying social sciences in isolation limits appreciation of their complex nature and only through holistic analysis and investigation can one seek the answers to the questions of the past, present and future.

Hence I feel that my insatiable thirst for knowledge and my desire for understanding the imperative concerns of our world mean that such a combination is suited to both my academic and personal passions.

Universities applied to:

- Oxford: Offer
- Warwick: Offer
- Durham: Offer
- Bristol: Offer
- St. Andrews: Rejected

Good Points:

This statement is especially strong in its lack of superfluous content: each point is well-developed and contributes to the image of the student and their academic interests and abilities. It shows a well-rounded student with a passion for political economics. They clearly convey their areas of interest and use each book mentioned to its full advantage, detailing why they chose to read it and how it affected their thinking.

Bad Points:

The student focuses overwhelmingly on politics and some related economics, with only a cursory exposition of some philosophical ideas that interest them, which was not linked to the rest of the ideas discussed. The student also suffers somewhat from a lack of extra-curricular activity. While their political interests seem to be broad, they don't discuss anything non-academic, which can be worrying for tutors reading the statement. Discussing hobbies, responsibilities, and interests outside of PPE gives an impression of a well-rounded person and shows a healthy balance between academic and non-academic pursuits. Discussion of these parts of their life can also be used to show time management, leadership abilities, and other desirable qualities.

Overall:

This statement would be exceptional if the student were applying for a Politics and Economics degree. The philosophical parts discussed, however, are poorly integrated and the student appears to have put far less time into their study of this discipline. They also fail to discuss anything besides academic pursuits. The political and economic interests mentioned, though, are discussed excellently, and clearly demonstrate the student is more than capable to take on a joint honours degree.

NOTES

Subject: Philosophy, Politics, Economics (PPE)

I have always had a fascination with risk and whilst I enjoy a good game of poker, managing an imaginary portfolio of stocks has proved to be a more sustainable long-term strategy. Whilst the use of trends and technical indicators is important, an overall view of the economy is vital and I read the news in print and online daily to stay on top of it. The financial crisis of 2008 was when I first became aware of the economy and I have closely observed it since. The various measures put in place to produce the subsequent period of austerity and recovery have slowly but surely succeeded, ultimately achieving a rate of recovery unmatched since WWII. The past half a decade or so has been an interesting time to live through and is sure to serve as a case-study for years to come.

The intrinsic link between politics and economics became particularly obvious recently with the turbulent scene in the UK surrounding the referendum for Scottish independence. Aside from the pound's decline and rally at the time, there were far-reaching potential consequences for the country as a whole both politically and economically. In particular, had it not been for the economic quagmire predicted for an independent Scotland, it's likely that the Yes voters would have come much closer to a majority. Looking at politics through the lens of philosophy has enticed me and studying Hobbes' state of nature, contemplating a time when the states that run the world today didn't exist, is both thought-provoking and useful for modern thinking. The premise of the pursuit of felicity caught my attention and reading into the concept of egoism, I was amazed by the parallels with the theory of evolution and The Selfish Gene made long before Darwin's time. All these ideas reduce the human to a selfish vehicle for genes and reveal the deterministic nature of our actions. Ultimately, they demonstrate that there has been no transcendence between us and the matter from which we are made.

This conclusion ties in with Nihilism, the mesmerising doctrine that drove me to look into philosophy as a whole. I thought Blackburn's "Think" was a fantastic introduction; the highlight for me was the discussion of senses as primary and secondary. Seeing the secondary senses of smell, taste etc. washed away by objectivity and even the primary senses of extension, motion etc. eradicated by the lack of a proper idea of solidity reminded me of Nihilism. I found the doctrine analogous to this transition to the realm of the noumenal because, in essence, Nihilism simply suggests that purpose and morality, among other things, are human abstracts that do not exist in any objective sense. Furthermore, just as Hume and Berkeley go on to refute the most basic property of the world around us – solidity – some nihilists additionally negate knowledge and reality as impossible and non-existent respectively.

During my free time, I was an editor for my school's weekly paper, contributing opinion articles and also writing a column that I started, with one of my articles being featured in the XZR International magazine. Additionally, I won one of my school's essay prizes with a piece on ethics and went on to present my ideas at an interschool lecture event. An avid public speaker, I have debated economics and given numerous talks. I have also had a strong involvement in voluntary work, helping at Mencap, the Patients Association and my local hospice. Furthermore, I have honed my leadership and teamwork skills, completing all three Duke of Edinburgh awards and captaining my house's football team.

Although my formal education has been based in science, my aptitude for questioning and analytical thinking in tandem with my keen interest in the way that society functions ought to serve me well in the study of PPE. The transition from definite answers to more abstract concepts and conclusions has given me great satisfaction outside of classrooms and I look forward to further embracing it within them.

Universities applied to:

- Oxford: Offer

Good Points:

The writing style is natural and flows well. The student does well in linking the three subjects together and explaining why studying them all as a joint degree is a worthwhile pursuit. They have a clear idea of what areas of Philosophy they're interested in, and demonstrate a relatively developed understanding of some of the ideas they discuss. Though some aspects of the statement are impersonal (as discussed below), the chronological nature of the progression of their private study is a nice insight into exactly how these ideas have developed, which is a telling insight into them as a student. They adequately address their formal academic background in the sciences and emphasise the private study they've done that leads them towards a degree in the social sciences and humanities.

Bad Points:

Although the student shows a good grasp of the economic climate that has surrounded them for the past few years, they do little to make it personal or to why this has made them want to study PPE. Instead, the statement reads more like a summary of recent political events and how they relate to some schools of philosophy. The third paragraph lets down the rest of the statement; its ideas are confused and expresses rather simplistic philosophical ideas in an academic language that tries to impress. It summarises ideas with no attempt to link them to the student's particular interest in them or to their desire to study PPE. They would also do better to discuss in a little more detail what they have gained from their extra-curricular activities, rather than simply listing them.

Overall:

This statement shows an intelligent student who has already actively developed their views in some areas relevant to their degree and a good understanding of how current events relate to it. Their statement is somewhat impersonal, however, and reads as a list of schools of thought in politics and philosophy with some brief explanation of how they relate to each other, rather than an explanation of why they personally are interested in them.

NOTES

Subject: Philosophy, Politics, Economics (PPE)

Studying economics, I found that its analysis is most effective when considered in the context of other disciplines such as politics and philosophy. The strong links between economics and these fields is the most appealing aspect to me of studying PPE at Oxford.

Reading Gigerenzer's 'Risk Savy', I was particularly interested in the irrational decisions that can be made when a common concept such as risk is misunderstood. His call for a simplification of risk portrayal by specialists, such as converting probabilities into natural frequencies, and a revolution of the way risk is taught in schools struck me as a convincing thesis in how to reduce the damaging decisions that ignorance of risk can lead to. My interest in the way human behaviour affects our economic decisions led me to read 'Irrational Exuberance' by Robert Shiller that proved helpful in developing my economics prize essay. There I analysed the debate between Shiller and Fama over whether the market price was always the best indicator of an asset's value and if so whether we could predict asset price bubbles. I found Fama's belief that all economic agents are rational when faced with new information on the worth of an asset was undermined by Shiller whose persuasive analysis of situations in which human nature leads us to act irrationally therefore aiding the occurrence of bubbles.

Equality as a concept that can be approached through all three subjects is one that I became concerned with. Pickett and Wilkinson's 'The Spirit Level' advocated a much more equitable society emphasising the economic benefits to future sustainable growth, and although I found this convincing I was sceptical of the tenuous link between inequality and social problems such as mental illness and teenage pregnancies. These doubts were reinforced by Snowdon's 'The Spirit Level Delusion' where he demonstrates that many social wrongs such as homicides are not linked to inequality and have in fact been falling as inequality rises. I attended Picketty's recent talk at the LSE, and although I agreed with his call for greater equality I was not persuaded by his proposal for a heavily progressive tax system, as it appeared politically implausible. On the other hand Nozick's equally extreme belief that redistributive taxation is akin to forced labour, I perceived to be unfair because that it would result in wealth being concentrated in the hands of the skilled, leading to great inequality that would be detrimental to the whole of society.

After reading 'An Introduction to Political Philosophy' by Wolff and 'Justice: What's the right thing to do?' by Sandel, I have become increasingly more concerned with the relationship between the citizen and the state and the question of the power the state has over the individual. This led me to read Mill's 'On Liberty' in which I found his view that the individual is sovereign over his body and thus his liberties, an unrealistic state in which individuals could live. The potential clashes that would occur between individuals over their desire to retain all their liberties seemed contradictory to an ideal society. However I found the view of Rousseau, in his 'The Social Contract', that the individual must sacrifice his natural rights to the community in order to preserve his liberties, a more compelling view on the relationship between the citizen and the state, allowing the state to limit our rights in order to preserve our other liberties and society as a whole. The 'moral and collective body' that this association creates seems to me a more persuasive representation of the ideal relationship between the citizen and the state.

I am an active member of the school community playing 1st XI football and being a school prefect. I am on the committee of the schools Economics Society where I invite, and have the opportunity to discuss with influential professionals in their respective fields.

ULTIMATE OXBRIDGE PERSONAL STATEMENT GUIDE — EXAMPLE STATEMENTS – PPE

Universities applied to:

- Oxford: Offer
- Bristol: Rejected
- Edinburgh: Offer
- Exeter: Rejected

Good Points:

The student makes it clear why they wish to study PPE as a joint honours, all the while underlining their passion for Economics and how it informs their study of the other two subjects. They show a wide range of reading around the subjects and mention a few more unusual books that they've found interesting (though students shouldn't aspire towards obscure readings above all else, it helps not to only mention books on the Oxford recommended preparatory reading lists – Think by Blackburn is mentioned by a huge number of PPE applications, for instance). More importantly, they outline their particular areas of interest, show a good understanding of the ideas they discuss, and outline why they found them interesting.

Bad Points:

They completely separate their discussion of political, economic, and philosophical ideas. While they mention in the introduction why they wish to study them together, they fail to go on to make a particularly compelling case for this. Instead, it reads like three mini-personal statements – one for each of the disciplines. Although they show an interest in various areas of PPE, they say very little about why they want to study them further or, more importantly, what makes them a good candidate for study. This is particularly evident in the paragraph outlining their non-academic interests, which is simply a brief list of things they do in their spare time. The statement reads more like a summary of their political, philosophical, and economic views, rather than a proposal to study at a university. Most egregiously, the candidate makes explicit mention of wanting to study at Oxford in their statement, this is an unnecessary inclusion which all-but ensures that universities besides Oxford will reject the application, and Oxford may also (as this indicates poor critical thinking skills on the part of the applicant.)

Overall:

It is evident from the statement that this is a very capable and well-developed student, however, the statement could be improved by tying the three subjects together more substantially opposed to just a throwaway line in the introduction. The student could have also spoke more about who they are as a person and a student, their strengths, and why they, in particular, should study PPE.

NOTES

Subject: War Studies / Politics

This world is a bleak place; and a change is what it needs. Not the type offered during the General Election Campaign of 2019, but the type offered by the inspirational Mahatma Ghandi and Martin Luther King Jr. It was between the ages of four to seven, during my stay in Bangladesh, that I saw poverty at my door step and corruption at every corner. Then I did not understand why this was so and honestly, I still do not. Today, as a passionate member of the pressure groups Amnesty International and Avaaz, I have tried to find my voice and channel it into something that is productive by signing many e-petitions against International Government actions such as stoning women and freeing political prisoners.

My interest in Politics was initially provoked by the daily reading of national newspapers during my GCSE years, the study of Hitler's Germany as well as the Middle East crisis; the complexities of such international conflicts also further intrigued me. This then led me to study both History and Politics at 'A' level. However, I had never anticipated that I would come to admire them both so much. Politics has taught me to be cynical, but has also shown me that it can also be the path to positive change. Meanwhile, History has taught me some painful truths and that there is no end to knowledge; we can never know enough. Studying Sociology at 'A' level as well, has helped me attempt to understand why society does what it does while my English Lit. 'A' level gives me the words and skills to artfully explain myself.

During the General Election of 2019, I found myself supporting a political party with such loyalty, that after the election I had joined the party. Through this membership I have attended local meetings to understand the issues of my constituency and get more involved. I have also attended a conference in London before the election with guest speakers including Nick Clegg and Jack Straw the then Justice Secretary. During this conference I led the way to scrutinising their claims by questioning their policies; to which I was given a much expected diplomatic reply. This then only enhanced my curiosity for the subject.

I wanted to experience the Political workings to see if I was truly made for this and so I ran for the Charities Officer post in the Student Council. This required three weeks of campaigning just like the politicians during an election, making public speeches and publishing my own mini manifesto. I kept to my morals and still managed to have won. This confirmed for me that studying Politics at a greater depth and becoming a Politician was what I wanted with a serious passion. Furthermore, as a member of the Council, I have learned a great deal; how to organise my time effectively so I could reply to every request made by students and staff promptly as well as helping to organise social events such as the Summer Ball. I am also held accountable, just like MPs, by the electorate and therefore I have to take every step in my decision making very carefully so that it is justifiable.

Along with the responsibilities I have in the council, I am also a member of the Politics Society in which I am continuously leading very heated debates about current political issues. I am also a member of the Amnesty Society within college and a member of the Jazz Choir as singing has always been a hobby. My political debates do not end in college, but continue over the dinner table and even on social networking sites. Even during my part time work as a sales assistant on Saturdays, I find myself teaching my colleagues and even my manager how politics works and what is happening right now worldwide. I see the future that I want and the world needs, and I am willing to give it my all. I am an ambitious, responsible, independent young woman with determination to bring about change; all I need is the opportunity.

Universities applied to:

- King's: Offer
- SOAS: Offer
- Queen Mary's: Offer
- Cambridge: Interview + Rejected

Good Points:

This statement is intensely personal and makes for an interesting read, which offers a telling insight into the student's life. They explain their personal reasons for wanting to study War Studies / Politics and makes a compelling case for their worth as a student by explaining what they've gained from both their formal education and their political activity. They also describe in detail what they want to gain from the further study of Politics and what they hope to do with their degree.

Bad Points:

It would have been nice to see them discuss the development of their political thought through their academic and political activities, as this is more relevant to study at university and would give the student an opportunity to discuss any more focused academic work they had done in preparation for the demands of further education (reading around the subject outside of class, for instance). The writing is also somewhat clunky. Additionally, the line in the introduction regarding channelling political beliefs into signing e-petitions is weak; remember that this is going to be viewed alongside, and compared to, hundreds of other statements from students who may be channelling their political beliefs into more direct action. By contrast, signing petitions is very little evidence of political drive and seems especially superfluous given what they go on to discuss.

Overall:

This student excels in demonstrating their passion for the subject. Their extensive political activity makes for a very strong statement and presents them as a well-developed young adult, which will interest, in particular, universities who interview candidates. It could, however, benefit from some content on their political beliefs, or at least their way of thinking, and on more academic work they had done to prepare. That said, this is very common in personal statements and their extra-curricular politically-driven activities are sure to stand out.

NOTES

CAMBRIDGE SAQS

What is the SAQ?

Applying to Oxbridge is not like applying to any other university; there are a number of extra hurdles to jump through. For those applying to the University of Cambridge, this includes, but is not limited to: picking a college; interviews; admission tests; and the topic of this section, the SAQ.

The SAQ stands for the Supplementary Application Questionnaire. On submitting a UCAS application for the University of Cambridge, Cambridge will email you within forty-eight hours with login details for the SAQ. The SAQ is their way of gathering information that is not collected in the UCAS form, in order for them to form a more detailed picture of you as an applicant.

The deadline for submitting and completing the SAQ is usually a week following the deadline for Oxbridge UCAS applications, however you will be informed of the exact date and time in the email where you receive your login details. You do not have to fill in the application in one go, you can login as many times as you like and edit and save your application up until when you choose to submit it.

Why does Cambridge want it?

If we take a look at Cambridge's FAQ page for Undergraduate Admissions (*https://www.undergraduate.study.cam.ac.uk/applying/saq/faq*) you will find this response:

"The Supplementary Application Questionnaire (SAQ) was developed to ensure that we have complete and consistent information about all applicants. It also enables us to collect information that's not part of the UCAS application but is helpful when assessing applications. The SAQ asks for details such as topics covered as part of your AS/A Level (or equivalent) courses (which helps our interviewers decide which questions to ask), UMS marks obtained in any modular AS/A Level units, and registration numbers for admissions assessments (if applicable)."

The majority of applicants to Cambridge are highly qualified, and deserving of a place to study at the University. They have the highest grades, a number of varied extra-curriculars, and excellent recommendations from their schools. This means that the information supplied by UCAS sets most candidates on a more or less equal footing, which is not helpful for the University when they have multiple students applying for each spot.

Therefore, Cambridge has to find a way to differentiate between applicants, and it does this by assessing you in various different ways beyond the simple UCAS form. Admissions tests are an example, as are interviews. The SAQ is yet another way of trying to gather more detail about your academic and personal record so they can better decide if you are best suited to study there. The information they collect is used in a holistic way alongside a number of other factors (interview scores, admissions test scores, personal statement, etc) in deciding whether they should offer you a place.

Some sections in the SAQ are not compulsory to fill out, such as the additional personal statement, similarly, there is often no minimum limit on the information you need to provide, however when providing information about your education, you should be as in-depth as possible. The detail you provide may not help you secure a place at Cambridge, but there is always a small chance that it might. If you provide the minimum amount of information, then the chances of communicating anything that boosts your chances are minimal, equally though writing a poor additional personal statement will definitely harm your chances, so you must exercise a degree of judgement, and make sure that if you are going to provide extra information, you do it in a way that is relevant. This section is going to cover how you can do your best to fill the SAQ effectively.

What do I need with me when I fill out the application?

Cambridge recommend having the following at hand when you fill out your SAQ:

- Your UCAS personal ID number
- A digital passport style photo of yourself
- Your BMAT registration number if you are medical applicant
- A high school/university transcript if required
- Details of the AS/A level units you have taken and UMS marks
- Details of Scottish/Advanced Highers you have taken and band scores

A full guide on filling out your SAQ, along with images of each page of the application, has been published by Cambridge and can be found here:
https://www.undergraduate.study.cam.ac.uk/files/publications/saq.pdf

What are the different sections of the SAQ and what information do they ask for?

As we've read in the statement supplied by Cambridge, they ask for extra information such as your UMS marks, and topics you covered in your A-levels. However, this is not all they ask for, so let's go through each of the eight sections of the SAQ in more detail:

Section 1 - Application Type

Here they ask for more detail on your application e.g. if the course you have applied for has multiple pathways then they will ask which track of the course you want to follow. They also ask whether you have any extenuating circumstances to declare, and direct you towards the form to do so.

If you are attending a school outside the EU, or have applied for an Organ Scholarship then you will be asked to submit an additional form called a COPA (Cambridge Online Preliminary Application), and you again will be directed towards this form.

Section 2 - Photograph

It is compulsory to submit a passport-style digital photo of yourself. It does not have to be an actual passport photo, however it must adhere to a number of guidelines similar to that for a passport photo. The full guidelines can be found on this page of the application form.

THE ULTIMATE OXBRIDGE PERSONAL STATEMENT GUIDE — SAQ

The photograph is used to identify you during interviews, and also to help them remember you when discussing you and assigning scores afterwards. If you are successful in gaining a place at Cambridge, this photo will also be used as the photo on your Cambridge student ID card – so make sure it's one you like!

Section 3 – Personal Details

In this section they ask for more information about you, such as your preferred name and where you live. They also ask you to list any dates that you would be unavailable for an interview. It is important to recognise that Cambridge expect you to be free during their interview period (usually last week of November and first three weeks of December). If you cannot attend certain dates within this period, you are asked to explain why, and acceptable reasons include religious commitments or long-standing hospital appointments. Holidays, or events for extra-curriculars are not considered valid reasons.

Section 4 – BMAT number

This section is only relevant for Medicine applicants. You are asked to enter your BMAT number so that they can track your results and apply them to your profile once they are published.

Section 5 – Education

This section asks for more detail on your education; your grades and where you have studied. You are also asked to give the month and year you graduated school, or are expected to graduate.

A transcript is a record of your education and academic achievement to date. If you are currently at University, you will need to upload a University transcript. If you are at school, you may be asked to upload a High School transcript.

You are also asked what subjects you took for AS/A-level, and whether there are other subjects you were not able to sit but would have liked to, and if there were any difficulties with the teaching at your school. This section also asks you to provide details of your class sizes and the main topics you covered during sixth form. It is important to fill out this in detail as they use this list of topics in order to formulate questions for your interview, it's also invaluable for providing information about any extenuating circumstances which may have affected your learning.

Section 6 – Qualifications

If you are taking modular AS and A-levels, you are asked to provide details of which subjects you are taking, and which awarding body you are sitting. You are then asked to provide your UMS scores for any modules you have already sat, and to list which modules you have yet to complete. If you have already sat a module, you must provide your UMS score and it must be accurate; if you are successful in gaining a place your College will ask for evidence of your marks.

If you have taken Scottish Highers/Advanced Highers, then you are required to submit your grade and band for each subject in this section.

Section 7 – Additional Information

This is where you can attach a transcript if needed, and provide information if you require financial assistance. This is also the section where you have the option to submit an additional personal statement.

As mentioned earlier, although this is optional, it is recommended you fill this out. More information on what you should include in this statement can be found below.

Section 8 – Submit

Here you are asked to provide information about your immigration status, declare any visa information, and finally, submit your SAQ.

The optional personal statement – what should you write?

Section 7 of the SAQ gives you an option to submit an optional personal statement (maximum 1200 characters including spaces). There is also a second box which asks you to write down anything else you would like Cambridge to know (maximum 600 characters including spaces).

So, what should you write here, if anything? Cambridge state that not providing an additional personal statement will not disadvantage you. However, as mentioned earlier in this post, while it may not disadvantage you, it will also not advantage you. You may be missing a valuable opportunity to expand upon your UCAS personal statement with Cambridge-specific details. However - a bad personal statement in your SAQ will *certainly* harm your application, so you must make sure that if you do choose to fill it out, you contribute something meaningful to your application, beyond what you've said in your UCAS personal statement.

When writing your personal statement for UCAS, you need to keep the information general, and applicable to each of your university applications. For some of the more esoteric courses in Cambridge, such as Land Economy or ASNC (Anglo-Saxon, Norse, and Celtic) the SAQ is a crucial opportunity to talk specifically about the course and your interests pertaining to it. However even for the more popular courses, such as English or Medicine, this is still an great opportunity for you to display your Cambridge-specific interest in the subject.

Let's take Medicine as an example. For your UCAS personal statement you need to write about the work experience you have done, the hours of volunteering completed, and why you are interested in a vocation centred around helping people. All universities require this of their medical applicants, including Cambridge. However, Cambridge are not only interested in producing tomorrow's doctors, they also want to train a cohort of clinicians interested in academic research. The course at Cambridge is geared towards this, with three years of highly scientific study before any patient contact, and they are looking for applicants suited to this style of study. As such, the SAQ is the perfect opportunity for an applicant to describe why they want to specifically go to cambridge, with a focus on their research interests and academic pursuits. It is the perfect place to demonstrate your interest in research and science, and to prove to the admissions team why you are suited to the Cambridge medical course.

This is applicable to any Cambridge course, not just medicine. Talk to current Cambridge students, the course lead at Open Days, and the Director of Studies at your college in order to find out what makes the Cambridge course different from other universities. Take that information and use the optional personal statement to explain and prove why you are best suited to the Cambridge-specific style of teaching. This will also demonstrate to the admissions team that you have done your research on the course and have taken the initiative to find out as much as possible about it, which is something they are keen to see in applicants.

Most importantly, prepare this optional personal statement just like you prepared your UCAS personal statement. As you know it's coming, start drafting it even before you receive your SAQ login details. Plan it carefully, make sure you gather the information needed, and get a teacher or parent to read your drafts over. You must make sure that you don't repeat information you have already provided through UCAS, and that your SAQ statement provides information unique to your Cambridge application and *relevant to* the admissions tutors.

FINAL THOUGHTS

In conclusion, the SAQ is an opportunity for Cambridge to gather more details about you, and also a chance for you to convince Cambridge that you are the right candidate for them to offer a place to.

Make sure you fill out the form early – don't leave it until the last minute! Gather all the documents needed to fill out the SAQ and prepare the optional personal statement in advance. Get a parent or teacher to read through your application and proof-read it for you. And finally, make sure you keep a copy of your application, especially the additional personal statement. Any information you provide here will likely be asked about at interview – make sure you are prepared for these questions!

EXAMPLE SAQS AND ADMISSIONS TUTOR COMMENTARY

Neha Iyer – Modern and Medieval Languages

I am attracted to the Cambridge course for a variety of reasons. I am particularly interested in linguistics and the impact of language on culture, rather than solely literature. For example, as I researched the details of the Russian course at Cambridge, I was impressed by the possibility of studying grammar through a "comprehensive training system", including register, syntax and idioms. I also welcome the opportunity of having access to a "non-standard Russian class", where an authentic manner of Russian speech is taught. I believe that I can benefit from the Cambridge tutorial system, as I think it will be an efficient way of developing speaking spills and becoming fluent. One area of specialist interest to me is the collective work of Pedro Almodovar. Therefore I am interested in the research conducted by the head of the Department of Spanish and Portuguese, focusing on the director and his cultural impact. Moreover, the Spanish course includes an exploration of Latin American and Catalan cultures and politics. I believe that studying the latter in detail will give me a tremendous insight into the current political situation in Catalonia.

SAQ review:

The author has managed to convey several pieces of information through this SAQ. First, they start by establishing that they are particularly interested in the Cambridge course. This is important as the SAQ is an opportunity for the student to let Cambridge know how interested they are in their course in particular. The author talks about how they are 'particularly interested in linguistics and the impact of language on culture, rather than solely literature' and explains why their interests are best suited to the Cambridge course. The author goes on to prove her interest by letting the reader know that she has researched the course structure in detail. By mentioning the 'comprehensive training system including register, syntax, and idioms,' and the '"non-standard Russian class" where an authentic manner of Russian speech is taught' she has proven that she has not just applied to Cambridge on a whim. These details are important to convey to the reader that the student has researched the course, is committed to their choice, and knows they are well suited to the style of teaching. The author hammers this point home by establishing 'I believe that I can benefit from the Cambridge tutorial system, as I think it will be an efficient way of developing speaking spills and becoming fluent.'

Next, the author goes above and beyond a classic SAQ submission. Most students recognise that they have to demonstrate a special interest in their choice of Cambridge course, and they normally do so by mentioning course structure detail. However, this author has gone a step further in proving their dedication by mentioning specific lecturers and department heads, which will greatly impress the reader. 'One area of specialist interest to me is the collective work of Pedro Almodovar. Therefore I am interested in the research conducted by the head of the Department of Spanish and Portuguese, focusing on the director and his cultural impact.' This is an excellent addition to her SAQ as it offers a level of detail about the Cambridge course that most other candidates would not be able to demonstrate.

Finally, the author has also highlighted her specific areas of interest. She mentions 'the Spanish course includes an exploration of Latin American and Catalan cultures and politics. I believe that studying the latter in detail will give me a tremendous insight into the current political situation in Catalonia.' This is an excellent addition as it gives an insight into the author's personality and interests. It gives the author individuality, and makes her application stand out amongst others that do not offer personal details. It also shows that the author is more mature than the usual sixth form applicant. When at school, you are given a curriculum to study and are awarded no extra points for developing your own areas of interest. The opposite is true of a Cambridge course. Cambridge students are expected to develop their own specific interests and shape them into constructive work, and the reader will be greatly impressed by a candidate who is already displaying these skills.

Courtney Ewart - Economics

The areas that the Cambridge Economics course covers are things that I fine extremely interesting. The first year political and social aspects of Economics is a paper I know I would really enjoy; I attend the Politics society in my school and I have made presentations about issues that link the two subjects such as Donald Trump's "Trade Wars". The opportunity to take more political papers later on is also something that greatly appeals to me about the Cambridge course, and the way that many of them relate back to Economics which is something not all universities offer. I feel that the most important thing to me is having an Economics course that will allow me to be well rounded in my knowledge and the compulsory and optional papers attracted me to the Cambridge course as they will allow me to achieve this.

SAQ review:

The author begins her SAQ by establishing that she is particularly interested in the Cambridge course. 'The areas that the Cambridge Economics course covers are things that I fine [sic] extremely interesting.' The SAQ is an opportunity for the student to let the reader know why they want to attend Cambridge over other universities, and so this is a key addition. While the typo undoubtedly reduced her chances of success, it doesn't detract from the fact that it is vital to demonstrate that you are familiar with the Cambridge course and able to meet its demands. The author continues her SAQ by describing specifics of the Cambridge Economics course, demonstrating her knowledge of the course, while simultaneously stating that she enjoys these areas. By doing this, the author has let the reader know that not only has she done her research, but that she has also put thought into deciding if the course suits her. This is important, as Cambridge wants to offer places to students who will thrive during their course and enjoy it.

The author goes on to mention, 'I attend the Politics society in my school and I have made presentations about issues that link the two subjects such as Donald Trump's "Trade Wars".' This is a strong statement for two reasons. First, she has mentioned ways in which she has developed her interest in the subject outside of the school curriculum. Cambridge students are expected to self-study and read well beyond the information provided in lectures, therefore an admissions tutor will be very impressed by a demonstration of these characteristics in an applicant. Second, she has mentioned specific areas of interest, mentioning topics she has given presentations on. Through this, the author has directed the reader towards a source of interview questions, making it likely that during her interview she will be asked to discuss her interest in these topics further, or will even directly be asked academic questions on these topics. As she has helped shape this likely source of questions, she will now be able to prepare for them in advance.

The author finishes her SAQ by explaining why she wants to attend Cambridge over other universities and explains her reasoning for this by referring to the course structure. This is essential to include in an SAQ, as Cambridge's application process is designed to find those that will academically flourish during the course. Although other parts of her application will test this, namely the interview, it is essential that a candidate takes every opportunity they are given, such as the SAQ, to prove that they will suit the Cambridge course.

Catherine Ofori – History

My fascination with the Cambridge History course came after attending the shadowing scheme in February. During the scheme I attended a Civil Rights Movement lecture, focusing on the idea of reconstruction and exploring the vulnerability of American history that resulted in some of the events that took place in the Jim Crow era. Prior to the lecture I had only studied Civil Rights in regards to the different attitudes people held at the time, however this taught me the importance of looking at history from different perspectives and examining the many different factors that can influence this. It was this deeper insight that initially inspired me to study History.

Looking deeper at the course offered by Cambridge, I am intrigued by the wide range of topics on offer. This appeals to me because, although previously showing a passion for British and African history, I am also looking to explore more of the different events that have taken place around the world, such as in North America and Greece.

As a Historian, it is important to have your ideas and views challenged, and I believe the supervision system will allow me to develop this and explore my ideas further.

SAQ review

The author has individualised her SAQ by mentioning a number of personal details and interests. This is an excellent way to write an SAQ, as it helps the author stand out compared to other applicants. It makes the candidate more memorable, and also provides interesting points for discussion at interview. By mentioning specific details, the author is also helping shape potential interview questions, which she can then prepare for in advance.

The author demonstrates a strong commitment to Cambridge, and the path she has taken to develop this. First, she states that she has attended the shadowing scheme, which instantly lets the reader know that the author has been preparing her Cambridge application well in advance, and that she has researched the course. It proves that the author did not just apply on a whim, but that she sought out information about the course structure and made sure it was suited to her. Cambridge is looking for applicants suited to their teaching style, and therefore it is advantageous for a candidate to already be able to prove that they enjoy the course structure and teaching methods.

Second, she demonstrates that she is capable of exploring new ideas and perspectives, and that she is keen to learn. This tells the reader that the author is a flexible thinker, has passion for her subject, and is able to adapt to new ways of learning. These are extremely important skills for a Cambridge student to have, especially as the course places so much emphasis on supervisions and small group classes where students are expected to debate and develop their ideas. The author makes sure this point has been conveyed to the reader, by stating, 'it is important to have your ideas and views challenged, and I believe the supervision system will allow me to develop this and explore my ideas further.'

This SAQ could have been improved by the author describing how she shows interest in her subject. Although she has mentioned the shadowing scheme, this seems to prove her interest in applying to Cambridge rather than her specific love for the subject of History. It would have been good to see her listing ways she pursues her passion for History outside the school curriculum e.g. by mentioning specific books she has read, lectures she has attended, and projects she has undertaken.

Hui Taou Kok – Natural Sciences (Physical)

Cambridge has been ranked among the very best in Physical Natural Sciences by many reputable world university ranking bodies. This speaks volumes of the education and research quality at Cambridge. Many Nobel Prizes in Chemistry have been awarded to Cambridge affiliates since 1904, 24 in total with 6 recipients since the turn of this century alone, the most recent one being in 2017. This reflects the depth and relevance of the Cambridge course and its impact to the world. I aspire to be an accomplished and outstanding research chemist, standing out among peers and making significant contributions to the world. Applying to, and hopefully being accepted by the University of Cambridge is a vital step to realise my aspiration. To excel in Chemistry, I must learn from the very best and this to me the University of Cambridge. Cambridge develops critical thinking skills and enhances analytical abilities. Understanding fundamental principles is vital to applications in the real world. The lectures and tutorials provided by professionals will definitely guide me throughout my course. I am also interested in the history of this wonderful place and its unique blend of international cultures.

My particular field of interest in Chemistry is nanotechnology, which, to my limited understanding at this stage, is about different ways to transform materials into solutions to solve problems. I sincerely hope that through the study opportunity that may be granted to me by the University of Cambridge, I may be able to advance my knowledge in this field and contribute to its advancement in the future as I progress in my learning.

SAQ review

The author spends a considerable portion of this SAQ detailing what he admires about the Cambridge course. He is heavy on detail, and demonstrates that he has done his research. The reader can be confident that the author is very impressed with the academic status and global ranking that Cambridge holds. While it is important to recognise that many candidates are attracted to Cambridge due to its excellent reputation, one should be wary of placing too much import on this. It may accidentally be interpreted as that the author is only interested in Cambridge *because* of its status, and has no real commitment or love for the specific course structure. Cambridge is far more interested in hearing why an applicant is suited to their course, and a successful SAQ should focus on this. It's also worth bearing in mind that the admissions tutors will *know* the key facts about Cambridge's academic performance, so you shouldn't expend space or effort telling them things that they already know!

The author does eventually move beyond Cambridge as an institution by praising the course and providing his reasoning for applying to Cambridge. However, the focus is overwhelmingly on Cambridge's reputation, and in its current state, this SAQ statement does more harm than good.

The author proceeds to describe the course structure, and the focuss on the way Cambridge 'develops critical thinking skills and enhances analytical abilities' really enhances this. It shows good insight into the specific advantages of the course, and he begins to describe why learning these skills will be useful. An improvement to this SAQ would be if the author expanded upon his point by specifically describing why this understanding would be useful to him. The author also mentions that he is 'interested in the history of this wonderful place and its unique blend of international cultures,' adding some much-needed individuality to his SAQ.

The author also takes the opportunity to add some further details to his application by describing his particular field of interest. This provides a potential topic for interview questions, allowing the applicant to help shape what areas they are likely to be asked about at interview. This SAQ could have been improved with more detail about how he has developed his area of interest, as it would demonstrat that an applicant has the ability to self-study and that they show passion for their subject.

Sameer Aiyar Majeed – Natural Sciences

Natural sciences at Cambridge excites me because of the opportunity to study more than one science to a high level without sacrificing rigour or depth. The Cambridge course is more flexible than most and I can combine options with fewer limitations in a way which will broaden my scientific horizons. It fosters greater collaboration between the sciences because there are no single science degrees on offer. This degree is long-established, so the institution has great experience in teaching and administering it as a combined course.

I am also drawn to the research aspects of the degree and to practical work that goes beyond the mainly prescriptive methods of A-level. I would enjoy the unique tutorial system as it is an excellent platform to air ideas and explore interesting problems with experts in their fields. I like investigating problems and asking questions beyond the syllabus, such as thinking of a method to calculate the mass of ATP used daily, understanding why the phosphorylation of ADP is counterintuitively endothermic, and asking why photosynthesis is feasible despite a negative change in entropy. Pursuing questions like this during my degree will be exciting.

SAQ review

The author begins his SAQ by describing the Natural Sciences course structure at Cambridge. By describing it as 'is more flexible than most' and explaining that the course 'fosters greater collaboration between the sciences', he demonstrates he has researched the course and put thought into his application. He also takes this opportunity to link the course structure to why he is applying to Cambridge. He mentions that the course will 'broaden my scientific horizons' and that he will have the 'opportunity to study more than one science to a high level without sacrificing rigour or depth,' telling the admissions tutor that he has not only done his research, but also put thought into deciding if the course suits him. Many applicants appear qualified for a place at Cambridge, but only a few are actually suited to the Cambridge style of teaching. The application process is designed to weed out those who will not do well with course, and therefore a successful applicant must take every opportunity to demonstrate that they will academically flourish at Cambridge. He hammers this home by explaining that he 'would enjoy the unique tutorial system as it is an excellent platform to air ideas and explore interesting problems with experts in their fields.'

The author also mentions specific areas of the course he is interested in, showing off his research skills and eagerness to study beyond the syllabus. Cambridge expect their students to read well beyond what is delivered on the course, and an admissions tutor will be very impressed by a demonstration of this characteristic in an applicant. Second, the author has directed the reader towards a source of interview questions. Now that he has mentioned these topics, it is likely that during his interview he will be asked to discuss his interest further, or even asked academic questions on these topics. If he prepares well, this is a great opportunity for him to be able to practice in advance for questions on a topic that is now likely to come up. Of course, this could backfire on him if he does not revise the topic, and the interviewer finds he does not know much about these areas when he claimed otherwise in his SAQ. This is level of detail is excellent in an SAQ, however when writing their submission, one must be careful not to exaggerate or overstate, and must be prepared to prove at interview any claims they have made.

Sarah Buddle – Natural Sciences (Biological)

(Applied in 2015-2016 academic year)

Since I was selected for a visit to Cambridge in year 10, I've been attracted by the high-quality education it offers. This inspired me to return twice in the past year to learn more about the exact content and style of the course and to ascertain that it was the right choice for me. The Tripos system really appeals to me. The Natural Sciences course would allow me to gain a good grounding in biology, chemistry and maths, whilst not compromising the level of depth in later years, a feature unique to Cambridge. This flexibility will enable me to pursue the field which best suits my interests and abilities, as I will be able to make a more informed choice about my specialisation once I have studied the sciences to a higher level. It would be a privilege to take part in supervisions with an expert in the field. Though these small group sessions I would learn about the topics in much more depth and receive lots of individual feedback, allowing me to maximise my potential.

As well as reading scientific periodicals and books by authors such as Dawkins, I've undertaken work experience in a hospital and a pharmacy. I am particularly interested in the science behind drug design and this has led me to attend a lecture on new cancer treatments at Bath University.

SAQ review:

The author starts her SAQ by establishing that she is particularly interested in the Cambridge course. This is important, as the SAQ is an opportunity for the student to let the reader know why they want to attend Cambridge over other universities. The author has written about how often she has visited Cambridge and demonstrates that she has researched the course. This is crucial as it proves dedication to the application and shows that the author has not merely applied on a whim, it's also valuable as a demonstration that the applicant knows what the true demands of the course are when they say that they can meet them.

The author then talks about how the Natural Sciences Tripos system appeals to her, demonstrating knowledge of the course structure. This shows that the author believes she is well suited to the Cambridge course, and explains her reasoning. This is a good addition to her SAQ, not only to further prove that she has researched the course, but also because Cambridge wishes to take people who will thrive through their teaching style. Although the author will be tested at interview as to whether they are indeed best suited to Cambridge's teaching method, it is useful for the reader to know the author already believes they are.

The author also mentions her interests in 'scientific periodicals and books by authors such as Dawkins' and the 'science behind drug design.' This gives an insight into the author's interests, although mentioning particular books does not add anything valuable. Her exploration of her interests through work experience is useful though as, if accepted onto a Cambridge course, students are expected to develop their own specific interests and explore them. The author has successfully proved she is already displaying these skills by making steps to find out more and educate herself about her areas of interest.

Although this is a good SAQ, there are ways it could have been improved. For example, on mentioning her interests, this would have been a perfect opportunity for her to expand upon her points by linking her interests to why she has pursued a place at Cambridge. For example, when talking about her passion for drug discovery, she could have then mentioned how the Cambridge Natural Sciences course places a lot of importance on this topic, which is why she wants to study there.

THE ULTIMATE OXBRIDGE PERSONAL STATEMENT GUIDE | ADMISSIONS TEST PREP

ADMISSIONS TESTS

Admissions tests are one of the most important components of your application to Oxbridge.

We would have liked to include practice papers for every test here, but no one will let us print a book that long. Instead, you can examine the table below and use it to determine which tests you should be preparing for, and what the best resource for that would be! All of our resources provide world-leading preparation with more questions and information than ever before. You can get them all from https://www.uniadmissions.co.uk/our-books/.

OXFORD

Test	Subject	Best resource
BMAT	• Biomedical Sciences • Medicine	The Ultimate BMAT Collection
CAT	• Classics • Classics and English • Classics and Modern Languages • Classics and Oriental Studies	Expert help from world-leading consultants can be found here: https://www.uniadmissions.co.uk/admission-tests/
ELAT	• Classics and English • English Language and Literature • English and Modern Languages	The Ultimate ELAT Guide

MLAT	<ul><li>Classics and Modern Languages</li><li>English and Modern Languages</li><li>European and Middle Eastern Languages</li><li>History and Modern Languages</li><li>Modern Languages</li><li>Modern Languages and Linguistics</li><li>Philosophy and Modern Languages</li></ul>	Expert help from world-leading consultants can be found here: https://www.uniadmissions.co.uk/mlat-tuition/
OLAT	<ul><li>Classics and Oriental Studies</li><li>European and Middle Eastern Languages</li><li>Oriental Studies</li><li>Religion and Oriental Studies</li></ul>	Expert help from world-leading consultants can be found here: https://www.uniadmissions.co.uk/admission-tests/
MAT	<ul><li>Computer Science</li><li>Computer Science and Philosophy</li><li>Mathematics</li><li>Mathematics and Computer Science</li><li>Mathematics and Philosophy</li><li>Mathematics and Statistics</li></ul>	The Ultimate MAT Guide
TSA	<ul><li>Economics and Management</li><li>History and Economics (TSA section 1 only)</li><li>Human Sciences</li><li>Philosophy, Politics, and Economics (PPE)</li><li>Psychology (Experimental)</li><li>Psychology, Philosophy, and Linguistics</li></ul>	The Ultimate TSA Collection
PAT	<ul><li>Engineering Science</li><li>Materials Science</li><li>Physics</li><li>Physics and Philosophy</li></ul>	Expert help from world-leading consultants can be found here: https://www.uniadmissions.co.uk/pat-tuition/

HAT	• History • History (Ancient and Modern) • History and Economics • History and English • History and Modern Languages • History and Politics	The Ultimate HAT guide
LNAT	• Law (Jurisprudence) • Law with Law Studies in Europe	The Ultimate LNAT Collection
	• Philosophy and Theology	Expert help from world-leading consultants can be found here: https://www.uniadmissions.co.uk/admission-tests/

THE ULTIMATE OXBRIDGE PERSONAL STATEMENT GUIDE — ADMISSIONS TEST PREP

CAMBRIDGE

Test	Subject	Best resource
BMAT	• Medicine	The Ultimate BMAT Collection
CTMUA	• Computer Science	Expert help from world-leading consultants can be found here: https://www.uniadmissions.co.uk/ctmua-tuition/
ECAA	• Economics	The Ultimate ECAA Collection
ELAT	• English	The Ultimate ELAT Guide

ENGAA	• Chemical Engineering via Engineering • Engineering	The Ultimate ENGAA Collection
NSAA	• Chemical Engineering via Natural Sciences • Natural Sciences • Veterinary Medicine	The Ultimate NSAA Collection
TSA	• Land Economy	The Ultimate TSA Collection

THE ULTIMATE OXBRIDGE INTERVIEW GUIDE

OXBRIDGE INTERVIEWS

Oxbridge interviews are frequently the source of intriguing stories. You'll frequently hear tales of students who were asked seemingly obscure questions e.g. "Why do we have two nostrils but only one mouth?", or impossibly difficult ones e.g. "How many grains of sand are there in the world?"

If taken in context, both of these are very fair Oxbridge interview questions. The first would naturally lead to a discussion concerning the evolution of sensory organs and the pros/cons of having multiple mouths e.g. reduced risk of infections vs. inability to eat and speak simultaneously etc.

The latter question would test a candidate's ability to breakdown an initially very large problem into more bite-sized chunks in order to manage it e.g. surface area of the Earth, percentage of the Earth covered by land, percentage of land covered by sand, average depth of sand and so on.

Oxbridge interviews are not about testing your knowledge. Instead, they are about testing what you can do with the knowledge you already possess. Remember, once you're at university, you will rapidly assimilate a great deal of new information (so much so that you will start to wonder what all the fuss A-levels were about).

This is the main reason why it's not particularly useful for interviewers to ask purely knowledge-based questions e.g. "What is the normal plasma concentration of magnesium?". Knowledge of isolated facts is neither necessary nor sufficient for a successful Oxbridge interview. Instead, it is the application of some basic facts to novel situations that is the hallmark of success.

To help demonstrate what we mean a little further, Rohan is going to talk through his interview experiences.

INTERVIEW ONE

This was my first science interview and the interviewer was delighted when he found out I studied physics at A2. His opening question was "What have you read recently?" I explained I'd been reading about the new drug Rosuvastatin – a statin that was being recommended for everyone above a certain age (regardless of their actual cholesterol levels). The follow-up questions were what you would expect e.g. "How do statins work?" (Ensure you know the basics of any topic that you voluntarily bring up), "What are the risks/benefits of giving them to everyone?"

This led to a discussion on how I would convince someone that this drug was useful for them, followed by how I would convince someone that blue light was more damaging than red. I struggled with this for a while, bouncing ideas back and forth (with each of them sequentially shot down) until I finally stumbled onto Einstein's $E=hf$. This led to a discussion about why the sky is blue and sunsets can be a myriad of colours. All of this culminated in the classic- "What colour is the Sun in reality?" (Hint: It's not yellow, orange or red!) This is the question that tabloids would take out of context to make the interview seem like an array of bizarre questions when in fact this was perfectly reasonable giving the preceding questions.

This interview serves as a perfect example of a non-scripted interview, i.e. one where the interviewer was happy to bounce ideas between us and forced me to think about concepts in ways I never had. I'm certain that if I had offered a different answer to the initial question about my reading, the discussion would have gone along a significantly different route.

INTERVIEW TWO

My second interview was more scripted – the interviewer had a pre-set agenda with corresponding questions that he wanted to discuss. Given that this person is known to ask the same interview questions annually, I've refrained from including specifics in order to not spoil the plot for everyone and to unfairly put future applicants at an advantage (or disadvantage!).

After going through my BMAT essay very briefly, he asked me to draw a graph on his whiteboard. This was no easy task. I spent fifteen minutes struggling with this graph due to its unusual axis. Like many candidates, I made the mistake of learning about excessively complex topics like the Complement Membrane attack complex and ignored many of the core A-level topics like human physiology. This meant that I wasn't completely sure about a basic fact that was required for the graph. This was a tough interview and at the end of it, I was certain I had flunked it. This was compounded by the fact that other candidates were bragging about how they had got the correct graph in only thirty seconds.

When you're in the waiting room with the other candidates, it may appear that many of them are far smarter than you and know a lot more. Again, remember that the entire point of an interview is to assess your ability to apply knowledge.

People get nervous and lose confidence whilst waiting for interviews. One of the ways they try to feel more secure is by exerting their intellectual superiority. In this example (although there were some exceptions), the students who tended to arrive at the answer very quickly were unsuccessful. This is likely because they had previous knowledge of the question from their school/extra reading. Although this allowed them to get the correct answer quickly, they were unable to clearly *show their thinking*, i.e. they knew the topic but didn't understand it.

LEARNING POINTS

As you can see, I made lots of errors in my interview preparation. Please learn from them. Good students learn from their mistakes but great students learn from others' mistakes.

1. Don't be put off by what other candidates say in the waiting room. Focus on yourself – you are all that matters. If you want to be in the zone, then I would recommend taking some headphones and your favourite music.
2. Don't read up on multiple advanced topics in depth. Choose one topic and know it well. Focus the rest of your time on your core A-level syllabus. A medic is not expected to know about the features of Transverse Myelitis, but you will be expected to be able to rattle off a list of 10 cellular organelles.
3. Don't worry about being asked seemingly irrelevant questions that you'll often hear in the media. These are taken out of context. Focus on being able to answer the common questions e.g. "Why this university?" etc.
4. Don't lose heart if your interviews appear to have gone poorly. If anything, this can actually be a good sign as it shows that the interviewer pushed you to your limits rather than giving up on you as you clearly weren't Oxbridge material.
5. Don't give up. When you're presented with complex scenarios, go back to the absolute basics and try to work things out using first principles. By doing this and thinking out loud, you allow the interviewer to see your logical train of thought so that they can help you when you become stuck.

Good Luck!

Dr Rohan Agarwal

THE BASICS

WHAT IS AN OXBRIDGE INTERVIEW?

An interview is a personal session with one or two members of academic staff from Oxford or Cambridge, usually lasting anywhere between 20 and 50 minutes. The interviewers will ask questions and guide the applicant to an answer. The answers usually require a large degree of creative and critical thought, as well as a good attitude and a sound foundation of subject-specific knowledge.

Why is there an interview?

Most of the applicants to Oxbridge will have outstanding grades, predicted exam results, sample course work and personal statements. Interviews are used to help determine which applicants are best-suited for Oxbridge. During the interview, each applicant has a unique chance to demonstrate their creativity and critical thinking abilities - skills that Oxford and Cambridge consider vital for successful students.

WHO GETS AN INTERVIEW?

At Cambridge, any applicant who might have a chance at being accepted to study will be called for interview. This corresponds to approximately 90% of applicants. At Oxford, odds of getting interviewed are lower, due to a mixture of factors including applicant numbers and selection criteria, and you're on average about 40% likely to be invited to interview. No one is offered a place to study without attending an interview.

WHO ARE THE INTERVIEWERS?

The interviews are conducted by a senior member of staff for the subject you've applied to; usually this person is the Director of Studies for that subject. There may often be a second interviewer who takes notes on the applicant or also asks questions. Interviewers describe this experience as just as nerve-wracking for them as for the applicants, as they are responsible for choosing the right students for Oxford and Cambridge.

WHEN IS THE INTERVIEW?

Interviews are held in the beginning of December and some applicants may be invited back in January for a second round of interviews at another college. There are usually multiple interviews on the same day, either for different subjects or at different colleges. You will normally be given 2 weeks' notice before your interview- so you should hear back by late November, but it is useful to begin preparing for the interview before you're officially invited.

THE ULTIMATE OXBRIDGE INTERVIEW GUIDE — BASICS

WHERE IS THE INTERVIEW?

The interviews are held in Oxford and Cambridge at the college you applied to. Oxford applicants may have additional interviews at another college than the one applied to. Cambridge applicants may get 'pooled' – be required to have another set of interviews in January at a different college. If you are travelling from far away, most Oxbridge colleges will provide you free accommodation and food for the duration of your stay if you wish to arrive the night before your interview.

Very rarely, interviews can be held via Skype at an exam centre- this normally only applies to international students or for UK students in extreme circumstances. During a pandemic, interviews are usually held on Microsoft Teams.

HOW SHOULD I USE THIS SECTION?

The best way to gain the most from this collection is to let it guide your independent learning.

1. Read through the General Interview section.
2. Read the Subject Interview chapter for your subject.
3. Read other Relevant Chapters corresponding to your subject.

Your Subject	Also read chapters on:
Biology	Psychology, Chemistry, Psychology, Maths
Medicine	Psychology, Chemistry
Psychology	Biology, Maths
Chemistry	Biology, Physics, Material Sciences, Maths
Physics	Chemistry, Engineering, Material Sciences, Maths
Engineering	Chemistry, Physics, Material Sciences, Maths
Material Sciences	Chemistry, Physics, Engineering, Maths
Computer Sciences	Maths
Economics	PPE & HSPS, Maths
English	History, Modern Languages
Earth Sciences	Biology, Chemistry, Physics
History	HSPS, English
PPE	HSPS, Economics, Maths
Politics	PPE, History, HSPS
HSPS	History, Psychology
Classics	Modern Languages, History
Modern Languages	Classics, English

Finally, work your way through the past interview questions – remember, you are not expected to know the answers to them, and they have been included here so that you can start to appreciate the style of questions that you may get asked. It is not a test of what you know – but what you can do with what you already know.

OXBRIDGE TUTORIALS & SUPERVISIONS

Hopefully, by this point, you're familiar with the unique Oxbridge teaching system. Students on the same course will have lectures and practicals together. These are supplemented by college-based tutorials/supervisions. A tutorial/supervision is an individual or small group session with an academic to discuss ideas, ask questions, and receive feedback on your assignments. During the tutorial/supervision, you will be pushed to think critically about the material from the course in novel and innovative ways. To get the most out of Oxbridge, you need to be able to work in this setting and take criticism with a positive and constructive attitude.

The interviews are made to be model tutorials/supervisions, with an academic questioning an applicant and seeing if they can learn, problem-solve, demonstrate motivation for their subject. It is by considering this ultimate goal of the interview that you can start to understand how to present and prepare yourself for the Oxbridge interview process.

WHAT ARE INTERVIEWERS LOOKING FOR?

There are several qualities an interviewer is looking for the applicant to demonstrate during the interview. While an applicant may think the most 'obvious' thing interviewers are looking for is excellent factual knowledge, this is already displayed through exam results. Whilst having an excellent depth of knowledge may help you perform better during an interview, you're unlikely to be chosen based solely on your knowledge. The main thing an interviewer is looking for is for the applicant to demonstrate critical thought, excellent problem-solving skills and intellectual flexibility, as well as motivation for the subject and suitability for small group teaching. It is also important for them to see that the applicant is willing to persevere with a challenging problem even if the answer is not immediately apparent.

HOW TO COMMUNICATE ANSWERS

The most important thing to do when communicating your answers is to think out loud. This will allow the interviewer to understand your thought processes. They will then be able to help you out if you get stuck. You should never give up on a question; show that you won't be perturbed at the first sign of hardship as a student, and remain positive and demonstrate your engagement with the material. Interviewers enjoy teaching and working with students who are as enthusiastic about their subject as they are.

Try to keep the flow of conversation going between you and your interviewer so that you can engage with each other throughout the entire interview. The best way to do this is to just keep talking about what you are thinking. It is okay to take a moment when confronted with a difficult question or plan your approach, but ensure you let the interviewer know this by saying, "I'm going to think about this for a moment". Don't take too long - if you are finding the problems difficult, the interviewers will guide and prompt you to keep you moving forward. They can only do this if they know you're stuck!

The questions that you'll be asked are designed to be difficult, so don't panic up when you don't immediately know the answer. Tell the interviewer what you do know, offer some ideas, talk about ways you've worked through a similar problem that might apply here. If you've never heard anything like the question asked before, say that to the interviewer, "I've never seen anything like this before" or "We haven't covered this yet at school", but don't use that as an excuse to quit. This is your chance to show that you are eager to engage with new ideas, so finish with "But let's see if I can figure it out!" or "But I'm keen to try something new!". There are many times at Oxbridge when students are in this situation during tutorials/supervisors and you need to show that you can persevere in the face of difficulty (and stay positive and pleasant to work with while doing so).

TYPES OF INTERVIEWS

There are, at Cambridge and for some Oxford subjects, several different types of interview that you can be called for. Every applicant will have at least one subject interview. Applicants to some courses may also have a general interview, especially if they are applying for an arts subject. Either way, you will be asked questions that touch on the course you are applying to study. It may be useful to look at your interviewers' teaching backgrounds and published work as this could potentially shed some light on the topics they might choose to discuss in an interview. However, there is absolutely no need to know the intricacies of their research so don't get bogged down in it. Interviews tend to open with easier and more general questions and become more detailed and complicated as you are pushed to explore topics in greater depth.

USING THE PRACTICE QUESTIONS

This book contains over 900 practice interview questions. They are all actual questions that successful Oxbridge applicants were asked in their interview. However, it is important you take these with a pinch of salt.

They are taken out of context and only included to give you a flavour of the style and difficulty of real Oxbridge interview questions. Don't fall into the trap of thinking that your interview will consist of a series of disconnected and highly specific knowledge-based questions.

> OXBRIDGE INTERVIEWS ARE **NOT** ABOUT YOUR KNOWLEDGE
>
> THEY ARE ABOUT WHAT YOU CAN DO WITH THE KNOWLEDGE YOU ALREADY POSSESS

Thus, it does little benefit to rote learn answers to all the practice questions in this book as they are unlikely to be repeated. Instead, follow our top tips, take inspiration from the worked answers and put in some hard work – you'll be sure to perform well on the day.

GENERAL INTERVIEWS

A general interview is a get-to-know-you session with senior admissions tutors. This is your chance to demonstrate a passion for Oxbridge; that you have understood the Oxbridge system, have a genuine interest in being a student, and could contribute to Oxbridge if you were admitted. These are more common for arts and humanities applicants, but all applicants should nevertheless be prepared for a general interview.

- This will be less specific than the subject interview. The interviewers will focus more on your personal statement, any essays you may have submitted or have completed on the day of the interview and may discuss your SAQ form if you are applying to Cambridge.
- One of the interviewers may not be a specialist in the subject you've applied for. Don't be put off by this – you aren't expected to have any knowledge of their subject.
- Ensure that you have read your personal statement and any books/journals that you've claimed to have read in your application. You will seem unenthusiastic and dishonest if you can't answer questions regarding topics and activities that you claim to know about. Remember that it is much better to show a good understanding of a few texts than to list lots of texts that you haven't properly read.
- Read and re-read the essays you have submitted (if you have done). Be prepared to expand on the ideas you have explored in them. Remember that the interviewers may criticise what you've argued in your submitted essays. If you believe in it, then defend your view but don't be stubborn.
- You will normally be asked if you have any questions at the end of the interview. Avoid saying things like, "How did I do?" – Instead use this as an opportunity to show the interviewers the type of person you are e.g. "How many books can I borrow from the library at one time?"

WHAT TYPE OF QUESTIONS MIGHT BE ASKED?

The three main questions that are likely to come up in an Oxbridge interview are:

- Why this university?
- Why this subject?
- Why this college?

You may also get asked more specific questions about the teaching system or about your future career aspirations. This will also be the time for discussing any extenuating circumstances for poor exam results and similar considerations.

To do well in a general interview, your answers should show that you understand the Oxbridge system and that you have strong reasons for applying there. Thus, it is essential that you prepare detailed answers to the common questions above so that you aren't caught off guard. In addition, you should create a list of questions that could potentially be asked based on your personal statement or any submitted work.

THE ULTIMATE OXBRIDGE INTERVIEW GUIDE | GENERAL

WORKED QUESTIONS

Below are a few examples of how to start breaking down general interview questions- complete with model answers.

Q1: How did you choose which college to apply for?

This question is a good opportunity to tell the interviewer about yourself, your hobbies, motivations, and any interesting projects you have undertaken. You can demonstrate that you have read about the College thoroughly and you know what differentiates your College from the others. The decisive factors can include a great variety of different things from history, alumni, location in the city, community, sports clubs, societies, any positive personal experiences from Open Day and notable scholars.

This is a warm up question – an ice-breaker – so just be natural and give an honest answer. You may not want to say things like, "I like the statues in the garden". The more comprehensive your answer is, the better.

Good Applicant: I chose which college to apply for based on a number of factors that were important to me. First of all, I needed to consider how many other students at my college would be studying the same subject as me; this was important to me as I want to be able to engage in conversation about my subject with my peers. Secondly, I considered the location of the college as I wanted to ensure I had easy access to the faculty library and lecture theatres. Thirdly, I am a keen tennis player and so looked for a college with a very active tennis society. Finally, I wanted to ensure that the college I chose would feel right for me and so I looked around several Cambridge colleges before coming to my conclusion.

This response is broken down into a set of logical and yet personal reasons. **There is no right answer to this question** and the factors which influence this decision are likely to be unique for each individual. However, each college is unique and therefore the interviewer wants to know what influenced your decision. Therefore, **it's essential that you know what makes your college special** and separates it from the others. Even more importantly, you should know what the significance of that will be for you. For example, if a college has a large number of mathematicians, you may want to say that, by attending that college, it would allow you to discuss your subject with a greater number of people than otherwise.

A **poor applicant** may respond with a noncommittal shrug or an answer such as, "my brother went there". The interviewers want to see that you have researched the university and although the reason for choosing a college won't determine whether or not you get into the university, a lack of passion and interest in the college will greatly influence how you are perceived by the interviewers.

THE ULTIMATE OXBRIDGE INTERVIEW GUIDE — GENERAL

Q2: Why have you chosen to apply to study at 'Oxbridge', rather than another Russell Group university?

This is a very broad question and one which is simply designed to draw out the motives and thinking behind your application, as well as giving you an opportunity to speak freely about yourself.

A **good applicant** would seek to address this question in two parts, the first addressing the key features of Oxbridge for their course and the second emphasising their own personality traits and interests which make them most suited to the Oxbridge system.

It is useful to start off by talking about the supervision/tutorial system and why this method of very small group teaching is beneficial for studying your subject, both for the discussion of essay work and, more crucially, for developing a comprehensive understanding of your subject. You might also like to draw upon the key features of the course at Oxford and Cambridge that distinguish it from courses at other universities.

When talking about yourself, a good answer could take almost any route, though it is always productive to talk about which parts of your subject interest you, why this is the case, and how this ties in with the course at Oxford/Cambridge. You might also mention how the Oxbridge ethos suits your personality, e.g. how hard work and high achievement are important to you and you want to study your chosen subject in real depth, rather than a more superficial course elsewhere.

A **poor applicant** would likely demonstrate little or no knowledge of their course at Oxford/Cambridge and volunteer little information about why studying at Oxbridge would be good for them or why they would be suited to it. It's important to focus on your interests and abilities rather than implying that you applied because Oxbridge is the biggest name or because your family or school had expected you to do so.

Q3: What do you think you can bring to the college experience?

This is a common question at general interviews and **you need to show that you would be a good fit for the College** and that you are also really motivated because you have researched the college's facilities, notable fellows and alumni, societies and sports clubs etc. You can mention that you have looked at the website, talked to alumni and current students.

This question also gives the interviewer an excellent opportunity to learn about your personality, hobbies and motivations. Try to avoid listing one thing after the other for 5 minutes. Instead, you should try to give a balanced answer in terms of talking about the College and yourself. You should talk about your skills and give examples when you had to work in a team, deliver on strict deadlines, show strong time-management skills etc. You should also give a few examples from your previous studies, competitions or extracurricular activities (including sports and music).

Q4: Tell me about a recent news article not related to your subject that has interested you.

This can be absolutely anything and your interviewers just want to see that **you are aware of the world in which you live** and have a life outside of your subject. You could pick an interesting topic ahead of time and cultivate an opinion which could spark a lively discussion.

THE ULTIMATE OXBRIDGE INTERVIEW GUIDE

GENERAL

Q5: Which three famous people would you most like to be stuck on a desert island with?

This is a personal question that might be used by your interviewers as an 'ice-breaker' – you can say absolutely anyone but try to have a good justification (and avoid being melodramatic). This is a really **good chance to show your personality and sense of humour**. This is also a good question to ease you into the flow of the interview and make you feel more comfortable.

Q6: Do you think you're 'clever'?

Don't let this one faze you! Your interviewers are not being glib but instead want to see how you cope with questions you may not have anticipated. You could discuss different forms of intelligence, e.g. emotional vs. intellectual, perhaps concluding that you are stronger in one over the other.

Q7: What experiences do you have which suggest to you that you'll cope well with the pressures of Oxbridge?

The **interviewers want to hear that you know what you're signing up** to and that you are capable of dealing with stress. If you have any experience of dealing with pressure or meeting strict deadlines, this would be a good opportunity to talk about them. Otherwise, mention your time management skills and your ability to prioritise workloads. You could also mention how you deal with stress, e.g. do you like running? Yoga? Piano? Etc.

Q8: Why are you in this room?

There are hundreds of potential responses to this type of question, and the interviewer will see this as a chance to get to know your personality and how you react to unusual situations.

Firstly, **take the question seriously**, even if it strikes you as funny or bizarre. A good response may begin with: "There are many reasons why I am in this room. There are lots of smaller events and causes that have led up to me being in this room". You might choose to discuss your desire to attend Oxbridge, the fact that you have travelled to the college to take your interview. You might choose to discuss the interviewer or college's taste and budget when it came to allocating rooms for interviews, as that determined why and how you have come to be sitting in that room, rather than anywhere else.

A weak response to this type of question would be to dismiss it as silly or irrelevant.

Q9: Let's say you're hosting a small private party, and you have a magical invitation that will summon anyone from time and space to your dining table. Who's name do you write on the invitation?

This is a fairly straightforward question to get in a general interview, so use it to show your personality and originality, and to talk about something you are passionate about.

If you are asked a question like this, give an answer that is relevant to your application. This is not the time to start talking about how you are a huge fan of Beyonce and would just love to have dinner together! You should also avoid generic answers like "God".

If you would love to meet Barack Obama and know more about him, consider what that would be like. Would he be at liberty to answer your questions? Might you not get more information from one of his aides or from a close friend, rather than the man himself? As this is a simple question, try to unpick it and answer it in a sophisticated way, rather than just stating the obvious.

Q10: What was the most recent film you watched?

This question seems simple and appears to require a relatively short answer. However, a good candidate will use a simple question such as this as an opportunity to speak in more depth and **raise new and interesting topics of conversation**: "What I find particularly interesting about this film was... It reminded me of... In relation to other works of this period/historical context, I found this particular scene very interesting as it mirrored/contrasted with my previous conceptions of this era as seen in other works, for example... I am now curious to find out more about... This film made me think about...etc."

Whilst it is extremely important to respond accurately to the questions posed by the interviewer, do not be afraid to **take the conversation in the direction led by your personal interests**. This sort of initiative will be encouraged.

Q11: How do you think the university will evaluate whether or not you have done well at the end of your degree, do you think that this manner of assessment is fair?

This question invites you to show your potential and how diverse your interests are. There are three aspects of this question that you should consider in order to give a complete answer: "end of your degree", "evaluate" and "done well". You may want to discuss your hobbies and interests and potential achievements regarding various aspects of university life including academia, sports, student societies, jobs, volunteering etc.

Then you may want to enter into a discussion about whether there is any fair measure of success. How could you possibly compare sporting excellence to volunteering? Is it better to be a specialist or a generalist? This ultimately comes down to your personal motivation and interests as you might be very focused on your studies or other activities (e.g. sports, music). Thus, multiple things would contribute to your success at university and your degree is only likely to be one way to measure this. Finally, it might be a great closing line to mention that getting your degree might not be the end of your time here.

Q12: Tell me why you think people should go to university.

This sounds like a very general question at first but it is, in fact, about your personal motivations to go to university. You don't need to enter into a discussion about what universities are designed for or any educational policy issues as the interviewer is unlikely to drive the discussion towards this in a general interview.

The best strategy is to **discuss your motivations**- this could include a broad range of different things from interest in a certain field, inspiring and diverse environments, academic excellence, opening up of more opportunities in the future and buying time to find out more about yourself etc. As it is very easy to give an unfocused answer, you should limit yourself to a few factors. You can also comment on whether people should go to university and whether this is good for society.

> # THE ULTIMATE OXBRIDGE INTERVIEW GUIDE — GENERAL

Q13: I'm going to show you a painting, imagine that you have been tasked with describing this to someone over the phone so that they can recreate it, but you only have a minute. How would you describe the painting in order to make the recreation as close to the original as possible?

This question is very common and surprisingly difficult. You can take a number of approaches. Ensure that you have a concrete idea of the structure you will use to describe the painting. For example, you could begin with your personal feelings about it, then the colours and atmosphere the painting creates, then the exact objects, then their respective position and size. It does not matter which approach you take but this question is designed to test your way of organising and presenting your ideas.

You could also comment on the difficulty of the task and argue that human language limits you from adequately describing smell, taste, sound, and vision. Modern language applicants may have read about Wittgenstein, in which case, they can reference his works on the limitations and functions of language here.

Q14: Which person in the past would you most like to interview, and why?

This is a personal question but try to **avoid generic and mainstream answers**. Keep in mind that you can find out much more about a particular period or era by speaking to everyday citizens or advisors for politicians or other important figures. It is much more important to identify what you want to learn about and then set criteria to narrow down the possible list of persons. This question opens the floor for developing an analytical, quasi-scientific approach to your research.

Q15: What's an interesting thing that's been happening in the news recently?

Whilst this question may be asked at a general interview, it's a good idea to come up with something that is related to your course. Instead of going into technical detail with an interviewer who may be from a completely different discipline, it is better to give a brief overview of the article and then put it into a broader context.

For example, an economics applicant may want to discuss the most recent banking scandal. A physics applicant may want to discuss a recent discovery.

A **good** candidate might say something like "That's a great question, there are a lot of really interesting things which have happened recently. For me, I think the most interesting one is the confirmation of increased magnetic movement in muons at the Fermi National Accelerator in America.

This is mainly interesting for two reasons, I think that it is always interesting when you have examples of the standard model perhaps not working as it should. It's seemed like there have been problems with the way we understand everything working for some time now, but actually being able to perhaps find a new force, and write new laws of physics is incredibly exciting! The other reason this in particular is interesting is because it shows some of the strengths and weaknesses of the scientific process. Even though this magnetic movement has been detected in multiple experiments for over twenty years, it is still not something which we can consider confirmed, because this movement has not been confirmed to the five-sigma level of certainty needed to announce an actual discovery. This rigour helps ensure that we don't have incidents like the Pons and Felischmann Cold Fusion scandal, but does also mean that we will have waited more than two decades to start re-writing the textbooks at the point that this can be confirmed, assuming of course that it ever is. Events like this one really show how thorough and reliable scientific work can be, but also that in areas like theoretical physics things can be very slow to change."

The answer should not be a complete analysis of the issue but an intuitive and logical description of an event, with a good explanation of why it is interesting to you, personally. They really want to see here your enthusiasm for the topic of the article in question (and hopefully the topic of your chosen course) as well as your ability to reflect in a mature way on its most general themes.

Q16: Can people be entirely apolitical? Are you political?

In general, you should avoid expressing any very extreme views at all during interviews. The answer, "I do not" is not the most favourable either. This question invites you to **demonstrate academic thinking in a topic which could be part of everyday conversations**. You are not expected to present a full analysis of party politics and different ideologies. It doesn't matter if you actually have strong political views; the main point is to talk about your perception of what political ideas are present and how one differs from the other.

With such a broad question – you have the power to choose the topic- be it wealth inequality, nuclear weapons, corruption, human rights, or budget deficit etc. Firstly, you should **explain why that particular topic or political theme is important**. For example, the protection of fundamental human rights is crucial in today's society because this introduces a social sensitivity to our democratic system where theoretically 51% of the population could impose its will on the other 49%. On the other hand, it should be noted that Western liberal values may contradict with social, historical and cultural aspects of society in certain developing countries, and a different political discourse is needed in different countries about the same questions. Secondly, you should discuss whether that topic is well-represented in the political discourse of our society and what should be done to trigger a more democratic debate.

Q17: One of the unique features of Oxbridge education is the supervision system, one-on-one tutorials every week. This means a heavy workload, one essay every week with strict deadlines. Do you think you can handle this?

By this point, you should hopefully have a sound understanding of the supervision/tutorial systems. You should also be aware of the possibility of spending long hours in the library and meeting tight deadlines so this question should not be surprising at all. It gives you an opportunity to **prove that you would fit into this educational system very well**. Firstly, you should make it clear that you understand the system and the requirements. On average, there is one essay or problem sheet every week for each paper that you are reading which requires going through the reading list/lecture notes and engaging with wider readings around certain topics or problems. Secondly, you should give some examples from your past when you had to work long hours or had strict deadlines etc. You should also tell the interviewer how you felt in these situations, what you enjoyed the most and what you learned from them. Finally, you may wish to stress that you would not only be able to cope with the system but also enjoy it a great deal.

Q18: If you had to live in the world of a book you have read, which book would it be, and whose role would you take?

This question is an ice-breaker- the interviewer is curious to find out what type of novels you read and how thoroughly you are reading them. You want to show that you are capable of thinking on your feet, talk them through why you've chosen their particular world, does it have advantages which outweigh its pitfalls. For example, if you say you like Robin Hood, it is a world in which you could carry out noble deeds in an idyllic setting, but you also have to deal with poverty, homelessness, and a brutal regime. If you would like to live here, then tell them why. As for the character, centre in on who you want, for instance Robin himself, explain his situation briefly as becoming an outlaw, resisting the authorities, and aiding the poor and his fellow men. Would you like to take his role because you would like to do the things he did, or do you feel that you could 'be' him differently, or even better? Would you be able to learn or grow from entering your chosen world, and being a certain character - think of what course you are applying to, and see if there are particular skills which you think this experience could teach you, empathy, if you're applying for medicine, or social responsibility, if you're applying for economics & management, as examples.

The main point is to be able to **give a very brief summary of the character and the world in which they live**, (especially if you choose a less well-known work), and have a good and interesting justification for choosing them.

Q19: Do you think that we should give applicants access to a computer during their interviews?

This is a classic open question for an insightful debate. The most important thing to realise here is that **Oxbridge education is about teaching you how to think** in clear, structured and coherent ways as opposed to collecting lots of facts from the internet.

Internet access would provide each candidate with the same available information and therefore the art of using information to make sound arguments would be the sole decisive factor. On the other hand, the information overload can be rather confusing. In general, a brain dump is not helpful at the interview as it does not demonstrate in-depth understanding and analysis of any problems. At the end of the day, it comes down to the individual candidate, i.e. what would you look up on the Internet during the interview? Would you want to rely on unverified knowledge? How reliable is that information on the internet? How could you verify this information?

Q20: What was your proudest moment?

This is another chance to highlight your suitability for the course, so try to make it as subject-relevant as possible. "I felt proud to be awarded first place in a poetry competition with a sonnet I wrote about..." (if you're applying for English). "I recently won the Senior Challenge for the UK Mathematics Trust.", "Achieving a 100% mark in my AS-level History and English exams – an achievement I hope to emulate at A2".

Of course, it's not easy to pick one achievement and this is not a question you might have expected. You could also argue that you can't really compare your achievements from different fields e.g. your 100% Physics AS-level and football team captaincy. This will allow you to bypass the question's number limit and mention more than one achievement so that you have more opportunities to impress the interviewer.

Q21: Would you ever use a coin-flip to make a choice, if so, when?

This question can be quite tricky and aims at revealing how you make decisions in your life, your understanding of abstract concepts, rationality and probabilities. You should begin with answering the question from your perspective, you can be honest about it but give a justification even if you never want to make decisions based on luck. Try to **give a few examples when tossing a coin could be a good idea**, or would cause no harm. Then you can take the discussion to a more abstract level and argue that once all yes/no decisions are made by tossing a coin in the long run, the expected value should be fifty-fifty so you might not be worse-off at all and you could avoid the stress of making decisions (although this is very simplistic).

You could also reference the stock markets where high returns may be purely luck-dependent. On the other hand, **rational decision-making is part of human nature** and analysing costs and benefits would result in better decisions in the long-run than tossing a coin. In addition, this would incentivise people to conduct research, collect information, develop and test theories, etc. As you see, the question could be interpreted to focus on the merits of rigorous scientific methodology.

Q22: If you had omnipotence for a moment, but had to use it to change only one thing, what would it be?

This question tests your sound reasoning and clear presentation of your answer and the justification for it. There is no right or wrong "one thing" to choose. It is equally valid to choose wealth inequality or the colour of a double-decker bus if you argue it well! It should be noted that if you've applied for social sciences, it is a better strategy to choose a related topic to show your sensitivity to social issues.

Firstly, you should choose something you would like to change while demonstrating clear thinking, relevant arguments. Secondly, you are expected to discuss how, and to what extent, you would and could change it. Again, a better candidate would realise that **this is not necessarily a binomial problem** – either change it or not – but there may be a spectrum between these two extremes. Once you've identified the thing you'd like to change, talk them through why. A good way to make sure you always do this is by thinking aloud, and walking the interviewer through the way you would reach this conclusion yourself.

Q23: Oxford, as you know, has access to some very advanced technology. In the next room we actually have the latest model of time machine, if we gave you the opportunity to use it later, when would you go?

This is a question where you can really use your imagination (or draw on History GCSE or A-level). **You can say absolutely any time period** in the past or the future but you must have a good reason for it which you communicate to the interviewer. This doesn't necessarily need to be linked to your subject.

For example, *"I would love to see a time when my parents were little children and see where and how they grew up. I'd ideally like to stay for some time to gather as much information as possible. This would be really valuable to me as I'd get to see them when they were people without children, just as they themselves were developing, and could give me opportunities to better understand them. I think understanding one's parents is often a good way to help you understand yourself. The pursuit of self-understanding never stops, but this opportunity would give me a unique chance to improve that."*

Choosing something personal or creative will make you stand out and you are more likely to get interesting questions from the interviewer if you are able to involve them in an intriguing conversation. It is also fine if you choose a standard period like the Roman Empire or a time which has not yet come to pass, say the year 4000, if you have a good reason.

THE ULTIMATE OXBRIDGE INTERVIEW GUIDE

GENERAL INTERVIEW QUESTIONS

The following pages contain real examples of interview questions that our tutors were asked at their general interview. At first glance, they may appear rather obscure and intimidating. However, remember that you are unlikely to be asked these questions in series. They will only be asked because the topic being discussed naturally led to the question or if you alluded to it earlier. E.g. "Why are flowers not green?" may precede or follow a discussion of chlorophyll or the evolution of colour vision.

Thus, whilst going through these questions is excellent practice, ensure that you don't get too bogged down in the knowledge aspects of these questions.

Interviewers are far more interested to see what you can do with the knowledge you already possess.

1. Should Interviews be used for selection?
2. Would you ever choose to go to a party rather than write an essay for university?
3. Who do you think has the most power: Biden, Merkel or Adele?
4. What would you say was "your colour"?
5. What shape is man? What shape is time?
6. Do things have to have specific names?
7. Do you read any international publications, do you think there is a value to doing so?
8. Can you hear silence?
9. You mentioned having good thinking skills in your personal statement, can you tell me how many golf balls can you fit in a Boeing 787 Dreamliner?
10. How would you work out the number of flights passing over London at this moment?
11. How many deliveries are made in the UK every day?
12. Have you been to this college before?
13. Do you think that Oxford/Cambridge will suit you?
14. What do you think you'll be doing in a decade? How about in two decades?
15. What is your favourite activity outside of school?
16. How will your fellow college residents see you?
17. Why do you think we structure the course in the way that we do?
18. What would you say was your single greatest weakness?
19. You have mentioned a number of personal strengths in your statement, which is your greatest?
20. How will your experiences from the Duke of Edinburgh scheme benefit you during your time at university?
21. Why choose Oxford or Cambridge, if you know that other universities are less competitive, and may mark your work much more generously?
22. Cambridge is very intense; do you think your current approach to time management will be sufficient?
23. What have you read in the last 24 hours?
24. What would you say was your greatest personal challenge in life? How did you handle it?
25. Do you think that the impact of a good teacher can stretch beyond the walls of a school? Who do you think was your best teacher?
26. What are your long-term plans in life?
27. If you had to name your three greatest strengths, what would you pick?

THE ULTIMATE OXBRIDGE INTERVIEW GUIDE — GENERAL

28. How much should you charge to wash all the windows in London?
29. How many piano tuners are there in Europe?
30. India introduces a new population control policy to address the gender imbalance. If a couple has a girl, they may have another child. If they have a boy, they can't have any more children. What would be the new ratio of boys : girls?
31. Why are manhole covers round?
32. How many times per day does a clock's hand overlap?
33. You are shrunk down so you're the size of a matchstick and then put into a blender with metal blades. It is about to be turned on – what do you do?
34. You are given 7 identical balls and another ball that looks the same as the others but is heavier than them. You can use a balance only two times. How would you identify which is the heavy ball?
35. What is your favourite number?
36. Who am I? (Always read up on your interviewers!)
37. Is there any question that you wished we had asked you?
38. What are you looking forward to the least at this college?
39. Who has had the largest influence on your life?
40. If you were me, would you let yourself in?
41. What do you think my favourite colour is? Why do you say that?
42. What is a lie? How do I know what you just said isn't a lie?
43. If you could keep objects from the present for the future, what would they be?
44. What is more important – art or science?
45. If you could have one superpower – which one would it be? Why?
46. Would you ever go on a one-way trip to Mars? Why/Why not?
47. Does human nature change
48. Define 'success' in one sentence.
49. Is there such a thing as truth?
50. You are shrunk down so you're the size of a matchstick and then put into a blender with metal blades. It is about to be turned on – what do you do?

SUBJECT INTERVIEWS

Subject interviews are where subject-specific questions are asked to test critical thinking and problem-solving skills. These interviews are very likely to follow the format of tutorials/supervisions. You will be interviewed by one or two senior academics from the college you applied to. They will be experts on the subject you've applied for and will ask academic questions around a central theme. The questions are intended to be difficult so as to push you and test your critical thinking abilities in a learning situation. You are not meant to know the answers, but to use your existing knowledge to offer creative and original thoughts to address the questions.

Here are some general tips to keep in mind:

- Apply the knowledge you have acquired at A-Level and from your wider reading to unfamiliar scenarios.
- Stand your ground if you are confident in your argument- even if your interviewers disagree with you. They may deliberately play the devil's advocate to see if you are able to defend your argument.
- However, if you are making an argument that is clearly wrong, and you are being told so by the interviewers - then concede your mistake and revise your viewpoint. Do not stubbornly carry on arguing a point that they are saying is wrong.
- Remember, making mistakes is no bad thing. The important point is that you address the mistake head on and adapt the statement, with their assistance where necessary.
- The tutors know what subjects you have studied at A-Level so don't feel pressured to read EVERY aspect of your subject.

In the chapters that follow, each subject is discussed in detail – including common types of questions and model solutions to previously asked interview questions. This collection is not intended to be an exhaustive list of all that you need to know for your Oxbridge interview (that's impossible!) Instead, it is designed to guide your learning by exposing you to the style and difficulty of questions that might come up and how to best approach them.

THE SCIENCES

BIOLOGY & MEDICINE

There is a large degree of overlap between the biological sciences and Medicine at Oxbridge. Thus, biologists may be asked straight biology questions, medical questions, or questions from a related subject, such as chemistry.

In contrast, medical interviews at Oxbridge are much more likely to focus on the human side of biology (physiology, pathology, pharmacology etc). One of the medical interviews may be a 'general' one- similar in style to the classical medical interviews (with questions like "how do you deal with stress?" etc). The advice that follows is applicable to both biology and medicine applicants due to their similarities.

In general, you'll be **tackling a large question with many smaller sub-questions** to guide the answer from the start to a conclusion. The main question may seem difficult, impossible or random at first, but take a deep breath and start discussing different ideas that you have for breaking the question down into manageable pieces.

The questions are designed to be difficult to give you the chance to **show your full intellectual** potential. The interviewers will help guide you to the right idea provided you work with them and offer ideas for them to steer you along with. This is your chance to show your creativity, analytical skills, intellectual flexibility, problem-solving skills, and go-getter attitude. Don't waste it by letting your nerves overtake or from a fear of messing up or looking stupid.

For biology, the questions will usually take one of **five possible forms** based on the skills necessary to 'think like a biologist':

- Observation-based questions ("Tell me about this...")
- Practical questions ("How would you determine that...")
- Statistical questions ("Given this data...")
- Ethical questions ("Are humans obligated to...", "What are the implications of...")
- Proximate causes (mechanism; "How does...") and ultimate causes (function; "Why does...")- usually both at once.

The questions also have recurring themes because they are important for biological theory and research: Natural and sexual selection, genetics and inheritance, human body systems, global warming and environmental change, and general knowledge of plants, animals, bacteria and pathogens.

Medical Ethics

Medical applicants are commonly asked medical ethics questions, so it's well worth knowing the basics. Whilst there are huge ethical textbooks available– you only need to be familiar with the basic principles for the purposes of your interview. **These principles can be applied to all cases** regardless of what the social/ethnic background the healthcare professional or patient is from. The principles are:

Beneficence: The wellbeing of the patient should be the doctor's first priority. In medicine this means that one must act in the patient's best interests to ensure the best outcome is achieved for them i.e. 'Do Good'.

Non-Maleficence: This is the principle of avoiding harm to the patient (i.e. Do no harm). There can be a danger that, in a willingness to treat, doctors can sometimes cause more harm to the patient than good. This can especially be the case with major interventions, such as chemotherapy or surgery. Where a course of action has both potential harms and potential benefits, non-maleficence must be balanced against beneficence.

Autonomy: The patient has the right to determine their own health care. This, therefore, requires the doctor to be a good communicator so that the patient is sufficiently informed to make their own decisions. 'Informed consent' is thus a vital precursor to any treatment. A doctor must respect a patient's refusal of treatment even if they think it is not the correct choice. Note that patients cannot demand treatment – only refuse it, e.g. an alcoholic patient can refuse rehabilitation but cannot demand a liver transplant.

There are many situations where the application of autonomy can be quite complex, for example:

- **Treating Children:** Consent is required from the parents, although the autonomy of the child is taken into account increasingly as they get older.
- **Treating adults without the capacity** to make important decisions. The first challenge with this is in assessing whether or not a patient has the capacity to make the decisions. Where patients do lack capacity, the power to make decisions is transferred to the next of kin (or Legal Power of Attorney, if one has been set up).

Justice: This principle deals with the fair distribution and allocation of healthcare resources for the population.

Consent: This is an extension of Autonomy- patients must agree to a procedure or intervention. For consent to be valid, it must be voluntary informed consent. This means that the patient must have sufficient mental capacity to make the decision and must be presented with all the relevant information (benefits, side effects and the likely complications) in a way they can understand.

Confidentiality: Patients expect that the information they reveal to doctors will be kept private- this is a key component in maintaining the trust between patients and doctors.

You must ensure that patient details are kept confidential. Confidentiality can be broken if you suspect that a patient is a risk to themselves or to others e.g. terrorism, suicide.

Ensure that you don't immediately give an answer – consider both sides of the argument (pros and cons) and discuss them in detail before arriving at a balanced conclusion.

Worked Questions

Below are a few examples of how to start breaking down an interview question, complete with model answers.

Q1: Why do we see colour blindness in women less than men?

[Extremely clear-headed] Applicant: *Well, I know that women are much less likely to be colour-blind than men. Why don't I start by defining colour-blindness and working out why there is a gender difference using Mendelian inheritance, and then think about mechanisms of colour-blindness which may not be accounted for in this method. I noticed you specified females in relation to males, so I'm going to suggest that whatever this mechanism is, it is sex-dependent.*

Now, being this clear-headed is unlikely to happen when put on the spot, unless you practice a lot, but it shows that the question can be broken down into sub-parts, which can be dealt with in turn. At this point, the interviewer can give feedback if this seems like a good start and help make any modifications if necessary. The applicant would realise that colour-blindness is inherited on the X-chromosome and the second female X-chromosome may help compensate. Although a single defective X-chromosome would lead to colour-blindness, having two defective X-chromosomes does not necessarily mean that a woman would be colour-blind as the defects might be opposites and therefore cancel each other to lead to normal colour vision. The details are unimportant, but the general idea of breaking down the question into manageable parts is important.

The interviewer is not looking for a colour-blindness expert, but someone who can problem-solve in the face of new ideas. Note that this is a question about Proximate Causes in disguise; although the question begins with 'Why', it is actually asking 'how' or which mechanism is causing this discrepancy.

A poor applicant may take a number of approaches unlikely to impress the interviewer. The first and most obvious of these is to say, "We never learned about colour-blindness in school" and make no attempt to move forward from this. The applicants who have done this only make it worse for themselves by resisting prompting as the interviewer attempts to pull an answer from them, saying "fine, but I'm not going to know the answer because I don't know anything about this", or an equally unenthusiastic and uncooperative response. Another approach which is unhelpful in the interview is the 'brain dump', where instead of engaging with the question, the applicant attempts to impress or distract with an assortment of related facts: "Colour-blindness mainly affects men. You can be completely colour-blind or red-green colour-blind. Many animals are colour-blind, but some also see a greater number of colours." Having gotten off to this start isn't as impressive as a more reasoned response, but the interview can be salvaged by taking the interviewer's feedback on-board. Many of these facts could start a productive discussion which leads to the answer if the applicant listens and takes hints and suggestions from the interviewer.

Q2: Do you think we have an ethical obligation to stop climate change?

This is a question about Ethics. To answer a question like this, the important thing is not to have a strong opinion that you defend to the death, but to be able to discuss the different viewpoints based on different understandings of right and wrong, and always with a sound understanding of the underlying issues- both scientific and humanitarian.

One way to break down this question would be to consider whether an ethical obligation extends only to other humans or to other organisms as well, and whether it applies in any situation or only when contributing to a situation that wouldn't occur naturally. Similarly, one could also discuss whether humans as a whole are obliged to halt global warming or just a select few members of the human race. Showing an ability to think flexibly about abstract concepts is always good, but don't forget to then argue for the different cases using knowledge of past and present climates and environments, as this is the subject-relevant part of the question.

For instance, as you are a scientist, don't waste time discussing if climate change is a reality – the scientific community has already reached a consensus. However, if you would like to argue against an ethical obligation instead, discuss the natural climate variations which have occurred on Earth in the past. Use probable climate change-driven events, like the Perma-Triassic extinction when 96% of species died out 250 million years ago, to argue that humans have no ethical obligation to save other species from anthropogenic extinction, because even without human presence there are climate-driven extinctions. Or argue the opposite, that despite past extreme environmental change being a reality, humanity is pushing the Earth further than it has ever sustained humans, and that we are obligated to do our part to leave a habitable Earth for people in other parts of the world and the future. Alternatively, argue completely that there can be no ethical obligation because everyone contributes to the problem in their own way and everyone will face the consequences. Or that only those who contribute more than they suffer are in the wrong for dumping their consequences onto others. Whichever argument you put forward, be sure to include scientific examples so that your discussion doesn't veer away from the question.

Remember that climate change is not the same as global warming and your discussion could include pollution (trash, toxins, chemicals, light and sound pollution, etc.), agriculture and monoculture, invasive species, hunting and fishing, deforestation and habitat fragmentation, or any of the other issues beyond the Greenhouse Effect which affect the environment.

Similarly, global warming is not just about fossil fuel use and carbon dioxide, but a range of gases and their effects on weather, ocean acidity, desertification, pathogen spread, etc. Show that you have a deeper understanding of these issues than you could get from skimming the headlines of the Daily Mail.

THE ULTIMATE OXBRIDGE INTERVIEW GUIDE

BIOLOGY & MEDICINE

Q3: Why do we find DNA inside the nucleus, instead of mitochondria?

This is a question mainly about Ultimate Causes. While you could attempt to answer this by explaining proximate causes; how DNA is used and that it can't be in mitochondria, by giving reasons like "transcription occurs in the nucleus so it has to be there", you would be missing the important why part of this question. It is asking for an ultimate reason. In this case, for the evolutionary history which led mitochondria to have their own separate reproduction. Although you are unlikely to know about this in detail, it is important that you engage with this part of the question so that the interviewer can guide you.

Applicant: DNA can't be stored in the mitochondria because the mitochondria are genetically separate from the host cell. When the cell replicates its DNA and divides, the mitochondria separately replicate their own genetic material and reproduces to populate the new cell. The reason for the mitochondria having separate and distinct genetic material not identical to that of the host cell has been proposed to lie in the evolution of eukaryotes. The Endosymbiotic Theory suggests that cell organelles, particularly energy-producing chloroplasts and mitochondria, were originally separate prokaryotes that were engulfed by larger prokaryotes. They are believed to have begun a symbiotic relationship where perhaps the host cell receives energy and the mitochondria receive a safe environment for reproduction. As this symbiotic relationship evolved, the cells have exchanged some genetic material to coordinate their life-cycles and now cannot survive independently. This explains both the distinct genetic material of mitochondria and the double membrane which surrounds them in the cell – one the original prokaryotic membrane and one from being engulfed by the host. If they were originally a separate organism this explains why cell DNA cannot be stored there.

Q4: How would you determine the function of a human gene?

This is a question about the practical applications of genetics and experimental techniques – it is asking you to use your knowledge of genetics and research methods to come up with some practical ways of answering this. There are many ways you could answer this question, so take an approach that will allow you to use many examples which show off your knowledge, experience or extra reading about this subject.

If you only know about Mendelian genetics, you could suggest searching the genome of relatives to a person known to have the gene to see if those with the gene share traits. This would be a good time to mention a technique if you know it e.g. PCR. However, it may not be possible to isolate gene function this way because:

- The gene would need to be active
- Any trait it contributed to would need to be single locus to really see an effect
- It could produce a hidden condition that isn't apparent in a pedigree
- The gene could be essential and thus present in all relatives
- The sample size is so low that making spurious correlations is very likely
- This would only be a correlation study and not an experiment that determined cause and effect (experiments requiring human breeding are, at best, inconvenient)

If you are more familiar with genetics you may have other ideas; perhaps a cross-species survey looking for the gene in other species to judge its age and specificity to human life, or knock-out genetics with a closely related species possessing the gene to see if its presence is vital or has a direct effect.

The gene could be added to a bacterial genome using plasmids to see which protein is produced. No matter what your answer is, the important part of this question is to take a practical and self-critical approach which plays to your individual knowledge base.

A poor applicant would disregard that the question is asking for a practical solution and instead tell the interviewer about the general function of genes, or would ignore the specifics of the question- treating it as if it could be solved through Mendel's pea-flower approach. A poor applicant would not be self-critical and would not point out the flaws and limitations of their proposed ideas.

Q5: How would you prove the existence of life on Mars?

Applicant: I would want to know what is meant by 'life'- whether it means something Earth-like, or a more general definition. Then I would want either direct or indirect evidence. Direct evidence would be observing life itself, and the indirect would be observing some marker for this life based on how it was defined. Thus, I'll start by thinking about how I would define life and then think about potential markers for it.

This is a practical question that aims to set out what the hypotheses would be for future experiments. It is not about describing one precise experiment, but how you would design a series of experiments. With that in mind, it's important to ensure that suggested evidence is precisely defined, observable and measurable or quantifiable and repeatable because these features open the door to a great variety of experiment types. Thus, the response, "I'd like to see something that's alive" isn't quite detailed enough. You can suggest something which is currently impossible, such as wanting to observe a specimen drilled from one kilometre down on Mars, but should include some practical ideas as well.

One approach would be to define life as an ability to create chemical disequilibria. Through respiration and other basic life functions, organisms shuffle electrons and molecules and create small disequilibria that are later used to power life functions (consider photosynthesis and the shuffling of electrons from donors to acceptors using sunlight to power the process). The surface and atmosphere could be studied for disequilibria, starting with those associated with life on Earth.

There are many other possible approaches, but the general idea is to define the question more specifically and then suggest possible evidence which could be found in a range of experiments. You should suggest multiple experiments as it is necessary to have a sizeable data-pool before reaching a conclusion on such a broad question.

Q6: Why don't we have more than two eyes? Why do we only have one mouth?

This is a question that involves disentangling ultimate and proximate causes. When answering this question, it is important to show that you can approach a question from a variety of perspectives, including both Proximate Causes about how the mechanism influences the observed condition, but also Ultimate Causes about why this may be and what function this serves- particularly from an adaptive standpoint.

For a complete answer to this question, both types of cause are important. Take a moment to consider this from a few perspectives:

- A mechanistic approach through which eyes and mouths work.

- An evolutionary approach by considering adaptation and fitness/survival and its impact on biological designs.
- An anthropological approach by considering evolutionary history and how our ancient ancestors influence the bodies we have today.

How many eyes and mouths we have is a matter of trade-offs: one eye provides an image of the surroundings, but depth perception is only possible with two or more. The slightly different angle from each eye allows us to determine how far away each object is. A very close object will project a very different image in each eye, while distant objects will look the same. The brain is then able to compare the differences in the images in order to estimate distances.

Having an extra eye and being able to integrate the two images is metabolically expensive energetically as a significant amount of neural processing is required. The gains from coordination in capturing prey and escaping predators offsets these costs, allowing for the second eye. A third eye could be helpful as it would allow vision ahead and behind simultaneously. However, each additional eye would be increasingly costly as its image would need to be integrated with the other eyes. Thus, the gains from escaping predators or spotting prey wouldn't be offset.

However, you might also point out that given rampant obesity and other signs that humans have great amounts of spare energy, it would now make sense to have an extra number of eyes. Similarly, for common prey, the metabolic costs of an additional eye could be offset by increased survival.

A mouth is the point of access to the digestive system and only one is required to ingest nutrients. Thus, having more mouths would mean an increase to the rate at which we could ingest food. However, a larger mouth could achieve similar results, so the energetic costs of growing a second fully-functioning mouth are not supported. In addition, introducing another mouth would increase the risk of infections.

There is another dimension to this question than the how and why- the was. Humans can't just grow another mouth or gazelles another eye because our ancestors did not have these. We have no genes to produce this extremely complex and divergent phenotype. It does not matter whether the prey would benefit from the third eye or not- they just can't grow one instantly because the path to that design is too difficult to attain from the present two eye setup.

In general, it is not easy to make such drastic physical changes (even over long periods of time). For example, consider the opposite case: if our ancestors had evolved a three-eye-system. The species would be more likely to become extinct rather than transform to a two-eye system.

A poor applicant would miss the point of this question- it is not to delve deeply into the workings of 3D vision and the digestive system, or even into trade-offs in an adaptation that lead to limits on designs. The point is to show that there are many perspectives which must be integrated to fully consider a question as complex as this.

Q7: Can you liken DNA to sheet music?

A question like this is a great chance to demonstrate your lateral thinking skills. In any comparison question, you should directly relate one thing to the other. For example:

- DNA consists of different patterns of amino acids; sheet music consists of different patterns of 12 notes.
- DNA describes the order in which mRNA should be produced; sheet music describes the order in which the music should be played.
- DNA and sheet music can both contain instructions on how and when to repeat sections.
- Mistakes in reading DNA can result in harmful mutations – mistakes in reading sheet music can result in a ruined melody/chord.
- Mistakes in reading DNA can sometimes be beneficial and lead to useful mutations; mistakes in reading sheet music can also rarely make the piece better than it was originally written.

Q8: Do you have a favourite protein?

This question allows you to demonstrate your enthusiasm for the subject. All answers are perfectly acceptable as long as you can justify them. Do not waste a question like this on an answer which doesn't show specific biological knowledge.

For example, you might like haemoglobin because it is very important as it facilitates oxygen transfer, or because there are many interesting diseases associated with it, e.g. Sick Cell, Thalassaemia. Alternatively, you might like insulin because of its importance in blood glucose homeostasis or its relationship with diabetes.

Q9: Why should we care about the Hayflick Limit?

Firstly, if you do not know what the Hayflick Limit is, ASK! It is impossible to answer this question if you do not know this technical definition. The Hayflick Limit is the theoretical limit to the number of times a normal human cell can divide. A good approach to this question would be to start by defining the Hayflick Limit and suggesting proximate reasons for its existence e.g. shortening telomeres with each cell division until they reach a critical length. Then, if you have any suggestions for ultimate reasons, discuss those, e.g. older DNA is more mutated, so older cells are less healthy and less related to the original than younger cells. If you have time, you could show an interest in biological issues by discussing some implications you may know about deriving from this topic, referencing articles or other media e.g. documentaries or the highly recommended TED talks available online.

Examples of things that are relevant would be the stability of clones derived from mature DNA, the possibility of immortality with finite cell rejuvenation, or problems with cancer cells that exceed the Hayflick Limit. You aren't expected to have any significant knowledge of these – the interviewers would guide you throughout the process.

Q10: Why is the liver on the right side of the body?

This is another classic question about disentangling ultimate and proximate causes, mechanisms and functions. The actual answer doesn't matter - only that you can show that you are able to approach biological questions from different perspectives. You could take a proximate mechanism approach and argue that there is a reason the liver can only work in that position - perhaps it needs to be in a specific orientation to allow the other organs to fit into the human body in this right-hand configuration.

From an ultimate perspective, you could argue there is an evolutionary advantage to this configuration. Maybe it is advantageous to have the vital liver on the opposite side of the body to the equally vital heart in case of severe injury to one side. You could take an evolutionary history approach- that there is no advantage to having the liver on the right, but some ancient ancestor had a right-left asymmetry with right-hand organs which became the liver. The important part of this answer is to show you are not locked into one perspective, but that you can see the variety of biological factors which may be at work.

The last example to drive this point home would be the question, *"Why are flowers usually never green?"* You could argue this from a proximate perspective- that flowers aren't photosynthetically active and thus don't have green chlorophyll. Alternatively, you could approach it from an ultimate perspective- flowers are meant to be attractive to pollinators and thus need to stand out from the foliage. Therefore, their functionality would be diminished if they were green.

Q11: Why do humans have two ears?

This type of question is often asked because all good candidates should be able to arrive at the correct answer (even if they haven't heard of it before). Therefore, it is useful to talk through your thought process, which will also allow the interviewer to guide you if necessary. A good place to start is to recognise that there must be a distinct evolutionary advantage of having two ears, so it must allow for functions that are not possible to the same extent with only one ear.

Having two ears allows you to compare differences in stimuli. How could comparing the sound you hear in each ear be useful? The properties of this sound would include amplitude, frequency, and timing – why would these differ between the ears?

If sound is coming from one side of the head then it would reach one ear before the other, so the timing of the sound would differ between the ears. Similarly, the amplitude would also differ between the ears if the source was not equidistant from them. Finally, if a moving sound source is closer to one ear than the other, then its frequency will differ between the ears (an extrapolation of the Doppler Effect).

Therefore, a comparison of the timing, amplitude, and frequency of sounds in each ear provides the brain with enough information to allow sound localisation, which is a powerful evolutionary advantage.

Q12: Can you explain how the brain works in a single word?

The challenge of this question is that the brain is such a complex organ that no single word could ever summarise how it works. It is important to make it explicit to the interviewer that you recognise this. Secondly, you need to recognise that the question is about 'how' the brain works, so the best answers will talk about a process and not simply the architecture that allows it to work. For example, answering 'plasticity' would be more appropriate than answering 'synapses' or 'circuits'. Whatever word you choose, the crucial thing is that you try to reasonably justify your answer.

A good student who chose 'plasticity' might then say: "this is because plasticity at the synaptic level encompasses processes like long-term potentiation and long-term depression. These are crucial in how the neural circuits that underlie brain function develop. Thus, they're ultimately responsible for modulating how one neuron responds to another neuron's firing and so how the circuits as a whole function. The crucial role of plasticity has been demonstrated in numerous brain functions; including learning, memory, emotions, sensation and the recovery from injury".

Q13: Is cancer inevitable?

This question is purposefully vague, so it is up to you to specify what you think they are asking. It also gives you scope to pick an angle for your answer through which you can best demonstrate your knowledge. You could take a 'nature vs. nurture' approach, discussing how there is a genetic component to cancer that predisposes to or protects vs. cancer.

You should make it clear that it is the predisposition to cancer that could be considered inevitable, not cancer itself. Mention any examples you may know of, such as the association of mutation in the BRCA1 gene with breast cancer.

In general, cancer is a disease of ageing and the risk of most cancers increases with age. Thus, one could argue that if most people lived long enough, they would eventually get some type of cancer. Alternatively, you could argue that whilst getting cancer is inevitable at the moment (like getting an infection), medical advances may change this in the future. The important thing is to define the question so that you are able to tackle it rather than giving a one-word response.

Q14: Why do second messenger systems exist?

You may have learned about this topic in A-levels but may not have thought about why it is the way it is. The interviewer would give you a quick explanation of 2nd messengers if you hadn't heard of them before. Again, they are interested in how you deduce your answers logically and using first principles.

It is useful to think about why secondary messenger systems would have evolved and what alternative systems are conceivable. One such alternative is signalling chemicals that pass into the target cells and interact directly with effector proteins (such as steroid signalling). What advantages are conveyed by having an extra step in the signalling cascade?

This is best thought about in the context of an example, such as the cyclic adenosine monophosphate (cAMP) system and gives you an opportunity to display what you know about these systems. Having a system that requires binding of a primary messenger (e.g. acetylcholine) to a cell surface receptor (e.g. G-protein coupled receptors) allows for signals to be determined by receptor density to a certain extent.

Similarly, a variety of intracellular signalling can affect the levels of a secondary messenger, allowing even finer control of the ultimate intracellular signal and response.

Perhaps most importantly, second messengers help to amplify the cellular response. For example, a single molecule of Acetylcholine (primary messenger) can result in millions of downstream 2nd messengers. This setup allows cells to react to small stimuli very rapidly.

Q15: Over the past century, which medical advancement would you judge to be the most significant?

There is no single right answer for this question- you just need to be able to justify your response. It is a good idea to pick something you may have read a little about so that you can add detail to support your answer. Some good options include antibiotics, population-scale vaccines (smallpox, polio and MMR are good examples), evidence-based analysis (placebo-controlled, blinded, randomised-controlled trials; meta-analysis), advances in blood typing/banking/infusion.

For example, "I think that the development of a huge array of antibiotics since the discovery of penicillin is perhaps the most important medical advance in the last 100 years. This is because bacterial infections are very common and affect most of us at some point in our lives. Before antibiotics, even very small infections could be life threatening. The discovery of antibiotics represented a paradigm shift in medicine whereby a huge number of very harmful infectious diseases (such as tuberculosis, diphtheria, typhoid) became treatable. Furthermore, antibiotics made surgery a lot safer, by reducing the risks of post-operative infection.

Your answer to this question may determine the future line of questioning for the remainder of the interview so choose carefully! For example, this particular response may lead to a discussion of how antibiotic resistance develops or why multi-drug resistant bacteria are a problem.

Q16: How would you plot a graph of drug concentration in the blood against time, for a drug partially removed by the kidneys prior to each subsequent dose?

You haven't been given enough information to allow you to draw the graph accurately e.g. the rate of absorption, the rate of elimination, and the time between each dose. However, you can still draw the general shape - as the drug is absorbed from the gut, the concentration of drug in the blood (called plasma drug concentration, or C) will rapidly increase.

When the majority of the drug has been absorbed, the rate of drug elimination will exceed the rate of absorption. Thus, there will be a turning point where C starts to decrease. C will continue to drop until the next dose.

Since the dose isn't fully eliminated, the lowest value of C will still be greater than zero. It will then again rapidly increase because the new dose is being absorbed.

Therefore, over several successive doses, C will become progressively greater to eventually give a graph shaped like below:

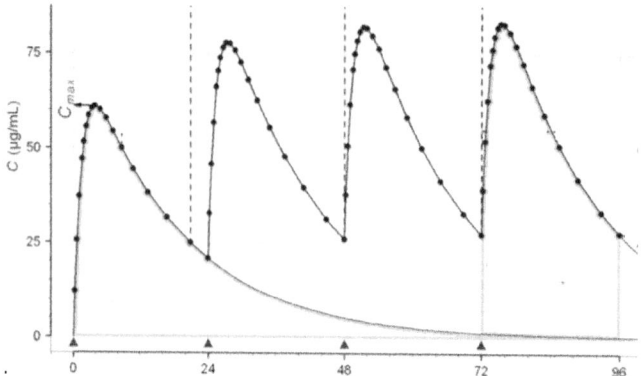

Q17: What does the nocebo effect tell us about how patients respond to treatment?

A good place to start with answering this question is to make it clear that you understand the difference between the 'nocebo effect' and negative iatrogenic side-effects produced by treatments. The key difference is that there is no physiological reason for the side-effects with the nocebo effect. You can then compare this to the well known 'placebo effect', where positive effects are experienced in response to 'drugs' (often completely inert sugar pills), despite there being no physiological explanation for this.

It is thought that the placebo effect is due to the patient's expectation of positive effects from the drug. Therefore, you could suggest that in nocebo, it is likely that some expectation of negative side effects could precipitate the perception of these negative side effects. Both these effects show that there is a psychological aspect to how patients respond to their treatments. This is very important when doctors consider how to manage patient expectations about how a treatment will affect them. It introduces an interesting ethical dilemma about keeping patients fully informed about the potential negative side effects of a treatment – it is important to let patients know the risks. However, doing this could cause them to experience negative side effects due to the 'nocebo effect'.

Q18: Why do humans rely on negative feedback?

You will know of examples of negative feedback from A-level Biology, such as homeostatic mechanisms like temperature control and the maintenance of steady blood glucose levels using insulin and glucagon. Although it's good to start by describing the role of negative feedback in these processes, it is crucial that you go on to discuss why homeostasis is necessary in the first place.

At the system level, you can discuss how using negative feedback to keep such parameters within a small range allows for larger physiological responses to relatively small changes in the environment. At the cellular level, the internal environment must be tightly regulated by negative feedback to allow enzymes to function efficiently e.g. temperature and pH.

A poor candidate would just list examples of negative feedback rather than discussing its significance.

Q19: What happens when the adrenal glands become hyperactive?

Your ability to answer this question will depend on if you know what hormones are produced by the adrenals and what their function is. Again, the interviewer will prompt you if you get stuck. The adrenals produce catecholamines such as adrenaline and noradrenaline as well as other steroid hormones like cortisol and aldosterone. Therefore, a 'hyperactive' adrenal gland would produce excess amounts of these hormones.

Catecholamines increase the heart rate and cause peripheral vasoconstriction. So increased catecholamine production from a hyperactive adrenal gland would lead to all of these features. You could also think about what would cause the adrenals to be 'hyperactive' e.g. an adrenal tumour or increased stimulation from the nerves innervating the adrenal gland.

Similarly, if you were aware of the effects of increased steroid hormones, then you should describe what actions they have and what would happen if there were increased production of them.

NB: This is an interesting area of clinical medicine and if you're interested in endocrinology – you are advised to do some background reading on *Cushing's Syndrome* and *Conn's Syndrome*.

Q20: What diseases do you think we should screen for?

This ethical question gives you an opportunity to demonstrate an understanding of resource allocation and knowledge of any screening programmes that you are aware of. You can discuss how it is important that the resources are used to achieve the most benefit for the most people (utilitarian argument). This is often measured using quality adjusted life-years (QUALYs) by the National Institute of Health and Care Excellence (NICE). They perform these calculations in order to decide if screening is appropriate. So for screening to be appropriate and cost-effective:

- The disease must be an important health problem
- The disease should be treatable
- There should be a simple screening test for the disease
- The test should have low false positive and false negative rates
- The test should be cost-effective

You could then offer your opinion on which diseases would satisfy these criteria. For completeness, current screening programmes include:

- Pap smears vs. Cervical Cancer
- Mammograms vs. Breast cancer
- Faecal Occult blood test vs. Colorectal cancer
- Foetal blood tests for Down's Syndrome

Biology & Medicine Interview Questions

1. What makes a cheetah so fast?
2. Why is an elephant's foot structured as it is?
3. What makes a horse's leg so well-suited to running?
4. Why do you want to be a vet/doctor?
5. How do fish respire? How is this different from mammals?
6. Tell me about your favourite animal.
7. Describe the function of an electron microscope.
8. How do reflexes in the leg work? How would this be affected if the spinal cord were damaged at the level of the neck?
9. What mutations could shorten or lengthen RNA or DNA?
10. How do you test which colours Rats and Octopuses can see?
11. Why do bats and moles have different brain:body ratios?
12. I see from your personal statement that you do a lot of sports. What effects does lactic acid have on the body and brain?
13. Take a look at this skull. What can you learn about it?
14. What experiment would you design to test whether Female deer select their mates based on the size of their antlers if older deer have bigger antlers?
15. Male deer show-fight when competing for mates, rather than fighting to the death - is there an evolutionary point to this?
16. How do dolphins regulate their body temperature?
17. Tell me the number of petrol stations in Europe.
18. How many molecules of gas are in here?
19. In a completely dissociated aqueous sulphuric acid solution at pH 2 - how many sulphate ions are there?
20. Please draw as many compounds as possible using C_4H_8O, placing emphasis on the different chemical groups involved.
21. What do you know about the bonding in a benzene ring?
22. An ice cube is floating in a glass of water. What happens to the water level when it melts?
23. How is aspirin synthesised? What organic reaction takes place?
24. Draw the full chemical structure of DNA.
25. Why are diamonds so expensive?
26. What is entropy?
27. Why are bacterial infections easier to treat than viral infections?
28. Does the molecular structure of glycine change with pH?
29. How long is a gene?
30. How many genes are in a cell?
31. Give an example of when specialist biological knowledge has helped a global issue.
32. Was Lamarck right?
33. How would you mass-produce insulin?
34. How would you tell if a mouse could differentiate between the smell of an apple and the smell of chocolate?

35. Should all stem cell therapy be legalised?
36. If senses work only because our brain interprets electrical signals, what is reality?
37. How many guinea pigs would you use in an experiment?
38. Is 'euthanasia' too vague to be useful?
39. What range of things could euthanasia refer to?
40. Do you believe that patients should have autonomy?
41. How much of a spending priority should the NHS attach to palliative care?
42. Is it fair to call the NHS the 'crown jewel of the welfare state'?
43. Can you adequately compare public and private healthcare?
44. Do you think otherwise terminally ill patients should be allowed to test unproven drugs?
45. What is the nature and value of clinical trials?
46. What is the importance of 3D printing to medicine?
47. What makes radiotherapy more effective against cancer than regular cells?
48. I'm going to give you one billion pounds - but you can only spend it on research in a specific area. What do you choose?
49. What would you say was the biggest medical breakthrough of the last decade?
50. How do ECG's work?
51. Could it be justifiable to legalise the drug known as ecstasy?
52. Do you think every hospital should have an MRI machine?
53. What are the ethical implications of genetic screening in-utero?
54. Where do you think it is appropriate to use placebos?
55. Without trying them, how would you tell the difference between salt and sugar?
56. How would you discretise perception, self-awareness and consciousness?
57. If a psychologically ill person commits a crime, are they a criminal?
58. If you had to give human rights to one of either chimpanzees, dolphins or elephants, which would you choose?
59. How much blood does a human heart pump over an average lifespan?
60. Why do men often go bald, but women rarely do?
61. Why is there no cure for the common cold? How does the flu vaccine work?
62. Why does the cardiac cycle work in the sequence it does?
63. Why don't we just release energy from glucose directly?
64. What is the value of DNA fingerprinting to forensics?
65. What is health? What is normality?
66. What is the DSM? How do you think doctors should responsibly use the DSM?
67. Has modern medicine blocked human evolution?
68. How can we cure global warming if environmental measures fail?
69. Why are stomata on the bottom of leaves?
70. Why are so few flowers and animals coloured green?
71. Radiation can cause cancer, yet we commonly use radiotherapy to treat cancers. Surely this doesn't make sense?
72. How would you find out what function a gene has in humans? What about in plants?

73. There is a test which is 99% accurate and specific (the probability of a positive test given a patient is ill is 99%, and the probability of a negative test given the patient isn't ill is also 99%). It's estimated that approximately 1% of the country has a live infection, so everyone is tested. Given that your patient gets a positive test, what are the chances that they have the illness?
74. What is your favourite pathogen?
75. What is the difference between bacteria and viruses?
76. How does a caterpillar transform into a butterfly?
77. Why do some habitats support higher biodiversity than others?
78. Why do so many animals have stripes?
79. Here's a cactus. Tell me about it.
80. If you could save either the rainforests or the coral reefs, which would you choose?
81. Is it easier for organisms to live in the sea or on land?
82. Why do only some lions have manes?
83. How many millilitres of beer (5% alcohol by volume) would an average person have to drink to be above the legal limit of 50mg alcohol / 100ml of blood?
84. Would it matter if tigers became extinct?
85. Why do cats' eyes appear to 'glow' in the dark?
86. What do you think the impact of epigenetic research is on medical treatment?
87. Do you think the NHS should advocate vegetarianism or veganism as a means to combat public health issues with obesity?
88. How do stem cells become specialised?
89. The Pernkopf Topographic Anatomy of Man is often regarded as the most comprehensive book of human anatomy in the world and is of immeasurable value to surgeons and other medical professionals as a result. It was also developed through human experimentation under the Nazis. Should we stop using or publishing it?
90. Define neurotransmitters
91. Why have deaths from infectious diseases dropped in the UK?
92. What is a gene?
93. Why can you stay balanced whilst cycling, but not on a stationary bike?
94. Why are BAME people more likely to die of Covid-19 than the general population were.
95. Will the global population continue increasing indefinitely? What factors might affect the ongoing population growth?
96. What are the problems with the current taxonomy system?
97. Draw a graph of how a bacterial population changes over time and one for the human population. Why is there a difference?
98. I have just injected myself with an unknown substance. Work out what it is doing to my body by asking me simple questions. (Answer= it blocked the function of motor neurons).
99. What is the mass of nitrogen in this room?
100. What is the most important technology available in medicine? Why? How could it be improved?
101. Is humour a useful skill for a doctor?

102. If you lived in the 18th century, how would you prove that different areas of the brain have different functions?
103. How do archaeologists decide which fossils are 'people' and which are something earlier?
104. Why is glass transparent but the sand that it's made from not?
105. Will the population of mankind ever stop increasing?
106. Why do people have different gaits when they walk?
107. How do you measure blood pressure?
108. Talk about a piece of recent scientific research. Why was it important and how could it be improved?
109. How could you measure how much blood is in your body right now?
110. How do you know if someone has a mental illness? How would you tell if they didn't?
111. Should we be trying to cure conditions such as autism or Downs syndrome?
112. Describe and draw a Volume/Pressure curve of a balloon and compare it to the workings of the lung.
113. You are with a nurse who takes blood and makes a labelling mistake on a patient who has a needle phobia. What do you do? What do you say to the patient and what do you say to the nurse?
114. Describe how the human nose is adapted anatomically and physiologically to perform its function?
115. How would you classify diseases?
116. What do you understand by the term 'apoptosis'?
117. Why is the heart so well adapted to performing its role?
118. What are QALYs?
119. Draw a schematic diagram of the heart and tell me about the circulatory system.
120. The interviewer places a skeleton foot on the table. What is this?
121. Is this a left or right foot? How do you know which side the foot is?
122. How do you know it is a foot and not a hand?
123. Describe the processes that occur at a synapse.
124. What causes the common cold?
125. What is cerebral palsy?
126. What is an amino acid?
127. How do amino acids bond to form a peptide?
128. Please look at this picture (brain slice after a stroke). What does it show?
129. What are the two main types of stroke?
130. What can cause strokes in young patients?
131. What are fluid balance charts used for?
132. What are the most important characteristics of a good doctor?
133. Is it more important to be competent or compassionate?
134. What will you do if the senior doctor is not at the hospital and you have to perform a life-threatening procedure for the first time to save someone's life?
135. Are disabled lives worth saving?
136. You're a metre underwater, breathing through a straw - why do you drown?
137. Discretise meiosis and mitosis

138. Considering genetics, why aren't we mostly banana?
139. What's the point of lungs?
140. What's the main cause of obesity?
141. How do birds fly?
142. How do you express the relationship between fluid flow and vessel diameter?
143. What is your pulse?
144. Why do you drown faster in sea water than fresh water?
145. What mechanisms allow blood to travel from your feet to your heart?
146. Why do blue veins bleed red?
147. How do humans maintain balance without vision?
148. How would you go about telling a farmer that his cow is dead?
149. Here's a snorkel - can you use it to explain the respiratory system?
150. Why is cellular compartmentalisation a reality?
151. Are meals today far removed from biology?
152. How do you think cocaine affects blood flow to the brain and heart?
153. Do you think Humans or Chimpanzees are more suited to their environment?
154. How would you tackle obesity?
155. How would you stop the spread of Ebola?
156. Does any human behaviour come from our genes?
157. Why is it so hard to be sustainable?
158. What problems are posed by an ageing population? Is age a disease?
159. Do humans need brains?
160. What's the point of your kidneys?
161. Why does exercise elevate our heart rate?
162. Besides treating the sick, what do doctors do?
163. You can afford 1 heart transplant or 100 hip replacements. Which do you choose?
164. I have been diagnosed with Huntingdon's disease, and I don't want my family to know about it. What are the ethical dilemmas here?

PSYCHOLOGY

A psychologist will likely be asked questions on biology, experiment design or statistics and data-handling. The interviewers understand that some applicants may not have studied psychology before – be prepared to explain why you think you want to study psychology and show through extra-curricular reading or activities how you've fostered your interest.

The questions below are specific to psychology, but **there is no guarantee that 'psychology' questions will be asked** in a psychology interview. Be prepared to answer questions that are open-ended, require some knowledge of popular psychology topics (e.g. well-known psychiatric conditions), require you to demonstrate an interest in psychology, require you to design experiments or metrics, and that show you can use statistical or other objective approaches to answer subjective questions. Remember that **neuroscience is a part of psychology**, so you may be asked about cognitive functions or sensory systems.

Worked Questions

Below are a few examples of how to start breaking down an interview question, complete with model answers.

Q1: What do you know about learning in infants?

There are a number of different ways this question could develop, and it is open-ended enough that it is possible to steer towards areas of particular knowledge or interest. Taking a neurological approach could mean discussing neuronal mechanisms involved with learning and memory (e.g. forging new synapse connections). It could also involve discussions of cognitive pathways, for instance, the functioning of normal versus impaired language centres in the cortex, and language acquisition.

Taking a psychological approach could involve discussing normal human developmental milestones and Piaget's learning stages. It could also involve a discussion of different types of conditioning (e.g. Pavlov), and how feedback from consequences and rewards influence behaviour. A social psychological discussion may include how individuals take cues from parents and society to learn (though remember the question specifies babies). This is also a chance to discuss any recent research encountered. For instance, a new study showing that mother rats lastingly pass down their specific fears to their babies through the scents they emit when reacting to specific triggers.

Q2: How would you go about measuring intelligence?

This is a question about metrics and there are several ways you could start this answer off. You could define intelligence in any way you like, and then set up some systems for measuring that definition of intelligence, or you could start by discussing the concept of intelligence and suggest some ways to constrain both the definition and level of intelligence simultaneously. For instance, you could define intelligence as a set of mental abilities, such as logic, spatial awareness, numeracy and memory, and suggest tests of each ability. Or you could mention current intelligence metrics and discuss which abilities they measure and ignore, whether they are representing different societal ideas about intelligence and intelligent figures, and if they work cross-culturally and through time.

For example, using IQ testing as a starting point, you could discuss the different types of questions it presents and which people will score high and low (e.g. spatial questions can be a large component of some versions of the test and men often have better spatial reasoning skills). You could discuss some of its advantages (e.g. that it scores on a bell curve with 100 at the centre to normalise a sample of test-takers) and disadvantages (e.g. that it is not an absolute scoring system so comparisons may be false). You could discuss related effects, such as the Flynn Effect (apparent rising of IQ over time as modern test-takers score above average on older IQ tests), and whether these work in the favour of these tests as valid metrics.

Remember that however you argue, you are not setting out to defend a personal viewpoint, but are discussing the strengths and weaknesses of a number of definitions and metrics from different perspectives, including recognising those ways of thinking which may be Western-centric.

Q3: Are diseases like schizophrenia caused more by nature or nurture?

This is a classic nature-nurture question with a psychology twist. A good way to start this question is to define nature and nurture as the genes inherited from parents and the environment exposed to during development. At this point you can showcase some knowledge of schizophrenia; you could perhaps cite the rates of incidence in relatives of schizophrenics versus the general population, or some adoption studies monitoring the incidence of the disease in children raised by their schizophrenic parent or by unaffected adoptive parents. If you have no knowledge of schizophrenia, you could ask if you can generalise the question to similar psychiatric disorders.

To continue, you might want to discuss the different ways you could be affected by nature and nurture. For instance, you could inherit genes that directly predispose you to schizophrenia or to conditions which make you vulnerable to schizophrenia, such as a related condition or a neurotransmitter imbalance, etc. You could also be epigenetically affected through the impact of schizophrenia on lifestyle, for instance, leading to damaged DNA in gametes or the transmission of phobias and anxieties in DNA, as has been shown possible in some recent studies. For nurture, you might want to mention in vivo effects of drugs and alcohol or stress and poor nutrition on a developing baby. Also after birth, the effects of having an ill parent, such as poor care or trauma as an infant, learning bad habits by imitation or other conditioning to an unhealthy mental state. Or having a generally bad childhood potentially leaving an individual more disposed to psychiatric conditions. The important part of this question is breaking down the effects of nature and nurture in a thorough discussion, rather than demonstrating perfect knowledge of schizophrenia.

Q4: Can you define synaesthesia? What is its importance?

The first part of this question would allow you to show that you have taken an interest in psychology, particularly if you haven't studied psychology at school, and the second part would show how you reason about the brain. Synaesthesia is a famous neurological abnormality where stimulation of one sensory or cognitive pathway leads to the automatic stimulation of another, particularly one not usually associated with the first. For instance, the letter 'S' may always seem red or the number '1' may sound like the note middle C. Synaesthesia is a favourite of the popular neuroscientist, V.S. Ramachandran. If you haven't heard of synaesthesia, say so, you can still answer the second part of the question. Synaesthesia is thought to be caused by cross-activation of brain regions, so the most common forms hint at which brain regions are adjacent.

This can then be used for cortex mapping. It also may hint at which cognitions and sensory concepts are processed in similar ways, as the prevalence of some forms and directions of synaesthesia over others may suggest that those cognitions and sensory concepts are encoded similarly in the brain.

Q5: How can we identify our 'known unknowns'?

This question is designed to push you to think in the abstract; to show that you can work on a problem where all definitive answers are off the table and to see what unique thoughts you can have. Any approach to this question will be individual and rely on your ability to think originally. Some ideas you might want to consider in your answer, if you are stuck, are distinguishing between individual and societal knowledge (e.g. knowing what you don't know by comparing to other members of society), or specific instances of definable ignorance versus an overall lack of knowledge (e.g. not knowing someone's phone number versus not knowing there is a great concept in our understanding of physics completely untouched, such as quantum mechanics in the 19th century). You could also take a neurological approach, discussing how the brain fills in gaps in knowledge automatically to reconcile reality to what the brain 'knows', perhaps citing an instance where this malfunctions and renders a situation unknowable.

For instance, in anosognosia, where, for example, people suffering from a paralysed limb believe that they are not paralysed due to a failure in reconciling the dissonance between the command to move a paralysed limb and the visual feedback that no movement is occurring. Whatever the approach to this question, it is important to show an understanding of the different types of knowledge and the different ways we can understand knowledge, both in our own minds and academically.

Q6: Which animal would you say was the most conscious?

This question is clearly aiming at consciousness and our understanding of it, which is known to be the 'hard question' of psychology. It is important to define whether by 'animal' the interviewer means only non-human animals. Should that be the case, the interviewer does not necessarily expect a 'right' or a 'wrong' answer. It is very difficult to assess whether a chimpanzee or a dolphin is 'more' conscious than the other. Indeed, it is very difficult to assess the consciousness of anyone that is not us, even our fellow human beings: the only reason we assume they are conscious is because they tell us so.

A good answer would take into account the difficulties of defining consciousness and assessing it in non-verbal creatures. It is also important not to get confused and equate consciousness with intelligence: there might be a good reason to believe that a monkey is 'more conscious' than a goldfish, but it is necessary to define the relationship between intelligence and consciousness and not conflate the two. Should the interviewer include humans in the question, it might be worth discussing the evolutionary importance of consciousness, how it may have developed in humans, and whether 'proto-consciousness' can be found in animals. Again, a few sentences highlighting the difficulties of defining and assessing consciousness are needed.

Q7: Is IQ a valid measurement of intelligence?

Intelligence is a complicated construct that most people have an opinion of, which makes it difficult to discuss in psychological terms. The question seems to be aiming at two things: first, provoking a discussion on our understanding of intelligence, the many different things it can mean, and how it can mean different things to different people. For example, in some cultures, intelligence may be regarded as something different than what many people in the Western world equate with intelligence. Indeed, upon inspection, there might be a large divergence in what individuals within a culture believe intelligence to be. Some issues that may come up are whether there is one intelligence or many, whether intelligence is learned or inherited, whether intelligence can change over time. The second point the question is trying to get at, which is closely related to the previous points, is regarding the measurement of intelligence. If you know about IQ and how it is quantified, here is your opportunity to demonstrate your knowledge. Always take into consideration, however, that you have to answer the question and not get side tracked. If you do not know much about IQ, it is your opportunity to deduce what it is from an intelligent conversation: if you had to invent a way to measure intelligence, how would you do it? The interviewer will help you if you get stuck, and once you do it, try to steer back the conversation to see if the new method wholly covers what you believe is intelligence, examining what the possible pitfalls may be.

Q8: What do we mean when we discuss 'activity in the brain'?

This question is double-edged: on one hand, it is an opportunity to demonstrate your knowledge of different brain scanning techniques. If you know a little about functional magnetic resonance imaging or other methods to scan for brain activity, here you have the opportunity to demonstrate your knowledge and discuss them. If you happen to not know much about brain scanning methods at the point this question is asked, do not panic for the interviewers are more interested in how you engage with difficult issues rather than looking for any concrete knowledge that you may or may not have.

It is indeed a bit of a philosophical question: if we see brain activity in a certain brain region during a certain task, what does it really mean? In many experiments, people are told to do a certain task while their brain activity is measured, and certain inferences are made based on the outcome. For example, the amygdala has become known as the fear centre of the brain for its strong activity during fear-related stimuli. But does this tell us that amygdala activation is both necessary and sufficient for experiencing fear? The brain is an extraordinarily interconnected system, is it really possible to isolate individual parts? More importantly, is it possible to isolate psychological processes, such as fear or attention? Just because we subjectively feel that they are isolatable does not mean that they actually are.

Q9: What would you say was the ideal personality for a world leader?

This sort of question may arise as a prompt to discuss personality or as an interesting discussion point in places where students are able to study both psychology and politics. Given the priority on psychology, it would be recommended that the answer begins with a definition of personality, what it means, what people usually understand it to mean, and perhaps on how it can be measured. Once you feel you have covered your bases, it would be interesting to incorporate the answer as to what a world leader would require. World leaders, be it in business or politics, generally need to be charismatic and able to convince people to work for them. Does this mean that they have to have a highly empathetic personality? On the other hand, these leaders often have to make difficult decisions that involve considerable sacrifices. Does this mean they need a particular sort of psychopathy that helps them understand individuals but not care about them? If we assume so, how does this fit into the personality structures that exist? How would one measure this? World leaders are often (but by no means always) thought to be intelligent: is intelligence part of a personality?

Q10: Would you say that questioning users of psychedelics produces useful data on cognition?

In the early days of psychology, a lot of research was performed on subjective reports of individuals. The problem with this research was that it was difficult to verify and confirm, and was not objective due to its very nature. Psychological research then attempted to move on to more objective measures, such as behaviour, which many people believe was a very important step towards establishing the validity of psychology as a science. On the other hand, interesting psychological constructs, such as consciousness, are very difficult to experiment on objectively. Drugs are interesting because by chemically altering the way the brain works, experimenters can make deductions about how the brain works. For example, most psychotropic substances alter time perception, which could be used to determine whether time perception depends on a specific part of the brain, or whether it is a broader function involving several parts of the brain. In addition, if a particular substance affects both certain types of vision and certain types of movement, it could be assumed that the two are somehow linked together. That being said, there are ethical questions raised by reliance on psychotropic substances in a research setting, such as their almost ubiquitous illegality or their effect on health, which should be taken into account before research is done in this way.

Q11: What can autism show us about the way we understand others?

Autism spectrum disorder is characterised by a wide variety of cognitive and behavioural symptoms, most characteristically problems in social issues. For example, people with autism are often thought to be highly interested in routines and numbers (e.g. a train schedule) whereas they seem to show very little interest towards other human beings or other games children like to play, like role-playing games. By studying the problems that people with autism have, we can perhaps get an insight into how healthy people think about others. It is well known that people with autism have trouble identifying and understanding human emotion from a very early age.

This can tell us many things, perhaps the most important of which is the realisation that it is surprisingly intuitive and easy for us to perform highly complicated tasks such as understanding what other people are feeling and why. By studying the development of autistic children and identifying the errors that they make compared to the errors of healthy children, we might be able to identify the mental processes that are behind our intuitive social appraisals and understand at what point and why they start to differ.

Q12: How can we determine whether we are capable of thought?

This question can be answered in a vast variety of ways, my answer will approach it from an evolutionary psychology point of view. First of all, I would like to point out that it is possible to dispute the premise of the question: we indeed know that we think, but often we overestimate exactly how aware we are of our mental processes. Psychology researchers looking at decision-making have discovered that human beings are quite unaware of how they come to decisions and how extraneous factors, such as the irrelevant number they had been presented earlier, can affect their decisions. This is important, for one could also argue it is better to ask: "why do we think we know that we think".

Nonetheless, it is safe to assume that we do indeed have a certain degree of awareness of our own thoughts and I propose two reasons why this may have developed. First, this awareness may have developed in human beings because it helps us understand why we behave in the way we do, which facilitates complex tasks like making tools or solving problems (i.e. I am looking for sharp stones so I can make an arrow that can kill an animal which I can then eat). Secondly, humans are highly social animals and knowing why we do things may help us understand why others do things, which can provide us with a competitive advantage.

Q13: Can you reliably learn about someone's personality by asking them about it?

First of all, it is necessary to distinguish what the question means by personality. The construct of personality is defined in myriad ways, but it is generally believed to be a group of individual characteristics, usually thought to be relatively stable over time, which can be used to predict and explain behaviour. Taking that into account, most personality tests, such as the Big 5, take the approach of asking individuals a set of questions and scoring the answers in order to place the individual along different dimensions of personality or in different groups. This has some merits: the resulting values are quite stable over time (if you take the same test a week apart you get the same result), between individuals (if you take the test and a good friend takes the test answering he or she thinks you would, you can expect the results to be quite similar) and can be used to predict behaviour to a certain extent.

However, there are a few downsides to asking people questions to determine their personality. First, it assumes that people are aware of what their personality is. Cognitive psychological research, particularly in decision-making, has demonstrated that people are very unaware of many things we would intuitively consider to be consciously accessible information. Secondly, it assumes that people will answer accurately questions relating to personality (they may be biased to answer in a certain way or to please the person asking, or to stick to cultural norms). Other, new methods, such as those which rely on using behavioural footprints online, have recently become increasingly accurate in predicting the personality of individuals.

Q14: Do you think individuals all behave similarly in controlled situations?

This question is hinting at the person-situation debate in psychology, in which psychologists long debated whether an individual's personality or the situation is more predictive of behaviour. On one hand, influential studies like Stanley Milgram's electrocution experiments and Phillip Zimbardo's Stanford prison experiment showed that ordinary individuals are prone to act in extraordinary ways in certain circumstances, supporting the claim that the situation is more important than the person. On the other hand, as many other researchers pointed out, not even in those experiments did everyone behave in the same way, and there are various reasons to believe that the methodology of the study did not quite support the arguments made by the original researchers. For example, people who are keen to participate in a "prison experiment" are likely to be different from most people. Of course, it seems to be true that both factors matter: both the person and the situation.

Overall, different people often behave similarly in similar situations because in most cases it makes sense to do so: if we had to think explicitly about what to do every time we do something, everything we do would involve a significant amount of effort. Therefore, it makes sense to copy others or follow certain behavioural schemas in many situations, not least because it is expected from us by other people. That being said, it is fairly evident that different people do tend to behave differently in the same situation, which is perhaps evidenced by the range of different behaviours interviewers witness in the interview setting.

Q15: Why do we have auditory hallucinations, and how do they relate to schizophrenia?

What we perceive the world to be is not so much what is actually out there but rather the reality that our brain constructs out of our sensory inputs: our vision, our hearing, our tactile input, etc. This is an extraordinarily complex process as there is a lot of noise in the world and our brain is constantly engaged in separating the useful information from the less useful information, and to do so, it often makes inferences such as assuming that an unheard word was based on the context.

In some cases, these inferences are incorrect, even for healthy individuals, for example, when one wrongly thinks someone said your name. Importantly, these inferences are dependent on a considerable amount of prior beliefs such as what sort of word fits in a particular sentence or what sort of things people say.

Schizophrenics are known to sometimes have auditory hallucinations, often appearing in the form of persecutory voices. It is possible that schizophrenics hear voices that are not there because they have trouble making the correct inferences, perhaps confusing their own internal beliefs with outside stimuli. In this case, auditory hallucinations might be the product of a highly effective but imperfect system (hence the mistakes made by healthy individuals) which is incorrectly calibrated in the case of schizophrenia.

Coursework Interviews

When applying to do Biological Natural Sciences (including Experimental Psychology) at Cambridge, or possibly Biology or Psychology at Oxford, an applicant may be asked to submit coursework and be called for a coursework interview. Usually, in the morning on the day of the interview, this work is submitted and read by the interviewer. The work is used as a basis for discussion of research and experimental methods and analysis.

The interviewer may open by asking for a summary of the piece of work, the methodology behind it, and the results obtained. They may then ask some follow-up questions related to the work or the subject matter. This part of the interview will be very individual and depend on the nature and subject of the work submitted.

After the discussion of the work, the interviewer will probably guide the conversation toward some questions about experimental methods and analysis to test the applicant's ability to think like a scientist. For example:

Q16: What experiment would you design to determine whether rats can differentiate colours?

Answering this question would involve suggesting model experiments and how to analyse the data. Perhaps the rats could be presented with different coloured tiles, and when they step on one of the colours they receive a treat. As the tiles are removed and replaced in new positions, the number of times the rats stepped on the food-giving colour could be counted, and this data analysed for a significant correlation. The point of these questions is to suggest different ideas and to show an understanding of their strengths and weakness and an ability to use data usefully.

Q17: Why do bats and moles have the same sized body, but different sized brains?

Those of you knowledgeable about bats may immediately think of their brain-power-demanding echolocation and it's OK to say this idea, but remember to think like a scientist and make sure you aren't jumping to conclusions. This is a chance for you to ask testable questions which may constrain the answer. Ask first: Which brain is bigger? Is the whole brain bigger or is one part, such as the cortex, disproportionately large? Then perhaps: is it that the brain is too large/small for the animal's body size or the body which is too large/small for the brain size? You might then use specific knowledge of the mole (e.g. lives in dark) and bat (flies) life-habit, and of brain function in relation to size to give all of the possible justified answers to these questions, and maybe design simple tests to rule out certain answers or favour others.

PSYCHOLOGY

Psychology Interview Questions

1. Describe phantom limb syndrome?
2. How would you approach treating phantom limb syndrome?
3. What made you choose psychology over a related subject like medicine?
4. Here's a graph showing the perception of pain against stimulation - why does perception of pain level off while stimulation continues to increase at the top?
5. How would you model the brain?
6. Why are faces so important?
7. What did you find interesting about the book you read?
8. What is the appeal of experimental psychology to you personally?
9. Take a look at this data from a psychology experiment - how would you try to interpret this?
10. Do you think computers could ever be as complicated as a human brain?
11. What is the most interesting thing about Psychology?
12. Does phenotype depend on nature or nurture?
13. Do you think you are born with a high IQ, or develop one?
14. What is sentience? Prove to me that you are sentient.
15. Can fish hear sound?
16. What marks the boundary between neuroscience and psychology?
17. What effect does heroin have on the brain?
18. Do you agree with Freud?
19. Can machines think?
20. Would you give chimpanzees human rights?
21. Do you think interviewing university applicants is a good idea?

PHYSICAL SCIENCES

The core of a subject interview in the physical sciences, mathematics or engineering is almost certain to be technical questions based on the subject material. Usually, these are not the odd or general questions that Oxbridge is rumoured to pose, but precisely defined questions that **test your technical knowledge of your subject and your ability to apply it**. The problems may be new to you, or may push problem-solving skills further than school questions, but for most questions it will be clear what the task is and you will have to use knowledge from school to get to an answer.

There is no absolute formula for how to approach these questions as they are highly subject to change and the method for one isn't transferable to others. A general point is to never give up – once you are there at the interview, all you can do is try your hardest; giving up means certain failure. Nevertheless, this doesn't mean you shouldn't prepare! By working through the questions in this collection, you'll get a much more comprehensive understanding of what admissions tutors are looking for as well as the style & difficulty of the questions you might get asked.

Remember that you may have interviews in other related subjects - not just for the subject you are applying for. This is particularly important if you've applied for Natural Science at Cambridge, so read all the relevant sections to ensure you don't get caught out.

Unusual Questions

Beyond questions relying on specialist knowledge, you may be asked questions to test your reasoning and problem-solving skills. These may test numeracy, logic or estimation abilities, where you are expected to rely on your wits rather than anything specific you learned in school. **Estimation questions are particularly important for scientists and engineers** as they show a command of skills essential to these disciplines. Solving an estimation problem requires an ability to co-opt general day-to-day knowledge, and most importantly, to use simplifying assumptions and where possible correct for these. For any science or engineering problem, it is never possible to account for every variable- assumptions must be made (e.g. 'assuming no air resistance'). The ability to make sensible and helpful assumptions without radically changing the problem is essential to all work in science. Though applicants are often warned about 'weird' questions, even an unexpected question will almost certainly be relevant to the subject or the ongoing discussion in an interview.

Worked Questions

Below are a few examples of how to start breaking down an interview question, complete with model answers.

Q1: How did the Ancient Greek astronomer, Aristarchus, determine how much further the Sun is from the Earth than the Moon is?

This question is already giving you a big hint by mentioning the moon – asking you to compare two linear distances; Earth-Sun and Earth-Moon. This already suggests that this may be a question about triangles. You may be given the second hint you need by your interviewer if your mind hasn't already wandered to the most apparent lunar phenomenon – the phases of the moon.

This may have seemed like a random or difficult question at first, but once you have brain-stormed and are thinking both about triangles and the phases of the moon, how to answer this question may be obvious. If you still aren't sure what the phases of the moon have to do with this question, consider why they occur (and don't say something stupid like 'the shadow of the Earth on the moon', because what is a lunar eclipse?). Draw a diagram of how the phases of the moon work including the sun, Earth and moon in the figure. Recognise that there is a time (quarter-moon) when Sun-Moon-Earth forms a right-angle. Remember also <u>that the sun and moon can be in the sky together</u>, and at this time, you can measure the angle Sun-Earth-Moon. Work out the Sun-Earth distance using a sine function of the angle and the Earth-Moon distance.

Aristarchus found the distance from the Sun to Earth to be more than 40 times Earth to Moon, which is more than an order of magnitude too small but is the right method. End with a discussion of which assumptions your model made (e.g. the sun is close enough that the angle of light on the moon and Earth is measurably different) and what the sources of error for Aristarchus would have been (e.g. the sun is very bright so hard to measure, it's hard to say when exactly it is quarter-moon, the measured angle would be very close to 90 degrees, etc.).

Q2: How would you calculate the weight of the Earth?

This is a fantastic illustration of the power of simplifying assumptions. It is possible to <u>get extremely close to the correct answer with no specialist knowledge</u>. Consider this approach:

Method 1:

I'm going to use $Mass = Density \times Volume$

The interviewer would tell you that the Earth's radius is approximately 6,000 Km.

Thus, Volume of the Earth $= \frac{4}{3}\pi r^3 = \frac{4}{3} \times \pi \times (6,000,000)^3$

You can approximate π to 3 to give: $V = 4 \times 216 \times 10^{18} \approx 10^{21} \, m^3$

The majority of Earth's core is made up of iron and since that is very dense, it probably contributes the most to the Earth's average density. I know that the density of water is 1,000 kg/m³ and I'll assume that iron is 10 times as dense as Water.

Thus the average density of Earth $\approx 10^4 \, kg/m^3$

Therefore, the Mass of the Earth $\approx 10^{21} \times 10^4 = 10^{25} \, kg$

THE ULTIMATE OXBRIDGE INTERVIEW GUIDE — PHYSICAL SCIENCES

Method 2:

A good physics student should also be able to use the fact that the moon orbits the Earth to calculate its mass.

Since the moon is approximately the same distance away from the Earth during its orbit, the <u>resultant force acting on the moon must = 0.</u> Thus:

Gravitational Attraction between Moon and Earth = Centripetal Force

$$\frac{Gm_1 m_2}{r^2} = \frac{m_2 v^2}{r}$$

$$\frac{Gm_1}{r} = v^2$$

Therefore, Mass of the Earth, $m_1 = \frac{v^2 r}{G}$

At this point, the interviewer would probably stop you as the only thing stopping you from proceeding is knowing the moon's velocity and the distance between the Earth and moon.

A harsh interviewer may not give these to you immediately in which case you might have to use some general knowledge- e.g. it takes light one second to travel from the moon to Earth.

Thus, $r = 1 \; 3 \; x \; 10^8 = 3 \; x \; 10^8 m$

If you assume that the moon has a circular orbit, you could also use this to calculate the moon's velocity:

$$Orbital \; Velocity = \frac{Orbital \; Distance}{Time \; for \; one \; Orbit} = \frac{2\pi r}{1 \; month}$$

$$v = \frac{6 \; x \; 3 \; x \; 10^8 \; metres}{1 \; x \; 30 \; x \; 24 \; x \; 60 \; x \; 60 \; seconds} = \frac{1.8 \; x \; 10^9}{2.6 \; x \; 10^6}$$

$$= 0.7 \; x \; 10^3 = 700 \; ms^{-1}$$

Finally: $m_1 = \frac{v^2 r}{G} = \frac{(700)^2 x \; 3 \; x 10^8}{6.67 \; x \; 10^{-11}}$

$$m_1 = \frac{4.9 \; x \; 10^5 x \; 3 \; x 10^{19}}{6.67} = \frac{15 \; x \; 10^{24}}{6.67}$$

$$= 2.25 \; x \; 10^{24} kg$$

[Real Answer: $6 \; x \; 10^{24} kg$]

Q3: In a family of five, what are the odds that two of them share a birthday?

This is a probability question that is testing two things: 1) basic numeracy, in this case, a grasp of probability, 2) the ability to interpret words into equations. This second point is very important to physical scientists, engineers and mathematicians alike, but particularly to physicists and engineers who must, throughout their degree, take real-world problems and interpret them as equations which can be solved mathematically. So being able to demonstrate this ability is essential. It is also necessary to make simplifying, yet not strictly true, assumptions, such as that all birthdays are equally likely (babies are more likely to be born on days favourable for tax reasons and less likely to be born on 'unlucky' dates).

To solve the problem, consider the complementary case that no-one shares a birthday. The likelihood of the second person not sharing the first person's birthday is 364/365. The likelihood of the third person not sharing either of the first two birthdays is 363/365, etc. As the events are independent, they are multiplied to find the overall probability that none share a birthday, about 97/100. The chance that any do share a birthday is thus 3/100.

Q4: Three prisoners stand in a line. They can look at the men ahead, but cannot turn to see those behind themselves. A hat is placed on each man's head from a bag they are told contains three red and two green hats. If any man can say the colour of his own hat, which he cannot see, all three will go free, and if any man gets the answer wrong, they will all be executed. The third prisoner gives no answer when asked and neither does the second, but the first man says, "I know the colour of my hat." What colour did he say?

This is a classic 'hat problem' logic puzzle. In answering this question, you can show that you can approach a problem logically and methodically, and choose an appropriate method which will lead to an answer. You can also demonstrate that you can interpret and extract the important pieces of a chunk of verbal information.

One approach is to list and eliminate the possible hat combinations given the problem statement. There are eight possible hat combinations for three people: RRR, GGG, RRG, GGR, RGR, GRG, GRR and RGG. GGG is not possible as there are only two green hats, leaving seven options. The third prisoner can see the two in front of him but remains silent. If both hats he could see were green, he would know that his is red, so it cannot be RGG (assuming prisoner three is on the left). Prisoner two can see prisoner one. If the first prisoner had a green hat, the only options remaining would be GRG and RRG, either of which gives prisoner two a red hat. He remains silent, so these are eliminated. All remaining options (RRR, RGR, GRR, GGR) give the first prisoner a red hat so he says, "My hat is red."

Practising these questions is both easier and harder than subject-related questions. If you struggle with using logic and reasoning, these questions may be very difficult for you, even with practice. On the other hand, they are easy to practice and make-up in day-to-day life and if you get the reasoning skills down, you can apply them to many questions. As you go about your day, ask yourself little questions to practice: How much does that tree weigh? How many gumballs are in that machine? Or get yourself a book of riddles and logic problems and have a go on the way to school. You may already be familiar with a shorter version of this type of question from Thinking Skills Assessment (TSA) practice.

Experimental Interviews

The specific interview types and testing procedures vary from college to college, but it is possible that a physical scientist or engineer will be called for an Experiment-based interview or a coursework interview. This type of interview is based on experimental work done at school. The applicant will submit a project or Experiment Logbook written at school or be asked to bring it to the interview. The interviewer will ask questions using this work as a basis.

This type of interview can go in many directions as it is personalised to the student. Be prepared to discuss a favourite experiment or one of the interviewer's choosing. A discussion of an experiment may start with your description of the aims and general method. You may be asked detailed questions about the methodology. It is likely that you will be asked about your conclusions and discussion. This is not the time to try to cover up your mistakes or make your conclusions seem exceptional.

This is your chance to be self-critical and correct your own mistakes and errors to show that you are capable of thinking like a scientist. Don't worry about pointing out your own errors to your interviewer – they have almost certainly already noticed them and this is your chance to show that you noticed them too and would know how to improve if you had another chance. When pointing out mistakes, highlight the ones that you wouldn't make again because you have grown as an experimenter or because you later realized a flaw in the methodology. Don't, however, point out your own sloppiness or laziness; that time you rushed the experiment because you wanted to leave; or you got the wrong answer because you couldn't be bothered to get out your ruler and calculator.

The discussion may diverge from your own work to general questions about experimental design or theory questions about topics covered. If asked about designing your own experiments, have many suggestions and critique your own ideas. The point of these questions isn't to come up with the perfect experiment, but to show that you can have original ideas and that you can see the strengths and weaknesses of different approaches.

CHEMISTRY

In your chemistry interview, your knowledge of a range of topics could be tested as well as your ability to apply your understanding of specific cases to other situations. The questions could be drawn from any part of the curriculum, so there is no way to revise just the area you will be tested on. There is no specific way to prepare for the example types of questions given in this chapter, or the similar styles of questions that could be derived from other parts of the curriculum. The important thing is to have a <u>sound</u> **understanding of not just specific instances you have rote-learned for exams, but the chemical principles that underlie them.** When you do your revision for your interview, make sure you always ask why certain results are achieved – don't just learn that a certain compound is less reactive, make sure you know why that is. If you don't know, then ask your teacher about the underlying principles, or even better, try to figure out the answer yourself to practice this way of thinking.

For instance, you could be asked questions about chemical formulae and their relation to structure and physical or chemical properties. For this style of question, you may be asked to **draw the chemical formula** for an ionic compound and a covalent compound, and then asked to draw the formula for something in-between like Al_2O_3. You could also be asked to draw in detail each atom with electrons and describe their distribution in the shells and Bohr's theories explaining this behaviour.

Alternatively, you could be asked to draw an organic compound from the formula and asked about the physical properties you would expect. This could be a compound you are expected to be familiar with. Then, you could be asked to draw other compounds with similar properties, or how you would alter the original compound for a new property. You could be given a made-up chemical formula and be asked to draw a suggestion for how it may be structured to have certain properties. You could be questioned about the **nature of any bonds** or how properties might change for enantiomers.

Your knowledge around the subject might be tested by asking about a well-known case, such as Thalidomide or hydrocarbon fractionation. Moving away from chemical structures and properties, you could be asked **calculation-based questions** such as molar equations or thermodynamics (entropy and enthalpy, reaction rates, phase changes, etc.). Given the nature of the interview, you are unlikely to get an in-depth calculation-based question.

However, knowledge of these topics might be necessary to answer questions such as: How would you balance these reactions? Which reaction would proceed faster? Which reaction would you expect to occur spontaneously? Would you expect either to reach equilibrium? Which conditions would you alter to change your answer? The important thing is not to have the right answer, but to show you can reason through unfamiliar examples using your knowledge of the principles.

As it is an experimental subject, your knowledge of experimental techniques and examples could be tested. Make sure you **revise the material and methods used in experiments and practicals at school**, in case you are asked specific questions about designing an experiment or interpreting results. An example of this is being asked to design an experiment to identify an unknown organic acid. This might involve an understanding of titration curves for mono-, di-, and tri-protic acids and how to generate them in the lab, or a number of other topics you may have covered in experiments.

As an extension of this, be familiar with the techniques that were used to discover the facts and theories in your textbooks as you could be asked how they were discovered or how you would verify they are true.

One Maths question is also likely to come up in the interview. Maths represents a significant portion of most Oxbridge science courses and skills like sketching, differentiating and integrating are skills that will be necessary throughout much of your scientific education. Thus, it is advisable to also read the mathematics section in this collection.

Worked Questions

Below are a few examples of how to start breaking down an interview question, complete with model answers. They are by no means an exhaustive list but they give a sense of how A-level material can be used as a basis for questions that require independent thought and problem-solving skills. Use these examples as a guide of what topics to revise and the style of questions that may arise.

Q1: How did we find out the composition of the sun?

This is a common example, so you may be expected to be somewhat familiar with it. Don't be discouraged if you are not though, the interviewer may be even more impressed if you can reach a reasonable answer all on your own. The gist of this question is to use spectral analysis and knowledge of the theories underlying it to determine the sun's composition using its own light. Spectral analysis is based on Bohr's work – as light passes through an atom, the energy in the photons passes to the electrons in the outermost shell, shifting them to higher energy levels. As they return to their original position, they release the energy.

Since energy levels in the atom are discrete, from Einstein's photoelectric effect, the energy is known to produce a specific frequency of light. The atoms which make up the sun are being constantly energised to plasma, so the frequencies they would have emitted as their electrons returned to their original positions are absent from the spectrum of light the sun emits. By comparing the spectra emitted by known elements to the gaps in the sun's spectrum, it is clear that hydrogen and helium are the main elements. This question only relies on basic knowledge of vital chemical principles but requires the applicant to use these in practice. Being familiar with common experimental techniques is helpful.

Q2: You receive a small sample of a human bone of unknown age and place of origin. How might you constrain these parameters?

Hopefully, seeing the word 'age' instantly makes you think 'isotopes' - this is a question about radiometric dating and isotope fractionation. To answer the first part, you might want to start with a description of isotopes and radioactivity and write an expression for radioactive decay. But the question asks for something more – it is pushing you to explain experimentally how you determine the age. This includes choosing an appropriate isotope system (in this case Carbon has an appropriately long half-life) and describing how mass spectrometers are used to find isotopic ratios. This is a difficult question if you have no knowledge of experimental techniques, but even if you don't know the specifics, show that you understand the difference between general theory and practice.

The second part of this question, the place of origin, is a chance to show you have cross-subject knowledge or ideas even when you are out of your depth. One sample answer is to look at the ratio of Carbon-12 and Carbon-13. Recent bones from North America will contain more C-13 relative to C-12 than European bones because of the much greater use of corn. Those with biology knowledge may remember that corn is a C4 plant that takes in a higher proportion of C-13. This is just one example that shows how you can integrate your specific knowledge base into an original answer.

Q3: Which of the two molecules below is more acidic? What factors make this the case?

(A) CH_3-OH vs.   (B) $(CH_3)_3C-OH$

This question is introducing the candidate to the idea that the <u>concept of acidity</u> can be applied to more molecules than just the classic "acids" you learn at school.

A good candidate would first define acidity:

$$HA \rightleftharpoons H^+ + A^-$$

Then need to <u>highlight the key reactive areas</u> on each of the molecules and assign how each of the molecules would perform when behaving as an acid. In this case, both molecules form RO- + H+ as the products. The crux of this problem is that the stability of MeO- is greater than (Me)3CO- which is because the O- is more stable in A.

Methyl groups are electron-donating groups and in molecule (B) there are three Me groups pushing onto the carbon bonded to the oxygen, therefore, this carbon is more electron-rich than molecule (A) so destabilises the O-. Consequently, the equilibrium for molecule (B) in water is more shifted towards ROH rather than RO- so molecule A is more acidic than molecule B. A good candidate will also then link this to equilibrium constants.

$$K_a = \frac{[H_3O^+]_{eq}[A^-]_{eq}}{[HA]_{eq}}$$

This question should not be too difficult - good students would be expected to give a comprehensive answer that synthesises multiple chemistry principles from the A-level syllabus. This question tests how comfortable people are with these principles and if they can use them in different scenarios.

Q4a: How do these two molecules react? Draw the mechanism.

$$\text{CH}_3\text{FC}=\text{C}(\text{CH}_3)\text{Cl} + \text{Cl-Cl}$$

This should be a really simple question to start with. The candidate should acknowledge the rich area of electron density in the alkene will attack a Cl atom in the symmetrical Cl-Cl causing the bond to break and form a Cl— anion.

Then the candidate needs to explain why the double bond breaks in such a way to leave the positive charge on the carbon with one Me group and one Cl atom. This is because the Me groups are electron donating, so push electron density onto that carbon and stabilise the positive charge. They also need to comment that F is more electronegative than Cl, therefore, the Cl-C bond is less polar.

THE ULTIMATE OXBRIDGE INTERVIEW GUIDE — CHEMISTRY

The route that is normally taught in A-level is that the Cl- anion then quenches the positive charge which is then localised on that carbon and forms the product.

This, however, is not strictly the case. A standard candidate should be able to answer this question, the second part, however, will assess a standard candidate compared to a good one.

Q4b: The reaction drawn above is not complete. What else can quench that positive charge instead of the Cl? Explain the new path mechanistically.

Here the candidate should recognise that the Cl- anion is not the only nucleophile and the Cl atom in the molecule can donate a lone pair of electrons and stabilise the reactive intermediate. It forms a <u>cyclo intermediate</u> with the positive charge now more delocalised but, strictly speaking, primarily localised on the Cl atom. A good candidate will remark that this intermediate happens almost immediately when the carbocation is formed because <u>intramolecular reactions happen faster than intermolecular reactions</u>, as intermolecular reactions require a collision between the two molecules.

This cyclised intermediate is then attacked by the Cl- anion and relieves the steric strain of the 3 membered ring. The reaction still takes place on the same carbon because it has a lower activation energy than if the ring was opened up the other way. This forms the same product as in the original reaction mechanism. This question is a typical example of taking what a student already should know and analysing something a bit deeper.

Q5: Ketones and aldehydes in aqueous solution are typically hydrated following the mechanism below. The extent to which a ketone/aldehyde is hydrated is dominated by numerous factors. Discuss the extent of hydration of each of the molecules below and order them from most hydrated to least.

The addition of water is reversible and happens via proton transfer. The candidate should recognise the thermodynamic stability of the carbonyl versus the hydrate, which will determine the percentage of hydrate at equilibrium. This reaction is under thermodynamic control. The candidate should first discuss the percentage of hydrate for an aldehyde vs. a ketone.

Ketones are less likely to be hydrated than the equivalent aldehyde, this is because of a greater steric hindrance in molecule (B) vs. molecule (D). There is repulsion between the two Me groups as they are so close in space when the hydrate is formed as they are forced together on forming a tetrahedral hydrate. This causes the equilibrium to be towards the starting material for molecule B.

For molecule C, the candidate should acknowledge that there is a lot of strain in cyclopropanone, the C=O forces the molecule to be in the same plane and the bond angles to be very small. With the addition of water to molecule (C), the steric strain is released and it can form a more stable tetrahedral molecule with an increased bond angle of 109.5°. Therefore, the equilibrium constant for this reaction is extremely large.

For molecule (A) the candidate should comment on the effects of three Cl atoms, which are electron-withdrawing groups due to being more electronegative than C. The inductive effect of the Cl atoms increases the reactivity of the C=O (a larger δ+ on the C) as less electron density on neighbouring carbon atom (CCl3) and so the water is even more strongly attracted the C in C=O and therefore has a large hydration constant.

Therefore the ordering is as follows: C, A, D, B

The discussion here is more important in some respects than the ordering. But it is also testing candidates' ability to assess the dominance and importance of different factors. It would also be advisable that the candidate draws out the whole mechanism as this will show that they understand how this reaction happens and also will actually help them answer this question.

Q6: Explain mechanistically how the following reaction happens?

The candidate needs to analyse what will attack the acid, "H+", i.e. what is the best nucleophile in the system. The Br-Br bond is not going to break by itself so it is not that so has to be the ketone. The lone pair of electrons on the oxygen attacks the H+.

The resulting molecule can be stabilised by losing the relatively acidic proton alpha to the C=O. Thus creating an enol, ketones in acidic conditions are always in equilibrium with their enol form. The stability and where the equilibrium lies depends on the molecule. The enol form, however, can go on and actually productively react with Br2.

This molecule here can then attack Br-Br. Like with electrophilic addition, the electron density is going to come from the double bond and break the Br-Br sigma bond. In this instance, there is an additional driving factor; the lone pair on the oxygen can feed into the double bond and kick start the reaction with Br2.

At this point, the candidate is basically there and just needs to point out that Br- can attack the protonated ketone and form the product. This reaction step is not in equilibrium. Unlike the enolisation, once the enol has reacted with Br2 it is irreversible.

Q7: Order these atoms in decreasing first ionisation energy: Al, Ba, S, O, P and Mg.

It is first necessary to define first ionisation energy: $X(g) + e^- \rightarrow X^-(g)$. The candidate should remark that O and S are both in group 16, Mg and Ba are both in group 2 Al and P are in the same row as each other as well as S and Mg. Recognition of this will help the candidate compare each of the atoms and have a nice structure.

There are two factors in this question and the candidate has to weigh them out. The first factor is that, in general, the ionisation energy across a period increases, due to an increase in effective nuclear charge. The nucleus is becoming more positively charged with the increase in protons and the outmost electrons are experiencing a similar shielding effect as they are filling up the same principal quantum number. The valence electrons are attracted more strongly and pulled in closer to the nucleus. The other factor here is that the first ionisation energy decreases as you go down a group. Although the nuclear charge increases, the valence electrons are shielded by the greater number of inner electron shells. Thus, the valence electrons are further away from the nucleus.

A **poor candidate** may get confused at the last point and predict that the ionisation energy increases down a group, the interviewer will check to see that they are comfortable with these two factors.

With this, you can thus conclude that O will have a higher first ionisation energy than S and Mg will have a higher first ionisation energy than Ba. Ba is last because the first ionisation energy means that a valence electron is removed from 6s orbital which is much more shielded than for Mg [He]3s² which loses an electron in 3s, [Ar]3s². You can also conclude that Mg has a lower ionisation energy than Al, [Ar] 3s²3p¹ which in turn has a lower ionisation energy than P and S, P [Ar] 3s²3p³ and S [Ar] 3s²3p⁴.

The last factor that needs to be deduced is comparing P and S. P 3p³ vs S 3p⁴. The candidate needs to recognise that whilst S has a larger <u>effective nuclear charge</u> than P, in fact, the first ionisation energy for P is larger than that of S. p energy level is comprised of 3 orbitals, p_x, p_y and p_z, Phosphorus had 3 electrons each in the three respective p orbitals, Sulphur 3p⁴ has 2 single electrons and one orbital has paired electrons. This is a less favourable electronic configuration, undergoing ionisation removes the <u>electron-electron repulsion</u> and so is rather favourable.

Q8: Draw the shapes of the following: CH4, PF5, SF6, ClF3 and SF4.

The logic for working out each of these shapes is the same. First, work out the <u>valence electrons</u> on the central atom. This tells you the area of negative charge around that atom. Then work out how many electrons each other atom gives to the central one – in single covalent bonds, it is 1 electron that is being donated. Pair the electrons up and work out the number of areas of negative charge around the atom and then this will indicate the shape of the molecule.

The first 3 molecules should be quite easy and will test to see if the candidate understands the basic principles; which can then be used to solve the latter molecules.

<u>CH₄:</u> Carbon 4 electrons, 4 x 1 e⁻ from each H. Therefore, 4 areas of negative charge, no lone pairs. So the shape is tetrahedral.

<u>PF₅:</u> P 5e⁻, F 5 x e⁻ so 5 areas of negative charge so trigonal bipyramidal.

<u>SF₆:</u> S 6e⁻, F 6 x e⁻ so 6 areas of negative charge so octahedral.

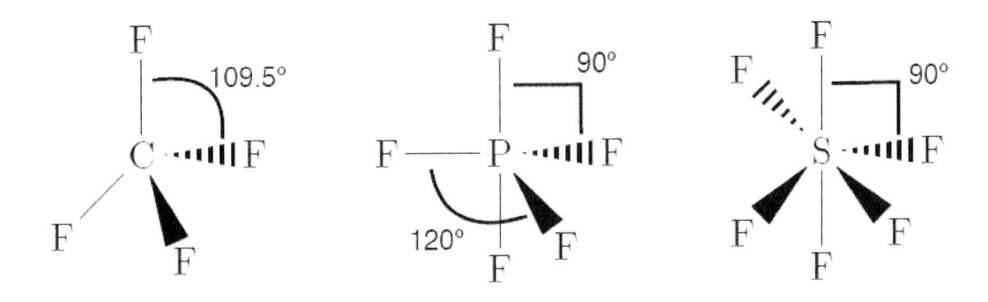

THE ULTIMATE OXBRIDGE INTERVIEW GUIDE — CHEMISTRY

<u>ClF₃</u>: Cl 7e⁻, F 3 x e⁻, 5 areas of negative charge, two of which are lone pairs, so is a trigonal bipyramidal structure but lone pair–lone pair repulsion greater than bond pair–lone pair and bond pair–bond pair, therefore, the two lone pairs take up more room, creating a 't-shaped' molecule

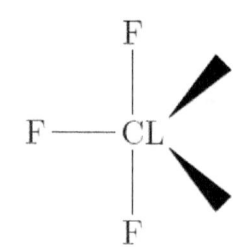

<u>SF₄</u>: S 6e⁻, F 4 x e⁻, so 5 areas of negative charge, this time one lone pair of electrons. A good candidate should remark that the lone pair of electrons goes in the equatorial position as it is statistically further away from all other bond paired electrons. Again this shape is based on trigonal bipyramidal but is called a "seesaw" molecular structure.

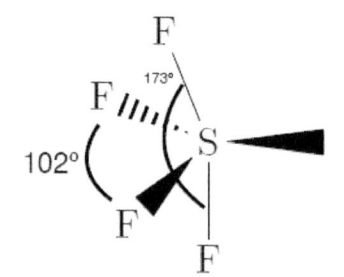

Q9: Why are metals, in particular, transition metals, coloured?

Octahedral splitting for transition metals:

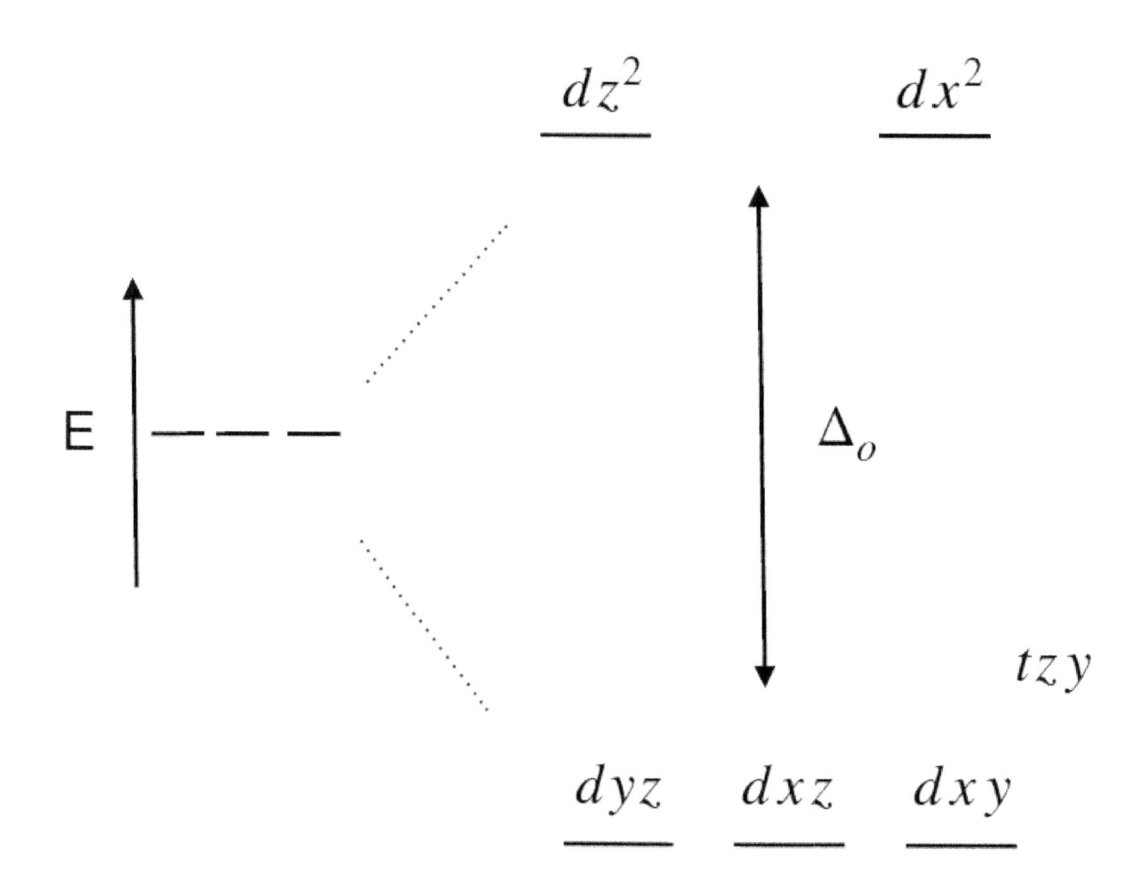

Candidates may comment on the following features:

- <u>Changes in oxidation state</u> lead to different colours - as the oxidation state changes, so do the configuration of electrons in the d-orbitals.
- The <u>absorption of white light</u> can lead to different colours. In aqueous solution, the d-orbitals split into two, but are still relatively close together. When certain wavelengths of light are absorbed, electrons in lower energy levels are excited to higher ones as they have the right energy match. The remaining photons then pass through and cause the metal to be coloured.
- The <u>shape of the molecule</u> affects the colour as it results in different electron arrangements in the d-orbitals. i.e. tetrahedral complexes are different colours to that of octahedral.
- The <u>nature of the ligand</u> itself will affect the colour – the greater the splitting of the d-orbitals, the more energy will be needed to promote electrons in the lower d-orbitals to the higher ones.

The <u>wavelength of light:</u> shorter wavelength absorption means that the colour of the complex will tend towards the blue end of the spectrum.

Q10: Draw for me and describe a phase diagram for a hydrocarbon, pointing out key characteristics of the graph and what you can deduce from it.

A Phase diagram shows the melting, boiling and sublimation curve of a substance and also the triple point. Candidate should end up discussing all of the points highlighted below on the graph. The important thing to note is that <u>the substance is in equilibrium between gas and liquid</u>. If they do not know what one is, the examiner may draw the graph and then expect the candidate to analyse it. A question on differentiation may also be asked to calculate the melting point.

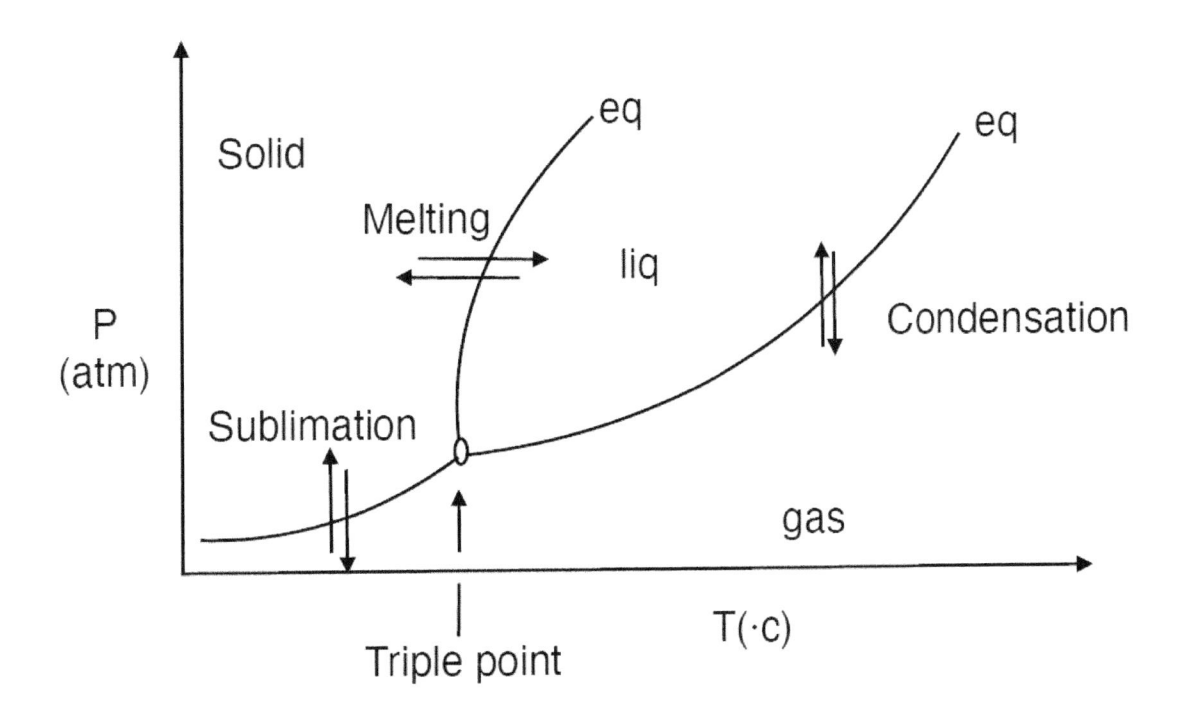

Q10b: What would this diagram look like for water?

This is slightly discussed at A-level so shouldn't be too challenging, but the phase diagram may not have been drawn before. The key thing to note is that ice takes up more volume than water (liquid), this is due to hydrogen bonding. This intermolecular force is very strong and favourable and causes the H2O molecules to align themselves in a certain arrangement so each molecule can have two hydrogen bonds each. When ice melts, these hydrogen bonds are broken and so the water molecules can get closer together. This should then lead to the negative gradient of the melting equilibrium line.

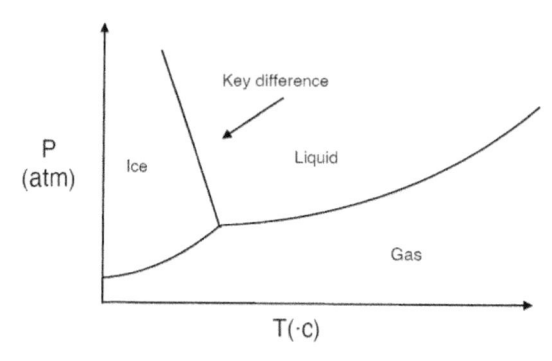

Q11: Describe for me what a ball in a 2D box (or well) would be like if it could only move along the x-axis and was between two infinitely high potential energy walls. Therefore, only potential energy is applicable on the ball. What would happen to the ball?

The candidate should start by drawing a potential well, drawing the y-axis and noting that it has infinite potential energy. The ball (analogy of a particle in a 1D box of Schrodinger's equation) can only move in the x-axis direction and since only potential energy is acting on the particle, it will vibrate back and forth.

Key things for candidates to note are that the ball will not be able to move out of the 2D box. When it approaches the y-axis, there is an infinitely large potential force acted on it and thus is repelled. Also note that the ball's potential energy would stay at the same level since no other force is acting on it.

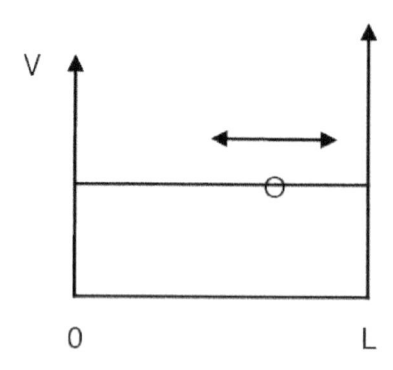

Q11b: Where is the ball statistically most likely to be found inside this potential well?

Here we are treating the ball as a particle and therefore if you label the x-axis say 0 to length L then the most probable place of finding the ball would be in the middle of the box i.e. L/2. This is applying a classic physics principle in what is a quantum physics problem. The ball passes through the middle the most and so is therefore most likely to be found here.

Chemistry Interview Questions

1. Describe the bonding in Al2O3
2. How do the double bonds in this hydrocarbon affect its solubility?
3. Can you draw an alkane where every carbon atom is in a different NMR environment?
4. How might playing in a band help you with Chemistry?
5. Compare and contrast electronegativity and ionisation energy.
6. Why is life carbon based and not silicon based?
7. The nucleus and electrons are oppositely charged. Why do electrons not crash into the nucleus?
8. What is the significance of bonding in benzene?
9. How do you make aspirin?
10. What is the difference between diamond and graphite?
11. What is the cause of le chatelier's principle?
12. What does pH stand for?
13. Estimate the mass of oxygen in this building.
14. What determines whether an acid is 'strong' or 'weak'?
15. What is your favourite element and why?
16. Why are the transition metals so colourful?
17. How many isomers of C4H8 can you draw?
18. Why are the transition metals good catalysts?
19. How many moles of water are there in this bottle?
20. What is the density of air in this room? What about outside? What about in Beijing?
21. What's the difference between entropy and enthalpy?
22. How do glow sticks work?
23. Why does food taste better when it's hot?
24. Why do we use water to dilute solutions?
25. Compare and contrast hydrochloric acid to phosphoric acid.
26. Why is Vanadium so special?
27. Where does chemistry end and physics begin?
28. Can you change an endothermic reaction into an exothermic one?

PHYSICS

Depending on which college you have applied for, the day of your physics interview will look different. At most Oxford colleges, the day will start with a general meeting with all physics applicants to go through the day's events and expectations before having **Subject Interviews**. At any college you may sit a short test; the questions you choose to answer in the test may form the foundation of the interviews later. Try to view these tests positively – they are letting you choose your strongest topics for the interview. Test or not, you will have one or more subject interviews for physics and you may have an interview in a related subject, such as maths or chemistry (particularly if you're applying for Natural Sciences), an **Experimental Interview** or a **General Interview**.

Questions in a physics interview may take a few forms but are most likely to be detailed and technical physics problems drawn from a range of topics you may have studied at school. There may also be more general questions which use basic physics concepts and reasoning skills to solve a physics-related problem, or there may be general questions testing numeracy, logic and estimation skills.

Most questions asked at interview will be open-ended technical questions and may be quantitative or qualitative. You will need to use your knowledge of maths and physics to attempt problems that may be quite different from those you have encountered at school. The point is not to solve the problem perfectly, but to show you are able to use your understanding of maths and physics concepts to create expressions which model physical systems. Many questions are also intended to test your physical intuition, whether you can get the right 'feel' for a system and its parameters, and whether you can tell if equations make physical sense.

While there are many topics that could come up in the interview, some are more prevalent and most questions will involve a generally similar approach. Mechanics questions appear to be favoured over other topics, particularly questions about gravitational systems ('If you jumped into a tunnel running straight through the centre of the Earth to the opposite side, what would happen?') and projectiles ('If you aimed a gun at a monkey hanging from a branch and it let go at the exact moment you fired, would the bullet hit the monkey?'). Waves and lenses also come up often ('How would the fringe pattern from a Double Slit experiment change if you put a sheet of glass against the slits?'), as do a range of physics-related questions about computers, engines ('How do wind turbines work?'), refrigerators and the like ('How would you create artificial gravity in a spaceship?').

Questions about electronics and magnetism are less common, but if you have covered these topics in school, be prepared to answer questions, as you should be for any topic you've covered.

No matter the question, there is a standard approach to questions about physical systems that is nearly always applicable.

Always start by making a **quick sketch** and giving a qualitative assessment of the situation (what does your common sense tell you the likely outcome will be? – you are setting out a hypothesis to test with the next steps); there are almost no questions where this is unhelpful, and even if it proves to be unnecessary for the question, it shows the interviewers you have a good standard approach to physics problems.

State any assumptions you are making as you go along (infinitely small points, no air resistance, parallel rays of light, etc.). Next, expand your sketch to a full labelled diagram, including all bodies and the forces/energies/etc. from different bodies.

Evaluate how these forces work together in this system and which are most relevant – think about what type of question it is: whether you are dealing with momentum, gravitational forces, conservation of energy (use the information given in the question as a tip, sometimes whether you are given distances, velocities, energies, etc. can tell you what type of question you are dealing with).

Write expressions for the forces/etc. you have marked on you figure; always work with variables, only substitute numbers where absolutely necessary or where it will greatly simplify expressions.

Return to the question statement to remind yourself what the precise aim of the question is before writing equations using the expressions from your figure.

Even if you can't reach a final answer, you've shown you know how to approach a physics question, which is arguably **more important**. This approach can be used for a range of questions so is a good go-to method.

To answer the questions at interview, there is a range of specific skills you may need to practice beyond general problem-solving. You will need to know how to make **quick and simple sketches**, both for physical systems and for changes in physical quantities relative to each other (e.g. velocity-time diagrams). You will need to be able to demonstrate that you can interpret words to figures and figures to equations.

You will need to be able to work in the abstract, using variables rather than numbers and it is helpful if you can apply calculus concepts to physics. For instance, considering acceleration as the second derivative of displacement with respect to time, which allows you to work more freely and generally when writing expressions. It is uncommon, though possible, to be asked to derive well-known equations ('Find an expression for the distance between fringes generated by Young's Double Slit apparatus'), and you can be asked to find general expressions for a certain system, but most commonly, you will be asked to **show you can use physical and mathematical expressions** to model reality.

You will need to demonstrate that you have a physical intuition for building models and that you can explicitly recognise the assumptions and limits of your models. Some questions may be even more open-ended, testing how you apply physics to more general physics-themed problems.

An interviewer may reasonably expect a physics applicant to have **general knowledge of physics fields** (e.g. astronomy), and **popular current research topics** (e.g. the hunt for exoplanets). Particularly, if an applicant has expressed any interest in space in the personal statement, it would not be impossible for a question such as 'How are exoplanets detected?' to be asked at interview. It would be quite difficult to reason yourself to the answer that planets in orbit gravitationally shift their stars, moving them closer and further from the Earth and creating a Doppler shift in their light which can be used to make a basic description of the planet. However, with interviewer guidance, this may be possible. It would be helpful, though, to have a basic understanding of this and other popular research topics to pull ideas from.

Finally, one Maths question is also likely to come up in the interview. Maths represents a significant portion of most Oxbridge science courses and skills like sketching, differentiating, and integrating, are skills that will be necessary throughout much of your scientific education. Thus, it is advisable to also read the mathematics section in this collection.

Worked Questions

Below are a few examples of how to start breaking down an interview question, complete with answer outlines and model answers.

Q1: The track for a high-speed train can be modelled as a very long beam (the rails) supported by an elastic foundation. The vibration of the rails away from a moving train is governed by the following partial differential equation:

$$EI\frac{\partial^4 y}{x^4 \partial} + Ky + M\frac{\partial^2 y}{\partial t^2} = 0$$

Q1 (i) Look at this equation and tell me about the structural behaviour associated with each term.

This is a very interesting question because it tests concepts related to mechanics, stresses and strains, and calculus.

Recommended Approach:

It should be obvious that y corresponds to vertical displacement. This suggests that the term to the right – with mass M times the second time derivative of y (i.e. acceleration) – corresponds to inertia for vertical motions.

The middle term is simply Hooke's Law, describing the elastic foundation. (K is the stiffness of the foundation.)

However, the term on the left is tricky, so most people would find it hard – but don't worry, it's meant to push you so you shouldn't feel scared. This is meant to test you and push you to think outside the box.

Let's break down the problem: E is Young's modulus, relating stress to strain. Although this is not part of the A-level syllabus, it is worth reading up a little about it. The symbol I corresponds to the second moment of area. And finally, there is the fourth derivative of y with respect to x.

The answer is that this is the bending stiffness of the beam. The interviewers will prompt you along the way and hope that you come to this result.

Q1 (ii) If a train runs at constant speed V and only the steady-state deformed shape of the track is required, do you think this partial differential equation can be reduced to an ordinary differential equation?

Recommended Approach:

This might seem very tricky but it is actually quite an easy question! Have a look below at how it can be approached, simply by understanding the relationship between distance and velocity:

$$\frac{d}{dt} = V\frac{d}{dx}$$

This means we can replace $M\frac{\partial^2 y}{\partial t^2}$ with $MV^2 \frac{d^2 y}{dx^2}$

We are now left with an ordinary differential equation that can be solved without difficulty.

# THE ULTIMATE OXBRIDGE INTERVIEW GUIDE — PHYSICS

Q2: The diagram to the right shows an idealisation of a tapered concrete chimney. It is desired to represent the dynamic behaviour in the fundamental mode by an equivalent single-degree-of-freedom system, using the approximate mode shape. In this context, think of dynamic behaviour as its response to a disturbance and single degree-of-freedom simply means it can only move in 1 direction.

$$\Psi = \frac{(3\lambda^2 - \lambda^3)}{2} \qquad \text{Where } \lambda = \frac{z}{L}$$

Q2 (i) What are the boundary conditions in this scenario?

This is a question that tests your ability to think intuitively on the spot. Kinetic constraints are not taught explicitly at A-level, but the knowledge required to come up with them should not be beyond you – especially with prompts and hints from the interviewer. *Remember, the interviewers are not there to see what you CAN'T do; they are there to see what you CAN do. If you're struggling, ask them for a bit more information to help you along.*

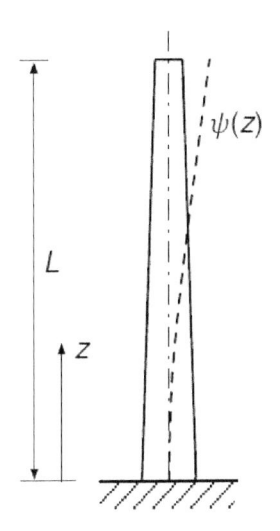

Recommended Approach:

Firstly, let's deal with the boundary conditions. We expect the slope at z = 0 to be zero because the beam is fixed into the ground*.

The displacement will also be zero at z=0. You will be expected to come up with this using your intuition, but the next two boundary conditions are not immediately obvious (although you will hopefully be able to get to them after a few hints from the interviewer).

The shear stress* and bending moment are zero at z = L.

Q2 (ii) Do you think the assumed mode shape satisfies the kinematic constraints of the problem?

This is another way of asking whether the boundary conditions in (i) are satisfied.

Given that $\Psi = \frac{(3\lambda^2 - \lambda^3)}{2}$ and $\lambda = \frac{z}{L} \rightarrow d\lambda = \frac{dz}{L}$

421

Differentiate:

$$\Psi' = \frac{1}{2L}(6\lambda - 3\lambda^2)$$

$$\Psi'' = \frac{1}{2L^2}(6 - 6\lambda) = \frac{3}{L^2}(1-\lambda)$$

$$\Psi''' = -\frac{3}{L^2}$$

z = 0 corresponds to λ = 0. Clearly, we must have ψ=0 at λ=0 in order for the displacement to be zero, i.e. for the first boundary condition to be fulfilled.

Likewise, the first derivative of ψ corresponds to the slope. This, too, must be zero at λ=0.

This next part is the tricky bit: the shear stress is the third derivative and the bending moment is the second derivative. But don't worry – this is beyond what you'd be expected to know, so the interviewer will help you along. We can test these boundary conditions at z = L:

λ=0 → ψ = ψ' = 0   : Both Satisfied

λ=1 → : ψ" = 0 Satisfied but ψ'" = 0 Not Satisfied

Check Normalisation: λ = 1 → ψ = 1

The "check normalisation" simply refers to the fact that the displacement is non-zero at z = L.

Conclusion:

The mode shape is NOT ideal but represents a reasonable compromise between accuracy and ease of use. In short, we have assumed a mode shape that might correspond to the deformation of the chimney. This allows us to analyse the problem, and thus to work out the values of interest – displacement, slope, etc. – to a reasonable level of accuracy.

Additional Tips:

- Do some research on the differences between simply-supported, fixed-ended, and free-ended structures.
- Search online for shear stress and try to understand what is going on conceptually.

Q3: Cavitation is the formation of vapour cavities in a liquid – i.e. small liquid-cavitation-free zones ("bubbles" or "voids") – that are the consequence of cavitational forces acting upon the cavitational liquid. It usually occurs when a liquid is subjected to rapid changes of pressure that cause the formation of cavities where the pressure is relatively low. When subjected to higher pressure, the voids implode and can generate an intense shockwave.

A therapeutic ultrasound transducer is to be designed to deposit heat without producing cavitation. The desired peak heating rating is 16W/cm3. At 1 MHz, the cavitation threshold of tissue is determined to be 2 MPa (peak rare fractional pressure). Assume linear propagation, plane wave relationships, sound speed 1500 m/s, density 1000 kg/m3, and specific heat 3700 J/(kg K).

THE ULTIMATE OXBRIDGE INTERVIEW GUIDE — PHYSICS

Q3 (i) For 1 MHz ultrasound, determine the value of tissue attenuation at which heat can be generated without producing cavitation.

This question is particularly important for Physics candidates, as it explores concepts related to wave propagation and energy. It is also relevant for mechanical/biomedical engineering candidates.

Recommended Approach:
Step 1: Find the intensity, using the maximum value of pressure (which is the pressure that causes cavitation) and the values of density and speed that would be given to you.

Peak allowable pressure: $\tilde{p} = 2$ MPa

$$I = \frac{1}{2} \frac{\tilde{p}^2}{\rho_0 c_0}$$

$$= \frac{1}{2} \frac{(2 \times 10^6)^2}{1.5 \times 10^6}$$

$$= \frac{4}{3} \times 10^6 \, \frac{W}{m^2}$$

Step 2: Rearrange the expression for the heating rate to obtain the attenuation α. Np is the dimensionless unit Neper, which is commonly used to express the attenuation.

Heating rate: $Q = 2\alpha I$

$$\alpha = \frac{16 \times 10^6 \; W/m^3}{2 \times \frac{4}{3} \times 10^6 \; W/m^2}$$

$\alpha = 6 \, Np/m$

Note: You would be given all the formulae above. The symbol *I* refers to the intensity.

Q3 (ii) Using the value of attenuation from part (a), determine how much extra heating could be realised if the frequency is increased to 4 MHz. Account for the frequency dependence of both attenuation and cavitation.

Recommended Approach:

At 4MHz, cavitation threshold will double. Therefore α will quadruple. Thus, $\alpha = 24 \, Np/m$

$$\dot{Q} = 2 \times 24 \frac{Np}{m} \times \frac{(4 \times 10^6 \, Pa)^2}{1.5 \times 10^6 \, Pa} = 256 \; W/cm^3$$

Thus, there is a sixteen-fold increase in heating rate.

You will be told the relationship between frequency and pressure and between frequency and attenuation, although the latter might be discernible, intuitively, to some candidates. Pressure is proportional to frequency squared, so the pressure doubles. The attenuation is directly proportional to frequency and hence quadruples.

Conclusion:

A small change in frequency can lead to a very large change in the heating rate.

Q3 (iii) If the pressure were increased to generate cavitation, what are the advantages and disadvantages with respect to heating?

Increasing the pressure to produce cavitation will result in higher heating rates and shorter treatment times as the cavitation bubbles do work on the tissue. Disadvantages are that controlling cavitation is difficult and so the heating rates are unpredictable. If cavitation grows out of control, it will grow towards the transducer, shielding the target region: this will mean very little therapeutic effect at the focus and damage in undesired regions.

Q4: In a BOD (biochemical oxygen demand) test, a 50 ml sample of treated sewage is placed in a 300 ml bottle. The bottle is then completely filled with clean water at 20°C containing inorganic nutrients and dissolved oxygen at a concentration of 9.0 mg/litre. After 5 days storage at 20°C, the dissolved oxygen concentration in the bottle is measured and found to be 4.5 mg/litre.

Q4 (i) Calculate the five-day biochemical demand (BOD5) of the sewage. If the deoxygenation coefficient of the treated sewage at 20°C is 0.25/day (to base e), calculate the ultimate BOD of the treated sewage.

This question is related to environmental/chemical/production engineering and several applied physics topics.

Solution:

	Volume (ml)	Oxygen Concentration (mg/litre)	Oxygen Mass (mg)
Effluent sample	50	0	0
Clean water & nutrients	250	9	2.25
Mix at 5 days	300	4.5	1.35
Oxygen consumed	50	18	0.9

The ultimate BOD is 18 mg/litre.

The key to this question is to work out the mass of oxygen consumed **by the 50 ml sample.** It is trivial to obtain oxygen masses from oxygen concentration given that we know the volumes. A simple subtraction will then give the mass consumed to 0.9 mg. Finally, we need to multiply by 20 to get the amount that would be consumed by a 1-litre sample.

THE ULTIMATE OXBRIDGE INTERVIEW GUIDE

PHYSICS

Q5: Discuss the use of sedimentation in waste water treatment and derive a formula for the overall removal of solids from wastewater in a rectangular sedimentation tank.

The second part of this question is very good for testing the student's understanding of core concepts related to physics or engineering. The first part is aimed at those interested in environmental/chemical engineering or similar topics within physics.

Recommended Approach:

Sedimentation is used for the following:

- To remove grit and coarse solids.
- To remove finer organic solids in primary settling tanks.
- To remove sludge from the effluent from trickling filters and the activated sludge process.

Idealised settling tank

Horizontal velocity, $V_h = Q / (H B)$

Residence time, $t = L / V_h$

$t = (H B L) / Q$

To reach sludge zone at the end of the tank:
Vs = H/t

But t = BHL/Q

Thus, Vs = Q/BL

I.e. Settling velocity Vs > Vo the hypothetical upward velocity- the overflow rate Vo.

$$Overall\ removal = (1 - x_o) + \frac{1}{v_o} \int_0^{x_o} V_s dx$$

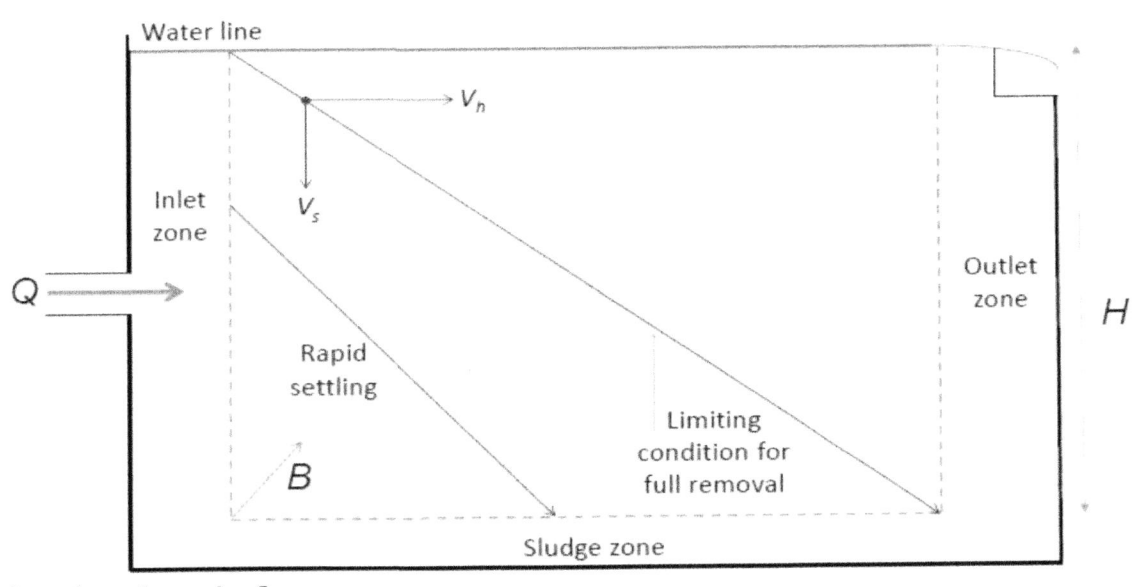

(continued overleaf)

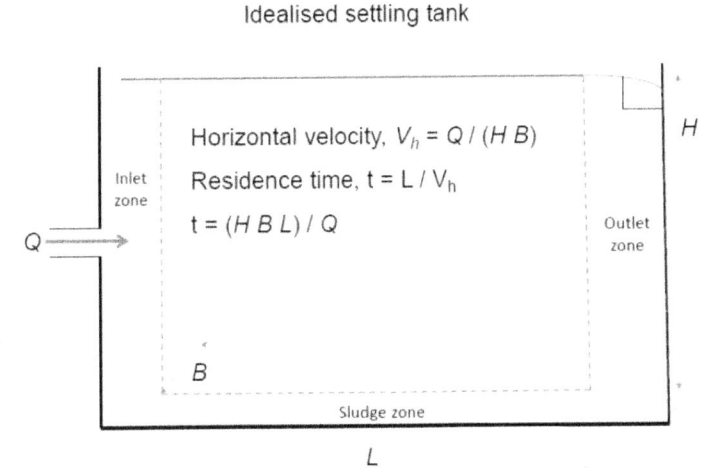

THE ULTIMATE OXBRIDGE INTERVIEW GUIDE

PHYSICS

$V_s = h/t$
but $t = BHL/Q$
and $V_o = Q/BL = H/t$
$h/H = V_s/V_o$

Inlet zone

Outlet zone

Fraction removed = h/H

Sludge zone

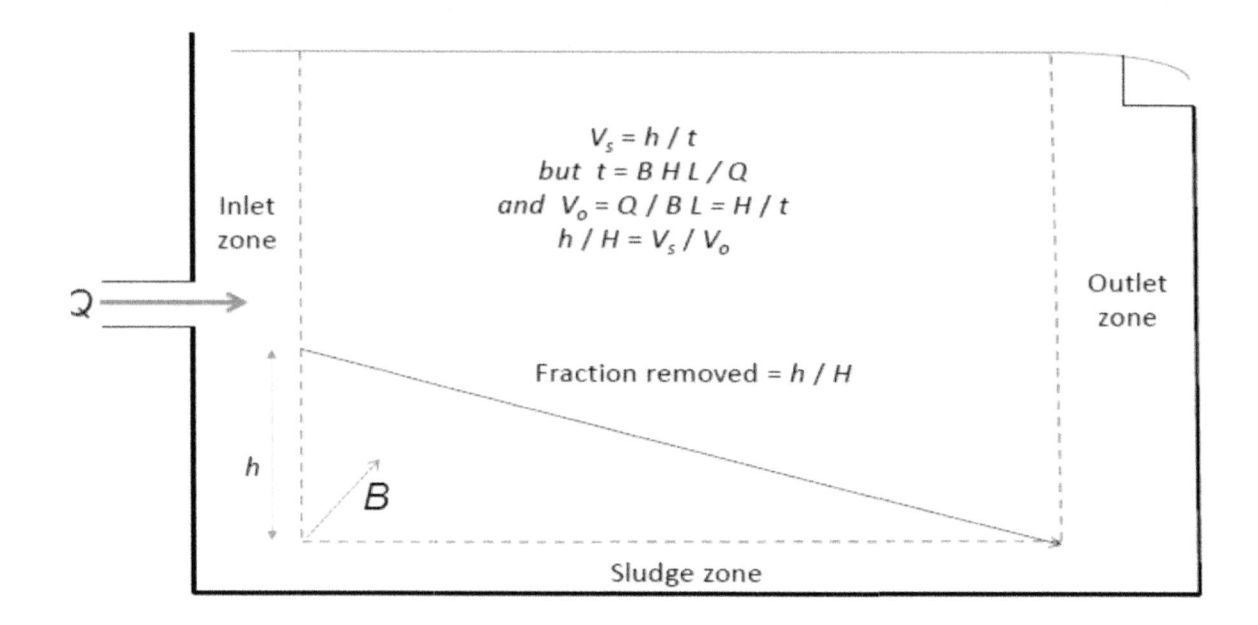

Q6: Determine the forces acting on all the bars below and label them on a sketch.

This question tests general mathematical skills, such as resolving forces, in addition to mechanics. The interviewer could give you a diagram like this and ask you to simply resolve the forces. Some people like to talk through every step while others like to work on it a bit first before telling the interviewer their working. Any approach where you aren't talking through your working from the very beginning constantly risks going off track, without giving the interviewer a chance to steer you back, so talk through every step.

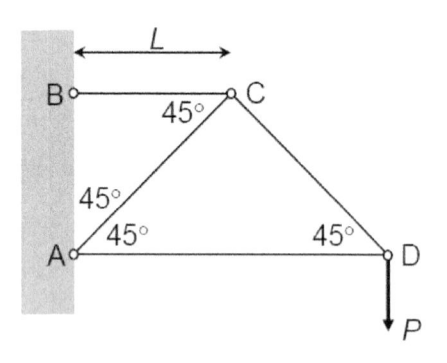

Solution:

Work with one joint at a time. Starting with D, resolve for the forces vertically.

This gives: $CD\cos 45 = P$

Thus, $CD = P\sqrt{2CD\cos 45}$

Next, resolve horizontally at D.

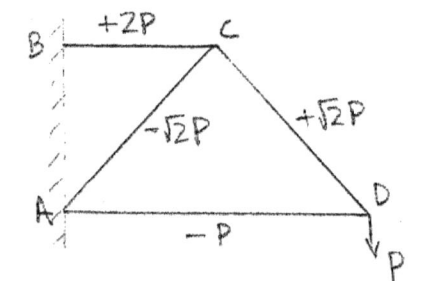

This gives AD = -P

Employ the same method at joint C.

The key here is equilibrium: the net force and moment at each joint is zero. We stay away from joints A and B because we don't know the reaction forces, so we avoid having to deal with them.

THE ULTIMATE OXBRIDGE INTERVIEW GUIDE — PHYSICS

Q7: A pulsating sphere radiates spherical waves into air, where the frequency is 100 Hz and the intensity is 50 mW/m2 at a distance of 1m from the centre of the sphere. The sphere has a nominal radius of 10cm.

Q7 (i) What is the acoustic power radiated?

Comment: This tests your understanding of power vs. energy and how this can be related to the wave theory.

Solution:

$$\dot{W} = I \times 4\pi r^2$$
$$= 50\ mW \times 4\pi \times (1m)^2$$
$$= 0.628\ W$$

The symbol I is the intensity, which is given in the question.

Q7 (ii) How are sound waves different to electromagnetic waves?

Sound needs a medium to propagate through, unlike electromagnetic radiation which can propagate in a vacuum.

Q8: The resolving power of a light microscope can be calculated by: Resolution = $\dfrac{0.61\lambda}{n \sin\emptyset}$

Q8 (i) Define each term in the equation.

λ is the wavelength of the light used.

n is the refractive index.

∅ is half the angular width of the cone of rays collected by the objective lens.

Q8 (ii) Explain why better resolution can be achieved by illuminating the sample with violet light.

The frequency of violet is higher than visible light:

$$c = f\lambda$$

This means the wavelength of violet is greater. This, in turn, means the resulting resolution is smaller.

N.B. Smaller resolution is better!

Q9: The linear dispersion equation for water waves on constant depth is:

$$\omega^2 = kg\,\tanh(kd)$$

Starting from the dispersion equation, show that for waves on deep water, the phase speed is twice the group velocity but for waves on very shallow water, the phase speed and group velocity are equal. w is the angular frequency, k the wave number, g gravity, and d depth below water.

This question tests calculus and algebraic manipulation.

Solution:

As d tends to infinity, the tanh term tends to 1. This leaves w² = kg. The phase speed, which is w/k, is, therefore, g/w. (Formulae would be given.)

The group velocity, $\dfrac{dw}{dk}$ is $\dfrac{g}{2w}$

To get this, simply differentiate w with respect to k and then substitute back in for k.

For shallow water, d tends to zero and tanh(kd) tends to kd.

This leaves w²=k²gd.

Next, take square roots to get $w = k\sqrt{gd}$. The phase velocity, w/k, is $\sqrt{gd}$.

Differentiate to find $\dfrac{dw}{dk}$: this, too, is $\sqrt{gd}$.

Q10: What is meant by wave breaking? Indicate the important parameters that determine wave breaking on a natural beach.

This question is related to hydraulics and coastal/offshore/geotechnical engineering, but the second part is really just a test of intuition.

Recommended Approach

Waves break when the water particles begin to move faster than the wave celerity.

(Note: The group velocity of a wave is the velocity with which the overall shape of the waves' amplitudes – known as the modulation or envelope of the wave – propagates through space.)

Wave breaking depends on the following:

- Bed slope
- Local water depth
- Offshore wave conditions

THE ULTIMATE OXBRIDGE INTERVIEW GUIDE

PHYSICS

Physics Interview Questions

1. How would you determine the distance to the sun?
2. What is the mass of nitrogen in this room?
3. You're in a boat in a closed harbour when you throw your anchor overboard. What happens to the water-level?
4. What are electromagnetic waves? How are they transferred through space?
5. If a sand timer was turned over onto a mass balance, would there be any fluctuations in the mass displayed as the sand fell through?
6. You're sat in the back seat of a car, going to a birthday party. You're carrying a helium balloon (of course). As the car accelerates, how does the balloon behave?
7. What physics allows some aircraft to fly upside-down?
8. Two particles enter a uniform magnetic field and are accelerated in a circle until they hit a detector while travelling perpendicular to their original direction of motion. Derive an expression for the distance between the points where they're detected based on sensibly defined particle properties.
9. Walk me through your calculation for the total number of atoms in the world. Tell us what information you need to begin, and then tell us the answer.
10. Sketch a graph of $y = \frac{x}{\cos(x)}$
11. What is internal energy? How does the internal energy of a system vary as pressure/temperature/volume is varied?
12. When skydiving you must deploy your parachute by the time you're 1.5km above the ground. What height would a person have to jump from to reach terminal velocity just before they deploy their parachute?
13. How could ammonia be used to manage energy supply from renewable such as wind or solar power?
14. Derive the equation for integration by parts. Hence, integrate $e^x \cos(x)$
15. What do you think caused the Titanic to break in half as it sank?
16. What is centrifugal force? How does it affect how fast cars can drive around corners? Why is this affected by weather conditions?
17. Heat rises. Why?
18. How would you derive the water pressure at the bottom of the ocean? What about air pressure at sea level?
19. What is wave/particle duality - how can light exhibit this?
20. What do you think the greatest advance in physics in the 21st century has been?

ENGINEERING

Engineers can expect to have a few **Subject Interviews** and possibly a **General Interview**. Questions may be detailed maths and physics questions, general questions testing estimation, logic and numeracy skills, questions about physical situations where the applicant may display the ability to 'think like an engineer', or questions about the subject and applicant. An engineer may be asked to sit a test before the interview with topics such as pure maths, mechanics and electricity. Discussing the answers given in this test will then be the starting point for the interview, so try view tests positively as they may allow you to choose your strongest topics for the interview.

The subject interviews are technical interviews with questions usually centred in physics and maths, but which may also have an engineering twist. Remember, a question aims to test your ability to apply maths and physics concepts in practice and your **ability to think about designs and real-life imperfections** while showing enthusiasm for engineering. You will need to be fluent in expressing core mathematics and physics concepts mathematically. Since engineering is not a subject usually taught at school, the interview will also test how quickly you think and assimilate new ideas and how you apply your foundation knowledge in new situations. All of these skills are vital for engineering students.

The **questions you will be asked will likely be too difficult for you to answer outright**, so you will need to approach each question methodically to help you build from your base knowledge to an answer, with guidance from the interviewer. When given an engineering question (e.g. "How would you design a gravity dam?"), a helpful first step is to repeat it back in your own words to make sure you have digested what your task is (e.g. "How would I design a free-standing dam utilising only gravitational forces?"). A good second step is to draw a quick sketch of the system and make a qualitative/descriptive assessment of the situation (e.g. 'The dam would need to be able to withstand the force of the water without falling over and have some measures to prevent this').

Once you have sketched the system, write some simple maths and physics expressions to model the system. These will often be for mechanical or electronic forces and energies because engineering is a practical design subject at heart, so real systems are often considered. Use the expressions you jot down to set up equations describing the system if possible, or if you aren't sure, give a verbal assessment of how the expressions dictate how the different elements of the system will interact.

Make sure to explicitly **recognise any assumptions** you are making; while in physics these assumptions may be largely ignored, in engineering it is not always possible to ignore simplifying assumptions (e.g. no air-resistance when designing an aeroplane). So, you must be aware of which assumptions you make in order to recognise how they may fail in the real world.

An engineer needs to be able to recognise potential problems to a system, including those which you may not have considered previously in school (e.g. sliding, seepage, non-plastic behaviour, uneven surfaces, etc.). Once you have a working model, address potential problems. Don't be afraid to poke holes in your own model – **your interviewer will already have noticed the weaknesses in your ideas**, they are more interested in whether you will!

Many questions will be similar in style to those for physics interviews, so it may be useful to read the section on **Physics** above as well. Despite the emphasis on maths and physics in the interview questions, don't forget that you are in an engineering interview and need to think like an engineer, not like a physicist. You may even be asked a question such as "What are the differences between Physics and Engineering?"

Any applicant to engineering should be prepared to discuss their choice of subject. Interviewers are aware that students won't have studied engineering before, so applicants should be able to justify their interest in the course as well as demonstrate an interest in the subject through extracurricular reading, projects, internships, etc. An applicant may also be expected to demonstrate an interest in the subject through well-thought-out answers to questions about the role of engineers in society.

Maths represents a significant portion of Engineering; skills like sketching, differentiating, and integrating, are skills that will be necessary throughout much of your scientific education. Thus, it is advisable to also read the mathematics section in this collection.

Worked Questions

Below are a few examples of how to start breaking down an interview question, complete with model answers.

Q1: (i) Could you explain what is meant by osmotic pressure?

Recommended Approach:

Always start by drawing a diagram of some sort, if applicable.

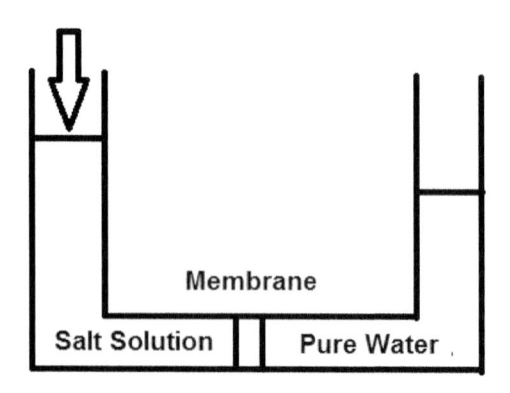

In the above schematic drawing, the osmotic pressure is the minimum pressure exerted on the salt solution that prevents pure water from moving through the semi-permeable membrane and entering the salt solution.

Q1 (ii) The molecular weight of NaCl is 58.5. What is the concentration of physiological saline (0.9% w/v NaCl solution)?

This is a question aimed at anyone who might have stated an interest in chemical/manufacturing/systems engineering in their personal statement. However, as with most Oxbridge interview questions, the interviewer is testing your intuition; the question is, therefore, appropriate for any engineering or applied sciences discipline.

Recommended Approach:

w/v corresponds to the mass of solute (g) times 100, divided by the volume of solution (ml). (Note: You would be told this if you were not studying Chemistry at A-level.)

We are told that the w/v concentration is 0.9. Assuming a 1000ml volume of solution (as we write concentration as moles/litre), this implies $0.9 = \text{mass} \times \frac{100}{1,000}$. Therefore mass = 9g. We are also given the molecular weight = 58.5.

$\frac{9}{58.5} = 0.154$ moles/litre.

Q2: Positive autoregulation (PAR) occurs when the product of a gene activates its own production. PAR is a common network motif in transcription networks but occurs less often in the E. coli network than negative autoregulation. (Network motifs are patterns in transcription networks that occur more often than at random. Transcription is the first step of gene expression, in which a particular segment of DNA is copied into RNA by the enzyme RNA polymerase.)

In positive autoregulation, a gene product activates its own transcription. A model which takes the following form has been proposed:

$$\frac{dx}{dt} = \beta + \beta_1 x - \alpha x$$

Q2 (i) Explain the different terms in this equation.

This question is aimed at students who might have mentioned biomedical/bioprocess/cellular/tissue engineering in their personal statement. However, the calculations involved are related to calculus and, therefore, could be asked to all engineering applicants, especially if this is the interviewer's field of interest.

$\frac{dx}{dt}$: The production rate of x

β: Basal Transcription rate

β_1: Transcription rate on activation

α: Degradation/Dilution rate

You are not expected to know the technical terms, e.g. 'basal transcription rate'. However, it should hopefully be intuitively obvious that <u>the basal rate</u> is the <u>rate of continuous supply</u> of some chemical or process. Like this, try to explain what you think is going on qualitatively.

N.B: Brush up on transcription, translation, etc., if you have mentioned anything related to this topic in your personal statement.

Q2 (ii) What is the condition so that the steady-state concentration of x is positive?

Recommended Approach:

Steady-state simply means the derivative with respect to time is zero. Rearranging the terms, we get the following:

$$x_{ss} = \frac{\beta}{\alpha - \beta_1} > 0 \text{ Requires } \alpha > \beta_1$$

Q2 (iii) How do you think we might try to quantify the response time of this reaction?

Recommended Approach:

The response time is actually defined as the time to reach half of the steady-state concentration.

$$T_{\frac{1}{2}} = \frac{\ln 2}{\alpha - \beta_1}$$

An equally acceptable answer would be to solve the differential equation and find the time constant.

Q2 (iv) When might positive autoregulation be biologically useful?

Recommended Approach:

Positive autoregulation is important for processes that take a long time, such as developmental processes due to its slower response time. However, instabilities can arise with positive autoregulation. Negative autoregulation, on the other hand, is typically more robust and leads to a faster response.

Q3: Explain how nanotechnology might be exploited for preventing and reversing chemical and microbiological contamination of water.

This is very topical at the moment. Think of the properties associated with nanotechnology and how these are relevant to answering the question, e.g. the precision that nanotechnology introduces.

The recent introduction of nanotechnology holds great promise preventing and reversing the effect of water contamination.

1. **Remediation.** The very high reactivity of nanoscale iron in terms of inducing redox reaction is being used for the dehalogenation of ubiquitous contaminants such as TCE. It is also being used to immobilise toxic heavy metals such as mercury.
2. **Detection** of contaminating chemicals (organics and metals). Nanoscale sensors are available which prove real time in situ measures of the presence of chemical contaminants and microbial pathogens.
3. **Nano-filters** with pore size ranging from 0.001-0.0001 μm are effective for removing pesticides.
4. **Nanomaterials** such as silver and titanium have huge potential for killing microbial pathogens in water. The nanoscale is non-toxic and only becomes toxic when it is activated with UV, which causes the short-lived free oxygen particles which are toxic. The nanoscale silver damages the cell's membrane, negatively impacting on respiration and penetration, thus disrupting metabolite transfer.
5. **Magnetic nanoparticles** have the potential to attach to cells for targeted kill and removal, as well as isolation of strains that could be exploited in biodegradation.

Q4: Tell me a bit about the potential of plants for improving soils damaged by anthropogenic activity.

This is also very topical – particularly within civil engineering, where an understanding of the soil properties is crucially important to the design of the structure.

The way plants can improve soils that have been damaged by industrial activity is by fixing carbon and pumping this out of the roots. This improves the nutrient status of the soil, stimulates beneficial activities and encourages the migration of new plant species which contribute to the cycle of soil recovery.

THE ULTIMATE OXBRIDGE INTERVIEW GUIDE — ENGINEERING

- **Phytoextraction**, extraction of toxic metals out of the soil by plants that are then harvested.
- **Phytotransformation**, plant uptake and degradation of organic compounds within the plant.
- **Phytostabilisation**, roots exudates precipitate the pollutant heavy metals and in the process making them less bioavailable and toxic.
- **Rhizofiltration**, uptake of metals into the plants
- **Phytovolatilisation**, plants evapotranspiration of metals such as mercury and hydrocarbons.
- **Vegetative cap**, rainwater is evapo-transpired by plants to prevent leaching contaminants from disposal sites.

Try to describe the engineering/physics principles at play behind some of these, if possible, too. What are the properties of toxic heavy metals? What features of soil do you think would be desirable in a civil engineering context? How might slope instability be prevented? Etc.

Q5: If intrinsic rates of contaminant degradation in a habitat are slow, what engineered interventions can be applied to stimulate microbial bioremediation of the site and how do they work?

This question will take most candidates by surprise. It is certainly effective in getting the candidate to think outside of the box and apply engineering concepts to solve real world problems.

The most common reasons for slow degradation include:

The concentration of the contaminant is so high it kills those cells that could potentially degrade them. In the case of soils, this problem can be overcome by diluting contaminated soil with clean soil or another substrate, such as sawdust. Bioslurping is another approach that is commonly used. (Bioslurping combines the two remedial approaches of bioventing and vacuum-enhanced free-product recovery. Bioventing stimulates the aerobic bioremediation of hydrocarbon-contaminated soils. Vacuum-enhanced free-product recovery extracts Light Non-Aqueous Phase Liquids from the capillary fringe and the water table.)

There is insufficient oxygen to stimulate the favoured aerobic mode of biodegradation. In deep groundwater aquifers, this can be alleviated by sinking wells and injecting air or oxygen release granules.

There are insufficient microbial populations with the genetic capacity to degrade the contaminant or resistant to the toxicity of co-contaminants. This is a rare situation, which when it does occur can be overcome by bio-augmentation of specifically selected populations originating from culture collections, other sites and even genetically modified. These can be injected into soils or introduced into sunken wells in the case of aquifers.

Heterogeneity of contaminant distribution on the site. In this case, the contaminant is present unevenly as hot spots. At such high concentrations, they kill or inhibit all the cells present. Alternatively, other spots are clear of all contamination or present at such low concentrations that degradation activity is not expressed. This condition can be alleviated by several physical mixing approaches, including electrokinetics; a technique of using direct electrical current to remove organic, inorganic, and heavy metal particles from the soil by electric potential. The use of this technique provides an approach with minimum disturbance to the surface while treating subsurface contaminant

THE ULTIMATE OXBRIDGE INTERVIEW GUIDE

ENGINEERING

Q6: The diagram below shows a simple model of a two-storey steel moment-resisting frame building. Write down the equations of motion for free vibrations.

This question tests mechanics, a topic that is almost certain to play an integral part of a physics/engineering interview.

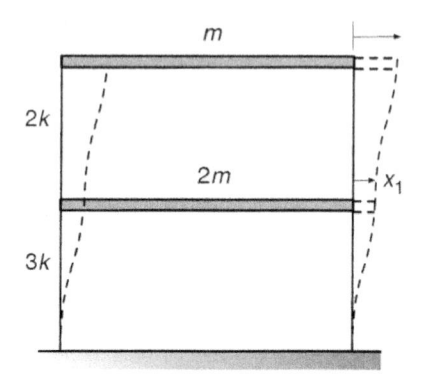

Recommended Approach:

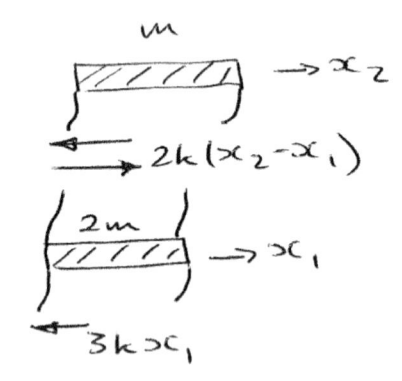

STEP 1: Treat the two storeys separately (you will most likely need prompting with this).

STEP 2: Resolve forces for each storey, bearing in mind that the forces must cancel at the point where the cut is taken.

STEP 3: Write out the equations.

$m\ddot{x}_2 = -2k(x_2 - x_1)$

$2m\ddot{x}_1 = 2k(x_2 - x_1) - 3kx_1$

STEP 4: Write in the equivalent matrix form.

$$\begin{bmatrix} 2m & 0 \\ 0 & m \end{bmatrix} \begin{bmatrix} \ddot{x}_1 \\ \ddot{x}_2 \end{bmatrix} + \begin{bmatrix} 5k & -2k \\ -2k & 2k \end{bmatrix} \begin{bmatrix} x_1 \\ x_2 \end{bmatrix} = 0$$

Q7: A cell suspension is concentrated in a batch MF process from 1% to 10%. Due to an effective back-shock method, the flux remains at 100 l/m2h. The fermenter has a volume of 1m3 and the membrane area is 1.5m2. Calculate the batch processing time assuming that the membrane has a rejection of 100%.

Although this question is referring to a cell suspension, it could apply to any engineering process or system.

Solution:

Solids retained 1 x 1% = V j x 10% m³. This implies V j = 0.1.

Therefore, final volume = 0.1 m³.

Change in volume = 1 - 0.1 = 0.9m³ = Throughput of membrane

$Flux = 100 \ lm^{-2}h^{-1} = 0.1 \ m^3 m^{-2} h^{-1}$

$Time = \dfrac{Throughput}{AxFlux} = \dfrac{0.9}{1.5 \times 0.1} = 6h$

Q8: I'm going to ask you about a cell culture medium that contains two types of cells, A and B, in a ratio of 1:3 by numbers. The mean cell doubling time is 6 hours for type A cells and 8 hours for type B cells under the prevailing cultivation conditions. What is the expected ratio of type A to type B cells in the culture after four days?

This question would be well-suited to any discipline of engineering/physics.

Solution:

STEP 1: Note that the growth rate is to the power of 2.

$N_A = 1 \times 2^{4 \times \frac{24}{6}} = 65,536$

STEP 2: Note that both species will double 4 or 3 times a day.

$N_B = 3 \times 2^{4 \times \frac{24}{8}} = 12,288$

STEP 3: Note their different concentrations: $\dfrac{N_A}{N_B} = 5.3$

ENGINEERING

Q9: I'd like you to draw a diagram, briefly outlining the main components in the signal pathway of a diagnostic ultrasound imaging system. Also, if you can, explain what is meant by time-gain compensation (TGC).

This might appear to be a biomedical engineering question, but it is really testing your electronics.

Recommended Approach:

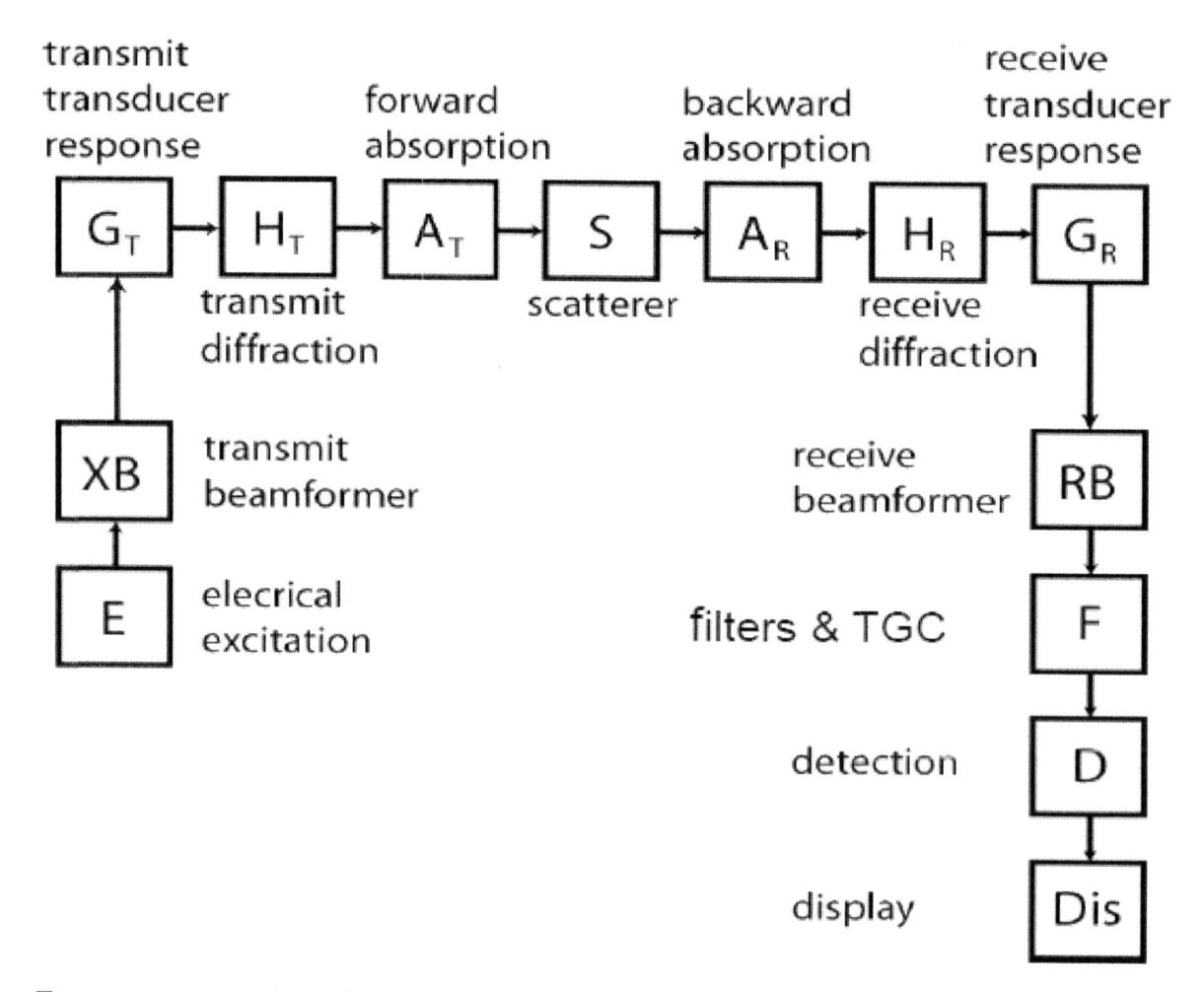

```
transmit                                              receive
transducer    forward              backward           transducer
response      absorption           absorption         response

 [G_T] → [H_T] → [A_T] → [S] → [A_R] → [H_R] → [G_R]
          transmit        scatterer    receive
          diffraction                  diffraction
   ↑
 [XB]   transmit                     receive         [RB]
        beamformer                   beamformer
   
 [E]    electrical                   filters & TGC   [F]
        excitation
                                     detection       [D]

                                     display         [Dis]
```

Time-gain compensation refers to the use of increasing amplification of the beam-formed RF signal received with increasing time of flight to account for the fact that the signal emanating from greater depths within the tissue will have experienced greater attenuation, both on transmit and on receive.

From an engineering point of view, what ultimately limits your ability to image deeper and deeper into tissue?

As the imaging depth is increased, the echo <u>signal received</u> by the imaging array eventually <u>drops</u> below electrical noise levels. The only option is then to <u>start increasing the transmit signal amplitude</u> so as to achieve greater signal-to-noise ratio on receive, but this can only be done up to a point.

As the amplitude is increased, two non-linear phenomena (non-linear propagation and acoustic cavitation) cause transfer of some of the energy carried out by the transmitted pulse into higher harmonics, where it is readily absorbed into heat. Furthermore, cavitation activity occurring in the propagation path will shield the region of interest deep within tissue, causing a further reduction in signal-to-noise ratio.

Q10: Specify typical procedures for the collection and transportation of soil samples from the site for triaxial testing.

This question is related to civil/geotechnical engineering.

Recommended Approach:

Know the main differences between using triaxial testing, the cone penetrometer test, and the shear vane test. No need to know any of the details, but no harm being familiar with the different methods. This displays your enthusiasm and shows that you have carried out research beyond your A-level syllabus.

Install bore-hole to 8m depth using an auger or light percussion drilling rig with clay cutter. Collect sample by driving a U 100 sample tube into the ground. If the clay is soft and sensitive, consider using a Shelby tube instead. In this case, the tube is carefully jacked into the soil at the base of the borehole. The sample tube is removed from the ground and brought to the surface. The ends of the sample are waxed and the tube wrapped in plastic. It is then transported to the testing lab.

Describe two of the main sources of error in the determination of undrained strength using the triaxial test. How can these errors be minimised?

The restraining effect of the membrane surrounding the sample increases the radial stress. This can be accounted for by applying a correction to the measured deviator stress.

Small samples (e.g. the 38 mm diameter samples that are often used) may not provide an appropriate representation of the soil fabric and any fissure that may be present. Conduct the test on larger samples instead.

THE ULTIMATE OXBRIDGE INTERVIEW GUIDE

ENGINEERING

Engineering Interview Questions

1. Can you explain the principles underlying Earthquake proofing?
2. How would a circular hole behave in a sheet of metal as it was heated over time?
3. How do heavy ships remain afloat?
4. What are the difficulties with connecting the UK and USA by road or rail?
5. What is the significance of superconductors?
6. What would you invent first?
7. Derive an equation connecting voltage, charge and capacitance.
8. How are cricket bowlers able to 'swing' and 'reverse-swing' their bowl?
9. What mechanical components does a wind turbine have? Why do wind turbines appear stationary in high winds?
10. What is the hardest naturally occurring material why? How would you cut it?
11. Is it better to build bridges on concrete or soil, explain your answer.
12. How would you derive the formula for a circle's area?
13. What is Moore's law and is it likely to continue? What limits the size of a computer chip?
14. What principles govern an aeroplane's flight? What allows some planes to fly upside down?
15. How do you tell if a website is slow because it has lots of visitors or because it is hosted in Australia?
16. How does a train handle a bend in the tracks?
17. What separates a gun from a rifle? Why do many firearms fire bullets which spin?
18. Sketch the graph of $y^2 = \sin(x^2)$
19. You can see a ladder leaning against the bookshelf behind me. How far do you think I can safely walk up it before it might slip?
20. What do you think you would have to consider if you were designing a remote-controlled drone?
21. You have a circuit with a DC non-ideal battery and a load output (which can be modelled as a resistor), as well any other circuit components you need. How would you maximise the power transferred to the output?

MATERIAL SCIENCES

Material Science interviews generally follow the formula of one maths question, one mechanical reasoning question, one materials-based question. Thus, you are strongly advised to also read the mathematics section in this collection.

Materials Science is a hands-on subject and requires an ability to explain and visualise potentially abstract concepts clearly; sketching is therefore encouraged (you will be given a pen and paper).

It should be stressed that, while specifics are given in the answers below, the interviewers are rarely looking for you to arrive at a correct final answer. They simply want to see how you approach unfamiliar and potentially daunting problems, and how you reason. The interview aims to achieve one thing: **to determine if you have the intellectual capacity, creativity and curiosity to thrive in the tutorial system**.

Finally, skills like sketching, differentiating and integrating will be necessary throughout much of your scientific education. Thus, it is advisable to also read the mathematics section in this collection.

Worked Questions

Below are a few examples of how to start breaking down an interview question, complete with answer outlines and model answers. The answers are by no means exhaustive; the points given could be used by the interviewer as prompts and to encourage lengthy discussion of certain topics.

Q1: What should we build a fusion reactor out of?

This question emphasises the multidisciplinary nature of material science. A well-read candidate who's keeping up-to-date with the biggest recent scientific news will know that a fusion reactor uses the process of nuclear fusion to produce energy which we can use on the electrical grid.

This knowledge is not presumed though and so this definition can be given as an initial prompt. From there, a good answer should split the question into two distinct parts.

The first is based on the physics of nuclear fusion. Fusion involves bringing together nuclei to create an element with higher atomic number. This involves overcoming the electrostatic repulsion of two positively charged nuclei and so requires huge temperatures and pressures (a good candidate might give the example of hydrogen fusing in our sun to give helium and the energy which powers our earth). A prompt may be given to explain that fusion reactors use deuterium and tritium rather than hydrogen nuclei as this gives the most efficient release of energy. Thus the candidate would be expected to say that the products of such a reaction are α-radiation and high-energy neutrons.

The second part of the answer should take the environmental conditions which arise in the first part of the answer (i.e. high temperature, high pressure, α-radiation and high-energy neutron bombardment) and use these to decide upon issues which come with materials selection. High temperature might suggest the use of ceramics (higher melting points than metals); high pressures might suggest the use of metals (more ductile than brittle ceramics). Strong candidates, after prompting, may be able to explain the effects of <u>α-radiation and high-energy neutron bombardment</u> on any materials used. α-radiation are just helium nuclei; these could penetrate a metal lattice structure and form helium gas bubbles; the effect of these bubbles on the strength of the metal could be likened to the difference in strength between expanded and non-expanded polystyrene. High-energy neutrons displace atoms in the metal lattice, leading to the formation of dislocations; dislocations are the reason for plastic deformation; simply put, more dislocations means more deformation which isn't great for the structural integrity of our fusion reactor.

Q2: I give you a vial with a black powder in it. I tell you the sample is pure and made of carbon. How do you determine what the black powder is?

There is a lot of scope in this question for a good candidate to make use of knowledge of characterisation techniques learnt in both Chemistry and Physics. A good answer will give solid reasoning for employing each technique plus knowledge of what the technique involves, rather than covering as many techniques as possible. By no means an exhaustive list of potential techniques is given below:

- Heating to determine <u>melting point</u> (good candidates might suggest that there's the possibility the sample will sublime rather than melt).
- (Time-of-flight) <u>mass spectrometry</u>: the sample is ionised and accelerated using an electric field before being bent round a corner using a magnetic field. Heavier species fly slower; particles with a greater charge fly faster. We end up with a plot of relative intensities with respect to the mass-to-charge ratio (m/z) of each species.
- <u>Infrared spectroscopy</u>: infrared radiation causes covalent bonds to vibrate at characteristic frequencies. When the applied IR radiation is in resonance with the vibration of the bond, then we know which bond is present.
- <u>Nuclear Magnetic Resonance</u> (NMR) spectroscopy: protons have a property called spin, which can be thought of as a tiny bar magnet. When an external magnetic field is applied, this determines the direction the spin 'points' in. Switching off the magnetic field leads to the spin decaying to its previous unaligned state and giving off radio-frequency radiation in the process. The local environment of a proton spin (i.e. where the hydrogen atoms are in a molecule) gives detectable changes in this signal. A good candidate will note that if this is a pure carbon sample then there are no hydrogen atoms present and that 13C NMR spectroscopy has to be employed instead.
- <u>Liquid Chromatography</u>: if the sample can be dissolved in a solvent then different methods such as thin layer chromatography (TLC), column chromatography, and high-performance liquid chromatography (HPLC) can be employed. Different species have different retention times and so can be identified if we know what our stationary and mobile phases are.

- Being a pure sample made of carbon, candidates should be aware that this must be an allotrope of carbon (such as diamond). Not being transparent, it cannot be diamond, so it could be graphite or amorphous carbon (allotropes candidates should have heard of these). Leading on from graphite, the interviewer can prompt to suggest that the sample could be graphene, explaining what this is if need be. Transmission Electron Microscopy (TEM) could be employed on such thin samples.

Q3: What is a Formula-1 car made from and why?

A common favourite given the incredible engineering which goes into making such a car. Good candidates should identify the solution to such a question involves identifying the requirements of the materials given the environment they're in, and then choosing suitable materials whose properties fit the desired function. It is this principle on which Materials Science rests as a discipline.

The main focus of the answer should be the chassis of the vehicle, although given the general nature of the question, mention could be given, for example, to the rubber in the tyres (how vulcanisation affects how hard or soft they are and when you might want to use each type) and the metals used in the suspension (balance between strength and lack of plastic deformation).

An F-1 car needs to be light. Carbon-fibre has an excellent strength-to-weight ratio but is no good by itself on impact as it absorbs energy by bending before potentially splintering. Thus a metal support could go beneath an outer layer of carbon fibre. Light metals include aluminium and titanium (good candidates will consider which is easier to process and cheaper to make). But bulk metal is heavy. Therefore, we could employ a hexagonal structure; hexagons are strong (cite the example of a beehive) and the resulting large air gaps significantly reduce the mass of the structure.

Q4: The temperature in a jet engine can exceed 1500°C. This is higher than the melting point of the nickel-based superalloys which are used to make the turbine blades. Why don't the blades melt?

This should be an unfamiliar concept to most candidates. Three types of answers could be given, for which most candidates will probably need prompts:

- Serpentine cooling: the introduction of an internal system of cooling channels in the blade. Cool(er) air flows through the channels; heat transfers from the blades to the air. Suggestions of using liquid instead of gas are no good as the liquid will not withstand the heat and could also lead to corrosion effects. Comparing this system to the operation of a radiator shows an understanding of what's going on. The surface area of the channels should be increased, but too many channels will compromise the structural integrity of the blades.
- Thermal barrier coatings: a thin layer of highly heat resistive material could coat the outer surface of the blade. Good candidates should note such a material would be a ceramic. With prompts, the efficacy of this thermal barrier coating could be improved by increasing its surface area; this is achieved by giving the coating a fin-like structure (as seen in certain systems in the body, such as the lungs).
- Good candidates should comment on what a superalloy could possibly be. An alloy is a mixture of metals whose properties are different from its constituent elements. A metal melts when its atoms have enough thermal energy to break free of the lattice structure in which they find themselves.

The addition of certain elements to a metal lattice may affect the movement of the atoms in the lattice (e.g. because of their differing size).

Q5: How does a touchscreen work?

A ubiquitous technology to which many of us never give much thought. Prior knowledge is not assumed, but insight can be gained into how this physical system works. There are two simple systems to consider:

Resistive screens:

These are made up of two conductive layers on top of the normal glass surface, which are separated by tiny spacers and through which passes a well-defined current. A scratch-resistant layer is applied on top of all this to keep the system safe. The upper conductive layer is flexible. When a local force is applied, this upper layer bends and comes into contact with the lower conductive layer, thus resulting in a voltage drop. A good candidate should note that one instance of stimulus requires two measurements, one in each of the x- and y-directions, and thus that a voltage is dropped separately across each of the x- and y-directions – the entire process taking a time shorter than is humanly perceptible.

Capacitive screens:

A conductive layer coats the top of the glass of the screen and this is again covered with a protective layer. As above, the conductive layer has a well-defined current running across it but it is not flexible. Instead, when your finger touches this layer, its charge can be transferred at the point of contact to your finger which is capacitive (it can store an electric charge). This leads to a change in the flow of current and can be detected appropriately. Good candidates should suggest that this is why some touchscreens don't work when you are wearing gloves (as the material in most gloves cannot hold a charge).

Q6: What's so special about carbon?

A deliberately broad question and impossible to answer in full in an interview. Candidates should draw from their Chemistry knowledge to talk about carbon's four valence electrons. These can bond with other carbon atoms in a dazzling array of ways to form many different structures. Organic chemistry arises because of carbon's ability to bond to itself and to other atoms: the building blocks of life, as well as polymers (derived from the hydrocarbons of the oil industry), are built in this way. Focus should be kept on <u>carbon's ability to bond with itself</u> to give unique structural forms known as allotropes.

Candidates should be aware of diamond (all four electrons bonded in a tetrahedral structure, thus giving strength and transparency) and graphite. In graphite, only three electrons are used in bonding to give planar hexagonal sheets which interact weakly each other (van der Waals forces are weaker than covalent bonds) and so can slide over each other – hence why we use graphite as pencil lead. There is also a free electron in graphite which leads it to be an electrical conductor. With prompts, extend the conversation to graphene (single graphite sheets) and what properties it might have (electrical conductivity, strength etc.). Particularly strong candidates might be asked as well/instead to consider <u>fullerenes and carbon nanotubes</u> – what is unique about their electronic structures and what properties might these materials have?

THE ULTIMATE OXBRIDGE INTERVIEW GUIDE — MATERIAL SCIENCES

Q7: Computer chips are intricate patterns of circuitry on silicon wafers, where the smallest features are of the order of 6nm. How do we make them? And how do we know we've made what we think?

Candidates should first identify that circuitry means "paths along which electricity conducts" – thus, this material should be a good conductor (suggestions of metals with their free electrons e.g. copper which is used in macroscopic circuitry, but gold and silver have higher conductivities). Hints and prompts should be given to engage in a discussion about likely never-before-encountered processes such as lithography, electron-beam milling, masking etc.

Masking involves the protection of certain areas with a material durable to the etching process – for example, a layer of gold may be sputtered onto the surface of the silicon and selectively covered where the circuitry will lie; an etch then gets rid of the non-protected gold before a further wash gets rid of the protective layer and leaves the desired micro-circuitry behind.

Characterisation of the product can be achieved using microscopy. Candidates should notice that optical microscopy is of no use for imaging the smallest features on these chips and so we have to move to electron microscopy (arguments for this citing the difference in wavelengths between electrons and photons are encouraged). Transmission electron microscopy (TEM) should be discounted as this requires extremely thin samples (which the microchip is not). Scanning electron microscopy (SEM) and scanning tunnelling microscopy (STM) can be used for topographical information. Strong candidates might spot that SEM can give both topographical information (from secondary electrons near the sample surface) and compositional information (from back-scattered electrons deeper within the sample).

Q8: I lay a Coke can on its side and balance a 2p piece on its edge on top. At what angle does the coin fall off?

An exact answer is not the aim of this question. Emphasis should be placed on the candidate setting up the problem well and contemplating all variables at each step, rather than diving in head first to get an answer. Making reasonable assumptions to help make the calculations manageable is an invaluable skill used every day in the physical sciences.

Such preliminary assumptions might talk about the coin not falling flat on its face, the start velocity of the coin (is it given a push?) and the coefficient of friction between the coin's edge and the can's surface. How do we define the angle at which the coin falls off? How do we analyse the effect gravity has on the coin's velocity as it begins to roll? It is the candidate's ability to discover why this is a complex problem and then trying to solve it methodically using familiar mechanical concepts which is what should be looked for.

Q9: I place an apple in a bowl of water and find that it floats. How much of the apple is above the waterline?

Again, the interviewer is not looking for an exact answer; rather a methodical approach to a seemingly simple question. The topic of buoyancy requires consideration of an object's mass and volume, and so its density too. There are two approaches to this question.

In the first, the candidate considers the Archimedean principle that an object will sink in water until it has displaced an amount of water equal to its own mass (this is independent of the size or shape of the object).

If the object has a volume greater than the volume of water displaced, then the object floats. The point of such a discussion is to get the candidate to say that how much of the apple is above the waterline is dependent on its density (which we are not told). Since it floats, it must be less dense than water. The closer its density to that of water, the more of it lies below the waterline.

The second approach involves looking at the forces involved. Gravity acts on the apple (F = mg) downwards. A buoyancy force acts to hold the apple up; this can be thought of as the force of gravity acting on the mass of water equal to the volume displaced by a fully submerged apple. Again this demonstrates the <u>dependency of the answer on the density of the apple</u> (the force of gravity is dependent on the apple's mass; the buoyancy force is dependent on the apple's volume).

Q10: I give you the definition of the hyperbolic sine function: $sinh(x) = \frac{e^x - e^{-x}}{2}$. Sketch sinh(x). Using only your sketch, sketch the derivative of sinh(x).

Whilst Further Maths A-Level students should have come across hyperbolic functions, the teaching of sketching visually is generally poorly taught in pre-university education. It is an essential skill in the physical sciences.

To sketch sinh(x), candidates need only one building block: the sketch of e^x. Candidates should be encouraged to split the problem into bite-sized chunks. First, sketch e^x (intercepting the y-axis at 1; asymptotic along the x-axis for x→-∞; exponential increase to y = ∞ for x→∞). e^{-x} can then be sketched as a reflection in the y-axis. The latter then needs to be taken away from the former. This can be done by considering three key regions of the sketch: x=0, x→-∞ and x→∞. At the infinite extremities of the x-axis, we are subtracting y-values of infinity from zero and vice versa, to give y-values of -∞ and ∞ respectively. At x = 0, y = 1 is subtracted from y = 1 (or y=½ from y=½ if the candidate had already included this from the definition of sinh(x)) to give a point at the origin. The symmetry of the problem also tells the candidate that the gradient at the origin is 1. Using this information, the sweeping curve of sinh(x) can be sketched with its rotational symmetry of order 2.

Stronger candidates should then be asked to sketch the derivative of sinh(x) on the same set of axes <u>without carrying out any symbolic differentiation</u>. As previously mentioned, the gradient at the origin is 1. Again, the x-axis extremities should be looked at. In both cases, the gradient is positive and exponentially increasing. The leap to sketching the derivative, cosh(x), with its reflection in the y-axis shouldn't be great.

The very strongest candidates might then be asked to divide their two sketches by one another: $\frac{sinh(x)}{cosh(x)} = tanh(x)$ before sketching its derivative ($sech^2(x)$). <u>All without algebra</u>.

Material Sciences Interview Questions

1. What differentiates carbon and carbon fibres?
2. What materials do we make rockets out of? Why?
3. What are the uses of graphene? Are there any weaknesses to using graphene?
4. Why do you think carbon is so widely used and versatile in carbon fibre, carbon-nano tubes, fullerenes etc...? Is this something we can do with other materials?
5. How do materials fail? What can materials scientists do to prevent this?
6. What's the tallest you could build a Lego tower by stacking single bricks one above the other?
7. How could you calculate a theoretical value for density based on knowledge of the arrangement of the atoms in a lattice? How do you think this would relate to an empirical density calculation?
8. How do crystals form? How does the formation process affect their properties?
9. Sketch the graph of $y^2 = e^{\sin(x)}$
10. How do electrons move through wires? What do you think the main considerations are when attempting to make ever smaller computers?
11. What are submarines made of and why? Why aren't the hardest metals used?
12. If you need a strong, low density material and you have one material which is strong but heavier, and one which is weaker but lighter – how would you decide between them?
13. What is a polymer? Why are they so useful? How are polymers tailored to their intended purpose?
14. What do you think the biggest challenges which will need to be solved by materials scientists are?
15. Why is gold so valuable?
16. What do you know about 3D printing? What do you think are the biggest opportunities and challenges it poses?
17. A new compound is found at a meteor crater. How would you work out what it is?
18. What would you expect an alien spaceship to be built from?
19. What is the difference between material sciences and engineering?
20. There are lots of materials which are strong in tension and weak in compression (or vice versa). How does this happen?
21. How do you think components are tested to ensure quality and avoid material failure in industry?

MATHEMATICS

A mathematician may be called for a **General Interview** or several maths **Subject Interviews** which can be difficult to prepare for. Unlike other subjects where an ability to think critically about the subject may be enough, maths interviews will require technical knowledge of all of the mathematics you have studied as well as an extensive complement of mathematical abilities and techniques.

Mathematics interviews will almost always take the form of questions outright testing if you are familiar with mathematical concepts and techniques. While there are several topics more likely to come up, **any topic covered in school until the day of your interview could come up** and you would be expected to show that you can solve these problems. This section will give some pointers on which questions may appear and which techniques any applicant should be familiar with, but the only real way to succeed is by being incredibly skilled and intuitive in solving mathematical problems. These are perhaps not the most encouraging words for an applicant, but Oxbridge has an exceptionally high bar for mathematicians, and the reality is that only gifted mathematicians will be accepted. Given that you have gotten as far as the interview, Oxbridge believes that you have the necessary technical knowledge of mathematics to interview successfully. So, at this point, you need only practice how to best present your answers and deal with the strange questions which may be asked (as well as revise all your school material!)

The form the interview takes can vary from college to college. You may or may not be asked to sit a test first, and if you are, this test is often used as a foundation for the interview, so the expectation is usually that the applicant will answer a few questions fully rather than all the questions on the test. The interview may build on the problems in the test or discuss techniques, etc. Try to view these tests positively – they are letting you choose your strongest topics for the interview. Test or not, the interviewers (usually) try to make the interview less frightening by **starting slowly with some easier questions and working up to some harder problems**.

The most popular topics that appear in subject interview questions are:

- Integration and Differentiation (e.g. differentiate $y = x^x$)
- Imaginary Numbers
- Trigonometry (e.g. Euler's Formula)
- Probability
- Combinatorics and Series

Any technically difficult question is almost certain to be about integration, differentiation, trigonometry, and complex numbers in some combination.

The interview is much less likely to thoroughly test topics from earlier years in school such as logarithms, solving lower polynomial equations or geometry. However, knowledge of these is assumed to be basal to higher topics, so you may be asked questions which assume knowledge of these or an 'easy' starter question about one of these topics. Double-check you are still familiar with these topics; as you revise you can use them to make your own practice questions for some of the techniques discussed later, such as practice proofs (e.g. prove the Pythagorean Theorem is true or why 100=99).

THE ULTIMATE OXBRIDGE INTERVIEW GUIDE — MATHEMATICS

The advanced topics listed above would be used to test the ability of the applicant to solve problems of a high technical level, but mastery of important mathematical techniques and reasoning may also be tested. An applicant may be asked to demonstrate techniques on either advanced or rudimentary topics.

For instance, **proofs will almost never be required for advanced topics**. Interviewers will usually be testing how you think about concepts and present mathematical solutions, so **often ask deceptively simple questions**. Prove that there is an infinity of primes, prove that some given value is the sum of two squares, or prove than $4n-1$ is a multiple of three, are examples of this type of question. This is not about demonstrating advanced knowledge, but about showing that you can use an appropriate method to approach a problem and present your solution in a logical way with proper use of mathematical language. You may be asked to prove something specifically by contradiction, so be prepared.

You may also be asked a similar style of question (e.g. "Why is the product of four consecutive integers always divisible by 24?"), but even when not asked to give a formal proof, present your answer well, laying it out in an attractive and logical way. The companion to proof questions, but for more advanced topics, are the 'Show that'/'Derive' questions. You could, for example, be asked to show that a trigonometric identity is valid or to derive an expression for differentiation from first principles.

The most common technique you will be asked to demonstrate is **graph sketching**. It is likely that you will first be given functions you are expected to be familiar with [e.g. e^x and $\sin(x)$], and then some function combining these (e.g. $e^{\sin(x)}$), or a new function (e.g. x^x). You would be expected to find the intercepts, stationary points, asymptotes, and maybe inflection points. Sketching is almost certain to come up, so check that you still remember how to sketch graphs for all the main types of functions and that you know how to combine functions when sketching graphs. It is probably safest to revise this from the basics, not just rely on the memory of how each function looks.

It is not uncommon to be asked a question which tests your ability to interpret word problems as equations. These may be physics-type questions of the 'Two trains leave two stations heading for each other at…'-type, or probability or geometric questions, or any number of other problems which are simple to solve once the equations are set up right. Rarely, you might also be asked a question where you need to 'brain dump' in a constructive way. An example is 'Tell me what you know about triangles', where you need to think through your approach carefully in order to lay out what you know in an **appropriate order and a way which emphasises the most important points**.

In general, the best preparation is to revise all the topics you have studied at school, taking particular note of the ones listed above. Make sure you understand how all these topics are constructed, both the specific derivations of concepts you have studied and how mathematicians systematically added these ideas to the body of mathematical knowledge through methodical work and proofs.

Worked Questions

Below are a few examples of how to start breaking down an interview question, complete with answer outlines and model answers.

Q1(i): Do you know why $det(AB) = det(A) det(B)$?

The Fibonacci numbers are defined as $F_{n+1} = F_n + F_{n-1}$ with $F_0 = 0$ and $F_1 = 1$. Can you show that
$$\begin{pmatrix} F_{n+1} & F_n \\ F_n & F_{n-1} \end{pmatrix} = \begin{pmatrix} 1 & 1 \\ 1 & 0 \end{pmatrix} \begin{pmatrix} F_n & F_{n-1} \\ F_{n-1} & F_{n-2} \end{pmatrix}?$$

The determinant can be thought of as the scale factor of the transformation. So when we write down det(AB), we can think of it as doing the transformation A and then the transformation B. The scale factor of a composition of transformation is the same as the product.

One can also achieve this by doing the algebra on two general 2x2 matrices.

The first part follows directly from the definition of matrix multiplication and then using the definition of the Fibonacci numbers.

The question seems to be guiding us to the fact that:

$$det \begin{pmatrix} F_{n+1} & F_n \\ F_n & F_{n-1} \end{pmatrix} = det \begin{pmatrix} 1 & 1 \\ 1 & 0 \end{pmatrix} det \begin{pmatrix} F_n & F_{n-1} \\ F_{n-1} & F_{n-2} \end{pmatrix}$$

Q1(ii): Hence show that $F_{n+1}F_{n-1} - F_n^2 = (-1)^n$

We know that the determinant of the first matrix is -1 so iteratively apply this identity and use the fact that for $n = 1$ the determinant is -1 to get $(-1)^n$.

Q1(iii): Can you think of an alternative way of showing this?

Alternatively, induction works here, $F_{k+2}F_k - F_{k+1}^2 = (F_{k+1} + F_k)F_k - (F_k + F_{k-1})^2 = -(F_{k-1}F_{k+1} - F_k^2)$, as required.

Q2: A rectangle's four corners touch the edge of a circle. What is its largest possible area?

There are two ways to do this. Taking a <u>geometric approach</u>, consider the diagonals of the rectangle. We know that the diagonals of the rectangles pass through the centre of the circle. The diagonals form two angles, ϑ and π-ϑ. The area of the inscribed rectangle is, therefore, sin ϑ + sin (π-ϑ) = 2 sinϑ, either from the angle addition formulae or just knowing that sin (π-ϑ) = sinϑ. Thus this area is maximized when ϑ = $\pi/2$, and this is a square. This area will then be 2.

Alternatively, you can <u>approach it computationally</u>. If we look at the circle $x^2 + y^2 = 1$ we know that the rectangle has vertices (a, b), (a, -b), (-a, b), (-a, -b). Consider the *square* with vertices (±(a + b)/2, ± (a + b)/2). This has area (a+b)². Compare the area of this circle to the area of the rectangle, it has area 4ab. But, $(a + b)^2 \geq 4ab$ (as $(a + b)^2 - 4ab = (a - b)^2 \geq 0$). Thus the square is bigger and it only gets larger when we consider the square projected out onto the circle.

THE ULTIMATE OXBRIDGE INTERVIEW GUIDE

MATHEMATICS

Q3: What is integration?

Integration is two possible things: a good candidate will discuss both of them. Integration can be considered *the inverse of differentiation* or it can be considered a process to *find area*.

For the first, we know the fundamental theorem of calculus that states $\int f'(x)dx = f(x) + C$ where $\int$ is considered the indefinite integral (or $\frac{d}{dx}\int_a^x f(t)dt = f(x)$). Such a definition makes sense whenever what we are integrating has a closed form anti-derivative. However, a candidate who has done S1 should be aware that there is no anti-derivative for exp (-x²), and thus an approach to integration should be more flexible than simply computing the function that differentiates to it. Throughout such an explanation, a candidate may be asked to prove one variant of the fundamental theorem of calculus (they would probably be encouraged towards the second of these) and proof should be given.

For the second, we have some notion of 'area' under a curve, typified by the area under rectangle, or the area under a straight line. Such an approach leads to the definition of definite integration, e.g., $\int_a^b f(x)\,dx$ is the 'area' under a curve. This may be made more precise, eg, a candidate may be expected to recall the trapezium rule (or lower/upper Riemann sums if these have been seen before), e.g., we can *approximate* the integral by taking sums of this form.

Q4: What is differentiation? Can you explain why d/dx x^n = nx^(n − 1)?

Differentiation is the act of finding the gradient of a curve at a point, e.g., taking a curve and then considering its tangents. We then map *x* to the gradient of the tangent at this point.

More formally, we consider $\frac{f(x+h)-f(x)}{h}$ where we think of *h* as very small. This gives a *secant* of the curve. We then take *h* closer and closer to zero and come up with some notion of the limit. This is then defined to be the derivative.

$$\frac{(x+h)^n - x^n}{h} = \frac{hnx^{n-1} + \frac{h^2 n(n-1)}{2}x^{n-2} + \cdots}{h} = nx^{n-1} + q(x)$$

where *q* is some polynomial in *x* (and *h*). So, on taking *h* to be extremely small, the second term vanishes.

Note that for both of the above questions, attempting to define differentiation or integration in terms of its <u>action on polynomials</u>, e.g., in terms of what $\int x^n dx$ and $\frac{d}{dx}x^n$ is possible. However, one needs to be a lot more careful than one thinks one would have to be. It is possible that such a situation would not end well, e.g., it is probably a poor candidate who attempts to define integration and differentiation in terms of x^n. Such an issue may also arise with questions of the type 'differentiate x^x', another staple interview question.

The response $x\,x^{x-1}$ is very incorrect and implies a misunderstanding of what differentiation is. (Bonus: $\frac{d}{dx}x^x = \frac{d}{dx}e^{x\log x}$ apply the chain rule with $u = x\log x$ to get $x^x(\log x + 1)$. Since $xx^{x-1} = x^x$ we (in fact) get a bonus, the 'wrong' answer is right if and only if log *x* = 0, eg, *x* = 1. Thus it's incorrect everywhere, which is pretty bad).

THE ULTIMATE OXBRIDGE INTERVIEW GUIDE — MATHEMATICS

Q5: Which is harder, differentiation or integration?

Both. You can think of either as harder (and successfully argue it!) but the general rule is, for A-level students, integration is harder. For undergraduates, differentiation is harder.

<u>Differentiation is harder</u>: The issue is that one can integrate a function such as f(x) = 1 for x > 0 and 0 for x > 0. What you get is $\int_{-\infty}^{x} f(t)dt = t$ for $t > 0$ and 0 for $t < 0$ (and $t = 0$ at $x = 0$). This shows that we can integrate functions that have 'jumps' in them. We note that for both of the definitions of integration we have given above (including the one based on differentiation) this works, e.g., the integral of $f(x)$ legitimately is this thing. So, there are functions you can integrate but not differentiate, e.g., differentiation is harder.

<u>Integration is harder</u>: The issue here is that whenever you have a nice explicit function, e.g., $\tan[e^{-x^2}\log(\sin x)]$ we could instantly write the derivative of this down. It's not a pleasant thing to do; however, it reduces to repeated applications of the chain rule and the product rule. So, any function with an explicit 'formula' (whatever that means) can easily be differentiated. This is different for integration: $\int e^{-x^2} dx$ is the most commonly known example. There is no expression of this integral in terms of elementary functions. This is because (ultimately) integration is not as algorithmic. Substitution and by parts are *rules* that may simplify the integral, or may not.

A good candidate will pick one and argue it well (following the rough outline here, these are two most sensible interpretations of the question). The interviewer may prod the candidate in the other direction, e.g., by drawing the function f(x), or writing down e^{-x^2} and encouraging through.

Q6: What is the area of a circle? Prove it.

As to be expected, the area of a circle is πr^2, where r is the radius of the circle. At this point, the interviewer would ask the candidate for a definition of π. One has various retorts: however, there are two sensible ones. The first is that it is the ratio of the circumference of a circle to its diameter. The second is that it is the smallest non-zero root of sin x (in essence, every other definition in terms of a trigonometric function is the same).

Again, various proofs exist of which two are now shown: If $x^2 + y^2 = r^2$ we have that $y = \sqrt{r^2 - x^2}$, where $\sqrt{}$ can take positive or negative signs. We take the positive sign, eg, we get the semi-circle. Then the area of the circle = $2\int_{-r}^{r}\sqrt{r^2 - x^2}\, dx$. We set $x = r\cos\theta$ and then $\frac{dx}{d\theta} = -r\sin(\theta)$, and the integral equals $2\int_0^{\pi} r\sin(\theta)\sqrt{r^2(1-\cos^2\theta)}\, d\theta$. Then, since $\sqrt{(1-\cos^2\theta)} = |\sin\theta|$ we get that the integral = $r^2\int_0^{\pi}\sin^2\theta\, d\theta$. Integrating $\sin^2\theta$ is a tricky business: however, nothing that $1 - 2\sin^2\theta = \cos(2\theta)$ allows us to conclude that the area of the circle = $r^2\int_0^{\pi}(1-\cos(2\theta))d\theta = \pi r^2$. (Here we are using the retort that π is the smallest root of the sin function).

Another <u>integration-based proof</u> is called the onion proof: you can consider the circle as a union of rings going outwards. Each ring has an area equal to the *diameter x a little bit*, so when we integrate we get that area = $\int_0^r 2\pi t\, dt = \pi r^2$. This proof uses that fact that π is the ratio of the circle's circumference to its diameter. Although technically correct, it is not a particularly good proof as making all the intermediary steps precise is a gargantuan task.

THE ULTIMATE OXBRIDGE INTERVIEW GUIDE — MATHEMATICS

Q7: If $f(x + y) = f(x) + f(y)$ and f is differentiable, what is $f(x)$?

If $g(xy) = g(x) + g(y)$ and g is differentiable, what is g?

If $h(x + y) = h(x)h(y)$ and h is differentiable what is h?

If $f(x)$ is differentiable, consider:

$$f'(x) = \lim \frac{f(x+h)-f(x)}{h} = \lim \frac{f(x)+f(h)-f(x)}{h} = \lim \frac{f(h)}{h} = f'(0).$$

So f has a constant derivative, e.g., $f(x) = Ax + B$ where $A = f'(0)$. Note that $f(x + 0) = f(x) + f(0)$, eg, $f(0) = 0$, and therefore $B = 0$.

For $g(xy) = g(x) + g(y)$, consider $g(e^u e^v) = g(e^{u+v}) = g(e^u) + g(e^v)$ e.g., the function $G(y) = g(e^y)$ satisfies the first part. We thus have that $g(e^y) = Ay$, e.g., $g(x) = A \log x$.

The same trick works for h, except consider $\log(h(x))$. This is of the form Ax, eg, the solution e^{ax}.

This question is straight forward, however, each stage requires somewhat of a jump. The candidate would be expected to *know* the answers and then be guided. The first step of using the derivative is not obvious, and there are various false starts a candidate could make (and various not so false starts). Obtaining that f(0) is good, using the fact that f is differentiable is good, writing down the Taylor Series works. Using the fact that f is differentiable is good, writing down the Taylor Series works. Using that $f(n) = nf(1)$, and $f(\frac{1}{n}) = \frac{1}{n}f(1)$ can be helpful too. The issue of "are there any functions other than the ones listed" is an interesting one. For such a function to exist, it would have a lot of bad properties.

Questions 8-16 are fairly straightforward questions that might be asked at the start of the interview and wouldn't take longer than 2-5 minutes. They also frequently come up in science interviews e.g. Biology, Chemistry, Material Sciences, Physics and Engineering.

Q8: If x is odd, show that x2 – 1 is divisible by 8.

$x^2 - 1 = (x - 1)(x + 1)$. If x is odd, $x - 1$ and $x + 1$ are both even. Since the difference between $x - 1$ and $x + 1 = 2$ and they are both even, one of them must be divisible by 4. Any multiple of 4 multiplied by another even number will result in a number that is divisible by 8.

Q9: If x is a prime number > 3 show that x2 – 1 is divisible by 24.

$x^2 - 1 = (x - 1)(x + 1)$. Since x has to be odd, $x^2 - 1$ must be divisible by 8 (see Q8 above). We now look at the remainder when we divide by 3, it is clear that we can't write x as $3n$, so either $x = 3n + 1$ or $x = 3n + 2$. Thus, either $x + 1$ or $x - 1$ is divisible by 3.

Q10: Can you define a prime number? Can you show every number is either prime or a product of prime numbers?

We proceed (surprisingly) by induction. We claim that every number above 1 is either prime, or is a product of primes. Suppose it is true for all m < n. Then either n is prime, in which case we are done, or there is some prime number p that divides n. So, consider n/p, which is strictly smaller than n. But then, by induction, we are done.

453

Q11: How many zeroes are there in 10? What about 100?

The number of zeroes is determined by the number of 5's, 10's, and 25's in the factorial. Thus, 5 has one zero, 10 has two zeros etc...

25 can be expressed as 5 x 5 so contributes two zeroes. Similarly, all multiples of 25 contribute two zeroes. This can be extrapolated to give:

Number	Zeros	Number	Zeros
100	2	95	1
90	1	85	1
80	1	75	2
70	1	65	1
60	1	55	1
50	2	45	1
40	1	35	1
30	1	25	2
20	1	15	1
10	1	5	1
Total	**12**	**Total**	**12**

Thus, there are 24 zeroes in total.

Q12: If I have a square of paper that is 10cm by 10cm, I cut out squares from the corners and fold up the result to form a cuboid. What is the largest cuboid by volume I can form?

Denote the length that has been cut out by a. When we fold it up, we get a cuboid of base length and width $10 - 2a$. It has height a. So the volume is $a(10 - 2a)^2$. Expand and differentiate, the volume is $4a^3 - 4a^2 + 100a$. Differentiating with respect to a, and setting equal to zero to find the maximum, we get $12a^2 - 80a + 100 = 0$, which we can factorize as $4(a - 5)(3a - 5) = 0$. $a = \frac{5}{3}$ is the solution we want, and thus the volume is $\frac{5}{3}\frac{400}{9} = \frac{2000}{27}$.

Q13: Suppose Alice, Bob and Charlie work together, digging standard-sized holes. It is assumed that Alice, Bob and Charlie do not affect each other when they work. It is known that Alice and Bob can dig a hole in 10 minutes, Bob and Charlie can dig a hole in 15 minutes, and Alice and Charlie take 20 minutes to dig a hole. How long does it take Alice, Bob and Charlie to dig a standard-sized hole?

Suppose that digging a hole involves doing 60 units of work. Alice and Bob thus work at a rate of 6 units per minute, Bob and Charlie work at a rate of 4 units per minute, and Alice and Charlie work at a rate of 3 units per minute. So, if we denote the rate of work that someone does by the first letter of their name, $A + B = 6, B + C = 4$ and $A + C = 3$. Adding all of these together and dividing by 2 gives that $A + B + C = \frac{13}{2}$. So, it takes Alice Bob and Charlie $60/(13/2) = 120/13 \approx 9$ minutes 20 seconds.

Q14: Integrate $\cos^2 x, \cos^3 x, \cos^4 x$

$2\cos^2 x - 1 = \cos(2x)$, e.g., $\cos^2 x = \frac{1}{2}(1 + \cos 2x)$. Thus, $\int \cos^2 x = \frac{1}{2}\left(x + \frac{1}{2}\sin(2x)\right) + C$. We have that $\cos^3 x = \cos^2 x \cos x = \frac{1}{2}(\cos x + \cos x \cos 2x)$. Then by the product to sum formula, $\cos x \cos 2x = \frac{1}{2}(\cos x + \cos 3x)$. Putting this in and integrating gives $\frac{1}{12}(9 \sin x + \sin 3x)$. At this point, it is quite likely that the interviewer would stop you as the principle is seemingly obvious at this point, $\int \cos^4 x \, dx = \int \frac{1}{4}(1 + \cos 2x)^2 = \frac{1}{4}\int 1 + 2\cos 2x + \cos^2(2x) \, dx$.

Expanding (again) gives $\frac{1}{4}\int (1 + 2\cos(2x) + \frac{1}{2}(1 + \cos 4x))dx$. Integrating we get $\frac{1}{32}(12x + 8\sin 2x + \sin 4x)$. There are a couple of other approaches to this question; De Moivre's theorem springs to mind, and we could also split and integrate by parts if we were looking for a general $\cos^n x$.

Q15: Integrate and differentiate x log x.

$\frac{d}{dx}(x \log x) = 1 + \log x$. For $\int x \log x \, dx$ we integrate by parts, $\int x \log x \, dx = \frac{x^2 \log x}{2} - \int \frac{x}{2} dx = \frac{x^2}{2}\left(\log x - \frac{1}{2}\right) + C$.

Q16: Integrate sin²x

The first key point to notice is that you cannot integrate this straight away and will need to manipulate sin²x in order to integrate this. A poor candidate will not notice this and will proceed to say that the answer is -1/3cos³x. When asked to differentiate this, they would hopefully realise that this is incorrect.

Knowledge of the trigonometric Identity $\sin^2 x + \cos^2 x = 1$ would be a good starting point. You could then use the double angular formula $[\cos(a + b) = \cos a \cos b - \sin a \sin b]$ as this can be used to remove cos²x.

As with all of these type of questions, it is essential that you talk through your working as much as possible. If you get stuck, then suggest formula and you might get reminded of the trigonometric identities.

Once you've identified the identities, you can then substitute back in and solve by the following:

$\int \sin^2 x \, dx = \int \frac{1}{2}1 - \cos 2x)dx$

$= \frac{1}{2}\int 1 - \cos 2x)dx$

$= \frac{1}{2}\left(x - \frac{1}{2}\sin 2x\right) + C$

$= \frac{x}{2} - \frac{1}{4}\sin 2x + C$

Whilst it is not mandatory to know how to do this straight away, the interviewer would expect you to be able to complete this once you're given the two identities.

Q17: As you may or may not know, $\sum_{i=1}^{k} i = \frac{i(i+1)}{2}$. As you may not know, $\sum_{i=1}^{k} i^2 = \frac{1}{6}i(i+1)(2i+1)$. As you may or may not know, $\sum_{i=1}^{k} i^3 = \frac{i^2(i+1)^2}{4}$. As one may guess, there is a general rule lurking here, $\sum_{i=1}^{k} i^n$ is an $n+1$ degree polynomial in k. Can you prove this?

(Hint: Consider $\sum_{i=1}^{k}[(i+1)^{n+1} - i^{n+1}]$)

We proceed by induction and use the hint. The question tells us that the answer is true in the case $n = 1$ (and 2 and 3) so we only need to show that the truth for all $n < p$ implies the truth for $n = p$. To see this $\sum_{i=1}^{k}[(i+1)^{p+1} - i^{p+1}] = (k+1)^{p+1}$, as every term apart from the last cancels identically. However, it also equals $\sum_{i=1}^{k} \sum_{j=1}^{p} \binom{p+1}{j} i^j$ (by expanding the binomial series $(i+1)^{p+1}$. If we write $S_j = \sum_{i=1}^{k} i^j$ we get that this equals $\sum_{j=1}^{p} \binom{p+1}{j} S_j = (k+1)^{p+1}$. So, $S_p = (k+1)^{p+1} - \sum_{j=1}^{p-1} \binom{p+1}{j}$. But now we're done, the right-hand side is a polynomial of degree $p+1$. This, in fact, gives an explicit expression for the polynomial, which was not required.

THE ULTIMATE OXBRIDGE INTERVIEW GUIDE

MATHEMATICS

Maths Interview Questions

1. It is estimated that 5% of the population in a country have a contagious disease, so everyone is tested. You test positive. Based on your test result, there is a 50% chance that you actually have the infection. How accurate is the test?
2. Plot $\frac{x^2}{1-x}$
3. Plot ln(xx)
4. Prove $\sqrt{3}$ is irrational
5. Find the roots of the curve $y = \sin(x^2) - x$
6. Do you have a favourite number, if so what is it?
7. Why are so many functions in maths approximated to sine and cosine?
8. Given that $y = \cos(t)$ and $x = t^{2t}$ Find $\frac{dy}{dx}$
9. $e^x = yx$. Does this curve have roots? If it does, find them.
10. Can you prove the irrationality of e?
11. Can you show us how you'd derive π?
12. Show us your proof that any integer is either prime, or can be expressed as prime factors?
13. I drove to this interview with speed, v, and will drive the same route back. How quickly would I have to drive home for my average speed over both journeys to be 2v?
14. What's the sum of all the positive integers?
15. There are 30 people in one room. What is the probability that exactly 2 of them have the same birthday?
16. Integrate ysiny with respect to x.
17. What can you tell me about... Fermat's Last Theorem?
18. Derive the equation for the volume of a sphere. ($V = \frac{4}{3}\pi r^3$)
19. Sketch the graph of $y = e^{(x^x)}$
20. Sketch the graph of $y = x^{e^e}$

COMPUTER SCIENCES

Prior to the interview stage, you will have undergone a preliminary assessment to test your aptitude; for Oxford, this assessment is the Mathematics Admissions Test (MAT) and, for Cambridge, it is the Cambridge Test of Mathematics for University Admissions (CTMUA). Upon satisfactory performance within the relevant examination, you will be invited to interviews at the respective university – the process of which can run over a few days, which will also give you time to fully explore the college you've applied to and is the perfect opportunity to make some new friends. On average, a student has three interviews at Oxford and two at Cambridge – it should be noted that you may have more than this number, which is not something to worry about as it is a sign that you're under serious consideration. Most importantly, it is often common for students to feel anxious at this stage – but it's useful to remember that, in essence, this is a conversation regarding a subject you feel passionate about. Although it may be with an expert in the field, they don't expect you to know everything or to never make a mistake.

The interviews themselves last approximately half an hour (though they can range from 20 to 50 minutes) – in this time, you may be faced with two or three people, who will chat with you to help you get comfortable. This could involve questions about your personal statement or just general questions about you. There may be paper or a whiteboard available to you during the interview – it is incredibly important that you use these resources as visualisation is key in most questions and may help show the interviewers your understanding of the concept even if you struggle to explain it verbally.

By undertaking the preliminary examinations, you will have learned the significance of mathematics in the study of Computer Science. Mathematics forms a foundation for the subject and, therefore, you must be suitably proficient in it. For this reason, it is recommended that you read the mathematics section of this collection. Your interview will mainly comprise of mathematical and logical questions, with some discussion of qualitative topics also.

The questions in the interview could involve basic ideas from school or may contain content you are unfamiliar with. They may also require you to bring together several different concepts you're familiar with in a way you haven't before. The point of the interview is to test your problem-solving skills – essentially, to see how you think – and so, it's very important that you communicate your thoughts well throughout the interview. Knowing the answer is good, but the interview is about demonstrating and explaining the process required to arrive there.

Your knowledge of **problem decomposition** into logical, computational steps will be tested and a methodical, systematic approach should be applied to every technical question – try to avoid applying the 'brute force' method to questions and look for a cleaner and more **efficient** solution.

Begin by breaking the problem down; you can **simplify** the question to something you're familiar with and then gradually work your way up to the question in hand. As long as you're explaining your steps, the interviewers will likely advise you if they see you're struggling or beginning to go astray, so don't be afraid to explain your thoughts and discuss the question openly.

A single question may contain many sub-questions within it and may even invoke a discussion – after obtaining an answer for one question, they may push you a step further and ask you to **generalise** the end result by changing the conditions outlined in the initial question. This is often just a generalisation of the process you just applied – again, break down each step and explain how you'd modify it for the new situation. This algorithmic approach demonstrates your ability to problem-solve and create/adapt algorithms for a given scenario.

Additionally, you may link certain problems to specific **algorithms** you've previously studied at school or ones you've researched. This knowledge will surely impress the tutors; especially if the algorithm is quite advanced.

There may be some standard questions towards the start to help ease you into the interview. These could be **standard mathematics** questions, for example, to **plot functions** – these will most likely be more complicated than the regular functions you've been dealing with, but there is a **simple, systematic** approach: simply evaluate the value of the function for different inputs in a table. Additionally, you can identify any asymptotes, roots or stationary points of the function to help you further. Then, simply plot the function using this information. You could also be asked to an **estimation** question – this is just a matter of accuracy and mathematical evaluation. Make sure your final answer seems reasonable physically.

The next type of question is **logical:** they want to test your deductive and reasoning ability. These questions can vary in difficulty – it could be as simple as constructing a **Boolean expression** or a **logic circuit** from a truth table, or it can be a very complicated problem which might possibly take up your entire interview. You could also be asked to decipher ciphertext (break a code) and solve visual **puzzles** – these problems are all about the identification of **patterns**.

The key to these more difficult questions is visualisation, so make sure you draw a clear diagram at the very start. Sometimes, it might not be immediately clear what the diagram should look like – to get started, you should understand the **entities** in the question and how they **interact** with one another. This can help you create a suitable diagram which clearly illustrates these relationships.

To solve the problem, take clear, logical steps and explain your reasoning; this is obviously dependent on the question itself but, generally, you must start from a fact given to you and deduce further facts from it and other information presented to you – these questions can appear difficult at first but essentially just require a **sequence of logical steps** to get to the solution. Don't make any assumptions or form conjectures in the process – every step needs to be purely derived from the previous step(s).

The last type of question is more of a **discussion** regarding a specific topic – it may begin with a question, but it will be very open-ended and will not have a simple answer. The point is to exhibit your knowledge and demonstrate your passion of the topic. This will most likely link to a topic you mentioned in your personal statement as the interviewers will assume you're comfortable with the subject and have researched it in your own time. Therefore, ensure you're **confident** with with everything you mentioned in your personal statement and remain **up-to-date** with the field.

It is very important that you're aware of recent advancements in the field of computer science as it's rapidly developing. Of course, you don't need to know everything, but you should be conscious of the progressive nature of the field and understand the effects of its rapid change on our modern world. If you don't typically feel confident discussing such topics in depth, practise often with your friends and family, or even in front of the mirror.

Additionally, you should try to get familiar with the **terminology** of the field – for example, the hardware of a computer system includes the processor, main memory (RAM), hard drive, solid state drive, etc. Being familiar with these will help make sure you can handle a wide range of questions fluidly.

THE ULTIMATE OXBRIDGE INTERVIEW GUIDE — COMPUTER SCIENCES

Worked Questions

These are a few examples of how to approach the kinds of questions that have been outlined in the previous section.

Q1: The real-valued function f(x), defined for $0 \leq x \leq 1$, has a single maximum at x = m. If $0 \leq u < v \leq m$ then f(u) < f(v), and if $m \leq u < v \leq 1$ then f(u) > f(v). You are told nothing else about f, but you may ask for the value of f(x) for any values of x you choose. How would you find the approximate value of m? How accurately could you find m if you could choose only 10 values of x for which to evaluate f(x)?

This question appears a lot more difficult than it is! The second sentence which involves the inequalities is actually just a re-statement of the first sentence; in other words, it's just telling you that before a maximum, the value of f(x) is increasing until it reaches its maximum value. After this peak, the value of f(x) begins to decrease. The u and v simply refer to two x-points and compare the function's value at these points before and after the peak.

Recommended approach:

It is clear to see from the diagram below, that before the peak, if u is smaller than v, then f(u) will be smaller than f(v). By a symmetrical argument, after the peak, if u is smaller than v, then f(u) will be bigger than f(v).

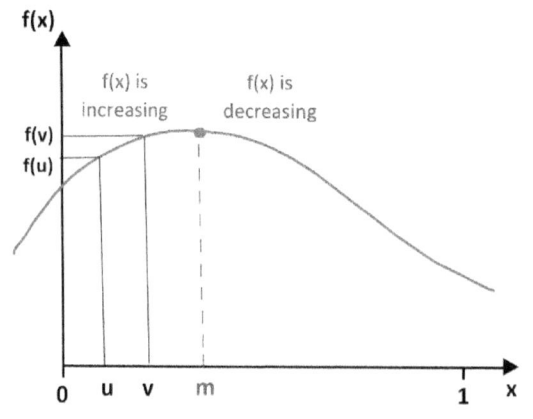

Now, the actual focus of the question is on the value of m (the x-coordinate where f(x) is a maximum). We don't know the value of m, but we do know the function's <u>behaviour</u> around m. That is the key to this question. Firstly, we know that m cannot be smaller than 0 or greater than 1, because that is the only region where f(x) is defined.

To <u>approximate</u> the value of m, we essentially need to know where the function starts to decrease. The question specifies that we can ask for the value of f(x) at any value of x we desire.

So, which value do we want to find f(x) for?

Well, guessing at random values will not be useful – in fact, finding the value of x-coordinates is only useful when we can compare it to another's value. This is where the initial inequalities become useful.

THE ULTIMATE OXBRIDGE INTERVIEW GUIDE — COMPUTER SCIENCES

By picking a u and v (where our value of u is less than our value of v), we can see whether f(u) is greater than f(v) or not. If f(u) is greater, we know that we have passed our maximum point: therefore, that u is greater than or equal to m. If f(u) is smaller, then we know that u is less than m and v is less than or equal to m.

Evidently, increasing our number of points where we evaluate f(x) <u>improves</u> our value of m as we're obtaining more information about the function's behaviour. If we know from our initial f(x) of our chosen x-value, that m is less than or equal to u, then we will keep our upper bound as u but choose another point as our lower bound.

By repeating this procedure and adjusting the bounds accordingly, we find a much smaller interval that m could be placed in. As our number of x-values increase, our interval (or bound for m) becomes smaller.

For 10 values, you can imagine that we're systematically splitting the interval into halves each time – therefore, giving us an accuracy of 1/(2^10).

Q2: An urn contains 23 white beans and 34 black beans. A monkey takes out two beans; if they are the same, he puts a black bean into the urn, and if they are different, he puts in a white bean from a large heap he has next to him. The monkey repeats this procedure until there is only one bean left. What colour is it?

This seems like a probability question but is a purely logical question – it will involve some diagrams to help simplify the situation.

Recommended Approach:

Below, I've created a diagram which illustrates every possible outcome for the situation. The monkey can either get different beans or two white/black beans – then for each case, I've specified the losses and gains for each colour afterwards.

	Different		Two Whites		Two Blacks	
White/Black	W	B	W	B	W	B
Loss	-1	-1	-2	0	0	-2
Gain	+1	0	0	+1	0	+1

From this diagram, it's clear to see that when the beans are different, there is no change in w (number of white beans) and one less of b (number of black beans).

Therefore, I obtain the following two equations:

$w = w$ and $b = b - 1$

Similarly, for when there are two white beans, I obtain the two following equations:

$$w = w - 2 \qquad\qquad b = b + 1$$

And for two black beans:

$$w = w \qquad\qquad b = b - 1$$

Now, the initial information included the number of white beans and black beans before the monkey meddled with its contents. There were 23 white beans and 34 black beans. As the initial number of white beans was <u>odd</u> and the equations for number of white beans in the bag only shift it by 2, we can conclude that the number of white beans will <u>remain odd throughout the process</u>. Therefore, it will eventually get to 1 but will not reach 0, whereas the number of black beans will eventually reach zero.

The answer then is that the white bean is the <u>last bean</u> remaining.

Q3: Alice, Bob and Charlie are well-known expert logicians; they always tell the truth.

In each of the scenarios below, Charlie writes a whole number on Alice and Bob's foreheads. The difference between the two numbers is one: either Alice's number is one larger than Bob's, or Bob's number is one larger than Alice's. Each of Alice and Bob can see the number on the other's forehead, but can't see their own number.

(i) Charlie writes a number on Alice and Bob's foreheads, and says "Each of your numbers is at least 1. The difference between the numbers is 1."

Alice then says "I know my number." Explain why Alice's number must be 2. What is Bob's number?

Recommended Approach:

The first question is quite straightforward – the number on both their foreheads must be greater than or equal to one and the difference is also one. If Alice immediately knows her number by reading Bob's number, then that means there's no ambiguity about her number – it is a definite value.

For this to be possible, there must only be one possible value for her number (at all other values, there are two possible values for her number and so she couldn't know it exactly). This occurs only at 1 – as then Alice can only have the number 2. Therefore, Bob has the number 1 on his forehead.

(ii) Charlie now writes new numbers on their foreheads, and says, "Each of your numbers is between 1 and 10 inclusive. The difference between the numbers is 1. Alice's number is a prime."

Alice then says, "I don't know my number." Bob then says, "I don't know my number." What is Alice's number? Explain your answer.

A prime number is a number greater than 1 that is divisible only by 1 and itself. Therefore, the only prime numbers between 1 and 10 inclusive are 2, 3, 5 and 7 as these satisfy the condition for a prime number. The difference between both of their numbers is again one. That means Alice's number is either ahead or behind Bob's number by one.

We can construct a table to help visualise this information, as shown on the right. Alice says she doesn't know her number, therefore, she doesn't have an exact value for her number. Similarly, for Bob, the number doesn't have an exact value. This immediately rules out 1, 2, 3 and 8 for Alice and 3, 7 for Bob. Therefore, only one possibility is left – Alice must have the number 5.

B	A
1/3	2
2	3
4	3/5
6	5/7
7	7

(iii) Charlie now writes new numbers on their foreheads, and says "Each of your numbers is between 1 and 10 inclusive. The difference between the numbers is 1."

Alice then says "I don't know my number. Is my number a square number?" Charlie then says "If I told you that, you would know your number." Bob then says "I don't know my number." What is Alice's number? Explain your answer.

Alice initially says she doesn't know her number, therefore, Bob cannot have 1 or 10 and, consequently, Alice cannot have 2 or 9. The only possible square numbers for Alice between 1 and 10 inclusive are 1 and 4 (as we just ruled out the possibility for 9).

If Charles told Alice that her number is a square number, then she would know which number she has. But Bob would not know his number. This is only possible when Alice has the number 4 as if she had the number 1, Bob would immediately know that he has the number 2. Because Alice has 4, Bob could have 5 or 6 and is therefore not sure of his exact number.

We could have equally achieved this result by drawing the diagram on the right. We know Bob's number cannot be 1 or 10, as we discussed previously. Because of Charlie's statement, it is inferred that that Alice's number (Bob's number plus or minus one) is a square number. The possibilities are listed in the diagram. If Alice had the numbers 1, 3, 2, 6, 7 or 9, then Bob would have immediately known his number. Therefore, Alice's number must be 4.

B	A
2	1/3
3	2/4
5	4/6
8	7/9

Q4: Prime factor decomposition: can you write a pseudocode algorithm that, given a number as an input, outputs its prime factors?

You may not be familiar with the term 'pseudocode' – however, you do not need any programming experience in order to answer this question. Pseudocode is essentially the steps of an algorithm; you do not need to write it exactly as you'd input it into a computer. It's just supposed to demonstrate the logical steps of the solution. The only operator you will need for this question that you may not be aware of is 'MOD' which give you the remainder when you divide by a number. For example, 6 mod 4 is 2 because 6/4 is 1 with a remainder of 2.

Recommended Approach:

The first is problem decomposition. We've been doing prime factor decomposition since we were young, but what are the actual specific steps we use to do this? This is very important for any algorithmic problem; you have to be clear of all the steps involved in the process.

For prime factor decomposition, we try to break down the input into a product of another two integers to reduce the problem. We then repeat this process until we cannot reduce the numbers any further (they are therefore primes as they do not have any other factors – other than 1 and themselves). There is an example of this process on the right – the input is 42 in this case.

```
    42
   /  \
  2    21
      /  \
     3    7
```

THE ULTIMATE OXBRIDGE INTERVIEW GUIDE — COMPUTER SCIENCES

So, how do we write this process as a series of steps? Well, it is quite easy to write is as 'instructions' for someone or a computer to follow – you just have do what we did above but be more specific in your instructions. Write each step in more detail and describe it fully without making any assumptions of knowledge of the follower.

Steps for prime factor decomposition:

- If the number is even, then keep dividing by 2 until it is no longer divisible by 2. The number of times you could can divide by 2 is how many factors of 2 the number has.
- Now we can divide by each odd number from 3 (as 1 does not count) up to the square root of the number (as this is the biggest that the factor can be).
- If the remainder of this division is zero, it is a prime factor of the number.

To turn this into pseudocode, we need be even more specific with these steps – but, now, we have to apply control loop structures and variable names to make the process more systematic and organised. The pseudocode is not very different to the actual code although it's independent of a programming language. Your pseudocode should be clear enough for a computer to follow it – it needs to be well-defined and thorough.

So, converting our qualitative steps into pseudocode will look like the following – note N is our input number and X is our control variable.

Q5: You are given 10 boxes, each large enough to contain exactly 10 wooden building blocks, and a total of 100 blocks in 10 different colours. There may not be the same number in each colour, so you may not be able to pack the blocks into the boxes in such a way that each box contains blocks of only one colour. Show that it is possible to do it so that each box contains at most two different colours.

```
INPUT N

WHILE N MOD 2 IS 0

    OUTPUT 2 (AND A SPACE)

    N = N/2

END WHILE


FOR X FROM 3 TO SQRT(N) IN STEPS OF 2
```

As with all problems, the first step is visualisation! Read the question carefully and create an accurate image in your head based on the description given.

Recommended Approach:

You've been told you have 10 boxes and 100 blocks – these blocks can come in one of 10 possible shades. If there were 10 of each colour, it would've been easy! Each colour would've been in its own box. The slight difficulty is that they 'may not be the same number'.

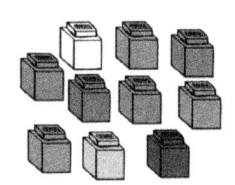

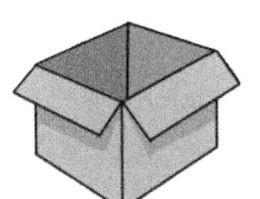

Well, you know the <u>average</u> number of blocks of each colour is 10 as there are 100 in total and 10 possible colours (100/10=10). In reality, some colours may be more popular (above average, so more than 10 blocks) or less popular (below average, so fewer than 10 blocks). We can use this idea to answer the question!

We want to show that it's possible to organise the blocks so that each box contains two different colours at most. Well, we know that every colour has around 10 blocks; the ones which have 10 exactly can go into their own boxes because we want to show that each box contains at most two different colours – this means that one colour is fine too!

So, we've gotten rid of all colours that have the exact average number of blocks. Now, the remaining colours have either above or below the average number of blocks.

If we begin by putting a colour which has less than the average number of blocks into a box, then we'll have some space for more blocks. Therefore, we can put in a colour with more than the average number of blocks to fill in the rest of this box and fill some of the next box.

By <u>repeating this process</u> (pairing less than average colours with more than average colours), we get rid of the colours one at a time whilst still only having, at most, two colours in each box. This works because we know that the total number of blocks sums to 100. Therefore, the additional amounts of blocks in some colours equals the loss in other colours.

Now we have the solution! It is possible for each box to contain at most two different colours. Some boxes will have a single colour (if they have 10 blocks exactly or if they have more than 10 blocks). Others will have a combination of two different colours (when we pair a less than average colour with a more than average colour).

Q6: Eleven lily pads are numbered from 0 to 10. A frog starts on pad 0 and wants to get to pad 10. At each jump, the frog can move forward by one or two pads, so there are many ways it can get to pad 10.

How many different ways are there of getting from 0 to 10?

Recommended Approach:

For example, it can make 10 jumps of one pad, 1111111111, or five jumps of two pads, 22222, or go 221212 or 221122, and so on. We'll call each of these ways different, even if the frog takes the same jumps in a different order. As always, a systematic approach is best – however, instead of attempting the brute force method, it's more effective to simply look at the problem as a whole and generalise the circumstances. In this example, we could simply try listing all the possible combinations that we can think of – however, you will most likely make a mistake or miss a solution which is not the point of these questions. The solution should be complete and thorough.

To achieve this, let's simplify the situation. Imagine there was just a single lily pad – in that case, there would evidently be just one way to get to it. If we generalise this to 'n' lily pads, then the number of ways of getting to it is going to be obtained by adding together the number of ways of getting to the (n-1) pad and the (n-2) pad. This is because we made our initial jump and then travelled down n-1 more pads, or equally, we jumped onto the second pad and travelled down n-2 more pads.

To summarise, the number of different ways (W) to get to the nth pad is given by:

$$W(n) = W(n-1) + W(n-2)$$

This is actually the definition of the Fibonacci sequence – a sequence which often comes up in patterns found in nature – and is given by: 1, 1, 2, 3, 5, ... It is clear that the nth term is the sum of the previous two terms.

Extension:

- What if the frog wasn't restricted to jumps of only one or two lily pads? What if it could jump up to m lily pads with every leap? How would that affect the result?

Well, it actually leads to a further generalisation of the sequence – it is called the m-step Fibonacci sequence. I've provided the list below up to five as the general trend is quite easy to see. As m (the number of lily pads the frog can leap to at once) varies, the series begins to diverge more quickly, which should be expected as there are more possible ways for the frog to get to every lily pad further down the pond.

m	Name of the sequence	Sequence
2	Fibonacci	1, 1, 2, 3, 5, 8, 13, 21...
3	Tribonacci	1, 1, 2, 4, 7, 13, 24...
4	Tetranacci	1, 1, 2, 4, 8, 15, 29...
5	Pentanacci	1, 1, 2, 4, 8, 16, 31...
m	Name of the sequence	Sequence

In standard summation notation, this result is written as:

$$W_m(n) = \sum_{i=\max(0,n-m)}^{n-1} W_m(i)$$

This is essentially the formulation for an m-step Fibonacci sequence, as explained above. The equation is simply saying that for m possible jumps we need to sum up from the (n-m)th pad. It is just an extension of our simple case with one or two jumps.

Q7: Imagine you are given a list of slightly less than 1,000,000 numbers, all different, and each between 0 and 999,999 inclusive. How could you find (in a reasonable time) a number between 0 and 999,999 that is not on the list?

There is more than one way to answer this question. Below, I'll outline two possible methods.

Recommended Approach:

The question is greatly simplified if the list is already ordered (increasing, decreasing, etc). If not, we shall form an ordered list out of the data. Now, by looking through the list or by programming a computer to do so, you can compare each element of that list and spot missing numbers. This means you'll have to go through every single element in the list to ensure your check has been thorough and you haven't missed out values.

In every case, you'd have to go through every value. Thus, this algorithm has linear time-complexity $O(n)$.

Suppose we half the ordered list into two separate lists, right from the middle value of the list. Now, our new lists comprise of 0-499,999 and 500,000-999,999. If either list is full (has 500,000 elements within the list data structure), then clearly no numbers are missing in that interval.

For whichever list that has less than the full number of elements, we keep halving the list to create two new lists. We again check the size of both lists and split the list with less than the full number of elements. If more than one sub-list has this property, then we can split it also, separately.

By repeating this procedure, you eventually obtain a list with only two elements, in which a third element is missing. By observing the two numbers, you can immediately note the missing number between then. You can do this for all the lists you've decomposed in this way and, therefore, you'll obtain the full set of missing numbers from the original list. So, essentially, you break down the lists until you isolate the missing numbers.

The time complexity of this algorithm is given by $O(n \log n)$. It is not $O(\log n)$, which is the time complexity of a regular binary search algorithm, as you must implement the binary search on n lists simultaneously – because we may have more than one missing value, we must have more than one list. Therefore, the time-complexity is multiplied by n.

We haven't checked through every element in the list. We've broken it down into chunks, by halving it repeatedly, to identify which intervals contain the missing numbers. This means we didn't have to waste our time going through the elements that we already knew didn't include the missing values. So it would seem that we've improved on our previous time-complexity.

However, when we plot both time- complexities, we find that the first algorithm (shown in red) performs less operations on a given number of elements in the list than the second algorithm. This means it ore time-efficient than the second algorithm.

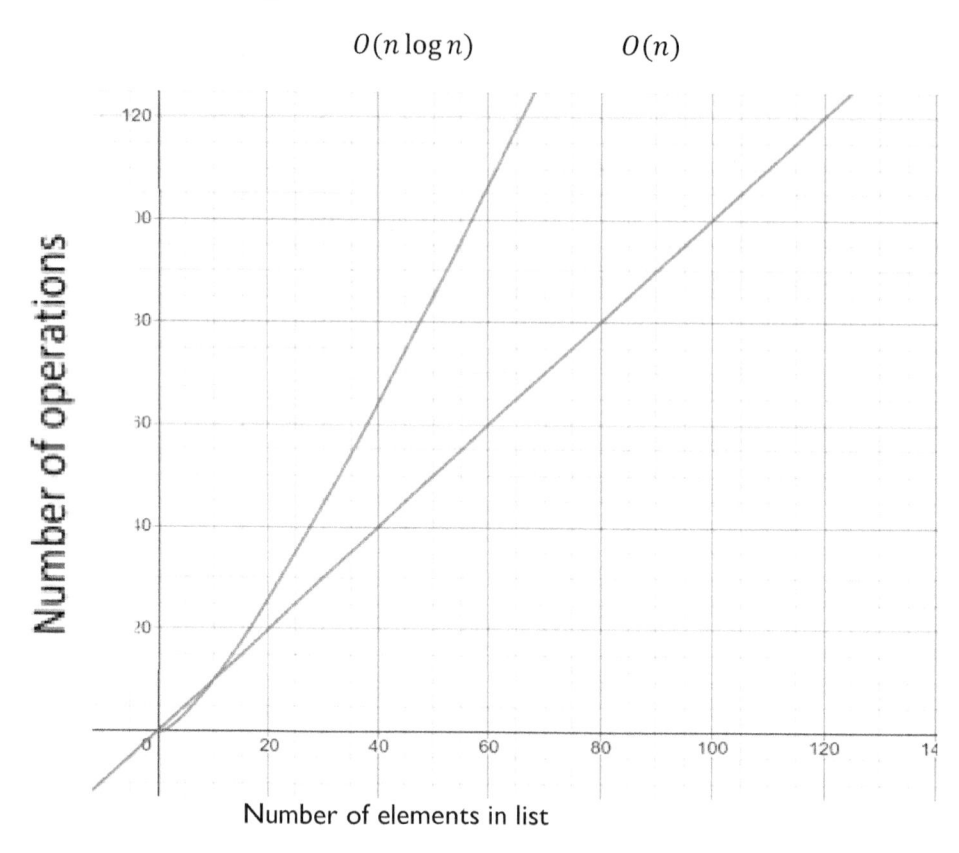

$O(n \log n)$ $O(n)$

(Graph: Number of operations vs Number of elements in list)

Q8: You are locked in a room with your worst enemy. On a table in the centre of the room is a bar of chocolate, divided into squares in the usual way. One square of the chocolate is painted with a bright green paint that contains a deadly poison. You and your enemy take it in turns to break off one or more squares from the remaining chocolate (along a straight line) and eat them. Whoever is left with the green square must eat it and die in agony. You may look at the bar of chocolate and then decide whether to go first or second. Describe your strategy.

This question is very easy to visualise, (I've chosen the standard 6 by 4 chocolate bar as an example) – and the scenario, although unrealistic, is quite simple conceptually. In this situation, going first or second could result in life or death; so it's very important for us to understand how that could affect us and develop a strategy accordingly.

THE ULTIMATE OXBRIDGE INTERVIEW GUIDE — COMPUTER SCIENCES

Recommended Approach:

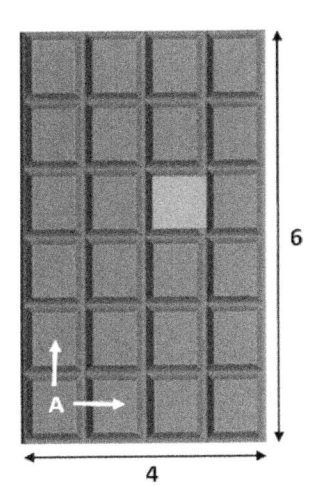

Now, there's only two people involved – you and the enemy – so either you go first or they go first. This restricts the other player's move as you can only break off the squares in a straight line. So, let's imagine we start: by breaking off an edge piece at A, the opponent can choose to head upwards or to the right. After this, the pattern is very easy to distinguish – no matter which side either of you decide to break off from, the opponent will definitely break off the last piece from the perimeter of the outer box of chocolate squares. This is because there are an even number of chocolate squares (16) and 2 players. So, after 8 turns (16/2), the entire outer edge will have been eaten.

Now, we've reduced the problem to a smaller block of dimensions 4 by 2. So, who gets to break off the block first? Well, it must be you because you started and there's been an even number of blocks since. It's obvious from the diagram that there are 8 pieces of chocolate left – this is an even number, which means your opponent will get the last piece (which will hopefully be the green piece so long as you don't choose it). So, all you have to do is pick any piece other than the green for four turns and then you've won!

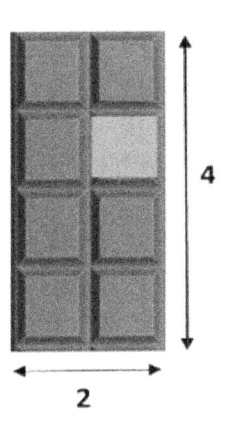

Extension:

- What if the opponent had started instead?

Well, in that case, we would've had the last piece on the outside perimeter and, consequently, for the smaller block, we'd get the green piece as our final piece. Therefore, to win, it is crucial that you start first.

- More generally, if we had an a by b chocolate bar, how would this affect the result?

If a*b was even, then our result wouldn't change (only the number of turns would change). If a*b was odd, then it depends on the number of 'outer perimeters' we have. If there's just one, then the person who started also ends that outer box, meaning the other player begins the next box.

If this inversion happens an even amount of times before the final block, then the first player will break off the first piece of the final block and, therefore, win the game. Otherwise, the opponent will win.

Q9: What is the Fetch-Decode-Execute cycle? Which factors affect the execution of this cycle and, consequently, the performance of the computer?

This is a question testing knowledge or discursive topics – you should make sure you are comfortable with these types of questions as they can come up quite often.

Recommended Approach:

The Fetch-Decode-Execute cycle is quite clear from its name: the central processing unit (CPU) of all computer systems follows this cycle constantly. The CPU fetches data and instructions from some form of main memory, such as cache memory or random-access memory (RAM). It then decodes the instruction and executes it on the data.

The data and results from the execution are stored temporarily in dedicated registers within the CPU. The instructions which can be executed by a CPU forms an important set called the instruction set of the processor.

From this information, we can consider which factors affect how quickly and effectively this cycle is undergone by the processor. As this is the CPU of the computer system which is in charge of all operations, the speed at which it completes the cycle governs how quickly the computer system can process.

Firstly, the form of main memory matters – cache memory is located very close to the CPU and is therefore easier to fetch data from than the RAM. So, increased cache memory would help.

Secondly, the data is transferred via buses – there is the address, data and control bus – and the amount they can store can affect the performance of the computer greatly. If, for every execution of the cycle, more data can be fetched, then less cycles are needed for the same amount of processing.

Increasing the number of cores is also beneficial as more of the cycles can be executed simultaneously.

To summarise, these are some of the factors affect the performance of a computer system:

Number of cores

- Using faster forms of memory, such as cache memory
- Size of the buses
- Size of the instruction set of the CPU

Q10: Binary search - can you create a flowchart demonstrating how a name can be found from a list of names using a binary search?

For the interviews, you should be quite comfortable with the common searching algorithms and their principles of operation. Writing their algorithms and creating equivalent flowcharts can be good practise to ensure you understand how they work.

Recommended Approach:

Firstly, you need to understand how a binary search works.

A list of any data type can be inputted – in this example, it is names which are strings of characters. To order this data type, the computer compares the names alphabetically where a has a lower index than z.

Below, there is an example of an ordered list of names and beneath them are their indexes. Note that index can begin at 0 or 1.

Bob	Chris	Hailey	Lee	Mariam
1	2	3	4	5

Let's say we were searching we were searching to see if 'Lee' was in the list. Clearly, we can see that it is – so let's see how the binary search confirms this.

You begin by halving the list to get to the element in the middle (black arrow) of the list, which is 'Hailey' in this case. Is Lee greater than or less than Hailey? Well, L is after H in the alphabet so Lee is indeed greater than Hailey.

Therefore, looking at the sub-list on the right of Hailey, we again half it and find the element in the middle (asterisk) – which is 'Lee' in this case. By comparison, we can confirm that Lee is in the list and has an index of 4.

If we had searched for 'Daniel', then we would've got to Hailey initially, and looked to the sub-list on the left as Daniel comes before Hailey in the alphabet. Then, by comparing with Chris, we would know Daniel must be to the right of Chris and to left of Hailey. No such element exists – therefore, Daniel is not in the list.

To create a flowchart, you must understand what the varying shapes represent; a parallelogram represents input and output, a rectangle represents a calculation and a diamond represents a decision.

So, firstly, let's write the algorithm in simple steps – although you may not need to undergo this step, it can help to clarify the process and make it easier to create your flowchart:

- Add the start index and end index, then divide this by two. This is the index of the middle name of the list.
- If the name is equal to the desired name, we can stop here.
- Otherwise, compare middle element to the desired name – if greater, repeat entire process for the sub-list on the right side of the middle element. If less, do it for the left side.

THE ULTIMATE OXBRIDGE INTERVIEW GUIDE — COMPUTER SCIENCES

COMPUTER SCIENCE INTERVIEW QUESTIONS

1. What factors might impose limits on the storage capacity of a computer?
2. Sketch the following function over the domain $-\pi \leq x \leq \pi$:
3. What was the first computer, and why?
4. In a game of Allamaraine, tiles are numbered 1-9. In turn, you and a second player remove a tile and add it to your collection. The one to obtain tiles summing 15 wins, do you play first or second?
5. Can AI produce art?
6. Construct a truth-table and logic circuit for the following Boolean output. Demonstrate how the expression can be reduced.
7. Jack needs to divide 10 red marbles and 10 blue marbles into two boxes in a way such that the probability of picking the red marble is maximized. How can he do this?
8. What is big data? How can we store and analyse such data?
9. What is the greatest possible value of the following function? $f(x) = (4\sin^2(2x+11) - 3)^2$.
10. You have a 7-litre jug and a 3-litre jug. How would you measure out 5 litres exactly?
11. Explain how a calculator evaluates a mathematical expression that is inputted by a user. Can you write the pseudocode for the algorithm?
12. Can machine learning predict the lottery?
13. What do we mean by flash memory? How does this form of memory work?
14. Imagine a unit sphere. If you randomly chose four points which lie on the sphere, what is the probability that the centre of the sphere lies within the tetrahedron formed by those points?
15. If you're offered a stack of pennies as tall as the Eiffel Tower, would you be able to fit them in a normal-sized room?
16. Sketch the following function over the domain $-4 \leq x \leq 4$: $f(x) = \frac{x^2+5x+3}{x^4}$.
17. How do you think technology will evolve over the next century given the trends in the past century? Why do you think this?
18. You have 10 boxes that contains balls with each of the ball weighing exactly 10 grams; one of the boxes has defective balls weighing 9 grams each. You have a scale to measure the weight but it is only single-use. Can you determine which box contains the defective balls?
19. Complete the following sequence: 1, 11, 21, 1211, 111221, __?
20. To what extent do you agree with the statement that humans are biological machines? Is our DNA equivalent to code? Justify your opinion on this.
21. Can you work out how many times the hour and minute hands of a clock overlap in a single day?
22. How many solutions does the following equation have given that $0 \leq x \leq 2\pi$ and n is an integer greater than equal to 1? $\cos^n(x) + \cos^{2n}(x) = 0$
23. There are three ladybirds sitting on the corners of an equilateral triangle. Each of the ladybirds chooses a random direction and begins crawling along that edge of the equilateral triangle. What is the probability that none of the ladybirds end up crashing into each other?
24. Explain how a transistor works. Why is this important for computer systems?
25. Ali, Yen and Molly run at constant speeds and are having a race over a hundred metres. Yen beats Molly by twenty metres and Ali beats Yen by 20 metres. How many metres does Ali beat Molly by?

THE ULTIMATE OXBRIDGE INTERVIEW GUIDE

COMPUTER SCIENCES

26. How many real solutions does the following equation have? $8^x + 4 = 4^x + 2^{x+2}$
27. How many squares are on an eight-by-eight chess board?
28. Can you explain how sounds are digitally stored and played back on your devices? What makes audio sound more realistic to us?
29. Four people must cross a bridge - unfortunately, they have only one torch to see and the bridge is too dangerous to cross without one. The bridge is only strong enough to support two people simultaneously. Each person can cross the bridge in 2 min, 4 mins, 9 mins and 14 mins for each person respectively. What is the shortest time needed for all four of them to cross the bridge?
30. For which values of x is the following inequality satisfied? $x^4 < 8x^2 + 9$
31. How would you attempt to decrypt a foreign ciphertext? What would be your strategy? Why is this your chosen strategy?
32. Could quantum computing be a reality in the near future?
33. Sketch the following function over the domain $-2\pi \leq x \leq 2\pi$: $f(x) = (\tan x)x$
34. A four-centimetre cube of metal is covered with white paint on all six sides. Then the cube is cut into smaller one-centimetre cubes; the new one-centimetre cubes have either three white sides, two white sides, one white side, or no white sides. How many of each will there be?
35. What are the different forms of memory? How are they used in the construction of computer systems and what are their uses?
36. How many distinct solutions are there to the following equation? $\log_{x2+2}(4 - 5x^2 - 6x^3) = 2$
37. Why do computer systems work in binary? Is it possible for them to work in another base, such as hexadecimal? Would this be beneficial?
38. Could a machine be capable of independent thought?
39. The four digit number 2652 has the special property that any two consecutive digits from it make a multiple of 13. Another number N shares this property – it starts with a 9 and is 100 digits long. What is the last digit of N?
40. What's the fastest way to transfer data between networks? What method does the Internet use? Do you think this is efficient?

THE ARTS

ECONOMICS

This interview will require you to demonstrate passion and a genuine desire to study your chosen subject. You can be asked to discuss a source extract, a diagram or a mathematical problem.

In E&M interviews, business-related questions will also feature, where applicants have to tackle basic problems related to the operation and management of a firm.

An economist may be asked economics-related questions or questions from a related subject, such as mathematics, business or even politics and history. An applicant for Economics and Management will be asked questions on both economics and business/management. (The **interviewers understand applicants may not have studied economics** before – be prepared to explain why you think you want to study economics and show through extra-curricular reading or activities how you've fostered your interest). Before the interview, it should be clear which subject will be the focus of any interview.

Candidates are not expected to have studied the subject they are applying for previously at A-level. Instead, candidates should have good general knowledge and to demonstrate interest in and enthusiasm for studying economics (and business in the case of E&M applicants), to demonstrate logic and critical thinking, and to communicate clearly and effectively.

Many of the questions asked in the interview will be a larger question, with many smaller sub-questions to guide the answer from the start to a conclusion. The main question may seem difficult, impossible or random at first, but take a breath and start discussing with your interviewer different ideas you have for breaking down the question into manageable pieces. Don't panic. **The questions are designed to be difficult** to give you the chance to show your full intellectual potential. They will help guide you to the right idea if you provide ideas for them to guide.

This is your chance to show your creativity, analytical skills, intellectual flexibility, problem-solving skills, and your go-getter attitude. Don't waste it on nervousness or a fear of messing up or looking stupid.

For economics, the questions will usually take one of a few possible forms based on highlighting skills necessary to 'think like an economist'. The six main question types are:

- Critical reasoning questions ("Tell me what your view on ... is").
- Normative questions ("Should the government do the following?").
- Practical questions ("How would you determine that...").
- Statistical questions ("Given this data...").
- Questions about proximate causes (mechanism; "How does...") and MultiMate causes (function; "Why does..."), usually both at once.
- Quantitative questions for example from game theory or economic principles.

The questions also have recurring themes because they are also prevalent topics for economic and management theory and research: markets, money, development economics, profit maximisation of a firm, game theory, unemployment and inflation, growth theory and international trade.

Worked Questions

Below are a few examples of how to start breaking down an interview question along with model answers.

Q1: I'm going to give you £50. You have to offer some of it to another person, but you won't get to keep a penny unless they accept the offer, with that in mind, how much of your £50 would you offer to them?

This is a mathematical question that will, therefore, require a numeric answer. The most important feature of a strong candidate is the ability to answer the question directly and from an analytical point of view the interviewer set through the phrasing of the question.

Applicant: So, I'm looking for a nominal value between 0 and £50 to be offered to the other person. This seems to be a question related to the field of game theory; the area that focuses on understanding optimal strategic decisions and their modelling. Unfortunately, I'm not familiar with the tools of this discipline but I will try to tackle the question using my basic economic intuition and mathematics. I understand that economics primarily deals with incentives, and here the two participants have very different incentives. Let me consider both of them and then outline who will get their way or what kind of a compromise they will reach. Both me and the other person want to get as much money as possible, but we both can't get the £50, **there is a trade-off**.

We also have different ways of achieving our aims: I set the amount, the other person decides whether to accept or not. The other person can stop me from having any money whatsoever; this seems to be a strong tool against me. So I will have to make the other person happy otherwise we will both walk away without anything. Given this, how can I get the best outcome for myself while navigating through my dual objective: getting money, but satisfying the other one? I have to give the person something, even though I don't want to.

Anything I give should make the other happy since the alternative is 0. Therefore, mathematically, I should probably offer the least amount: £1. But would that be acceptable? At this point, I could consider other, alternative methods to understanding cooperation that can better deal with phenomena like envy, fairness, altruism, etc.

Assessment: The student immediately sets the context and frame of the question, which suggests a very strong candidate who is not trying different things but knows the direction of the answer. Identifying the relevant area in Economics for the question is a nice touch that doesn't require extensive prior knowledge of that particular field, but still shows that the student has a general understanding of what belongs to the subject.

The interviewers don't expect you to be an expert in a niche field. Instead, they want you to apply your existing knowledge and experience to a new problem.

A good candidate will always **draw from multiple disciplines** and apply the seemingly most relevant knowledge they have. Structuring the answer is always key, most importantly, to make it easier for the interviewer to help with the solution. If they know what the plan of attack is, they can guide the applicant in the direction that leads to the correct answer most easily. An outstanding candidate goes beyond conventional wisdom and demonstrates real outside-the-box thinking by having the ability to challenge seemingly fundamental assumptions. In this particular example, the candidate could point out that there are many people to whom getting the highest amount of monetary gain might not be a primary goal, hence making the simple mathematical analysis problematic.

Q2: You've mentioned globalisation in your personal statement, how would you define it, and what would you say the benefits of it might be to ordinary people?

The main challenge in this question is clearly the broadness of the topic. This is a subject hundreds of academics and other pundits have written hefty books on. How does one answer this question in 2-3 minutes so the response has sufficient content but is still structured?

The important thing to keep in mind here is that sometimes the applicant's first response serves only as a discussion starter. There is no need to include everything you would want to talk about in excruciating details, the interviewers only want to hear a few points they can start from. Then they will drive the discussion in a direction they want to.

Applicant: Let me start by clarifying the concept of globalisation. It's a household concept by now, but I'm not sure we have a universal agreement on what is meant by it. To me, globalisation is the process through which national and regional borders become increasingly irrelevant, as a result of culture, business and general economic activity all become more homogeneous and are formed by actors unrelated to any single country. This definition allows me to capture the different aspects of globalisation each of which requires a different analytical perspective: sociology, economics, politics, international relations, etc.

From an economics point of view, **the average citizen gains in two main ways from globalisation**. First, the citizen benefits from the diversification of products and services available for consumption at lower prices. Second, the broadening of opportunities allows citizens to have a better match between their skills and their occupation.

I will first consider the benefits of free trade. The emergence of transnational corporations and wider political movements supporting globalisation have put increasing pressure on governments to allow for greater freedom in international trade. This has resulted in an unprecedented expansion of consumption goods and services available for all customers. Just think about all the exotic fruits, spices, and craft goods one can buy even in their local Tesco. International competition, another benefit of globalisation, has furthermore allowed all goods to be priced competitively on a global scale, leading to significant price drops. This process clearly benefits the average citizen.

My second point relates to the tendency that globalisation comes with the **expansion of cross-border mobility** too. This happens for a range of reasons: better and more easily available information about opportunities abroad, the internationalisation of communication (English as lingua franca) and the transnational HR procedures and multinational corporations. The average citizen benefits from being able to find a position more ideally suited for them than before globalisation had emerged.

Having said that, I believe it's important to note the likely negative consequences of globalisation too: the threat of dumping in developed countries, the threat of exploitation in developing countries or diminishing cultural diversity are just a few on the list.

Assessment: The interviewers most likely have already interrupted the interviewee by this time somewhere. They might be interested in a discussion on free trade, the applicant's thoughts on multinational corporations, etc. But by presenting a clearly outlined structure in the beginning, the applicant ensured that the interviewers know that a strong and well-argued presentation would follow had they not interrupted. It is also advisable with such a complex question to take some time before starting the answer, this allows any applicant to articulate any thoughts in a more organised manner. A focus on the economic arguments is also important as this is an economics and not a sociology interview, and the points, therefore, need to be chosen accordingly.

Q3: I'm going to show you a teapot. Feel free to examine it in as much detail as you'd like - once you've done that, tell me about whether you could value it.

An odd question that clearly is not interested in specific knowledge, but rather pushing the applicant way out of their comfort zone. A question like this can easily appear on both an Economics and a Management interview as it requires out-of-the-box thinking and independence to solve challenging, unfamiliar problems, crucial in both fields. Each student would answer this question differently; the only important point is to show confidence and originality in an answer.

Straight Economics Applicant:

I can certainly look for a suitable price for this teapot from my perspective. However, the valuation different individuals assign to the same product often vary significantly and also with changing circumstances too. Therefore, my monetary valuation is not going to be a universal one.

I would start by stating that the monetary value of the teapot will fundamentally be linked to the concept of a market. I am not looking for the intrinsic value (i.e. the 'usefulness' of the teapot) but the ideal monetary amount it should be exchanged for. Thus I turn to the basic knowledge I have about the market and try to understand how those will determine the optimal exchange price of the teapot. There are two key factors on a market: supply and demand. I will consider both of them in relation to our example.

I know that if goods are supplied widely, its prices or monetary value will be lower than of goods in limited supply. Consider the example of water vs. diamonds. It's not that diamonds are more 'useful' than water, but that they are only available in a very limited amount; hence their supply is constrained. Whereas, water is essential for life but is abundant in supply. Consequently, diamonds have a much larger monetary value than water. In our case, a teapot can probably be bought in any large department store, however, its cracks and tea marks on its side make it unique. Therefore, one could argue that the supply of this teapot is extremely limited, indicating a high monetary price.

Equally, demand for the teapot is also probably fairly limited. While these qualities are visually pleasing, it is probably fair to assume that there aren't many who could appreciate its artistic beauty. Modest demand suggests a low monetary value, as people would not be willing to pay much for the item. This **concept of willingness-to-pay** is a central one for our analysis, and we would have to conduct a more thorough investigation into the existing demand for an artistically cracked teapot.

The two sides (supply and demand) put together suggest that **this teapot should be valued similarly to other niche products** with both small demand and supply. Such products include pieces of art, rarities or unique luxury products (e.g. custom made sports cars or watches).

Assessment: This is an economist's take on the question who tries to analyse the problem with the tools provided by the discipline. The question provides a great opportunity to enter a discussion on markets and prices, complemented by a basic summary of the forces present on a market. With such a question, a specific, numeric answer is not necessarily required as the process of understanding the determinants of prices is much more important. A clear outline, clarification of definitions and real life examples all add to the answer and the image communicated to the interviewers. But once again, many alternative answers could be presented here. The important point is that the applicant shouldn't feel intimidated by a seemingly unrealistic and unsolvable question.

Finally, if the starting point of the question is already ridiculous, then the applicant is free to make unrealistic assumptions too, as long as those can be defended somehow (e.g. the artistic cracks on the teapot add extra monetary value to it).

Economics and Management Applicant:

From a firm's perspective, it is crucial to understand the underlying processes that determine the monetary value of a product. In our situation, the monetary value is equivalent to finding the price of the teapot. I am going to consider three methods to establish that value:

- Pricing based on competition
- Pricing based on cost
- Psychological pricing

The first method seems to be the most obvious to me as it simply builds on the competitive tendencies in a market. This would require us to look at any other seller of similar teapots and record their prices. Afterwards, we simply have to decide if we want to undercut them or simply price it according to their set monetary valuations. Online retailers and, in this particular case, used goods' resellers can both provide a starting point.

Secondly, I could simply figure out how much it costs me to produce it if I'm a decision-maker in the company involved in the creation of the product. Then I would add some profit margin on my costs and that would give me the monetary valuation of the teapot. The **production costs,** in this case, could include raw materials (porcelain, paint, etc.), labour costs, electricity, rent for the workplace and so on. A profit margin is required to make it worthwhile running the business and provide a payout to the company's owners.

Finally, I have read about behavioural economics before, for example in the book *Freakonomics* or in *Predictably Irrational*. These books showed me how psychological factors play a crucial role in our perceptions of prices. The idea about the **relativity of prices explains the lack of a fundamental link between products and their monetary value**.

Therefore, the **prices of this teapot could be anything in a wide range,** depending on the psychological connections I create, through procedures such as *anchoring*.

Assessment: The student always has to tailor the answer to the subject of the interview. One of the most important requirements of an interview is to show that the applicant is capable of analysing problems from the perspective of the given discipline. Thus, in this case, the student had to demonstrate the ability to consider the firm's view, collecting thoughts around basic concepts that an applicant might be familiar with: costs, competition, etc. The brightest candidates shine through their ability to complement the basic materials with extra reading and real-life examples.

Q4: Considering recent events, do you think that the creation of the Eurozone was a good idea?

A good response: "For me, the main objectives of the Eurozone were to improve trade between European nations and to provide more economic stability for those nations involved. I think the European Union has been successful in the first of these goals, however, when addressing the latter, it is clear that the last two decades have been rather turbulent for all Eurozone countries, especially considering the issues with the COVID-19 vaccine rollout. Proponents of the Euro may argue that weak nations such as Greece would never have survived the economic crisis of 2008 without the presence of the Eurozone, but others may argue that a lack of control over individual countries' monetary policy contributed to the severity of the recession. One interesting aspect of the Eurozone process is that it has highlighted the high geographical mobility of labour in many European nations…"

Assessment: This is an extremely open-ended question, which provides the candidate with the opportunity to talk about a multitude of topics and issues. It is easy to get side-tracked with such an unstructured question, but the applicant should make sure they answer the question. However, there is potential for them to talk about areas that interest them, and display their enthusiasm for the subject in doing so.

Candidates should, however, be wary about trying to suggest they have substantial knowledge of areas that they don't, in reality, know much about.

This question may be followed up with further questioning by the interviewer on more specific aspects of the questions, and the least helpful thing a candidate can do when trying to impress a tutor is try to falsify knowledge of certain topics and then get 'caught out' doing so.

It is worth bearing in mind that not only is the tutor looking for intelligence; **they are looking for someone that they are happy to teach for the next few years**. Personality can be a factor in determining their decision: arrogance or attempting to deceive a tutor may not be looked upon fondly.

Q5: What would you say if someone used the fact that people who went through higher education get higher wages to argue that going to uni makes you rich?

This question invites the applicant to address a situation closest to what an economist is qualified for. Take a dataset and form a hypothesis. Then test the hypothesis using the dataset to form a conclusion and thus, provide policy recommendations. In an interview, a student might be asked to perform any part of the above process, or to give an account of an understanding behind the approach in its entirety. In this case, an externally formed hypothesis and policy recommendation should be evaluated. The key, once again, is not to go into a detailed discussion about econometrics, but to demonstrate some basic aptitude for numerical analysis.

Assessment: In my answer, I am going to focus on the plausible conclusions that can be drawn from a statistical result – in this case, that individuals who go to university have a higher average salary than those who don't – while I am going to take the statistical result itself as given. We could, and ideally should discuss the methods used to arrive at that result and, of course, their validity, but this would be too time-consuming in the current circumstances.

We can illustrate the result on a graph that would look something like this. [Draws a simple x-y diagram with a 45-degree line from the origin and with scattered points around it. The axes would be labelled: earnings and education]. More education is *correlated* with higher earnings.

This is an important result; making us wonder about the likely benefits of education towards people's wages and their living standards, which is one of the government's primary objectives.

However, as we know it well, **correlation is not causation**. While the former simply means that two variables change their values similarly, the latter means the changes in one variable lead to changes in the other variable. Basic statistical methods, such as a simple graphical illustration as seen before, are only able to show us *correlation;* we don't know why education and wages are high at the same points. More advanced statistical analysis would allow us to go into further details and hopefully enable us to form statements about *causation,* too. With the information given in the question, it could well be that there is **reverse causality**; a situation where causation actually runs reversely. Those who are richer might decide to go to university as they can afford not to earn wages while studying.

Equally, it could be that there is a third, unknown variable that affects both variables. For instance, the geographic area individuals live in: urban citizens can have both higher wages and better access to higher education when compared to rural inhabitants.

In both of these cases, we would see a correlation between education and wages, but that would not mean that education causes higher wages. Therefore, I would say we need to **further investigate the data** to understand whether in this case, there is indeed a causal effect running from university education to higher earnings.

Assessment: This question allowed the applicant to demonstrate a number of vital skills. First of all, priorities needed to be set. The applicant had to understand that there is no time to address all aspects of the question, from data analysis to recommendations.

Second, the applicant could make use of graphs, the confident use of which is a fundamental skill any aspiring economist or management student should have. Third, the basic notion: **correlation is not causation** was required for the answer. This is a concept all applicants should feel comfortable about as it's the basic principle of statistics.

The interviewee could also shine by bringing in originality in trying to come up with reasons other than education → wages. In an interview situation, the interviewer would likely specifically ask about this rather than expecting the applicant to feel the need to list examples, but the importance of original thoughts is evident nonetheless. Finally, the applicant needed to remember that the question was: "What would you say?", therefore, the answer needed to be specific. Had the applicant stopped before the last paragraph, their response would have been far less strong for not directly answering the question.

THE ULTIMATE OXBRIDGE INTERVIEW GUIDE — ECONOMICS

Q6: Do you think the government should privatise the NHS?

This question provides an opportunity for the applicant to present their understanding of the issue, but they must be wary not to be drawn into giving a political argument. The focus should be placed on the economic impacts of privatisation, rather than personal opinions. The applicant has to formulate an argument about a topic that is both important and probably relatively unfamiliar for most A-level students. As always, it is not the factual knowledge of healthcare economics that's important, but **good structure and critical thinking**.

Applicant: Privatisation is the act of transferring assets from public ownership (effectively state ownership) to private owners through the sale of the assets. Political parties from the left and the right have had a long-standing debate over the desirable extent of public ownership of certain strategic companies and sectors, e.g. schools, hospitals, utilities or public transportation operators. Out of these, the transfer of the healthcare provider, the NHS, has been one of the most controversial topics in UK politics, effectively since the creation of a universal healthcare provider shortly after WWII.

There are strong reasons for both supporting and opposing the transformation of the healthcare system into a market-driven system. However, I still believe that the arguments against it are stronger, thus I would not support the privatisation of the NHS. I have **three main reasons** to believe so: adverse effects on doctor-patient relationships, social injustice, and insecurity of continuous provision.

Firstly, I have always thought that **doctors choose their profession very differently** from what economists assume about rational agents, who only care about monetary reward. They are dedicated to helping the sick and doing everything they can to do their jobs best. If the NHS was privatised, there is a good chance that the business owners of hospitals would introduce measures to motivate doctors to think more business-mindedly. This could endanger the personal trust patients need to feel when they see their doctor about their health.

Secondly, allowing private owners to supply healthcare services would create a considerable risk that services would **seek profits above patient care**. They could increase prices of services as demand for basic health services is inelastic (we are all willing to pay nearly anything for the health of our loved ones). While the well-off could probably still pay for their healthcare, with higher prices many would not be able to purchase even basic services.

Finally, a private owner might decide to continue the supply of profitable services and cut back on others or even shut down loss-making hospitals in less developed areas. This could mean that **healthcare is not universally available across the UK**, undermining citizens' inalienable right to equal treatment.

Of course, privatisation doesn't have to take such an extreme form and it can also be heavily regulated to improve some of the above-mentioned areas. Yet, the potential problems raised by the lack of checks and balances against private agents are so serious that **even if the NHS is an expensive service which costs the State a lot, it should remain in the public domain.**

Assessment: The applicant started by placing the question in a historical and political context, which is always a good idea with questions of this sort. It shows the interviewer that the applicant didn't just memorise arguments for topics but actually understands how things come together. A clear structure and a strong stance are also qualities of a strong applicant. Of course, such a question is bound to lead to a discussion where the interviewer challenges the applicant and comes up with strong counter-arguments. The applicant is expected to respond to those challenges, but not to give up their stance unless factually proven wrong.

Another good response: "There are economic benefits and costs of privatisation, which would be particularly emphasised in the case of a large institution like the NHS. The benefits of privatisation may include the potential for improved competition between healthcare providers, improving efficiency and quality of service. However, it could be argued that this is a welfare issue and that health care would be underprovided to poorer citizens in a free market. It may also be reasoned that the high barriers to entry make healthcare provision a natural monopoly and that privatisation would lead to one firm dominating the market and exploiting its powers to overcharge. I would not support privatisation of the NHS as I do not think healthcare is a good that should be made excludable based on price."

Q7: Let's say I'm the CEO of a major company, what do you think my biggest concern will be?

The applicant has to show the ability to 'think like a manager' and to analyse questions from that perspective. With such an open-ended question, the challenge is not to find something to talk about but to be able to make a proper case out of it with valid reasons. There is no wrong answer, only insufficient reasoning.

Applicant: Chief Executive Officers are the people in charge of the overall business and with the final say on most daily issues, where the Board of Governors doesn't intervene. The pressure and responsibility on them are tremendous and finding a way to prioritise their tasks and problems is crucial. CEOs serve as the **ultimate link** between the company's employees, owners and customers. Therefore, rather than any individual task of their own, I think it's the management of opposing incentives and goals which are the biggest problem facing CEOs.

The workers in the company strain themselves to achieve better working conditions and higher wages. Shareholders seek a return on their investment. Thus, they expect the CEO to deliver growth and, most importantly, profit which is already in conflict with higher wages and better conditions. Customers care the most about price and quality.

The former needs to be low to attract customers, but high to have profits and pay wages. The latter is costly to produce and requires stringent work effort. Finding the perfect middle ground is challenging and requires constant monitoring and re-evaluation from the CEO.

This is a big problem for CEOs because other challenges are one-dimensional, e.g. developing future growth plans, creating more equality between workers, fighting competition, etc. Whilst these are all difficult areas, the desired outcomes are obvious. In the case of managing different interest groups, it's often **unclear what outcomes CEOs need to achieve**.

Assessment: After demonstrating familiarity with the main stakeholders in a firm (CEO, Board, workers), the applicant took a clear stance and named a topic thought to be the most difficult. This was then analysed from the point of view of the CEO or any other business professional. The applicant didn't lose track of the question. And by mentioning other potentially important topics, a wider familiarity with the subject could be highlighted. After this intro, the interviewer would likely invite the applicant to further discuss those other areas and compare their relative importance.

Q8: Would you be able to tell me about the relationship between restrictive monetary policies and the bond market?

A good response: "I may be wrong but I believe that restrictive monetary policy involves raising short-term interest rates. I don't know if there is any formal relationship between interest rates and bond prices, but if I was investing in bonds at a time with high interest rates, I would expect higher returns in order to stop me from investing the money in a bank instead. Therefore, I would imagine that the **price of bonds would probably fall** in order to make them more attractive to investors who might otherwise save their money in a bank."

Assessment: The main point of this question is to identify an interviewee's ability to determine relationships between two ideas and their understanding of how economic mechanisms allow policies to work. The candidate shows the interviewer that they are not completely certain on the topic, but this is perfectly acceptable – the tutor is attempting to test thinking skills and not knowledge. The logical, step-by-step approach shows that the candidate remains calm and methodical even when presented with unfamiliar information. Given the testing nature of the Oxbridge courses offered, it is important for tutors to establish the ability of potential students to work under pressure.

Q9: You're the new Chancellor of the Exchequer - you've been appointed on the promise of growing the economy, would you pursue this from the demand side or supply side?

A good response: "Classical economists believe in a vertical long-run average supply curve, and thus would argue that demand side policies are useless in stimulating growth. However, I feel like the Keynesian model is more realistic and demand side policies can be effective when an economy is not at full employment. Despite this, I believe that supply side policies usually stimulate more long-term sustainable growth rather than one that boosts to economic performance. If a government is seeking growth, I think supply side policies would be preferable."

Assessment: This answer is good and comes to a solid conclusion, but seems to lack the depth to impress an Oxbridge tutor. To improve, the candidate could spend more time analysing why a government may disagree with their viewpoint, and then providing evidence to support their own argument.

Another extension to the answer may be to consider the circumstances under which one approach is more suited than another. Questioning the context surrounding the question shows an inquisitive nature and shows that the candidate is analytical of information presented to them. In this case, a conclusion along the lines of "if a government is facing *situation x*, it should pursue *policy y*…" may add some substance to the arguments presented.

Q10: Tell us about Classical economic theory, how do you think it compares to the theories of economists like Keynes?

Keynesian economists believe that the immense resources of the state should be deployed during periods of economic slowdown (recession). Classical economists, on the other hand, believe that the interference of the state distorts the working of the market to an extent that any well-intended policy will actually further hinder economic recovery and that, where possible, government spending should be limited and taxes cut.

It would be good to use a relevant example from current affairs. In 2008, Gordon Brown used a **fiscal stimulus** (Keynesian) to attempt to kick-start the economy – he brought forward capital spending and cut VAT to boost consumption. While in 2010 the Chancellor George Osborne began austerity in an attempt to restore confidence in UK public finances and reduce the budget deficit while shifting growth from public to private industries through the reduction of interest rates to facilitate business lending.

Who are classical economists? Friedrich Hayek *A road to serfdom*, Milton Freeman (negative income tax), Adam Smith *The Wealth of Nations*.

Who are Keynesian economists? Paul Krugman or Nicholas Kaldor (and obviously John Maynard Keynes).

Q11: Have you ever heard of the term 'rational agent' used to describe a consumer - can you think of examples of consumers being 'irrational'?

A good response: "To answer the question, we must first understand what rationality is. In my view, a rational decision seems sensible to the decision-maker, based on the information presented to them. An example of irrational consumption that springs to mind would be addiction. In the case of addiction, the facts available to the addict are the feeling which their addiction gives them – which may be seen as benefits, and the associated costs of the addiction.

If the benefits to the addict outweigh these costs, then it may be argued that addiction is rational. However, it could be suggested that an addict has a distorted view of these costs and benefits, and, therefore, their ability to think rationally is compromised."

Assessment: This response is well-structured and focuses on attempting to answer the question at hand. By initially outlining a definition of rationality, the candidate displays that they fully understand the question and are engaging with it critically. The response shows a consideration of both sides to the argument without being side-tracked into an irrelevant discussion. One area for potential improvement is the conclusion where no definitive answer is given. Tutors will be looking for students who can articulate their own opinions, and the lack of a conclusive response may suggest that an interviewee does not possess these skills.

Q12: Inflation is often talked about as a bad thing, but governments don't try to prevent inflation from taking place, why do you think this is?

A good response: "0% inflation may seem like a good idea as lower prices provide consumers with the opportunity to get more for their money. Price increases are often poorly received by consumers as they have to reduce what they buy. However, there is often a **trade-off between inflation and economic growth**, and aiming for zero inflation may lead to stagnation in an economy, which is undesirable in most Western economies which desire constant growth. Inflation only forces a reduction in consumption when prices are rising faster than wages. In that case, a government may compromise on inflation – such as the Bank of England have done with their 2% target – in order to ensure that economic balance is being achieved."

Assessment: The candidate effectively pre-empts, and dispels, arguments in favour of 0% inflation goals. Given that this is probably a topic that the interviewee has never had to tackle before, it is advisable to ensure they can present a structured logical argument before attempting to answer. This may involve asking for a moment to think, and a good candidate should not be discouraged from doing this as it gives themselves a moment to collect their thoughts.

This response is clearly well organised and thought through, which is clearly preferable to a rushed and illogical answer, even if it comes at the expense of a momentary pause. The candidate has the opportunity to show the extent of their understanding by referring to current policies or additional knowledge from further reading.

Q13: Economics is often thought to sit between the humanities and the sciences, do you think economics should be classed as a social science?

A good response: "I would define a social science as any academic discipline that studies human interactions using scientific methods. Economics seems to fit this definition. Firstly, it is clearly the study of a human phenomenon; the core issue at the heart of the subject is how humans allocate resources. The methodology used is what provides the science part of the description in my view. Economics is based on quantitative analysis and modelling, and much of the theory is built upon scientific methods. Some people might disagree with the description of economics as a social science. They may argue that it has no real scientific grounding given that there is often very little irrefutable evidence to prove an economic theory. However, I believe that this is inevitable in any study of humanity as **human behaviour is so unpredictable** – and that if economics is not a social science, then neither is any other field of study."

Assessment: A clear definition, even if it is one the candidate has concocted rather than one taken from a textbook, shows a real understanding of what the question is asking. This is a very difficult question to answer given the vague nature of a 'social science' and the difficulty in pigeonholing an entire subject such as economics. However, by considering how well certain criteria are met and assessing contradictory points of view, the interviewee is able to display their ability to grapple with testing problems and use logical reasoning to answer the question at hand. The answer may have been improved by suggesting alternatives to the description provided (e.g. "perhaps a better description of economics is as a series of 'fads and fashions'...") and then assessing the credibility of those alternatives.

Q14: How much do you think CEOs should be paid?

A good response: "I do not know a lot about current CEO pay levels, but it would seem to me that any **employee should be paid based on their contribution** to the firm. If the CEO has a serious positive impact on the business, for example, if they are responsible for securing high levels of profits, then they deserve a large salary. However, if they have no greater impact than any other employee, then they should not be compensated any more generously. If the cost of paying a CEO outweighs the benefits they bring, they are being overpaid."

Assessment: The candidate is honest in their response, acknowledging the fact that this is a topic they know little about. However, by applying more general economic intuition, they are able to provide a concise argument, and more importantly, demonstrate their ability to engage with unfamiliar concepts. This is a very attractive skill to an Oxbridge tutor and is preferable to an interviewee who attempts to deceive an interviewer into believing they know a lot about the subject.

Q15: Moving away from the UK, let's take a look at OPEC - do you think that a cartel is a wise choice for running a global market?

A good response: "Am I right in the understanding that OPEC is the organisation that maintains oil prices?" [Interviewer: "*Yes, that's right.*"] "In that case, I believe that OPEC has run the oil market relatively well. However, I do not believe that the market has even been close to efficiency as many OPEC members have made large profits on the back of the cartel, and in a perfectly efficient market, these profits would not occur. Large price fluctuations, particularly the fall in oil prices, in the last 18 months suggest to me that OPEC does not have as much control over the industry as it would like…"

Assessment: Asking for clarification on a question is not something a candidate should be afraid to do. It displays a willingness to fully understand the concepts that they are dealing with, and so would not be frowned upon in most scenarios.

If the topic in question was of a very basic level, there may be some questions raised, but tutors will not expect a candidate to know about every economic issue and will be expecting some gaps in their knowledge. In this case, the student was right to establish exactly what the question was before attempting to answer. Bringing in **knowledge of current affairs** regarding oil prices also displays interest in the subject, and this enthusiasm for the subject will be taken well by interviewers.

Q16: The economy of scale is a widely acknowledged concept, where average unit costs decrease as a company's output level increases - do you think the opposite, a 'diseconomy of scale' if you will, could ever exist?

A good response: "If average costs are rising as output increases, this suggests that it would be beneficial for firms to stay small. I think we can see plenty of examples of cases where it is beneficial for a firm to stay small. If a company would have to increase its spending on marketing greatly in order to sell any additional goods produced, then the average costs of those products may rise and the company would be suffering from diseconomies of scale.

Assessment: Some applicants, particularly those who have previously studied economics, will have a good understanding of this topic whilst others will have almost none. However, the interviewer is not using this question as a test of existing knowledge, but rather will be looking at the way in which it is approached. The ability to apply theory to real-life is important and this question may be designed to test that ability. The candidate excels by showing good real-world knowledge.

Q17: What do you think is the difference between a floating currency and a pegged currency, what difference would switching to a pegged currency have?

A good response: "A pegged currency is when a country chooses to set its own currency as a direct proportion of that of another economy, usually when a less developed economy aligns with the exchange rate of a more established currency.

This means that an economy has more stability in their exchange rate, which can lead to less volatility in the balance of payments. However, it means a government cannot use economic policies to affect its exchange rate, so they are more susceptible to shocks from external factors – particularly from the nation they are pegged to. It also means that government policy elsewhere has an impact, so the pegged country needs to ensure congruence between the two nations' objectives."

Assessment: The candidate clearly shows a great understanding of the topic, which may not have been covered in any real depth during A-Levels or equivalent. They are able to present a balanced argument even in a short answer and draw on a variety of ideas. To improve, the applicant could refer to real life examples, which shows that they have read around their subject and can be an indication of enthusiasm for the subject. However, in a situation where they don't know any examples, then considering the types of nation that might use pegged currencies – "a less developed economy" – is a good alternative which still displays good understanding.

Economics Interview Questions

1. Would 0% inflation be a good thing or a bad thing?
2. A lot of economics revolves around the use of economic models, do you think these are used too much?
3. If economics is a social science, does it follow that sociology is a valuable tool for studying economics?
4. How do we measure GDP - do you think this is reflective of reality?
5. If you were evaluating the UK's productive potential, what would be the main influences on it which you could identify?
6. What, if any, is the value of government debt?
7. Should you or I be bothered by inequality?
8. If there's a national deficit in the balance of trade, should this trouble the government?
9. Is the Keynesian approach to market intervention correct?
10. Do you think that it would be reasonable to say that a failure of regulation caused 2008's financial crisis?
11. Let's suppose that due to a mainframe error, the value of the American Dollar and the Japanese Yen are exchanged instantaneously - what do you think the main outcomes would be?
12. Sadly we aren't allowed to just sit down with you and play a game of Monopoly, but if we did, how would you try to win? Would your strategy also work in the real world?
13. There are a wide range of materials which we go to considerable effort to extract from the Earth, one of the most expensive is diamond, while one of the cheapest is steel - why do they have their respective values?
14. You are the CEO of new airline, which only flies directly between London and Tokyo - this is a route which no one else in the world currently provides, so how would you work out how much to charge in order to maximise your profits?
15. Tell me about the golden ratio - why do people at banks and investment companies care about it?
16. How would you try to predict economic changes, if you could, do you think this would help you avoid depressions?
17. Do you think that a country which can fund its own space programme should receive international aid from countries like the UK?
18. How would you assess the scale of the divide between communist and capitalist ideologies?
19. What do you think are the main factors driving the increasing privatisation of once-public large services like the Royal Mail or NHS?
20. On Oxford high street there are three coffee shops belonging to the same brand on a single street - why do you think this happens in populous cities?
21. You have been tasked with getting rid of the UK's national debt - how?
22. Why do we use public money to provide healthcare to the elderly?
23. What do you think are the main push and pull factors behind human migration?
24. Here in the UK - we have a fairly well-established system of taxation which is used to fund a range of programmes. How do you think that places like Dubai, which don't use taxation at all, are able to grow at all, let alone so quickly?

THE ULTIMATE OXBRIDGE INTERVIEW GUIDE — ECONOMICS

25. You are the infamous pirate captain "Dread {YOUR SURNAME}" and you have a standing rule where if more than half of the crew publicly disapprove of your tactics, they can execute you. You've just seized a large haul of gold and have to divide it up. How would you distribute the wealth in such a way that you maintain the favour of your crew and get the largest possible share of the booty?

26. Why do people decide to change careers? If they are moving from a career which relies on extensive higher education to one which requires extensive vocational training, where do you think responsibility for funding their re-education lies?

27. Do you think that you could ever build an economy which was based entirely on service industries?

28. Is global overpopulation a problem?

29. Do you think that the buying and selling of sports players by teams and managers around the world is similar to the buying and selling of people as slaves? Explain why.

30. Why is a film actor wealthier than a theatre actor?

31. Why is deflation a scare to the UK?

32. You run a sweet shop next-door to a rival sweet shop - you've both been able to drum up considerable loyalty in your customers who will flat-out refuse to shop anywhere else, provided you keep your prices below a tenner per sweet. You each have 10 such loyal customers - but there are 100 potential customers on the street who don't care as much and will buy from whoever is cheapest. With this in mind, at what price point would you have to reach for it to be more valuable to sell everything for ten pounds?

33. Why are the Chancellor of the Exchequer and the Governor of the Bank of England different jobs? What are the differences between them?

34. What would be the economic consequences of Scotland gaining independence from the UK? What about Wales?

35. How do you predict oil prices will change in the next decade? How about the next century?

36. What makes the US economy so strong?

37. Could you explain to a layman the perceived value of the G8? How would you discretise it from the G20?

38. What are the main similarities and differences between the Chinese and Indian economies?

39. Take a look at this graph. It shows the price of salt since 1800. You'll notice that it follows a recurring pattern. How can this have been sustained in the face of events like the Great War, the Great Depression, and The Second World War?

40. How does the job of a manager differ from that of a director, executive, or leader?

41. How might we begin to work out the ROI from Christopher Columbus's expeditions?

42. Is it possible to calculate ROI for exploratory organisations, like NASA?

43. A dramatic election leads to the formation of a new country in Central Africa, which promptly develops and introduces a new currency. How is this currency then valued on the international market?

44. Why didn't the UK adopt the Euro?

ENGLISH

The English interview will require you to demonstrate passion and a genuine desire to study English. Make sure you have thought, at least vaguely, about your answer to a wide question like: "Why English?" or "Why English at Cambridge?"

You will usually be asked to discuss an unseen extract from a play, poem, or piece of prose; this will enable the interviewer to see whether you can think on your feet, both in terms of subject-related knowledge (of literary forms, techniques, and genres) and forming your own critical opinions on the spot ("Is this a good poem? Why?").

Apply the knowledge you have acquired at A-Level and from wider reading to unfamiliar scenarios. You may not recognise the text you have been asked to read, but that is probably deliberate: **embrace this chance to experiment,** make mistakes, and show off your imaginative readings of new texts. Indeed, the Cambridge English course places a strong emphasis upon Practical Criticism, which encourages you to explore unseen texts in isolation from their context (by erasing the writer's name or the date written) in order to understand how the form of a text influences themes and meanings.

If you are making an argument that the interviewers are telling you is clearly wrong, try to revise your viewpoint and expand your argument in light of this information. Remember, **making mistakes is no bad thing**; in fact, it can be very constructive to be wrong, since changing your argument shows real intellectual flexibility. The important point is that you address the mistake head on and attempt to revise your thinking with the assistance of the tutors where necessary. For instance, perhaps a tutor has asked you to try and place a poem in its literary context – say, a sonnet by John Donne from the Renaissance – and you have given it the wrong date – perhaps thinking that it could be a Romantic sonnet instead.

This guesswork can be used as an exciting springboard for a fresh discussion. How did knowing the real date of this poem change the way you viewed the themes and message? You might find it interesting that enduring features of the sonnet form existed both in the Renaissance and in the eighteenth century –what subtle changes in genre might you notice, and are these conventions ever subverted? Try and think creatively and use this correction as the basis for a wider conversation about how the sonnet form has evolved over the centuries.

The tutors know what subjects you have studied at A-Level. They will try to theme your interview around the texts and periods that you have studied. However, they may ask you about certain literary periods that you have not studied in depth or detail. If so, be open-minded and respond to the information that you are given. If you are given Wilfred Owen's 'Anthem for Doomed Youth' and you have not studied any war poets before, you can still apply techniques and ideas you have learned. While you should discuss the poem with fresh eyes, analysing the form, the metre, and imagery as you would do with any unseen poem, feel free to make connections with other texts.

For example, you may have studied Tennyson's 'The Charge of the Light Brigade'; what can this earlier poem, which uses powerful rhetoric to valorise patriotism and male honour, illuminate about Owen's more nihilistic sonnet? Such **connections show that you are thinking actively** and enjoying the challenge of approaching new texts.

What Questions Might Be Asked?

Most of the questions asked in the interview will disguise a larger question within a network of smaller sub-questions to guide the answer from the start to a conclusion. The main question may seem difficult, weird, or random at first, but take a breath and start discussing different ideas you have for breaking down the question into manageable pieces. Don't panic.

The questions are designed to be challenging to give you the chance to show your full intellectual potential. They will help guide you to the right idea if you provide ideas for them to guide. This is your chance to show your creativity, analytical skills, intellectual flexibility, problem-solving skills, and your willingness to be challenged. Don't waste it on nervousness or a fear of messing up or looking stupid: think aloud and work together with the interviewer.

An interviewer may question any decision you come to in response to a question, and it is possible that in the course of the ensuing conversation your original views will alter as your thinking becomes more nuanced. Do not panic! This is perfectly okay and shows an ability to adapt to new information and ideas and respond to them. Similarly, you should not feel the need to quickly agree with anything coming from an interviewer's mouth in order to appease them. An interview is a discussion and a chance to show the interviewer how you think and respond to the thoughts of others.

To quote Robinson College's English admissions advice, you should show:

"A readiness to respond to challenges to your opinion, holding firm and arguing your case where appropriate, but also modifying your opinion in the light of contradictory evidence."

Worked Questions

Below are a few examples of how to start breaking down an interview question along with model answers.

Q1: Take a look at these extracts from a piece of literature, do you think they were written by someone identifying as a man, or as a woman? On what basis could you determine this, and once you have done, does it matter?

This seemingly complex question can be broken down first into a critical exercise in analysing an unseen text, followed by a wider discussion of whether biographical information is important in literary criticism: is the author 'dead'?

Your starting point for this question might be your initial gut-reaction to the two contrasting texts: **do they seem more 'masculine' or 'feminine' to you**, and how would you define these adjectives? Since the interviewer is asking you to guess this information without expecting you to know details about the authentic author, you might realise that they are interested in the assumptions that literary critics bring to bear upon texts seen out of context: *why* does this seem like a male writer wrote it?

For example, let's say you were given an extract from Ernest Hemingway's *The Old Man and the Sea*. Most obviously, the themes focus upon the traditional male pursuit of fishing, or hunting, and centre upon nature in the vein of Romantic poets like Byron or Coleridge. You might describe the main stylistic features as abrupt punctuation and short, factual statements. Perhaps you notice the lack of floral language or poetic set-pieces, and a simplistic texture. Hemmingway uuses efficient and controlled prose without stylistic excess. This lack of explicit emotion might strike you as 'masculine', reminding you of stereotypically reticent male discourse. Then, maybe the second extract is a piece from Virginia Woolf's *Mrs Dalloway*.

Initially, it may be clear that the text is centred around a female character, her emotions and feelings. Moving deeper, you might describe the prose as smooth and fluid, linked by flowing connectives, perhaps recognising this to be an experiment in stream of consciousness. Maybe you feel that the author prioritises chaotic human psychology and internal thoughts rather than linear events. The way she moves by association through clusters of images, impressions, and sensations in a way that reminds you of lyrical poetry more than realist prose, striking you as a more 'feminine' way of writing. You could, of course, equally be presented with work by William Burroughs and have no way to tell either way! In a case like that, talk the interviewer through the difficulties you're having in identifying the author's gender, and suggest ways you could break this impasse.

However, you may argue none of the above and analyse these two texts in a completely opposite way, arguing for the femininity of the Hemingway piece and showing the masculinity of Woolf's prose (which is even more interesting). In a way, it doesn't matter: the interviewers just want to see you <u>argue your case for the author's gender with a detailed, analytical piece of prose analysis.</u>

Once this starting point is established, they might ask you to reassess your answers, pushing you to define these gendered observations and defend your argument. Is there — as Woolf discusses — a specifically 'feminine' or feminist, style? Can a text ever have a neutral or androgynous style, mixing both genders?

Finally, the interviews are likely to steer this discussion towards a final twist: <u>does the gender of the author matter?</u> Should we celebrate anonymity? Does biographical information restrict or generate meaning? The interviewers are inviting you to think broadly about texts and contexts. You might have come across theories like Roland Barthes' *Death of the Author* or be aware of *New Criticism*, which argues for texts as self-contained units of meaning liberated from biographical constraints. Maybe you have touched upon the 'intentional fallacy', a phrase coined by critics Wimsatt and Beardsley, and recognise the difficulties involved in interpreting a text solely in terms of what the author meant. Even if you have not formally studied any of these theories, it is likely you will voice some of these central ideas as you debate, aloud, whether biographical knowledge in literary criticism is useful, limiting or both. As you can see, from these two short extracts, you have covered an enormous amount of ground, both technical, in terms of analysing prose, and theoretical, asking huge questions about the author and the text.

THE ULTIMATE OXBRIDGE INTERVIEW GUIDE — ENGLISH

A <u>poor applicant</u> may take a number of approaches unlikely to impress the interviewer. The first and most obvious of these is to say "I don't know who wrote these texts", or similarly uncooperative responses. In fact, the whole task assumes you won't know who wrote the texts, but rather invites you to speculate about unseen extracts in order to investigate your assumptions about the relevance of gender or biographical information when studying literature. Another approach which is unhelpful in this interview situation is the 'brain dump', where instead of engaging with the question, the applicant attempts to impress or distract with an assortment of related facts. For instance, you might offer a fantastic standalone stylistic analysis of these prose extracts, listing the different ways in which Hemingway uses punctuation, or how Woolf uses connectives in her languid sentences. However, unless this is used to strengthen your final argument about the gender of each author and why you think that, then this is irrelevant information. Instead, listen and respond to your interviewers as they prompt you further, continually asking you to extend and defend your analysis by asking: "why?", or "so why do these connectives make the prose seem feminine to you?" These <u>observations should be pieces of evidence in a reasoned argument for authorial gender</u>, which will provide a basis for productive discussion of whether this biographical information is important or irrelevant in the task of literary criticism.

Q2: Is Fifty Shades of Grey literature? Why?

This question invites you to think about the sets of criteria used to evaluate what is 'literature', what is a 'classic' or the 'canon'. Does popularity diminish the cultural prestige of art? Does the audience matter? Can EastEnders ever be 'literature' in the same way as works by Samuel Beckett or James Joyce? Begin to criticise and re-evaluate these throwaway terms that you use every day, imagining how a dictionary might define them: what do we really mean when we categorise texts as 'canonical' or 'literature' and what (or whose) criteria are we using? Can a contemporary novel ever be a classic? Think about the rise of English Literature as a respected academic pursuit and your own A-Level syllabus, and the influence of criticism like F.R. Leavis's *The Great Tradition*: what has been included, and, more significantly, what is excluded, marginal, and devalued? Ask questions and probe your own answers in what will become a lively two-way discussion.

This is a playful, provocative question which introduces the theme of popular culture, of 'high' and 'low' art, asking you to analyse shifting or enduring artistic standards and tastes of 'art' or 'entertainment'. What about the way in which Shakespeare meshes 'high' tragic art and 'low' comedic clowns? You might want to approach this in terms of obscene or taboo subject matter across the ages. Why do institutions study John Donne's most erotic poetry – 'To His Mistress Going to Bed' – or obscene Elizabethan pamphlets, but neglect this exceedingly popular novel?

You could explore the idea of censorship by linking Fifty Shades to D.H. Lawrence's *Lady Chatterley's Lover*: perhaps the book deserves to be seen as a historically-interesting celebration of artistic freedom and liberated female sexuality?

Q3: What makes a tragedy?

The interviewers are pushing you to explore one of the <u>most famous literary genres in an imaginative fashion</u>.

Perhaps you might start with the classical formulation of 'Tragedy' that you might have come across in your A-Level studies, including Aristotle's tragic precepts (hamartia, hubris, peripeteia, anagnorisis, catharsis etc.). However, use Aristotle's definitions as a starting point, a springboard, not the answer. What does it really mean to have a tragic 'catharsis'? Can you think of modern examples that reinforce or subvert these ideas – what about Arthur Miller's The Crucible, or Death of a Salesman? Think about plays you have studied that illustrate or undermine this term in practice. You could then move on to how these precepts manifested themselves in later literary movements, discussing Shakespearean tragedy and the moments that you think illuminate these aspects.

There is no 'correct' answer: this is an exercise in probing the boundaries of a 'genre'. What about women? Does Shakespearean tragedy prioritise the aristocratic male at the expense of the poor or female characters? What about class? What about other media – can cinema, comic books, paintings, television soap operas, news programmes, or Twitter statuses ever be tragic? Your interviewer might ask similar questions, maybe discussing iconoclastic critics like Raymond Williams who argued for a more egalitarian view of the tragic. Perhaps you might agree with George Steiner who famously argued for the 'death of tragedy' – is tragedy dead, or is it still alive and kicking? You don't have to recognise or have read these critics, but respond and be interested when their ideas are mentioned – do you agree, or not? If not, why? Use examples that spring to mind from your reading and be as varied as you like.

Q4: Do you think the ending of [Novel] is poor?

This question invites an explanation of your verdict and a consideration of what makes a 'good ending'. What is the point of a conclusion? Is it to provide a final commentary on the preceding themes to tie up any loose ends of the plot, to introduce a parting thought for the reader to mull over? Do different genres demand different things of their endings? Should endings have certain qualities to help the overall structure of a novel?

For example, if you were asked to comment on the conclusion of 'Mill on the Floss', you may answer that it is a poor ending as the sudden destruction of two characters both jars and frustrates the reader. The flooding incident was unprecedented and random, and in a way gimmicky. The preceding novel focused so much on character development and the effect of human actions, that the sudden 'act of God' disrupted the style of the book. Moreover, having invested time and energy into the heroine's struggles, the reader may well feel frustrated and betrayed at receiving such an unsatisfactory resolution for Maggie. One could argue that the ending felt lazy and that the final note that follows the drowning is sentimental. George Eliot could stand accused of having not provided a proper conclusion to her work, and opting for an easy way out of dealing with the mess Maggie's life was now in. The sudden flood could be compared to the often mocked "and it was all a dream" ending.

Alternatively, one could argue "no", as the unexpected flood was a representation of the cruelty of the world, of the ultimate futility of human struggle. Our frustrated expectations and shock could be argued as a testimony to the strength of the ending: the power it has to compel the audience to react makes it not 'poor', but great. One may argue that an ending does not have to satisfy if it is able to teach us something new. Or perhaps the horror of this incident justifies the work as something tragic, and in its way is true to its genre.

There is also room to discuss <u>what constitutes an ending</u>. The discussion includes the flood in understanding George Eliot's conclusion, but another person may argue the final epilogue is the ending, or demands more attention than the deadly incident. Moreover, one can explore the idea of endings and link it with the idea of literature itself: if literature is meant to please, provoke, or has different purposes in different situations, what does this mean for endings?

Q5: What do you think differentiates a short story from a novel?

This question asks you to consider the nature of form and the impact it has on a piece of literature. A weaker answer will state the obvious: "a short story is shorter than a novel". A stronger answer will take this into account and then consider how length will affect the treatment of a story's content. For example, one may consider if the significance of individual words is affected by the total word count within a work. Or they may discuss how characterization is affected by having fewer words to explore a person within a narrative and argue that short stories must establish protagonists and antagonists in ways novels are not necessarily constricted by. The answer could contrast the characters of Edgar Allen Poe to those of Jane Austen and note the differences in the way they present individuals in the plot.

One may also talk about <u>how structure differs between a longer and a shorter work</u> and how the latter needs a clearer, more concise plot, whereas the former has more space to meander and add multiple episodes within the narrative. Again, this idea could then be corroborated through examples provided by the candidate's reading. A candidate could also consider the difference between a novel and a collection of short stories, and consider how the overarching theme of a novel is explicit, whereas a theme across the group of stories is more implicit.

Q6: Tell me about a novel you've read recently.

A <u>weaker candidate</u> will simply summarise a text, whereas a stronger one will analyse it. For example, if a candidate has recently read 'Oliver Twist', they could discuss it within a context: for example, how does this collection differ to other Dickensian novels or Victorian novels, or even modern novels the candidate has read? What do they think of the story's use of comedy or perhaps the characterization of Nancy or Oliver himself? Why do they think this is considered a 'classic'? How do they think the structure affects the story and does a consideration of the novel's roots – as a serial printed in instalments in a magazine – affect the way the candidate reads the novel as a whole? Does the movement from segments to a single volume improve the work or do they think something has been lost in the translation?

A candidate is invited here to show the <u>thoughts that have arisen through their reading</u> and to make a judgment. They can explain what they find interesting or enjoyable, or why they disliked a work or found it uncomfortable. Beyond simply having a reaction to the text, a stronger candidate will also explore their reaction to the text: if they felt frustrated with a certain character, why do they think this was? Was it the author's intention or a limitation in their skill? Does the context of a work affect its reception – do Dickens's idealised characters charm a certain audience and not another, and is this due to different time periods or social, economic or religious contexts?

Whatever time or location a text originates from, consider it on its own in comparison with other things you've read within its context, and consider why and how it elicits a reaction from you as a reader.

The answer does not necessarily have to mention all these different aspects, but it should mention the title and then an analysis of the text, showing what the interviewee finds interesting about the piece of literature, whether he or she likes it or not.

Q7: How would you begin to define the difference between poetry and prose, in English literature?

An applicant may wish to begin with the difference between the two by thinking about their respective formal qualities: poetry and its use of metre, for example. They may then wish to think if this alone is a simple distinction, prompting them to discuss prose-poetry and explain whether they believe it belongs either to prose or poetry, or is a separate category in itself, and crucially why this is so. One may also want to discuss other elements associated with either poetry or prose specifically and see if these elements define them (or why they do not).

For example, 'poetic devices' such as metaphor and alliteration can be found in prose. In any given subject matter, one may go on to explain that this can be explored through both: love can be discussed in *Tess of the d'Urbervilles* or in Robert Burns's *My Love is Like a Red, Red Rose*. If they then dismiss other possible differences, they could again reaffirm their original thoughts on the definition that separates poetry from prose. If in the process they then wish to add to their original statement, they can do this. The movement from the original idea to a discussion of it, backed with examples and a consideration of the answers other people may provide to this question, will lead to a nuanced response to the interviewer.

Q8: Do you think that the gender of a lead character in any piece of media is meaningful?

An applicant may first wish to define gender – e.g. "the state of being male or female – normally used to in a social or cultural context as opposed to a biological one."

An applicant may then say "yes" and describe the manifest ways gender affects a text: either by informing character or influencing the plot. They may go on to use many examples to explain this: for example, Jane Eyre would not have a romantic attachment with Rochester if she was a man and so all the events relating to their relationship would not have happened, and the plot of Jane Eyre would be non-existent. If she was a man, and she and Rochester shared a homosexual love, it would be an entirely different book.

Moreover, one's relationship to the world can be seen as partially defined by their gender. Cathy (the elder) in Wuthering Heights believes her way of achieving a greater rank is through marriage to a wealthy man, whereas if she were herself a male, she might have gone the way of Heathcliff who found his fortune through mysterious enterprises. One cannot simply dismiss her gender as irrelevant: her identity is bound in the societal expectations and legal status of women of her time and this limits her expectations of what she could achieve and forces her to retreat into the status of desired marital object in order to pursue her worldly ambitions.

The treatment of women/men in different periods and places will also be visible in any work as it will inform the writer's viewpoint and so inform the book. As there is still a perceived difference between men and women, gender identity is still important to recognise and modern books still see the importance of gender in defining a character's history, relationship to others, and awareness of their place in the world. One may then go on to question how different Harry Potter would have been if Harry were a girl.

Of course, one may argue that men and women are equally capable of feeling and acting and that a female protagonist for a novel like Harry Potter is entirely possible. It could be argued that believing in the equal rights of men and women, gender should cease to be a definitive aspect of the character. However, "should" is very different than "is", and though feminism has come a long way in changing attitudes towards women's rights, society is not ignorant of the individual's gender. There remain preconceptions and arguments relating to notions of a female or male identity. If a girl was fighting Voldemort, different associations would arise in the reader's mind than they would when reading a boy battling the Dark Lord.

One may also argue that certain characters within plays are considered quite gender neutral, and can be performed by either male or female cast (for example, though Ariel is a man in The Tempest, he is often played by a woman). The counter-argument to this is that, though this ambiguity exists, once the neutral body is gendered through the performer, it again elicits a reaction specific to that gender.

One could argue that, on the page, a character could be considered gender-neutral, but then this absence of gender may be of importance, the "neutrality" becoming a third gender to consider, and eliciting a different reaction than the other two.

The answer could also go on to discuss the idea of a transgender protagonist.

Q9: Is there a book you think you should not have studied?

The question invites an exploration of what the purpose of literary study is. An applicant will look at the books they have read for schoolwork and consider and answer truthfully if they think they were all valid choices, or if one was not. Having clarified this, the candidate may then explain what he or she thinks is a requirement for a book to be worthy of 'study' – what merits does a text require to validate its place in education?

Having clarified what these qualities are – or indeed if there are any requirements for a book to be worth studying – they can then compare the works he or she has read for class against these requirements. If they decided that everything is worth study, the applicant can then discuss the idea of this further and explain the value of any text within a classroom, providing examples to corroborate their argument. This discussion may then lead to a greater analysis of the purpose of literature: is what makes a text worth studying what makes it worth reading, or is there a difference between books that should be pursued in leisure time as opposed to academic time?

Q10: Is literature inherently moral?

If the applicant answered "no", he or she may go on to explain that, although literature can be a source of moral edification, it should not be unified by an ethical cause because there are a variety of purposes that can inform a text. It could be written simply to be beautiful (and the candidate may then talk about aesthetic criticism of literature) or perhaps to hold "a mirror up to nature" and capture something of reality or the human condition – whether this is through naturalism or through another expression of an emotional state.

One may argue, for example, that Waiting for Godot would be rendered absurd if a moral was added: its purpose is not to provide ethical education, and the complexity of the piece would be crudely simplified. It would be turned from a challenging work to a didactic one; simple to understand but with all its original intention and meaning deleted. One could question if literature 'should' ever be or do anything.

One may, however, question whether literature that can be considered immoral can also be considered harmful. The relationship depicted in the 50 Shades series is often considered abusive and one may wonder if this sets a bad example for impressionable readers who will go on to idealise this couple.

The candidate may then argue that <u>responsibility lies in the reader</u> and the censoring of work is in itself troubling. He or she could go on to name any number of banned books and then demonstrate their value as opposed to their potential to damage.

Q11: How would you define the words lie, deceive, and mislead? What do these words tell you about the English language?

An applicant should begin with explaining one of these on their own: for example, to "lie" is to deliberately say something the speaker knows to be contrary to the truth, such as "trees are made of purple cheese". To "deceive" is not, however, necessarily to lie: it is to lead someone to believe in something that is not true. The word is <u>more to do with intent</u>; the desire to make another believe in something false than the action of simply stating something that is not true. There are also other uses of the word – one can "deceive oneself" or an object may give a mistaken impression – which gives it different meanings, and one may wish to consider these. However, one should ensure the differentiation between "deceive" and "lie" is clearly stated. To "lie" describes an action; to "deceive" describes an action coupled with intent.

Having established the meanings of these two words, the candidate may then compare these to the definition of "mislead".

Often "mislead" is treated as a synonym of "deceive", with dictionaries using one to define the other. However, the subtle difference may be that <u>one can "mislead" unknowingly</u>. If we take "mislead" to "cause someone to have the wrong idea or impression" or to "lead astray", we can see that someone might "mislead" without intent, but purely by error. For example, if one believes he or she knows the quickest way to a location but is mistaken, that person may have misled a group of friends without meaning to at all. One can definitely mislead with intent, but one does not necessarily have to.

This is a question that <u>demands careful attention to the nuances of words</u>, so it is good to constantly compare the differences between these three terms. For example, one can say you might "mislead" without lying. One may even deceive without lying, by refraining from revealing crucial information that would lead to a fuller understanding of the scene. For example, if someone wanted to make you believe Mr X killed Mrs Y, he or she might say "Mr X went to Mrs Y's house an hour before the crime", and then neglect to mention that he left the same house two minutes later and went across town. One might then discuss whether one can "lie by omission" and how this would again affect the relationship between "to lie" and "to deceive."

Q12: Why do critics exist? Is there a value to criticism?

If one was to answer "yes", they could argue there is a dual purpose to criticism. Firstly, it can introduce new ideas to the reader, ones they may not have considered alone. Perhaps the critic has a <u>novel interpretation</u> of the words that inspires a new train of thought.

For example, WH Auden's description of Twelfth Night as a "nasty" play may encourage his reader to reconsider the nature of the comedy within the drama and potentially find darkness where previously they saw only light humour. The second purpose of criticism could be seen as confirming the reader's thoughts.

If the critic offers an idea that reaffirms their previous views, or that the candidate is annoyed by / disagrees with, it helps them to <u>solidify their own views on literature</u>. For example, Oscar Wilde's comment that "All art is quite useless" may be so infuriating that it provokes a strong reaction, and this reaction allows the reader to clarify his or her own understanding of the purpose of a text.

One may argue that analysis does not necessarily require a critic. For example, a look at the historical context of a work can inspire thought. One may also refer to the use of Practical Criticism, which asks the reader to simply respond to an unseen text and discuss the potential merit of this exercise. It is useful to respond to a text without your mind being coloured by another's critique. However, once one has gained this perspective, it can be argued that considering another interpretation can further deepen his or her analysis. Using several approaches to a text ensures a more nuanced understanding of it.

Q13: You mentioned that Hamlet was your favourite Shakespeare play. In it, Hamlet speaks directly to the Ghost; what significance does this have?

Firstly, you should explore "speaks to the Ghost". Another character has attempted to engage the Ghost in conversation but significantly, the spectre did not respond. Should we make a distinction between being "spoken to" and "spoken at"? Are we looking at the fact that Hamlet is speaking or at that there is communication between the two figures?

If we are looking at the fact that they have a conversation, there are several ways to look at this significance depending on how one interprets the figure of the Ghost. Hamlet himself is unsure at first whether this is truly the spirit of his father or some demonic being tempting him to sin. If the latter, this conversation means potential damnation and implies peril for Hamlet's soul. If the former, we may see this dialogue as an insight into the familial relationship between father and son.

As Shakespeare shows the father calling on the living for revenge, he portrays a character who foists the burden of vendetta onto his offspring, potentially risking Hamlet's chance of reaching Heaven, and dooming Hamlet to Hell. This conversation can be used to define the characters via their relationship with one another.

One may look at this conversation as a manifestation of madness: though others spot the ghost at first, he is crucially neither seen nor heard by Gertrude in the bedroom scene. Perhaps we can then dismiss the earlier sightings as a sort of group hysteria by a bunch of men on watch, not really there at all. Or maybe we can divide the Ghost into two: one which can be seen by others and one that solely haunts the guilty, addled mind of Hamlet. Again, the fact that only Hamlet can communicate with the spectre of his father may suggest madness, a reality which is solely his and inaccessible to any other.

<u>How 'real' the ghost is can be debated</u> because of these two very different impressions - a spectre that is seen by some, but utterly invisible to the dead man's wife. One may then go on to say that the Ghost does not wish to be seen by Gertrude, only by his son, and this in itself is significant. One may also wish to speak about how the audience can see the ghost and wonder if this implies Gertrude alone is in the dark about his presence, or whether we are being granted access to Hamlet's vision, and so his mind; something other characters cannot access.

If we decide that the phrase "speaks to" is simply the action of Hamlet trying to initiate contact, one might say the significance here is of a son who desperately wants contact with his father, who overcomes his fear of the potentially dangerous spectre due to his great need to speak to his dad. Hamlet remarks that he does not set his life at a "pin's fee", so does his conversation with the deathly spirit also suggest a desire to join it in death, a rejection of the living? As Hamlet speaks to the Ghost alone on stage, we see a living man forming a relationship with a dead one. This image is worth analysing.

Renaissance ideas on ghosts, damnation, and superstition differ to the predominant beliefs in 21st Century Britain, and this may also be taken into context and used to describe how a Shakespearian audience's understanding of ghosts would affect how one would witness a scene.

Tests, Essays & Personal Statements

Written Tests

It is crucial to have a toolkit or checklist of techniques at your fingertips for analysing poetry, prose, and drama effectively in order to compare, contrast, and comment upon different extracts. You should always be thinking about how to explore form and structure (syntax, metre, versification, scansion) as well as language (imagery, motifs, similes, metaphors). Try and practice your timed essay technique and find ways to use your observations as evidence for a powerful argument, noticing what links are apparent rather than just a list of random feature-spotting. Remember, these selected texts will be set because the examiners want you to notice distinctive features, make connections and interesting arguments: look for overlapping themes or juxtaposing techniques, keeping an eye out for examples of the traditional and the subversive. You could pick up an anthology of poetry, prose or drama and pick interlinked texts at random to practice: what is similar or different about them?

Essay + Personal Statement Discussions

Read and reread your personal statement and make sure you have interesting things to say about your ideas and chosen texts. Try to pre-empt off-kilter interview questions, which will be designed to steer you away from pre-packaged speeches learned before the day itself. Make sure you have a deep awareness of different periods and prepare by using anthologies to gain a rough sweep of chronological developments. For instance, if you mention liking T.S. Eliot's poetry, you might be asked which other modernist poets you have read and how these have deepened your understanding of what it really means to be a 'modernist poet'. Is this a useful categorisation or not?

Expect the interviewers to undermine your arguments and to push you into defending or adapting your beliefs. Go back over texts you might not have studied for a long time and try and develop, or argue against, your ideas, which might have changed over time if you have read more widely.

Be Inventive

The interviewers may have heard forty interviewees discuss revenge in *Hamlet* or the radicalness of Jack Kerouac's *On the Road*. Why not talk about *Pericles* or *Timon of Athens* or Shakespeare's poetry – *The Rape of Lucrece* is an excellent accompaniment to *Titus Andronicus* – instead? If you are fascinated by the Beat Generation, look further than the obvious texts: make an effort to explore the writing of other groundbreaking writers like Hunter S. Thompson or William Burroughs, comparing and contrasting how their formal techniques can be used to investigate similar themes. Follow your natural interests to the furthest extreme and you will be surprised at how enjoyable the interview can be.

Branch out from your set texts and you will show off your own drive to read and study. Talk about different mediums if you feel they illuminate your discussion from films to plays, to song lyrics. For example, you could talk about how a certain set design or production aesthetic changed your understanding of a play, such as the recent all-female *Julius Caesar* at the Donmar Warehouse.

THE ULTIMATE OXBRIDGE INTERVIEW GUIDE

English Interview Questions

1. What is the point of studying English?
2. What do you think you'll get out of an English degree?
3. How would you define 'Literature'?
4. What is prose? How does this differ from poetry?
5. What was the last thing you read?
6. Do you think leaders would benefit from studying English?
7. Why do you think literature dating from before living memory is still studied, does it hold value?
8. How much value would you attach to the gender of a protagonist?
9. Let's say that you are a director, and you are preparing a modern performance of Shakespeare's Hamlet, a play you've mentioned. You have recently learned that modern audiences often prefer shorter plays, so how would you abridge it?
10. Do you think we should ever draw comparisons between literary characters and real people? Can the story of Christ's birth be used to evaluate the current prime minister, for example?
11. You mentioned King Lear, would you agree that it is a tragedy?
12. Our course is structured by period, we start with very early works of English literature, and move towards the present. Why do you think we do this?
13. Some texts are highly spatial, they focus on a particular place. Have you ever been to a place which is heavily referred to in a text you have read? Do you think that visiting somewhere like that would have an effect on the way you read the text, and should more people do it?
14. Who do you think wrote Shakespeare's plays?
15. What poems have you read by [insert poet here]?
16. How would you explain the differences between a Sonnet and a Haiku to someone who hasn't studied English?
17. Every year we have applicants who mention that the structure of our course is flawed in one way, or another. Given the chance, what would you change about this course?
18. What do you think makes a tragedy?
19. How would you go about classifying the genre of the Holy Bible? Would you class it as a work of fiction?
20. Do you think that fiction should always include a lesson on morality?
21. What do you mean when you say [X] about [X – poet/author] in your personal statement?
22. Do you feel that the best way to express and communicate ambiguities or questions about the nature of particular words is through poetry?
23. What would you say were the most significant similarities and differences between The Lord of the Rings trilogy, and the Harry Potter series?
24. It looks like you had to study Romeo and Juliet in GCSE English, did you think that Romeo was a rebel? Would you say that Romeo shared much in common with Shakespeare?
25. Do you read other people criticisms of works you have read? Why?
26. Who is your favourite character?
27. If we were to hand you a carrot, and ask you to use it in a prop in an impromptu performance of one of Hamlet's soliloquies, would that vegetable become 'theatrical'?
28. Do you think the ending of [X] is poor?

29. What is your all-time favourite novel?
30. Is the ending of [Novel] is poor?
31. What was your coursework about?
32. You mentioned that Hamlet was your favourite play before, what would you say was the importance of family in Hamlet's plot?
33. Considering what you know about Hamlet, what do you think the Ghost has to do with madness?
34. When Hamlet gives his famous soliloquy 'to be, or not to be' who do you think the audiences are?
35. Take a moment to read this poem – and tell us your thoughts.
36. How would you explain the difference between a novel and a short story?
37. Do you think that poets make their work hard to understand on purpose?
38. Do you think the way we use English in writing is different to how we'd speak it?
39. From the perspective of an English student, what do you think is the significance of Coronation Street being on air for five decades?
40. Why do we study English Literature?
41. Would you be able to link poetry to music and other forms of media?
42. What do you think about ambiguity?
43. If you could make up a word, what would it be?
44. Can literature be bad for you?
45. What makes a classic a 'classic'?
46. Is an aptitude for rhythm valuable when writing poetry or prose?
47. Do you think that English students should learn about the life of an author when evaluating their work?
48. If you had to choose between a novel and a poem, which would you rather be?
49. Can stories be intrinsically immoral?
50. What is your favourite word?
51. How would you define poetry, and can you think of any 'poems' which don't fit your definition?
52. Do you think that language can change the way that people think? Would exclusively speaking English make us in any way different from people who speak another language?
53. How do you think not having a written language would change the way that English is used?

GEOGRAPHY AND EARTH SCIENCES

If you're applying to Geography, it is important that you prepare for both human and physical geography questions since you could be asked questions on either sub-field. If you're applying for Natural Sciences at Cambridge (with the aim of studying Earth Sciences) or Earth Sciences at Oxford, you are also likely to have a course-work related interview.

- This interview will require you to demonstrate passion and a genuine desire to study your chosen subject. You will be asked to discuss a source extract, a diagram, or even an object depending on the subject you are applying for. You may not recognise the text you have been asked to read, but that is probably deliberate.
- The tutors know what subjects you have studied at A-Level. They will not ask you for detailed knowledge about areas of your subject that you are not familiar with. Nobody knows every aspect of their subject.
- **Apply the knowledge you have acquired** at A-Level and from your wider reading to unfamiliar scenarios. Feel confident to make references to academics whose works you have read, this shows that not only did you read widely, but you can also pinpoint specific researchers and apply this to questions they ask.
- If you begin by answering and you realise that you actually want to take a different direction, ask to start again. It's ok to change your mind. In order to help you avoid making any unnecessary comments, always take a few seconds to think about your response before saying it out loud. This will give you time to formulate your thoughts and arrange them in a logical order that you can then present before the interviewers.
- Remember, making mistakes is no bad thing. The important point is that you address the mistake head-on and attempt to revise the statement, perhaps with the assistance of the tutors where necessary.
- The interviewers want to see students are willing and able to elaborate on their answers, so if you have something crucial to add when responding to a question, make sure to include it. At the same time, make sure not to keep on rambling when you have noted all the crucial points that directly address the question asked.

Being accepted into Oxbridge is not determined by how much you know, but by how well you can communicate your thought processes in a way which shows your analytical skills.

What Questions Might be asked?

Most of the questions asked in the interview will begin with a larger question, followed by many smaller sub-questions to guide the answer from start to end. The main question may seem difficult, impossible or random at first, but take a breath and start discussing with your interviewer different ideas you have for breaking down the question into manageable pieces. Don't panic. **The questions are designed to be difficult** to give you the chance to show your full intellectual potential. They will help guide you to the right idea if you provide ideas for them to guide.

THE ULTIMATE OXBRIDGE INTERVIEW GUIDE — GEOGRAPHY & EARTH SCIENCES

This is your chance to show your creativity, analytical skills, intellectual flexibility, problem-solving skills, and aptitude for challenges. Don't waste it on nervousness or a fear of messing up or looking stupid. It is also important to remember that especially for a subject like Geography, **answers are often more complex and multifaceted than a simple yes or no**. This should give you some reassurance during the interview process that your responses can take one direction but also refer to anomalies or include instances where the response would be different. If this is the case, make sure to elaborate on why a response could be both yes and no, and under which circumstances.

Geography

For Geography, at some point in the interview, questions **will likely draw on data** (for example graphs, diagrams or photographs). These types of questions are used to test whether you are able to analyse trends, make sense of the information and therefore apply it to a real-world context. It is worthwhile using a two-step process to answer data-related questions which will give you time to think of a response if you are unsure of what to say, as well as allowing you to provide a clear and well-formulated answer. The first part of your response should describe what you see, for example; 'this graph demonstrates an X trend with a greater clustering of points towards a certain axis'. The second part of your response should comment on why the graph looks that way; for example, why does one trend rise as the other falls?

For geography, in particular, **questions have recurring themes** because they pose critical issues for both geographical research and policy makers: climate change, glacial melt, and also questions exploring the overlap between human and physical geography, for example, conservation and ecosystem loss. The interviewers want to see that you can think analytically (meaning how well you can unpack a given question and how you think of varying possibilities and topics relevant to the response), and how you can think critically (meaning whether you can identify the flaws in certain arguments or data sets and what reasons could be provided for these).

Coursework Interviews

When applying to do Geography or Earth Sciences/Natural Sciences at Cambridge, an applicant may be asked to submit coursework and be called for a coursework interview. Usually, in the morning on the day of the interview, this work is submitted and read by the interviewer. The work is used as a basis for discussion of research and experimental methods and analysis.

The interviewer may open by asking for a summary of the piece of work, they might open a discussion about certain ideas that you mention, or they might want to understand how you reached your conclusions. They may then ask some follow-up questions related to the work or the subject matter. This part of the interview will be very individual and depends on the nature and subject of the work submitted.

After the discussion of the work, the interviewer will probably guide the conversation toward some questions about a related topic to test the applicant's ability to think like a Geographer/Earth Scientist.

Worked Questions

Below are a few examples of how to start breaking down an interview question, complete with model answers.

Q1: This map displays a distribution relating to a natural hazard event. What do you think the natural hazard is and what do you think the map is showing in relation to it?

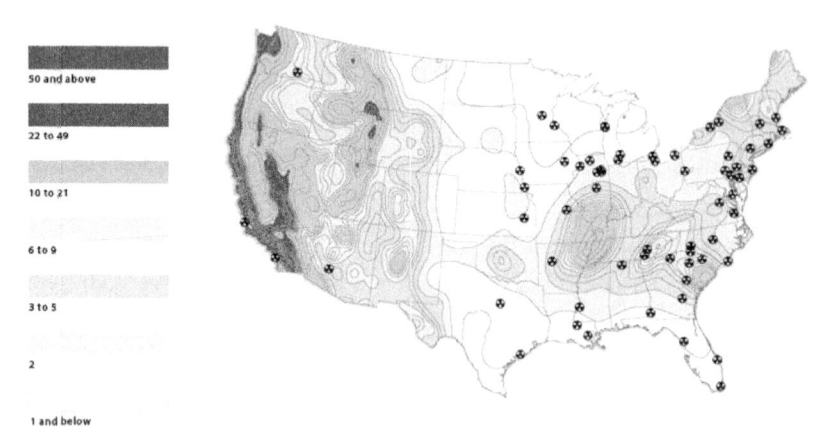

[Extremely clear-headed] Applicant: Well, I can tell that this is a map of North America. At a purely descriptive level, it is evident from the map that there is a higher concentration of the natural event on the west coast than on the east coast. There is also a notable hotspot located on the continent's south-western region. It could be that darker shades represent a higher incidence of events in particular areas like the California region. On the other hand, darker colours could also refer to places in which the effects of the hazard are more pronounced.

Before suggesting what the natural hazard could be, I want to first provide a definition of the term. The definition of natural hazards on the World Meteorological Organisation website is useful for an overall definition, refers to 'events that occur naturally in all parts of the world, with some regions being more vulnerable to certain hazards than others'.

From my knowledge of common natural hazards in California, I would say this map shows the distribution of earthquake events. Darker zones probably point to areas where earthquakes are more common. A different distribution which the colours may represent could be the regions most affected by ground shaking following an earthquake, and those that are less affected.

The details are unimportant, but the general idea of breaking down the question into manageable parts is important. Notice how a better applicant begins by describing what he sees in order to provide directions for his upcoming explanation and to guide his interviewer through his thought process. The interviewer is not looking for a natural hazard expert, but someone who can problem-solve in the face of new ideas. Note that even though the question begins with 'What', it is actually expecting you to consider 'Why' certain distributions look the way they do. The point of these questions is to suggest different ideas and to show an ability to use data usefully.

A poor applicant may take a number of approaches unlikely to impress the interviewer. The first and most obvious of these is to say "We were not taught about natural hazards in America at school" and make no attempt to move forward anyway. It is worth providing some sort of logical response rather than giving up completely. The interviewer is likely to help you by asking follow-up questions, especially if they see you showing a genuine interest and if you make an obvious attempt at some sort of response that is headed in the right direction (for example, even just providing a description of what you see will be better than giving up altogether).

Another approach which is unhelpful in the interview is the 'brain dump', where instead of engaging with the question, the applicant attempts to impress or distract with an assortment of related facts: "Natural hazards are geographical events that occur naturally across the world. These become natural disasters when there is a chance for populations to be affected/at risk". This isn't as impressive as a more reasoned response.

Nevertheless, the interview could be salvaged by taking feedback from the interviewer. This would depend on the applicant's attentiveness and ability to take hints and suggestions from the interviewer.

Q2: Where does the Venn diagram of human geography and physical geography overlap?

A question such as this is a classic way of integrating the two main streams found in Geography, and to test whether you can provide a concise response to a very broad question.

You could begin by speaking about how each stream is integral to the other, resulting in them both being inherently intertwined.

While human geography strives to understand how societies organise and why they organise in certain ways, physical geography strives to understand how natural systems operate and why they function in certain ways. To understand topics more cohesively, such as conservation and climate change, you need an appreciation of how physical and environmental systems function, as well as how these understandings can be applied to societies in social, political, and economic terms.

At the same time, it is important to consider the manner in which human societies affect their environments and what the short, medium, and long-term implications are of these social activities.

It would be useful to note the real-life instances in which these two streams overlap, for example, when policy makers use scientific information to implement policies that affect our lives (i.e. encouraging the use of public transport rather than personal vehicles to reduce CO_2 emissions).

A more advanced response may touch on the gap that exists between both streams, as social and natural scientists often fail to communicate effectively with one another. One example of this may be evident in the plethora of research on climate change existing today, and the lack of ability to communicate this to much of the population in ways that makes them understand the implications of their actions. You could then briefly discuss what other implications this gap may pose for societies.

Q3: How important is the concept of 'space' to geographers?

This is an example of a more theoretical/philosophical question that could be asked in an interview situation, and certainly during your undergraduate career. Start with more simple and basic concepts and build from there.

First, address the concept of space. The more obvious notion of the term implies a <u>physical or rooted place/location</u>. This is important in Geography in terms of pinpointing certain locations and analysing their physical facets.

At a closer look, we can say that the concept of space in Geography is important for understanding how humans interact with the physical features of the land. For example, one place can be used differently by different people and for various purposes. Therefore, understanding space is vital in order to understand the meaning of why certain relations arise between people, arise in specific locales, and how they impact on economic and political institutions.

Q4: Why is it that in some countries, like the United States and Kenya, slums form near wealthy neighbourhoods?

There are certain patterns evident across most developing countries. The emergence of slums in these countries largely refers to informal settlements in urban areas characterised by substandard housing and squalor, including unreliable sanitation services and electricity. Often, the people living in slums have arrived from rural regions of the country in search of better employment and other opportunities. The only places they can afford to live in are the ones they create themselves.

By positioning themselves near wealthy hubs, poorer settlements are able to benefit from access to various established services such as electricity and water, which they could even tap into. They also have <u>easier access</u> to employment, healthcare, and educational opportunities than they would if they were in poorer neighbourhoods.

Q5: How would you go about estimating the mass of the world's oceans, and what would your final figure be?

You can state at the beginning that calculating this accurately depends on the data you have to work with. Since this is an estimation question, you don't need to worry about being precise – rounding numbers is perfectly acceptable. An interviewer wants to see what your thought process is - they are less concerned with receiving a specific number. <u>It's the journey- not the destination that matters</u>.

The key part to providing a coherent response is knowing which key factors you need to identify for the calculation to be made. Start by breaking down the question:

Firstly, recall that Mass = Density x Volume

You should know that the density of water is 1,000 kg/m3.

The Volume of the oceans is trickier. The easiest way is to make a series of assumptions:

The Surface Area of a sphere $= 4\pi r^2$

You could then ask the interviewer for the Earth's radius (6,000 km) or use a sensible estimate.

Approximate π=3 to give:

$$Area = 4 \times 3 \times (6 \times 10^6)^2$$

$$Area = 12 \times 36 \times 10^{12}$$

$$= 432 \times 10^{12} \approx 4 \times 10^{14} \, m^2$$

Approximately 75% of the Earth's Surface Area is covered by the Oceans, so the surface area of the oceans = $4 \times 10^{14} \times 75\% = 3 \times 10^{14} \, m^2$

Finally, you need to convert the area into a volume by multiplying it via an average depth of the oceans. Again, any sensible estimate would be fine here (100 m – 10,000m).

Volume of Oceans = $3 \times 10^{14} \times 1,000 = 3 \times 10^{17} m^3$

Thus, Mass of Oceans = $3 \times 10^{17} \times 1,000 = \mathbf{3 \times 10^{20} kg}$

Real Answer: $1.4 \times 10^{21} \, kg$

Q6: How do mountains originate?

Geography Applicant: It is important to note at the outset that mountain formation is a phenomenon unique to the specific geography and previous conditions of a given location. That said, there are specific processes that, in general, lead to the formation of mountains.

One example is mountains originating from fault-line movements. For example, if a fault exists where both sections push against each other and one rock mass is moving up while the other is moving down, then the upward moving rock mass may form a mountain as it gets pushed up.

Mountains can also originate from volcanic eruptions. This can occur as rock builds up from an explosion, as magma solidifies, and thirdly, as the earth's crust heaves upwards (due to the pressure of the explosion), eventually forming a mountain. Triggers for fault line movements and volcanic eruptions are often unknown and may be the result of several processes occurring within deeper layers of the earth's structure.

In all cases, it is important to note that for mountains to form there needs to be an external trigger that allows for sufficient matter and mass to mobilise in order to create such a phenomenon. Also, while in most cases the process is rather gradual (fault-mountains), in some, the process can be more sudden (volcanic eruptions).

Earth Sciences Applicant: Answering this question would involve suggesting possible scenarios and important parameters. For example, a candidate could begin by explaining that mountain formation is associated with large-scale movements of the earth's crust (making a distinction at the onset between the layers of the earth which could result in such formations). Then one could discuss the various factors that lead to mountain formation, for example, volcanic eruptions and tectonic movements, perhaps providing a brief description/example of how these processes result in mountain formation.

It would then be useful to comment on the timescale and explain how mountains tend to organise over a very long timescale (e.g. due to gradual tectonic movements) or can be formed more suddenly (e.g. during volcanic eruptions). The point of these questions is to suggest different ideas, and to show an understanding of their strengths and weaknesses, as well as an ability to use data usefully.

Crucially, the point of these types of questions is for you to address the key terms (notably volcanoes, global climate), first by defining and describing them, and later by explaining their influences in a logical manner.

Q7: Why do we bother with conservation?

Before considering the aim of conservation, it is important to first understand that it is a loaded term. As such, it could be argued that a loose definition is most appropriate to explain the term. Many definitions include a normative judgment about how the world should be, in other words, what nature should be like given human relations to natural environments. Perhaps one of the most all-encompassing definitions refers to conservation as a "social practice that reflects choices about relations between people and nature".

Given this preliminary understanding, we can see that the 'point' of conservation is very context-specific. Therefore, its aim very much depends on the people carrying out conservationist activities and the ecosystem in question. Given this, conservation aims will include various parameters such as the economic betterment of involved actors, or the environmental preservation of local species, or perhaps the social inclusiveness of local people in environmental programmes.

To summarise, I would say that the point of conservation encompasses the enhancement of relations between nature and people, and the maintenance of this interaction. That said, this heavily depends on the motives of players involved in conservationist activities and the environment in question.

Q8: Are humans ethically obligated to stop global warming and environmental change?

This is a question about Ethics. To answer a question like this, the important thing is not to have a strong opinion that you defend to the death, but to be able to discuss the different viewpoints based on different understandings of right and wrong, and always with a sound understanding of the underlying issues- both scientific and humanitarian.

One way to break down this question would be to consider whether an ethical obligation extends only to other humans or to other organisms as well, and whether it applies in any situation or only when contributing to a situation that wouldn't occur naturally. Similarly, one could also discuss whether humans as a whole are obligated to halt global warming or just a select few members of the human race. Showing an ability to think flexibly about abstract concepts is always good, but don't forget to then argue for the different cases using knowledge of past and present climate and environment, as this is the subject-relevant part of the question.

For instance, don't waste time discussing whether climate change is a reality – the scientific community has already reached a consensus. However, if you would like to argue against an ethical obligation instead, discuss the natural climate variations which have occurred on Earth in the past. Use probable climate-change driven events, like the Permo-Triassic extinction when 96% of species died out 250 million years ago, to argue that humans have no ethical obligation to save other species from anthropogenic extinction, because even without human presence there are climate-driven extinctions. Or argue the opposite, that despite past extreme environmental change being a reality, humanity is pushing the Earth further than it has ever sustained humans, and that we are obligated to do our part to leave a habitable Earth for people in other parts of the world and the future.

Alternatively, you could argue the complete opposite - that there can be no ethical obligation because everyone contributes to the problem in their own way, and everyone will face the consequences. Or that only those who contribute more than they suffer are in the wrong for dumping their consequences onto others. Whichever argument you put forward, be sure to include scientific examples so that your discussion doesn't veer away from the question.

Remember that climate change is not the same as global warming, and your discussion could include pollution (trash, toxins, chemicals, light and sound pollution, etc.), agriculture and monoculture, invasive species, hunting and fishing, deforestation and habitat fragmentation, or any of the other issues beyond the Greenhouse Effect which affect the environment.

Similarly, global warming is not just about fossil fuel use and carbon dioxide, but a range of gases and their effects on weather, ocean acidity, desertification, pathogen spread, etc. Show that you have a deeper understanding of these issues than you could get from skimming the headlines of the Daily Mail.

Q9: What effect does an increase in sea level have on coastal morphology, and why does this impact vary geographically?

The area that will see the greatest morphological impact from sea level rise is the shore and beach area since it is subject to wave action. Sea level rise is caused to the greatest extent by ocean thermal expansion and glacial melt. Since characteristics of coastal zones vary considerably worldwide, due to: a) the rate of relative sea level rise, b) the type of coastline, and c) human stresses, the geographical impact of sea level rise on coastal morphology varies.

Coastal landforms are extremely sensitive to changes in sea level. The likely outcome of increased sea level rise will be that submerging coastlines will become more extensive and erosion rates will increase along most coastal areas. However, other coastlines, mainly around previously glaciated regions, may see a fall in sea level and as a result, may see coastlines growing rather than retreating. In turn, we see that different types of coastlines respond differently to increasing sea level rise, depending on the sensitivity and resilience of the coastline, as well as the human interference implemented. Furthermore, since sea level rise is not uniform across the globe, the response of coastal areas will change depending on the region in question.

It is also essential to consider that existing models of coastal morphology are inadequate in determining responses to sea level rise as they do not take into account the variety of responses and interconnectedness of different processes. Thus, fully determining the extent of geographical variation in coastal geomorphology as a result of sea level rise remains difficult, making it subject to continuing research.

Q10: What is 'risk'?

The field of risk is influenced by two major streams: positivist and normative. The former stream sees risks as real events or dangers that can be approached objectively and calculated using probabilities. Meanwhile, the second stream sees risks as being socially constructed. In this sense, the notion of risk becomes a way of dealing with hazards and insecurities. Such variation in opinions makes it difficult to define what a general 'understanding' of risk really is.

Today, in particular among policy makers, the emphasis within risk still relies on it being something calculable, with science remaining at the basis of attempts to reduce the vulnerability of certain populations in the face of hazards. However, this idea that science can provide an understanding of future risk through mathematical predictions is being increasingly challenged, particularly by academics of the social sciences and within the geographic discipline. This is especially because quantitative analysis tends to overlook the short and long term influence of communities likely to be affected by various risks.

According to one of the most prominent risk theorists, Ulrich Beck, risk can be defined as 'the anticipation of catastrophe'. Alongside other social scientists, Beck has played a key role in advancing a social understanding of risk so that the term can be easily understood by the societies it influences. Therefore, it is becoming increasingly clear that with time, the definition of risk is changing at its core to incorporate the social aspects of the term.

Q11: What is sustainable development?

The definition which I think best encompasses the idea of sustainable development is the one provided by the Brundtland Commission in 1987. It refers to the term as "development which meets the needs of current generations without compromising the ability of future generations to meet their own needs". This definition foregrounds careful management of resources in order to facilitate a high quality of life for current and future generations as well.

It is important to remember that sustainable development does not oppose the idea of humans' use of resources and manipulation of natural environments. Sustainable development, in fact, supports such activities, though in a manner which ensures that the integrity of nature's processes is preserved. The preservation of such processes is important since it allows the reproduction of key biological resources and cycles on which humans depend for sustenance.

Furthermore, it is necessary to consider that sustainable development can be divided into separate but intricately connected subdivisions. For example, development may be economically sustainable, though socially unsustainable. Therefore, for development to be considered truly sustainable, it must encompass the following pillars; social, economic, political, and environmental.

Q12: How do cities act as sources of resilience in an era of heightened risk?

Before providing a response, you need to address two key aspects of the question: the <u>definition of resilience</u> and an understanding of what an 'era of heightened risk' refers to. Martin and Sunley (2006) define resilience as the capacity to bounce back to some previous state following a disruption to the system. Resilience is also about a system being able to withstand total collapse, during which some parts will inevitably become damaged and others will remain intact. Resilience is not just about the ability to recover to a previous state, it is also about reaching a new state that is arguably more robust than the previous by learning from previous catastrophes and incorporating solutions into the urban environment through infrastructures and by educating citizens. Crucially, redundancy and slack are a key aspect of resilience, referring to the idea of leaving space for the unexpected, having spare capacity. Furthermore, questions of resilience have gained new prominence in our era of heightened risk. This new era of global risks is largely the product of human activities and is worsened by the nature of the interconnected global economy in which we live.

I think the main way in which cities act as sources of resilience in today's world is by combining three central factors: resilient communities, smart infrastructures, and intelligent governance. The first makes references to societies that are characterised by solidarity and altruism in the face of a crisis. The second refers to the hardware, and software, that underpins the functioning of our cities, for example, sewage systems and electricity grids. Intelligent governance is the factor that brings the first two characteristics together, including city leaders, academic communities, and researchers. Resilience then becomes the product of a combination of sophisticated modelling, information-based governance, and strong, clear and intelligent urban leadership that creates a sense of community.

In conclusion, we can see that <u>resilience is the product of humans and non-humans coming together</u>. Though the relative balance of each factor varies from city to city, and in turn, creates different forms of resilience in each urban community.

Q13: What can we learn by hazard mapping? What can't we learn?

Hazard mapping displays the distribution of hazards according to their geographical location. Such maps are typically created for natural hazards such as earthquakes, volcanoes, landslides, flooding, and tsunamis.

Even so, hazard mapping has several limitations. I will discuss two specific issues. Firstly, and perhaps most importantly, these maps often make no reference to hazards' <u>potential social impact</u>; either in terms of human life or economic loss.

At times, this renders hazard maps less useful or understandable for local communities. Another issue is attributable to the uncertainty inherent within natural hazards themselves, in turn, compromising the accuracy of hazard maps. For example, we are still <u>unable to predict the timescale</u> of certain hazards, such as volcanic eruptions, given that we cannot always identify which forces trigger their manifestation. Furthermore, inaccuracies in modelling tools create uncertainties in mapping, again, limiting the applicability of such maps for use in warning communities.

Q14: Does cost-benefit analysis (CBA) helps us make difficult decisions with regards to the environment?

This isn't a simple yes/no question – it requires that you address both sides of the argument.

A cost-benefit analysis is a useful tool for making difficult decisions regarding the environment since it breaks down issues into separate factors. These can then be quantified with the numerical values of each benefit and cost being used to consider the overall soundness of the project in question. This type of analysis is also good for identifying which players are involved in decision-making and who will win or lose from the proposed project. While this type of analysis is helpful for making difficult decisions, it has its downfalls which must be considered if such a tool is adopted for decision-making. Perhaps the core issue of CBA is that some environmental issues cannot be quantified. For example, it may be difficult to quantify the aesthetic and spiritual value of environments to their indigenous populations. Furthermore, the outcome of the CBA will largely depend on the player that is carrying out such analysis, with an economic developer likely to place greater positive weighting on the economic benefits of a project, rather than the need for environmental preservation.

Overall, we can see that CBA is a useful tool for helping us make difficult decisions about the environment. Even so, it may be necessary to adopt supplementary tools for analysing environmental questions in order to make up for CBA's shortfalls.

Q15: Do you think that access to education lies at the heart of development?

Development loosely refers to processes of social change or class that aim to transform national economies, particularly in formerly colonised countries or countries situated in the global south. Access to education is an important part of a country's development, though, given the complexity of the subject, it's not possible to isolate one factor that will, on its own, help a country improve economically, politically, and socially. Furthermore, since each country begins at a different stage of development, its educational needs will vary. For example, in certain countries, the state of healthcare may be so dire that economic productivity may suffer significantly. In this case, healthcare would be a more urgent factor for targeting development. Therefore, education doesn't lie alone at the core of development because the process itself is multifaceted and because it is dependent on the country.

That said, and as also stated by the Campaign for Global Education in 2010, education remains a focal point for development initiatives since it is an important catalyst for national economic and social growth. For example, national expenditure on education can be seen to promote development if the investment results in improvements in the quality of labour, which in turn raises GDP over the long term. The importance of education is reiterated by its status as a millennium development goal and it being one of the dimensions for measuring the Human Development Index (HDI). Furthermore, access to education has the capability of acting as an important force for social change and even political transformation (you may wish to reference specific case studies here).

In summary, since development cannot be distilled to one factor alone, it may be more useful to consider in what ways access to education can be used to propel development rather than trying to weigh its relative importance within the development field.

Q16: When it comes to climate change, does the past help us predict the future?

If we look at current publications regarding climate change, there is no doubt that the data collected about past climate trends has been instrumental in making future projections. This is because paleo-climactic evidence from the past sheds light onto the emergence and functioning of the Earth's climate system, and what changes it has experienced. This, in turn, suggests what path it might follow in future. In his writings on Paleoclimatology, Bruckner states that past climate reconstructions can then be 'integrated with observations of the Earth's current climate and placed into a computer model to deduce the past and predict future climate'. Additionally, in a social context, using past records is important for identifying what exposes certain physical and human vulnerabilities; which is crucial for climate change forecasting.

While the past is useful in predicting the future, it is important to keep in mind that reasons for changes in climate can be attributable to various sources. In the case of climate change, we must very carefully analyse the impacts of humans in creating new, unusual climatic patterns, and the potential consequences of these for society. Following from this, it is important that we are aware that the past will not provide a precise analogue of the future given inherent uncertainties in nature and inaccuracies in our modelling tools. Thus, uncertainties in measurements and forecasting must be acknowledged to ensure that inappropriate actions aren't taken by policy makers.

In sum, while the past is crucial in helping us to understand the potential future trajectory of climate change, various social factors and discrepancies in data need to be accounted for to ensure that projections about climate change's trajectory are more accurate and relevant to today's societies.

Q17: How can volcanic eruptions change global climate?

Answering this question can begin with recognition of the meaning of global climate. Since our planet's climate is comprised of a complex mixture of processes and elements, any significant influence to this system has the potential to change the climate.

You should then address how volcanic eruptions, given their nature and force, are able to influence global climate. First, you must note the types of elements ejected by volcanoes during an eruption, including the release of vast amounts of ash and gases into the atmosphere, as well as flows of lava and ash covering the ground. You could suggest that lava cover on the ground can have some effect on regional (though perhaps not global) climate, and how the most important influence on climate comes from volcanic gases released into the atmosphere, e.g. sulphur dioxide. The cloud formed by the gases and ash can reduce the amount of solar radiation reaching the earth. This can result in the Earth's surface temperature decreasing significantly.

Changes in one region's climate can result in climate changes in other regions. You can also launch a discussion of how the deep earth and biosphere are linked through the carbon cycle. For example, erupting magma releases CO_2 into the atmosphere. Years of weathering remove most of this gas – causing it to end up in the oceans as calcium carbonate sediment. Therefore, an excess of this from eruptions can offset the balance of CO_2 in the system.

The idea of timescale is also important here. Ash cover created by volcanic eruptions can have an immediate impact on a region's climate. Contrastingly, changes in the carbon cycle can result in long-term impacts.

Geography Interview Questions

1. Why do you think that temperatures rise more quickly at the poles than near the equator?
2. How would you define 'Culture'?
3. Do you have any ideas about why the rate of glacial melt isn't linear?
4. Can you describe the relationship between population and carbon dioxide in the atmosphere?
5. Please plot a graph of CO2 emissions over time, from 900AD onwards.
6. Why did India progress more quickly through the DTM than the countries it was based on originally?
7. In the modern world of smartphones, what is the value of a map?
8. Why do climate change deniers exist?
9. Can you think of examples of how computer technologies can help us understand geographical processes, or natural hazards?
10. Is nature still 'natural'?
11. What's the impact of a volcanic eruption on the global climate – how much time does it take for this impact to be felt?
12. Can you think of some obstacles to disease transmission?
13. What do you know about Malthus's ideas regarding population?
14. Why do levels of biodiversity vary around the globe?
15. Is it important to quantify the diversity of living species?
16. Draw the carbon and water cycles, how do they connect?
17. Can you identify the impacts of economic policy on social inequality?
18. What would you say is the central component of development, education?
19. What proportion of all the water in the world can be found in a watermelon?
20. If atmospheric pressure is 10,000 Pa., what is the total mass of Earth's atmosphere?
21. Can you predict the fallout from an asteroid impact in the Pacific? Let's say the asteroid is ten kilometres across.
22. What separates a volcano from a mountain?
23. If you could only save one, which of the Antarctic or the Amazon would you choose?
24. How do we know what the Earth's core consists of?
25. How do you think our ancestors determined that the earth wasn't flat?
26. Suggest methods by which we could work out how old things are.
27. Imagine that Earth had a second moon, identical to Luna – what would this change?
28. Do you think you'd survive for longer in the arctic or Sahara desert?
29. What would happen if pandas became extinct?
30. How could we measure sea levels, what would be some issues with this?
31. How would you go about proving man-made global warming?
32. What are the geographic impacts of globalisation and multi-national corporations?
33. If you could take a non-geographer anywhere in the world to convince them geography was important, where would you take them and what would you say?
34. It is often said that we know more about the surface of the moon than the depths of our oceans – do you think this is true, and if it is how would you fix it?
35. Why is there a wider range of living organisms in rainforests than there are in deserts?
36. What geological phenomena can you think of which have had significant impacts on people?

HISTORY

The subject interview for History can take several different formats as each college has their own way of conducting interviews. The Admissions Office for your college will let you know what format your interview will take in good time. If you have any questions about it, it's best to contact them directly.

It may be the case that you have prepared extensively for one aspect of your interview, but aren't given a chance to draw on that preparation. For example, they might not ask you about anything on your personal statement, even if you are very keen to talk about it. If this happens, try not to let it rattle you. The interview process can be unpredictable, so try to remain as calm and flexible as you can.

In a standard history interview, the interviewers will ask you a **series of questions pertaining to your subject**. Some of these will be related to topics you have studied before. Others will be related to certain areas of historical methodology.

The interviewers know what subjects and what areas of history you have studied at school from your application. For example, they will know if you have studied modern history or ancient history. They will **not** ask you for detailed knowledge about areas of your subject that you are not familiar with. However, questions on topics you've studied are fair game.

Draw on the work you have done at school to answer these questions, but be prepared that the conversation might go beyond your syllabus. Avoid saying things like 'we haven't covered this in school yet' – just try your best to answer each question.

The interviewers will also have read your personal statement (and your SAQ form, if you applied to Cambridge). They are likely to ask you questions about the academic sections of it.

For example, if you have mentioned that you furthered your understanding of historical practice by reading Richard Evans' *In Defence of History*, then they may ask you to summarise an aspect of the book or ask whether you agree with the author on a certain issue. If you have mentioned work experience in a museum, they might ask you about the work you did there.

Worked Questions

Below are a few examples of how to start breaking down an interview question, complete with model answers.

Q1: Does the study of history serve any practical purpose?

Applicant: This question covers quite a lot of potential areas, so I will start by looking at the study of history in the context of university/higher education as that seems most relevant. Firstly, I will evaluate a few potential arguments. Studying history at university serves many practical purposes, both for the student and society as a whole. The student gains many skills such as research and formulating an argument. Society gets to benefit from these skills when they graduate. But these benefits are not unique to history alone as this description could also cover other humanities subjects such as Classics or Sociology.

The other argument is that <u>history teaches lessons</u>, without which history would simply repeat itself and humanity would go on making the same 'mistakes'. This is also not a particularly convincing view in my opinion. Though, there can be similarities between different historical events as all historical events are unique, which I believe undermines the idea that history constantly repeats itself. I think this idea is based too much on hindsight as it is easy to see similarities between events after they have happened.

Instead, I think that historical causation (what makes events happen) depends above all on the context in which those events take place. This means that we cannot necessarily learn specific practical 'lessons' from history to apply in the future because the context of the future will be completely different.

However, this does not mean that history does not serve any practical purpose. Even though I don't think one can learn concrete 'lessons' from history, being able to understand how a certain problem came about can make it easier to find a solution. This means that the <u>skills gained by studying history can have a positive practical impact</u> on policy-making. Aside from that, the study of history also serves to educate and entertain the public. Most historical works are written by historians at universities and TV documentaries are usually made with the input of historians.

<u>Analysis:</u> You will not be expected to answer questions as fully as this. This answer is an indication of some of the things you might be expected to talk about in response to a question like this, but the interviewer will help you along the way with additional questions and comments. The merit of the answer is that it <u>breaks down the question</u> into manageable chunks and proceeds through an answer while signposting this process to the interviewer. These are good skills for you to try to develop, but remember that the interviewer is there to help get the best out of you.

<u>Poor applicant:</u> A poor applicant could begin by saying "we haven't studied this in class", and make no effort to further the conversation. He or she might then, if pressed, express a vague opinion that history serves a practical purpose in that it teaches people lessons for the future. As discussed, this is not a very strong interpretation because historical events depend on a specific configuration of circumstances. It would be difficult to gain a concrete and specific 'lesson' from one historical situation that could be applied in another historical situation as no two historical situations are the same.

A <u>poor applicant</u> may also respond to this question by saying that there is no practical purpose to history at all. Unless you have a very good argument to back this up, this would be a bad answer to this question because it would overlook the practical benefits that a historical perspective can bring to various areas of public life. It would also be a bad answer because it would imply that there is no practical purpose to the career to which your interviewers have dedicated their lives, as well as the degree to which you are applying.

Q2: Is it ever possible to find out 'what really happened' in the past?

A <u>good applicant</u> will recognise the complexity of this question. Throughout school, one is encouraged to assume that every statement written in a history book is a statement of fact. But at university level, it becomes clear that sources are subjective, historical interpretations are subjective, and the idea that history is just a series of events and facts seems a little simplistic. With a question like this, a good way to break it down is to focus first on one side of the argument and then on the other before coming to a conclusion. If you do this, you might choose to say to the interviewer, "first I will look at the idea that it is not possible to find out 'what really happened' in the past", so they know the approach you are taking.

Then you might choose to discuss the fact that you can never really know whether a source is telling the truth because <u>historical sources are inherently subjective</u>. A diary entry or letter about a certain event is only written from one person's perspective and they might not have had a full understanding of events or may be recording them in hindsight, having forgotten some of what happened. Even official documents are subjective; they might have an agenda behind them or be subject to censorship. When it comes to more distant historical events, the source material is necessarily subjective because it depends on a large extent on what documents have survived.

So, in many ways, it may be impossible to find out 'what really happened' in the past – there are too many obstacles in the way and history is only ever an interpretation of past events, rather than an objective statement of fact.

On the other hand, however, it would be unfair to say that this means all interpretations are equally invalid. While historical sources are subjective, it is possible to come to a reasonable interpretation of past events by using a wide variety of sources that corroborate each other. If all available sources say the same thing about a certain event, we can be reasonably sure that this is correct. This is how we can determine certain facts that are beyond interpretation. For example, the French Revolution occurred in 1789. Therefore, it is possible to find out some aspects of what really happened. Even though sources and interpretations are subjective, <u>history is not fiction</u>.

Q3: Is history increasingly the study of ordinary people?

In many ways, the answer to this would be quite straightforward. Yes, history does seem to be moving away from the study of great men to that of ordinary people – whereas in the early 20th century, 'history' was almost synonymous with '<u>political history</u>' and focused largely on politicians and generals. History seems to have democratised in recent decades. Scholarship in recent years appears to have focused more than ever on people who had not been represented by historical studies before such as women, ethnic minorities, the working classes, etc.

A good answer may, therefore, challenge this obvious response in a few ways. While all of the above is true, it would be worth mentioning that some <u>parts of history still focus disproportionately on 'great men'</u> rather than 'ordinary people'. Political history still occupies a big part of university history curricula while 'popular history', such as TV documentaries and historical bestsellers, are more often than not focused on 'great men' (or great events or occasionally, great women such as Elizabeth I) rather than 'ordinary people'.

A good answer would also recognise the secondary question implicit in this question – <u>Why is history moving away from the study of great men to that of ordinary people?</u> Answers to this would perhaps include a discussion of how minority rights movements often initiate new historical interest in minorities or a discussion of the democratisation of education in recent decades (e.g. African-American civil rights or second-wave feminism).

Q4: How would a biography of a major political figure written during their lifetime differ from one written after they had died? Which would be more accurate?

This type of question is a great one to get as it gives you a lot of scope to be creative and to bring in your own knowledge. The interviewers may ask this in response to a political biography you have listed in your personal statement, which would allow you to speak about a topic you are familiar with and passionate about.

However, assuming you are asked this question hypothetically without a specific biography in mind, there are several ways to approach it- even if you are not familiar with any biography of a major political figure yourself.

First, it would be sensible to tackle the first part of this question in isolation and leave the additional question ("which would be more accurate?") for later in the discussion. A biography of a major political figure written during their lifetime would be likely to differ significantly from one written after their death.

The biographer may have had access to meetings with the political figure or the biography may even have been written with the input of the political figure. This may make the text richer in its detail, but may also mean that it is coloured by the politician's political agenda and desire to manage his image and reputation. A biography written after the politician's death may have access to newly released sources not available during the figure's lifetime. There are many possible answers to this question.

In response to the second part of the question, a weak candidate may have a strong opinion on this, saying something like "a biography written during their lifetime would be more accurate because the biographer would know the politician, so they would tell the truth" or alternatively, "a biography written after their lifetime would be more accurate because the biographer would have the benefit of hindsight". Both of these answers fail to take the complexity of the situation into account.

A stronger candidate would investigate both options more fully and would not take too dogmatic a view on what is a complicated question without a clear answer. After considering the merits and weaknesses of each type of source, a stronger candidate may conclude that one cannot deem either type of source more accurate than the other. This is because it would depend entirely on the specific biography and biographers in question, or may conclude that it would be best to draw upon both sources to get the most accurate depiction of the politician in question.

Text/Source-Based Interview

If your college decides to give you a text- or source-based interview, you will be given a piece of academic text to look at before the interview. You may also need to write a summary or commentary; the Admissions Office will tell you if this is the case. It is likely that the text you are given will be unfamiliar to you, on a topic or area of history you have not studied before. Do not be daunted by this – you are not expected to have any detailed factual knowledge related to the text.

The interview will then be based on the contents of the extract, and the issues surrounding it. Things to keep in mind:

- When reading the text in advance, pay attention to the author, the date of publication, and the nature of the work. It may be a historical source or an extract from a work of historiography by a theorist such as E.H. Carr or Richard Evans. It may be an introduction from a history book on a topic you have never encountered before.
- Try to pick up on aspects of the publication that are unusual or revealing (e.g. was it written anonymously? Is it a revision of an earlier text? Is it clearly written in response to another text or another writer's view? Who is the intended audience?)

- When reading the text, pay attention to the argument it is making. Is it a strong argument or a weak argument and why? Can you think of any counter-arguments?
- Does the text relate in any way to any other area of history and historiography that you -are familiar which can be drawn upon in the interview?

What Questions Might Be Asked?

For this type of interview setting, the interviewers will ask questions about the text and the broader historical issues that the text raises. Questions about the text directly will range from content comprehension (what is the author arguing? What does the author mean by X?) to interpretation (do you agree with the author's characterization of X?) to questions of historical methodology (why has the author approached this subject in this way? Is the author's method valid?)

The thing to remember when answering these questions is not to panic! The questions are designed to be difficult to give you the chance to show your full intellectual potential. The interviewers will help guide you to the right idea if you provide ideas for them to guide. This is your chance to show your creativity, analytical skills, intellectual flexibility, problem-solving skills and your go-getter attitude. Don't waste it on nervousness or a fear of messing up or looking stupid.

Q5: You are given an extract from an introduction to a historical work that is based entirely on oral sources, such as Robert Fraser's 'Blood of Spain'.

Can one ever understand a historical event from oral history sources alone?#

This question is asking you to evaluate a particular type of source. A good way to approach a question like this would be to look firstly at the ways in which this type of source can help to understand an event, then to look at the weaknesses of this type of source, and then to come to a conclusion. There are lots of aspects of a historical event that could be understood through oral history sources alone. Using the example of the Spanish Civil War, oral history allows one to understand what the war was like in terms of lived experience, as in a fairly decentralised state with low levels of literacy and high levels of censorship. Oral history can bring a perspective to the war that is lacking in other types of sources and official documents.

Furthermore, seeing as oral histories are generally collected in interviews after the event in question, this type of source allows the historian to understand not only the event itself but also its aftermath and long-term effects on those who lived through it.

However, there are several drawbacks to oral history. While it is a useful way to understand what it was like to live through an event, it only shows the perspective of those interviewed, which may not be representative of the people of Spain as a whole. It also would not take into account political, economic or international factors influencing the course of events, which can only be illuminated by other types of sources. Oral history is also fallible, in that people are interviewed about events that happened years or even decades earlier. Therefore, recollections of events may not be entirely reliable.

A good conclusion to this question would be that while certain aspects of historical events could be understood from oral sources alone, no one type of source is comprehensive enough to encapsulate every aspect of an event. For the best understanding of the Spanish Civil War, it would be necessary to use as wide a variety of sources as possible, including oral history.

Q6: You may be given an extract from an introduction to a history book on a very specific topic about which you know very little about, and asked to comment on the historian's proposed method. For example, it may be an extract from a work that looks at Georgian England from a woman's perspective, such as Vickery's Behind Closed Doors: At Home in Georgian England.

This work looks at Georgian England from a feminist perspective. Do you think it is acceptable to analyse a period through the lens of a concept that didn't exist during the period under study (i.e. feminism)?

This would be a difficult question to be presented with at an interview. It is important to stay calm and be open-minded, and the interviewers will help guide you to an answer. It would be useful to analyse both sides of such a question before coming to a conclusion. You might start by looking at the drawbacks of analysing a certain period through the lens of a concept that was not contemporary to the period you are looking at.

There are several problems with analysing Georgian England through a feminist framework (for example). Many historians argue that it is better to analyse the past through terminology that was in use in the period under discussion.

By looking at Georgian England through a feminist perspective, you may be imposing ideas onto the past that are incompatible with the period under study. You could argue that this is not so much history as sociology, as it is putting more of an emphasis on the modern concept (feminism) than on the period you are supposed to be studying (Georgian England).

However, there are also benefits to this type of historiography. Part of the purpose of history is to look at the past through a new perspective. Even if this perspective would not have been understood by the people who lived in the period under discussion, it may still illuminate aspects of the period that have not yet been covered by the scholarship.

Q7: You may be given an extract from a work about a certain aspect of historical theory, such as Niall Ferguson's Virtual History or Richard Evans' Altered Pasts, both of which deal with counter-factual history.

What, if any, is the value of studying counter-factual history?

Counter-factual history is the history of *what if?* It challenges the historian to consider what would have happened had something else occurred. A common counter-factual investigated by Ferguson is *'what if Great Britain had never entered the First World War?'*

A good answer to this question would reflect on the merits and limitations of this type of history and the basis of the information given in the source.

There are several merits to studying counter-factual history. It allows one to focus on crucial turning points in historical events. You may only really be able to understand the consequences of a certain event (such as Britain entering the First World War) if you have gone through the process of imagining how things might have turned out if this one event had gone differently. It may also help in thinking about causation in history. You may come to the realisation that a certain factor was a key cause in a certain event only by considering whether the event would have gone ahead without the factor. *What If?* History can also be entertaining and engaging and may be a good way of inspiring interest in history.

However, there are also problems associated with studying counter-factual history. Many counter-factual hypotheses (such as *'what if Britain had not entered the First World War?'*) can be taken too far. It's one thing to reflect on such a question in order to analyse the importance of what did happen and the consequences of Britain's entry into the war. It's another thing to imagine a complete parallel universe in which a hypothetical scenario (Britain staying out of the war) is extrapolated into a completely different historical narrative. Perhaps counter-factual speculation is a useful historical tool when used in moderation but can easily slide into fiction.

Essay-Based Interview

Some colleges at Oxford and Cambridge will ask you to submit one or two essays with your application. The details for this will be made clear in the application process. One of your interviews may, therefore, be based in part on the contents of your essay. This is a chance for you to demonstrate your detailed factual knowledge about an area of history you are familiar with, as well as to show your passion for the subject.

The interviewer may open by asking for a summary of the piece of work, of the methodology behind it, and the conclusion reached. They may then ask some follow-up questions related to the work or the subject matter. This part of the interview will be very individual and depend on the nature and subject of the work submitted. Here are some things to keep in mind if you are submitting essays as part of your application:

- Ensure that any work you are submitting is your own. You will not be able to justify an argument you make in an interview if that argument was written by your tutor or teacher. The interviewers will be able to tell if this is the case.
- Ensure that any work you are submitting is on topics that you feel comfortable talking about in detail (e.g. something you have studied at AS-level, rather than something you have only just started studying)
- Of course, ensure that the work you submit is of a high standard that you believe reflects your academic abilities. If it is a piece of work you are proud of, you will better be able to defend it in your interview.
- Re-read the essays you have submitted before the interview so they are fresh in your mind.
- While it is good to remain flexible and open to revising your arguments, try not to disagree with your own essay! If the interviewer asks about a certain aspect of the essay and you respond by saying "I wrote this ages ago, I don't think it's very good", that won't come across well. On the other hand, if you have a very solid reason for revising your argument, this is something you can bring up in your interview.

Example Questions

These questions are likely to be **tailored to the individual essay you've submitted**, so it is likely that the answers given are not relevant to the topics covered in your own essay. However, it is useful to read them anyway and think about the *types* of questions you might be asked.

Q8: The questions are likely to build on the essay you have written or they will prompt you to investigate an aspect of the topic your essay has not covered fully. A candidate who has written an essay on the topic 'Did Napoleon bring an end to the French Revolution' in which he/she has argued in the affirmative could be asked the question: "When did Napoleon bring an end to the French Revolution?"

A good answer to a question such as this should firstly acknowledge the complexity of the question. In this case, this would require recognising that there are many potential answers to the question. One could argue that Napoleon ended the French Revolution in 1799 when he became First Consul, or in 1802 when he declared himself Consul for life, or in 1804 when he made himself Emperor. You may have a strong opinion in favour of one of these interpretations, but before making your case, it would be good to show that you are aware that there are many possible arguments that could be made.

If you believe that the French Revolution ended when Napoleon made himself Emperor in 1804, you would need to explain why. In this type of question, factual detail and a command of the material is crucial as the topic on which you have written an essay should be one with which you are very familiar. You may, for instance, talk about this event from a constitutional perspective and argue that this is the point at which leadership of France technically returns to the type of monarchical system the Revolution had aimed to overthrow. You may mention that the Pope takes part in Napoleon's coronation ceremony, showing that the anti-Catholic nature of the Revolution has been reversed. Whatever you decide to argue, you must show clear factual evidence to back up your interpretation.

A poor candidate may respond to this question in a number of ways. The most obvious mistakes to be avoided would be to reply, "I don't know" or to say "1804" and refuse to explain your answer. It would also be unwise to reverse the argument you originally made in your essay by saying "Napoleon didn't bring an end to the French Revolution" (unless you have very good reason, for example, new research to back up this revision).

Q9: A candidate who has written an essay on the Enlightenment could be asked a question such as "Why do you write 'the Enlightenment' in your essay, rather than 'enlightenment'?"

A good answer will recognise the complexity of the question. It is not a question about grammar and formatting at all. Instead, it highlights the issue of whether the Enlightenment (or enlightenment) can be seen as a movement that was clear and homogeneous enough to warrant being labelled with a proper noun (The Enlightenment) rather than a vaguer descriptive term (enlightenment).

A good answer would then talk this through with the interviewers, with reference to factual evidence you are familiar with. You could talk about how the Enlightenment was a very diverse movement, encompassing ideas as varied as Rousseau's *The Social Contract* to enlightened absolutism in the Habsburg monarchy. This might, be better characterised through a descriptive term rather than a proper noun as The Enlightenment makes these ideas seem more uniform than they were in reality. However, you might on balance argue that it should still be categorised as The Enlightenment because many of its thinkers referred to themselves in these terms.

A <u>weaker candidate</u> may simply say "My teacher said it was The Enlightenment" or "My textbook says The Enlightenment" and refuse to engage with the topic. A weak candidate may also say "I had never really thought about it" and leave it at that. If you have genuinely never considered an idea that you are presented with in the interview (which is very likely to happen), it is fine to say so. But then do go on to engage with the idea critically, e.g. "I had considered that but it's a very interesting point".

History Interview Questions

1. Do you think that we should be careful when examining colonial history in a postcolonial world?
2. Can you think of any examples of a student protest having a significant impact on the path of history?
3. Do you think that historical eras have tangible meaning, should the 'Progressive Era' be capitalised?
4. Why do you want to study history?
5. Should we exclusively teach British history in British schools?
6. Can you learn real history from films and television programmes?
7. How can we justify public funding of the study of history to the taxpayer?
8. Do you think history can have any practical purpose?
9. Do you think that it's possible to learn lessons from history?
10. Currently, history is largely treated as contiguous – should we separate ancient history from modern?
11. What would you say differentiates modern and classical sources?
12. Should we ever take ancient accounts literally?
13. Do you think that the concept of race is useful for historians?
14. Can you identify patterns or cycles in history?
15. What is the significance of medieval history in the modern world?
16. Define 'revolution'
17. Do you think that ideology exists in history?
18. How can we ever really know what people in the past thought or felt?
19. Do you think that class is valuable as an analytical tool for historians?
20. What's the value in studying contemporary history?
21. Do you think historians should just tell the story of the past in the plainest terms, or should they add their own input?
22. Do you think that religion remains important for historians of the modern world?
23. You mentioned being fascinated by historiography in your personal statement. What does that word mean?
24. What do you think is the value of gender-history?
25. Is Marxist history still worth studying?
26. Do you think written sources are less useful to historian than verbal ones?
27. You mentioned working on the French Revolution for your EPQ, can you compare it with a modern event of your choosing?
28. Do you think that the events of the 11th of September, 2001 changed the way that we approach history in the West?
29. What separates mythology from history?
30. How do you think people were able to justify slavery on the grounds of the economic benefits?
31. How do you think we should commemorate the Great War?
32. Is all history is the history of great men?
33. What do you look at when determining how reliable a source is?
34. Should economic history be purely quantitative?
35. What could you learn about a past society from a pair of shoes?

36. What separates a terrorist and a patriot?
37. If you could invite someone from the past to dinner, who would you choose and why?
38. What is a nation?
39. Does nationalism have negative connotations?
40. Can the study of history be scientific?
41. To what extent can historians ever be unbiased?
42. When do you think the British Empire had the most power?
43. At what point would you say that the English monarchy was at its height?
44. All historical records in the world are lost to a natural disaster. All that remains are historical records on sports. How much of the past could we relearn?
45. You're transported back in time with one goal – stop Hitler. How do you accomplish this?
46. Where is the end of history?
47. What are the main differences and similarities found in the French and Russian revolutions?
48. What elements were continuous between the Great War and World War II? What elements had changed?
49. How might history be written by the loser?
50. Why did Europe not follow America's example and form a USE?
51. Do you think that Napoleon was a better leader than Alexander the Great?
52. What can we learn from 18th century warfare which is applicable in the modern world?

PPE & HSPS

A politics applicant may be asked a question relating to politics or questions from a related subject, such as sociology. Despite stating a previous knowledge in one particular area of HSPS or PPE on your application, you may be asked a question on any of these subject areas. However, you will not be expected to demonstrate specific detailed knowledge in an area not studied previously, you will simply be expected to apply your own point of view and understanding to the topics.

HSPS & PPE interviews generally consist of a large question with many smaller sub-questions to guide the answer from the start to a conclusion. The main question may seem difficult, impossible, or random at first, but take a breath and start discussing with your interviewer different ideas you have for breaking down the question into manageable pieces. Don't panic.

The questions are designed to be difficult to give you the chance to show your full intellectual potential. They will help guide you to the right idea if you provide ideas for them to guide. This is your chance to show your creativity, analytical skills, intellectual flexibility, problem-solving skills and your go-getter attitude. Don't waste it on nervousness or a fear of messing up or looking stupid.

The interviewer wants to see what you know and what you are capable of, not what you don't know – "positive interview".

When answering a question, you should be responsive to the interviewer and take on board their prompts and suggestions. If you are making an argument that is clearly wrong, then concede your mistake and try to revise your viewpoint – it is ok to say 'I didn't think of that' when taking on board a different viewpoint. Do not stubbornly carry on arguing a point that they are saying is wrong. **Making mistakes is not a bad thing** – if you can show that you have addressed a mistake and attempted to revise your argument upon the realisation of more information, you are showing a skill crucial to getting through essays and supervisions at an Oxbridge university.

Due to the amount of subjects available under the HSPS and PPE courses, **there are no set patterns to the questions you can get asked**. Most questions, however, will focus on a topic for which it is possible for any individual to have an opinion without previous knowledge of the area. This is to test the way you think about a topic and to test whether you are able to apply your own experiences and knowledge to an unknown subject area. These skills are important when studying HSPS/PPE as the courses are essay-based and rely strongly upon the ability to construct an argument based on the information provided. Many questions are related to society today and may require the individual to be familiar with current affairs and big events in the news.

A sociologist may be asked sociology questions or questions from a related subject, such as politics. An archaeologist will likely be asked questions on archaeology, history, and anthropology. Given the very broad nature of the course, candidates are required to have a general interest in all aspects of the course, but which subject will be the main focus of any interview should be clear beforehand.

The questions will usually take one of a few possible forms based on highlighting skills necessary to 'think like a social scientist.' **Five main questions types** are:

- Why do we need... (borders, welfare state, international institutions, museums etc.)?
- Compare X to Y... (normally based on your essay or personal statement, so something you are familiar with)
- Distinguish between... (state and nation, race and ethnicity, liberalism and libertarianism etc.)
- What do you think about... (the current British school system, nature vs. nurture debate etc.)?
- Why is there... (gender inequality in the workplace, poverty etc.)? How would you solve it?

Questions also have recurring themes that appear because they are important for social sciences: legitimacy and role of government, human rights, poverty, feminism, international institutions, the purpose of education and different educational systems, voting systems, inequality and social classes.

Worked Questions

Below are a few examples of how to start breaking down an interview question, complete with model answers.

Q1: Can a violent protest ever be justified?

[Extremely clear-headed] Applicant: Well, I know that the law states that violence against other people or property is not acceptable, and yet I also know that violent protests still occur and this makes me wonder why. There must be a reason that people feel the need to turn to violence. This might be because of their personality or it may be something deeper such as the feeling of having no choice. If a point is important and the protest is for a serious reason, such as fighting for human rights, and all other forms of protest have been avoided, then maybe the only way to be heard is through violence. However, I don't think a violent protest can ever be justified. For example, take the 2011 UK Riots – violence didn't solve anything – it is a way of being seen and heard, but a horrific one. I don't think being heard for doing something that is wrong is the right way to be recognised.

This shows that the question can be broken down into smaller-parts, which can be dealt with in turn. At this point, the interviewer can give feedback if this seems like a good start and help make any necessary modifications. In this particular case, the applicant might be asked to expand on the reasons a person might resort to violence in protests and to give an example if possible. They may also be asked to provide a suggestion as to a better way to be heard than a violent protest. The details are unimportant, but the general idea of breaking down the question into manageable parts is important. The interviewer is not looking for an expert, but someone who can problem-solve in the face of new ideas.

A poor applicant may take a number of approaches unlikely to impress the interviewer. The first and most obvious of these is to simply answer 'yes' or 'no' with little justification or reference to an alternative point of view and with no attempt made to move forward. The applicants who have done this only make it worse for themselves by resisting prodding as the interviewer attempts to pull an answer from them, saying "fine, but I'm not going to be able to expand because I don't know anything about this", or equally unenthusiastic and uncooperative responses.

Another approach which is unhelpful in the interview is the 'brain dump', where instead of engaging with the question, the applicant attempts to impress or distract with an assortment of related facts or events: In this case, reeling off the law on violence or a list of historical riots and their outcomes.

Having gotten off to this start isn't as impressive as a more reasoned response, but the interview can be salvaged by taking feedback from the interviewer.

Many of these facts could start a productive discussion which leads to the answer if the applicant listens and takes hints and suggestions from the interviewer.

Q2: How do you know the moon isn't made out of cheese?

[Extremely clear-headed] Applicant: What I am first going to think about is what needs to be considered when deciding whether or not something is true. This raises questions like "Is it patently absurd?", "Is it backed up by evidence?", and "What types of evidence do we require?". Next, I consider whether it is reasonably possible that this statement fits with other associated and established pieces of knowledge, e.g. the formation of the planets, stars, and satellites. If the claim is at odds with established knowledge, then I may be more inclined to believe it untrue. However, this does not necessarily prove anything. For example, in this case, what is meant by cheese? If we are talking poetically, or aesthetically then it may be considered reasonable to make the above claim.

Moreover, whose reality are we talking about, and indeed does the result vary depending on this? I mean, is it really possible to 'know' anything, or are we just making educated guesses based on a set of assumptions married with some data – and does this count as 'real'? Essentially, when I first looked at the statement I thought it was completely absurd and previously proven otherwise. However, after consideration of perspective, definition, reality, and knowledge, I am now not so convinced.

This is a step by step answer. The applicant has broken down their thoughts and provided the interviewer with a stream of their own workings of their mind. This allows the interviewer to understand how the individual is breaking down the question and gives an opportunity for the interviewer to intervene with further questions if required.

A poor applicant may state something like "Well because it obviously isn't" – without any further justification. The point of a question like this is to consider the many different ways in which we experience reality and develop our understanding therein. If the applicant fails to address more than the superficial, then they are unlikely to show an understanding of the point of the question.

Q3: Despite knowing the health implications of smoking, why does it remain legal in the UK?

Good Applicant: I'd like to think about what other areas are considered by the legislators of the UK when they allocate legal status to things, as it can't just be health implications. With regards to smoking, there are a number of vested parties including tobacco companies and smokers themselves. Tobacco companies rely on smoking being legal in the UK for their income. If smoking were made illegal, then these companies would lose 100% of their UK revenue, which in turn, may impact the economy as a whole (these sales are far from insubstantial). Secondly, when thinking about smokers who are 20% of the UK's adult population (equating to around 10 million people), they represent a large fraction of the potential electorate.

Therefore, banning smoking would have significant implications for political intervention due to unpopularity, loss of freedom, etc.

As another point, smokers may claim that they have an addiction which is difficult to stop. They may also argue that smoking was legal when they first started to smoke. Thus, the government may face a legal battle if they were to suddenly make the product illegal. This may make a total ban on smoking impractical and a breach of an individual's right to choose. However, banning smoking on a more gradual basis may be feasible and is happening today; for example, it is now against the law to smoke in cars, in the workplace, and in public areas. Maybe phasing out smoking is more realistic, and is therefore what is being attempted in the UK. This would imply that it is not the case that legislators are unaware or uncaring of the health implications of smoking, but that they are attempting to reduce smoking in a less disruptive manner.

A poor applicant might fail to address the reasons why smoking has not been made illegal. It is not simply a case of saying "smoking is bad, therefore the government should ban it". The question of whether it should be banned impacts many people and showing an understanding of different perspectives and potential arguments is important for answering this question sufficiently.

Q4: Politicians often claim that a 'nuclear deterrent' is vital in averting war, if every country had nuclear weapons, does it follow that there would be no war?

A Good Applicant: We all have learnt how dangerous nuclear weapons can be when Hiroshima and Nagasaki were destroyed at the end of World War 2. The threat to the environment, human lives, and even future generations is known, and the risk is too high. Nuclear weapons should not be used at all. On the other hand, it is true that there was no direct war between the USA and USSR during the Cold War and both had nuclear weapons. It seems possible that countries with nuclear weapons do not engage in war with one another as the high risk of a catastrophe deters them from using nuclear weapons, and hence the proliferation of nuclear weapons may prevent wars.

This shows that the candidate understands the question and is able to draw on some examples from A-level History. A better candidate would then engage in a discussion with the interviewer about the moral aspect of the topic or may choose to draw on a broader range of examples and realise that although proliferation of nuclear weapons may deter another world war, it could lead to more frequent small-scale wars. Examples of wars in Iraq, Vietnam, Afghanistan, and Korea during the Cold War demonstrate that there were, in fact, wars, and the USSR and USA backed smaller countries in war. So, the proliferation of nuclear weapons may have led to small-scale wars, yet prevented another world war. If every country had their own nuclear weapons, this could either serve as an effective deterrent to war, or ensure world annihilation, depending on the trust we place in our assumption that the reason the Cold War remained cold was the proliferation of nuclear ordnance. Making a moral case against any use of nuclear weapons, for instance, referring to the experience from Hiroshima and Nagasaki shows sensitivity about the topic.

A poor applicant may make a moral argument against the use of nuclear weapons before providing any insightful analysis and attempting an answer to the question. Another approach which is unhelpful is focusing too much on providing a yes/no answer to the question, and hence missing the point that the proliferation of nuclear weapons is a gradual process with various political, moral, and economic difficulties, and it is not plausible that all countries could get nuclear weapons overnight. The question is very broad and raises many interesting arguments for discussion, but 'brain dump' is not helpful here.

Q5: When we make contact with an extra-terrestrial civilisation, what should we tell them is humanity's greatest achievement?

[Extremely clear-headed] Applicant: The concept of humanity's greatest achievement is very subjective. It can either be measured in terms of effort needed to accomplish it, or in terms of impact. In the first case, humanity's greatest achievement could be the pyramids, since they required a tremendous amount of work with little technology, and are still standing today after thousands of years. In terms of impact, humanity's greatest achievement could be the discovery of penicillin for example. I think that it makes more sense to focus on a ground-breaking achievement from the past, rather than the most recent accomplishments of humanity.

If I were to tell an extra-terrestrial civilisation about penicillin, however, I would also have to provide an explanation on humanity's problems which it solved. Finally, I would have to take into account the aim of my message: am I trying to impress, intimidate, or simply inform?

A good applicant will understand the true aim of the question: creating an abstract situation in which he is encouraged to problematise the subjective concept of 'greatest achievement' and make an argument.

A poor applicant could misinterpret the question, and focus on the extra-terrestrial civilisation, talking about space technology and means of communication. Alternatively, they could choose an accomplishment and fail to justify his answer, or provide a lot of facts on the subject without problematising the concept of 'greatest achievement'.

Q6: In a democracy, can the majority impose its will on the minority?

[Extremely clear-headed] Applicant: First, I am going to think from the practical point of view: if by 'minority' we mean 'the ruling elites', does the majority have the actual ability to impose its will? The population only gets to make decisions on rare occasions: elections and referenda. Most of the time, decisions are made by a small group of people: the government. In 2002-2003, there were mass protests against the war in Iraq, but this did not stop Tony Blair from sending troops. It seems that once a government is in power, there is little that the majority of the population can do before the next elections. Secondly, we could think about the question from a normative point of view: should the majority be able to make most decisions in a democratic system? There is a difference between democracy and populism, where power is held by the masses. The latter could be problematic. If by minority we understand things such as small ethnic or religious groups, in a populist system they would have no say and could end up being oppressed. In a democratic system, minorities are protected by laws. However, we can see that the system is sometimes flawed. For example, in the US, there are only two major political parties: people with different agendas than Republicans or Democrats are pushed away from power.

This question can be answered in a number of ways, but a good candidate will show their capacity to deconstruct it, and think for a moment before replying. They will support their points with examples.

A poor applicant will rush into an answer without thinking and might end up getting confused between the different aspects of the question. They will either make generalisations without giving examples, or focus exclusively on a single real-life case, giving a lot of facts but without any argument or acknowledgment of a different point of view.

THE ULTIMATE OXBRIDGE INTERVIEW GUIDE — PPE & HPS

Q7: Why is there social inequality in the world? How would you resolve this issue?

[Extremely clear-headed] Applicant: I do not think that there is a single reason for social inequality in the world. Of course, it is not normal that 1% of the population controls almost 50% of its wealth. Greed and self-centeredness increasingly govern the apportionment and use of the world's resources. However, I also think that there are other underlying factors behind social inequality. I cannot imagine a society in which everybody would have the same proportion of wealth and the same professional opportunities. People live in different places, speak different languages, and simply have different talents and skills. Thus, I do not think that social inequality can ever be fully resolved. Attempts to resolve this through communism have proven unstable, and generally collapse. Nevertheless, I think I would try to solve this issue through more progressive taxation, and diversion of funds from supporting businesses and industries to supporting individuals.

A good applicant can have a different opinion on the subject, but will take into account other points of view, and will identify the difficulties associated with resolving such a complex problem, supporting their argument with solid A-level type factual knowledge.

A poor applicant could focus on only one of the two questions. They might give a 'trendy' answer such as "It's all because of the rich" or "Humans are bad so there is nothing you can do", without giving any real explanation or evidence, and refuse to engage fully with the questions.

Q8: To what extent is taxing the rich likely to lead to greater equality in society?

[Extremely clear-headed] Applicant: There is a big disproportion in terms of wealth between a small group of the 'rich' and the 'poor' majority. Therefore, it would seem logical to find a way of redistributing that wealth. As we can see, altruism does not suffice, since the problem persists despite a few notable examples of rich people giving big proportions of their fortune to charity, for instance, Bill Gates. Taxation does seem like a good solution. However, it needs to be designed efficiently. For instance, we must make sure that such a tax does not affect the economy negatively, for example, by forcing companies out of business. Secondly, public funds can be misused equally as often, as seen in America in 2017, and Somalia in the 1990s. It might be necessary to establish an international body of experts to design and monitor the implementation of projects funded by this tax.

A good applicant will be able to identify both the positive and the negative sides of such a policy. Regardless of whether he has any knowledge on the subject, he will provide a well-structured, logical answer.

A poor applicant might be intimidated by the question and refuse to answer by saying something like "I don't know anything about taxes". Alternatively, he might provide an answer which focuses only on one side of the coin, making it very vulnerable to counterarguments.

Q9: Is alcohol addiction always a result of the social environment, peer pressure, and negative role models?

[Extremely clear-headed] Applicant: Alcohol addiction is more widespread in certain social environments or countries: for instance, it is a much bigger problem in Russia than in the UK. I don't think that it would be appropriate to argue that nationality or ethnicity inherently determines the likelihood of alcohol addiction.

This is why explanations such as peer pressure and negative role models are very useful. Indeed, peer pressure can become integrated into culture. For example, drinking alcohol in large quantities on a teenage trip abroad or on an American Spring Break has become almost a ritual. In some cultures, drinking vast amounts of alcohol can be considered as a mark of virility, or politeness, which is conducive to alcohol addiction. However, we should not generalise. It is possible for someone to develop an alcohol addiction in an environment where drinking is frowned upon or rare, just as it is possible to remain abstinent while being surrounded by alcoholics. If an individual's parents and friends do not drink, and yet he becomes an alcohol addict citing a musician with questionable habits as his role model, it seems reasonable to assume that other factors, perhaps psychological, were at play. Thus, while the social environment is a very potent explanation for alcohol addiction, ignoring the possibility of other factors could have negative consequences, such as failing to properly address the issue.

A good applicant will note the use of the word 'always', and attempt to come up with a counter-example.

A poor candidate might fall into the trap of agreeing with the statement without thinking of other points of view. He could refuse to reply stating his lack of knowledge on the topic, or give anecdotal evidence from his experience or environment without constructing an argument.

Q10: Imagine you are a historian a hundred years in the future, looking back on today. What aspects of society would you focus on?

[Extremely clear-headed] Applicant: I do not think that any aspect of history should be discarded as unimportant. However, I am most interested by politics and geopolitics. It is basically impossible to predict the future, and very hard to fully understand the present and its implications. A hundred years from now, we will have a much better understanding of some of today's unanswered questions. For instance, how successful are international organisations in fostering cooperation and preventing conflict? After all, the UN and the EU are relatively recent constructs, and did not fully exploit their potential until the end of the Cold War.

Determining whether international institutions have any real influence or whether they are just tools in the hands of self-centered states is one of the big debates in the study of international relations. Secondly, it would be interesting to see whether in the age of mass information and communication, humanity is able to learn from its previous mistakes. Parties of the extreme right are currently gaining a lot of votes in Europe, due among others to economic hardship. Will European countries suffer a fate similar to the Weimar Republic?

A good candidate will demonstrate a certain degree of knowledge on the current topic of his choice, and will be able to identify the way in which it might be perceived by a historian.

A poor candidate might avoid the question by saying something like "I think that humanity will destroy itself within a hundred years so there will be no historians left". He could also lose track of his argument by trying to impress the interviewer with his factual knowledge on a current topic, or attempt to make unjustified predictions of future developments.

Q11: What are the main reasons for persistent unemployment in the UK?

Extremely clear-headed] Applicant: I think that people are often tempted to look for simple explanations behind complicated issues. This is why extreme political parties are so successful: they provide the population with easily identifiable scapegoats such as 'the current government', 'immigrants', or 'the EU', and blame them for every economic and social problem. In reality, issues such as unemployment have many reasons. One of them could be the discrepancy between supply and demand: what type of jobs people are prepared for at schools and universities, and what type of jobs are offered on the market. For instance, in Scandinavian countries, when an unemployed individual cannot find work for a certain period of time, he is offered courses which allow him to perform a different type of work, where there is more demand.

Another reason could indeed be globalisation, with the international economic crisis, and many companies moving abroad to reduce costs. However, this does not justify oversimplifying the issue by blaming solely external factors such as foreigners or international organisations. Instead, efforts should be made to better adapt the national system to the realities of the globalised world.

A good candidate will try to provide a balanced and well-argued answer, regardless of his political or moral stance. He will stay away from generalisations and normative statements based on little or no evidence.

A poor applicant might refuse to engage with a question on which he has little previous knowledge. Alternatively, he may make sweeping generalisations or provide an exhaustive list of factors without really explaining any of them.

Q12: Should prisoners have the right to vote?

[Extremely clear-headed] Applicant: I think that in a democracy, voting is one of the citizen's basic rights. The question is: should prisoners still be considered as citizens? It could be said that when they break the social contract of norms governing the society, their rights are also revoked. However, if a prisoner is deprived of all his rights, his eventual reintegration into society will be even harder. In my opinion, the right to vote should be granted to those prisoners who have not committed the gravest of crimes, such as murder or rape.

Moreover, in some countries, the issue of 'political prisoners' is still prominent, for instance, in China or Ukraine. If someone is imprisoned for disagreeing with the regime and has no right to vote for a different party or candidate, then there is little chance of change and the system moves one step further towards authoritarianism.

A poor applicant could focus too much on providing a yes/no answer based on personal beliefs or anecdotal evidence, without trying to engage with alternative perspectives on the question.

See Question 10 in the Law Chapter for a more legal perspective.

Q13: Is there such a thing as national identity in the world of globalisation?

[Extremely clear-headed] Applicant: In my opinion, while borders are becoming more and more permeable and people can communicate and travel from one part of the world to the other, national identity is not necessarily losing its potency. According to the Marxist theory, national identity was supposed to disappear, giving way to an international movement of workers. This was not really accomplished, and the communist countries which survived the longest such as the Soviet and Chinese systems, were those which mixed communism with nationalism. While from our 'Western' perspective it might seem that national identity is dying, this might be related to the fact that we live in relatively peaceful times: there has been no war on the current territory of the EU for decades.

However, in times of conflict, national identity becomes very powerful. We can see this on current examples such as Ukraine and Russia, but also in post 9/11 USA. I think that in times of external threat, people tend to unite under a symbol which differentiates them from the 'other'. Since the nation state remains the main actor in international relations, most conflicts are likely to oppose one nation against another, thus reinforcing the sense of national identity.

A good candidate can argue either way, but should be able to acknowledge both sides of the coin. He should be able to support his ideas with some factual A-level type knowledge.

A poor applicant might fail to engage properly with the question, instead of trying to impress the interviewer by dumping facts. Alternatively, he could make broad generalisations without supporting his argument with any real evidence.

Q14: What areas of Philosophy are you interested in?

[Extremely clear-headed] Applicant: I am interested in theories of the state. Many thinkers have attempted to tackle this issue throughout history, ranging from Plato, through Hobbes and Rousseau, to Marx. They all have very different visions of what an efficient political system should look like, whether the human being is inherently good or bad, and who should have the right to rule. What is interesting in this area of Philosophy is that the thinkers have often actually affected the reality.

The writings of Marx are the best example of this phenomenon since they have been used and abused by activists in many countries, leading to the October Revolution in 1917 and the establishment of the USSR, one of two systems dominating the international system for decades. I think that there are many interesting questions in this area of Philosophy. Is it possible to design a system which would be applicable to any setting and society? Do philosophers have a responsibility over how their writings are understood and used?

A good candidate will show both a certain degree of knowledge and of genuine interest in the topic of his choice. He will identify some of the big questions related to the field.

A poor candidate might give an exhaustive list of areas of Philosophy without going into depth on any of them. Alternatively, he could try to demonstrate his extensive factual knowledge of the writings of a single author, without engaging with the wider question on the area of Philosophy.

Q15: Tell me about some political texts that you have read.

[Extremely clear-headed] Applicant: I have looked at some political theory texts, such as Plato's Republic. In this text, the author is describing a perfect political system, an ideal city led by a philosopher-king. He also talks about other flawed political systems, such as tyranny or democracy. I think that this text is very interesting and useful for understanding political systems from the past, and has also inspired other, more recent authors. However, it is important to note that Plato writes from the perspective of Ancient Greece, and many of his concepts are outdated. I think that the term 'political text' could also apply to other types of documents, for example, party programmes, but even literary fiction. I recently read Bulgakov's Master and Margarita, a novel with fantasy themes such as the devil and witchcraft, written in the Soviet Union. Its focus on religion and the occult was also a hidden critique of the atheistic Soviet society. Similar things could be said about the Animal Farm or 1984.

A good candidate will try to go beyond simply giving factual knowledge on a text studied in class. He will try to come up with a critical approach towards the text showing a certain degree of independent thought, or problematize the term 'political texts'.

A poor candidate might panic if he has not studied texts of political theory in school, instead of making the best of it by trying to come up with different types of political texts. Alternatively, he might opt for dumping a lot of factual information on a text, instead of showing his understanding of it or demonstrating a critical perspective.

HSPS INTERVIEW QUESTIONS

1. How would you discretise the concepts of ethnicity and race?
2. Would you argue that the society and the state are inseparable? If not, what separates them?
3. A Roman magistrate appears on your doorstep, and asks you to tell him about the United Nations – how would you compare it to his Empire?
4. Some of us think that the poor live in poverty because they don't try hard enough – what would you say to that?
5. What do you think lies behind the recent resurgence of Nationalism in Europe?
6. You're redesigning a map of the world, how would you go about deciding on national borders?
7. Do you think that you have free will? Does free will as a concept relate to the notion of the state of nature?
8. Do you think that primates, like chimpanzees, should be given the same rights as ordinary people?
9. What do you think is one of the most fascinating facts about where you come from, what makes that so interesting?
10. Take a look at these cave paintings, how might you analyse them for meaning?
11. Do you think love exists?
12. On the course we are introducing a new paper this year in which we can teach you about any part of the world you like – which part of the world do you think you will pick?
13. Can you think of anything happening in the news at the moment which you feel is a particularly good example of a larger significant issue?
14. You are an archaeologist in the year 2500, excavating Cambridge – what material culture might you expect to find from my present?
15. Do you think that one's culture can shape one's perceptions? Is the way we see colour the same as someone from a different culture would?

PPE Interview Questions

1. You've been presented with an unknown symbol - how might you go about trying to decipher its meaning?
2. What makes you human?
3. How would you go about assessing the number of people in here?
4. Do you think you know anything?
5. You run a sweet shop next-door to a rival sweet shop - you've both been able to drum up considerable loyalty in your customers who will flat-out refuse to shop anywhere else, provided you keep your prices below a tenner per sweet. You each have 10 such loyal customers - but there are 100 potential customers on the street who don't care as much and will buy from whoever is cheapest. With this in mind, at what price point would you have to reach for it to be more valuable to sell everything for ten pounds?
6. You mentioned that you read [a philosophy book], tell me about it!
7. What do you think would happen if inflation was impossible?
8. Do you feel that economists trust models too much?
9. Do you think that sociology would make a valuable background for an Economist?
10. What is GDP really? Do you think it can ever truly be measured?

THE ULTIMATE OXBRIDGE INTERVIEW GUIDE — PPE & HPS

11. What would you say are the major influence on the productive potential of a country?
12. Is there any particular value to the national debt?
13. Should you or I care about inequality?
14. You're a politician in charge of the country, and you've accumulated a considerable deficit in the national balance of trade - is this an issue?
15. Do you believe that the market should be completely free, or should government intervene?
16. What would you say to someone who argued that 2008's Credit Crunch can only be blamed on regulators?
17. Let's say that the value of the Yen and the Dollar exchange places overnight, what do you think the impacts of this would be on the global market?
18. Do you think that property tycoons should pay more attention to how you win in monopoly? Why?
19. What makes diamonds so much more valuable than raw steel?
20. Many industries are outsourcing less and less as it is disincentivised by government policy, do you think this is a bad thing?
21. How do you go about valuing a unique commodity? Let's say you're setting prices for a unique air-route, how would you decide how much to charge to make as much money as possible? How would you determine what price to set tickets at to ensure maximal profit?
22. Why do you think financiers and financial institutions are so preoccupied with the golden ratio?
23. How would you go about trying to identify the warning signs of an economic recession - if you could spot it soon enough, can you think of a way to avoid depressions?
24. Do you think that India, which has a substantial space programme, should still be getting aid payments from other countries?
25. How would you judge the extent of the differences between a capitalist and a communist system?
26. Your friend is running a struggling corner shop, she knows you've done some work on economics and asks for your advice - they have £25 they'd like to spend on developing their sales, what three things would you recommend that they do, with or without that money?
27. Do you think the separator between a global company and a failed company is innovation, or are there other factors at play?
28. What do you think were the main factors driving the American Great Depression - do you think that understanding its causes could teach us valuable lessons?
29. What attracted you to the PPE course?
30. Is there an area of politics that you are most interested in?
31. What have you seen on the news recently that has interested you?
32. Why do you think some countries are rich and some countries are poor?
33. What makes a nation "successful"?
34. Do you think it's important to represent minorities in democracies?
35. How can we achieve minority representation in a democracy?
36. Do you think that democracy is the only acceptable form of government?
37. Why do you think some countries go to war?
38. How far do you think governments should interfere in the lives of their citizens?
39. What do you think are the key differences between the UK and US forms of government?
40. What do you think causes a rise in populism?

41. Why do you think political parties might have increasingly similar policies, most of which sit at the centre of the political spectrum?
42. Do you think that countries should interfere in the running of other countries when human rights are at risk?
43. Do you have a particular philosopher whose work interests you?
44. How do you think we can know that something is right or wrong?
45. Consider the following case: There is a train running down a track. There is a fork in the track a short way from where the train currently is. On the right-hand track at the fork there is tied one person. On the left-hand track at the fork there are tied five people. Currently the train will go to the left-hand fork. Whichever track the train runs down, anyone on that track will be killed by the train.

    Should the train driver switch tracks so that the train kills one person rather than five people?
46. Consider the following case: You are a Doctor with 5 patients who need immediate organ transplants; they have conditions which have been brought on by entirely natural causes. All patients have a very rare blood type, so they have been unable to find organ donors. A patient comes in to see you for a routine check-up. This patient has the same rare blood type as your other 5 patients but is otherwise entirely healthy.

    The doctor could kill the healthy patient in order to donate her organs to the 5 patients. If the doctor did this, all 5 patients would live.

    Do you think the case is different in any significant way to the Trolley Problem?
47. Do you think that you freely chose to apply to this PPE course?
48. If humans don't have free will, and knew that they didn't, do you think that would make any difference to how society functions?
49. Do you think that you can trust what your eyes are telling you?
50. Consider the following case Smith and Jones have both applied for the same job. The hiring manager for the job has told Smith that Jones will get the job. Smith has also counted the coins in Jones's pocket and has found there are 10 coins there. Based on this evidence, Smith makes the following assertion:

    (1) The person who will get the job has 10 coins in his pocket.

    As it turns out, Smith actually gets the job and has 10 coins in his pocket, although he didn't count these coins before he got the job. This means that (1) is true.

    Do you think that we can say that Smith knew that (1) was true? (Gettier Case)
51. What do you think makes a strong philosophical argument?
52. Can you see any problems with the following argument?
    1: Samantha can't get a job where she's currently living.
    2: Samantha got a job in London.
    Conclusion: Samantha will move to London.
53. Can you see any problems with the following argument?
    1: All men are mortal.
    2: Socrates is a man.
    Conclusion: Socrates is mortal.

CLASSICS

Classics applicants will typically be asked **questions about the Classical world**, but usually not about things they have studied in detail at A-Level. This is to avoid some candidates gaining an advantage by simply having studied the topic in question since *interviews are designed to assess how you think and how you adapt to new information, not what you know.*

The interview will usually consist of a large question with many smaller sub-questions that the interviewer will ask in order to guide the applicant to an answer. The main question may seem difficult, impossible or random at first, but take a breath and start discussing with your interviewer different ideas you have for breaking down the question into manageable pieces. Don't panic. **The questions are designed to be difficult** to give you the chance to show your full intellectual potential. They will help guide you to the right idea if you provide ideas for them to guide. This is your chance to show your creativity, analytical skills, intellectual flexibility, problem-solving skills and your go-getter attitude. Don't waste it on nervousness or a fear of messing up or looking stupid.

Often questions will pick up on a theme from your written work or your personal statement and take it in an unexpected direction. For example, if you mentioned visiting the Parthenon in your personal statement, an interviewer may well ask you to talk about a particular frieze from the building and what you consider its significance to be, what its purpose might be, and who might have commissioned it. In this scenario, they would not expect you to know anything about the frieze in question, but simply to **make sensible suggestions based on the given information** and talk the interviewer through your thinking process.

The only other main section of the interview process is the language test for Cambridge candidates with Latin, Greek or both, conducted in one interview. The interviewer will allow you to study a Latin or Greek text for a few minutes and then ask you to translate it aloud, giving you assistance with vocabulary and grammar as appropriate.

This will usually be a difficult and obscure piece to ensure that no candidates are better prepared than others. Again, the emphasis is on showing a good working method for working out the meaning of a sentence, rather than knowing lots about grammar or vocabulary - remember to think aloud and ask about any vocabulary you don't know.

Worked Questions

Below are a few examples of how to start breaking down an interview question, complete with model answers.

Q1: Why might it be more useful to study ancient texts in their original languages, as opposed to in translation?

A good applicant might begin by acknowledging the benefits of texts in translation, i.e. that they are more accessible and retain most of the content, but then go on to examine how translations can present difficulties. For example, discuss that some ways of thinking and figures of speech simply do not translate into English and, hence, can only be understood in the original language. A very good candidate might then broaden this into a discussion of how far it is necessary to study ancient texts in their original context and how far they can be considered to be stand-alone works, and what the merits of these different approaches might be for a scholar.

It is often useful to break the question down into sub-parts, which can be dealt with in turn. At this point, the interviewer can give feedback if this seems like a good start and help make any modifications necessary. In this particular case, the interviewer may well begin to ask further questions to direct the discussion once the candidate has made an initial survey of the issues. You would seldom be expected to talk about a topic unguided for a lengthy period as interviewers will always be keen to challenge your thinking and see how you react to new information.

A poor applicant may take a number of approaches unlikely to impress the interviewer. The first and most obvious of these is to say, "We never learned about that in school" and make no attempt to move forward with the discussion. In this event, the interviewer will likely try and prod the candidate to make an inroad by asking subsequent questions, in which case the important thing to do is make an effort to make sensible conjectures and not worry about whether you know any facts. Another typical tactic of poor applicants to avoid is the 'brain dump', where a candidate simply spouts all of the knowledge they have on the question topic without considering whether it is relevant. It is important to remember *that interviews are about giving thoughtful answers to questions which demonstrate your thinking process, not about demonstrating knowledge.*

Q2: What can we learn about Roman emperors from the depictions of them on statues and coins?

A good applicant will likely begin by narrowing the question to a manageable dimension. For example, talking about a specific depiction(s) or a specific emperor(s) (it is also likely that the interviewer will provide some visual stimuli to help you).

One might then explore what these items could tell us about how the emperors wanted to be seen (e.g. how widespread they are, how the emperor is depicted upon them, what the inscriptions say). It also informs us about how the emperors were seen by people in a given area (e.g. statues were often commissioned by local dignitaries in the provinces, what message did they want to send by putting up a statue of, say, Augustus?). It also tells how this might be compared with other sources, such as the written accounts of Tacitus and Suetonius. The interviewer would be likely to offer the candidate information and examples to help them test their theories, as well as asking further questions.

Outlining the concepts in this way would provide a good starting point to mention any relevant reading you have done. For example, if you have read Suetonius' biography of Claudius, you might be able to contrast his depiction in that work with his depiction in a statue or coin you have seen and suggest why that might be and what we could usefully learn from it. This type of proactive and thoughtful approach to the question is likely to impress the interviewer, but it is still important to listen to their directions and interjections carefully to ensure that you answer their question fully.

THE ULTIMATE OXBRIDGE INTERVIEW GUIDE — CLASSICS

A poor applicant would be more likely to protest that they don't know anything about statues or coins, or attempt to offer a shallow and relatively pedestrian statement of the obvious. For example, they might hypothesise that such artefacts can tell us what the emperors looked like and then struggle to conjecture anything any further when asked for more suggestions by the interviewer. The worst thing to do in these situations is to seem unreceptive and attempt to derail the interviewer. Seeming interested in the topic and being seen to make an effort to consider your answers to the questions carefully is often half the battle.

Q3: What is literature? Why do we value it?

This is a very open-ended question and one to which there are no wrong answers, the key is to cut a sensible path through the material.

A good applicant would quickly seek to address the broadness of the question and state their angle of approach. The most useful tactic would be to try and develop a theory of literature which differentiates it from other types of written material. Such a theory might try to establish how far authorial intent goes and how far audience reception determines what literature is, as well as addressing the role of form (e.g. poetry or prose) and the question of whether anything can be said to be entirely literature or not. Other peripheral questions may be posed by the interviewer such as "Does literature have to be written down or can it be an oral culture?" - you should attempt to address these and incorporate them into your theory to provide nuance to your answer.

The good applicant might then tackle the question of why we value literature with reference to their theory of what constitutes literature, since how we define literature likely tells us about why we prize it. Such an answer is likely to make reference to a variety of ideas, possibly focusing on the allegorical and didactic powers of literature, i.e. its potential benefits to society, versus its more intrinsic goods, e.g. beauty, the human condition and so forth. The interviewer will be looking for candidates to make a lively, intellectual, and sensible approach to the question but will by no means expect revolutionary or fully-formed analyses of such large concepts.

A poor candidate is, therefore, likely to try and be dismissive of the question with a brief answer such as "books and poems" or "I don't know" and fail to engage with the scope of the topic. They may also attempt to avoid making useful analyses by simply listing things which are and aren't literature, or erring from the main point of the question by talking about their love for literature and/or its value to them. Some of these points may complement a good answer but they are highly unlikely to form the cornerstone of a good response.

Q4: Who wrote the Iliad and the Odyssey?

This question is looking to see how applicants analyse what might, superficially, seem to be a very simple question and tease out its hidden complexities and potential difficulties.

A good applicant would likely begin by acknowledging that these works are attributed to the poet we know as 'Homer' but in reality, the situation is more complex. An interesting avenue to start with would be what we mean by 'wrote' since we know that the works in question were an unwritten oral tradition for the first 400 or so years of their lives, which were eventually written down in Athens around the fifth century BC.

Building on this, we might suggest that to posit a single author for works with a long oral tradition is inherently problematic since a work which is purely performed as an unwritten tale must be subject to constant change and reimagining by those performing it - even if the core of the works originate from 'Homer' himself.

Very well-read applicants may even be able to go further and discuss scholarly theories that the origins of the *Odyssey* are different from those of the *Iliad*, or the aspersions cast on the Homeric authenticity of some later books of the Odyssey - but this would only serve as the icing on the cake.

A poor applicant would be one who attempts to give a very short and overly factual answer to the question, which fails to be analytical. For example, to reply simply "Homer" would hardly impress the interviewer since this basic factual knowledge would be expected.

The interviewer is looking for evidence of analytical abilities in terms of how we think about texts, and, hence, would be more than likely to provide the candidate with additional information about the provenance of the works in the event that this is not something the candidate has previously encountered. If you find that you know very little about a topic on which you are questioned, feel free to admit this and ask specific questions, but be sure to do so in such a way that it shows an analytical method rather than resignation to failure. A good question to ask would be something like: *"Is there any historical evidence about the origins of the works?"*

Q5: Would you argue that the Greeks left a bigger impact on the culture of today, or the Romans?

This question is another broad one and is looking for candidates to demonstrate an ability to analyse the Classical world within its wider context in a way that is less similar to the way in which they are taught at school.

A good applicant could take any number of successful approaches, though useful topics to cover will be language, politics, art (including literature and architecture) and possibly something more nebulous such as 'identity'. In light of this, it may also be useful to make a distinction about what you take 'culture of today' to mean: Britain? Europe? The world? Feel free to define it as you wish, but it may be prudent to restrict yourself according to your knowledge.

Linguistically, one could make a number of points about more words in English being Latin-derived than Greek, but also that Latin developed largely from Greek origins. This might tie in with a discussion of how strictly we can define Greece and Rome as civilisations, given the great deal of influence Classical Greece had on Classical Rome and the Roman rule of Hellenistic Greece.

You might also like to speculate on what effects Roman rule (until c. 400AD) had on modern Britain, from the law to roads and our sense of national identity - is the Roman past a matter of pride for Britons?

Literature is an extremely broad topic and could take any number of directions, but you could usefully begin by listing some widely read works of ancient literature and why you think they are culturally significant (or not). Perhaps with reference to the influence they may have had on more modern literature - e.g. could we have Milton without Homer or Virgil?

The key thing with this question is simply to demonstrate some sort of analytical route through the vast material which resembles an argument. The interviewer will probably question your hypotheses - responding to these with your own examples and arguments will serve you well. A <u>poor applicant</u> would be more likely to give a short answer about how we were never ruled by the Greeks and so the Romans were probably more influential. Such an answer, whilst making one useful point, demonstrates a lack of engagement with the breadth of the question and a pedestrian mode of thinking which is unlikely to impress the interviewer.

Q6: Is historical record reconcilable with mythology?

This question is a little more specific in scope than some of the previous but still leaves substantial scope for interpretation. A <u>good applicant</u> would likely begin by defining terms that pertain to the central issue of the question, i.e. what do we mean when we say myth or history and how neatly can we divide the two concepts from one another?

The key issue to tackle in the question is how we <u>interpret the idea of 'compatible'</u> since myth and history might be of very similar significance or hardly differentiated between in the ancient world. For example, the Roman foundation myths were notionally regarded as 'historical' in ancient Rome and certainly had the cultural significance of real historical events, though they were known to be largely fictitious.

In Greece, one might argue that the question is even more vexed given that the line between myth and history is so blurred, e.g. the question of the extent to which the Trojan war is a historical fact and the extent to which it is a myth. Further, one might question whether such a distinction is relevant to the Trojan war since its significance to Greek literature and culture is unchanged in either case. Moreover, one might also discuss whether all history is a myth. For example, if 'all history is written by the victor', how far can we be sure that any 'historical' account of events is not, in fact, a biased mythologisation?

The most important thing with a question like this is to attempt to <u>pull the question apart</u> and ask to what extent its premises are valid by dissecting what we mean by the various terms and how far these terms can truly be said to be distinct from one another. This demonstrates an ability to think in a critical and original way and is likely to impress the interviewer.

A <u>poor applicant</u> would likely make some more pedestrian distinctions about history and myth being incompatible because history is about things which really happened, whereas myths are simply fairy tales and fictions, without digging much into the wider significance of the question.

Classics Interview Questions

1. What languages can you speak?
2. What is the value of classics degrees to the taxpayers who fund them?
3. You mentioned a passion for Roman history – would you use Sulla as an example when explaining tyranny?
4. What are the main similarities and differences between ancient Greece and Rome?
5. How would you discretise the Latin and Grecian pantheons?
6. When did the Roman Republic collapse? Why?
7. Did Alexander the Great earn his epithet?
8. You mentioned studying the expansion of the Roman empire outside of school time. What does the work surrounding the Numidian king Jugertha tell us about Roman foreign policy?
9. How is the study of classics useful to the modern world?
10. As a classicist, how do you tell fact from fiction?
11. How would you end the siege of Troy?
12. How accurate is the film '300'?
13. What's the meaning of Stonehenge?
14. Why is it important that we pay attention to changing artistic style between the republic and mid empire?
15. Do you think that the triumvirate was a success?
16. Was Alexander the Great gay? Is this unusual for the time period?
17. What can we learn about Roman Society from the practice of gladiatorial combat?
18. To what extent could you describe the Persian empire as 'civilised'?
19. What makes a 'classic'?
20. Based on your study of Greek, what is a neoteric?
21. Should Classicists study contemporaneous texts to Greek and Latin from other areas of the world?
22. Was the Roman invasion of Britain a success?
23. Should we study modern retellings of classics?
24. Latin and Greek are dead languages, yet have been preserved through various means for millennia. With this in mind, how would you use this to prevent the extinction and total loss of some modern languages?
25. If you were offered the opportunity to learn Cuneiform, would you? And regardless of yes or no, why?
26. Is Classical archaeology more important than the study of Classical texts?
27. What is the difference between complex and simple societies? Do you think there are any examples of simple societies still left in the world today?
28. Who would you reason was the most important Greek god in Greek society and why?
29. You studied Catullus at A-Level – what does his sparrow symbolise?

LAW

A law applicant may be asked legal questions or questions from a related subject, including history, politics, or current affairs with a legal slant. None of the questions asked of you will assume any previous legal knowledge, as the interviewers understand that applicants will likely not have studied law before. Be prepared to explain why you want to study law and show through extra-curricular reading or activities how you've fostered this interest.

The interview will usually consist of a large question with many smaller sub-questions that the interviewer will ask in order to guide the applicant to an answer. The main question may seem difficult, impossible, or random at first, but take a breath and start discussing with your interviewer different ideas you have for breaking down the question into manageable pieces.

The questions are designed to be difficult to give you the chance to show your full intellectual potential.

For law, the questions will usually take one of a few possible forms based on highlighting the skills necessary to 'think like a lawyer'. Five main question types are:

- Observation-based questions ("tell me about...")
- Practical questions ("how would you decide if...")
- Statistical questions ("given this data...")
- Ethical questions ("are humans obligated to...")
- Questions about proximate causes (mechanism; "how does...") and ultimate causes (function; "why does..."), usually both at once.

Questions also have recurring themes which appear in many questions because they are central to jurisprudential thinking: the workings of the English legal system, problems of access to justice, the centrality of morality in legal development, the future of the legal profession, the impact of international treaties and legal institutions, looking carefully at words and drawing fine distinctions, building up an argument and applying that to examples.

Worked Questions

Below are a few examples of how to start breaking down an interview question, complete with model answers.

Q1: In a society of angels, is the law necessary?

Applicant: Well, an angel could be defined as someone who is always inclined to do what is good, just, and moral in any situation. If I thought that the sole purpose of the law was always to achieve what is good, just, and moral, I might conclude that in a society of such creatures, law would not be necessary as angels would already be achieving this goal on their own. Why don't I continue by giving my own definition of the purpose of the law in society, taking account of the law's function as a social coordinator and as an international arbitrator? Perhaps I should also add a brief of what it means for something to be necessary and apply that definition to my discussion at hand. I may even expand this discussion further and think about what a society without any laws would look like, or indeed, if such a society would be at all possible.

This shows that the question can be broken down into sub-parts, which can be dealt with in turn. At this point, the interviewer can give feedback and help make any modifications necessary. In the case of the above interview, the applicant will realise that the function of the law is not just to promote what is good, just, and moral, but also to act as a method of social cohesion. The details are unimportant, but the general idea of breaking down the question into manageable parts is important. The interviewer is not looking for an expert in legal philosophy, but someone who can problem-solve in the face of new ideas.

A poor applicant may take a number of approaches unlikely to impress the interviewer. The first and most obvious of these is to say "I don't know anything about societies of angels" and make no attempt to move forward.

Q2: What are the advantages and disadvantages to a non-written constitution?

This question is looking to see if you understand something of the nature of the British constitution and whether you can lay down pros and cons of an argument, with a conclusion that comes down on one side or the other of the debate.

Perhaps begin by defining what is meant by a written and a non-written constitution and try to give examples of countries with each (e.g. the UK and the USA). A constitution could be defined as a legal contract which states the terms and conditions under which a society agrees to govern itself, outlining the functions, powers and duties of the various institutions of government, regulates the relationship between them, and defines the relationship between the state and the public.

Problems of a non-written or uncodified constitution – firstly, it is difficult to know what the state of the constitution actually is, and secondly, it suggests that it is easier to make changes to the UK constitution than in countries with written constitutions, because the latter have documents with a 'higher law' status against which ordinary statute law and government action can be tested. Is the problem then more with the perception of our constitution than the legal status of the constitution itself?

Are they really so different? The American constitution may be elegantly written and succinct, but it can be amended or reinterpreted or even broken as the times demand, in the same way that the UK's unwritten constitution can be. Furthermore, even a written constitution is supplemented by unwritten conventions and most countries' constitutions embody a mixture of the two. This line of argument could lead you to conclude that the issue here is really only with semantics as there isn't any real difference in governance.

This question could lead to a discussion of the ways the UK constitution allows for laws to be made – e.g. "should judges have a legislative role?"

A poor applicant would not attempt to address both written and non-written constitutions, instead, sticking staunchly to whatever they have read on either subject.

THE ULTIMATE OXBRIDGE INTERVIEW GUIDE — LAW

Q3: How would you clarify the meaning of the words intention and foresight?

The question is looking for your ability to give accurate definitions of two principles central to criminal law. Intention could be defined as an aim or a plan, whilst foresight could be defined as the ability to predict what will happen. Thinking about the way these subtly different definitions might be applied in a legal context, we see that one might foresee that doing X will lead to the death of B but that consequence was not necessarily intended.

This intuitive distinction is mirrored in criminal law in the UK. There are two different types of intention: direct intent which exists where the defendant embarks upon a course of conduct to bring about a result which in fact occurs, and oblique intent which exists where the defendant embarks on a course of conduct to bring about a desired result, knowing that the consequence of his actions will also bring about another result.

A particularly topical example of the application of this distinction in practice can be seen discussing "the doctrine of double effect". This doctrine is only really applied in medical cases. Consider this example – a doctor who administers a lethal dose of painkillers to their terminally ill patient in order to relieve their suffering also foresees that such a dose will kill the patient. Should this doctor be guilty of the murder of her patient? Ultimately, the doctrine says that if doing something morally good has a morally bad side-effect it's ethically OK to do it providing the bad side-effect wasn't intended. This is true even if you foresaw that the bad effect would probably happen.

A poor applicant would fail to distinguish the two and would fail to see how these definitions are applied in modern criminal law.

Q4: Does a computer have a conscience?

Intuitively, we want to answer this question with a resounding "no" as it seems obvious that only living things can have consciences. Computers are creations of man and therefore merely act according to our needs, having little or no agency of their own. A poor applicant would only be able to articulate this very basic intuitive response and would be incapable of digging further.

In fact, the answer depends entirely upon which definitions you choose to give to the key terms in the question. Conscience could be defined as a moral sense of right and wrong which is viewed as acting to a guide of one's behaviour.

A computer is an electronic device which is capable of receiving information and performing a sequence of operations in accordance with a predetermined set of variables. Given these two definitions, it could be possible to program a computer with a conscience.

You could discuss the distinction between having a conscience and being 'sentient'- the former being a form of moral compass, whilst the latter is merely the ability to perceive or feel external stimulus. Do you think "artificial intelligence" is possible? Is it dangerous? If a computer does have a conscience, what might this mean for data protection laws? Freedom of expression? Ownership? Would this mean that computers should have rules protecting them from abuse, e.g. Computer Rights?

Q5: What is justice?

It might be good to begin with a succinct definition of 'justice' like 'behaviour or treatment which are just' with 'just' meaning 'equitable, fair and even-handed'.

You might then want to expand on this initial definition. Perhaps an exploration of what justice means in the context of criminal law which might go as follows:

Firstly, custodial sentences are used for their deterrent effect. Secondly, decisions on the form and duration of the sentence focus upon the crime itself rather than looking at how the punishment will best rehabilitate the offender, appease the victim, and benefit society as a whole. This judicial inflexibility which we see in the sentencing of criminals reflects a right-wing conception of justice based on the maxim 'an eye for an eye'.

You might put forward that an alternative conception of justice might achieve fairer results - perhaps one which takes a utilitarian approach to punishment. Such a conception would necessitate finding the best possible outcome for the largest number of people.

However, the counter argument to this would be that this approach would not allow for the idea of 'moral forfeiture', the principle that in committing a crime, you give up some of your rights. This contextual approach gives us a taste of just how difficult it really is to define justice, even in such a narrow context.

We often hear the term 'social justice' which is another context in which the term is applied. The concept in this context is very difficult to reconcile with justice as vengeance in the criminal context. Social justice too has several definitions; one might be socioeconomic equality amongst all members of any given society, whilst another might be more meritocratic and insist upon greater social mobility and fairness in general. We see that, upon examining this wider application of the idea of justice to non-criminal contexts, that the conception of justice itself is made even more difficult to define.

To conclude, we have proven that our initial definition of justice was not sufficient. The concept seems to defy any coherent definition as it is so broad and subjective.

Q6: Should the aim of the law be to make people happy?

One might argue that the aim of the law is to generally make everyone's lives better. Indeed, improving the quality of citizens' lives is the explicit focus of much of the policymaking and regulatory work done by many governments around the world. If we accept this, the next question would be 'what does better really mean?' One account could be that to make someone's life "better" we should render that person more able to get what they want. Another account might be that the quality of someone's life depends on the extent to which they do well at the things that are characteristically human to do. This difficulty in defining what it might be to make any one person's life better and therefore making them happy is one difficulty with placing this as the law's overarching aim – happiness is internal – how can we accurately know what anyone is feeling, and therefore truly know how well the law is working?

Perhaps one way to combat this problem could be to develop a method of measuring subjective happiness – a type of well-being analysis. How might we do this? Well, we could introduce a system of weekly online surveys which would be answered by a representative portion of society on how happy they were able to make particular administrative decisions. Over time, such large masses of data would allow us to accurately pinpoint just what really makes people happier and just how the law can shape itself to better achieve this.

Q7: Which laws are broken most frequently? Are they still laws?

Millions of people who declare themselves law-abiding citizens actually commit seven crimes on average per week. The most common offences are things like speeding, texting while driving, dropping litter, downloading music illegally, or riding bicycles on the pavement. Many of these more common 'minor crimes' are committed so regularly that they have almost become legal, which might be the reason so many people aren't fazed when they do break these laws.

Are these 'minor laws' still laws? You might argue that a law is a law even if it's not followed. The definition of a law, as a law, lies in the process by which it is enacted, i.e. the legislative process. This line of argument would lead you to believe that all laws are of the same importance because they become law by the same process.

However, you might not necessarily think that is the case. For instance, most people would think that killing someone would be much worse than accidentally dropping your train ticket and therefore littering. This would suggest that there is a hierarchy of laws, and therefore, that some laws are more important or that some laws are more immoral. This would lead you to conclude that 'minor laws' are still laws, but merely a lower class of laws, perhaps because the repercussions of infringement in these cases is lesser or the infringement is seen as less immoral and therefore are less thoroughly enforced.

Q8: After you have been to the hairdressers and had all of your hair cut off, do you still own your hair?

Intuitively, we believe that when our hair is attached to our heads, we do own it. The law supports this and if someone were to cut off your hair without your consent, you would be entitled to compensation.

However, where you have consented to your hair being cut off, the situation is very different and there is very little precedent to go on. You might argue that if you hadn't expressed an interest in maintaining your ownership of your hair once it had been cut off, it would be for the hairdresser to dispose of as he saw fit, in line with common practice in a hairdressers. You might think that the hairdresser's use of your hair would be of no consequence to you, but what if he sold it on eBay? What if it was used in an art exhibition to make a political point with which you disagreed? Would you then have a claim to your hair in these cases?

This question might lead on to a discussion about whether or not we own our own bodies. Surprisingly perhaps, we have no legal right to decide what happens to us when we die – instead, we can only express preferences and there are some things that the law will not let us do (e.g. leave your body to be used as meat for the dogs in Battersea Dogs' Home). We may contrast this with the approach the law takes to our other possessions after we die – in the case of all other property, your wishes are absolute. This contrast would suggest that we do not have the same legal relationship with our bodies as we do with our toasters, our cars, or our pocket-watches- but the really interesting question is – *should we?*

Q9: Should prisoners have the right to vote?

The European Court of Human Rights has ruled that Britain's blanket ban on voting for all convicted prisoners is a breach of their human rights. Allowing only some prisoners to vote would be ok, states the Court, but refusing the vote to all convicted prisoners is unacceptable.

Prison is generally considered to serve three key purposes; 1) to protect the public, 2) to serve as a deterrent, 3) to rehabilitate. Most prisoners have not committed crimes that warrant a life sentence. Most will eventually be released from prison. It's in everyone's interest that once out of prison, they do not commit any further crimes, but instead, become useful members of society. That involves reform whilst still in prison, and rehabilitating offenders to think - and act - more positively about their civic duties and responsibilities. One of the most important contributions a citizen can make to society is to take part in democracy and vote – removing a prisoner's civic duty does not, therefore, seem to accord with the aims of putting them in prison in the first place.

Alternatively, one might argue that all citizens of a country have implicitly agreed on a set of rules that gives them, and those around them, certain rights. It is the duty of every citizen to protect this framework and to respect the rights of others. If a person is in prison, it is because they broke the rules, and hence, in a way, forfeited their rights. The citizenship of prisoners can be seen as temporarily suspended along with all their rights.

Human rights do not mean that someone cannot be suitably punished or imprisoned for a crime once fairly tried and convicted. Human rights means that all humans deserve them, and the State protects them from abuse of their basic civil rights. If the State can be allowed to abuse humans – any humans, for any reasons or excuses – then how can we justify laws against humans abusing other humans? How the State behaves must be reflective of how we want all humans to behave.

Human rights are meant to be universal, which means the rights apply to all humans without exception; to you and to me; even to criminals and foreigners, and even to those humans we do not like. Once we take basic rights away from one human, we start to erode the basic protections for all humans.

Q10: Should 'immoral' or 'evil' laws be obeyed?

Note: if candidates are unsure of what the question means, interviewers can share Victorian jurist Dicey's famous example: should Parliament legislate for all blue-eyed babies to be killed, the law would still be a valid law but citizens would be 'mad' to obey it.

This question requires candidates to take a step back and consider the purpose and basis of the law. A good candidate would be able to make some comment about legal normativism versus legal positivism, but this is not essential. It is more important that they can engage with concepts and ideas, not get bogged down in technical terms.

A sensible place to start would be a discussion on why people obey the law -- out of a sense of moral obligation independent of the law (e.g. if I think stealing is wrong, I will not steal regardless of what the relevant statute precisely says), versus wishing to adhere to social norms (i.e. not being "looked down upon" or shunned by one's peers for being involved with illegal activities), versus actually fearing legal sanctions (e.g. avoiding recreational drugs while travelling in the Far East because I fear the death penalty being applied to me as a 'trafficker'). This should lead to strong candidates taking a step back and addressing to what extent morality should be the basis of law in a liberal society.

Candidates are free to proceed in a number of ways. It is only essential that they show that they have thought about the topic and have read some appropriate material. However, they must highlight that such 'immoral' laws would attract political criticism, and be conscious of the fact that political and legal mechanisms must work in tandem to protect basic constitutional values and civil liberties.

Q11: Given that juries consist of untrained people who do not have to give reasons for their decisions, are juries inherently inefficient and unreliable?

Candidates may not be aware of precisely what role juries play in the British justice system. It may be necessary to simply state that juries decide questions of fact but not law, which are used in certain more serious criminal trials, and jury members are picked at random from all adults on the electoral roll (except for members of certain professions, such as solicitors or MPs).

Candidates must be aware of the fundamental constitutional significance of trial by jury, an institution dating back to the time of the Magna Carta: being tried in front of a body of one's peers is purported to be central to democracy as they are held to be fairer and more objective than a single judge, as the jury is drawn from members of all strata of society, and thus, better able to understand the lifestyle of the ordinary man (as opposed to the white, middle-aged, male and upper-middle-class views of most judges). Juries can also play a role in repudiating repugnant, undemocratic laws. Not having to give reasons, the jury may refuse to convict if they believe the law was enacted to be overly harsh.

Candidates should also be aware that jury trials are expensive and inefficient. A balance between these two competing factors is necessary, and being able to provide sensible reasons for their preference is all that is needed.

However, strong candidates should question whether unelected juries ought to have a de facto power to ignore the legislation of the elected parliament if they think the law is repugnant. They should also consider whether or not jury decisions are even reliable.

Q12: Is the British monarchy antiquated and undemocratic? What reasons are there for either keeping or abolishing this institution?

This question is general and superficially familiar to any British applicant. However, it is one which hints at the complex, uncodified nature of the British constitution.

Candidates should know that a large range of powers are vested in the Monarch nominally. However, the Monarch does not exercise these powers independently as a matter of convention: there is no legal requirement that the Monarch must take the advice of the Prime Minister in, for example, giving Royal Assent to any Act duty passed by the elected Parliament. However, it would be unthinkable that she would refuse such advice, and, if she were to exercise such powers arbitrarily, it is likely that legal sanctions would be enacted to severely curtail the Monarch's power or to abolish the Monarchy altogether. There must be an awareness that what is right and wrong in law is not what is right or wrong generally and that the law is not the sole control of behaviour in society.

It would not be wrong for candidates to discuss the advantages or disadvantages of constitutional monarchy vs. republicanism in general, but they should not waste time discussing something not strictly pertinent to the question asked.

Strong candidates must frame their answer with reference to the tension between the theoretical anachronisms and empirical modernity which exist in the British constitution. A balanced approach is crucial, or, minimally, one which at least acknowledges the popularity (and therefore quasi-democratic mandate) of the Monarchy, and the importance of the Monarch as uniting numerous Commonwealth countries (e.g. Australia, New Zealand, Canada and the Bahamas), and how the removal of the Monarch in the UK would force citizens of many other countries to change their constitutional arrangements, possibly against their will.

Q13: Should publications like Charlie Hebdo be free to circulate uncontrolled? What kinds of restrictions on the media are compatible with freedom of speech?

If candidates are unfamiliar with the Charlie Hebdo killings, they would be told that Charlie Hebdo is an 'irreverent' French magazine which published inflammatory cartoons of the Prophet Mohammed. Outraged by these 'blasphemous' cartoons, Muslim extremists stormed the Charlie Hebdo office and killed a number of cartoonists. Many reacted with horror and immediately highlighted the importance of the freedom of speech. However, a smaller number of voices, while decrying what had happened, also highlighted the importance of responsible journalism.

Obviously, this is connected to ideas about Freedom of Speech. More generally, this raises fundamental questions about the nature of rights, and how rights are balanced against one another, as well as how the rights of the individual need to be balanced against the rights of the community.

A sensitive, nuanced approach would consider the overtones of Islamophobia which have tainted discourse on this case. In contrast, many simply speak about 'the right to offend' and the 'terror of extremism' with reference to this case.

A candidate who is able to think laterally may talk about how, in the UK, one's personal reputation is strongly protected by the UK's vigorous defamation laws. In contrast, offending or defaming an entire religion does not have such protection. Some consideration should be made of the role and position of religion in a secular, liberal society.

Q14: In the UK, the age of minimum criminal responsibility is 10, but the age of sexual consent is 16. A 15-year-old boy caught kissing a 14-year-old girl on the mouth could thus be convicted of various sexual offences. Is this satisfactory?

This question mixes together two anomalies in British criminal law. England has one of the youngest minimum ages of criminal responsibility in the Western world (it is 12 in Canada, Scotland, France, Germany, and Ireland), and the UN has recommended that all countries raise the age of minimum criminal responsibility to 12. Further, England has one of the highest minimum ages of consent for sex: it is typically 12 to 14 in Western Europe (but 18 in most of the US).

A good candidate must talk about whether or not the low age of criminal responsibility and high minimum age of sexual consent is justified. However, a strong candidate must interact with the question and be aware of the 'double whammy' effect these laws have.

One tension that must be identified is that the law must be reasonable and realistic. If the law were to criminalise activities which one is unlikely to be arrested for (which is inherent to the clandestine nature of underage mutually consensual sex), it may bring the law into disrepute.

Candidates must have a balanced view, however, and acknowledge how a high minimum age for sexual consent can protect the vulnerable and how a low minimum age of criminal responsibility is politically popular separately, but the interaction between the two can be problematic. It may be helpful to talk about how law is influenced by culture and the 'traditional' British attitude towards law and order and openness about sex.

Ultimately, a successful candidate must interact with the question and come to a sensible, thoroughly-considered opinion. A range of conclusions are acceptable, namely that the law should protect the young from harmful overly-early sexualisation, and because a 10-year-old facing a charge will not go to an adult jail (the emphasis being on rehabilitation). It could be suggested that the minimum age of criminal responsibility should be raised for the sake of compliance with international norms and the rights of the child, acknowledging their psychological immaturity and the sheer iniquity of charging children in an adult court. Also, that the age of sexual consent could be lowered so that the law should keep up with current societal norms, or some other combination of reform and consistency.

Q15: What are the fundamental differences between US and British Law? What are the implications of this?

It would be unfair to expect any technical knowledge from the candidate, so this need only be answered in general terms.

Primarily, we are concerned with the fact that the US has a codified constitution, and that there is, therefore, a clear separation of powers and the legislature, unlike in the UK, is not 'sovereign'. This means judges have the power to overturn unconstitutional legislation, and that in the US, the supreme source of authority is the constitution, not the will of Congress.

Another pertinent point is that the UK is a constitutional monarchy, but the US has a President. Though the monarch nominally has vast discretionary powers, these are never exercised by the monarch per se. In contrast, the elected President can and does use his considerable powers. This can be linked to the earlier point about the UK's uncodified constitution and that constitutional conventions play an important role in the UK.

A further point that can be mentioned is that the US is a federal system with each state having equal and defined powers, whereas the UK uses a devolution system where full power nominally remains with Westminster, not, say, the Scottish Parliament.

All these points must be linked to basic ideas about the rule of law, legal certainty, the separation of powers, and good governance. How exactly the implications of each of these differ is not essential. Rather, a strong candidate should demonstrate evidence of further reasoning, consider a number of perspectives, and show depth and clarity of thought. It would be helpful if they comment on whether or not the US or UK model is better, and whether or not the US model ought to be applied to countries with very different histories.

Q16: In France, if a person sees somebody drowning, they have a legal obligation to help them. Should this be the case in the UK?

This is about 'Good Samaritan Laws'. The duty to rescue, however, is necessarily a limited one in practice. Candidates should consider this when analysing the actual legal effect of such laws.

Ideas about liberty and an understanding that it is fundamentally more restrictive to force someone to do something as opposed to preventing them from doing certain things (the basic premise of most law) are fundamental to this question.

It must be acknowledged that such laws are morally attractive to prevent repugnant events such as healthy adults ignoring a two-year-old drowning in a paddling pool.

In balancing the two, the role of the law in society and the influence of morality on law must be considered. The practical limits of such a law must be analysed too: it would be unreasonable to expect a man who cannot swim to try to save a drowning person. However, as the rescuer's ability to rescue decreases and the danger involved in rescuing increases, the line to draw becomes blurred and a sensible legislature would generally give the benefit of the doubt to the rescuer, the one whose liberty is being restricted.

Ultimately, a nuanced, thoughtful response which weighs the two competing considerations is necessary. To be successful, links must be made to real-world implications, rather than just theoretical, philosophical considerations.

Q17: Is it fair to impose a height restriction on those wanting to become firefighters?

This is a general question posed within a specific scenario. Ideas about non-discrimination and EU law are relevant. However, it must be highlighted that functional job requirements do not constitute discrimination. Moving on from this, an intelligent candidate ought to question whether or not a height requirement is a genuine job requirement as technology may be used to overcome this. Strong candidates may be aware that public bodies are required to act 'reasonably' (which they must define).

Though their entire response need not be legally-related, this question really tests a legal style of reasoning. This means that they must be able to weigh up and consider a number of factors and be aware of the context of the supposed 'discrimination'.

Q18: Your neighbour noticed your roof had become damaged while you were away, and fixed it, are you obligated to pay him for his work?

This question links to ideas about contract: a good contract is one which predicates upon mutual consent. One cannot make a contract unilaterally -- is this assumption valid? Is it necessary? However, though some traction may be given to such a line of query, it should be accepted that the basic premise of contracts is one of agreement between free agents, who should be at liberty to make decisions and negotiate according to their individual requirements.

With regards to this question, there is a <u>minor assumption</u> that must be challenged: did you ask your neighbour to perform this service and if so, was any payment expected by either party when the agreement was made?

However, given the fact that this question has arisen, it is likely that there was no agreement, or, at most, a casual request for a favour which may have been understood. In untangling these two possibilities, it must be acknowledged that this is not a business context, and that the intention to create legal relations is improbable given that such arrangements are made informally and between (presumably) amicable neighbours who may even regard one another as friends.

Ultimately, though, one may feel it appropriate to make some sort of contribution towards the cost of painting the fence, it must be acknowledged that this is not a business relationship. It would not be fair for the neighbour to do something unilaterally and expect payment had you not expressed a wish for him specifically to paint your fence. Even if I had simply wanted someone to paint the fence and casually mentioned this to my neighbour, it would be a pleasant surprise if my neighbour did this for free. It would not be appropriate, however, for my neighbour to demand payment unless previously stipulated, or else it would be unfair to the householder who may have been able to get a cheaper price or a more skilled painter if that was what he preferred.

The best answers should make some reference to the demands of <u>actual commercial transactions</u> and draw out appropriate principles that are necessary for the proper functioning of a capitalist society.

Q19: Why should we care about the rule of law?

This is a general question which invites the candidate to talk about a range of issues. A sound definition is required for the question to be answered successfully.

Strong candidates should be aware of the different conceptions of the rule of law. It goes beyond 'the law of rules' (that laws must be enacted by the appropriate authority), but is about a culture of fairness and fair-mindedness. The debate centres on to what extent values like human rights or democratic values can be 'read in' to legislation.

This should be linked to other constitutional values like the <u>separation of powers and parliamentary sovereignty</u> and how these sometimes-competing demands need to be balanced against each other, and must be considered with reference to the values of British liberal democracy.

Strong candidates would have a wealth of examples, e.g. the Belmarsh case.

Language Interviews

If you are applying for the French, German, Spanish, or Italian version of the course and are invited to Oxford for an interview, you should expect to be given a short oral language test as part of the interview process. Such a test is important and you must show the necessary linguistic competence. However, it is important to emphasise that the decision as to whether to offer a place on the four-year course is made first and foremost by reference to your potential as a law student, not by your performance in the oral language test.

The language test will be quite relaxed, normally with just yourself and a native speaker alone in a room. The **interview will likely be recorded**. You do not necessarily need to have a great deal of knowledge of the foreign legal system, but you should be able to articulate what it is specifically that interests you about that legal system and why you want to spend an extra year of your degree studying it. Real passion for the language, culture, and country will get you a long way too, of course!

If you are applying for the four-year Law with European Law course (to spend the year abroad in the Netherlands), you will not have this additional language interview as the course is entirely in English.

Q20: What is the difference between Course I and Course II (Law with Legal Studies in Europe) at Oxford?

Course II incorporates all the elements of course I – you will study all of the same topics in years 1, 2 and will have the same choice of options open to you when you return from your year abroad in your 4th year. The difference between the two courses lies in the additional element of the study of the foreign legal system.

In your first year, you will take weekly language classes (French, Italian, Spanish, German, or conversational Dutch). These classes will be around 2 hours per week. They are not obligatory but act as a really good way of allowing you to get to know the other students who you will be going abroad with in your 3rd year. They also help to keep up your language skills.

In your second year, you will take weekly introductory classes to your foreign legal system in the language of that legal system. These will be around 2 hours per week and there will rarely be additional work set. These are obligatory and provide a good basis on which you will build when you begin your studies on your year abroad.

In your third year, you will study abroad at one of the selected universities. You will have exams in your 3rd year but these marks will not count towards your final degree grade, instead, you must simply pass this year. You will likely be taking topics which first-year law students in that jurisdiction take, but your workload will likely be much lighter than the average law student. This year is an Erasmus year and you will be supported by grants from the Erasmus program. Furthermore, there are several Oxford-based grants which are available for students on Course II during their year abroad. You will be given the opportunity to completely immerse yourself in the local culture and custom, perfect your language, and get a real insight into how the law works in that country. You will also have much more spare time than you will have been used to in Oxford, given the significantly lighter workload. This means you'll have more time for travel and recreation. This is a fantastic year.

In your fourth year, you will be back in Oxford and your course of study will be exactly the same as that of someone on course I. You will not be examined on the foreign legal system in your finals.

Law Interview Questions

1. What is the rule of law?
2. Why should we care about the rule of law?
3. Is it fair to impose a height restriction on those wanting to become fire-fighters?
4. Your neighbour noticed your roof had become damaged while you were away, and fixed it, are you obligated to pay him for his work?
5. What does it mean to 'take' another's car?
6. If traffic wardens had the legal right to execute people caught parking in restricted areas, and as a result no one did, would this be considered a fair and effective law?
7. If we lived without malice and ill intent, would there be any need to have the law?
8. Do the girl scouts have a political agenda? Can any organisation be truly 'apolitical'?
9. Why do you want to study law?
10. If someone unintentionally commits a crime, are they guilty?
11. When should the state be allowed to violate your privacy?
12. Should anyone have the right to invade our privacy?
13. Do you think that the state should be more free to operate as it chooses than the media is?
14. What is the role of honesty in law?
15. Should the law protect people from themselves?
16. Can a law ever be truly just if it restricts our freedom to do something?
17. Should laws ever govern what we can and cannot say?
18. How would you place a value on life? Would you shoot a baby to save another person, to save a thousand people?
19. Do you think that euthanasia should be legal?
20. Should overweight people have to pay extra on planes if they need to take two seats?
21. Do you think it is legally justifiable to charge for access to a toilet in a closed environment like an aeroplane?
22. Should a jury of peers be selected based on the IQ of the defendant?
23. What would a country without law be like?
24. In France, you are legally obligated to help a person you see in distress, for instance, if they are drowning in a river. Why do you think we don't have a law like this, should we?
25. Should the law be absolute, or black and white, or should it be more flexible?
26. Should the law be based on morality?
27. Let's say that overnight, the Supreme Court took ownership of all judicial functions previously allocated to the House of Lords – what changes?
28. Should the legislature and executive be kept separate?
29. Do you think that judges should be elected?
30. Which legal barriers prevent daily wars?
31. A simple case, a cyclist is hit by a car, only they were cycling in a car lane rather than the adjacent cycle lane – who is liable? Does your answer change if the cyclist had taken no measures to be visible at night?
32. Which of the House of Lords and House of Commons has more power? What are the main differences between them?

33. Why do people who do some particular jobs get exemptions from jury duty.
34. When you become prime minister, what laws will you change?
35. Two people die as a result of their parachute failing due to a manufacturing flaw, would their deaths constitute murder or manslaughter?
36. If a person is convicted of a murder which did not take place, and upon release kills the original victim, can they be sentenced again?
37. What does it mean when something is "beyond reasonable doubt"
38. What are the legal implications of gay marriage?
39. What data should our government be able to find out about us? Should foreign citizens be treated any differently?
40. What is the significance of differences between American and British Law?
41. How would you advise a client who is refusing to attend court despite multiple summons?
42. A General orders a soldier to kill his squad mate. Would this be murder?
43. A doctor is asked by the wife of a patient to end the patient's suffering by killing them. Do you think this would be murder?
44. Which law is broken most frequently?
45. When people are tried by their peers, why bother with a judge?
46. You take shelter from a thunderstorm in an unlocked car – have you committed the offence of allowing yourself to be carried in a conveyance without the owner's consent?
47. How would you separate the words: Mislead, Deceive, and Lie?
48. Why are manslaughter and murder treated differently, what separates them?
49. Should stalking remain legal?
50. How do civil cases differ from criminal ones?
51. What would you say are the advantages and disadvantages of juries?
52. To what extent can you know how much you do not know?
53. What would you say differentiates solicitors from barristers?
54. If you were made Queen's Counsel tomorrow, what do you think your responsibilities would be? What would you have to do to be made a Queen's Counsel?
55. If a parent slaps their child, are they abusing them? Does your answer change if they bruised the child?
56. What prevents European nations from combining into a United States of Europe?
57. What impact did 9/11 have on western law?
58. Who can change the law, or make a new law?
59. If you could change any 3 laws, which ones would they be and what would you change?
60. To what extent did the NSA revelations impact on the British public?
61. What is the hierarchy of courts in the UK?
62. Which law do you think is broken the most often in the UK?
63. Do you think a mandatory uniform contravenes the rights of school children?
64. A man points a gun at you and says "If you don't shoot your friend or I'll kill you both". If you shoot your friend are you guilty of murder? Would you be guilty if, instead, the man had said "If you don't shoot your friend, I'll shoot you"? How about if he had said "If you don't shoot your friend, I will"?
65. Do we have an innate moral code, or are we taught it?

66. What compels us to obey the law?
67. What is the relevance of Roman Law to your course?
68. What law is broken most frequently?
69. Do you think that the state should pass laws governing what we can eat? What laws would you introduce to combat obesity?
70. What does law have to do with the environment?
71. What is a country?
72. Define a miracle.

MEDIEVAL AND MODERN LANGUAGES

At the start of a subject interview for Modern Languages, an applicant may be asked to discuss a short text in the target language which will have been presented to them shortly before the interview.

During the preparation time, you will have been expected to read through the text thoroughly and to **ready yourself for a short discussion** of its main ideas and features.

When reading through the text and preparing for discussion:

- If you don't understand every word in the passage you've been given, then don't panic. It is probably supposed to be difficult and applicants are not expected to have already achieved fluency in the language they wish to study.
- Apply the knowledge you have acquired at A-Level and from wider reading to unfamiliar scenarios. You may not recognise the text you have been asked to read, but that is probably deliberate.
- Think about the style of the text. You may not be told its source, so you will have to engage critically to decide what sort of text it might be. Does the style reflect that or an article or an extract from a novel? Does the type of language tell you anything about what time period the text might be from?
- Pick out parts of the text that you find interesting. The interviewers will be keen to see evidence of your personal response to the text. Is there an idiomatic phrase which you particularly like? Does a certain line remind you of another text you have already read? What effect does the passage and its use of language have on you as a reader?
- The interviewer will want to see that you've tried to read and comprehend the text as best you can, and also to have engaged critically with it.
- If there is a word or concept you don't understand, talk these harder texts through carefully and the interviewer will help you reach an answer. Be prepared to accept some help and assistance from the interviewer - that is no bad thing.
- Remember, making mistakes is normal. If you have misinterpreted a word or an idea, the important point is that you address the mistake head-on and attempt to revise the statement, with the assistance of the tutors where necessary.
- Following a short discussion of the text, subsequent questions will reflect the various different elements of the Modern Languages course.

This interview will require you to demonstrate passion and a genuine desire to study your chosen subject, so be prepared to voice your personal interests beyond those mentioned in your personal statement. Material mentioned in your personal statement can be used as a starting point for the conversation.

The tutors know what topics you have studied at A-Level within your chosen subjects. *They will not ask you for detailed knowledge about areas of your subject that you are unfamiliar with.* Nobody knows every aspect of their subject.

An applicant will most likely be asked about their reading/engagement with cultural material in their chosen language areas. It is worth emphasising that the Modern Languages courses at Oxbridge privilege the study of literature and applicants will be expected to have pursued their personal interests beyond the remit of their A Level/IB/Pre-U syllabus, even if they have not had the opportunity yet to study literature at school.

Learning a New Language

At both Oxford and Cambridge, there is the option to learn a new language *ab initio*. If one of the languages you have applied for is one which you have not previously studied, then you will be expected to demonstrate your curiosity and enthusiasm for learning it. You will not be expected to have developed knowledge of the language, but **you will be expected to have made a decent attempt at learning some of the basics** and engaging with the culture of its speakers.

What Questions Might Be Asked?

Most of the questions asked in the interview will be broad, allowing the candidate to use them as a springboard for discussing their personal interests.

Smaller sub-questions may be used by the interviewer to prompt and guide the candidate into an active discussion.

The main question may seem difficult, impossible or random at first, but take a breath and start discussing with your interviewer different ideas you have for breaking down the question into manageable pieces. Don't panic. **The questions are designed to be difficult** to give you the chance to show your full intellectual potential. They will help guide you to the right idea if you provide ideas for them to guide. This is your chance to show your creativity, analytical skills, intellectual flexibility, problem-solving skills and your go-getter attitude. Don't waste it on nervousness or a fear of messing up or looking stupid.

As well as specific questions about a book, the course or a topical issue in the language-speaking country, applicants may be asked questions of a more philosophical nature. These questions will not have one specific answer, rather they will serve as an opportunity for the applicant to consider an idea.

The interviewers will be looking for inquisitive minds that can engage creatively with new problems. Don't be afraid to present your trains of thought out loud- the interviewer will be just as interested in seeing *how* you tackle the question as to the response you give. Often, the interview is most concerned with **how** you think and how you tackle difficult and challenging problems.

Worked Questions

Below are a few examples of how to start breaking down an interview question, with model answers.

Q1: Is silence something we can hear?

With a more abstract question such as this, it is best to try and talk through your thought process, engaging with the question and applying logic as best as you can to work through your ideas. If you are thrown by a question, start by linking it back to your subject. Think about the question in relation to the study of languages.

It's a good idea to start by thinking about the subject of the question. A solid piece of advice for any humanities student- start by questioning the question:

What is silence? How do we define silence? How do we experience silence? What is the opposite of silence? Is silence a sound? Is silence a state independent of a listener? Does silence depend on an ear?

Asking these types of things out loud will demonstrate your active engagement with the original question.

Q2: How would you define language?

With broad questions such as these, it can be useful to draw upon specific examples to back up your argument. Try to analyse the role of language in day to day speech and how that compares, for example, to the *language* as seen in a poem/text you have recently read. What are the common defining features of language? What are the differences seen in its usage according to context?

Think about what constitutes a language, the uses and limitations of language, and the role and nature of communication structures.

Follow up questions may include: "Do you need more than one speaker for a language to exist?" And, "Is a language only a language if it is spoken?"

Q3: What does a nation's literature tell us?

This question provides an opportunity to demonstrate a real enthusiasm for critically engaging with literature - this is important as literature features heavily on the Oxbridge Modern Languages Courses.

With a question as broad as this, a strong response would use a framework in order to engage more incisively with the key issues at stake (the role of literature, the place of literature in the society, the relationship of literature to a given society). For example:

Nation and narration are inextricably linked. Literature creates a narrative for a society and its people. It can provide an aperture into new worlds: their cultural specificities, mindset, and histories.

From my initial engagements with literature from Latin America -namely readings of poems by Neruda- I have been struck by the ability of the writer to cast an eye onto the parallel worlds of his nation. In his verse, we find commentary on Chilean politics, embedded within a lyric which references the heritage of past civilisations.

I have read sections from the first and final parts of *Alturas de Machu Pichu* (1945). Here, in entering into a dialogue with his nation's ancestry, Neruda both celebrates the achievement of Machu Picchu and condemns the exploitative slavery that made it possible. Furthermore, In *Canto XII of his Canto General* - considered one of the greatest political poems of the last century- Neruda calls upon the dead to be born again and to speak through him. In doing so, he references the power of literature to connect us not only to the present but to a nation's past.

Q4: How would you discretise language from linguistics?

This question encourages a technical response, demonstrating the candidate's understanding of the broad theoretical terminology that underpins their subject.

A well-structured answer may begin by defining language and linguistics. The candidate will then draw the two definitions into dialogue in order to address the original question of 'difference'. The best responses may also reference eminent theorists of language.

Language is a system of signs which serves to enable the communication between beings. According to Noam Chomsky, language is a "set of sentences, each finite in length, and constructed out of a finite set of elements." And Aronoff states that "it is impossible to separate language from literature, or politics, or most of our everyday human interactions." (2007)

Linguistics is the scientific study of language. The difference is that as a discipline of study, it applies itself to language. It is to explain language; it references and analyses the working mechanisms of these systems of signs. According to Aitchison, linguistics "has a twofold aim: to uncover general principles underlying human language, and to provide reliable descriptions of individual languages." (1992)

Q5: Will automatic translation software make human translators redundant?

This question will allow a good candidate the opportunity to engage critically with pertinent questions in the current climate of language learning. It encourages the candidate to also consider its underlying question- what is the need for learning languages today?

Thanks to the internet, we live in an increasingly interconnected world. Technology has been said to 'shrink' the world, bringing us closer together through instant means of communication. What's more, technology has been employed for the purposes of transcending linguistic barriers to communication, through innovations in computerised translation.

The availability of devices such as Google Translate and other translation apps force us to consider whether machines will ever be able to fully replace human translators. However, because languages are complex and nuanced, words are often defined and understood according to a given context. It seems unlikely that a machine alone could ever replicate the job of the human translator.

Through an article I read on Foreign Tongues, The Market Research Translation Agency, I was introduced to a program called Unbabel, which is a combination of technology and crowd-sourced human translation.

Unbabel first uses computers to translate a customer's inquiry and then splits it into micro-tasks for its human translators to refine and check for errors. Unbabel then puts the text together and sends it back. Customers can send and receive their text through email, online or through Unbabel's API.

So, when it comes to documents demanding accurate translation to the level of a native speaker, it seems unlikely that software as rudimentary as Google Translate will ever be able to replace the human translator. Another way to engage with this question would be to implicate literature and the poetic voice.

Our use of language in accordance with aesthetic parameters (forms, rhyme, allegory, metaphor, simile, idiom) render literary language resistant to the face-value translations of the machine.

Q6: What do you think are the main differences between Latin American Spanish and European Spanish.

This question encourages both a historical contextualization and technical understanding of the Spanish language.

A good candidate will be able to demonstrate their understanding of this linguistic colonial legacy and its relation to the development of Latin American Spanish. They will also be able to cite some specific examples of the difference between Latin American and European Spanish:

When Spanish colonisers travelled the world, they brought with them a language that was in the process of changing back at home. A linguist called Marckwardt came up with the term "colonial lag" to describe a situation where the language spoken in colonies does not keep up with innovations in the language in its country of origin. An example in English would be the use of 'fall' in the USA and 'autumn' in Britain; when British colonisers went to America, 'fall' was more common than the Latin version in British English. The older, Germanic word 'fall' later became obsolete in Britain but has remained in common use in the USA. This process happens with vocabulary but also with grammar. Later on, immigrant groups from different parts of Europe brought linguistic traditions with them to Latin America. In turn, these groups met different local linguistic traditions, creating variations in local dialects.

One of the clearest examples of that process is the use of 'vos', primarily in Argentina, Paraguay and Uruguay. Originally, a second-person plural, vos came to be used as a more polite second-person singular pronoun among one's familiar friends. It was commonly used in Spanish when the language reached the southern cone of the Americas. It fell out of use in Spain but stayed in Rioplatense Spanish. Nowadays, just like 150 years ago, at a bustling Buenos Aires café, you are much more likely to be asked "¿de dónde sos?" than "¿de dónde eres?"

Then, there is the question of pronunciation: in many parts of Central America, 's' isn't always pronounced and in Argentina, the 'double-l' that is usually pronounced like the 'y' in yellow is pronounced like the 's' in measure.

Q7: What was the most recent film you saw?

General questions such as these are often posed towards the start of modern languages interviews to help make the candidate feel at ease. They provide an opportunity to demonstrate your interest in your subject beyond the school syllabus.

It goes without saying that the question refers to a foreign language film, most likely one in the target language being tested in the interview. A good answer to this sort of question (which could just as easily replace film with book, play, exhibition) will quickly progress from a direct response:

"I watched *La Haine*, a French film directed by Mathieu Kassovitz" to a more interrogative analysis/expression personal response:

"What I found particularly interesting about this film was its setting within such a brief timeframe- the film relays to its audience the 19 hours in the aftermath of a riot in the Parisian suburbs.

"The pace at which we observe the aimless daily routine of the three young protagonists draws us into line with their perspective on events as they struggle to entertain themselves and frequently find themselves under police scrutiny. When Saïd and Hubert are racially humiliated and physically abused, resulting in their missing the last train home and having to spend a night on the streets, the cinematic frame, as employed by Kassovitz, serves with a political agency to remind us of societal 'framing' and outcasting of these individuals. As such, this film has fed into my engagement with my A Level syllabus and our considerations of racism and integration in France, with respect to the riots in 2005 in Clichy-sous-Bois."

Q8: What have you been doing on your A Level course?

This is another example of a question that may be used to put you at ease. Good responses to these questions will not simply list the various tasks and materials engaged with on the course. Rather, they might draw upon one or possibly two areas which have been of particular interest and talk about these in more detail.

"This term we have studied a piece of literature for the first time. We are looking at Sartre's *Huis Clos*. I have particularly enjoyed engaging with the fundamentals of existentialist philosophy through the medium of theatre.

"In fact, during the half-term break, I went to see a production of the play in London in order to help conceive the text more fully as a dramatic piece. I was interested to see in the performance the use of space and shape formations between the three characters to demonstrate the relational power-shifts within the trio.

"I was also intrigued by the Valet, a character 'without-eyelids'. As the only character to move in and out of the closed room, entering with each of the characters, I thought we might read his unbreakable stare as a reflection of the unbreakable gaze within, of Estelle offering herself as a mirror and of the definition of self in relation to the other."

The interviewer may then pose further questions about the play, the eyelids, existentialism etc.

Q9: How would you say that your travel has affected relationship with language?

Questions about travel are frequently asked in modern languages interviews- which is not to say that extensive travel is by any means expected of a candidate. Evidently, those who have partaken in excursions, school trips, exchanges or gap year travels will be able to reference these experiences. However, an absence of these opportunities will not put a candidate at a disadvantage.

A question such as this, above all, seeks to engage with the motivations for learning another language. When drawing from travel experience -or thinking ahead to future travel aspirations- what the candidate should consider is:

- What does it mean to communicate - in its broadest sense?
- What does it mean to communicate with speakers of a different language?
- How much of a nation's culture manifests itself in language?
- Does language provide an access point to that culture? How?

Q10: How would you define language?

Here, the greatest challenge lies in the broadness of the question. This is a subject which has been central to philosophical interrogation.

The important thing to keep in mind here is that sometimes the applicant's first response serves only as a discussion starter. There is no need to include everything you would want to talk about, the interviewers only want to hear a few points they can start from. They will then drive the discussion in the direction they want to.

It is perfectly reasonable for the application to ask for a minute to consider the question and organise their thoughts.

Candidates should try to move beyond the 'system of communication' answer, perhaps by showing their awareness of theoretical problematizations of language:

- Estimates of the number of languages in the world: 5,000-7,000
- What constitutes a language? They can be spoken, signed, encoded.

Depending on their interests, the candidate may wish to reference the philosophy of languages, drawing upon the works of key thinkers of the 20th century: Wittgenstein, who argued that philosophy itself is really the study of language; or with regards linguistics, they could reference Saussure's distinction between sign and symbol or the work of Chomsky.

Q11: Can you tell me three reasons that reading could be considered dangerous?

Antagonistic questions such as this are often unexpected and as such, unprepared for. This is part of the exercise- to see how candidates respond and process a completely new stimulus. The interviewer will primarily be interested in the thought processes behind your response. With a question such as this, a stimulating response may manifest as a working through the various possible ways of interpreting the question:

"Of course, we could on one level, consider this question in terms of pure practicality: we don't know how badly it can affect our eyesight...although I'm quite certain that's more to do with Vitamin D and sunlight exposure... so perhaps reading is at its most dangerous when done inside. Then there is the environment, and increasing paper shortages.

"But it's not just the act of reading, it's also a question of the material being read. Propaganda is certainly dangerous. The disseminated written word, when imbued with malice or political agency, can become a potent form of contagion."

Q12: What was it about this book (mentioned in Personal Statement) that particularly caught your attention?

Questions framed in this manner are designed to elicit personal responses to cultural material. The interviewer will be interested to hear specifically about your reaction to the text in question. Giving opinions and backing them up with reference to parts of the text will be expected. The level of detail into which a candidate is able to go will demonstrate their level of preparation.

"Cien Años de Soledad" was unlike any other book I have ever read. Through it, I have been introduced to magical realism and its distinctive form of narrative. To me, it felt a bit like lucid dreaming.

"Despite having difficulty initially with keeping a firm grasp on the plot as it unfolded, due to the number of similarly-named characters, I learnt to stop resisting such confusions, but rather embrace them as a crucial and intentional part of García Márquez's cyclical narrative.

"For me, it was striking to encounter a textual narrative which allowed for forms of linear progression and other treatments of time, which perhaps can be seen to allegorise the metaphor of history as a circular phenomenon, seen through the recurrent characteristics in the six generations of José Arcadio and Aureliano.

"On a further note, Macondo's turn in the final chapter from a city of mirrors to a city of mirages can perhaps be read as a reflexive comment on the nature of literature itself."

It is likely that the interviewer will interrupt the candidate during this response, commenting in reaction to the points raised: "In what way did this compare to lucid dreaming?" or "What do you consider to be the effects of this cyclical narrative?" or "What do you mean by the nature of literature, how so?

FURTHER QUESTION AREAS

If the applicant has mentioned linguistics as an area of interest, questions to do with the nature of language itself may also be posed. It may be worth looking at recent controversies/new schools of emergent thought in this field.

It has also become common for interviewers to ask about the changing status of language in the modern world and the position/role/importance of multilingualism in an age of increasing globalisation. Consider crucial turning points in this narrative- the internet as a space for global communication etc. Think about why you still value the importance of learning new languages. What does it mean to study languages today?

MML Interview Questions

1. Why do you think we see such variation in the number of tenses between different languages?
2. Will the total number of languages in the world change over the next 100 years?
3. What can you learn from an accent?
4. How would you simplify English?
5. What's so complex about translating something like the Bible?
6. What are the differences and similarities between Spanish and Portuguese.
7. What do you think makes one language easier to learn than others?
8. What is the big deal about fluency? Isn't being able to be understood enough?
9. How does the German language shape people's mindsets in different ways to the Russian language?
10. What was the most recent film you saw?
11. What was it about this book in your statement which particularly caught your attention?
12. What is 'language'?
13. Has travelling changed the way you feel about language?
14. What would you say were the principal components of a language?
15. Would you agree with me that translation is reproduction?
16. What's the point of learning a language at all these days?
17. What's the relationship between the spoken and written word?
18. What draws you to other cultures?
19. You mentioned being fascinated by Latin American culture in your personal statement, but didn't elaborate on why - what would you say interests you the most about it?
20. What role does language play in our identity?
21. Tell me about the differences between French poetry and English poetry.
22. Do you think that poetry is a different language to that used in prose?
23. Would you say that the words we are exchanging now are in the same language as a work of great literature?
24. How do you feel about ambiguity?
25. What is your favourite word?
26. Make up a word for me – what does it mean?
27. What is the practical difference between Chinese whispers and translation?
28. How would you describe a cucumber to an alien whose translator can only understand Spanish?
29. Would you describe human thoughts as malleable?
30. Have electronic translators rendered linguists obsolete?
31. Newsflash! We are at war with Europe. The ministry of defence has asked for your advice on which languages their personnel should be taught, how do you answer?
32. What is the driving force behind the evolution of language – do you think this could be halted?
33. Where do accents come from?
34. Can culture shape vocabulary?
35. How do babies learn language?
36. You have a very short space of time to learn a new language, what is your strategy?
37. Do you think there's a limit on how many languages someone could learn, what do you think that limit might be?

38. What are the issues when studying multiple languages simultaneously?

39. What is used to convey the gender of a noun in German?

40. Do people from different parts of the world have different difficulties learning English? How would a German's experience of English differ from someone from Asia?

41. What steps would you take to make Google Translate a better service?

42. Do you have a favourite author? What is it you like about their work?

43. Is any language actually 'dead'?

44. Could a language exist using nothing but numbers, and without grammar?

45. What separates a modern language from a medieval one?

READING LISTS

The obvious way to prepare for any Oxbridge interview is to read widely. This is important so that you can mention books and interests in your personal statement. It is also important because it means that you will be able to draw upon a greater number and variety of ideas for your interview.

- **Make a record of the book**, who wrote it, when they wrote it, and summarise the argument. This means that you have some details about your research in the days before the interview.
- **Reading is a passive exercise**. To make it genuinely meaningful, you should engage with the text. Summarise the argument. Ask yourself questions like how is the writer arguing? Is it a compelling viewpoint?
- **Quality over quantity**. This is not a race as to how many books you can read in a short period of time. It is instead a test of your ability to critically analyse and synthesise information from a text – something you'll be doing on a daily basis at university.

BIOLOGY AND MEDICINE

- *Bad Pharma*: Ben Goldacre
- *Trust me I'm a Junior Doctor*: Max Pemberton
- *Genome*: Matt Ridley
- *The Single Helix*: Steve Jones
- *Bully for Brontosaurus*: Stephen Jay Gould

PSYCHOLOGY

- *The Man who Mistook his Wife for a Hat:* Oliver Sacks
- *How the Mind Works:* Steven Pinker
- *Predictably Irrational:* Dan Ariely
- *Thinking, Fast and Slow:* Daniel Kahneman

CHEMISTRY

- *The Disappearing Spoon*: Sam Kean
- *Uncle Tungsten*: Oliver Sacks
- *Reactions- The Private Life of Atoms*: Peter Atkins
- *Periodic Tales*: Hugh Aldersey-Williams

PHYSICS

- *A Brief History of Time:* Stephen Hawking
- *The Feynman Lectures on Physics:* Richard Feynman
- *Three Roads to Quantum Gravity:* Lee Smolin
- *Death by Black Hole:* Neil deGrasse Tyson

ENGINEERING

- *How do wings work?*: Holger Babinsky
- *Structures- or why things don't fall down*: JE Gordon
- *Remaking the World*: Henry Petroski
- *Sustainable Energy*: David MacKay
- *Truth, Lies, and O-Rings*: Allan J, McDonald

MATERIALS SCIENCE

- **Stuff Matters:** Mark Miodownik
- **The New Science of Strong Materials: Or Why You Don't Fall Through the Floor:** J. Gordon
- **Rust: The Longest War:** Jonathan Waldman
- **Nano Comes To Life: Now Nanotechnology is Transforming Medicine and the Future of Biology:** Sonia Contera

MATHS

- *The Man Who Knew Infinity*: Robert Kanigel
- *A Mathematician's Apology*: GH Hardy
- *Fermat's Last Theorem*: Simon Singh
- *Game, Set and Math:* Ian Stewart

COMPUTER SCIENCE

- **The New Turing Omnibus:** Alexander Dewdney
- **Data Science:** John Kelleher and Brendan Tierney
- **Elementary Number Theory with Programming:** Martin Lewinter and Jeanine Meyer
- **Computer Science: An Overview:** J. Glenn Brookshear

LAW

- *Learning the Law*: Glanville Williams
- *An Introduction to Your Future*: Richard Susskind Tomorrow's Lawyers:
- *The Rule of Law:* Tom Bingham
- *The British Constitution:* Anthony King
- *Letters to a Law Student: A Guide to Studying Law at University*: Nicolas J McBride
- *Just Law*: Helena Kennedy

MML

French:

- *French Grammar in Context*: Margaret Jubb and Annie Rouxeville
- *A Comprehensive French Grammar (Blackwell)*: Glanville Price
- *French Grammar and Usage:* Roger Hawkins and Richard Towell:

Spanish:

- *A Spanish Learning Grammar:* Pilar Muñoz & Mike Thacker (London: Arnold, latest edition)
- *Grammar Practice:* Uso de la gramática española - nivel elemental, Francisca Castro (Edelsa, Spain, latest edition).

German:

- *German Grammar in Context:* Carol Fehringer
- *Using German Vocabulary, (2004):* S. Fagan

CLASSICS

Texts in Translation:

- *The Iliad*: Homer
- *The Odyssey:* Homer
- *The Aeneid:* Virgil

Secondary Works:

- *The Oxford Classical Dictionary*: Oxford University Press
- *Classics: A Very Short Introduction:* Beard/Henderson, Oxford University Press
- Any scholarly works that take your interest, especially if relevant to texts you have read. E.g. Those interested in Roman History should consider reading Andrew Wallace-Hadrill.

GEOGRAPHY

- *The Global City: New York, London, Tokyo:* Sassen. S
- *The Wretched of the Earth*: Fanon. F
- *Nature Unbound: Conservation, Capitalism And The Future Of Protected Areas:* Brockington, Duffy and Igoe
- *A Geographical Perspective On Poverty-Environment Interactions. The Geographical Journal:* Gray, L.C. and Moseley, W.G.

HISTORY

- *What is History?*: E.H. Carr
- *In Defence of History*: Richard J. Evans
- *The Historians Craft*: Marc Bloch
- *The Practice of History:* Geoffrey Elton
- *The Pursuit of History:* Josh Tosh
- *A History of Modern Britain*: Andrew Marr

ECONOMICS:

- The Economist / The Financial Times
- *Freakonomics*: Steven Levitt
- *A Very Short Introduction*: Partha Dasgupta Economics
- *End this Depression Now!* Paul Krugman
- *The Worldly Philosophers*: Robert L Heilbroner
- *Predictably Irrational*: Dan Ariely

PPE:

- *On Liberty*: J.S. Mill
- *Defence of Usury*: Jeremy Bentham
- *The Ascent of Money*: Niall Ferguson

ENGLISH

Think about how your other subjects might illuminate your study of English. For instance, perhaps you study Psychology and can use this framework to criticise Freud's theory of the Oedipus Complex in relation to Hamlet. You might study History and find this invaluable when analysing Shakespeare's history plays, informing your arguments about the importance of myths and legends, the theme of nationality, or tropes of traditional kingship, and so on. Even more interestingly, you might have studied Physics, Music, or Maths: did these otherwise distinct subjects enhance your study of English in a more oblique way?

There are infinite guides out there for English reading, but the main thing is to follow your interests like a cultural sniffer-dog. A few useful guidelines are given below for general reading around the subject.

There are many anthologies which can give you an excellent overview of chronological literary periods and 'traditions'. Margaret Drabble's **Oxford Companion to English Literature** will provide a wide-ranging scope, while Andrew Sanders' **Short Oxford History of English Literature** is very useful too. For poetry, in particular, **The Norton Anthology of Poetry,** ed. by Ferguson, Salter and Stallworthy is good, while Christopher Ricks' **Oxford Book of English Verse** is a detailed spectrum of styles of poetry, with a fantastic introduction that he expands upon in his **The Force of Poetry** or **Essays in Appreciation**. Pair this with oft-studied essayistic collections **like** T.S.Eliot's **Selected Prose of T.S. Eliot**, or William Empson's **Seven Types of Ambiguity**, which will make you think deeper about the art of studying poetry and the difficulties of being a good critic.

It is worth investing in a meaty critical anthology **like** Bennett and Royle's *An Introduction to Literature, Criticism, and Theory* which will give you a rough but valuable guide to a chronological overview of critical history that you can dip in and out of easily for reference. **The Norton Anthology of Theory and Criticism** is another valuable guide. However, use these as rough outlines, and broaden your thinking with Terry Eagleton's **Literary Theory,** which will provocatively debate many of these terms and ideas. A more readable guide is James Wood's **How Fiction Works**, which is a broad but detailed examination of the novel as a genre.

It can also be useful to have a dictionary like Chris Baldick's **The Oxford Dictionary of Literary Terms**, which will have bite-size snippets of information in the form of comprehensive definitions.

Pair this with Raymond Williams' **Keywords**, which is in effect a radical literary dictionary designed to make you question and expand these straight-forward definitions. Brush up on your practical criticism and close reading skills with John Lennard's **The Poetry Handbook: A Guide to Reading Poetry for Pleasure and Practical Criticism** – a true classic, and very readable. Pair this with giving yourself exercises in close reading, setting yourself extracts, and thinking about what you might discuss or point out.

If you read any classics, read Homer's **Iliad** and **Odyssey**, Ovid's **Metamorphoses** and Virgil's **Aeneid** in any reputable translation if you have the time, preferably in the Penguin or Oxford World Classics editions: these are foundational, and will prove incredibly useful in deciphering allusions. The same applies to the **Bible** or at least a selection of the most pivotal sections: Genesis, Exodus, The Song of Songs, the gospels of Matthew, Mark, Luke, and John, Revelation, the Book of Job, the Song of Solomon, etc. If you find this theological approach interesting, go on to read John Milton's **Paradise Lost**, which is surprisingly absorbing in its poetic dramatization of Adam and Eve; Alastair Fowler has edited an excellent critical edition.

It may sound obvious, but read or watch as many of Shakespeare's plays and poems as you can; they really are foundational and will stand you in good stead throughout your course. A guide like **Reading Shakespeare's Dramatic Language: A Guide** by Hunter, Magnusson, and Adamson will provide a readable introduction to the specifics of Shakespearean verse. Think more about the practical aspects of staging plays and theatrical history, from stage building to props, aspects which are often neglected at A-Level: Tiffany Stern and Farah Karim-Cooper's **Shakespeare's Theatre and the Effects of Performance** is fantastic, as is Stern's **Making Shakespeare: From Stage to Page** and Andrew Gurr's **The Shakespearean Stage**. In general, Cambridge and Oxford/Blackwell Companions are always very good and provide strong leads for further reading, such as Hodgdon and Worthen's **A Companion to Shakespeare and Performance**, but feel free to use modern dramatic criticism like Peter Brook's **The Empty Space** to deepen your ideas.

BIOLOGICAL ANTHROPOLOGY

- *How Humans Evolved*: Robert Boyd and Joan Silk.
- *The Principles of Human Evolution:* Robert Foley & Roger Lewin.
- *The Fetal Matrix:* Peter Gluckman and Mark Hanson.
- *Nature via Nurture*: Matt Ridley.
- *The Origin of our Species:* Chris Stringer.
- *Guns, Germs and Steel*: Jared Diamond.

POLITICS

- *Imagined Communities: Reflections on the origins and Spread of Nationalism*: Benedict Anderson.
- *The Anarchical Society*: Headley Bull.
- *Setting the People Free: The Story of Democracy*: John Dunn.
- *The Prince*: Niccolo Machiavelli.
- *World Politics: Progress and its Limits*: James Mayall.
- *Politics of Good Intentions: History, Fear, and Hypocrisy in the New World Order*: David Runciman.
- *Seeing Like a State: How Certain Schemes to Improve the Human Condition Have Failed*: James C Scott.
- *The Evolution of International Society*: Adam Watson.

SOCIOLOGY

- *Sociology*: Nicholas Abercrombie.
- *Sociology (5th edition)*: Anthony Giddens.
- *Capitalism and Modern Social Theory*: Anthony Giddens.
- *Understanding Classical Sociology*: J.A. Hughes.
- *Sociology: Diversity, Conflict, and Change*: K.J. Neubeck and D.S. Glasberg.
- *The Blackwell Dictionary of Modern Social Thought*: W. Outhwaite (ed).
- *The New Culture of Capitalism*: Richard Sennett.

HSPS

- ***Communist Manifesto***: Friedrich Engels and Karl Marx.
- ***Social Psychology***: Hogg & Vaughn.
- ***Introducing Child Psychology***: Schaffer.
- ***Introducing Child Psychology***: Durkin Blackwell.
- ***Making Decisions About Children:*** Schaffer.
- ***Globalisation: A Very Short Introduction***: Manfred Steger.
- ***Globalisation: A Critical Introduction***: Jan Art Scholte.
- ***Why we Hate Politics***: Colin Hay.
- ***Politics and Fate***: Andrew Gamble.
- ***Democracy: A Very Short Introduction***: Bernard Crick.
- ***An Introduction to Social Anthropology***: Joy Hendry.
- ***Understanding International Relations***: Chris Browne & Kirsten Ainley.
- ***Sociology: A Short Introduction***: Nicholas Abercrombie.

FINAL ADVICE

BEFORE YOUR INTERVIEW

- Make sure you understand your curriculum; your interview will most likely use material from your school courses as a starting point.
- Remind yourself of the selection criteria for your subject.
- Read around your subject in scientific articles and books, visit museums, watch documentaries, anything which broadens your knowledge of your favourite topics while demonstrating your passion for your subject. They may ask you at the interview which articles you've read recently to check you are engaged with the subject. Scientists should try New Scientist's online articles to start you off; TED talks are also a great way to be quickly briefed on cutting-edge research, and it's more likely you will remember the name of the researcher, etc.
- Practice common questions or sample questions – this is better done with a teacher or someone you are less familiar with or who is an experienced interviewer.
- Make up your own questions throughout your day: Why is that flower shaped like that? Why is that bird red-breasted? Why does my dog like to fetch sticks? What did I mean when I said that man wasn't 'normal', and is this the criteria everyone uses? How do I know I see the same colours as others?
- Re-read your personal statement and any coursework or submitted essays you are providing. Anticipate questions that may arise from these and prepare them in advance.
- Read and do anything you've said you've done in your application – they may ask you about it at the interview!
- Check your interview specifications – what type of interviews you will have for which subjects, how many there will be, where, when, and with whom they will be so there are no surprises.

THE ULTIMATE OXBRIDGE INTERVIEW GUIDE — FINAL ADVICE

ON THE DAY OF YOUR INTERVIEW

- Get a good night's sleep before the big day.
- If you are travelling from far away, try to arrive the night before so that you're fresh in the morning. Getting up early in the morning and travelling far could tire you out and you might be less focused whilst being interviewed. Many colleges will provide you with accommodation if you're travelling from a certain distance away.
- Take a shower in the morning and dress to your comfort, though you don't want to give a sloppy first impression – most opt for smart/casual
- Get there early so you aren't late or stressed out before it even starts.
- Smile at everyone and be polite.
- Don't worry about other candidates; be nice of course, but you are there for you, and their impressions of how their interviews went have nothing to do with what the interviewers thought or how yours will go.
- It's OK to be nervous – they know you're nervous and understand, but try to move past it and be in the moment to get the most out of the experience.
- Don't be discouraged if it feels like one interview didn't go well – you may have shown the interviewers exactly what they wanted to see, even if it wasn't what you wanted to see.
- Have a cuppa and relax, there's nothing you can do now but be yourself.

> *The Most Important Advice...*
> - Explain your thought processes as much as possible – it doesn't matter if you're wrong. It really is the journey; not the destination that matters.
> - Interviewers aren't interested in what you know. Instead, they are more interested in what you can do with what you already know.

× **DON'T** be quiet – even if you can't answer a question. How you approach the question could show the interviewer what they want to see.

× **DON'T** rely on the interviewer to guide you every step of the way.

× **DON'T** ever, ever, ever give up.

× **DON'T** be arrogant or rigid – you are bound to get things wrong, accept them and move on.

× **DON'T** expect to know all the answers; this is different from school, you aren't expected to know the answer to everything – you are using your knowledge as a foundation for original thoughts and applications under the guidance of your interviewer.

× **DON'T** think you will remember everything you did/wrote without revising.

× **DON'T** be afraid to point out flaws in your own ideas – scientists need to be self-critical, and the interviewer has already noticed your mistakes!

× **DON'T** be defensive, especially if the interviewer is hinting that your idea may be on the wrong path – the interviewer is the expert!

× **DON'T** get hung up on a question for too long.

- ✗ **DON'T** rehearse scripted answers to be regurgitated.
- ✗ **DON'T** answer the question you wanted them to ask.
- ✗ **DON'T** lie about things you have read/done (and if you already lied in your personal statement, then read/do them before the interview!)
- ✓ **DO** speak freely about what you are thinking and ask for clarifications.
- ✓ **DO** take suggestions and listen for pointers from your interviewer.
- ✓ **DO** try your best to get to the answer.
- ✓ **DO** have confidence in yourself and the abilities that got you this far.
- ✓ **DO** be prepared to discuss the ideas and problems in your work.
- ✓ **DO** make many suggestions and have many ideas.
- ✓ **DO** show intellectual flexibility by taking suggestions from the interviewer.
- ✓ **DO** take your time in answering to ensure your words come out right.
- ✓ **DO** research your interviewers so that you know their basic research interests. Then ensure you understand the basics of their work (no need to go into detail with this).
- ✓ **DO** prepare your answers to common questions.
- ✓ **DO** answer the question that the interviewer has asked – not the one you want them to!
- ✓ **DO** practice interviews with family or teachers – even easy questions may be harder to articulate out loud and on the spot to a stranger.
- ✓ **DO** think about strengths/experiences you may wish to highlight.
- ✓ **DO** visit www.uniadmissions.co.uk/example-interviews to see mock interviews in your subject. This will allow you to understand the differences between good and bad candidates.

FINAL COMMENTS

Remember that the route to success is your approach and practice. Don't fall into the trap that *"you can't prepare for Oxbridge interviews"* – this could not be further from the truth. With targeted preparation and focused reading, you can dramatically boost your chances of getting that dream offer.

Work hard, never give up, and do yourself justice.

Good luck!

ACKNOWLEDGEMENTS

I wish to thank the many tutors for their help with compiling this mammoth book – it wouldn't have been possible without you all. I'm hopeful that students will continue to benefit from your wisdom for many years to come.

ABOUT US

We currently publish over 100 titles across a range of subject areas – covering specialised admissions tests, examination techniques, personal statement guides, plus everything else you need to improve your chances of getting on to competitive courses such as medicine and law, as well as into universities such as Oxford and Cambridge.

Outside of publishing we also operate a highly successful tuition division, called UniAdmissions. This company was founded in 2013 by Dr Rohan Agarwal and Dr David Salt, both Cambridge Medical graduates with several years of tutoring experience. Since then, every year, hundreds of applicants and schools work with us on our programmes. Through the programmes we offer, we deliver expert tuition, exclusive course places, online courses, best-selling textbooks and much more.

With a team of over 1,000 Oxbridge tutors and a proven track record, UniAdmissions have quickly become the UK's number one admissions company.

Visit and engage with us at:

Website (UniAdmissions): www.uniadmissions.co.uk

Facebook: www.facebook.com/uniadmissionsuk

Your Free Book

Thanks for purchasing this Ultimate Book. Readers like you have the power to make or break a book – hopefully you found this one useful and informative. *UniAdmissions* would love to hear about your experiences with this book. As thanks for your time we'll send you another ebook from our Ultimate Guide series absolutely FREE!

How to Redeem Your Free Ebook

1) Find the book you have on your Amazon

purchase history or your email receipt to help find the book on Amazon.

2) On the product page at the Customer Reviews area, click 'Write a customer review'. Write your review and post it! Copy the review page or take a screen shot of the review you have left.

3) Head over to www.uniadmissions.co.uk/free-book and select your chosen free ebook!

Your ebook will then be emailed to you – it's as simple as that!

Alternatively, you can buy all the titles at

Printed in Great Britain
by Amazon